A History of the Spanish Language

Second edition

Ralph Penny

CAMBRIDGE UNIVERSITY PRESS
Cambridge, New York, Melbourne, Madrid, Cape Town,
Singapore, São Paulo, Delhi, Tokyo, Mexico City

Cambridge University Press
The Edinburgh Building, Cambridge CB2 8RU, UK

Published in the United States of America by Cambridge University Press, New York

www.cambridge.org
Information on this title: www.cambridge.org/9780521011846

First published 1991
7th printing 2000
Second edition 2002
Sixth printing 2009

A catalogue record for this publication is available from the British Library

Library of Congress Cataloguing in Publication Data

Penny, Ralph J. (Ralph John), 1940–
A history of the Spanish language / Ralph Penny. – 2nd edn
p. cm.
Includes bibliographical references and index.
ISBN 0 521 80587 2 (hardback) ISBN 0 521 01184 1 (paperback)
1. Spanish language – Grammar, Historical. I. Title.
PC4101 .P46 2002
460.9 – dc21 2002025671

ISBN 978-0-521-80587-2 Hardback
ISBN 978-0-521-01184-6 Paperback

Content

Maps

Tables

Preface to the first edition

The aim of this *History of the Spanish Language* is to provide the reader with as complete a picture as possible of the development of Spanish over the last two thousand years. The book is concerned essentially with the internal history of Spanish (with what used to be called, rather forbiddingly, 'historical grammar'), although the external history of Spanish (the account of the circumstances in which Spanish has been spoken and written over time) is discussed at some length in the Introduction. In writing this book, I had in mind the needs of undergraduate and postgraduate students of Spanish and other Romance languages, but more advanced scholars will, I trust, find it a useful source of reference.

My indebtedness to other scholars will be evident on almost every page, but I have not sought to acknowledge this debt in detail at each moment; such acknowledgement is to be found in the list of references on pp. 332–40. Where I make reference in the text to the work of a particular scholar, it is with the specific aim of directing the reader to a source in which a more complete discussion may be found of the issue in question than is possible within the confines of a textbook.

Help in the writing of this book has come from many sources, from many cohorts of students who have participated over the years in my seminars on the history of Spanish, from colleagues with whom I have discussed many of the issues concerned, and from those who have read drafts of the text. I am indebted to the readers to whom the proposed book was referred by Cambridge University Press, and particularly to Professor Thomas J. Walsh, of Georgetown University, whose constructive and detailed comments brought about a host of improvements to the original version. All shortcomings, it need hardly be said, are entirely my own.

Preface to the second edition

The writing of this second edition has benefited significantly from a number of reviews of the first edition. Particularly helpful were those by Adelino Álvarez Rodríguez (*Analecta Malacitana*, 17 (1994): 405–27), Robert J. Blake (*Hispanic Review*, 61 (1993): 547–50), Steven N. Dworkin (*Canadian Journal of Linguistics*, 38 (1993), 91–4), John England (*Modern Language Review*, 87 (1992): 770–1) and Alf Monjour (*RLiR*, 56 (1992): 250–9). Similarly profitable were the detailed personal letters I received from Jerry Craddock, John England, Fred Hodcroft and Mª Jesús López Bobo, and the various suggestions for improvement made by the Spanish translator of the first edition, Ignacio Pérez Pascual. To all these friends and colleagues I am immensely grateful for their positive comments, for the errors and omissions they drew my attention to, and for their broader suggestions for improvement. The large majority of the points they make have received attention in this second edition, and if I have not attended to every single one, they will understand that, on a few points, I still think I was right.

Two other factors have motivated a rewriting of many sections of the original book. On the one hand, Hispanic and Romance linguistics have, of course, moved on since the first edition was written, and evidence of new thinking on the problems tackled here will be found in the revised list of references. On the other hand, I have received reactions and suggestions from colleagues in a number of countries who have used the book in connection with their teaching. These stimuli have led to the rewriting of many sections, most notably the complete redrafting of the sections on verbal morphology and syntax. They have also suggested an expansion of the introductory chapter on external history and the addition of a final chapter on the past, present and future of Spanish. However, it continues to be the case that little is written on the semantic development of Spanish, so that chapter 5, regrettably, remains essentially unchanged. While obviously indebted, in the writing of this second edition, to a host of scholars, and while I am immensely grateful for the help I have received, I naturally remain entirely responsible for the book's surviving shortcomings.

Abbreviations and symbols

Ar.	Arabic
Arag.	Aragonese
C. It.	Central Italian (including Tuscan)
Cat.	Catalan
CL	Classical Latin
Eng.	English
Fr.	French
GA	Golden Age
Gal.	Galician
Germ.	German
Gmc.	Germanic
It.	Italian
JSp.	Judeo-Spanish
Lat.	Latin
Leon.	Leonese
Moz.	Mozarabic
MSp.	Modern Spanish
N. It.	North Italian
Occ.	Occitan
OFr.	Old French
OPtg.	Old Portuguese
OSp.	Old Spanish
Ptg.	Portuguese
Rom.	Romanian
S. It.	South Italian
Sard.	Sardinian
Sic.	Sicilian
Sp.	Spanish
VL	Vulgar Latin
abl.	ablative
acc.	accusative

adj.	adjective
cons.	consonant
dat.	dative
fem.	feminine
fut.	future
gen.	genitive
imper.	imperative
imperf.	imperfect
indic.	indicative
inf.	infinitive
masc.	masculine
neut.	neuter
nom.	nominative
part.	participle
perf.	perfect
pers.	person
pluperf.	pluperfect
plur.	plural
pret.	preterite
sing.	singular
subj.	subjunctive
voc.	vocative

*	Reconstructed form or meaning (whose existence is claimed; see 1.1 (end))
**	Form or meaning whose existence is denied
x > y	*x* becomes *y* in the course of time
x < y	*x* is the descendant (reflex) of *y*
x → y	*y* is created on the basis of *x* (e.g. through derivation)
x~y	*x* coexists with *y* with equivalent function
Ø	Null segment (e.g. [h] > [Ø] = '[h] ceases to be pronounced')
á, é, í, etc.	Vowel carrying stress-accent
Ā, Ē, Ī, etc.	In Latin words (which appear in small capitals), a long vowel; any vowel not so marked in a Latin word is short
aː, eː, iː, etc.	In transcriptions, a long vowel
[xxxx]	Phonetic transcription
/xxxx/	Phonemic transcription
{xxxx}	Morpheme
<x>	Letter of the alphabet, grapheme

The phonetic and phonemic symbols used are those of the International Phonetic Association, but with the following modifications:

- [ǰ]is used for the mid-palatal fricative (as in *mayo*) to distinguish it from the (frictionless) glide [j] (as in *tierra*).
- [s̪] and [z̪] are used for all dental fricatives (whether predorsal, coronal, etc.), as used in Andalusia, America, etc., to distinguish them from the apico-alveolar [s] and [z], typical of central and northern Spain.

In the chart below, a symbol at the left of its box represents a voiceless sound, one on the right indicates a voiced sound. In the case of glides with double place of articulation, the symbol within parentheses indicates the secondary locus.

Table of phonetic symbols used

Consonants	Bilabial	Labio-dental	Inter-dental	Dental	Alveolar	Pre-palatal	Mid-palatal	Velar	Glottal
Plosive	p ⁝ b			t ⁝ d				k ⁝ g	
Fricative	ɸ ⁝ β	f ⁝ v	θ ⁝ ð	s̪ ⁝ z̪	s ⁝ z	ʃ ⁝ ʒ	ǰ	x ⁝ ɣ	h ⁝ ɦ
Affricate				tˢ ⁝ dᶻ		tʃ ⁝ dʒ			
Lateral			l̟	l̪	l		ʎ		
Vibrant					r				
Flap					ɾ				
Nasal	m	ɱ	n̟	n̪	n		ɲ	ŋ	
Glides									
Opening	ʍ ⁝ w						j	(ʍ) ⁝ (w)	
Closing	u̯						i̯	(u̯)	
Vowels						Front	Central	Back	
High						i		u	
Mid-high						e		o	
Mid-low						ɛ	ɐ	ɔ	
Low						æ	a	ɑ	

1 Introduction

Time-line

218 BC	Roman troops enter northeastern Spain.
206 BC	Defeat of the Carthaginians and capture of Cádiz, their Peninsular capital.
19 BC	Conquest of the remaining parts of the Peninsula (now Galicia, Asturias, Santander and part of the Basque Country), hitherto outside Roman control.
AD 76	Hadrian (Roman emperor 117–38) born, probably in Italica, near Seville.
410	The Visigoths establish (as *foederati)* a semi-autonomous kingdom in southwestern Gaul, with their capital at Toulouse.
early 6th c.	Visigoths expelled from Gaul by the Franks.
c. 560–636	Lifetime of St Isidore, archbishop of Seville and author of *Origines sive etymologiae*.
585	Swabian kingdom of the northwest absorbed into Visigothic Spain.
711	The Islamic invasion of Spain.
711–18	Muslims establish control over approximately three quarters of the Peninsula.
884	Reconquest of Burgos.
1035	Creation of the kingdom of Castile.
1080	Council of Burgos.
1085	Reconquest of Toledo.
1086	First Almoravid invasion.
1137	Merger of Aragon with Catalonia.
1154	Almohads gain control of Islamic Spain.
1212	Christian victory in the battle of Las Navas de Tolosa.
1236	Reconquest of Córdoba, followed by that of Jaén (1246), Seville (1248) and Cádiz (1250).
1244	Castile gains control of the kingdom of Murcia.
1252–84	Alfonso X the Learned, king of Castile and León.
1479	Union of the Crowns of Castile and Aragon.

1492 Granada captured by the Catholic Monarchs.
1492 Expulsion of Jews from Spain.
1492 Publication of Antonio de Nebrija's *Gramática de la lengua castellana.*
1492 Discovery of America.
1519–21 Conquest of Mexico.
1532–5 Conquest of the Inca empire.
c. 1535 Juan de Valdés completes his *Diálogo de la lengua.*
1521 Discovery of the Philippine Islands, incorporated into the Spanish Empire later in the sixteenth century.
1561 Madrid becomes capital of Spain.
1605–15 Publication of Miguel de Cervantes's *El ingenioso hidalgo don Quixote de la Mancha.*
1713 Establishment of the Real Academia Española.
1726–39 Publication of the Academia's three-volume *Diccionario de autoridades.*
1800–36 Wars of American Independence deprive Spain of almost all its American colonies.
1898 Spain loses its last American and Asian colonies (Cuba and the Philippines).
1936–75 Franco controls the Spanish state.
1978 Publication of the post-Franco constitution.

This history of Spanish is conceived as an account of the 'internal' development of the language, a discussion of the way in which its phonology, its morphosyntax, its vocabulary and the meanings of its words have evolved, and of the reasons for these developments (insofar as they can be established). It is therefore what used to be called a 'historical grammar' of the Spanish language. However, although it follows that the book is not essentially concerned with the social contexts in which Spanish is and has been used, it is appropriate to give a brief account of these contexts, by way of introduction to the main matter which follows. More detailed accounts of the 'external' history of Spanish (Lapesa 1980, Penny 2000) are available to the reader, and what is discussed here consists of an outline of the circumstances under which Spanish and its antecedents have been spoken over the centuries, an outline which is sufficient, one hopes, to explain the chronological and social terms used in later chapters.

1.1 Indo-European, Latin and Romance

Spanish is a member of the Indo-European family of languages, whose earliest reconstructible ancestor was spoken approximately 5,000 years ago in the area of the Black Sea (either, in keeping with the traditional view, to the north of that Sea, in the steppes of southern Russia, or, according to a more recent view (e.g. Renfrew 1998), to its south, in what is now Turkey). Speakers of

Indo-European gradually spread (perhaps in conjunction with the spread of farming) in various directions, and varieties of their speech came to be used in enormously broad areas: almost all Europe (where only Basque, Finnish, Sami (Lapp) and Magyar (Hungarian) do not have this ancestry), the greater part of the Indian subcontinent as far east as Bangladesh and Assam, and many territories in between (e.g. Armenia, Iran, much of Afghanistan). During this migration process, each group of Indo-European speakers inevitably lost contact with other groups, so that innovations and losses originating in one group could not spread to others and fragmentation was the natural result. However, the family resemblance has persisted over the millennia and the surviving members retain many structural similarities and a significant proportion of their core vocabulary in common. Scholars typically recognize nine surviving branches of the Indo-European family (Indo-Iranian, Slavonic, Germanic, Italic, Baltic, Hellenic, Armenian, Albanian and Celtic), while two branches (Tocharian and Hittite) have left substantial written records but are no longer spoken.

The most prominent member of the Italic branch of Indo-European is Latin. However, other members of this branch were spoken for centuries in Italy beside Latin. These included Oscan (in much of the centre and south of the Italian peninsula), Umbrian (in the area northeast of Rome), and Faliscan (immediately to the north of Rome), and were gradually replaced by Latin, as the political and cultural power of Rome spread from Latium to encompass the rest of the Italian peninsula. This process of assimilation was, naturally, long lasting, beginning in the fourth century BC, and not becoming complete until at least the first century AD. For example, some of the graffiti preserved on the walls of Pompeii (and therefore written shortly before the eruption of Vesuvius in AD 79) are best described as reflecting Oscan rather than Latin speech.

The spread of Latin outwards from Rome was not limited to the Italian peninsula, but continued into adjacent and eventually distant parts of the Mediterranean world and its hinterland. As a result of varying development in different parts of this territory, Latin evolved into the family of related dialects (some of which achieved the status of standard languages) known as the Romance language family. No classification of the Romance languages can be fully satisfactory because they form a continuum of overlapping varieties, which is broken only in the eastern Balkans, where the link between Italian and Romanian varieties has been severed by the incursion of Slavonic speech (modern Serbo-Croatian, etc.), and in the Alps, where northern Italian varieties are separated from Romansh by the expansion of German. The most prominent members of the family (those that came to be written and which constitute the standard languages within the group) are French, Occitan (once the literary language of southern French society, now a series of rural varieties), Italian, Romanian, Romansh (the fourth national language of Switzerland, spoken in the southeastern canton of the Graubünden), Catalan, Portuguese and Spanish. Dalmatian, spoken on the eastern Adriatic coast, has been extinct since the nineteenth century.

Latin is the ancestor of Spanish (and, by definition, of all other Romance languages) in the sense that there is an unbroken chain of speakers, each learning his or her language from parents and contemporaries, stretching from the people of the Western Roman Empire two thousand years ago to the present population of the Spanish-speaking world. An alternative way of expressing the relationship between Latin and Spanish is to say that Spanish *is* Latin, as Latin continues to be spoken in parts of Europe, Africa and America. Similar claims are of course justified in the case of Portuguese, Catalan, French, Italian, Romanian, etc., and the main reason the term 'Latin' is not used for these various kinds of speech and writing is one of convenience: some forms of contemporary Latin (i.e. some Romance languages) have become mutually unintelligible and it is inconvenient to use a single label for mutually unintelligible forms of language. Another, more powerful, reason for the use of distinctive labels such as 'Spanish', 'French', etc., is that the rise of nation-states in medieval and modern Europe led to the development of separate written standards and has come to demand a separate linguistic identity for each state, as an expression of its cultural and political identity.

It is self-evident that contemporary 'Latin' speech (in the sense used here to embrace what are otherwise referred to as 'the Romance languages') is not uniform, but it is equally important to recognize that Latin speech can never have been uniform. All language displays variation (and Latin speech can have been no exception) in three main ways: it varies diatopically (i.e. in space), diachronically (i.e. over time), and sociolinguistically (i.e. in the same place and at the same time it varies in accordance with factors such as the age, sex, education, occupation, etc. of the speaker). In addition, variation is inherent not only in speech-communities, but in individuals, in the sense that individuals normally vary their speech according to the circumstances in which they are speaking. The fact that we are deprived of the opportunity (for the most part) of observing such variation in the case of Latin should not blind us to the fact of its existence in the Latin-speaking world of two thousand years ago.

Evidence of diatopic variation in Latin is scarce, owing to the fact that those who wrote were trained to do so in a variety of Latin (an educated, literary variety, traditionally called 'Classical Latin') which by its nature rejected merely local characteristics. However, some evidence is available and, insofar as it refers to the Latin of Spain, it will be discussed in the following section (1.2). Evidence of diachronic variation is more plentiful, and comes from comparison of the language used by writers at different periods, and from comments made by Latin grammarians on the antiquated or obsolete status of certain features of the language.

It is the evidence of sociolinguistic variation that has received most attention from students of the Romance languages, although this aspect of variation is not traditionally described as 'sociolinguistic'. Since at least the nineteenth century, it has been known that the Romance languages do not descend from Classical (i.e. literary) Latin, but from non-literary varieties, often referred to collectively as 'Vulgar Latin'. To take a simple and well-known lexical example, the word meaning 'horse' in literary Latin is EQUUS, a form which is clearly not the ancestor of the Romance words for this concept (Sp. *caballo*, Ptg. *cavalo*, Fr. *cheval*, It. *cavallo*, Rom. *cal*, etc.). The latter forms descend from CABALLUS, which, where it appears in literary Latin, means 'nag; workhorse', but which in non-literary language was evidently used in the generic sense 'horse'.

Definitions of 'Vulgar Latin' have abounded, and many have rested on historical models that can now be seen to be mistaken. Thus, Romance linguists have long since rejected the notion that Vulgar Latin is a later form of Latin than the Classical variety, despite the fact that much of the evidence for Vulgar Latin comes from the later centuries of the Empire and despite the fact that many (but not all) of the features of Vulgar Latin are revealed as more 'advanced' than the corresponding features of Classical Latin.

Harder to die is the notion that Vulgar Latin and Classical Latin are sharply different codes, and that the two terms represent mutually exclusive concepts. This view cannot be sustained, since all varieties of Latin of which we have knowledge share most of their vocabulary, most of their morphology and most of their syntactical rules. The model adopted here is that 'Latin', like any language observable today, represents a gamut or spectrum of linguistic styles, ranging from the codified, literary register at one end to the raciest slang at the other, with a smooth gradation of intermediate styles. On this model, 'Classical Latin' occupies one extreme of the spectrum, representing essentially written varieties (unspoken except in 'performance' or 'reading aloud' mode), while Vulgar Latin represents almost the whole of the remainder of the spectrum, perhaps with the exception of the spoken language of the educated classes (for which a separate term is required) and with the exception of the language of marginal social groups at the other extreme, since the slang of such groups is known to be unstable and therefore unlikely to have affected the speech of the great mass of the population in any consistent way.

This view of Vulgar Latin, although expressed differently, is in broad agreement with one of the more satisfactory current definitions of the term, that adopted by Herman (2000: 7) and some predecessors: 'the set of all those innovations and trends that turned up in the usage, particularly but not exclusively spoken, of the Latin-speaking population who were little or not at all influenced by school education and by literary models'. However, it is important to make clear certain corollaries which flow from the definition of Vulgar Latin adopted here.

First, Vulgar Latin has no implicit chronological limits. It is contemporary with Classical Latin and as soon as it is meaningful to refer to Classical Latin (i.e. from the first century BC) it is also meaningful to use the term 'Vulgar

Latin', despite the fact that most evidence of the nature of Vulgar Latin comes from later centuries. At the other extreme, the term 'Vulgar Latin' ceases to be useful once locally divergent forms of language begin to be recorded in writing (the ninth century AD in northern France), and the term 'Romance' is then used for any or all vernacular descendants of Latin, written or spoken. However, some scholars also use the term 'Romance' to refer to the spoken language of earlier centuries, while other scholars use the term 'Proto-Romance' to indicate those forms of spoken language which constitute the ancestor of the Romance languages, and which by definition belong to a period prior to the appearance of texts written in Romance.

Second, there can be no such thing as a 'Vulgar Latin text'. Texts of all kinds are composed, by definition, by the educated and therefore in the codified or 'standard' variety of Latin in which such writers have inevitably been trained. This is not to say that textual evidence of spoken registers of Latin is unavailable (it will be outlined below); what we do find is that certain types of text contain a greater or lesser proportion of forms (spellings, words, constructions, etc.) which differ from the standard and which reveal particular features of spoken Latin. Such information is inevitably incomplete and cannot amount to a 'full' picture of Vulgar Latin.

Third, like 'Latin' considered in its entirety, Vulgar Latin is inherently variable. The term includes reference to all the chronological, local and social varieties of Latin as spoken by the majority of the relevant populations. It cannot therefore be described in the 'grammar-book' way that is appropriate to codified or standard varieties.

What then are the sources of information about the features of Vulgar Latin? Full discussion is inappropriate here (and can be found in works on Vulgar Latin such as Väänänen 1968: 39–49), but may be summarized as:

- Literary writing purporting to reflect popular speech (dramatists such as Plautus (*c.* 254–184 BC), Ennius (239–169 BC), Terence (*c.* 195–159? BC); satirists such as Petronius (d. AD 66)).
- Informal letters, such as those written to his father by Claudius Terentianus in second-century AD Egypt (see Adams 1977).
- Christian writings, which generally rejected the exclusivist standard language in favour of a style more suited to a proselytizing religion, especially those written for an unsophisticated audience (such as the late fourth-century account by a Spanish nun of her pilgrimage to the Holy Land, usually referred to as the *Peregrinatio ad loca sancta* or the *Peregrinatio Etheriae*).
- Technical writing, which because of its practical intent and the modest education of its intended readership was usually unpretentious in style and allowed the use of vocabulary and expressions belonging to speech; such writing includes works on cookery, farming, building, medicine, veterinary science, etc.

- Writing for various purposes, literary and non-literary, from the late Roman period (third to fifth centuries AD) and from the following centuries, when standards of education and culture among the literate were lower than they had earlier been and when writers consequently may lapse into non-Classical modes of expression.
- Informal inscriptions, including gravestones but especially including painted graffiti (such as those of Pompeii and Herculaneum, which include advertisements, announcements, slogans, obscenities, etc.) and *defixiones* (metal plaques on which magical spells are scratched).
- Writings of grammarians, especially insofar as they condemn forms as incorrect, since this assures us of their existence in speech; particularly noteworthy is the so-called *Appendix Probi*, a sixth- or seventh-century (see Robson 1963) list of 227 forms to be avoided in writing, in which each recommended expression is placed alongside its condemned equivalent (e.g. BACULUS NON VACLUS, AURIS NON ORICLA, GRUS NON GRUIS, TRISTIS NON TRISTUS); of almost similar importance, especially for Spain, are the linguistic observations of St Isidore, bishop of Seville (*c.* 560–636), in his *Origines sive etymologiae*.
- Glosses of various dates from the first century AD on, where some reader has inserted into a text interlinear or marginal equivalents for words or expressions which were obsolete and therefore posed difficulty for readers, the replacements sometimes being drawn from spoken registers.
- Borrowings made by Latin from other languages, and vice versa, in which the manner of adaptation of the borrowed word to the borrowing language may reveal features of pronunciation (e.g. German *Kaiser* reveals that when Germanic borrowed the Latin word CAESAR its initial consonant was articulated [k]).

Alongside this testimony drawn largely from ancient texts is to be placed the evidence deducible from the Romance languages themselves. We have already seen that by comparing certain Romance forms it is possible to deduce that in spoken Latin the word CABALLUS had the generic sense 'horse', and it is possible to apply this procedure to any linguistic feature, on the hypothesis that if the same feature is observed in a broad range of Romance languages then that feature belonged to spoken Latin. Thus, by comparing Romance words for 'green' (e.g. Sp., Ptg., It., Rom. *verde*, Fr., Cat. *vert*), it is possible to make the minimal deduction that their spoken Latin ancestor had no more than two syllables, despite the fact that the Latin word for 'green' that we find in writing suggests that it has three: VIRIDIS. On this occasion, our deduction is confirmed by the author of the *Appendix Probi*, who prescribes VIRIDIS NON VIRDIS. However, in a large number of cases, such confirmation from written sources is not forthcoming, and many forms have been deduced (on the basis of the comparison of Romance forms) as belonging to spoken Latin without their existence being confirmed by any written source. Thus, a comparison of the Romance verbs meaning 'to be' (e.g. Sp., Ptg. *ser*, Cat. *ésser/ser*, Fr. *être*, It. *essere*) reveals that their spoken Latin ancestor is likely to have had three syllables and that the last syllable was -RE, by contrast with the Classical Latin form ESSE 'to be'. On the basis of known facts about the development of each Romance language, it is possible to refine the deduced Vulgar Latin form to *ESSERE. It will be noted that in such cases an asterisk indicates the lack of confirmation from written sources, and therefore the hypothetical (but not necessarily doubtful) status of the word concerned.

1.2 The Latin of Spain

Latin came to be used in Spain as a result of the gradual incorporation of the Peninsula into the Roman Empire and of the consequent romanization of its diverse peoples and cultures. Romanization began in 218 BC, at the beginning of the Second Punic War, when Roman troops were disembarked in northeastern Spain to prevent reinforcement of Hannibal's army in Italy (following his famous march across the Alps) by Carthaginian troops from southern Spain, then part of Carthaginian territory. After the defeat of the Carthaginians and the capture of their Peninsular capital, Cádiz, in 206 BC, what had begun as a military enterprise became a process of colonization and settlement. This process was relatively slow, progressing in a westerly and northwesterly direction over the next two centuries and culminating in the conquest of the northern coastal area (now Galicia, Asturias, Santander and part of the Basque Country) in 19 BC (see map 1.1).

In the wake of conquest and settlement came latinization. The use of Latin was not enforced (and scarcely could have been), but was learned by the local populations, as a matter of convenience and prestige, from Roman settlers, administrators, soldiers, traders, etc. This process was rapid in some areas (the east and south, where Roman immigration was earliest and most frequent), slower in others (the centre, west and north), and is still incomplete in one area (the Basque Country). Any such language-change implies bilingualism over at least several generations, and since bilingualism persists today in the western Pyrenees it is likely that it persisted in other areas remote from the major Roman cities (that is, in parts of the north and west) at least until the end of the Roman period, in the fifth century, and in the remotest areas probably later. Such bilingualism, between Basque and Latin and between Celtic and Latin, has often been cited as the cause of certain changes which are evident in the Peninsular descendants of Latin (see 2.5.3.2, 2.5.6, etc., for discussion), and it is certain that it allowed the borrowing of certain words by Latin from the languages with which it coexisted (see 4.2). Latinization was evidently much more rapid in the east and south, where Iberian and Greek (in what is now

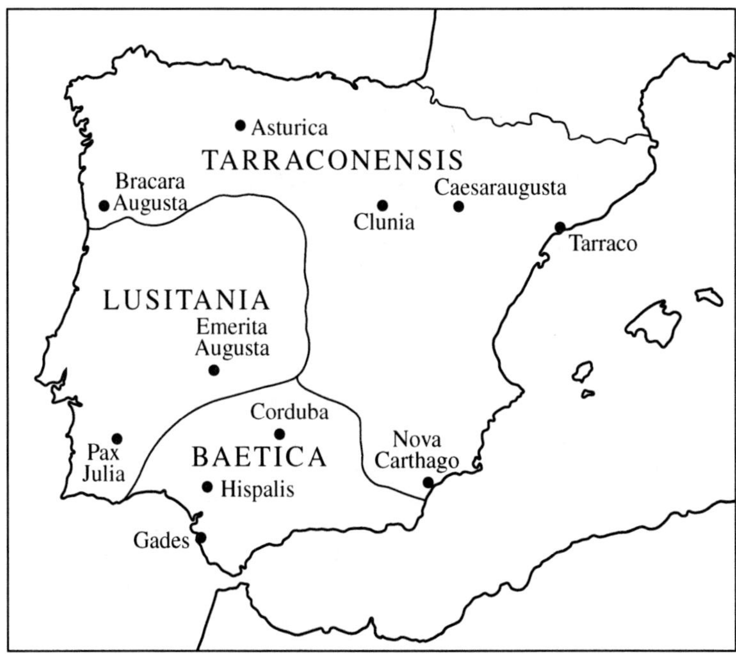

Map 1.1 Roman Spain in the first century AD

Catalonia and Valencia) and Tartessian (in Andalusia and southern Portugal) appear to have been displaced entirely by Latin by the first century AD at the latest.

The pace of latinization is probably correlated with geographical distance from the 'educated standard' of the 'average' Latin spoken at any given date. The factors which encouraged rapid latinization (close contact with central Italy, urbanization, good road communications, the consequent fostering of trade, etc.) are the same factors which encouraged the use of forms of Latin which were closer to the prestigious end of the sociolinguistic spectrum (see 1.1). It is therefore likely that the 'average' Latin spoken by people in the remoter, less developed, parts of the Peninsula was considerably further from the prestige norm (that of upper-class Rome) than was the speech of the eastern and southern cities. This factor is particularly relevant to the history of Spanish, since Spanish has its geographical roots in what is now the northern part of the province of Burgos, an area of the northern meseta which was remote from the centres of economic activity and cultural prestige in Roman Spain, which was latinized fairly late, and where the Latin spoken must consequently have been particularly remote from the prestige norm (that is, particularly 'incorrect') at the time of the Roman collapse. With the end of the Roman state came the effective removal of the linguistic model towards which, however distantly and ineffectually, speakers strove to adhere, so that any 'incorrect' features of local speech were likely to be perpetuated (unless challenged by some other prestige model, which was not to be the case in the Burgos area). Spanish has often been described as a rather idiosyncratic form of Peninsular Romance (even of Romance *tout court*), a view associated with Menéndez Pidal (1964a: 472–88) and developed in Penny (2000). Such linguistic idiosyncrasy can plausibly be accounted for in part by the conditions under which the northern meseta was latinized.

It is also appropriate to consider here the ways in which the Latin spoken in Spain differed from that spoken in other provinces. Such a consideration must not assume that the Latin of Spain was in any sense uniform; we have just seen that it was probably far from uniform. But it is at least arguable that there are some characteristics shared by all or most of the surviving varieties of Peninsular Romance (and which therefore belonged to the Latin spoken in most if not all of the Peninsula), which may be contrasted with the corresponding features of Gallo-Romance, Italo-Romance, etc. The characteristics which have been assigned to the Latin of Spain, at different times by different scholars, are its archaism, its conservatism and its Osco-Umbrian dialectalism. Paradoxically, there are a number of features which allow the Latin of Spain to be described as innovatory. Each of these characteristics will be considered in turn.

1.2.1 Archaism

The early date at which the latinization of Spain began (the end of the third century BC) implies that the Latin carried to Spain by the earliest soldiers, traders and migrants represents an earlier phase in the development of Latin than that represented by the language carried to other areas. For example, the latinization of northern Italy and southern Gaul begins in the second century BC, at a time when all of Spain but the northwest was under Roman rule, while the latinization of the rest of Gaul does not begin until the first century BC, and that of Dacia (approximately modern Romania) does not begin until the second century AD. On the hypothesis that colonized areas often retain features of speech which are abandoned in the parent-state (a hypothesis which finds some support in the history of English and Spanish in America, as elsewhere), it is predictable that Hispano-Romance will retain some features of third- and second-century BC Latin which were then abandoned in the Latin of Rome and other, more recently latinized, provinces. Such an argument may apply to the widespread appearance in Peninsular speech of bilabial [ɸ] (corresponding to the spelling F; see 2.5.6) rather than its successor, the labiodental [f], which is used in most of the rest of the Romance-speaking world. However, it is in the field of vocabulary that such archaism has been most closely studied. The following expressions are ones whose antecedents appear in pre-Classical writers (Plautus, Ennius, Terence, etc.) but not in the works of those writing in Rome from the first century BC onwards, facts which suggest that the words concerned had fallen out of use there (while continuing in use in the Latin of Spain):

- Sp., Ptg. *cansar* 'to tire' < CAMPSĀRE 'to bend, to round (a headland)', an early borrowing from Greek not found in literature after the second century BC.
- Sp. *cueva*, Ptg. *cova* 'cave' < the pre-Classical adjective COVA 'hollow', by contrast with CL CAVA 'id.', whence Fr. *cave* 'cellar', etc.
- Sp. *cuyo, -a,* Ptg. *cujo, -a* 'whose' < CŪIUS, -A, -UM '-id.', a form already obsolescent in the first century BC.
- Sp. *(a)demás*, Ptg. *demais* 'besides' < DĒMAGIS, not found in writing after the second century BC.
- Sp. *hablar*, Ptg. *falar* 'to speak' < pre-Classical FABULĀRĪ 'to converse'.
- Sp., Ptg. *querer* 'to wish' probably reflects the pre-Classical sense of QUAERERE 'to wish', found in Terence (early second century BC), but whose sense later became 'to seek'.

1.2.2 Conservatism

Conservatism cannot be sharply distinguished from archaism, since both terms refer to the retention of forms which elsewhere disappear. What is meant by the conservatism of the Latin of Spain is the retention of forms which appear in Classical Latin (and which were presumably once current in the spoken Latin of many areas besides Spain) by contrast with their eventual rejection in those areas which formed the cultural centre of the late Roman Empire (central and northern Italy and Gaul). Thus, the Latin numerals QUADRĀGINTĀ ... NŌNĀGINTĀ 'forty ... ninety', retain the stress on the penultimate vowel Ĭ (later > /e/) in their Spanish and Portuguese descendants: *cuarenta~quarenta ... noventa* (see 3.6.1), whereas in other Romance areas a stress-shift to the preceding syllable produced forms with tonic /a/: Fr. *quarante*, It. *cinquanta*, etc. But it is again in vocabulary that most evidence of conservatism is forthcoming; in the following cases, Spanish (together usually with Portuguese) retains a form which is normal in Classical Latin but which, if it appears outside the Peninsula, appears only in similarly 'remote' areas (e.g. the Alpine area, southern Italy, Sicily, Sardinia, Romania):

- Sp. *arena*, Ptg. *areia*, Rom. *arină* 'sand' < CL ARĒNA 'id.' (cf. Fr. *sable*, It. *sabbia*).
- Sp. *ciego*, Ptg. *cego*, Cat. *cec*, C. It. *cieco* 'blind' < CL CAECU 'id.' (cf. Fr. *aveugle*, N. It. *orbo*).
- OSp., Sard. *cras*, S. It. *crai* 'tomorrow' < CRĀS 'id.' (cf. Fr. *demain*, It. *domani*, Rom. *mîine*).

- Sp. *hervir*, Ptg. *ferver*, Rom. *fierbe* 'to boil' < CL FERVERE 'id.' (cf. Fr. *bouillir*, It. *bollire*, Cat. *bullir*).
- Sp. *hombro*, Ptg. *ombro*, Rom. *umăr* 'shoulder' < CL UMERU 'id.' (cf. Fr. *épaule*, It. *spalla*, Cat. *espatlla*).
- Sp., Ptg. *ir*, OSp., OPtg. *imos*, S. It., Sic. *immu*, OSp., MPtg. *ides*, Sp., Ptg. *ido*, forms of the verb 'to go' which descend from corresponding forms of CL ĪRE 'id.' (cf. Fr. *aller*, *allons*, It. *andare*, *andiamo*, Cat. *anar*, *anem*, etc.).
- Sp., Ptg. *mesa*, Rom. *masă* 'table < CL MĒNSA 'id.' (cf. Fr. *table*, It. *tàvola*, Cat. *taula*).
- Sp. *queso*, Ptg. *queijo*, C. It. *cacio*, S. It. *caso*, Rom. *caş* 'cheese' < CL CĀSEU 'id.' (cf. Fr. *fromage*, It. *formaggio*, Cat. *formatge*).
- Sp., Ptg. *rogar*, Rom. *ruga* 'to beg' < CL ROGĀRE 'id.' (cf. Fr. *prier*, It. *pregare*, Cat. *pregar*).
- Sp., Ptg. *sanar*, S. It., Sard. *sanare* 'to cure' < CL SĀNĀRE 'id.' (cf. Fr. *guérir*, It. *guarire*, Cat. *gorir*).
- Sp. *yegua*, Ptg. *égua*, Cat. *egua*, Rom. *iapă* 'mare' < CL EQUA 'id.' (cf. Fr. *jument*, It. *cavalla*).

It can be seen from these examples that there is a correlation between those varieties of Romance which preserve older forms and those which are located in peripheral parts of the Romance-speaking area, that is, those that were remotest from the trend-setting centres of the late Roman period. However, this correlation is not solely evident in the preservation and distribution of forms which also appear in Classical Latin. It is also evident in the distribution of Vulgar Latin innovations, where earlier innovations are typically found in peripheral regions and later innovations are observable in the central territories of Romance-speaking Europe. This distribution can be seen in the Vulgar Latin replacements of the synthetic forms of the comparative adjective (see 3.3.2), where the earlier innovation MAGIS (+ adj.) is preserved in Sp. *más*, Ptg. *mais*, Cat. *mes*, Rom. *mai*, by contrast with the later type PLUS (+ adj.) seen in Fr. *plus*, It. *più*. In vocabulary, this pattern is frequently repeated; e.g.:

- Sp. *hallar*, Ptg. *achar*, S. It. *acchiare*, Rom. *afla* 'to find' < AFFLĀRE 'to breathe out' (see 5.3.1) (cf. Fr. *trouver*, It. *trovare*, Cat. *trobar* < *TROPĀRE).
- Sp. *hermoso*, Ptg. *formoso*, Rom. *frumos* 'beautiful' < FŌRMOSU 'shapely' (cf. Fr. *beau*, *bel*, It. *bello* < BELLU).
- Sp. *pájaro*, Ptg. *pássaro*, Rom. *pasere* 'bird' < VL PASSAR (CL PASSER) 'sparrow' (cf. Fr. *oiseau*, It. *ucello*, Cat. *aucell* < AVICELLU).

For further details, see Rohlfs (1960).

1.2.3 Dialectalism

At the time that the latinization of Spain began, at the end of the third century BC, Latin was far from having ousted its Italic competitors (Oscan, Umbrian, etc.)

from central and southern Italy; there is evidence of the use of Oscan until at least the first century AD (see 1.1). And since it seems likely that many Roman soldiers and settlers who came to Spain were drawn from areas of Italy where Latin was spoken bilingually with Oscan or Umbrian, it has been claimed that the Latin of such speakers was likely to have contained non-standard features resulting from this bilingual contact. A detailed case of this kind can be seen in Menéndez Pidal (1960), where phonological changes such as MB > /m/ (see 2.5.3.2) and -LL-, -NN-, -RR- > /ʎ/, /ɲ/, /r/ (see 2.5.3.2.9) are assigned to this origin. Similarly, the tonic vowels of the ancestors of *nudo* 'knot', *octubre* 'October' and *cierzo* 'north wind' have sometimes been explained on the basis of interference between Latin NŌDU, OCTŌBER and CIRCIU and cognate Oscan or Umbrian forms with tonic Ū and Ĕ (namely hybrid *NŪDU, *OCTŪBER, *CĔRCIU), an interference which did not arise outside southern Italy and Spain (cf. NŌDU > Fr. *noeud*). The distribution of forms cognate with Sp. *dejar* 'to leave' (Ptg., Cat. *deixar*, Gasc. *dechà*, Sic. *dassari*, S. It. *dassare*, OSard. *dassare*), by contrast with descendants of LAXĀRE (OSp. *lexar*, Fr. *laisser*, It. *lasciare*) has sometimes been explained on the basis of a dialectal Latin form *DAXĀRE, whose D- would be due to interference from Oscan. A similar distribution of the meaning 'to arrive' associated with descendants of PLICĀRE (CL 'to fold'), such as Sp. *llegar*, by contrast with those Romance forms which retain the Latin sense (e.g. Fr. *plier*, It. *plegare*, as also Sp. semi-learned *plegar*), is also cited as a case of the dialectal nature of the Latin of Spain. However, it cannot be said that there is general agreement on the origin of any of the instances of putative Osco-Umbrian influence so far adduced.

1.2.4 Innovation

Despite the general characterization of Hispanic Latin as archaic and conservative, there are a number of features displayed by its descendants which reveal innovatory changes which were evidently limited to the Peninsula. Among these innovations can be counted the total merger of the Latin second and third verbal conjugations (see 3.7.6), so that infinitives like DĒBĒRE and VENDĔRE, originally distinct, became identical in type (Sp. *deber*, *vender*, Ptg. *dever*, *vender*), rather than remaining separate as they do in other varieties of Romance (e.g. Fr. *devoir*, *vendre*).

Some Hispanic innovations consist of new cases of word-formation, as in:

- CIBU 'food' → CIBĀRIA > *cibera* '(animal) feed, etc.', now only in rural use.
- CIBU 'food' → CIBĀTA > *cebada* OSp. 'feed', later 'barley'.
- AMĀRU 'bitter' → AMĀRELLU 'yellowish' > *amarillo* 'yellow'.
- ARGENTU 'silver' → ARGENTEU 'of silver' > OSp. *arienço* 'a (specific) coin, unit of weight'.
- CATĒNA 'chain' → CATĒNĀTU 'chained' > *candado* 'padlock' .

- CENTĒNI 'hundredfold' → CENTĒNU 'rye' > *centeno* 'id.'.
- COLUMNA 'column' → COLUMELLU 'canine (tooth)' > *colmillo* 'id.'.
- FŌRMO 'shape, mould' → FŌRMĀCEU 'mud-brick wall' > *hormazo* 'id.', now antiquated.
- PĀCĀRE 'to pacify' → ADPĀCĀRE 'to extinguish' > *apagar* 'id.'.

On other occasions the innovation consists of a change of meaning which is peculiar to the Latin of Spain and its descendants:

- CAPTĀRE 'to seize' > *catar* 'to look'.
- FRĀTRE GERMĀNU 'true brother (i.e. one who shares both parents)' > GERMĀNU 'brother' > *hermano* 'id'; thus also GERMĀNA > *hermana* 'sister'.

Other innovations of course include the borrowing of words from the pre-Roman languages of the Peninsula (see 4.2).

1.3 Conquest and Reconquest

1.3.1 The Visigoths

From the fifth to the early eighth century, Spain was controlled by a Visigothic monarchy and aristocracy. The Visigoths had forced an entry into the Roman Empire in the late fourth century and following their sack of Rome in 410 established (as *foederati*), a semi-autonomous kingdom in southwestern Gaul, with their capital at Toulouse. While remaining subjects of the Roman state, they expanded their territory to include much of the Peninsula, which, together with their lands north of the Pyrenees, became an independent kingdom on the collapse of Roman administration in the west (see map 1.2). Expulsion from most of Gaul by the Franks (early sixth century) was followed by the successful absorption (completed in AD 585) of the Swabian kingdom of the northwest (in modern terms, Galicia, northern Portugal, and the provinces of Asturias and Leon), and by the eventual expulsion (in the early seventh century) of the Byzantine forces who dominated parts of eastern and southern Spain on behalf of the Eastern Roman Emperor.

The Visigoths were partly romanized before their entry into the Peninsula and it is likely that from the first they spoke Latin, bilingually with their East Germanic vernacular. The latter never achieved the status of written language in Spain and Latin continued to be the language of culture and administration throughout the Visigothic period. The influence exercised by Visigothic upon the Latin of Spain was therefore small. Apart from a number of lexical loans (see 4.5), such influence is limited to a few morphological features:

- The introduction of a new noun-declension type in nominative -Ā, oblique -ĀNE (plur. -ĀNES), alongside the three types already existing in late spoken Latin (see 3.2.3). This pattern was mostly restricted to personal names of Germanic origin (e.g. OSp. *Froilán* < FROILANE, beside *Fruela* < FROILA,

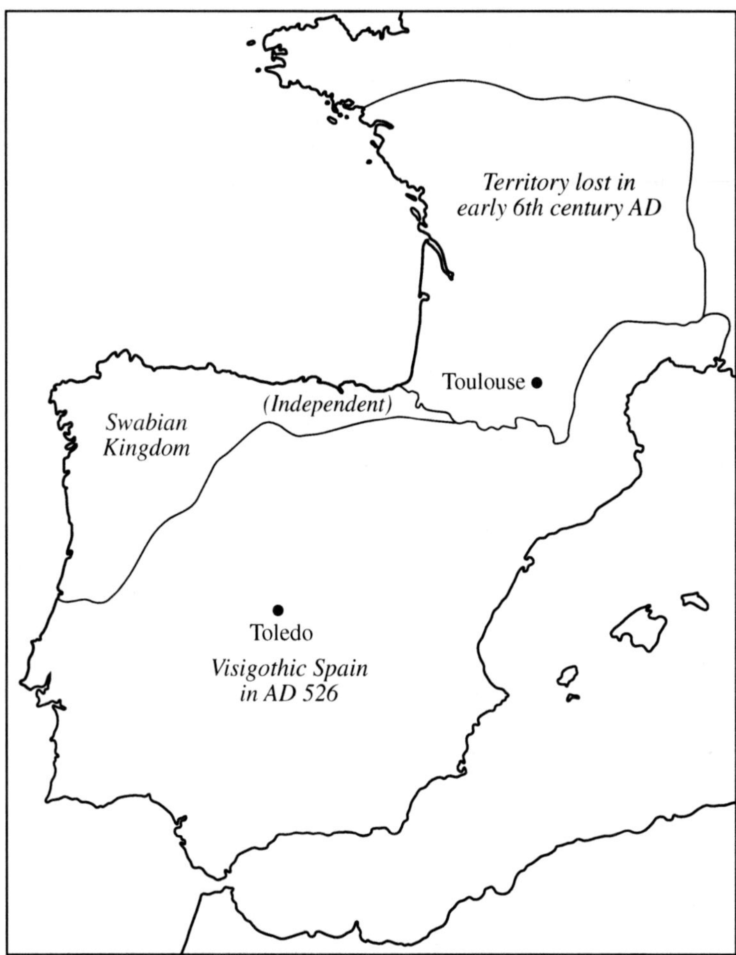

Map 1.2 The Visigothic kingdom in AD 476 and AD 526

both names applied to the same Visigothic monarch), but was occasionally applied to common nouns (usually personal, usually borrowed from Germanic). In one instance, Spanish shows descendants of both the nominative and oblique forms of this paradigm: *guardia* 'guard, policeman' < WARDJA 'guard(sman)', *guardián* 'guardian' < *WARDJĀNE 'id.'.

- The introduction of the suffix *engo* (< Gmc. -ING), for deriving adjectives from nouns. This suffix has always been of low productivity and is found in: *abadengo* 'belonging to an abbey', *realengo* 'belonging to the Crown', and, now substantivized, *abolengo* 'ancestry' (originally 'pertaining to one's ancestors').

- The possible introduction of the suffix *-ez, -oz,* etc., found in names which were once patronymic and are now surnames (e.g. *Rodríguez, Fernández, Muñoz*). The genitive of the latinized form of certain Germanic names in -IKS, e.g. RODERĪCĪ '(son) of Roderick', may explain certain patronymics (e.g. RODERĪCĪ > *Rodriz* > *Ruiz*). By comparison with the short form of the corresponding given name (e.g. *Ruy*), it was possible to extract an element *-z* with patronymic value, which could then be applied to other given names, including their 'full' forms: *Rodrigo* → *Rodríguez, Fernando* → *Fernández,* etc.

The ruling Visigothic group constituted a small fraction of the total population of the Peninsula, and despite their political supremacy, they sooner or later abandoned bilingualism and their speech became entirely assimilated to that of their subjects, who were not only numerically superior but, even in these 'Dark Ages', enjoyed a culture which was more prestigious than that of their rulers. Throughout this period, the large majority continued to speak Latin, no doubt with considerable and increasing variation between one locality and another.

It was probably this divorce between political power and cultural prestige which allowed centrifugal, linguistically diversifying, forces to gain the upper hand over centralizing and linguistically unifying forces. Despite the fact that the Visigoths eventually ruled the whole Peninsula, they presided over a period in which diatopic variation of speech was increased rather than diminished. However, there is one political event of this period which was to have great linguistic significance at a later date: the establishment of Toledo as the centre of government. For the first time in Peninsular history, the seat of political power was situated in the central meseta and, after the collapse of Visigothic Spain and the Moorish conquest of the early eighth century, Toledo therefore assumed great symbolic importance to the northern Christians, who to some extent saw their mission as the reestablishment of Christian Visigothic Spain. The fact that Toledo fell (in 1085) to Castilian reconquerors endowed Castilian speech with a prestige it might otherwise not have enjoyed, and can therefore be seen as an important factor in the rise of Castilian to national status (see 1.4).

1.3.2 Moors and Christians

The Islamic invasion of 711 had enormous linguistic consequences. It was not merely that it brought Hispanic Latin and its successors into contact with the language of a culture which was soon to be more developed and prestigious than that of Christian Europe, thereby creating the conditions for substantial lexical and semantic borrowing from Arabic (see 4.6, 5.1.5), for the modification of the syntax and phraseology of Hispano-Romance (see Galmés 1956; also Lapesa 1980: 156–7 for the Arabic origin of phrases like *que Dios guarde/que Dios mantenga, si Dios quiere, Dios le ampare, bendita sea la madre que te*

Map 1.3 Spain in the late eighth century AD

parió, etc.), and for occasional morphological borrowing (e.g. the suffix *-í*; see 4.14.2.1). The linguistic effects of the Moorish conquest were even more profound, since the dialectal map of Spain was entirely changed, and importance was given to varieties of Romance which, in the absence of this political upheaval, would have remained insignificant and peripheral. The reason is, of course, that the Moorish armies failed to conquer the entire Peninsula. Between 711 and 718 they established control over approximately three-quarters of its territory, but allowed the survival of Christian nuclei in the extreme north and northwest (see map 1.3). These were precisely the areas which had been remotest from standardizing influences during the Roman period and from such linguistic levelling processes as obtained during the period of Visigothic rule. It can therefore be argued that they were the areas of the Peninsula where speech was most distant from the 'norm' of eighth-century Hispano-Romance speech. This was no doubt particularly so in the case of Cantabria (modern Santander, northern Burgos and adjacent areas), the southern part of which is the area where Castilian has its origins and which was especially resistant to Roman and Visigothic rule and whose language in the eighth century is likely to have been particularly 'abnormal'. (It is recognized that there can have been no single accepted prestige-norm for speakers of eighth-century Hispano-Romance, and the term 'norm' here is a means of referring to those linguistic features which were common to most varieties of Hispano-Romance speech.)

The linguistic effects of the Christian Reconquest of the Peninsula are similarly great. Features of Hispano-Romance speech which had hitherto belonged to geographically peripheral and linguistically unusual varieties are extended southwards at the expense of those features which one can presume were previously the most prestigious and the most similar to those of the Romance spoken outside the Peninsula. And among these peripheral features of Hispano-Romance, it was those belonging to the most 'abnormal' variety, namely Castilian, which were to achieve the greatest territorial and cultural spread. At first typical only of the speech of the Burgos area of southern Cantabria, Castilian linguistic characteristics were carried south, southeast and southwest, in part by movement of population, as Castilians settled in reconquered territories, and in part by the adoption of Castilian features by those whose speech was originally different. The creation of the kingdom of Castile in 1035 no doubt sharpened awareness of the separate identity of Castilian speech and the capture of Toledo in 1085 (by Alfonso VI, king of both Castile and Leon) has already been noted as having considerable linguistic significance, by reason of the prestige that this success afforded to Castile and to Castilian speech (see map 1.4).

After what proved to be temporary setbacks at the hands of Almoravid and Almohad reformers of Islamic Spain in the late eleventh and twelfth centuries, the Castilian advance continued with the capture of the major cities of northern and western Andalusia (Córdoba 1236, Jaén 1246, Seville 1248, Cádiz 1250) and with control over the kingdom of Murcia (1244). By the mid-thirteenth century, then, Castile had expanded to comprise something over half of the Peninsular territory and Castilian speech was on the way to displacing its competitors, Arabic and Mozarabic, the latter term indicating those varieties of Hispano-Romance which had continued to be widely spoken in Islamic and ex-Islamic Spain. The contact between Castilian and Mozarabic produced some effects upon Castilian, largely restricted to borrowing of Mozarabic vocabulary (see 4.7), but perhaps including the development of the sibilant consonants in Andalusian (and, later, American) varieties of Castilian (see 2.6.3). However, it is likely that Mozarabic speech was assimilated to Castilian patterns (or was abandoned in favour of Castilian speech) during the thirteenth and fourteenth centuries. (For further discussion, see Penny 2000: 75–80.)

Between the mid thirteenth century and the end of the fifteenth, Islamic Spain consisted only of the mountainous southeastern parts of Andalusia, namely the kingdom of Granada. When this area was captured in 1492 by the Catholic Monarchs, Ferdinand and Isabella, it was largely resettled by speakers of Andalusian varieties of Castilian, so that in the course of six centuries Castilian

Map 1.4 Spain in AD 1150

had come to occupy a territory stretching from the Cantabrian coast to the Atlantic and the Mediterranean.

However, it should be made clear that Castilian speech characteristics were spread not simply to those central and southern Peninsular territories into which the kingdom of Castile expanded. At the same time as this southward development was taking place, people in neighbouring kingdoms were adopting Castilian manners of speech. In the case of Leon, the westward spread of Castilian features is firmly attested, in literary and non-literary writing, well before the definitive union of Castile and Leon in 1230. Unattested, but presumably no less real, was the northeasterly advance of Castilian at the expense of Basque. Similar encroachment of Castilian features upon Aragonese territory is observable in texts written in Saragossa in the fourteenth and fifteenth centuries, that is, before the union of the crowns of Castile and Aragon in 1479. At this stage, only Galicia and the Catalan-speaking areas (Catalonia, Valencia and the Balearics) remained, for the most part, outside the Castilian sphere of linguistic influence.

The reasons for this lateral spread and imitation of Castilian features lie in the political prestige of Castile, stemming from its increasingly predominant role in the Reconquest, and in the development of its literature (see 1.4), which had no comparable counterpart in the kingdoms of Leon and Aragon. The castilianization of these kingdoms was of course not rapid (although it was undoubtedly more swift among the educated than among the majority) and it is still incomplete today, in rural areas of Asturias, western Leon, northern Huesca, etc.

1.4 Standard Spanish

The creation of early standard Spanish is arguably the result of the work of one man, Alfonso X the Learned, king of Castile and Leon (1252–84). Writing by means of a spelling system which was able to specify vernacular pronunciation, by contrast with writing in Latin, goes back to the period following the reforms of the Council of Burgos in 1080 (see Wright 1982), and vernacular writing in the kingdom of Castile, both literary and non-literary, becomes ever more frequent in the late twelfth and early thirteenth centuries. However, until the period of Alfonso X, all writing can be seen to be dialectal, in the sense that the language used shows some features characteristic of the writer's region, rather than representing any supraregional variety. Thus, the late twelfth-century *Auto de los reyes magos* reveals features of the speech of Toledo (perhaps due to contact with Mozarabic) not shared with the rest of the kingdom, while the *Poema de mio Cid* displays a number of characteristics which locate its language in the east of Castile. Non-literary writing is no different in this respect; the *Fuero de Madrid*, which reached its final form in 1202, is recognizably from New Castile.

Such regional characteristics disappear, for the most part, in the later thirteenth century, as a result of the scholarly activities of the king and his collaborators. On the one hand, the use of Castilian as the vehicle of an enormous output of scientific, historiographical, legal, literary and other work, was bound to lend great prestige to the chosen medium, Castilian, by contrast with other varieties of Hispano-Romance, such as Leonese or Aragonese, which enjoyed little literary cultivation. On the other hand, the king's express concern over the 'correctness' of the language of his scholarly output is a witness to the creation of a standard form of Castilian. Certainly, as just stated, by the end of Alfonso's reign it is no longer possible to identify a specific regional flavour in the writing of Castilians. It is reasonable to assume that the new supraregional literary standard was based upon the speech of the upper classes of Toledo, a form of speech which, as we have seen, owed many of its features to varieties spoken in the Burgos area, which had become dominant in the speech of Toledo following the Reconquest of New Castile.

A further important aspect of Alfonso's activities was the consistent use of Castilian as the language of administration. Latin had been partly abandoned in the previous reign, but was now definitively superseded by Castilian, which had the culturally unifying advantage of being religiously neutral, by contrast with

Latin (or Arabic, or Hebrew). In Alfonso's reign, the entire business of the state was carried out in an increasingly standard form of Castilian and documents issuing from the royal chancery could stand as models of correctness in writing wherever they were read, copied or imitated.

The use of the Castilian vernacular as a medium of scientific, legal, administrative and other writing required the expansion of its expressive resources. The syntax of Castilian becomes considerably more complex and subtle during the Alfonsine period, and the vocabulary is enormously expanded, in part by borrowing from Latin and Arabic (see 4.3.4.6), in part by word-formation (see Penny 1987).

It should not be assumed, however, that the speech of Toledo, which we have seen forming the basis of the written standard, immediately provided the only spoken standard. Other cities were cultural rivals to Toledo, and the speech of their educated classes no doubt continued to pose a challenge to that of the central city. In particular Seville: at the time of its reconquest and for centuries thereafter, Seville was the largest and economically the most flourishing city of the kingdom. The speech of its educated classes must consequently have enjoyed great prestige in its region. This factor, together with the geographical remoteness of Seville from the central cities, was responsible for the establishment of a spoken norm which to some extent rivalled that of Toledo. This norm was characterized by a number of phonological features which sooner or later (but almost certainly by the sixteenth century) included *seseo* (see 2.6.3). Other features which contributed to the Sevillian 'norm' were *yeísmo* (see 2.6.6), preservation of the phoneme /h/ descended from Latin F- (which was eliminated from central Spanish in the sixteenth century under northern influences; see 2.5.6 and 2.6.4), weakening of syllable-final /s/ (see 2.6.7), and the weakening and merger of syllable-final /ɾ/ and /l/. At the morphosyntactical level, Sevillian Spanish was characterized by, among other features, etymological distinction of the pronouns *lo* and *le*, in contrast with central Spanish, which was *leísta* (see 3.5.1). Between these two varieties there were no doubt also considerable lexical differences, which are now difficult to reconstruct.

Therefore, at the time of the overseas expansion of Spanish, there were two main norms, that of Toledo (superseded in the 1560s by Madrid), rivalled by that of Seville (see Penny 2000:118–28). It cannot be claimed that they were of equal status, and in Spain the Madrid norm was to establish a firm priority during the Golden Age of Spanish literature. However, in areas outside the Peninsula to which Spanish was extended, the two norms continued in much more equal contention, as will be seen in the following section.

It is also during the Golden Age that Castilian becomes the main language of literature and of the educated in Galicia and the Catalan-speaking areas, giving rise to bilingualism in those parts of the Peninsula, a bilingualism which was intensified in the following centuries through the almost exclusive use of

Castilian as the medium of education. From the mid-nineteenth century onwards, however, and despite their suppression during the Franco era, Catalan (and to a lesser extent Galician) have regained the status of languages of literature and culture. From the sixteenth century, Basque has also acquired some literary and other written use, and now coexists bilingually with Castilian in Guipúzcoa, eastern Vizcaya, northern Navarre and the northern fringe of Álava.

1.5 Spanish overseas

In the fifteenth and sixteenth centuries, Spanish was carried outside the Peninsula to a number of other parts of the world, by soldiers, settlers, priests, colonial administrators, etc. The main areas to which Spanish was extended were the Canaries, America, the Mediterranean and the Balkans, and the Philippines.

1.5.1 The Canaries

The conquest of the Canary Islands and their incorporation in the crown of Castile was a fifteenth-century undertaking not completed until the reign of the Catholic Monarchs. The enterprise was launched and sustained from Andalusian ports and the participants were in all probability drawn from Andalusia; the clear evidence is that they were speakers of southern (i.e. Andalusian) Spanish and that the prestige norm by which they were influenced was that of Seville (see Penny 2000: 129–31). Thus Canaries Spanish is in all cases *seseante* (see 2.6.3); it retains the aspirate /h/ descended from F- (see 2.5.6, 2.6.4); at least in part of the relevant vocabulary and among many speakers, it suffers weakening of syllable-final /s/ (usually to [h]; see 2.6.7), and merger (among some speakers) of syllable-final /r/ and /l/, all features found to a greater or lesser extent in Andalusian and American Spanish.

The Canaries were an indispensable stepping-stone and staging-post on the route to and from America, in closer contact with the American colonies than was most of the Peninsula, and therefore sharing with American Spanish certain features which are absent, or largely absent, from Spain. Such features are often lexical (like the use of *guagua* 'bus'), but include other characteristics, such as the absence of contrast between second-person-plural informal and formal address (*ustedes* + third-plural verb is almost universal in Canarian Spanish, and is identical to the universal American usage and to that of parts of western Andalusia; see 3.5.1.1).

1.5.2 America

Columbus's route of discovery took him from southern Spain to the Canaries and thence across the Atlantic to the West Indies. Columbus's landings, on each of his four voyages to America, were in the Caribbean: the island of La Española (now the Dominican Republic and Haiti), Cuba, etc. He established small settlements in these islands and they became thereafter an essential staging-post for the conquest and settlement of the northern and southern continents. The conquest of Mexico by Cortés (1519–21) was launched from La Española, and eventually led to the acquisition by Spain of large parts of North America (now New Mexico, Texas, Arizona, California, as well as Mexico proper).

Following the discovery of the Pacific in 1513, the conquest of the Inca empire was carried out (1531–3) by Pizarro, who thereby extended the chain of communication from the Caribbean down the Pacific side of the Andes to Lima in Peru.

These routes of discovery and conquest then became the normal lines of communication between Spain and America and within America:

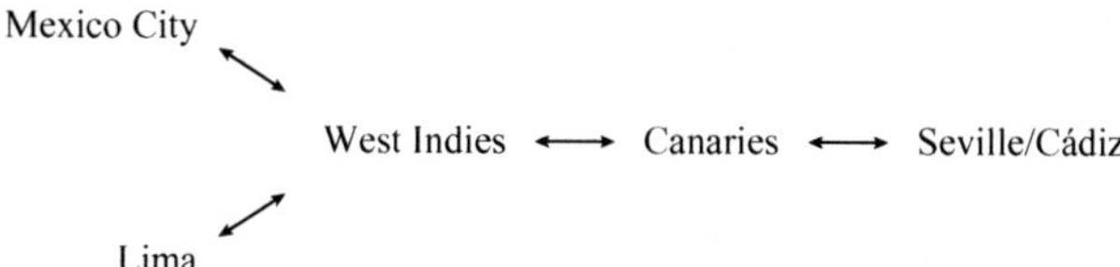

Mexico City and Lima became the main administrative and cultural centres of Spanish America. They were the seats of the king's representatives (the viceroys), the headquarters of the Church, and the places where the first universities in America were founded (already in the sixteenth century). From these centres, subsidiary lines of communication eventually came to feed the rest of Spanish America. But it should be noted that, except in the case of parts of the Caribbean, communication with Spain was for centuries effected only via Mexico and Lima. As a result, some areas (like Argentina/Paraguay/Uruguay, Central America, New Mexico) remained much more remote (geographically and culturally) than the territories connected by the main lines of communication. For example, until the nineteenth century, Buenos Aires was accessible only by an enormous overland journey down and across the southern continent (see map 1.5).

This pattern of conquest, settlement and communication, in addition to explaining the sources of most of the words which are borrowed by Spanish from Amerindian languages (that is, explaining why they are borrowed from the languages of the Caribbean, the Mexican plateau and the central Andes; see 4.9), also helps to account for the relative influence of the Seville norm and the Toledo/Madrid norm in the speech of different parts of America. Thus, the speech of highland Mexico and of Peru/Bolivia has remained closer to the central Peninsular standard, while, in areas remoter from the main cultural centres of colonial America, southern Peninsular features have been

Map 1.5 Spanish territories in the Americas 1784

more successful in establishing themselves. Such southern features have more easily spread through society in those areas, such as Argentina and Central America, which were geographically remote, in terms of sixteenth- and seventeenth-century communications, from the American centres which were responsible for radiating the central Peninsular norm (namely, Mexico City and Lima).

These similarities and dissimilarities from central Peninsular Spanish have sometimes been explained by reference to physical geography and choice of location by early settlers; it has been claimed that settlers from the Castilian meseta preferred the highland areas of America (the Mexican plateau, the Andean area), while lowland and coastal areas of America were preferred by Spanish settlers from lowland and coastal areas of Spain, principally including Andalusia. Since there is absolutely no evidence of the exercise of such preferences by settlers of the New World, it is preferable to explain the broad differences between varieties of American Spanish in the way here expounded, in terms of proximity or distance from the main centres of colonial government and the cultural influence (including linguistic influence) they exercised. In these centres, speakers from the centre of Spain would be sufficiently numerous and prestigious to set the linguistic tone for such cities and for the areas in easiest communication with them. It is in this context that one can explain the distribution of certain key features in American Spanish (for details of the distribution of phonetic features, see Canfield 1981, Lipski 1994, Penny 2000: 137–73). For example:

- Retention of syllable-final /s/ is typical of those areas of America which were under the greatest central Peninsular influence, namely Mexico (except the far south), Peru, Bolivia and Andean Ecuador. Most other areas show weakening and/or loss of the phoneme under these conditions, as in southern Peninsular and Canarian Spanish (see 2.6.7).
- Use of the pronoun *tú* as the singular informal mode of address, as in Spain, is found in a somewhat broader but essentially similar distribution: in Mexico and the southwestern United States, in most of Bolivia and Peru, but on this occasion including the Caribbean islands and the major part of Venezuela. Such *tuteo* contrasts with the use of *vos* (see 3.5.1.1), which occurs in those regions which were remote from the main lines of communication, either in competition with *tuteo* (as in Chile, Ecuador, Colombia, etc.), or as the dominant form of address (as in Argentina, Uruguay, Paraguay and most of Central America up to southern Mexico).

On the other hand, there are many features of American Spanish which demonstrate that southern Peninsular tendencies have successfully gained the upper hand in all or most of Spanish America. Such features include *seseo* (see 2.6.3), *yeísmo* (see 2.6.6), use of /h/ where standard Peninsular Spanish has /x/ (see 2.6.3–4), and *loísmo* (see 3.5.1). The result is the predominantly 'Andalusian' character of most transatlantic Spanish, a character which was traditionally 'explained' by the assumption that the majority of American settlers came from Andalusia. However, this notion was rejected by Henríquez Ureña (1932), on the basis that many colonists came from the north of Spain (they were Galicians, Basques, etc.) and that a majority were non-Andalusian. He therefore came to the conclusion that the similarities between American and Andalusian Spanish were due to separate but parallel developments on each side of the Atlantic, favouring a now discredited climatological explanation.

However, more recent and more detailed examination of the regional origins of American settlers, by Boyd-Bowman (1956, 1964), has led to broad acceptance of an amended version of the earlier theory. Boyd-Bowman concludes that the similarity between Andalusian and American Spanish is due to inheritance of Andalusian (and specifically Sevillian) speech characteristics and adduces the following facts in support of his contention. There was a large majority of Andalusians among the early settlers of the West Indies, 78 per cent in the first two decades of settlement, when colonies were limited to the Caribbean. Subsequent waves of settlers usually spent at least some time in the West Indies before passing on to new areas of settlement. And significantly, most of the Andalusians were from Seville, with a very high proportion of Andalusian women, who were likely to pass on their Andalusian speech-patterns to the following generation.

Another factor which is relevant here is the fact that groups of colonists from all over Spain gathered in Seville before their departure and were often kept there for months waiting for a ship. It is understandable that such emigrants, with their diverse linguistic backgrounds, should have gravitated towards a common linguistic denominator, most conveniently furnished by the popular speech of Seville. This process of dialectal adjustment is now well understood and it can now be said that such processes are normal, even inevitable (see Trudgill 1986). Even before setting out, then, prospective settlers from the centre and north of Spain had probably already acquired at least some of the characteristic features of southern speech. Similarly important is the fact that the sailors on the ships that made the Atlantic crossings were almost exclusively Andalusians. Owing to their prestige as experienced men who had travelled back and forth to America, their speech may well have influenced that of the emigrants who travelled with them.

Nor should it be forgotten that almost all contact between Spain and its American colonies was channelled through Seville (or its dependent port of Cádiz), which for centuries enjoyed a powerful trade monopoly with Spain's American empire. This dominant position of Seville in all dealings with America no doubt favoured the continuing spread of Andalusian linguistic features to America, while the material wealth that this monopoly brought would have served to enhance further the prestige of the city and its speech. Only in the viceregal centres of Mexico and Lima were there sufficient concentrations of speakers of central and northern varieties of Spanish to challenge this prestige.

1.5.3 The Mediterranean and the Balkans

At the same time as the beginning of the settlement of America, and the completion of the Reconquest of the Peninsula upon the fall of Granada, came the expulsion of the Jews of Spain, in 1492. Faced with conversion to Catholicism or expatriation, many thousands chose to leave Spain. Some settled at first in Portugal, until their later expulsion from the neighbouring country, some in the cities of north Africa (Fez, Algiers, Cairo, etc.), some in Italy, but the majority in the cities of the Ottoman Empire, which by the early sixteenth century included not only Syria and Asia Minor but what are now the Balkan states of Greece, Albania, Yugoslavia, Bulgaria and much of Romania. In Constantinople, Salonika, Sofia, Bucharest, Monastir, etc., the Spanish or Sephardic Jews established flourishing communities, which were later joined by Jews expelled from Portugal and those who found their way to the east via Italy. Within these communities, regional origins within the Peninsula (and probably also the associated dialectal differences) were at first distinguished; there were separate synagogues for those originally from Aragon, Castile, Portugal, Barcelona, Lisbon, Córdoba, etc. Merger of regional origins was no doubt accompanied by dialectal mixing, with the result that although the resulting Judeo-Spanish speech (also called 'Ladino', or 'Judezmo', or simply 'Espaniol') is predominantly of Castilian tradition, it shows a considerable admixture of features from other regions of the Peninsula, especially western or specifically Portuguese features, while among its Castilian features we find a number which are specifically southern or Andalusian, as well as features preserved with little change from general fifteenth-century Castilian.

Among the non-Castilian features of Judeo-Spanish can be cited the frequent absence of diphthong corresponding to Latin Ĕ and Ŏ (*quero* (= Sp. *quiero* 'I wish'), *preto* (= Sp. *prieto* 'black'), *rogo* (= Sp. *ruego* 'I beg')), in keeping with the non-diphthongization of Galician-Portuguese, although in other instances the diphthongs /ie/, /ue/ are found, and may even be analogically extended to unstressed syllables (e.g. *puedo* → *pueder*, standard *poder* 'to be able'; see 3.7.8.1.4.1 for parallel cases in the standard). In the Judeo-Spanish of the Balkans, the system of final vowels is /i/ – /a/ – /u/, similar to that of Portuguese and like many varieties of Leonese, and unlike Castilian /e/ – /a/ – /o/ (e.g. *vedri* (= Sp. *verde* 'green'), *fijus* (= Sp. *hijos* 'sons')). Again like Galician-Portuguese and most of Leonese (but also like Aragonese and Catalan), Balkan Judeo-Spanish often preserves Latin F- as /f/ (e.g. *fazer* 'to do', *furmiga* 'ant', *fambri* 'hunger' (= Sp. *hacer, hormiga, hambre*)), although eastern varieties of Judeo-Spanish (e.g. in Istanbul) most frequently show /h/ or no consonant (e.g. *hetcho*~*etcho* (= Sp. *hecho* 'done')). Again as in Galician-Portuguese and Leonese, Latin -MB- is widely retained as /mb/ (e.g. *palombika* (= Sp. *paloma* 'pigeon, dove')). Like Portuguese, syllable-final /s/ is palatalized (> /ʃ/), although in Judeo-Spanish the change only occurs before /k/ (e.g. /móʃka/ 'fly', /eʃkóla/ 'school' (= Sp. *mosca, escuela*)).

All the data so far considered argue for a substantial western Hispanic (and specifically Portuguese) input into the dialectal mixture which in the sixteenth

Table 1.1 *Sibilant development in Portuguese and Judeo-Spanish*

medieval		*modern*	
prepalatal	/ʃ/ /ʒ/	/ʃ/ /ʒ/	prepalatal
apico-alveolar	/s/ /z/		
		/s/ /z/	dento-alveolar
dento-alveolar	/t^s/ /d^z/		

century produced Judeo-Spanish. The Portuguese flavour of Judeo-Spanish is further emphasized by the outcome in these varieties of the medieval sibilants (see 2.6.2–3). The medieval Portuguese sibilant system was identical to that of Castilian, but changed less, producing a system which is identical to that of Judeo-Spanish, while the fundamental shifts of the Castilian system produce an outcome quite foreign to Judeo-Spanish. The Portuguese and Judeo-Spanish development can be summarized as in table 1.1, showing merger of apico-alveolar fricatives and dento-alveolar affricates into dento-alveolar fricatives (i.e. *seseo*), but preserving the contrast between voiceless and voiced phonemes.

Examples of these developments in Judeo-Spanish, in the order of the medieval phonemes as listed, include: OSp. *dixo, ojo, passo, casa, cinco, dezir* > JSp. /diʃo/ 'he said', /óʒo/ 'eye', /páso/ 'step', /káza/ 'house', /sinko/ 'five', /dezir/ 'to say'. However, it should be noted that the incidence of the phonemes concerned in Judeo-Spanish is generally the same as in Castilian (e.g. OCULU > JSp. /óʒo/ 'eye', by contrast with Ptg. *olho* 'id.'

A further case of agreement with Portuguese is the contrast made in some varieties of Judeo-Spanish between *b* and *v*, sometimes in the form /b/:/β/ as in north-central Portugal, sometimes in the form /b/:/v/ as in the standard. However, the argument for Portuguese phonological input into Judeo-Spanish is less strong in these cases, since sixteenth-century southern Castilian still showed the contrast /b/:/β/ (see 2.6.1), as do southern and Balearic varieties of Catalan.

In some respects, the phonology of Judeo-Spanish concurs with southern varieties of Castilian. The main instance of this agreement is the merger of /ʎ/ and /ǰ/ (see 2.6.6). Such *yeísmo is* typical of most Andalusian and Canaries speech and of much American and southern Peninsular speech, and is universal in Judeo-Spanish (e.g. *sevoya* 'onion', *fayar* 'to find' (= *cebolla, hallar*)). The resulting phoneme /ǰ/ is most frequently lost when adjacent to a front vowel: *ea* 'she', *amarío* 'yellow', *gaína* 'hen', *aí* 'there' (= *ella, amarillo, gallina, allí*)).

In some of its features, however, Judeo-Spanish can be regarded as archaic, preserving characteristics of fifteenth-century Spanish which have elsewhere disappeared. Because Judeo-Spanish was entirely cut off from contact with the Peninsula after the early sixteenth century, changes which have since then affected other varieties of Spanish have been unable to penetrate the language of the Sephardic Jews. This archaic character is clearly visible in vocabulary (see Zamora Vicente 1967: 361–77, Sala 1979), where Judeo-Spanish maintains in use words which were current in Spain in the Middle Ages, but which have since then become obsolete or restricted to regional use. All new vocabulary (except that originating in word-formation) is due to borrowing from a variety of other sources, Italian, French, Turkish, Greek, etc. However, archaism is not restricted to vocabulary but can also be seen, for instance, in the morpho-syntax of Judeo-Spanish. The second-person-plural verb forms show the variation found in fifteenth-century Spanish (see 3.7.3.1–3), but with palatalization of the final /s/ in the shorter forms: /kantáʃ/~/kantáis/, /keréʃ/~/keréis/. With the exception of this palatal development, the shorter forms are therefore identical to those used in most American areas of *voseo* (see 3.5.1.1). However, unlike all other forms of Spanish, the innovation *vuestra merced* (whence modern *usted*) is unknown in Judeo-Spanish, which contrasts informal *tú* (sing.), *vos* (plur.) with formal *el, e(y)a, e(y)os, -as* (see Malinowski 1983).

Despite its five hundred years' survival, Judeo-Spanish does not have a rosy future. The rise of nationalism in the Balkan states from the nineteenth century (together with the concomitant pressure towards language uniformity), followed by decimation of many Sephardic communities during the Second World War, has brought about a dramatic decline in the use of Judeo-Spanish. It continues to be used to some extent in the Balkan and Turkish cities where it has been spoken for centuries, but perhaps now survives best in Israel, as a result of further migration. There, however, it belongs essentially to the older generation, as is also the case in New York, the other principal destination of Sephardic Jews emigrating from erstwhile Turkish areas. (For more detailed discussion of the development and features of Judeo-Spanish, see Penny 2000: 174–93.)

1.5.4 The Philippines

Discovered by Europeans in 1521 and incorporated in the Spanish Empire later in the sixteenth century, the Philippine islands were administered via Mexico until Mexican independence in the early nineteenth century, and remained a Spanish possession until the war with the United States in 1898. By contrast with the Canaries and America, the Philippines were only superficially hispanized; Spanish became the language only of the ruling class, of civil and judicial administration, and of culture. By the time Spanish rule came to an end, Spanish was the language of approximately 10 per cent of the population, and although it has become an official language of the country (together with English and Tagalog), its use probably declined in the twentieth century (see Whinnom 1954).

Long contact between Spanish and local languages has given rise to a series of pidgins and creoles, the latter of which are the language of a substantial proportion of the Philippine population (see Quilis 1980, Whinnom 1956).

It is unsurprising, given the fact that communication between Spain and the Philippines was for centuries mediated by Mexico, that Philippine Spanish is similar in its broad lines to American Spanish (see 1.5.2), not only in vocabulary but in pronunciation and grammar. Although some speakers distinguish /s/ and /θ/ (as in central and northern Spain), and /ʎ/ and /ǰ/ (as some speakers do in the northern half of the Peninsula), Philippines Spanish is more generally characterized by *seseo* (see 2.6.3) and *yeísmo* (see 2.6.6). It also reveals retention of /h/ (from Latin F-), uses the same phoneme to correspond to standard Peninsular /x/ (see 2.5.6, 2.6.2–4), and shows some evidence of merger of syllable-final /ɾ/ and /1/. The atonic pronoun system is also similar to American Spanish (and to Canarian and Andalusian Spanish) in its preservation of *loísmo* (see 3.5.1.4). A local phonological development, under the influence of Tagalog, which lacks /f/, is the replacement of Spanish /f/ by /p/ (e.g. *Pilipinas* 'Philippines', *supri* 'to suffer').

1.6 'Castilian' and 'Spanish'

The terms *castellano* and *español* are now synonymous when they refer to the national language of modern Spain and of nineteen American republics. In this sense, their English equivalents, *Castilian* and *Spanish*, will be used interchangeably in this book. However, in other contexts the two terms are not synonymous, and some discussion of their meaning is called for. Much has been previously written on this topic (e.g. Alonso 1943, Alvar 1978) and remarks will therefore be kept to a minimum.

The language whose history is traced in this book is referred to in the Middle Ages as *castellano* or *romance castellano*, a term which at the written level can be contrasted with Latin, and at the written and spoken level with other varieties of Hispano-Romance (Portuguese, Aragonese, etc.), or, increasingly, with extra-Peninsular Romance (principally French and Italian). At this stage the term *español* (earlier *españón)* is rarely used of language; it is of course related to *España*, which in the early centuries of the Reconquest refers to Muslim Spain, then to the Peninsula as a whole (under the influence of Lat. HISPANIA?), and finally, after the union of the crowns of Aragon/Catalonia and Castile/Leon/Galicia, to the new nation-state.

It is in the sixteenth century that the term *español* is applied to the language of culture of Spain, and therefore becomes equivalent in this sense to *castellano.* The two terms have been used almost interchangeably since then, although political considerations have often led to preference for the older term (as in the current Spanish constitution and as in the usage of many American countries), in order to avoid the implication (sometimes seen as present in the term *español*) that the language concerned is the only language of the Spanish state or that the Spanish state has cultural hegemony over those, living in other states, who speak the same language.

There is, however, a further use of the term *castellano* (and of Eng. *Castilian)*, which may give rise to misunderstanding. This is the use of the term to mean 'the speech (or dialect(s)) of Castile', a sense in which *castellano* is opposed to *leonés, gallego, aragonés, catalán*, etc., but which naturally refers to a different portion of the Peninsula at different times in history. In the earliest period (the ninth century) at which the name *Castile* occurs (as *Castella,* then *Castiella*) it refers to a very small area at the eastern extremity of the kingdom of Oviedo, which then comes to include Burgos (884). Only in the tenth century does Castile expand as far as the Duero (912) and the Guadarrama mountains (*c.* 950). Even this territory is less extensive than what is now called *Old Castile* (*Castilla la Vieja*), since areas such as that which now comprise the province of Palencia fell outside Castile until the eleventh century. After the conquest of the kingdom of Toledo from the Moors in the late eleventh century, it becomes necessary to distinguish the newly acquired territory south of the Guadarrama (*New Castile*) from that to its north (*Old Castile*), and the maximum extent of *Castile* is achieved at the end of the twelfth century, when the Reconquest reaches the Sierra Morena. Beyond that, the term *Castile* did not apply; the territory to the south was, and is, *Andalusia.* In its more limited sense, then, *Castilian* can nevertheless refer, after 1200, to a considerable portion of the Peninsula.

1.7 Spanish in the present day

Spanish has today become a world language with more than 350 million speakers who are concentrated in Spain and the Americas, but who are also to be found in Africa and Asia. Approximate numbers of native speakers are shown in table 1.2.

Not all of these speakers have Spanish as their first language, although a very large majority does. Some speakers in Spain, although native speakers, use it bilingually with another language, which is dominant. Perhaps four million speakers of Spanish (in Catalonia, Valencia and the Balearic Islands) have Catalan as their dominant language, with possibly two million speakers in

Table 1.2 *Numbers of native speakers of Spanish*

Spain	39.5m
Equatorial Guinea	0.3m
Cuba	11.0m
Dominican Republic	7.3m
Puerto Rico	4.1m
Mexico	85.0m
Guatemala	10.0m
El Salvador	5.4m
Honduras	5.5m
Nicaragua	4.0m
Costa Rica	3.1m
Panama	2.5m
Colombia	35.8m
Venezuela	20.0m
Ecuador	10.0m
Peru	22.8m
Bolivia	6.9m
Paraguay	4.5m
Uruguay	3.2m
Argentina	33.0m
Chile	13.6m
US	25.5m
Philippines	2.0m
Total	355m

Galicia for whom Spanish is their second language. Likewise, an unknown proportion of the approximately 750,000 speakers of Basque have that language as their dominant one (see map 1.6).

In the Americas, several million speakers of native American languages use Spanish as a second language, in some cases in a genuinely native way and in others as a language learned in adulthood. The very large number of Spanish speakers in the United States (at more than 25 million, the US is the fifth largest Spanish-speaking country in the world) has arisen in part through the survival (principally in the southwest) of communities which were once part of Mexico, but mostly through immigration. Although immigrant communities are to be found in many parts of the US, the highest concentrations of Spanish-speakers are to be found in New York (mostly from Puerto Rico), Florida (mostly from Cuba) and the southwest (from Mexico and other Spanish-American countries).

Map 1.6 Present-day autonomous regions of Spain

In Africa, apart from north African cities such as Ceuta and Melilla (part of metropolitan Spain) or Tetuán and Tangier (Morocco), Spanish is spoken by part of the population of Equatorial Guinea. Spanish is the language of education and the press, and is the only common language in an otherwise linguistically diverse country. However, those who speak Spanish use it as a second language, often acquired in adulthood and therefore not always in a fully native manner.

2 Phonology

This chapter presupposes some knowledge of phonological theory, in particular of the concepts of the phoneme, the allophone, complementary distribution and neutralization. Useful discussion of these matters can be found in Lyons (1968: ch.3), and, with reference to Spanish, Alarcos (1965), Dalbor (1980), Macpherson (1975) and Quilis and Fernández (1969).

2.1 Phonological change

Phonological change is motivated in a number of ways, although scholars are not in agreement on the number or relative importance of the factors which provoke such change. Among the main types of phonological change are the following:

2.1.1 Conditioned change

Conditioned change is caused (initially, usually at the allophonic level) by a neighbouring phoneme or phonemes in the spoken chain. Such change is in most cases motivated by the unconscious need to save articulatory energy and may take a number of forms:

2.1.1.1 Assimilation

Assimilation is said to occur when a phoneme is modified in one or more of its features in such a way that the phoneme becomes more similar to a neighbouring phoneme. The most frequent case is that of **anticipatory** (or 'regressive') assimilation, in which the modified phoneme precedes the modifying unit, as in the case of Latin /k/ (see also 2.5.2.2). Lat. /k/, until about the first century AD, appears to have had only velar articulation ([k]), but thereafter, in the spoken Latin of most areas, the allophones of /k/ used before front (i.e. palatal) vowels themselves became attracted into the palatal area (becoming at first [tʃ], later further fronted to [t^{s}], etc., in some areas). Thus,

CĪNQUE (CL QUĪNQUE) ['kiŋkwe] > ['tˢiŋkwe]
CISTA ['kesta] > ['tˢesta]
CERVUS ['kɛrβos] > ['tˢɛrβos]

(ultimately appearing in Spanish as *cinco*, *cesta*, *ciervo)*, while, in cases where Lat. /k/ was followed by a non-front vowel, it remained unmodified and appears in Spanish as /k/:

CAPANNA > *cabaña*
CORŌNA > *corona*
CURRERE > *correr*

Assimilation less frequently results in modification of allophones under the influence of a preceding phoneme (this is termed **progressive** assimilation or assimilation 'by lag'). Thus, in cases where Latin presents the sequence /mb/, the second consonant is modified, in some areas, from non-nasal to nasal, producing /mm/ (later simplified to /m/, see 2.5.3.2.3):

PALUMBA > Sp. *paloma*
LUMBU > *lomo*

Thirdly, assimilation may be **mutual**; two adjacent phonemes each change, in one or more of their features, and merge in a pronunciation which is physiologically intermediate between the two original phonemes. Thus, the Latin diphthong /au/, in which the low vowel /a/ is followed by the (high) labiovelar glide, is resolved in many Romance languages (including Spanish) as /o/, a single phoneme whose aperture lies between that of the two original phonemes, e.g.

CAUSA > *cosa*
AUDĪRE > *oír*
TAURUS > *toro*

2.1.1.2 Dissimilation

Dissimilation springs from the difficulty of coordinating the articulatory movements required in the repetition, within a word or phrase, of a given phoneme. It arises especially when other phonemes intervene between the occurrences of the phoneme in question and leads (in one of the occurrences) either to **replacement** by a related phoneme or to **elimination**. Cases of vowel dissimilation can be seen in

ROTUNDU > *ROTONDO > *redondo* (replacement of back vowel by front vowel)
AUGUSTU > *agosto* (elimination of first occurrence)

and of consonant dissimilation in

*RŌBORE > *roble* (replacement)
ARATRU > *arado* (elimination of second occurrence)

2.1.1.3 Epenthesis

Epenthesis, the addition of a phoneme to a word, normally occurs in order to aid the transition from a preceding to a following phoneme. Thus the appearance of /b/ or /d/ in the following examples (where syncope first eliminates an intertonic vowel; see 2.4.3.3) is due to a need to facilitate the articulatory movement between the preceding nasal and the following /ɾ/:

HUMERU > *hombro*
INGENERĀRE > *engendrar*

2.1.1.4 Metathesis

Metathesis is less obviously energy-saving. It consists in the re-ordering of phonemes in the utterance; in some cases, at least, such re-ordering may be energy-saving. Cases of metathesis may involve the movement of a single phoneme:

PRAESĒPE > *pesebre*
CREPĀRE > *quebrar*

or the interchange of two phonemes:

early OSp. *parabla* > *palabra*
early OSp. *periglo* > *peligro*
GENERU > *yerno*

2.1.2 *Isolative change*

Isolative change is the term used to refer to cases in which a phoneme is modified, without apparent influence of environmental factors, in all or most of its occurrences. For example, Lat. /w/ (spelt v) is regularly modified in such a way that it appears in OSp. as /β/ (still spelt *v*):

VĪTA > *vida*
early Lat. COVA > *cueva*

The origins of isolative change are probably many: generalization of conditioned variants to all environments, influence from another language or dialect, etc.

It will be noted that individual changes of the types so far discussed do not, by themselves, create additional phonemes or otherwise alter the phonological structure of the language concerned. For structural changes, see the following section.

2.1.3 *Changes affecting the phonemic system*

Phonemes may be added to the system of a given language through the process of **split**, while the number of phonemes may be reduced through **merger**.

2.1.3.1 Split

Split requires two changes for its accomplishment. It is not common in the history of Spanish, but may arguably be seen in the following case. OSp. /h/ (spelt *f*) probably came to have, for reasons of assimilation, the following allophonic variation (see 2.5.6):

the glottal aspirate [h] was used before full vowels ([haˈβlaɾ], [ˈhondo], *fablar*, *fondo*)

the voiceless labiovelar fricative [ʍ] was used before the glide [w] ([ˈʍweɾte], [ˈʍwente], *fuerte*, *fuente*)

(There may well have been a third allophone [ɸ], used before consonants, which I shall ignore here; see 2.5.6.)

In some varieties of Spanish, [ʍ] > [f], perhaps spontaneously, perhaps under foreign (French?) influence, but so long as the conditioning factor (the following sound) remained stable, the unity of the phoneme /h/ was unaffected.

However, at a certain stage in later Old Spanish, the introduction of borrowings from neighbouring languages and from Latin created the possibility in Spanish of the sequence [f] + full vowel:

Lat. FŌRMA was borrowed as [ˈfoɾma]

Occ. *faisan* was borrowed as [fai̯ˈsan]

From this point on, both [f] and [h] could occur in the same environment (i.e. before full vowels) and could therefore serve to distinguish the meanings of separate words, whereupon the phonemic split was complete:

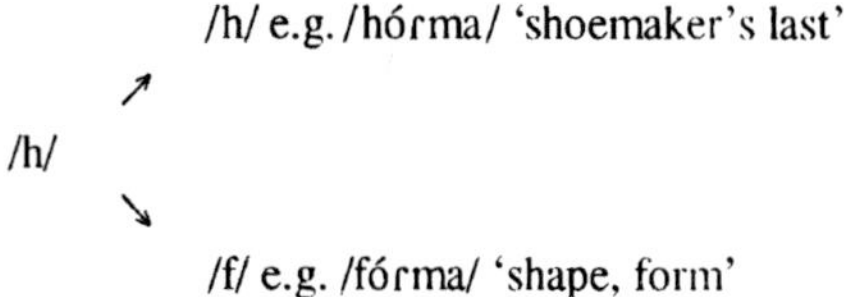

The ultimate loss of /h/ in most varieties of Spanish (including the standard) does not affect the substance of the split examined here.

2.1.3.2 Merger

Merger is more common in the history of Spanish and consists of increasing neutralization of originally distinct phonemes (for which see Alarcos 1965: 97–8, 18–5), until there are no phonetic environments in which the two units remain distinct. At this stage, the two have fully merged and are henceforth a single phoneme. Thus, in the case of OSp. /b/ (spelt *b*) and /β/ (spelt *v*), spelling evidence suggests that the two phonemes were neutralized when they occurred in consonant clusters; the spellings *alba* and *alva* (< ALBA) alternate, as do *enviar* and *embiar* (<INVIĀRE), with apparent freedom. Similarly, in

word-initial position after a nasal or pause, neutralization of /b/ and /β/ is also likely in OSp.; thus, in cases like the following,

lo han báxado *báxalo*
lo han vendido *véndelo*

it was probably true that realization of the phonemes /b/ and /β/ was uniformly [b]. Increasingly frequent neutralization in word-initial position was followed, in the fifteenth and sixteenth centuries, by neutralization of the two phonemes in intervocalic position; this is revealed in Golden Age verse, which increasingly allowed, say, *grave* to rhyme with, say, *sabe*. At this stage, the two original phonemes are no longer distinguished in any environment and the merger is therefore complete (see 2.6.1):

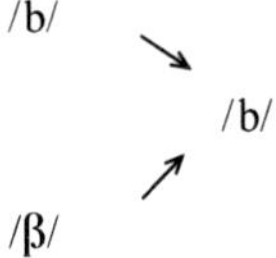

Further discussion of the reasons for phonetic and phonological change can be found in Bynon (1977) and Samuels (1972).

2.1.4 Change of incidence of phonemes

The particular phonemes which occur in a given word may be replaced, at any historical moment, by other phonemes. One motive for such change is popular etymology (see 5.2.3), but the main reason for this kind of phonemic replacement is **analogy**. A broad definition of analogy is 'the process by which related words become more alike in form', where 'related' can refer to relatedness either of meaning or of function. Analogical change of form motivated by relatedness of function will be of particular concern when morphological change is considered (see 3.1.1), and here we shall exemplify analogy motivated by similarity of meaning. The meaning relationships involved are many and include 'complementarity' and 'antonymy'. A well-known case of analogical change inspired by complementarity of meaning is that of Lat. SOCRUS 'mother-in-law' and NURUS 'daughter-in-law'; leaving aside the change of ending (for which see 3.2.2.2.1), these two words might be expected to give *suegra* and *nora (for tonic /o/ < Ŭ see 2.2.2.6); however, the outcome of the second word was *nuera*, where tonic /ue/ is due to analogy with the corresponding segment of *suegra*. Opposite meaning may also induce change of form; thus DEXTRU 'right' (whence OSp. *diestro* 'id.') has influenced SINISTRU 'left' to produce an Old Spanish form with /ie/ (*siniestro* 'id.'), when, in the absence of analogy, a form with /e/ is predicted (see 2.4.2.6).

2.2 Transmission

It is convenient at this point to introduce discussion of the difference between **popular**, **learned** and **semi-learned** words.

2.2.1 Popular words

Popular words are those which, in a given language, have a continuous oral history. In the case of Spanish, the term means that the word concerned has been transmitted from spoken Latin, generation by generation, by word of mouth, to modern Spanish (or until the word dropped out of use), undergoing in the process all the phonological and morphological changes which are characteristic of the development of Spanish. This book is largely concerned with the history of such popular words, but special reference will be made from time to time to words which have been transmitted to Spanish in other ways. The following are examples of popular transmission:

FABULĀRĪ > *hablar* 'to speak' (Note treatment of F- (2.5.6) and loss of pretonic vowel (2.4.3.3))

REGULA > *reja* 'ploughshare' (Note loss of post-tonic vowel (2.4.3.3) and /gl/ > /x/ (2.5.2.4))

2.2.2 Learned words

Learned words are ones which have been borrowed by Spanish from Latin (Classical or Medieval), through the medium of writing. Such borrowings were already frequent in the Middle Ages and have taken place at all times since then. The words concerned do not undergo the changes typical of popular words, but merely suffer minor modification of their endings in order to fit them to the morphological patterns of Spanish. Thus, *fábula* 'fable' (a borrowing of Lat. FABULA) reveals its learned nature by the retention of post-tonic /u/ (see 2.4.3.3) and by the appearance of /f/ (see 2.5.6). Likewise *regular* (Lat. REGULĀRIS) 'regular, poor, etc.' is best described as learned, because of its retention of pretonic Ŭ as /u/ and the consequent failure of /gl/ to evolve to /x/ (see 2.5.2.4). It should be noted that the term *learned*, as defined here, does not refer to the meaning or register of a word so described, but solely to the manner of its transmission from Latin to Spanish. Despite this, it is observable that many learned words have a sense that has remained fairly close to that of their Latin etyma, and are marked by having relatively high register (that is, they typically belong to a literary or elevated portion of the Spanish vocabulary).

2.2.3 Semi-learned words

Much dispute has taken place over the precise definition to be given to the term **semi-learned** (see, in particular, Wright 1976, Clavería Nadal 1991: 14–18).

The main definition adopted here is that of words which, although orally inherited (like popular words) from spoken Latin, have been remodelled, usually during the medieval period, under the influence of Latin, as read aloud in the church, the law-courts, etc. Because of their oral transmission, they undergo some (but, by definition, not all) of the changes typical of popular words; however, in other features, semi-learned words are unevolved. Thus:

- *Cruz* 'cross' (< CRUCE), despite showing the popular treatment of C^{e,i} (see 2.5.2.3), reveals its semi-learned status in its tonic /u/; in fully popular words, Lat. Ŭ appears in Sp. as /o/ (see 2.4.2).
- *Infierno* 'hell' (< INFERNU), although it shows the diphthongization of tonic Ĕ > /ie/ typical of orally transmitted words (2.4.2.2), nevertheless combines this popular feature with the consonantal group /nf/, which only appears in learned words or those influenced by the phonology of Latin as heard in church. In fully popular words, Latin -NF- is assimilated to Spanish /f/ (as seen in the medieval competitor of *infierno*, namely *i(f)fierno*; see 2.5.3.2.2).
- *Octubre* 'October', possibly from an Oscan-influenced form of Lat. OCTŌBER, namely *OCTŪBER (see 1.2.3), provided early medieval *ochubre*. As a result of influence from OCTOBER, as read aloud, *ochubre* was modified to semi-learned *octubre*.

However, the term *semi-learned* will also be used for words which (like learned words) have been transmitted to Spanish from written sources, but which (unlike learned words) have undergone some phonological change (in addition to the minimal morphological changes required of all additions to the Spanish vocabulary). Thus, Lat. REGULA, when borrowed by Spanish (as *regla* 'rule, ruler') underwent loss of the post-tonic vowel (see 2.4.3.3) as in popular words, but retained the resulting /gl/ group (which in popular words became medieval /ʒ/, now /x/; see 2.5.2.4).

2.2.4 Doublets

It will be evident from the examples given in the preceding sections that a given Latin word may be transmitted to Spanish by more than one means. Cases of double transmission are referred to as **doublets** and usually also show semantic differentiation, the popular form being associated with changed meaning, while the learned or semi-learned counterpart typically retains the Latin sense. Compare popular *reja* and semi-learned *regla* above, or learned *fábula*, above, with popular *habla* 'speech'. Among many other doublets we find *artejo* 'finger-joint, knuckle' and *artículo* 'article' (both from ARTICULUM); *raudo* 'fast-flowing' and *rápido* 'rapid' (both from RAPIDUS); *delgado* 'slender' and *delicado* 'delicate' (both from DĒLICĀTUS).

2.3 Suprasegmental features

The main feature of concern here is the accent, and, in particular, its position and nature in Latin and Spanish. The accent serves as one of the devices which aids word recognition, and in Spanish (but not in Latin) it also has a semantic role.

2.3.1 *Position of the accent*

Throughout the development from Latin to Spanish, the position of the accent is highly stable; the accent of a Spanish word falls on the same syllable it occupied in the Latin ancestor of that word. In Latin words of two syllables, the accent fell on the first, while in words of three or more syllables the position of the accent was determined by the length of the penultimate syllable; if the penultimate syllable was long, the accent fell upon it; if the penultimate syllable was short, the accent fell on the antepenultimate. Since a Latin syllable was long either because it contained a long vowel or a diphthong or because its vowel, although short, was followed by at least two consonants (the first of which combines with the short vowel to provide a 'long' syllable), Latin polysyllabic words can be said to fall into three accentual categories:

1 The penultimate vowel (and therefore the penultimate syllable) is long (the accent falls on it): DĒBĒRE (> *deber*), MOLĪNU(> *molino*), CONSUTŪRA (> *costura*).

2 The penultimate vowel is short, but is followed by two or more consonants (the accent falls on the penultimate): SAGITTA (> *saeta*), QUADRĀGINTĀ (> *cuarenta*). For one exception to this rule, affecting cons. + /r/ and cons. + /l/, see 3.2.3.

3 The penultimate vowel is short and is followed by a single consonant or by no consonant (the accent falls on the preceding syllable): VETULUS (> *viejo*), VIRIDIS (> *verde*), FĪLIUS (> *hijo*), CORRIGIA (> *correa*).

It follows from the above that the position of the Latin accent was determined by the phonological structure of the word concerned and never by its meaning. In Spanish, accent-position has acquired phonemic value, as can be seen in cases like *continuo* 'continual', *continúo* 'I continue', *continuó* 'he continued'.

As stated above, there are few cases of accent-shift in the history of Spanish; these fall into two main categories. On the one hand, words whose short penultimate vowel was followed by a consonant group whose second member was R were at first accented on the antepenultimate, because in such consonant groups the first element was syllable-initial (unlike the case of the majority of consonant clusters, in which the first phoneme was syllable-final) and could not therefore form a long syllable with the preceding (penultimate) vowel. Thus,

TÉNEBRAE, ÍNTEGRUM (see rule 3, above). However, in spoken Latin, it seems that these consonant groups came to be articulated like other groups, with the consequences that a preceding short penultimate was now in a long syllable and therefore *could* bear the accent (rule 2): TENÉBRAE, INTÉGRUM (whence Sp. *tiniéblas*, *entéro*).

The other main category of words in which accent-shift took place consists of those in which a stressed antepenultimate was in hiatus (see 2.3.2) with the penultimate (e.g. MULIĒRE, FĪLIOLUS, PUTEOLUS, TĀLEOLA). The instability of hiatus in spoken Latin (see 2.3.2 (end)) led to transfer of accent to the more open of the two vowels concerned (and reduction of the first to a glide): /muljɛ́re/, /filjɔ́lo/, /potjɔ́lo/, /taljɔ́la/ (> *mujer*, *hijuelo*, *pozuelo*, *tajuela*).

2.3.2 Nature of the accent

The nature of the accent, in various languages, is complex. Three main elements involved are pitch, energy and duration, with different prominence given to each in different languages.

1 Pitch refers to the relative frequency of the musical note adopted in articulating a vowel. The vowel which bears the accent will tend to have higher pitch than other vowels in the word.
2 Energy refers to the muscular force with which air is expelled during articulation (this force is sometimes called **stress**) and therefore governs the loudness of vowels. The vowel which bears the accent will tend to be louder than others.
3 Duration is, of course, a matter of relative length. The accented vowel may be longer than other vowels.

It is thought that early Latin had a type of accent in which pitch was the predominant element. In the case of this type of accent (so-called **pitch-accent**), relative heights of musical notes reveal where the accent lies, while energy is more uniformly deployed, so that all vowels have similar loudness. (The third element can never have been important in Latin, since length was a distinctive feature of the vowel system (see 2.4.1) and it is unlikely that length was associated with two separate values.) However, for reasons which remain obscure, spoken Latin underwent a change of accent-type and came to have an accent in which energy-deployment dominated. This type of accent (**stress-accent**) is the one which continues to characterize the Romance languages (including Spanish) and is also the type used by English. The consequences of this change of accent type can be seen elsewhere in the development of the Romance languages. The increasingly uneven deployment of energy over the word (more to the tonic, less to the atonics) accounts in large part for the different historical treatment of the Latin vowels in different positions. Concentration of energy on the tonic (and the greater audibility this brings) allows tonic vowels to be quite well differentiated and preserved, while lesser degrees of energy devoted, in decreasing order, to initial, final and intertonic vowels imply greater degrees of merger and loss (see 2.4.3) A second effect of the change to a stress-accent is the wholesale destruction of hiatus. Cases of hiatus (vowels which are adjacent but in separate syllables) were frequent in early Latin, but scarcely any survive in Spanish words of popular descent (among the few exceptions are *día, mía, vía*). For hiatus to survive, the vowels which constitute it must have similar degrees of energy/audibility, a condition which was precisely not fulfilled in later spoken Latin. Since adjacent vowels increasingly had different degrees of energy, cases of hiatus were generally reduced to monosyllabic pronunciation, either by loss of one of the vowels or by reducing the higher of the two to a (non-syllabic) glide (see 2.4.3.4).

2.3.3 The syllable

The other suprasegmental feature with which we need to be concerned is the syllable. The nature of the syllable will not be discussed here (see Abercrombie 1967: 34–41 for a good description), but only the matter of syllable-boundaries. Generally speaking, it seems that in the case of such boundaries Latin differed little from Spanish: a single consonant between vowels is syllable-initial (TE-PI-DUS), while in the case of groups of two consonants the boundary falls between the two (POR-CUS, DEN-TĒS, CUP-PA), except in the case of cons. + R and cons. + L, where the first consonant is syllable-initial (LA-CRY-MA, PE-TRA, CA-PRA). In groups of three consonants, the boundary falls after the first (AM-PLU) or after the second (CŌNS-TĀRE).

In discussing accent position, which follows closely from syllable structure, we have seen two types of syllable-boundary change, exemplified by ÍN-TE-GRUM > IN-TÉG-RUM (some groups consisting of cons. + R, originally syllable-initial, come to straddle the boundary) and MU-LI-Ē-RE > MU-LIĒRE (where the boundary fell between vowels it was almost always abolished, reducing two syllables to one, at the same time as converting the first vowel to a glide; see 2.4.3.4).

A further instance of syllable-boundary change (this time also affecting the word-boundary) occurs in the case of words which in Latin began with S + cons. Because the second consonant (typically P, T, C, QU or M) required maximum closure, speakers of Latin came to hear it as syllable-initial, preceded by an anomalous 'semi-syllable' consisting of /s/. This difficulty would be particularly noticeable where the preceding word, if any, ended in a consonant (e.g. AD SCHOLAM) and was resolved by turning 'semi-syllabic' /s/ into a full syllable, by means of the addition of a vowel (at first I, later evolving to /e/). Thus,

SPĒRĀRE > *esperar*
STĀRE > *estar*
SCHOLA > *escuela*

This remains a productive rule of Spanish, so that, when words are borrowed from languages which permit initial /s/ + cons., /e/ is added in the adaptation process:

Eng. *snob* > Sp. *esnob*
Eng. *smoking* (*-jacket*) > Sp. *esmoquin*

although this addition is not always noted in the spelling of neologisms (e.g. *snob*, *smoking*).

2.4 Development of the vowel system

2.4.1 *The Latin vowel system*

The early Latin vocalic system, perpetuated by the literary language, consisted of ten phonemes, which were contrasted on the basis of three distinctive features, aperture, locus and length. There were three distinctive degrees of aperture: high (/i/ /iː/ /u/ /uː/), mid (/e/ /eː/ /o/ /oː/) and low (/a/ /aː/). Front vowels (/i/ /iː/ /e/ /eː/) were distinguished from back vowels (/u/ /uː/ /o/ /oː/), with two vowels (/a/ /aː/) which were neither front nor back. Each point in this system was occupied by two vowels, distinguished on the basis of length (i.e. duration, indicated here by presence and absence of 'ː'); /iː, eː, aː, oː, uː/ were long, and /i, e, a, o, u/ were short. The system can therefore be represented as in table 2.1.

The Latin system of spelling generally ignored differences of length and used only five letters, each indicating both a long and a short phoneme. (Grammarians later devised a graphical distinction, using the macron (¯) over a long vowel and a micron (˘) over a short vowel; here the micron is omitted.) Despite the general lack of written distinction between long and short vowels, the contrast of length was (by definition) meaningful, as can be seen by the minimal pairs in table 2.2.

In addition to these ten simple vowels, literary Latin used three diphthongs (combinations of two vocalic elements belonging to a single syllable): AE [ai̯], OE [oi̯] and AU [au̯].

At the level of articulatory phonetics, it is likely that, within each pair of phonemes which shared the 'same' point of articulation, the long vowel was a little higher than the short vowel; that is, the distinctive feature of length was accompanied by a redundant distinction of aperture. Such relative raising of long vowels is observable in many modern languages. Taking into account this (small) difference of aperture (which does not affect the lowest pair of vowels), the ten simple vowels of literary Latin can be seen to have the

Table 2.1 *The Latin vowel system*

	Front	Centre	Back
High	/iː/ /i/		/uː/ /u/
Mid	/eː/ /e/		/oː/ /o/
Low		/aː/ /a/	

Table 2.2 *Minimal pairs based upon contrasts of Latin vowel length*

Long vowel		Short vowel	
HĪC	'here'	HIC	'this'
LĪBER	'free'	LIBER	'book'
LĒVIS	'smooth'	LEVIS	'light in weight'
VĒNIT	'he came'	VENIT	'he comes'
MĀLUM	'apple'	MALUM	'evil, misfortune'
ŌS	'mouth'	OS	'bone'
PŌPULUS	'white poplar'	POPULUS	'people'

following phonetic realizations (ignoring any allophonic variation stemming from environment):

Ī = /iː/: [iː] Ū = /uː/: [uː]
Ĭ = /i/: [ɪ] Ŭ = /u/: [ʊ]
Ē = /eː/: [eː] Ō = /oː/ [oː]
Ĕ = /e/: [ɛ] Ŏ = /o/: [ɔ]
Ā = /aː/: [aː]
Ă = /a/: [a]

Although the system just described appears to have persisted in educated speech, the vowel system of popular spoken Latin gradually underwent a number of fundamental changes. The earliest of these (no later than the first century AD) was the loss of the distinctive feature of length, the functional load carried by this feature being transferred to that of aperture. There is no consensus over the motivation for this change; a phonological account can be seen in Alarcos (1965: 210–18) and a substratum explanation is sketched in Lausberg (1965: 208–9). What is clear is that as length ceased to be meaningful, the pre-existing (and hitherto non-significant) differences of aperture between pairs of vowels such as Ī and Ĭ came to be the sole basis of distinction between the two vowels (and between the other pairs of vowels, except Ā and Ă, which simply merged). At this stage, then, after the transfer of distinctiveness from length to aperture and the merger of Ā and Ă, the vowel system of spoken Latin can best be expressed in terms of the following nine units:

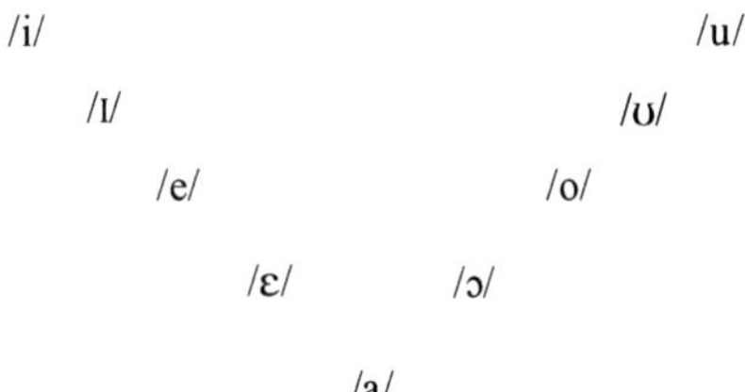

The effect of this change can be exemplified through a minimal pair such as HĪC/HIC (see above). While length continued to be distinctive, the contrast between these words can be represented as /hiːk/ vs /hik/; after the change, the contrast between the words can be shown as /hik/ vs /hɪk/.

The second major transformation of the Latin vowel-system is due to the change in the nature of the accent in spoken Latin (see 2.3.1). As a result of the differing degree of energy devoted to the different syllables of each word, the vowels of these syllables evolve differently. From this point on, we shall need therefore to discuss separately the treatment of vowels in **tonic** position (i.e. in syllables which receive the major word-stress), where there is a maximum of differentiation between phonemes, from their treatment in **atonic** positions (i.e. in syllables which do not receive the major stress), where mergers of phonemes are more frequent. Furthermore, we shall need to distinguish between various classes of atonic vowels, since merger is more extensive in some than in others. Among atonic vowels, those in **initial** syllables (the first syllable of the word, unless the main stress falls there, in which case the word has no initial syllable) preserve more distinctions than those in **final** syllables (the last syllable of the word, which in Latin may not bear the stress). Similarly, such final vowels preserve more distinctions than those in **intertonic** position (internal vowels, which may be further classified as **pretonic** (between initial and tonic) or **post-tonic** (between tonic and final). Vowels in intertonic position, because of the severely lessened amount of energy devoted to them in spoken Latin, suffer the greatest degree of merger and may be weakened to the point of effacement.

2.4.2 *Tonic vowels*

The nine-vowel system which emerged after the loss of the length contrast (see 2.4.1) was inherently unstable. Any system which depends upon the distinction of five tongue-heights (= five **degrees of aperture**) is likely to be modified, since the acoustic difference between the vowels concerned is probably too small for the accurate conveying of information. There is convincing evidence that, no later than the first century AD, there was a merger between tongue-heights 3 and 4, and a consequent reduction from nine phonemes to seven in tonic position:

5	/i/							/u/
4		/ɪ/					/ʊ/	
3			/e/			/o/		
2				/ɛ/	/ɔ/			
1				/a/				

4	/i/					/u/
3		/e/			/o/	
2			/ɛ/	/ɔ/		
1			/a/			

The seven-vowel system which emerged from this merger is often referred to as the 'Vulgar Latin vowel system', since it was evidently in use in much of the Latin-speaking world, including Spain. Notice that, in terms of spelling, the change just considered implies that, on the one hand, the phonemes written Ĭ and Ē have merged in /e/, and, on the other hand, the phonemes written Ŭ and Ō have merged in /o/. Like all mergers, these changes led to uncertainty of spelling among the less well educated. Among the graffiti of Pompeii, we find the misspellings VECES and MENUS (for VICES and MINUS) while the *Appendix Probi* (see 1.1) recommends the spellings TURMA, COLUMNA and FORMOSUS and condemns TORMA, COLOMNA and FORMUNSUS.

2.4.2.1 Metaphony

The vowels of the tonic system were subject, during the Vulgar Latin phase, to metaphony (assimilatory raising of vowels, in anticipation of a following, higher phoneme, typically a high vowel or a glide). Thus, in many areas, including the area where Castilian developed, the tonic vowels of Vulgar Latin were frequently raised, by one degree of aperture, through metaphony exercised by a following palatal glide [j] or [i̯] (see 2.4.3.2 and 2.5.2.4 for glide-formation) which occurred in the same syllable or in the following one, or by an /i/ in the final syllable. Naturally, the highest tonic vowels, /i/ and /u/, were exempt from this process. It is also true that the glide concerned sometimes combined early in spoken Latin with an adjacent consonant, thereby losing its identity and consequently failing to affect the preceding vowel; this is the case of the glide [j] preceded by Latin /t/ or /k/: in LENTEU > *lienzo* 'fabric', FORTIA > *fuerza* 'strength', etc. Spoken Latin /ɛ/ and /ɔ/ are here unaffected by metaphony and remain half-open vowels, later receiving the normal treatment of such vowels, namely diphthongization to [jé], [wé] respectively (see 2.4.2.2).

However, in the majority of cases, the glide survived longer (as is always the case with a final high vowel) and produced *in principle* the following raising effects on tonic vowels:

/e/ is raised to /i/: VINDĒMIA > *vendimia* 'grape harvest', FĒCĪ > *hice* 'I did' (cf. non-metaphonized PLĒNA > *llena* 'full')
/ɛ/ is raised to /e/: MATERIA > *madera* 'wood', VENĪ > *ven* 'come!' (cf. PETRA > *piedra* 'stone')
/ɔ/ is raised to /o/: FOLIA > *hoja* 'leaf' (cf. FOCU > *fuego* 'fire')
/o/ is raised to /u/: *CUNEA > *cuña* 'wedge' (cf. CUPPA > *copa* 'wine glass')
/a/ is raised to /e/: ĀREA > *era* 'threshing-floor' (cf. ANNU > *año* 'year')

We look in turn at the metaphonic effects of a glide and of final /i/.

The detailed effects of metaphony by the glide yod are complex (and are best studied in Craddock 1980), in that certain spoken Latin vowels sometimes escape raising, depending on the precise sequence of vowel, consonant and glide (or vowel, glide and consonant) which appears in a given word. In order to clarify the details of the way in which the spoken Latin vowels have been affected by metaphony, it is necessary to distinguish between five environments observable at the stage of spoken Latin:

1 The vowel is followed immediately by [i̯], by definition in the same syllable as the vowel. The glide may have arisen through one of a number of processes: reduction of /i/ in hiatus with the vowel concerned (see 2.4.3.4); loss of a consonant between the vowel and an atonic /e/ or /i/, which thereupon is reduced to [i̯] by the preceding process; metathesis of a glide from the following syllable (see 2.5.2.2(6)); or palatalization of a syllable final velar (see 2.5.2.4). Ultimately, the glide is absorbed by the preceding vowel and/or by the following consonant.
2 The onset of the syllable following the vowel concerned contains (as it still does) a glide [j] (from earlier atonic /e/ or /i/ in hiatus (see 2.4.3.4)), the intervening consonant(s) being /b/, /m/ or a group such as /bɾ/, /tɾ/, /mp/.
3 The vowel in question is followed by [ǰ] (from earlier [gj], [dj] (2.5.2.2(4), and in some cases from [bj] (2.5.2.2(5)). Ultimately, the consonant either survives intact or is absorbed by a preceding front vowel.
4 The vowel in question is followed by [ʎ] (from earlier [lj] (2.5.2.2(2)) or [kl], [gl] (2.5.2.4)). Ultimately [ʎ] becomes [ʒ] in Old Spanish and [x] in the modern language.
5 The vowel concerned is followed by [ɲ] (from earlier [nj] (2.5.2.2(3) or [gn] (2.5.2.4)), which remains unchanged from spoken Latin to the present.

These five environments are listed in accordance with the proportion of Latin vowels which undergo metaphony in each. Thus, in environment 1, four of the five susceptible spoken Latin vowels (/a/, /ɛ/, /ɔ/, /e/ and /o/) are affected, while in environment 5 only one vowel is clearly affected. Considering each relevant vowel in turn, the effects of metaphony can be seen to occur (✓) or not (×) in each environment:

/a/ 1✓ LAICU > *lego* 'layman'; CANTĀVĪ > spoken Latin [kan'tai̯] > *canté* 'I sang'; ĀREA > ['ai̯ɾa] > *era* 'threshing-floor', BĀSIU > ['bai̯so] > *beso* 'kiss', SAPIAM > ['sai̯pa] > *sepa* '(that) I know'; LACTE (CL LAC) > ['lai̯te] > *leche* 'milk', MATAXA > [ma'tai̯sa] > OSp. *madexa* > MSp. *madeja* 'skein'.

2× LABIU > *labio* 'lip', RABIA > *rabia* 'rage'; FLACCIDU > ['flatt^sjo] > OSp. *llacio* > *lacio* 'limp, lank'.

3× RADIU > *rayo* 'ray, spoke', (ARBOR) FĀGEA > *haya* 'beech tree'.

4× ALIU > *ajo* 'garlic', PALEA > *paja* 'straw'; NOVĀCULA > *navaja* 'knife, razor'; COĀGULU > *cuajo* 'rennet'.

5× ARĀNEA > *araña* 'spider', EXTRĀNEU > *extraño* 'strange'; TAM MAGNU > *tamaño* 'size'.

/ɛ/ 1✓ GREGE > ['ɡrɛe] > ['ɡrɛi̯] > *grey* '(bishop's) flock'; MATERIA > [ma'tɛi̯ra] > *madera* 'wood', CERESIA (CL CERASIA) > [ke'rɛi̯sa] > OSp. *ceresa* > *cereza* 'cherry'; DĪRECTU > [de'rɛi̯to] > *derecho* 'law; straight', LECTU > ['lɛi̯to] > *lecho* 'bed', INTÉGRU (CL ÍNTEGRU) > [en'tɛi̯ro] > *entero* 'whole'.

2✓ SUPERBIA > *soberbia* 'pride, vainglory', NERVIU > *nervio* 'nerve; strength', PRAEMIU > ['prɛmjo] > *premio* 'prize'. In TEPIDU, creation of the glide (through loss of /d/) presumably came too late to prevent /ɛ/ receiving its normal treatment, diphthongization, so that TEPIDU > ['tjeβeðo] > *['tjeβjo], whence *tibio*, under the double influence of preceding and following yod.

3✓ SEDEAT > ['seǰa] > *sea* (pres. subj. of *ser*).

4✓ SPECULU > [es'pɛʎo] > *espejo* 'mirror' (*pace* Corominas & Pascual 1980–91, s.v. *espejo*) (but VECLU [CL VETULU] > ['βɛʎo] > *viejo* 'old').

5✓ INGENIU > OSp. *engeño* 'siege engine' (although this single example should perhaps be discounted as semi-learned)

/ɔ/ 1✓ OCTO > ['ɔi̯to] > *ocho* 'eight', NOCTE > ['nɔi̯te] > *noche* 'night', COXU > ['kɔi̯so] > OSp. *coxo* > *cojo* 'lame'.

2✓ OSTREA > OSp. *ostria* 'oyster' (later *ostra*), NOVIU > *novio* 'fiancé'.

3✓ PODIU > *poyo* 'stone bench', HODIE > ['ɔǰe] > *hoy* 'today', FOVEA > *hoya* 'pit'.

4✓ FOLIA > ['fɔʎa] > *hoja* 'leaf', COLLIGIS > ['kɔllees] > ['kɔlljes] > ['kɔʎes] > *coges* 'you grasp', OCULU > ['ɔʎo] > *ojo* 'eye'.

	5×	SOMNIU > *sueño* 'dream' (unless this form is simply a semantic extension of *sueño* < SOMNU 'sleep').
/e/	1×	STRICTU > [es'trei̯to] > *estrecho* 'narrow', TĒCTU > ['tei̯to] > *techo* 'roof', CERVĒSIA > OSp. *cervesa* > *cerveza* 'beer', PIGNORA > ['pei̯nɾa] > *prenda* 'garment' (see 2.5.2.4 (end)).
	2✓	VINDĒMIA > [βen'demja] > *vendimia* 'wine harvest', LIMPIDU > ['lempeo] > *limpio* 'clean', SĒPIA > *jibia* 'cuttlefish', VITREU > ['βetɾjo] > *vidrio* 'glass'.
	3×	CORRIGIA > [ko'reǰa] > *correa* 'leather belt, strap', VIDEAT > ['βeǰa] > *vea* (pres. subj. of *ver*).
	4×	CILIA > *ceja*, CONSILIU > *consejo* 'advice', APICULA > [a'βeʎa] > *abeja* 'bee', TEGULA > ['teʎa] > *teja* '(roof)tile'.
	5×	LIGNA > *leña* 'firewood', SIGNA > *seña* 'sign'.
/o/	1✓	LUCTA > ['loi̯ta] > *lucha* 'struggle', TRUCTA > [trói̯ta] > *trucha* 'trout', MULTU > ['mou̯to] > ['moi̯to] > *mucho* 'much', AUSCULTAT > [as'kou̯tat] > [as'koi̯tat] > *escucha* 'he listens', VULTURE > ['βou̯toɾe] > ['βoi̯toɾe] > ['βoi̯tɾe] > *buitre* 'vulture' (see 2.5.2.4 (end)), IMPULSAT > [em'pou̯sat] > [em'poi̯sat] > *empuja* 'he pushes'.
	2✓	RUBEU > ['roβjo] > *rubio* 'fair-haired', PLUVIA > ['pʎoβja] > *lluvia* 'rain', TURBIDU > ['torβjo] > *turbio* 'cloudy'.
	3	(no example; the frequently cited case FUGIO > *huyo* 'I flee' is inconclusive, since tonic /o/ is excluded from the stem of *-ir* verbs (see 3.7.1.5))
	4×	CUSCULIU > *coscojo* 'kermes-oak gall', GURGULIŌNE (CL CURCULIŌNE) > *gorgojo* 'weevil' (a back-formation from **gorgojón*), GENUCULU > OSp. *enojo* ~ *(h)inojo* ~ *finojo* 'knee'.
	5✓	CUNEU > *cuño* 'die-stamp' (whence *cuña* 'wedge'), PUGNU > *puño* 'fist'.

Even this complex state of affairs leaves out of account certain recalcitrant data. In the following cases, /ɔ́/ or /ó/ (in environments 1 and 5) have combined with a following glide to produce ['we]:

CORIU > *cuero* 'leather'
SOMNIU > *sueño* 'dream'
AUGURIU > *agüero* 'omen'
CICŌNIA > *cigüeña* 'stork' (cf. *cuño*, *puño*, above)
SALE MURIA > *salmuera* 'brine'
VERECUNDIA > OSp. *vergüeña* 'shame'

Early textual evidence (*coiro*, *agoiro*, *salmoyra*, *cigoña*, *vergoña*, the latter forms perhaps representing [tˢi'ɣoi̯ɲa], [βeɾ'ɣoi̯ɲa]) suggests the following sequence: (1) /ɔ́/ is raised to /ó/ (['kɔi̯ɾo] > ['koi̯ɾo]); (2) /ói/ evolves to /ué/ in accordance with the Castilian avoidance of off-gliding diphthongs (see Malkiel 1976), thus forestalling any metaphonic effect of [i̯] on preceding /o/.

A possible (partial) explanation of the differential effect of yod on preceding tonic vowels is one based on the length of survival of the glide in different phonemic environments. Where [j] was absorbed early through assimilation to preceding /t/ or /k/, it has no metaphonic effect, but where it has survived to this day (environment 2), it affects all vowels except /a/. A similar deep effect is seen in environment 1 (four out of five vowels affected) and it is probably the case that the glide survived for centuries where it arose through palatalization of /k/ before /t/ and /s/, through metathesis, or through loss of an intervocalic consonant; French *nuit*, etc., and Portuguese *noite*, *leigo*, *madeira*, *beijo*, etc., provide evidence of its long survival in other territories.

Environments 3 and 4 represent chronologically intermediate positions; two vowels are affected (if *espejo*, rather than *viejo*, can be taken to represent the development of /ɛ́/), perhaps betraying a fairly rapid (but not immediate) absorption of the glide into the adjacent /d/, /g/ or /l/. Finally, environment 5 (in which only /o/ is affected) perhaps indicates that a glide adjacent to /n/ survived the shortest period (except for the glide following /t/ or /k/). There is also a case for separating instances like LIMPIDU (> *limpio*) and TURBIDU (> *turbio*) from environment 2, on the grounds that the glide of such forms can only be late in appearing (after the loss of -D-). And it has to be said that such a chronological account, although it receives some support from other Romance languages, is far from complete, since it fails to explain why particular vowels (and not others) are affected in a given environment.

Metaphony by final /i/ is less frequent than that caused by a yod, since the conditioning factor (/-i/) is relatively infrequent in Hispano-Romance. The main examples are:

/ɛ/ > /e/: VENĪ > *¡ven!* 'come!' (but HERĪ > *(a)yer* 'yesterday')
/e/ > /i/: VĒNĪ > *vine* 'I came', FĒCĪ > *hice* 'I made', MIHĪ, TIBĪ, SIBĪ > *mi*, *ti*, *sí* (see 3.5.1)

Metaphony can also be seen to operate in atonic syllables. The most usual case is raising of an initial vowel (see 2.4.3.1).

2.4.2.2 Diphthongization

In the late Roman period, the tonic vowel system underwent further modification in many areas, including the area where Castilian (and its immediate neighbours) originated. In this period, it seems there was a lengthening of tonic vowels in many regional varieties of spoken Latin; by contrast, the atonic vowels remain unlengthened. The reasons for this development are disputed (some see here the influence of Germanic speech on Latin, at a period when large numbers of Germanic speakers were allowed or forced their way into the Empire and were learning to speak Latin), but its effect on the tonic vowels was extensive.

There have been many accounts of the way in which this effect was exercised, and no single account has gained general acceptance. What follows is one of a number of possible sequences of events.

The immediate effect of the lengthening of tonic vowels was to raise most such vowels, since the added muscular tension required for lengthening will cause added tensing of the jaw muscles, with consequent raising of the jaw and of the tongue-position of the vowel being articulated. However, /i/ and /u/, because of their already high position, were not susceptible to further raising. Since raising of all vowels but the highest implies that the physiological and acoustic difference between neighbouring vowels is lessened, this process gave rise to potential confusion. Thus, e.g.

/ósso/ 'bear' (< URSUS)
/ɔ́sso/ 'bone' (< non-standard OSSUM)

must have become confusingly similar.

Any language so affected may seek some therapeutic device to preserve comprehension, and the device employed by some varieties of Romance, including Spanish, was a compensatory downward movement of the newly lengthened low-mid vowels, /ɛ/ and /ɔ/, leading to their fracture and the creation of incipient diphthongs:

/i/		/u/
/e/		/o/
/ɛ/ > [eɛ]		[oɔ] < /ɔ/
	/a/	

Further differentiation between the on-glide and the off-glide of these complex sounds led to the true diphthongs already observable in the earliest Spanish and no doubt by then interpreted as sequences of two vowel phonemes:

[eɛ] > [iɛ] > [je] (= /ie/)
[oɔ] > [uɔ] > [wo] > [we] (= /ue/)

e.g. BENE = /bɛ́ne/ > *bien* 'well'
PETRA = /pɛ́tra/ > *piedra* 'stone'
BONUS = /bɔ́no/ > *bueno* 'good'
OSSUM = /ɔ́sso/ > *hueso* 'bone' (thereby avoiding collision with *oso* 'bear')

Since the glide [j] may not in Spanish occupy syllable-initial position, the result of diphthongization of word-initial Ĕ (or HĔ) was a sequence of fricative consonant + /e/:

EQUA > *yegua* 'mare'
HERBA > *yerba* (later spelt *hierba*) 'grass'

The phonological effect of diphthongization is that, since two of the seven VL tonic vowels came to be interpreted as sequences, in each case, of two other vowels (or of consonant plus vowel), the number of tonic vowel phonemes in Spanish is reduced to five.

2.4.2.3 The Latin diphthongs

The three Latin diphthongs, AE, OE and AU, were reduced to simple vowels, although at different rates. AE > /ɛ/ and OE > /e/ in spoken Latin, that is to say, early enough for the product of AE to be involved in the diphthongization process discussed in 2.4.2.2. Thus,

POENA = /péna/ > *pena* 'grief'
FOEDUS = /fédo/ > *feo* 'ugly'
CAELUM = /kɛ́lo/ > *cielo* 'sky'
QUAERIT = /kwɛ́ret/ > *quiere* 'he wishes'

By contrast, in a few cases AE was reduced to /e/, giving rise to undiphthongized outcomes:

CAESPITE = /késpite/ > *césped* 'turf'
SAETA = /séta/ > *seda* 'silk'

Although there were a few cases of reduction in spoken Latin of AU > /o/ (e.g. *Appendix Probi:* AURIS NON ORICLA), this change was at first limited to non-patrician varieties and to certain words. It was not until later that reduction of AU became regular in Spanish (as happened in most Romance languages, but not all; cf. Gal.-Port. /ou/, Occ. /au/):

PAUCU > *poco* 'little'
TAURU > *toro* 'bull'
CAUSA > *cosa* 'thing'.

2.4.2.4 New diphthongs

As a result of the transfer of a glide into a preceding syllable (see 2.5.2.2(6)), certain new diphthongs came into existence in late spoken Latin or in Hispano-Romance. Where the new diphthong consisted of a front vowel or /a/ + palatal glide, there was a reduction of the sequence, through assimilation, to /e/:

MĀTERIA > /matɛ́ira/ > *madera* 'wood'
CASEU > /káiso/ > *queso* 'cheese'
SAPIAT > /sáipa/ > *sepa* (3rd sing., pres. subj. of *saber*)

Where the new diphthong consisted of a back vowel + palatal glide, it was dramatically modified to /ue/, in part, no doubt, because by this time the diphthong /ue/ (< tonic Ŏ) was extremely frequent and because diphthongs stressed on the first element were rare:

CORIU > /kɔ́iro/ > *cuero* 'leather'
DŌRIU > /dóiro/ > *Duero* (river name)
SEGŪSIU > /sagúiso/ > *sabueso* 'bloodhound'

It is possible, too, for a labiovelar glide to be transferred to a preceding syllable, combining with tonic /a/ to produce /o/, as in the case of primary AU (see 2.4.2.3). The only examples are certain irregular preterites (see 3.7.8.6.2 (1):

HABUĪ > /áuβi/ > OSp. *ove* (MSp. *hube*)
SAPUĪ > /sáupi/ > OSp. *sope* (MSp. *supe*)

2.4.2.5 Medieval developments

After diphthongization and the emergence of the system of five tonic vowels, there were no further modifications to this system either in the medieval or the modern periods. However, there were some modifications of individual vowels, of which the most frequent cases are the occasional reduction of /ié/ to /í/ and of /ué/ to /é/.

/ié/ was reduced to /í/ in Old Spanish principally when followed by /ʎ/, probably through assimilation of /e/ to the higher phonemes (/i/ and /ʎ/) by which it was surrounded (for the chronology of this change, see Menéndez Pidal 1958: 55–7, 1964a: 152–8):

CASTELLU > OSp. *castiello* > *castillo* 'castle'
CULTELLU > OSp. *cuchiello* > *cuchillo* 'knife'
SELLA > OSp. *siella* > *silla* 'seat'

However, this change may also occur before syllable-final /s/:

VESPERA > OSp. *viéspera* > *víspera* 'eve'
VESPA > OSp. *aviespa* > *avispa* 'wasp'

although this is not the case in *fiesta* (< FESTA), *siesta* (< SEXTA) or *hiniesta* (< GENESTA). There is also an ill-defined group of other words in which this reduction takes place, e.g.

MERULU > OSp. *mierlo* > *mirlo* 'blackbird'
SAECULU > OSp. *sieglo* (semi-learned) > *siglo* 'century'

Reduction of /ue/ to /e/ occurs in Old Spanish, probably for reasons of assimilation, after /ɾ/ or /l/:

FLOCCU > OSp. *flueco* > *fleco* 'fringe, tassel'
FRONTE > OSp. *fruente* > *frente* 'forehead'
COLOBRA > OSp. *culuebra* > *culebra* 'snake'

2.4.2.6 Summary of tonic vowel development

The developments studied in this section can be summarized in the following way:

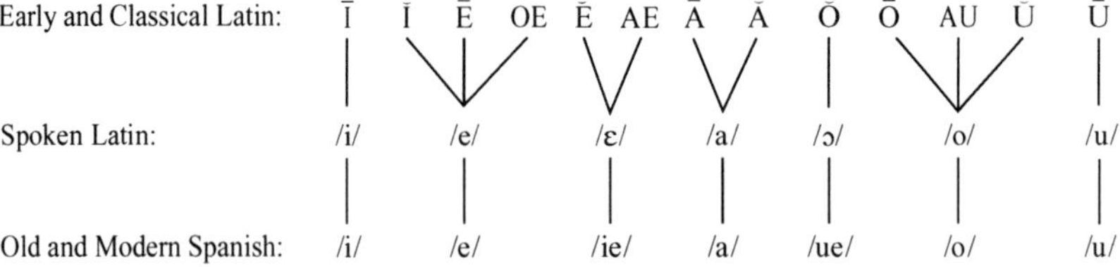

Examples of these developments, omitting the spoken Latin stage:

Ī > /i/: FĪLIU > *hijo* 'son'
FĪCU > *higo* 'fig'
VĪTA > *vida* 'life'

Ĭ > /e/: CISTA > *cesta* 'basket'
PILU > *pelo* 'hair'
SIGNĀS > *señas* 'address'

Ē > /e/ PLĒNU > *lleno* 'full'
ALIĒNU > *ajeno* 'alien'

OE > /e/: POENA > *pena* 'grief'
FOEDU > *feo* 'ugly'

Ĕ > /ie/ PĔTRA > *piedra* 'stone'
MĔTU > *miedo* 'fear'
SĔRRA > *sierra* 'saw, mountain range'

AE > /ie/: CAECU > *ciego* 'blind'
CAELU > *cielo* 'sky'

Ā > /a/ CĀRU > *caro* 'dear'
PRĀTU > *prado* 'meadow'

Ă > /a/ MANU > *mano* 'hand'
PATRE > *padre* 'father'

Ŏ > /ue/: ROTA > *rueda* 'wheel'
NOVE > *nueve* 'nine'
NOVU > *nuevo* 'new'

Ō > /o/: TŌTU > *todo* 'all'
FLŌRE > *flor* 'flower'
FŌRMŌSU > *hermoso* 'beautiful'

AU > /o/: MAURU > *moro* 'Moorish'
CAULE > *col* 'cabbage'

Ŭ> /o/: CUBITU > *codo* 'elbow'
CUPPA > *copa* 'wine glass'

Ū> /u/ FŪMU > *humo* 'smoke'
CŪPA > *cuba* 'vat'
ACŪTU > *agudo* 'sharp'

2.4.3 *Atonic vowel development*

As anticipated in 2.4.1, the different classes of atonic vowels have received different treatment, owing to the different degrees of energy with which they were articulated in spoken Latin. (See 2.4.1 for definitions of the various types of atonic vowels.) In broad terms, the development of the atonic vowel system can be summarized as follows (although further developments will be noted in 2.4.3.2 and 2.4.3.3):

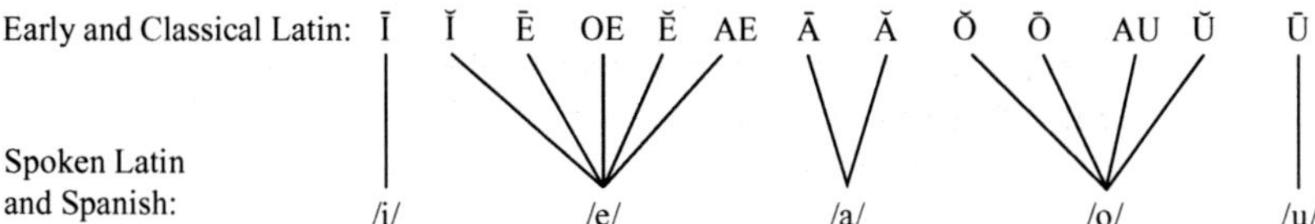

The main difference between tonic and atonic development is that in atonic syllables, Ĕ and Ŏ merged early with their long counterparts, so that the conditions for diphthongization (the need to keep the low-mid vowels, /ɛ/ and /ɔ/, separate from the high-mid vowels, /e/ and /o/) did not arise, and diphthongization could not therefore take place.

The further development of atonic vowels will now be discussed in accordance with their position in the word, beginning with the position in which they received most energy.

2.4.3.1 Initial vowels

Vowels in this category, less energetically articulated than tonic vowels, are the most energetic of the atonics. They therefore show a greater degree of merger than the tonics but less than other atonics. The ten vowels of early Latin (which appear unchanged in literary Latin) were reduced in spoken Latin to the five shown above (2.4.3), which were directly inherited by Old and Modern Spanish.

Although they probably began earlier, the mergers concerned are not clearly attested until the third century AD. They are then revealed by misspelling of the kind FRECARE (for FRICARE) and by statements in the *Appendix Probi* (SIRENA NON SERENA, SENATUS NON SINATUS).

These developments may be exemplified by the following items:

Ī > /i/: RĪPĀRIA > *ribera* 'riverbank'
Ĭ > /e/: PLICĀRE > *llegar* 'to arrive'
Ē > /e/: SECŪRU > *seguro* 'sure'
Ĕ > /e/: SENIŌRE > *señor* 'sir'
AE > /e/: PRAECŌNE > *pregón* 'announcement'
Ā > /a/: PĀNĀRIA > *panera* 'basket'
Ă > /a/: CAPISTRU > *cabestro* 'halter'
Ŏ > /o/: CORTICEA > *corteza* 'skin, rind'
Ō > /o/: NŌMINĀRE > *nombrar* 'to name'
AU > /o/: PAUSĀRE > *posar* 'to put down'
Ŭ > /o/: SUSPECTA > *sospecha* 'suspicion'
Ū> /u/: CŪRĀRE > *curar* 'to cure'

Metaphony, which has been studied in connection with tonic vowels (2.4.2.1), also occurs in the case of initial vowels. A following palatal glide (yod) may cause the raising of initial /e/ and /o/ to /i/ and /u/ respectively, from late spoken Latin onwards (i.e. after the mergers discussed earlier in this section), e.g.

RENIŌNE = [reˈnjone] > *riñón* 'kidney'
GENESTA > *hiniesta* 'broom'
CAEMENTUM > *cimiento* 'foundation'
TENEBRAS > *tinieblas* 'darkness'
COCHLEĀRE = [koˈkljare] > *cuchara* 'spoon'

COGNĀTU > [koi̯'nato] > *cuñado* 'brother-in-law'
MULIERE = [mo'ljere] > *mujer* 'woman'
CŌGITĀRE > [koi̯'dare] > *cuidar* 'to take care of'

Although in most cases the system of initial vowels has proved stable (the five vowels of late spoken Latin persisting unchanged, and with the same incidence, through Old Spanish to the modern language), there is some sporadic evidence of a drift towards a three-vowel system. There are few cases of minimal pairs in which initial /u/ and /o/ or /i/ and /e/ are the differentiating elements and historically there has been some unconditioned drift from /o/ to /u/. In the following cases, initial /o/ was normal in Old Spanish, usually until the fourteenth century, but was gradually replaced by /u/:

jogar > *jugar* 'to play'
logar > *lugar* 'place'
polgar > *pulgar* 'thumb'
roido > *ruido* 'noise'

2.4.3.2 Final vowels

Change in the nature of the Latin accent (2.3.2) brought severe decrease of energy to final syllables, with consequent intense merger and some loss. Where Latin final vowels survived into Spanish, they had the following outcomes:

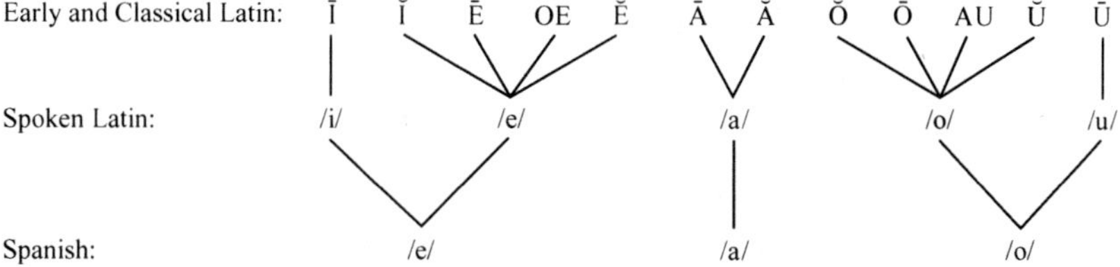

These developments may be exemplified by the following items:

Ī > /e/: VĒNĪ> *vine* 'I came'
Ĭ > /e/: IOVIS > *jueves* 'Thursday'
Ē > /e/: PATRĒS > *padres* 'fathers'
Ĕ > /e/: DE UNDE > *donde* 'where'
Ā > /a/: CANTĀS > *cantas* 'you sing'
Ă > /a/: CANTANT > *cantan* 'they sing'
Ŏ > /o/: CITO > OSp. *cedo* 'soon'
Ō > /o/: CANTŌ> *canto* 'I sing'
Ŭ > /o/: VĪNU > *vino* 'wine'
Ū > /o/: MANŪS > *manos* 'hands'

It is evident that the contrast between final /i/ and /e/ was maintained in spoken Latin. Not only is this contrast maintained in Italian, but the two vowels have different effects on preceding tonic vowels in Spanish: final /i/ (< Ī) gives rise to metaphony (2.4.2.1), while /e/ (< Ĭ, Ē, Ĕ, AE) does not. A contrast between final /u/ and /o/ is also evident in pre-literary Spanish (Menéndez Pidal 1964a: 168–72), and is required to explain Asturian and Cantabrian metaphony (Penny 2000: 98–102).

Of the three final vowels which appear in Old Spanish, /a/ and /o/ are relatively stable. /a/ is raised to /e/ (and occasionally lost) in Old Spanish when in hiatus with a high tonic vowel: *mía* > *míe* > *mi* 'my', *duas* > OSp. *dues* 'two (fem.)', *-ia* > *-ie* (imperf. endings of *-er*/*-ir* verbs). Final /o/ was lost in a few words which habitually preceded a noun or adjective: *primero* > *primer* 'first', *tercero* > *tercer* 'third', *santo* > *san* 'Saint', DOMINU > *don* (honorific), *segundo* > *según* 'according to', MULTU > **muito* > *muy* 'very'.

By contrast, final /e/ is highly unstable and suffered elimination in two periods of the history of Old Spanish. In pre-literary texts of the tenth and eleventh centuries (see Menéndez Pidal 1964a: 186–90), one can observe the loss of /e/ where it followed a dental or alveolar consonant (except /t/) which at that stage was ungrouped (i.e. preceded by a vowel):

PARIETE > *pared* wall
MERCĒDE > *merced* 'mercy'
PĀNE > *pan* 'bread'
MARE > *mar* 'sea'
FIDĒLE > *fiel* 'faithful'
MĒNSE = /mése/ > *mes* 'month'
PĀCE = /pát^{s}e/ > *paz* 'peace'

However, as noted above, the sequence /(V)te/ (always the product of Latin /(V)tte/; 2.5.3.2.4) did not at this stage allow this apocope of /-e/: SEPTEM > *siete*.

Later, especially in the thirteenth century, certain varieties of Castilian (urban, educated varieties, which are those reflected in writing) suffered sporadic loss of /e/ in other phonological environments. In this period, perhaps under the influence of French (see Allen 1976, Lapesa 1951, 1975, 1982), /e/ could be absent after almost any consonant or consonant group: *nuef (nueve)*, *nief (nieve)*, *siet (siete)*, *lech (leche)*, *noch (noche)*, *princep (príncipe)*, *mont (monte)*, *cuend (conde)*, *part (parte)*, *estonz (entonces)*, etc. The forms with /e/ never disappeared from the written record and it is likely that they continued to characterize popular styles of Castilian speech, which reasserted themselves towards the end of the thirteenth century and have been perpetuated into the modern language. Only in a handful of cases was this later loss of /e/ made permanent; where a consonant group preceding /e/ was simplified in later Old Spanish to /t^{s}/ = *ç* (through vocalization and assimilation of /-l/ or through assimilation of /-s/ to following /t^{s}/), forms without final /e/ were preferred, after long competition between apocopated and unapocopated forms:

CALCE > _coçe_ > _coz_ 'kick'
FALCE > _foçe_ > _foz_ > _hoz_ 'sickle'
FASCE > _façe_ > _faz_ > _haz_ 'bundle'
PISCE > _peçe_ > _pez_ 'fish'

This eventual solution no doubt occurred because, after loss of /e/, these words ended with the same (now ungrouped) phoneme as many other previously existing words (_paz_, _cruz_, etc.).

2.4.3.3 Intertonic vowels

Unstressed internal vowels are those which suffer most from the development of a stress-accent in spoken Latin (see 2.3.2). With the exception of the vowel /a/, whose inherent audibility ensured its survival, Latin intertonic vowels have been entirely eliminated. In certain environments (contact with /r/ or /l/, sometimes with /n/ or /s/), intertonics were frequently lost in spoken Latin. This conditioned loss, which is evident in all Romance languages, is attested in (amongst other sources) the _Appendix Probi_:

ANGULUS NON ANGLUS
CALIDA NON CALDA
SPECULUM NON SPECLUM
STABULUM NON STABLUM
VETULUS NON VECLUS
VIRIDIS NON VIRDIS, etc.

Later, in pre-literary Spanish (and before the loss of final /e/: HOMINE > _omne_ > _omre_ > _(h)ombre_; see 2.4.3.2), almost all surviving intertonics other than /a/ were eliminated. Examples of pretonic loss:

CATĒNATU > *_cadenado_ > *_cadnado_ > _candado_ 'padlock'
LĪMITĀRE > *_limedar_ > *_limdar_ > _lindar_ 'to border upon'
SEPTIMANA > *_setemana_ > _setmana_ > _semana_ 'week'
TEMPORĀNU > _temprano_ 'early'

and of post-tonic loss:

MANICA > *_mánega_ > _manga_ 'sleeve, hose'
RETINA > *_riédena_ > *_riedna_ > _rienda_ 'reins'
SANGUINE > _sangre_ 'blood'

Examples of survival of /a/ include:

CALAMELLU > _caramillo_ 'type of flute'
CANTHARU > _cántaro_ 'pitcher'
RAPHANU > _rábano_ 'radish'

Latin words with two pretonic vowels other than /a/ lose the vowel closest to the tonic:

INGENERĀRE > _engendrar_ 'to engender'
RECUPERĀRE > _recobrar_ 'to recover'

It will be seen that the consonants brought into contact by the loss of intertonic vowels frequently undergo modification. This will be discussed in 2.5.5.

2.4.3.4 Hiatus

In 2.3.2 it was noted that hiatus could not survive the change in the nature of the Latin accent. Once the accent had become predominantly a stress-accent, neighbouring vowels received markedly different degrees of energy, conditions which militated against hiatus, which requires that its constituent syllables should be of similar intensity. The result is, on the one hand, loss of the weaker vowel (see 2.3.2 for the concept of 'weaker'), a result which is almost regular where the two vowels were identical, or became identical in spoken Latin, through regular change (see 2.4.1–2.4.3.3):

PARIETE > PARETE > *pared* 'wall'
QUIĒTUS > QUĒTUS > *quedo* 'still'
DUŌDECIM > *doce* 'twelve'
MORTUU > *muerto* 'dead'

But note MULIERE > /muljére/ > *mujer* 'woman'.

On the other hand, hiatus was more frequently destroyed by converting the weaker vowel into a glide, thereby changing a sequence of two vowels (each belonging to a separate syllable) to a sequence of glide + vowel (both belonging to the same syllable). The weaker vowel normally happens to be the first and if it is a front vowel it is converted into the front (i.e. palatal) glide [j], while if it is a back vowel the result is the back (i.e. labiovelar) glide [w]. That is,

Ī/Ĭ/Ē/Ĕ (+ vowel) > [j] (+ vowel)
Ū/Ŭ/Ō/Ŏ (+ vowel) > [w] (+ vowel)

This change is evidently a case of neutralization; all front vowels came to be realized in the same way when one of them was originally the weaker member of a sequence of vowels in hiatus, and similarly all back vowels were neutralized under the same circumstances. Such a neutralization produced the usual uncertainty of spelling among the less well educated, and alternation between the spellings E and I, and between O and U, under these conditions, was common in non-literary Latin. In an attempt to redress this uncertainty, the *Appendix Probi* comments

ALIUM NON ALEUM
LANCEA NON LANCIA
VINEA NON VINIA
CLOACA NON CLUACA
PUELLA NON POELLA, etc.,

indirectly demonstrating the total confusion between the phonemes concerned under conditions of hiatus.

The effect upon vowels of the palatal glide created in this way has been anticipated in the discussion of metaphony (see 2.4.2.1 and 2.4.3.1), as has the appearance of new diphthongs created when a glide was transferred to a preceding syllable (2.4.2.4). The effect of the glide upon consonants will be seen in 2.5.2.2.

2.5 Development of the consonant system

2.5.1 The Latin consonant system

The consonants in use in spoken Latin until the first century BC, and in literary Latin for longer, were organized in the following system of three orders and six series shown in table 2.3.

To these thirteen phonemes, some would add two labiovelar phonemes /k^{w}/ and /g^{w}/, although the sounds spelt QU and GU in Latin can be regarded as sequences of the phonemes /k/ and /g/ followed by a non-syllabic (or glide) realization of the phoneme /u/. The productivity of the system was increased by the fact that most of these phonemes could appear, within the word, in **geminate** form (i.e. doubled), with the exception of /h/, which could not be geminated, and /f/, /b/, /d/, /g/, which rarely were in the native vocabulary, except at morpheme boundaries.

The spelling of Latin at this stage seems to have been broadly phonemic, with one letter for each phoneme, although, as we have just seen, both Q and C could be said to represent the same consonant.

2.5.2 Developments from Latin to Old Spanish: (1) The creation of the palatal order

Of these thirteen consonants, /h/ (which was strictly glottal rather than velar) was lost by the first century BC, as can be seen from Latin versification, misspellings and frequent direct comments by grammarians and others.

The twelve remaining phonemes have all survived into Old Spanish (and Modern Spanish), but have been joined by a number of others created along

Table 2.3 *The Latin consonant system*

	labial	dento-alveolar	velar
voiceless plosive	/p/	/t/	/k/
voiced plosive	/b/	/d/	/g/
voiceless fricative	/f/	/s/	/h/
nasal	/m/	/n/	
lateral		/l/	
flap		/ɾ/	

the way. The broad pattern of development of the system has been one of enrichment: the system grew in size and complexity until the late medieval period (after which a number of mergers reduced the range of phonemes).

The Spanish consonant system became more complex than the Latin system through participation in two very general Romance processes:

1 A new order of palatal consonants was created between the dento-alveolar and the velar orders (see 2.5.2.1–6). This process began in spoken Latin and is common to all Romance languages (Lausberg 1965, Lloyd 1987: 131–7, Pensado 1984).

2 A series of voiced fricatives was created (see 2.5.3), to match the pre-existing series of voiceless fricatives. This change includes the lenition process common to all Western Romance varieties (Jungemann 1955, Lausberg 1965, Lloyd 1987: 140–7, Martinet 1974: 421-61, Pensado 1984, Tovar 1952).

In each of these cases, a number of individual changes contributed to the restructuring, and we shall consider these changes in chronological order, beginning with those which contributed to the creation of the palatal order.

2.5.2.1 Consonantization of /i/

Word-initial /i/ before another vowel was non-syllabic from early times in Latin, no doubt articulated as the glide [j]. IĀNUĀRIUS was probably pronounced [jaːnuaːrius], and the same is likely to have been true in other morpheme-initial positions such as the case represented by CŌNIUGES. In spoken Latin, the frictionless glide [j] became a consonant, presumably the fricative [ǰ] or even the affricate [d$^{\check{j}}$] (in some areas [ʒ] or [d^{ʒ}]). The consonantal quality of I- under these circumstances is reflected in clumsy misspellings of the kind ZANUARIO (for IANUARIO), ZERAX (for HIERAX), SUSTUS (for IUSTUS), spellings which do no more than indicate the fricative or affricate nature of the initial phoneme. Word-initial I- may be regarded as a separate (voiced palatal fricative or affricate) phoneme in spoken Latin, and its appearance can therefore be considered the first step in the creation of a palatal order of consonants (and of the voiced fricative series; see 2.5.3). Further development of /ǰ/ will be considered together with that of /g/ (2.5.2.3), some of whose allophones merged with I-.

2.5.2.2 Palatal developments of consonant + [j]

The palatal glide [j] (emerging from atonic E and I in hiatus; see 2.4.3.4) was frequent in spoken Latin. Through the process of assimilation (2.1.1.1), this glide often modified the preceding consonant, changing its place of articulation by drawing it towards that of [j], and sometimes, in the process, changing its manner of articulation from plosive to affricate or fricative. Such an assimilatory process is referred to as **palatalization** and may or may not lead to the simplification of the two phonemes to only one. In general, the palatalizing influence of [j] is felt most readily on those consonants articulated closest to the palate (the dento-alveolars and the velars) but may be exercised at even greater distance (on the labials). We shall consider all the possible combinations of cons. + [j] (remembering that /h/ had been lost and observing that /f/, because it was rare in word-internal position, does not enter into combination with [j]) in the order in which, it seems, they were affected by palatalization.

1 /t/ + [j] and /k/ + [j]. The first stage of palatalization of these combinations (*c.* first century AD) produced

/t/ + [j] > [t^s] (PUTEU > ['pot^{s}o], MARTIU > ['mart^{s}o])
/k/ + [j] > [tʃ] (ĒRĪCIU > [e'ritʃo], CALCEA > ['kaltʃa]),

pronunciations which are hinted at by such misspellings as VINCENTZUS (for VINCENTIUS) and TERSIO (for TERTIŌ). However, although most Romance languages maintained the contrast between these two results, the Latin of Cantabria (the area where Castilian developed) allowed them to merge in [t^s]. This pronunciation survives into Old Spanish (spelt *c* or *ç*) when it was preceded by a consonant:

MARTIU > *març̧o* 'March'
CALCEA > *calça* 'stockings', later 'breeches'

However, where [t^s] was preceded by a vowel (and was therefore intervocalic) it was subject to lenition (2.5.3.2) and mostly frequently produced OSp. /d^z/ (spelt *z*):

PUTEU > *pozo* 'well'
ĒRĪCIU > *erizo* 'hedgehog'

although this voiced outcome is far from regular (see 2.5.3.2.6).

There is some evidence (see Malkiel 1971, Wilkinson 1976) that [tj] and [kj], when following a vowel, were at first treated differently in Old Spanish, [tj] producing OSp. /d^z/, but [kj] giving /t^s/. Many of the forms containing /t^s/ < [kj] were then modified to /d^z/, perhaps for reasons of analogy, since most of the relevant cases of /t^s/ occurred in suffixes (e.g. -ACEU > *-aço*), which were open to influence from similar inherited derivational elements which in a majority of cases displayed voiced consonants (see 4.14.2.1).

Geminate /tt/ and /kk/ were also palatalized by following [j], producing in spoken Latin the geminate [tt^s], at which stage there was a merger, in Cantabria, between the product of /tt/ + [j] and /kk/ + [j], on the one hand, and the product of /pt/ + [j], /kt/ + [j] and /sk/ + [j], on the other, all these groups giving [tt^s], later simplified (through lenition, like other geminates, 2.5.3.2) to OSp. /t^s/ (spelt *ç* or *c*):

MATTIĀNA > *maçana*, later *mançana* 'apple'
BRACCHIU > *braço* 'arm'
*CAPTIĀRE > *caçar* 'to hunt'
*DIRĒCTIĀRE > *adereçar* 'to prepare'
ASCIOLA > *açuela* 'adze'

2 /l/ + [j] widely became [ʎ] in spoken Latin, a sound which persisted in most areas. However, in the late spoken Latin of Cantabria or in pre-literary Castilian, this [ʎ] was modified to /ʒ/ (voiced pre-palatal fricative, comparable with *s* in Eng. *leisure, measure*). This development from lateral to central articulation may have resulted from a need to maintain contrast between words originally containing /l/ + [j] and those containing /ll/, since the latter was being transformed into [ʎ] in the Castilian area (e.g. GALLU > *gallo* 'cock'; see 2.5.3.2.9). However, this argument cannot be regarded as conclusive since Eastern Hispano-Romance (Aragonese and most of Catalan) allows the merger of /l/ + [j] and /ll/. Examples of the development of Lat. /l/ + [j] > Cast. /ʒ/ (spelt *j, i, g*) include:

ALIU > *ajo* 'garlic'
FOLIA > *foja, foia* (later *hoja*) 'leaf'
MOLLIĀRE > *mojar* 'to soak'
MULIERE > *mugier* (later *mujer*) 'woman, wife'
MELIŌRE > *mejor, meior* 'better'

3 /n/ + [j] underwent mutual assimilation in spoken Latin, producing [ɲ], which survives as OSp. /ɲ/ (spelt *nn*, or its contraction *ñ*):

ARĀNEA > *araña* 'spider'
HISPANIA > *España* 'Spain'
SENIŌRE > *señor* 'sir'
VĪNEA > *viña* 'vineyard'

4 /d/ + [j] and **/g/ + [j]** were everywhere palatalized in spoken Latin and merged, probably as the geminate [ǰǰ], thereby entering into a further merger with intervocalic -I-. The sound represented by I in words like MAIUS, PEIUS, etc., was evidently a geminate (no doubt [ǰǰ]) in spoken Latin; this conclusion is based on direct comment by Roman grammarians and on the spelling of such words in inscriptions with a double-height I (I *longa*). Whatever its source, spoken Latin [ǰǰ] was subject to reduction, in Western Romance, through lenition (2.5.3.2) and normally appears in OSp. as /ǰ/ (spelt *y*, also *i* in late Old Spanish, and early Modern Spanish):

PODIU > *poyo* 'hill, bench'
RADIĀRE > *rayar* 'to scratch, score'
EXAGIU > *ensayo* 'attempt'
FĀGEA > *faya* (later *haya*) 'beech tree'
MAIU > *mayo* 'May'
MAIŌRE > *mayor* 'greater'

Where /ǰ/ was preceded in early Old Spanish by a front vowel, the consonant was lost through assimilation to the vowel:

SEDEAM > *sea* (pres. subj. of *ser*)
VIDEO > *veo* 'I see'

CORRIGIA > *correa* 'leather strap'
PĒIŌRE > *peor* 'worse'

Where Lat. /d/ + [j] was preceded by a consonant, the result of the palatalization process was OSp. voiceless /t^s/:

HORDEOLU > *orçuelo* 'style'
VIRDIA > *berça* 'cabbage'
VERĒCUNDIA > *vergüença* (beside *vergüeña*) 'shame'

5 The labials **/b/ + [j]** and **/m/ + [j]** were largely unaffected by palatalization. Apart from the verbal case HABEAM > *haya* (pres. subj. *haber*), the place-name *Peñarroya* (< PINNA RUBEA), and possibly *hoya* 'pit' (< FOVEA), the consonants survive unchanged (apart from fricatization of /b/; see 2.5.3.2) into Old Spanish (and Modern Spanish). The merger of -B- and -V- in spoken Latin (2.5.3.1) must also be borne in mind. Examples include:

RUBEU > *ruvio* (later *rubio*) 'blond'
NOVIU > *novio* 'fiancé', etc.
PLUVIA > *lluvia* 'rain'
PRAEMIU > *premio* 'prize'
VINDĒMIA > *vendimia* 'grape harvest'

6 Lat. **/p/ + [j]**, **/s/ + [j]**, and **/r/ + [j]** were subject only to metathesis (see 2.1.1.4), without palatalization of the consonant. For the treatment of the glide, once transposed, see 2.4.2.4. Examples are:

CAPIAM > *quepa* (pres. subj. *caber*)
BĀSIU > *beso* 'kiss'
MANSIŌNE > *mesón* 'inn' (for NS > /s/, see 2.5.3.2)
AUGURIU > *agüero* 'omen'
FERRĀRIU > *ferrero* (later *herrero*) 'blacksmith'

2.5.2.3 Palatalization of syllable-initial velars

The Latin phonemes /k/ and /g/, when followed by a front vowel, were palatalized in later spoken Latin and contributed to the creation of the Old Spanish phonemes /t^s/, /d^z/, and /ǰ/, a process initiated by the assimilations discussed in 2.5.2.2.

As exemplified in 2.1.1.1, Lat. /k/ probably always had a fronted allophone ([ḱ]) used when the following vowel belonged to the front series (/i/, /e/, or /ɛ/). In spoken Latin, this assimilatory fronting process was continued and exaggerated, so that the allophone of /k/ used before front vowels came to be palatal ([tʃ]), and was further fronted in some areas (including Spain) to [t^s]. This phonetic adjustment, made possible by the absence of palatal phonemes from the Latin system, is reflected in occasional misspellings like INTCITAMENTO (for INCITAMENTO) and NISEAM (for NICEAM). However, the change is not merely phonetic, but has consequences for the phonemic system of Latin. In the first place, it implies neutralization, before front vowels, of /k/ on the one hand, and /t/ + [j] and /k/ + [j], on the other. Thus PĀCE [ˈpat^{s}e], and FACIE [ˈfat^{s}e] shared the same internal consonant.

In the second place, the sound [t^{s}] could now occur before any of the spoken Latin vowels, and was therefore well on the way to phonologization. For example, PRETIĀRE [preˈt^{s}are] 'to prize' was in minimal opposition to PRĒCĀRE [preˈkare] 'to beg', and the sound [t^{s}] can be seen before a range of vowels in ĒRĪCIU [eˈrit^{s}o], MARTIU [ˈmart^{s}o], CALCEA [ˈkalt^{s}a], ACUTIĀRE [akuˈt^{s}are], FACIT [ˈfat^{s}et], AMĪCĪ [aˈmit^{s}i], etc. Full phonologization of /t^{s}/ probably had to await the development of QUI-, QUE- > [ki], [ke] (see 2.5.7), at which stage /t^{s}/ contrasts with /k/ in all environments.

The treatment of Lat. /k/ is therefore a case of incipient split, /k/ remaining velar before non-front vowels and contributing towards the creation of the phoneme /t^{s}/ when it occurred before front vowels:

CIRCA > *cerca* (OSp. /t^{s}/) 'near'
CAELU > *cielo* (OSp. /t^{s}/) 'sky'
CAPANNA > *cabaña* (OSp. /k/) 'hut'
CORŌNA > *corona* (OSp. /k/) 'crown'
CŪPA > *cuba* (OSp. /k/) 'vat'

When spoken Latin /t^{s}/ (< /k/ or any other source) occurred between vowels, it was subject, in Spanish (as in other Western Romance varieties) to lenition (see 2.5.3.2), and therefore appears in Old Spanish as the voiced phoneme /d^{z}/ (spelt *z*):

DĪCIT > *dize* 'he says'
FACERE > *fazer* (later *hacer*) 'to do'
RACĒMU > *razimo* 'bunch of grapes'
VĪCĪNU > *vezino* 'neighbour'

Since Latin intervocalic /k/ before non-front vowels became voiced /g/ in Old Spanish (see 2.5.3.2.8), it can be seen that Lat. /k/ in this position split into two Old Spanish phonemes, /d^{z}/ and /g/:

FACIT > *faze* (later *hace*) 'he does'
IACĒRE > *yazer* (later *yacer*) 'to lie'
LOCĀLE > *logar* (later *lugar*) 'place'
IOCU > *juego* 'game'

The sequence QU, whether word-initial (see 2.5.7) or internal, retained its glide [w] following /k/ for a sufficiently long period to ensure that this /k/ is always treated like /k/ preceding a non-front vowel and never like /k/ preceding a front vowel: QUĪNDECIM > *quince* 'fifteen', SEQUERE (CL SEQUĪ) > *seguir* 'to follow'.

Note that although few words with geminate /kk/ before a front vowel have survived into Spanish, the Latin group /sk/ was frequent before such vowels. Both groups gave rise to a geminate /tt^{s}/ in the spoken Latin of Cantabria, thereby merging with the product of /kk/ + [j], /tt/ + [j], etc. (see 2.5.2.2(1)) and producing OSp. /t^s/ (spelt (*s*)*ç* or (*s*)*c*), through the usual Western Romance simplification of geminates (2.5.3.2):

FLACCIDU > *llacio* (later *lacio*) 'lank'
FASCĒS > *faces* (later *haces*) 'bundles (of corn, wood, etc.)'
PASCĒRE > OSp. *pascer~pacer*, later only *pacer* 'to graze'
PISCĒS > *peces* 'fish'.

The voiced velar /g/, like voiceless /k/, no doubt had always had fronted allophones when followed by any front vowel. As in the case of /k/, such fronted allophones were further fronted in later spoken Latin (a development made possible by the absence of palatal phonemes in Latin) and became the voiced palatal fricative [ǰ]. In word-initial position, therefore, the product of /g/ (before front vowels) merged with the product of non-syllabic I- (see 2.5.2.1), so that henceforth words like GENESTA and IĀNUĀRIUS had the same initial sound. This neutralization of phonemes is reflected in the usual confusion of spellings among less well-educated writers of Latin; we find GEIUNA (for IEIŪNA) and GENARIUS (for IENUĀRIUS or, more standardly, IANUĀRIUS).

Palatal /ǰ/ from these sources was sometimes preserved, in word-initial position, in Old Spanish, spelt *y*. Thus:

GEMMA > *yema* 'yolk, etc.'
GYPSU > *yesso* (later *yeso*) 'plaster'
IACET > *yaze* (later *yace*) 'he lies'

However, loss or modification of /ǰ/ was frequent in early Old Spanish, for a series of reasons. Sometimes, through analogy, word-initial /ǰe/ in an atonic syllable was replaced by /e/, since /ǰe/ was phonetically identical to the tonic syllable of words like *yegua* 'mare' < EQUA and *yerva* 'grass' < HERBA. But in *yegua*, *yerva*, etc. /ǰe/ owed its existence to the diphthongization process (see 2.4.2.2) and was therefore limited to tonic syllables and corresponded to /e/ in atonic syllables (e.g. *ervage* 'fodder'). For this reason the **atonic** /ǰe/ of words like **yermano* 'brother' (< GERMĀNU) or **yenero* 'January' (< IĀNUĀRIU) would have appeared anomalous and was brought in line with the prevailing morpho-phonological pattern by replacing /ǰe/ by /e/:

**yermano* > *ermano* (later *hermano*)
**yenero* > *enero*

Similarly, IACTĀRE > *echar* 'to throw', GENUCULU > OSp. *(h)inojo* 'knee', (non-standard) IINIPERU > *enebro* 'juniper', GELĀRE > *(h)elar* 'to freeze', GINGĪVĀS > *enzias* (later *encías*) 'gums'.

Early OSp. /ǰ/ was also occasionally lost for reasons of dissimilation before another palatal phoneme, e.g.

**yayuno* (< non-standard IAIŪNU) > *ayuno* 'fasting'

Finally, /ǰ/ was sometimes modified to /ʒ/ (spelt *j*, *i*), probably under the influence of Medieval Latin, as read aloud in the church and the law-courts:

IŪSTU > *yusto* > *justo* 'just'
IŪDICĒS > *yuezes* > *juezes* 'judges'

For a full account of the various medieval treatments of /ǰ/, see Penny (1988).

Intervocalic /g/ before front vowels was also palatalized, but in this position did not merge with non-syllabic -I-. The latter, it will be recalled (2.5.2.2(4)), corresponded to geminate /ǰǰ/, while the immediate product of spoken Latin intervocalic /g/ before front vowels appears to have been simple /ǰ/, which was rapidly eliminated, by total assimilation to the following vowel, or through the lenition process (2.5.3.2). It is probably this total loss that is indicated by occasional misspellings like TRIENTA (for TRĪGINTA) and by the *Appendix Probi*'s recommendation CALCOSTEGIS NON CALCOSTEIS. Certainly, this loss is characteristic of all Romance languages, including Spanish:

DIGITU > *dedo* 'finger'
FRĪGIDU > *frío* 'cold'
MAGISTRU > *maestro* 'master'
SAGITTA > *saeta* 'arrow'

To summarize, Lat. /g/ underwent phonemic split. In initial position, it gave palatal results (which merged with I- and then suffered further changes, including loss) before front vowels, but remained velar before other vowels:

GYPSU > OSp. *yesso* 'plaster'
GENERU > *yerno* 'son-in-law'
GALLĪNA > *gallina* 'hen'
GAUDIU > *gozo* 'enjoyment'
GUTTA > *gota* 'drop'

In intervocalic position, /g/ was palatalized and lost before front vowels, but before non-front vowels survived in some words as a velar (but a velar fricative, see 2.5.3.2.8), although elimination of this velar was frequent, so that the effects of the phonemic split are partially obscured:

RUGĪTU > *roido* (later *ruido*) 'noise'
DIGITU > *dedo* 'finger'
NEGĀRE > *negar* 'to deny' (but LIGĀRE > *liar* 'to tie')
AUGUSTU > *agosto* 'August' (but REGĀLE > *real* 'royal, real')

Where /k/ and /g/ occurred as the second element of an internal group in Latin, in principle they evolve, as is generally the case for consonants under these conditions, in the same way as in word-initial position (see above). Thus, in the case of cons. + /k/ (in which case the consonant may be S (see /sk/ above), L, R, or N), we observe the same phonemic split as in the case of initial /k/, namely /k/ before non-front vowels, OSp. /t^s/, MSp. /θ/ before front vowels:

SULCU > *surco* 'furrow'	DULCE > *dulce* 'sweet'
PORCU > *puerco* 'pig'	*TORCERE (CL TORQUERE) > *torcer* 'to twist'
IŪNCU > *junco* 'reed'	*VINCICULU > *vencejo* 'bond (for tying corn)'

However, in the case of cons. + /g/ the development of the velar is notoriously thorny, especially since many of the examples are verbs, where analogical interference with phonological development is likely to be involved (see Malkiel 1982 for a detailed account). Of the consonants that may be grouped internally with /g/ (L, R and N), only R and N occur with any frequency. For /ɾg/ the outcome is /ɾg/ before non-front vowels and (usually) OSp. /ɾd^z/, MSp. /ɾθ/ before front vowels:

SPARGŌ > OSp. *espargo* 'I strew' (remodelled as MSp. *esparzo*; see 3.7.8.1.3(2))

ARGĪLLA > OSp. *arzilla* > MSp. *arcilla* 'clay'

For /ng/ we predictably find no change when a non-front vowel follows:

TANGŌ> OSp. *tango* 'I touch' (remodelled as MSp. *taño* 'I play (an instrument)'; see 3.7.8.1.3(2))

But, before a front vowel, /ng/ gives no fewer than three results:

OSp. /nd^z/, MSp. /nθ/: GINGĪVA > OSp. *enzia* > MSp. *encía* 'gum'

OSp. and MSp. /ɲ/: RINGERE (CL RINGĪ) > *reñir* 'to scold'

OSp. and MSp. /n/ (i.e. with loss of /g/ when intervocalic before a front vowel (see above)): QUĪNGENTŌS > *quinientos* 'five hundred'

2.5.2.4 Palatalization of syllable-final velars

A further source of Old Spanish palatal phonemes was provided by /k/ and /g/ when grouped, within the word, with a following consonant. In Western Romance (and therefore in Spanish) such syllable-final velars were first fricatized (to /x/) and then modified to [i̯]. This off-glide had two effects which are observable in Spanish: on the one hand, through metaphony (see 2.4.2.1), it caused raising of the preceding vowel, often combining with it thereafter; and, on the other, it had an assimilatory effect on the following (syllable-initial) consonant, a process which gave rise to new palatal phonemes. The internal groups of spoken Latin whose first member was a velar were the following: -X- (= /ks/), -CT-, -CL- (occurring chiefly in words where the group was formed by loss of an intertonic vowel, e.g. SPECLUM for SPECULUM, see 2.4.3.3), -GL- (likewise formed through loss of an intertonic; cf. *TEGLA for TEGULA, etc.), and -GN-. In the first two cases, the processes outlined above produced entirely new (palatal) consonants:

-X- > /ʃ/:	DĪXĪ> *dixe* (later *dije*) 'I said'
	MATAXA > *madexa* (later *madeja*) 'skein'
	TAXU > *texo* (later *tejo*) 'yew'
-CT- > /tʃ/:	FACTU > *fecho* (later *hecho*), participle of *hacer*
	NOCTE > *noche* 'night'
	STRICTU > *estrecho* 'narrow'

The group LT, when preceded by U, has the same outcome as CT. Syllable-final /l/ was frequently velar in spoken Latin (as in Modern English; cf. *wool*, *wall*, *old*), and this characteristic was no doubt exaggerated after a back (velar) vowel. This velar allophone of /l/ was then treated like other syllable-final velars (see above):

(U)LT- > /tʃ/: MULTU > *mucho* 'much'
CULTELLU > *cuchiello* (later *cuchillo*) 'knife'

Note that where the vowel preceding -CT- was /i/ in spoken Latin, the glide (< -C) was quickly absorbed by the (homorganic) vowel and leaves the T- unaffected:

FRĪCTU > *frito* 'fried'
FĪCTU > *fito* (later *hito*) 'boundary-marker, target'

In the case of -CL- and-GL-, the result of palatalization of the second consonant was at first /ʎ/, an outcome which implies merger with the product of /l/ + [j] (see 2.5.2.2(2)) and the same Old Spanish outcome as that group:

-CL- > /ʒ/: LENTIC(U)LA > *lenteja* 'lentil'
NOVĀC(U)LA > *navaja* 'razor'
OC(U)LU > *ojo* 'eye'
VERMIC(U)LU > *bermejo* 'red'
-GL- > /ʒ/: REG(U)LA > *reja* 'ploughshare'
TEG(U)LA > *teja* 'tile'

Note that in the sequence -T(V)L- (where (V) indicates an intertonic vowel lost in spoken Latin), the first consonant was replaced by /k/ (*Appendix Probi*: VETULUS NON VECLUS, VITULUS NON VICLUS) and the group therefore shares the development of -CL-:

-T(V)L- > /ʒ/: *ROTULĀRE > *arrojar* 'to throw'
VETULU > *viejo* 'old'

The outcome of -GN- again shows merger, this time with the product of /n/ + [j] (see 2.5.2.2(3)):

-GN- > /ɲ/: LIGNA > *leña* 'firewood'
PUGNU > *puño* 'fist'
STAGNU > *estaño* 'tin'

The groups concerned here had the full evolution described above only if the second consonant remained syllable-initial. The final stage (palatalization) did not take place if the group was (or became) word-final, or if, through loss of an intertonic vowel (see 2.4.3.3), one of the consonant groups under consideration here came into contact with a following, third, consonant (for such secondary groupings, see 2.5.5). Under all these circumstances, the second consonant of the primary group necessarily ceased to be syllable-initial and became syllable-final. Since, throughout the history of Spanish, it has been impermissible for palatal consonants to occupy syllable-final position, a palatal result is precluded in this case. The glide which emerged from their velar consonant (see above) affects the preceding vowel but not the following consonant. Contrast the following cases with those quoted above (DĪXĪ > *dixe*, STRICTU > *estrecho*, MULTU > *mucho*, LIGNA > *leña*, etc.):

-X(C) > /(i̯)s/: FRAXINU > (pre-literary) *freisno* > *fresno* 'ash tree'
SĒX > *seis* 'six'
-CT(C) > /(i̯)n/: PECTINĀRE > *peinar* 'to comb'
LECTŌRĪLE > *letril* (later *atril*) 'lectern'
(U)LT(C) > /i̯t/: VULTURE > *buitre* 'vulture'
MULT(U) > *muyt* (later *muy*) 'very'
-GN(C) > /(i̯)n/: PIGNORA > *peyndra, pendra, prenda* 'pledge, garment'

2.5.2.5 Palatalization of -LL- and -NN-

One of the outcomes in Spanish of the lenition process was the palatalization of the Latin geminates /ll/ and /nn/. The motives for this change will be seen in 2.5.3.2, but we note here its contribution to the creation of the Old Spanish palatal order of consonants. While -LL- produced a new phoneme (we have seen (2.5.2.2(2), and 2.5.2.4) that late spoken Latin /ʎ/ (</l/ + [j] and -CL-, -GL-) was modified in early Spanish to /ʒ/, perhaps owing to the change now under consideration), -NN- merged with the product of Lat. /n/ + [j] (2.5.2.2(3)) and -GN- (2.5.2.4):

-LL- > /ʎ/: CABALLU < *cavallo* (later *caballo*) 'horse'
GALLU < *gallo* 'cock'
VALLĒS > *valles* 'valleys'
-NN- > /ɲ/: ANNU > *año* 'year'
CANNA > *caña* 'cane'
GRUNNĪRE > *gruñir* 'to growl, groan'

2.5.2.6 Palatalization of PL-, CL-, FL-

It seems likely that the /l/ of these groups had a palatalized pronunciation ([ʎ]) already in the spoken Latin of some areas (see Lausberg 1965: 332–5). In pre-literary Spanish, the initial consonant was in most cases assimilated to the following [ʎ] and was absorbed by it, although there are some popular words (e.g. PLATEA > *plaça*, later *plaza* '(town) square', CLAVĪCULA > *clavija* 'peg', FLOCCU > *flueco*, later *fleco* 'tassel'; for detailed discussion see Malkiel 1963–4) which shows retention of the group. Examples of the more usual (palatal) treatment are:

PL- > /ʎ/: PLAGA > *llaga* 'wound'
PLANU > *llano* 'flat'
PLICĀRE > *llegar* 'to arrive'
CL- > /ʎ/: CLĀMĀRE > *llamar* 'to call'
CLAUSA > *llosa* 'enclosed field'
CLAVE > *llave* 'key'
FL- > /ʎ/: FLAMMA > *llama* 'flame'
FLACCIDU > *llacio* (later *lacio*) 'lank'

Where these groups occurred internally following another consonant, the regular result was /tʃ/. In this case, it appears that the voiceless /p/, /k/ or /f/ devoiced the following /ʎ/ before being absorbed:

(cons.)PL- > /tʃ/: AMPLU > *ancho* 'broad'
IMPLĒRE > *henchir* 'to cram'
(cons.)CL-> /tʃ/: *MANCLA (CL MACULA) > *mancha* 'stain'
(cons.)FL- > /tʃ/: INFLARE > *hinchar* 'to inflate, swell'

The same treatment was accorded, in a few words, to initial PL-, a development which no doubt originated under circumstances where the word was preceded by another ending in a consonant and where the post-consonantal treatment was eventually extended (for unknown reasons) to all uses of the word:

PL- > /tʃ/: *PLATTU > *chato* 'snub-nosed'
*PLŌPPU (CL PŌPULU) > *chopo* 'black poplar'
PLUTEU > *chozo*, whence *choza* 'hut'

2.5.2.7 Summary of palatal developments from Latin to Old Spanish

As a result of the various processes considered in the preceding sections (2.5.2.1–6), Old Spanish came to have a palatal order of consonants, which had been lacking at first in Latin. In some cases (specifically, in the development of /t^s/ and /d^z/), although there had been an earlier palatal stage of development, the outcome was a new dento-alveolar phoneme. The Old Spanish phonemes created in these ways are listed in table 2.4, together with the various sources of each phoneme and a single example of each development. Cross reference is given to the earlier discussion of each change. (C) and (V) respectively indicate that a consonant or a vowel is a necessary conditioning factor but does not participate directly in the outcome.

2.5.3 Developments from Latin to Old Spanish: (2) The creation of the voiced fricative series

We come now to the second of the two major realignments which affected the consonantal system of spoken Latin. As anticipated in 2.5.2, a series of voiced fricative consonants (a series of phonemes lacking in spoken Latin) was created as the result of a number of separate processes, the main one of which is lenition (2.5.3.2). Some of these processes have already been considered, since they contribute to both the major readjustments, providing not just new **palatal** consonants but **voiced** palatal **fricatives**.

2.5.3.1 The appearance of /ǰ/and /β/

We have already seen how the voiced fricative /ǰ/ emerged, from initial non-syllabic I- (2.5.2.1) and intervocalic -I- (see 2.5.2.2(4)), and merged with /d/ + [j], /g/ + [j]. Just as non-syllabic I was consonantized in spoken Latin, so too was non-syllabic V, in words like VĪTA, AVIS, where the earlier Latin pronunciation

Table 2.4 *Sources of Old Spanish palatal consonant phonemes*

OSp. phoneme	Latin sources	Example	See
/t^s/	(C)/t/ + [j]	MARTIU > *marÃ§o*	2.5.2.2(1)
	(C)/k/ + [j]	CALCEA > *calÃ§a*	2.5.2.2(1)
	/tt/ + [j]	MATTIANA > *ma(n)Ã§ana*	2.5.2.2(1)
	/kk/ + [j]	BRACCHIU > *braÃ§o*	2.5.2.2(1)
	/pt/ + [j]	*CAPTIÄ€RE > *caÃ§ar*	2.5.2.2(1)
	/kt/ + [j]	*DIRÄ’CTIÄ€RE > *adereÃ§ar*	2.5.2.2(1)
	initial /k/(E/I)	CISTA > *cesta*	2.5.2.3
	/sk/(E/I)	PISCÄ’S > *peÃ§es*	2.5.2.3
	/kk/(E/I)	FLACCIDU > *lacio*	2.5.2.3
/d^z/	(V)/t/ + [j]	PUTEU > *pozo*	2.5.2.2(1)
	(V)/k/ + [j]	Ä’RÄªCIU > *erizo*	2.5.2.2(1)
	(V)/k/(E/I)	VÄªCÄªNU > *vezino*	2.5.2.3
/tÊƒ/	/kt/	FACTU > *fecho*	2.5.2.4
	(U)/lt/	MULTU > *mucho*	2.5.2.4
	(C)/pl ~ kl ~fl/	AMPLU > *ancho*	2.5.2.6
/Ê’/	/l/ + [j]	FÄªLIU > *fijo*	2.5.2.2(2)
	(V)/kl/	OC(U)LU > *ojo*	2.5.2.4
	(V)/gl/	TEG(U)LA > *teja*	2.5.2.4
/Êƒ/	/ks/(V)	MAXÄªLLA > *mexilla*	2.5.2.4
/Ç°/	initial /i/(V)	IACET > *yaze*	2.5.2.1
	(V)/i/(V)	MÄ€IU > *mayo*	2.5.2.2(4)
	initial /g/(E/I)	GYPSU > *yesso*	2.5.2.3
	/g/ + [j]	FÄ€GEA > *faya*	2.5.2.2(4)
	/d/ + [j]	RADIÄ€RE > *rayar*	2.5.2.2(4)
	initial /É›Ì/	EQUA > *yegua*	2.5.2.3
/É²/	/n/ + [j]	VÄªNEA > *viÃ±a*	2.5.2.2(3)
	/gn/	PUGNU > *puÃ±o*	2.5.2.4
	/nn/	ANNU > *aÃ±o*	2.5.2.5
/ÊŽ/	/ll/	CABALLU > *cavallo*	2.5.2.5
	initial /pl/	PLÅŒRÄ€RE > *llorar*	2.5.2.6
	initial /kl/	CLÄ€MÄ€RE > *llamar*	2.5.2.6
	initial /fl/	FLAMMA > *llama*	2.5.2.6

was the glide [w] ([wiËta], [aËwis]). And just as /Ç°/ (< I) entered into mergers with other phonemes, so too did the product of V, the voiced bilabial fricative /Î²/ (see VÃ¤Ã¤nÃ¤nen 1968: 92â€“3). In intervocalic position, V seems to have been identical to B in spoken Latin, as witnessed by the extraordinary frequency of interchange of the spellings *b* and *v* in this position: SIVI (for SIBI), VIBA (for VIVA), PLEBES NON PLEVIS (*Appendix Probi*), etc. The likely pronunciation was the voiced fricative /Î²/ for both, a pronunciation inherited by Old Spanish and spelt *v* or *b*:

CABALLU > *cavallo* (later *caballo*) 'horse'
BIBERE > *bever* (later *beber*) 'to drink'
NOVU > *nuevo* 'new'
VĪVERE > *bevir*, *bivir* (later *vivir*) 'to live'

With regard to initial B- and V-, ancient misspellings suggest that there was some neutralization of the two phonemes concerned in spoken Latin (after a word-final nasal, it would be difficult to distinguish a bilabial plosive (B-) from a bilabial fricative (V-)). Spellings like BIXIT (for VIXIT), BALIAT (for VALEAT), and the recommendations of the *Appendix Probi* (BACULUS NON VACLUS, VAPULO NON BAPLO) are evidence of this incipient (but unaccomplished) merger. However, it seems that in initial position the Latin phonemes represented by B- and V- maintained their contrast into the Old Spanish period, since Old Spanish spelling practice for the most part continues to distribute initial *b* and *v* according to whether the etymon had B- or V-:

BUCCA > *boca* 'mouth'
BENE > *bien* 'well'
VĪTA > *vida* 'life'
VACCA > *vaca* 'cow'

Only in a minority of instances does Old Spanish spelling show confusion of initial *b-* and *v-*, sometimes due to dissimilation of initial /β/ from a following /β/ (as in VĪVERE > *bevir* (see above), VĪVU > *bivo* 'alive', VERVĀCTU > *barvecho* (later *barbecho*) 'fallow', VOLVERE > *bolver* (later *volver*) 'to return') and sometimes no doubt through increasing neutralization of the two phonemes (e.g. *boz* for *voz* 'voice', *vando* for *bando* 'clan'). Full merger was not accomplished until the late medieval and early modern periods (see 2.6.1 and Penny 1976).

2.5.3.2 Lenition

Beginning in the last centuries of the Empire and continuing through the Dark Ages, Western Romance (therefore including Spanish) was affected by an interrelated series of consonantal changes, sometimes described as 'weakenings' and referred to by the name **lenition**. Almost all intervocalic consonants and all geminates were involved in these changes, one of whose major outcomes was the provision (in Old Spanish, etc.) of further voiced fricative phonemes.

The reason for the lenition changes is much disputed. Some have seen in them the influence upon spoken Latin of Celtic speech, since similar weakenings of intervocalic consonants are evident in the well-documented history of the Celtic languages, and since there is considerable (but not complete) correspondence between the areas of originally Celtic population and the areas of Romance speech where lenition is evident (Gaul, the Alps, northern Italy, western Spain); see Baldinger (1972: ch. 8), Martinet (1974: 365–420). Others (e.g. Alarcos 1965: 241–7) have sought purely Latin explanations: an increase

Table 2.5 *Increase in incidence of geminates*

Process	Evidence
RS > /ss/	DOSSUM for DORSUM; *Appendix Probi:* PERSICA NON PESSICA
PS > /ss/	ISSE for IPSE
PT > /tt/	SETTEMBRES for SEPTEMBRIS
MN > /nn/	ALUNNUS for ALUMNUS
MB >/mm/	*LUMMUS < LUMBUS; limited to central and S. Italy and to central and E. Spain; not attested until after the Latin period

in spoken Latin of the incidence of geminates (see below) led to an unbalanced consonantal system, an imbalance which was redressed by the simplification of the geminates, a process which had the consequence of causing a chain-reaction of further changes (voicing of voiceless intervocalics and fricatization/loss of voiced intervocalics).

It is certainly true that in spoken Latin there was a considerable increase in the incidence of geminates, resulting from a number of assimilations which affected certain common consonant groups. Of the following cases of assimilation (revealed by the spelling evidence quoted), not all affected all varieties of Romance; some were geographically widespread, others more limited, but all affected that variety of spoken Latin which gave rise to Spanish (see table 2.5).

Note that the group NS was reduced to the simple consonant /s/ (e.g. *Appendix Probi*: ANSA NON ASA, MENSA NON MESA, TENSA NON TESA), not a geminate.

Following these changes (in the opinion of some, *because* of them), the intervocalic consonants of Western Romance underwent a series of interrelated modifications, which, in principle, take the following form. Geminates were reduced to simple intervocalic consonants (perhaps because geminates are expensive in terms of physical energy and the incidence of geminates had, as we have seen, increased); e.g. /kk/ > /k/. This simplification put pressure on pre-existing intervocalic consonants to change, causing the simple intervocalics (if they were originally voiceless) to become voiced (e.g. /k/ > /g/), in order to maintain, by other means, the original contrast between geminate and simple. In turn, the voicing of voiceless intervocalic phonemes threatened merger with the pre-existing voiced phonemes, and the latter (if originally plosive) became fricative (e.g. /g/ > [ɣ]) in order to avoid the merger. The chain-reaction was completed when, in order to avoid merger with the new voiced fricatives (< voiced plosives), the pre-existing voiced fricative /ǰ/ (the result of the palatalization of /g/ before front vowels, for which see 2.5.2.3) was eliminated from the words in which it occurred.

This chain-reaction can be summarized, still in principle, in table 2.6.

Table 2.6 *Lenition in Spanish*

Process			Example
1 Simplification	geminate	simple	Lat. /kk/ > OSp. /k/
2 Voicing	voiceless	voiced	Lat. /k/ > OSp. /g/
3 Fricatization	voiced plosive	voiced fricative	Lat. /g/ > OSp. /ɣ/ OSp. /g/ > MSp. [ɣ]
4 Loss	voiced fricative	zero	OSp. /ɣ/ > MSp. /Ø/ Lat. /ǰ/ > /Ø/

In practice, it is important to know, in the case of Spanish, which of these processes were contemporary (and therefore mutually exclusive) and which were successive (allowing the output of one process to become the input of the next). Process 1 is contemporary with process 2; its output (a simple phoneme) never becomes the input of any of the other processes. Thus, Latin /kk/, having been reduced to /k/ by simplification (1) (e.g. SICCU > *seco* 'dry'), remains a voiceless plosive and is not affected by voicing (2), fricatization (3) or loss (4).

Process 2 may (specifically, in the case of the fricatives of spoken Latin) stand alone. Thus Latin -S-, having become /z/ (e.g. CASA = /kása/ > OSp. *casa* = /káza/ 'house'), suffers no further change. However, the output of process 2 may (specifically, in the case of the Latin voiceless plosives) become the input of process 3. Thus Latin /k/ suffers voicing to OSp. /g/, which is then fricatized to [ɣ] by about the thirteenth century (Lloyd 1987: 327) (e.g. SĒCĀRE > *segar* 'to reap', where *g* = [ɣ], as in Modern Spanish).

Process 3 may operate in isolation from the other processes, as can be seen in the treatment of spoken Latin -B-, fricatized (already in spoken Latin, see 2.5.3.1) but not lost (e.g. NŪBĒS > *nuves* 'clouds', where *v* represents the voiced fricative /β/, a word later respelt *nubes*). However, the output of process 3 may become the input of process 4. Thus, spoken Latin /g/, having been fricatized (process 3) is also, in a majority of cases, lost (e.g. RĒGĀLE > *real* 'royal', LĪGĀRE > *liar* 'to bind').

Finally, process 4 may operate in isolation. This is what happens in the case of the spoken Latin voiced palatal fricative /ǰ/ (< -G^{e,i}; see 2.5.2.3 (end)), which is eliminated (e.g. DIGITU > *dedo* 'finger').

Full exemplification now follows of the effects of lenition on Spanish intervocalic consonants. The consonant phonemes of spoken Latin are organized into nine groups, on the basis of their distinctive features.

2.5.3.2.1 Labial plosives (see table 2.7). We have seen (2.5.3.1) that Lat. /-b-/ merged with -v-, both giving OSp. /β/.

Table 2.7 *Lenition of labial plosives*

Latin phoneme	Old Spanish phoneme	Example
/-pp-/	/p/	CUPPA > *copa* 'wine glass'
/-p-/	/b/	CŪPA > *cuba* 'wine vat'
/-b-/	/β/	CIBU > *cevo* 'food' (later *cebo* 'bait')

Table 2.8 *Lenition of labial fricatives*

Latin phoneme	Old Spanish phoneme	Example
/-ff-/	/f/	SCOFFĪNA > *escofina* 'file'
/-f-/(<-F-, NF)	/h/	DĒFĒNSA > *defesa* (later *dehesa*) 'unenclosed pasture'
		CONFUNDERE > *cofonder* (Nebrija *cohonder*) 'to ruin' (later *confundir*)
	/β/	PRŌFECTU > *provecho* 'benefit'
		RAPHANU > *rávano* (later *rábano*) 'radish'
/β/ (<-V-)	/β/	NOVU > *nuevo* 'new'

2.5.3.2.2 Labial fricatives (see table 2.8). Internal /ff/ and /f/ were infrequent in Latin and the effects of lenition are obscured here by the characteristic Castilian treatment of this phoneme (see 2.5.6). It can be seen that the development of -F- depends upon speakers' perceptions of the morphological structure of the word concerned: where -F- is perceived to be morpheme-initial (DĒ-FĒNSA, CON-FUNDERE, etc.), it is treated as word-initial and avoids lenition; where it is perceived to be morpheme-internal (as in PRŌFECTU, since PRŌ- ceased to be a productive prefix), it undergoes the lenition process (see Pensado 1999). It will also be noted that Old Spanish at first had no labiodental phonemes, /f/ being a late medieval development (see Penny 1972a, 1990b).

2.5.3.2.3 Labial nasal (see table 2.9). This is the only case of a contrast between geminate and simple consonant which is lost in the course of the development of Spanish.

2.5.3.2.4 Dental plosives (see table 2.10). In general, then, the threefold Latin distinction between /tt/, /t/ and /d/ is maintained in Spanish in the form of a distinction between /t/, /d/ and /Ø/. However, there is a minority of cases in which Latin /-d-/ survives as /d/ in Old Spanish and which therefore

Table 2.9 *Lenition of the labial nasal*

Latin phoneme	Old Spanish phoneme	Example
/-mm-/	/m/	FLAMMA > *llama* 'flame' LAMBERE > *lamer* to lick (for MB > /mm/, see above)
/-m-/	/m/	REMU > *remo* 'oar'

Table 2.10 *Lenition of dental plosives*

Latin phoneme	Old Spanish phoneme	Example
/-tt-/	/t/	GUTTA > *gota* 'drop' RUPTU > *roto* 'broken'
/-t-/	/d/(= [ð])	CATĒNA > *cadena* 'chain'
/-d-/	/Ø/	SEDĒRE > *seer* 'to sit, be'

attest to occasional merger of Latin /t/ and /d/ (CRŪDU > *crudo* 'raw', NŌDU > *nudo* 'knot', NŪDU > *desnudo* 'naked', VADU > *vado* 'ford', etc.). Some of these forms are attested in Old Spanish without /d/ (*crúo*, etc.), and it is possible to view the /d/ of *crudo*, etc., as a case of the influence of Latin spelling (CRUDUS, etc.) on Spanish phonology, at a time when there was genuine vernacular hesitation between, say, *crudo* and *crúo*, leading to preference, in these cases, for the more conservative form of the two. However, Dworkin (1978) makes a strong case for phonotactic unacceptability as the reason for the rejection of *crúo, desnúo, *vao* and preference for the alternants with /d/.

Note that the contrast between /t/ and /d/ operates only in syllable-initial position. Where these phonemes came to occupy syllable-final (including word-final) position, through loss of an intertonic or final vowel, the opposition is neutralized in Old Spanish, as indicated by the free variation between the spellings *t* and *d* in this position. For example, the -T- of words like PARIETE, voiced to /d/ through lenition and then becoming final through loss of /-e/, appears in Old Spanish as a phoneme whose voice is irrelevant, witness the spellings *paret~pared*, identical to *mercet~merced* (the semi-learned descendant of MERCĒDE).

2.5.3.2.5 Dento-alveolar fricative. As can be seen from table 2.11, the spoken Latin contrast between geminate and simple phoneme persists into Old Spanish, but is transformed into a contrast between voiceless and voiced consonant, a distinction maintained until the sixteenth century (see 2.6.2). The

Table 2.11 *Lenition of the dento-alveolar fricative*

Latin phoneme	Old Spanish phoneme	Example
/-ss-/	/s/	OSSU > *huesso* 'bone'
		URSU > *osso* 'bear'
		IPSŌS > *essos* 'those'
/-s-/	/z/	ROSA > *rosa* 'rose'
		MĒNSĒS > *meses* 'months'
		(for NS > /s/, see above)

Table 2.12 *Lenition of the dento-alveolar affricate*

Latin phoneme	Old Spanish phoneme	Example
/-tt^{s}-/	/t^{s}/	*PETTIA > *pieça* 'piece'
(see 2.5.2.2(1))		*POST COCCEU > *pescueço* 'neck'
		RUPTIĀRE > *roçar* 'to scrape, etc.'
		COLLACTEU > *collaço* 'servant'
		*ASCIĀTA > *açada* 'hoe'
		CRESCERE > *creçer* 'to grow' (see 2.5.2.3)
/-t^{s}-/ (see 2.5.2.2(1))	/d^{z}/	MINĀCIA > *amenaza* 'threat' (2.5.2.2.(1))
		TRISTITIA > *tristeza* 'sadness' (2.5.2.2.(1))
		LŪCES > *luzes* 'lights' (2.5.2.3)

spelling contrast between *ss* (for /s/) and *s* (for /z/) was maintained, with hesitations in some texts, through the Middle Ages.

As in the case of /t/ and /d/, the contrast of voice between /s/ and /z/ is neutralized in syllable-final (including word-final) position, where only the spelling *s* occurs. Thus, MĒNSE (pronounced /mése/) > *mes* 'month', -ĒNSE > *-és* (the adjective suffix seen in *cortés*, *montés*, etc.), etc., where *s* descends from Latin /s/, show the same final unit as those words whose final consonant descends from /ss/, e.g. MESSE > *mies* '(ripe) corn'. It should be noted that when these words have added to them the plural morpheme {-es}, the opposition of voice between OSp. /z/ and /s/ (spelt *s* and *ss*) is reasserted, since the phoneme which was word-final (and therefore frequently syllable-final) in the singular form is syllable-initial in the plural form. Thus, *meses*, *corteses*, but *miesses*.

2.5.3.2.6 Dento-alveolar affricate (see table 2.12). As in the previous case, the spoken Latin distinction between geminate and simple consonant is maintained in Old Spanish as a contrast between voiceless and voiced consonant, spelt *ç* and *z* respectively. This contrast was lost in the sixteenth century (see 2.6.2).

Table 2.13 *Lenition of the palatal fricative*

Latin phoneme	Old Spanish phoneme	Example
/-ǰ ǰ-/ (see 2.5.2.2(4))	ǰ	RADIU > *rayo* 'ray, spoke'
		PLAGIA > *playa* 'beach'
		CUIU > *cuyo* 'whose'
/-ǰ -/ (2.5.2.3)	/Ø/	RĒGĪNA > *reina* 'queen'

Another similarity with the case of /s/ and /z/ is that syllable-final neutralization takes place between /t^s/ and /d^z/, the result of the neutralization being spelt *z*. Thus words like *faz* 'bundle' (< FASCE), *pez* 'fish' (< PISCE), where *z* is a reflex of spoken Latin /tt^s/, have the same final unit as words like *paz* 'peace' (< PĀCE), *fez* 'lees (of wine), etc.' (< FECE). It should again be noted that when these words have added to them the plural morpheme {-es}, the opposition of voice between OSp. /d^z/ and /t^s/ (with separate spellings *z* and *ç* respectively) is reasserted, since the phoneme which was word-final (and therefore frequently syllable-final) in the singular form is syllable-initial in the plural form. Thus, *pazes*, *fezes*, but *façes*, *peçes*.

The Old Spanish outcome of Latin /t^s/ is notoriously thorny (see Lloyd 1987: 259–63), and certainly less straightforward than just suggested, in that there are considerable numbers of Old Spanish words whose etyma have /t/ + [j] or /k/ + [j] and which show retention of voiceless /t^s/ rather than voicing: CAPITIA > *cabeça* 'head', PLATEA > *plaça* '(town) square', PŌTIŌNE > *poçón, poçoña* 'poison', CORĀCEA > *coraça* 'cuirass', etc. Some have suggested (e.g. Lausberg 1965: 395–7) that /t/ + [j] and /k/ + [j] were often subject to gemination, becoming /tt/ + [j] and /kk/ + [j], and therefore not subject to process 2, but only to process 1 (2.5.3.2). Later, in early Old Spanish, and as suggested in 2.5.2.2(1), it is possible that, since /t^s/ frequently occurred in derivational suffixes, it was analogically replaced by its voiced counterpart /d^z/, on the basis of the fact that other derivational suffixes most frequently contained voiced consonants (Malkiel 1971–2).

2.5.3.2.7 Palatal fricative (see table 2.13). The contrast between geminate and simple palatal fricative for the most part survives into Spanish (as a contrast between simple consonant and /Ø/), although when a front vowel precedes the contrast is lost, since, as noted in 2.5.2.2(4), under these circumstances the product of /ǰǰ/ was eliminated through assimilation (SEDEAM > *sea*, CORRIGIA > *correa*, PĒIŌRE > *peor*, etc.).

2.5.3.2.8 Velar plosives (see table 2.14). The velar plosives can be seen to evolve in precisely parallel fashion to the dental plosives. This similarity

Table 2.14 *Lenition of velar plosives*

Latin phoneme	Old Spanish phoneme	Example
/-kk-/	/k/	SICCU > *seco* 'dry'
/-k-/	/g/ (= [ɣ])	SECURU > *seguro* 'sure'
/g/	/Ø/	LĒGĀLE> *leal* 'loyal'

Table 2.15 *Lenition of /n/, /l/ and /ɾ/*

Latin phoneme	Old Spanish phoneme	Example
/-nn-/	/ɲ/	PANNU > *paño* 'cloth' (2.5.2.5)
/-n-/	/n/	DAMNU > *daño* 'harm' (for MN > /nn/, see 2.5.3.2)
		BONU > *bueno* 'good'
/-ll-/	/ʎ/	GALLU > *gallo* 'cock' (see 2.5.2.5)
/-l-/	/l/	MALU > *malo* 'evil'
/-ɾɾ-/	/r/	TURRĒS > *torres* 'towers'
/-ɾ-/	/ɾ/	PIRA > *pera* 'pear'

of treatment extends to the double Old Spanish outcome of /-g-/; whereas /Ø/ is the commoner result (thereby maintaining the contrast between Lat. /kk/–/k/–/g/ as Sp. /k/–/g/–/Ø/), in a few cases the Latin /g/ survives (as [ɣ]): *LEGŪMINE > *legumbre* 'vegetable', PLĀGA > *llaga* 'wound', NĀVIGĀRE > *navegar* 'to sail'. As in the case of /d/, survival of /g/ may be due to the influence of Latin on early Old Spanish, at a stage when /g/ was in the process of elimination and vernacular words could appear either with or without the phoneme. Awareness that the corresponding Latin word was spelt with G (and read aloud with [ɣ]) may have led in some cases (including the above) to preference for the vernacular form with /g/.

It should be noted that the /k/ of -QU- is subject to the same treatment as that spelt -C- (and occurring before A, O, U), whether or not the following glide [w] survives, as it does before /a/ but not before other vowels: AQUA > *agua* 'water', SEQUERE (CL SEQUĪ) > *seguir* 'to follow' (compare 2.5.7 (end)).

2.5.3.2.9 /n/, /l/ and /ɾ/ (see table 2.15). In these cases, there is evidently a departure from the general statement made about the operation of lenition (process 1) in 2.5.3.2. The geminates /nn/, /ll/ and /ɾɾ/ are not reduced to the corresponding simple consonants (as is the case with all other Latin geminates except /mm/). In these three cases, simplification does take place, but the resulting phoneme differs in one of its features from the predicted phoneme.

The reason for this difference of behaviour is probably that the Latin simple consonants /n/, /l/ and /ɾ/ do not qualify as the input of any of the four lenition processes (i.e. they are neither geminate, voiceless, voiced plosives, nor voiced fricatives) and therefore do not undergo any lenition change. The consequence of this lack of change is that straightforward simplification of the corresponding geminates would automatically bring about merger of /nn/ with /n/, /ll/ with /l/, and /ɾɾ/ with /ɾ/ (unless the scope of process 4 were extended to include /-n-/, /-l-/ and /-ɾ-/, contrary to what is observable throughout Western Romance, with the exception of Portuguese, where /-n-/ and /-l-/ are eliminated: LŪNA > *lua*, SALĪRE > *sair*). No doubt in order to preserve these distinctions, simplification of these geminates in Spanish leads to further change: /nn/ and /ll/ are simplified and made palatal, while /ɾɾ/ is simplified by changing the spoken Latin sequence of syllable-final /-ɾ/ + syllable-initial /ɾ-/ to the single syllable-initial vibrant /r/. It is acknowledged that this account begs the question of why /mm/ and /m/ were allowed to merge: the reason conceivably lies in the number of minimal pairs which relied upon the various contrasts of geminate vs single consonant, a number which it is now practically impossible to establish.

As noted in some previous cases, contrasts which function in syllable-initial position may be neutralized in syllable-final position. This is true of the contrasts between /ɲ/ and /n/, /ʎ/ and /l/, and /r/ and /ɾ/, and is witnessed, historically, by the fact that when, through loss of an intertonic or final vowel, spoken Latin /nn/, /ll/ or /ɾɾ/ came to occupy syllable-final position, their Old Spanish results were identical to those of spoken Latin /n/, /l/ and /ɾ/, respectively, i.e. OSp. /n/, /l/ and /ɾ/. Examples of this treatment of syllable-final geminates are listed in table 2.16.

Note that, as a result of this process, Old Spanish syllable-final /-n/, /-l/ and /-ɾ/ could occur in morphophonemic alternation with syllable-initial /ɲ/, /ʎ/ and /r/, respectively. Thus beside *mil cavallos* we find *mill omnes* (where the lateral is syllable-initial), spelt thus and probably pronounced /míʎ/ until the late Middle Ages, when the alternation was levelled in favour of /míl/ in all circumstances. Similarly, singular *piel* was flanked in early Old Spanish by plural *pielles*, when the singulars of *valles* and *calles* were *val* and *cal*. Levelling of *piel/pielles* to *piel/pieles* followed the same path as *mil/mill*, while *val/valles* and *cal/calles* were levelled in favour of the palatal (*valle/valles, calle/calles*), except in a wide range of place-names (*Valfermoso*, etc.). In the case of the rhotics, this morphophonemic alternation has left a residue in the contrast between CARRICĀRE > *cargar* and CARRU > *carro* 'cart', and probably once existed between singular *tor* and plural *torres* (< TURRĒS), later levelled in favour of the vibrant (*torre/torres*), except in place-names.

2.5.3.3 Further effects of lenition: consonant + R or L

The first phoneme of certain Latin consonant groups was affected by lenition, in the same way as intervocalic consonants were. Latin groups include those

Table 2.16 *Treatment of /nn/, /ll/ and /rr/ in syllable-final position*

Latin phoneme	Old Spanish phoneme	Example
/-nn-/	/n/	JOHANNE > *Juan* 'John'
		DOMNE (CL DOMINE) > */dónne/ (see 2.5.3.2) > *don*
		MĪLLE > *mil* 'thousand'
		PELLE > *piel* 'skin'
/-ll-/	/l/	GALLICU > *galgo* 'greyhound'
		CABALLICARE > *cavalgar* (later *cabalgar*) 'to ride a horse'
/-ɾɾ-/	/ɾ/	CARRICĀRE > *cargar* 'to load'
		TURRE *C(R)EMĀTA > *Torquemada*

Table 2.17 *Lenition of consonant* + R/L

Latin phonemes	Old Spanish phonemes	Example
/pɾ/	/bɾ/	CAPRA > *cabra* 'goat'
/pl/	/bl/	DUPLU > *doblo* > *doble* 'double'
/fɾ/	/bɾ/	AFRICU > *ábrego* 'south wind'
/tɾ/	/dɾ/	PATRE > *padre* 'father'
/dɾ/	/ɾ/	QUADRĀGINTĀ > *quaraenta* (later *cuarenta*) 'forty'
	/dɾ/	QUADRU > *quadro* (later *cuadro*) 'picture'
/kɾ/	/gɾ/	SOCRU > *suegro* 'father-in-law'
/gɾ/	/ɾ/	PIGRITIA > *pereza* 'laziness'
	/gɾ/	NIGRA > *negra* 'black'

which had long been in existence in spoken and literary Latin (sometimes called Classical Latin groups) and those which came into existence in spoken Latin through loss of intertonic vowels (see 2.4.3.3), a loss which in spoken Latin was normally limited to vowels in contact with R or L. The groups under consideration here are precisely those whose second element is R or L, but excepting the groups TL, CL and GL (formed through syncope in spoken Latin: VET(U)LU, OC(U)LU, TEG(U)LA, whence *viejo, ojo, teja*; 2.4.3.3), whose first consonant was palatalized to [i̯] (see 2.5.2.4) before the period when the lenition process operated, and so was exempt from this process. All other such Latin groups show lenition of the first phoneme (table 2.17).

2.5.3.4 Lenition of consonants in contact with a glide

When an internal consonant was preceded by a vowel and followed by a glide, or vice versa, at the spoken Latin stage, the effects of lenition on the consonant are inconsistent. Under these circumstances, the consonant was evidently in less than the ideal (intervocalic) conditions for lenition to operate, so that voicing of Lat. /p/, /t/, /k/ sometimes, but not always, fails to occur.

Preceded by [u̯], /t/ and /k/ fail to become voiced (AUTUMNU > *otoño* 'autumn', PAUCU > *poco* 'little'), while /s/ and /p/ show normal lenition (CAUSA > *cosa* 'thing' – with /z/ in Old Spanish – PAUPERE > *pobre* 'poor').

Followed by [w], almost the reverse is true: /k/ becomes voiced (PLACUIT > OSp. *plogo* 'it pleased'), while /p/ appears immune (SAPUIT > OSp. *sopo* > *supo* 'he knew', CAPUIT > OSp. *copo* > *cupo* 'it fitted'), although Italian *seppe* 'he knew' suggests that /p/ became geminate /pp/ before the glide in spoken Latin. It is unclear whether AQUA > *agua*, EQUA > *yegua*, and other cases in which -QUA- > *-gua-*, should be cited as cases of voicing of /k/, since they may have contained a unitary phoneme /k^{w}/ rather than a sequence /k/ + [w] (see 2.5.1).

Followed by [j], which in most cases became preceding [i̯] (2.4.2.4, 2.5.2.2(6)), /k/ again shows voicing (PLACEAT > obsolescent *plega* 'may it please'), but /p/ again remains voiceless (SAPIAM > *sepa* [pres. subj. of *saber* 'to know'], CAPIAM > *quepa* [pres. subj. of *caber* 'to fit']), APIU > *apio* 'celery'), although all three words may descend from spoken Latin forms with /pp/, showing gemination before [j], as is witnessed by It. *sappia* (= Sp. *sepa*). Sp. *jibia* 'cuttlefish' (< SĒPIA) is likely to witness Mozarabic rather than Castilian development (see 4.7).

2.5.3.5 The Old Spanish voiced fricative series

As a result of changes which began in spoken Latin and continued in subsequent centuries, and which are studied in previous sections, Old Spanish came to have a series of voiced fricative phonemes, a series originally absent from Latin (see 2.5.1–2). There were four phonemes in this series, which are given in table 2.18, together with the various sources of each phoneme.

2.5.4 Final consonants

Not all of the Latin consonants (2.5.1) could appear in word-final position. Of those that could, only /l/, /s/, /n/, and sometimes /m/ survive into Old Spanish in that position, while /ɾ/ becomes internal and the remainder were eliminated (table 2.19).

The -N of NŌN was occasionally preserved in Old Spanish (*non*~*no* 'no'), while -T (the third-person-singular verbal marker) was still apparently pronounced in the early thirteenth century, as witnessed by the forms cited. Final -M

Table 2.18 *Sources of Old Spanish voiced fricative phonemes*

Old Spanish phoneme	Latin sources	Example	See
/β/	-B-	CABALLU > *cavallo*	2.5.3.1
	-V-	CLAVE > *llave*	2.5.3.1
/z/	-S-	CASA > *casa*	2.5.3.2.5
	-NS-	MĒNSA > *mesa*	2.5.3.2.5
/ʒ/	L + [j]	MULIERE > *mugier*	2.5.2.2(2)
	(V)CL	NOVĀC(U)LA > *navaja*	2.5.2.4
	(V)GL	REG(U)LA > *reja*	2.5.2.4
ǰ	I- (+V)	IŪGU > *yugo*	2.5.2.1
	-I-	MĀIŌRES > *mayores*	2.5.2.2(4)
	Initial G (+E/I)	GYPSU > *yesso*	2.5.2.3
	G + [j]	EXAGIU > *ensayo*	2.5.2.2(4)
	D + [j]	PODIU > *poyo*	2.5.2.2(4)
	Initial (H)Ĕ	HERBA > *yerva*	2.5.2.3

Table 2.19 *Development of Latin final consonants*

Latin	Spanish	Example
-L	/-l/	FEL > *fiel* (later *hiel*) 'gall'
		MEL > *miel* 'honey'
		MINUS > *menos* 'less'
-S	/-s/	MONTĒS > *montes* 'mountains'
		TENĒS > *tienes* 'you have'
-N	/-n/	IN > *en* 'in'
-R	internal /ɾ/	QUATTUOR > *quatro* (later *cuatro*) 'four'
		SEMPER > *siempre* 'always'
-T	/d/ > /Ø/	SALĪVIT > *saliot/saliod* (> *salió*) 'he left'
		POTE(S)T > *puedet* (> *puede*) 'he can'
-D	/Ø/	AD > *a* 'to'
		ALIQUOD > *algo* 'something'
-M	/Ø/	IAM > *ya* 'now'
		SUM > *so* (later *soy*) 'I am'
		CANTĀBAM > *cantava* (later *cantaba*) 'I sang'
		NOVUM > *nuevo* 'new'
-C	/Ø/	ILLĪC > *allí* 'there'
		DĪC > *di* 'say (imper.)'
		NEC > *ni* 'neither'

was eliminated in the first century BC, except in a few frequent monosyllables, where it survives as /n/ (QUEM > *quien* 'who', TAM > *tan* 'so', CUM > *con* 'with').

As anticipated in 2.4.3.2, in certain cases a dental or alveolar consonant which was internal in Latin became final in Old Spanish through the loss of a final

Table 2.20 *Old Spanish final consonants*

Latin internal consonant	Spanish final consonant	Example
/-t-/	/-d/	AETĀTE > *edad* 'age'
/-d-/	/Ø/	FIDE > *fe* 'faith'
		PEDE > *pie* 'foot'
/-s-/	/-s/	MĒNSE > *mes* 'month'
/-t^s-/	/-t^s/	PĀCE > *paz* 'peace'
/-n-/	/-n/	PANE > *pan* 'bread'
		SINE > *sin* 'without'
/-l-/	/-l/	FIDĒLE > *fiel* 'faithful'
		MALE > *mal* 'badly'
/-ɾ-/	/-ɾ/	MARE > *mar* 'sea'
		SENTĪRE > *sentir* 'to feel'

vowel (usually /e/). Since such a consonant was preceded by a vowel (and therefore intervocalic), and since lenition occurred before the loss of final vowels (2.7), these consonants could be expected to undergo lenition changes (where relevant) before they became final. However, these changes are only visible in the case of -T- (> /d/) and -D- (> /Ø/), since -N-, -L- and -R- are unaffected by lenition, and its effects are masked in the case of Old Spanish final *-s* and *-z*, since neutralization of voice in syllable-final position (2.5.3.2.5–6) implies that any voicing of /s/ or /t^s/ brought about by lenition would have been reversed by neutralization. Examples are given in table 2.20.

By comparison of Old Spanish with Catalan, Portuguese, and Judeo-Spanish, it is possible to assert that in phrases like *más o menos* or *paz e guerra* the word-final *-s, -z* of *más, paz,* etc. (here syllable-initial because followed by a word-initial vowel) were pronounced [z] and [d^z] respectively, in accordance with the lenition process.

For /nn/, /ll/, and /ɾɾ/ made final by loss of /-e/, see 2.5.3.2.9.

2.5.5 *Secondary consonant groups*

Although the development of secondary consonant groups (sometimes called 'Romance consonant groups') involves the creation of no new phonemes, the incidence of phonemes is changed thereby, so that these clusters require some consideration. Secondary groups are those which came into existence, after the Latin period, through the loss of an internal (usually intertonic) vowel. It will be recalled (from 2.4.3.3) that there were two periods of loss of intertonics, the first in spoken Latin (which gave rise to new Latin groups, best regarded as primary, such as CL, GL; see also 2.5.2.4), and the second later. It is this second loss (e.g. SEMITA > *senda* 'path', VINDICĀRE > *vengar* 'to avenge') which gave rise to the groups now under consideration.

An important chronological principle underpins the development of secondary consonant groups: the intertonic vowel is lost *after* the lenition processes (2.5.3.2) have taken place, so that the consonants concerned will have undergone simplification, voicing, etc., where appropriate, *before* they are brought together in new groups. Similarly, the palatalization processes discussed in 2.5.2.2–5 precede the loss of intertonics. This chronological principle can be illustrated by means of a case like ACCEPTŌRE (CL ACCIPITER). The sequence of events was probably the following:

/akkeptóre/ > akkettóre/ (/pt/ > /tt/: 2.5.3.2)
/akkettóre/ > /att^{s}ettóre/ (palatalization of velars: 2.5.2.3)
/att^{s}ettóre/ > /at^{s}etóre/ (simplification of geminates: 2.5.3.2)
/at^{s}etóre/ > /at^{s}tóre/ (syncope: 2.4.3.3)
/at^{s}tóre/ > /at^{s}tóɾ/ (loss of final vowel: 2.4.3.2)
/at^{s}tóɾ/ > /at^{s}óɾ/ *açor* (later *azor*) 'goshawk' (secondary consonant group development: this section)

Similarly, in the following cases, we can see changes affecting internal consonants before the creation of secondary groups:

LITTERA > *letra* 'letter' (simplification of geminates)
SEMITA > *senda* 'path' (voicing)
DOMĪNICU > *domingo* 'Sunday' (voicing)
FLACCIDU > *lacio* 'lank' (palatalization and simplification of -CC^{e,i}; fricatization and loss of -D-)
CŌGITĀRE > *cuidar* 'to think', later 'to take care of' (palatalization of -G^{e,i}; loss of voiced fricative /ǰ/)

Where an intervocalic consonant of Latin, later grouped with preceding /l/ or /ɾ/, shows no change (e.g. SOLITĀRIU > *soltero* 'unmarried'), this usually indicates that the groupings occurred in spoken Latin (i.e. before lenition).

The consonant groups formed in this way, probably in the tenth to eleventh centuries, sometimes posed no articulatory problems and have survived unchanged. This is the case in the following instances, in some of which it is impossible to determine whether the group was formed in spoken Latin or later, given that intertonics could be lost in spoken Latin when adjacent to R or L (and sometimes S or N; see 2.4.3.3), and given that consonants grouped (in spoken Latin) with following R or L were subject to lenition in the same way as intervocalic consonants (2.5.3.2(end)). Note that ' indicates the loss of an internal vowel and Ć indicates that this velar consonant was followed by a front vowel (and was therefore palatalized; see 2.5.2.3).

R'M EREMU > *yermo* 'wilderness'
R'T VĒRITĀTE > *verdad* 'truth'
R'Ć MAURICELLU > *morziello* (later *morcillo*) 'black (horse)'

MP'R TEMPORĀNU > *temprano* 'early'
P'R PAUPERE > *pobre* 'poor'
B'R LĪBERĀRE > *librar* 'to set free' (OSp. /bɾ/, rather than /βɾ/, suggests early formation of the group)
F'R BIFERA > *bebra* (later *breva*) '(black) fig' (OSp. /bɾ/ again suggests early grouping)
T'R LATERĀLE > *ladral* (later *adral*) 'side-board (of cart)'
D'R HEDERA > *yedra* (later spelt *hiedra*) 'ivy' (retention of /d/ may indicate grouping took place in spoken Latin; cf. dialectal *yera*)
TT'R LITTERA > *letra* 'letter'
L'D SOLIDU > *sueldo* 'certain coin' (later 'salary') (for /d/, see HEDERA, above)
L'C ALIQUOD > *algo* 'something'
P'L POPULU > *pueblo* 'people, town'
MP'L POMPELONE > *Pamplona* (top.)
B'L NEBULA > *niebla* 'fog'
S'L *ĪSULA (CL ĪNSULA) > *isla* 'island'
S'N ASINU > *asno* 'donkey'
S'C RESECĀRE > *resgar* (later *rasgar*) 'to rip'
C'M DECIMU > *diezmo* 'tithe'
C'N DŪRACINU > *durazno* '(kind of) peach'

In some cases, the bringing together of the consonants concerned requires a minor phonological adjustment. Thus, neutralization of syllable-final nasals determines that if the first consonant is a nasal its place of articulation will become identical to that of the following consonant, a principle which is most evident in the case of M'cons., but applies equally to all nasals:

M'T SĒMITA > *senda* 'path', COMITE > *conde* 'count'
N'T BONITĀTE > *bondad* 'goodness'
N'C DOMĪNICU > *domingo* 'Sunday'

Likewise, where -LL-, -NN- or -RR- come to be grouped with a following consonant (and therefore become syllable-final), the phonological pattern of Spanish requires that they become /l/, /n/ and /ɾ/ respectively, rather than /ʎ/, /ɲ/ or /r/, since the latter are regularly neutralized with the former in syllable-final position (see 2.5.3.2.9 for examples).

A further case of minor adjustment is that of R when grouped with preceding N. In this (post-consonantal, syllable-initial) position, the flap /ɾ/ is impermissible in Spanish, so that R is here replaced by the vibrant /r/: HONŌRĀRE > *onrrar* (later spelt *honrar*) 'to honour'.

However, certain secondary groupings of consonants produced sequences which were contrary to the phonotactic rules of Spanish (i.e. such groups were at that stage unknown and therefore 'difficult') and necessitated some radical adjustment to bring them in line with these rules. The processes of adjustment employed are assimilation, dissimilation, metathesis, epenthesis, etc. (see 2.1.1 for these processes), although it should be noted that the same group, occurring in different words, may be treated in more than one way.

Assimilatory adjustment can be seen in:

D'N >	/n/:	FRIDENANDU > **Frenando* > *Fernando*
C'T >	*/d^{z}d/ > /d^z/:	PLACITU > *plazdo* > *plazo* 'time limit'
D'Ć >	/dd^z/ > /d^z/:	DUŌDECIM > *doze* (later *doce*) 'twelve'
PT'M >	/tm/ > /m/:	SEPTIMĀNA > *setmana* > *semana* 'week'

In the case of the following groups, the assimilation takes the form of the devoicing of the third consonant (if the second is voiceless), followed by loss of the middle consonant (for details, see Penny 1983b):

ND'C >	/ng/:	VINDICĀRE > *vengar* 'to avenge'
ND'Ć >	/nd^z/:	UNDECIM > *onze* (later *once*) 'eleven'
RD'Ć >	/ɾd^z/:	QUATTUŌRDECIM > *quatorze* (later *catorce*) 'fourteen'
NT'Ć>	/nt^s/:	PANTICE > *pança* (later *panza*) 'belly'
MP'T >	/nt/:	COMPUTĀRE > *contar* 'to count'
SC'P >	/sp/:	EPISCOPU > *obispo* 'bishop'
SP'T >	/st/:	HOSPITĀLE > *hostal* 'inn'
ST'C >	/sk/:	MASTICĀRE > *mascar* 'to chew'

Dissimilatory change can be seen (between nasals) in:

N'M >	/lm/:	ANIMA > *alma* 'soul'
	/ɾm/:	MINIMĀRE > *mermar* 'to lessen, shrink'
M'N >	/mɾ/:	HOMINE > *omne* > **omre* (> *hombre*) 'man'
NG'N >	/ngɾ/:	SANGUINE > *sangre* 'blood'
	/ngl/:	*ĪNGUINE > *ingle* 'groin'
ND'N >	/ndɾ/:	LENDINE (CL LENS) > *liendre* 'nit'

Metathesis is sometimes the solution to a 'difficult' secondary group:

T'N >	/nd/:	CATENATU > *candado* 'padlock', RETINA > *rienda* 'reins'
T'L >	/ld/	(in certain semi-learned words): CAPITULU> *cabildo* 'chapter (meeting)'
M'L >	/lm/:	CUMULU > *colmo* 'height (fig.)'
N'R >	/ɾn/:	GENERU > *yerno* 'son in law'
		VENERIS > *viernes* 'Friday' (see above, *honrar*, and below, *engendrar*)
F'C >	*[βɣ] > *[u̯ɣ] > [ɣw]:	-ĪFICĀRE > *-iguar* (e.g. SANCTĪFICĀRE > *santiguar(se)* 'to cross (oneself)')

Epenthesis is also employed (usually between nasal and liquid) to resolve a problematical sequence:

M'R > /mbɾ/: HUMERU > *(h)ombro* 'shoulder'
N'R > /ndɾ/: in the semi-learned treatment of INGENERĀRE> *engendrar* 'to engender'
M'N > /mɾ/ >/mbɾ/: FĒMINA > *hembra* 'female', HOMINE > *(h)ombre* 'man'
M'L > /mbl/: TREMULĀRE > *temblar* 'to tremble'

A further process of adaptation of 'difficult' secondary groups, adopted by later Old Spanish, is to replace the first consonant by the glide [u̯], which was absorbed if the preceding phoneme was a homologous (i.e. back) vowel. This is the process adopted when a labial came to be grouped with a following dental and when /l/ was preceded by /a/ and followed by /d^z/:

P'T CAPITĀLE > *cabdal* > *caudal* 'capital (sum)'
P'D CUPIDITIA > *cobdicia* > *codicia* 'covetousness'
B'T CUBITU > *cobdo* > *codo* 'elbow'
V'T CĪVITĀTE > *cibdad* > *ciudad* 'city'
B'D DĒBITA > *debda* > *deuda* 'debt'
L'Ć SALICE > *salze* > *sauce* 'willow'

When the first consonant of a secondary group was T or D, the Old Spanish result was at first the expected /d/ + cons. However, in later Old Spanish, neutralization took place between syllable-final /d/ and /d^z/, in favour of the latter, a process reflected in the replacement of the spelling *d* by *z*:

T'C PORTĀTICU > *portadgo* > *portazgo* 'transit tax'
D'C IŪDICĀRE > *judgar* > *juzgar* 'to judge'
T'M EPITHEMA > (semi-learned) *bidma* > *bizma* 'poultice'

Finally, note the treatment of CT, X and GN when they constitute the first two consonants of a secondary group of three (2.5.2.4).

2.5.6 *The development of Latin* F

Modern Spanish words which descend orally from Latin words in F- reveal that there are two treatments of the Latin phoneme, as exemplified by the following:

1 FĪCU > *higo* 'fig'
FĪLIU > *hijo* 'son'
FĪLU > *hilo* 'thread'
FARĪNA > *harina* 'flour'
FACERE > *hacer* 'to do'
FŌRMA > *horma* 'shoemaker's last'
FORNU > *horno* 'oven'

2 FORTE > *fuerte* 'strong'
FONTE > *fuente* 'spring'
FOLLE > *fuelle* 'bellows'
FRONTE > *frente* 'forehead'

Internal F was not frequent in Latin words. In those cases where speakers perceived F to be morpheme-initial (i.e. where it followed an identifiable prefix, e.g. DĒ-FĒNSA, OF-FOCĀRE, or where it headed the second element of a compound expression, e.g. CANNA FERULA, SANCTĪ FĒLICĪS), it was treated in the same way as word-initial F- (thus: *dehesa* 'unenclosed pasture', *ahogar* 'to suffocate', *cañaherla* 'wand', *Santelices* (toponym)). Where F was perceived to be morpheme-internal, it received the treatment appropriate to internal consonants (becoming simplified if geminate: SCOFFĪNA > *escofina* 'file'; becoming voiced if intervocalic: STEPHANU > *Esteban* 'Stephen', COPHINU > *cuévano* 'basket (carried on the back)', RAPHANU > *rábano* 'radish' (see 2.5.3.2.2); being preserved if post-consonantal: INFERNU > *infierno* 'hell').

In Old Spanish, all such words (except where voicing had previously occurred: *Esteban*, etc.) were spelt with *f* (*figo*, *fijo*, *filo*, *farina*, *fazer*, *forma*, *forno*, *defesa*, *afogar*, *fuerte*, *fruente*, *fuelle*), as were learned words drawn from Latin terms spelt with F- (*forma* 'shape', *falso* 'false', *fama* 'fame', *figura* 'image', etc). The modern spellings (*h* and *f*) reflect a phonemic split which will be discussed in 2.6.4, but it is arguable that until the late Middle Ages all the popular words concerned here had the same phoneme, with allophonic variation governed by the following phoneme.

The process by which Latin F- came to be eliminated from most popular Spanish words has been the subject of intense debate. An outline of this debate can be seen in Menéndez Pidal (1964a: 198–208), or in Baldinger (1972: 22–7). Discussion has been polarized between, on the one hand, accounts which appeal to substratum influence (exercised by Basque) on the Latin of Cantabria, and, on the other hand, those which seek purely intra-Latin explanations. The chief exponent of the former view is Menéndez Pidal (1964a: 198–233), who assembles data from medieval Hispanic documents, from modern Basque and from Gascon, to suggest that the absence of a labiodental phoneme /f/ from the pre-Roman language of northern central Spain and southwestern Gaul (i.e. Basque) had the consequence that, as speakers of Basque became bilingual in Latin, they replaced Lat. /f/ with sounds familiar in their native speech, of which the aspirate /h/ is the main survivor (in Gascon and Medieval Spanish, as in some modern Spanish dialects). The main objections to this theory are, firstly, that the development F- > /h/ is found in some (small) Romance territories where Basque influence is evidently impossible, and, secondly, that such a substratum account has difficulty in explaining why the words of group 2 (above) appear in Spanish with /f/ (see Trask 1997a: 424–9 for these and other objections). To expand on this second point, if Latin F- was replaced by /h/ in FARĪNA, etc., why was it not also replaced in FORTE, etc.? (The fact that rural dialects of Spain and America do indeed employ /huérte/ where the standard has *fuerte* does not answer the question why the standard shows /f/ in the words of group 2.) Adherents of substratum theory typically appeal to dialect mixing in order to explain the /f/ of *fuerte*, etc., seeing it as a phoneme borrowed from dialects spoken to the south of the area where Castilian originated (see 1.3.2), during the territorial expansion of Castilian which began in the early Reconquest.

Those who seek an internal Latin explanation for the loss of F- in Spanish have sometimes turned to regional Latin pronunciation (see, e.g., Penny 1972a and 1990b). It is possible that the spoken Latin of remoter areas (such as Cantabria) preserved a bilabial articulation (/ɸ/) of F-, which had earlier been normal in Latin but which had been replaced by labiodental /f/ in Rome and in those areas in closest contact with Rome. Such a bilabial articulation of F-, together with normal allophonic variation, governed by the nature of the following phoneme, may have led to a pattern like the following in the late spoken Latin of Cantabria:

/ɸ/ realized as [ʍ] in words where the initial phoneme was followed by the glide [w], whose appearance was due to diphthongization (see 2.4.2.2); e.g. FORTE > ['ʍworte] or ['ʍwerte];
realized as [ɸ] elsewhere: ['ɸrido] < FRĪGIDU, [ɸa'rina] < FARĪNA.

Through dissimilation of bilabial /ɸ/ to [h] before the (labial) vowels /o/ and /u/, the range of allophones was possibly increased, at an early period, to the following:

/ɸ/: [ʍ] before [w]: ['ʍwerte];
[h] before syllabic /o/, /u/ (i.e. not [w]): ['horno] < FURNU;
[ɸ] elsewhere (includes non-back vowels, the glide [j], /ɾ/, /l/): [ɸa'rina], ['ɸjera], ['ɸrido].

As a result of a process of generalization of the allophone [h], which operated in such a way that [h] came to occur before all syllabic vowels (rather than only before back vowels, as hitherto), the following situation was reached (which was probably that of Old Spanish, until about the thirteenth century, and is certainly that of many rural dialects of Spanish today, e.g. Santander, Extremadura, western Andalusia, varieties of American Spanish):

/ɸ/: [ʍ] before [w]: ['ʍwerte];
[h] before all syllabic vowels and [j]: ['horno], [ha'rina], ['hjero] < FERRU;
[ɸ] before /ɾ/ (FL- having been modified either to /ʎ/ (2.5.2.6) or to /l/): ['ɸrio].

It is only in later Old Spanish that the allophones [ʍ] and [ɸ] were modified to labiodental [f], principally in urban Spanish (which forms the basis of the standard). This change may have been initiated by Frenchmen (speakers of French and Occitan) who entered Spain in large numbers in the twelfth and thirteenth centuries, sometimes occupying positions of great social prestige. Such people, as they learned Castilian, would have had difficulty imitating the labiovelar [ʍ] and the bilabial [ɸ], and may have replaced them with the most similar sound of their native language (namely [f]), a practice which arguably then spread to native speakers of Spanish, particularly those of educated, urban background, who would have been in closest contact with Frenchmen (Penny 1972a). Note that speakers of twelfth-century French would have no difficulty in adopting the allophone [h], since contemporary French included such an aspirate. Following such a change, late medieval urban Spanish would have included the following sounds (still perhaps best regarded as allophones of a single phoneme, which is here arbitrarily designated /h/):

/h/: [f] before [w] and /ɾ/: ['fweɾte], ['fɾio];
[h] elsewhere (i.e. before syllabic vowels and [j]): [ha'ɾina], ['hoɾno].

We shall see (2.6.4) that these two allophones were eventually phonologized, providing Spanish with two distinct phonemes, /f/ and /h/, although the latter was being dropped from pronunciation in Old Castile in the later Middle Ages. This /h/-dropping continued to spread territorially and socially, until in the sixteenth century, /h/-less pronunciation became standard, a change which brought about the following pattern:

/f/: /fuéɾte/ *fuerte*, /fɾío/ *frío*, etc.
/Ø/: /aɾína/ *harina*, /óɾno/ *horno*, /ǰéro/ *hierro*, etc.

It should be remembered that all the words considered in this section (i.e. all the words descended from Latin forms in F-) were spelt with *f-* throughout the Middle Ages, obscuring phonetic and phonological change. It was not until the late fifteenth and early sixteenth century that the spelling *h* came to be used in the case of those words which at that time had initial /h/. Thus OSp. *figo*, *fijo*, *filo*, *farina*, *fazer*, *forma*, *forno*, etc., were replaced by *higo*, *hijo*, *hilo*, *harina*, *hacer*, *horma*, *horno*, etc., while *fuerte*, *fuente*, *fruente*, *fuelle*, etc., continued with their traditional spelling. It should be noted that the graphical change (*f* replaced by *h*) is not contemporary with the phonological change F- > /h/, which occurred centuries earlier. The spelling change sprang from the need (felt in the late Middle Ages) to provide distinct spellings for what were for the first time two separate phonemes, i.e. to distinguish pairs like /hóɾma/ 'shoemaker's last' and /fóɾma/ 'shape', hitherto both spelt *forma*. Indeed, by the time the use of *h* had become normal in *horno*, *hablar*, etc., a substantial proportion of Spanish speakers no longer used any consonant at the beginning of such words.

For a medieval orthographical experiment to distinguish /h/ and /f/, by using *ff* for /f/, see Blake (1987–8, 1988).

The spread (social and territorial) of an innovation should always be carefully distinguished from the cause(s) of that innovation. Although the causes of the change by which Lat. F- becomes Sp. /h/ are by no means fully clarified, the spread of the articulation [h] is reasonably well established (see Menéndez Pidal 1964a: 219–33). Up to the period of the beginnings of Castilian expansion (early tenth century), [h] was limited to the area of origin, Cantabria (Santander, northern Burgos, parts of the Basque country); other areas employed either [f] or [ɸ]. As the prestige of Burgos and its speech-forms grows in the early Reconquest (tenth to thirteenth centuries), [h] comes to be used throughout Old Castile, begins to encroach upon León and perhaps begins to extend over the Guadarrama. In the later Middle Ages and early modern period (thirteenth to sixteenth centuries), [h] becomes part of standard (Toledan) pronunciation and is extended to southern Spain, with the Reconquest, except for Portuguese- and Catalan-speaking areas. It also expands vigorously into Leonese territory. At the same time as [h] was enjoying this success in the south and west, it was being replaced by /Ø/ in Burgos and other areas of Old Castile. The sixteenth-century contrast between the Burgos pronunciation /ablár/, etc., and the Toledan pronunciation /hablár/, is well known. Following the establishment of the northern, /h/-less, pronunciation in Madrid in the 1560s, this style becomes the norm and is increasingly extended to all areas of Castilian speech, /h/ only surviving in remoter rural areas (western Santander, eastern Asturias, western Salamanca, Extremadura, western Andalusia, parts of America).

2.5.7 *Other initial consonants*

With the exception of /f-/ (2.5.6), and of the velars /k/ and /g/ when followed by front vowels (2.5.2.3), the Latin consonants in word-initial position were extremely stable, passing unchanged into Spanish in almost all instances. Only in the case of /ɾ-/, /s-/ and /k-/ (followed by non-front vowels) do we find departure from this norm.

It is observable that most initial consonants of Latin have an identical outcome in Spanish (and in other varieties of Western Romance) to that of their (necessarily word-internal) geminate counterparts. Thus initial /t-/ in TERRA and /tt/ in GUTTA both appear in Spanish as /t/ (*tierra*, *gota*) and both Latin /p-/ and /pp/ (PETRA, CUPPA) appear as Spanish /p/ (*piedra*, *copa*). However, in those instances where a Latin geminate is *not* reduced to its single correlate in Spanish (i.e. in the case of -LL-, -NN-, -RR-; see 2.5.3.2.9), there consequently arises a potential failure of this rule, and -LL- and -NN- do indeed have a different outcome in Spanish from L- and N-, despite some evidence in pre-literary Spanish (see Menéndez Pidal 1960: xcv–xcvii) of a move, ultimately thwarted, to palatalize initial L- and N- and thereby give them the same outcome as -LL- and -NN-. However, in the case of R- and -RR-, similarity of treatment of initial and geminate consonants is preserved, by changing the initial consonant's articulation from flap /ɾ/ to vibrant /r/. This phonological change, which is masked by absence of any corresponding spelling change, has no exceptions in Spanish.

Although initial S- normally appears in Spanish as /s/ (i.e., unchanged, since it is likely that the Latin S of many areas was apico-alveolar, a characteristic inherited by its descendants in the centre and north of the Peninsula), a few words showed hesitation, at the medieval stage, between /s/ and /ʃ/, and some of these found their way into the standard with the latter (prepalatal) phoneme. Such words, which later undergo the regular change /ʃ/ > /x/ (see 2.6.2), include: SAPŌNE > *xabon* > *jabón* 'soap', SŪCU > *xugo* > *jugo* 'juice', SĒPIA > *xibia* > *jibia* 'cuttlefish', SYRINGA > *xeringa* > *jeringa* 'syringe'.

Initial /k-/ is the other phoneme which shows departure from the rule that the initial consonants of Latin are preserved unchanged in Spanish, although in this case the change is sporadic. Indeed, most cases of Latin /k-/ before non-front vowels show /k/ in Spanish: CUPPA > *copa* 'wine glass', CAPRA > *cabra* 'goat', CORNU > *cuerno* 'horn', etc. However, in a few cases we find voicing of /k-/ (i.e. the same treatment as in intervocalic position; see 2.5.3.2.8): CATTU > *gato* 'cat', *CŌLOPU (CL COLAPHU) > *golpe* 'blow'.

Initial consonant groups were limited to /s/ + cons., cons. + /l/, cons. + /ɾ/, and /kw/. The first of these types, /s/ + cons., remained unchanged, except for the addition of a preceding vowel (see 2.3.3), while PL-, CL-, FL- frequently produced palatal results (see 2.5.2.6), although in the case of FL- the ultimate result was occasionally /l/ (FLACCIDU > *llacio* > *lacio* 'lank'). Other initial combinations of cons. + /l/ are BL- and GL-, of which the first is retained unchanged in Spanish (BLANDU > *blando* 'soft'), while the second most frequently shows elimination of the first consonant (i.e. the /g/ receives the treatment it most frequently receives in intervocalic position (see 2.5.3.2.8), as we have just seen occasionally occurs in the case of initial /k/): GLĪRE + suffix > *lirón* 'dormouse', GLATTĪRE > *latir* 'to throb, yelp', GLOBELLU > *luviello* > *ovillo* 'ball (of wool, etc.)' (with false separation of /l-/: *el luviello* > **el uviello*).

Cons. + /ɾ/ is highly stable and rarely undergoes change. Only in the case of CR- do we find occasional instances of voicing to /gɾ/, similar to those seen in the case of ungrouped Latin /k-/ (above): CRĒTA > *greda* 'chalk', CRASSU > *graso* 'fatty'. However, these cases may not represent a regular change in Spanish; they may descend from spoken Latin forms which already displayed GR-, in cases like *greda* because of the frequent Latin adaptation of Gk. κ as G-, and in the case of *graso* by analogical imitation of the initial group of GROSSU 'fat, stout' (whence *grueso* 'id.').

QU- (= [kw]) can be regarded in some sense as a group, consisting of the voiceless velar /k/ together with the opening glide [w]. Under almost all circumstances, the glide was lost (at a period prior to the appearance of written Spanish) and /k/ remained unchanged, although the digraph *qu-* was used before /e/ and /i/ in Old Spanish as well as in the modern language, and also sometimes before /a/ in Old Spanish:

QUAERERE > *querer* 'to wish'
QUĪNDECIM > *quince* 'fifteen'
QUĪNGENTŌS > *quinientos* 'five hundred'
QUATTUORDECIM > OSp. *quatorze* (*qu-* = /k/?) ~ *catorze*, MSp. *catorce* 'fourteen'

Table 2.21 *The Old Spanish consonant system*

	labial	dental	(dento-) alveolar	prepalatal	mid-palatal	velar
voiceless plosive/affricate	/p/	/t/	/tˢ/	/tʃ/		/k/
voiced plosive/affricate	/b/	/d/	/dᶻ/			/g/
voiceless fricative			/s/	/ʃ/		/h/
voiced fricative	/β/		/z/	/ʒ/	/ĵ/	
nasal	/m/		/n/	/ɲ/		
lateral			/l/	/ʎ/		
vibrant			/r/			
flap			/ɾ/			

*QUASSICĀRE > *cascar* 'to crack'
QUOMO (CL QUOMODO) > *como* 'as, how'

However, where QU- is immediately followed by tonic /a/, the glide was retained as well as the /k/. Old Spanish spelling employs *qu-* also in this case; the spelling *cu-* becomes the usual spelling only in the nineteenth century.

QUATTUOR > *quatro*, later *cuatro* 'four'
QUĀLE > *qual*, later *cual* 'which'.

2.5.8 *The Old Spanish consonant system*

As a result of the changes so far studied, the consonantal system of Latin (2.5.1) was transformed into the Old Spanish system, characteristic of the literary period (twelfth to fifteenth centuries), as shown in table 2.21.

2.6 Phonological change since the Middle Ages

The phonological changes that have affected Spanish since the late Middle Ages all belong to the consonantal system and in many instances are cases of merger.

2.6.1 *The merger of OSp. /b/ and /β/*

This case was studied in 2.1.3.2 to exemplify the process of merger, but will here be considered in more detail.

Relative consistency of spelling in Old Spanish, and rhyme in Old Spanish verse, suggest a contrast, in many positions, between a voiced bilabial plosive /b/ (spelt *b*) and a voiced bilabial fricative /β/ (spelt *v*). In intervocalic position this contrast is certain:

/b/: *cabe* (pres. ind. *caber*; < CAPIT)
/β/: *cave* (pres. subj. *cavar*; < CAVET)

It is also likely that this contrast applied in initial position, at least when the word was preceded by a vowel or by certain consonants:

/b/: *bienes* 'possessions' (< BENE)
/β/: *vienes* 'you come' (< VENĪS)

Had the products of Latin B- and V- merged before the Old Spanish period, it is unlikely that Old Spanish spelling could have achieved such a high degree of consistency in the distinction of *b* (< B-) and *v* (< V-). After all, Old Spanish spelling makes no attempt to distinguish the products of Latin intervocalic -B- and -V- (which had merged, in spoken varieties), but spells both with *v*.

However, in consonant clusters, confusion of spelling (e.g. *alba*~*alva* 'dawn') suggests neutralization, just as occasional hesitation between *b* and *v* in initial position suggests that, after certain phonemes, initial /b/ and /β/ were indistinguishable. To take the example of the *Poema de mio Cid* (early thirteenth century), initial *b* and *v* are contrasted, in most cases, in the expected way, but there is a minority of cases (see Menéndez Pidal 1964b: 172–3) in which initial *b* and *v* are muddled: *vando*~*bando* (*b* expected), *bistades*~*vestidas*, *ban*~*van*, *boz*~*voz* (*v* expected), etc. Working with knowledge of the modern language, it is possible to suggest that neutralization of initial /b/ and /β/ occurred when they were preceded by a pause or when the preceding word ended in a nasal: *un buey* 'an ox', *un viento* 'a wind', and commands like *¡baxa!* 'come down!' and *¡ven!* 'come!' were probably all articulated with [b].

Neutralization took a further step when /b/ (like /d/ and /g/) took on fricative articulation in a wide number of environments, notably when preceded by a vowel (see 2.5.3.2). In later Old Spanish, it is likely that phrases like *no me baxo* 'I'm not coming down' and *no me voy* 'I'm not going' showed [β] at the beginning of both verbs. By the end of the fourteenth century, it is likely that initial /b/ and /β/ were neutralized in all environments and that the phonemic contrast survived only in intervocalic position. It is in the fifteenth century that the merger is completed. Some poets of this period allow words like *cabe*, *recibo*, *acaba*, *sabe* and *arriba* to rhyme with words like *suave*, *bivo*, *matava*, *grave* and *viva*, and although some sixteenth-century poets, such as Garcilaso (under Italian influence?), maintain the old distinction, such practice was by then no doubt out of touch with everyday (including educated) speech. No poet born after 1550 avoids rhyming *b* with *v*. The merger was by then complete in all varieties of Spanish.

For more detailed discussion of this topic, see Alonso (1967: 21–61, 1962: 155–209), Penny (1976).

Despite the merger of /b/ and /β/, Spanish spelling continues to use both the letters *b* and *v*. In initial position, the modern use of these letters is the same as the medieval practice, except for the occasional adjustment, made for etymological reasons, such as *bivo* and *boz* replaced by *vivo* and *voz*. In intervocalic position, the descendant of Latin -B- was spelt *v* until the late eighteenth century, but

Table 2.22 *Spelling of voiced labials in Spanish*

Latin	Up to 1800	Since 1800
SAPIT	*sabe*	*sabe*
DĒBET	*deve*	*debe*
LAVAT	*lava*	*lava*

Table 2.23 *The sibilant phonemes of Old Spanish*

	Voiceless	Voiced
Dento-alveolar affricate	/tˢ/	/dᶻ/
Alveolar fricative	/s/	/z/
Prepalatal fricative	/ʃ/	/ʒ/

this letter was then replaced in the relevant words by *b*, again on etymological grounds. Medieval and modern use of intervocalic *b* and *v* can be summarized as in table 2.22.

2.6.2 *The Old Spanish sibilants*

The term **sibilant** refers to fricative or affricate consonants articulated in the dental, alveolar and palatal areas; Old Spanish (see 2.5.8) had seven such phonemes, of which we shall disregard /tʃ/, since it passes unchanged into the modern language. The remaining six phonemes were organized in three pairs (table 2.23).

In intervocalic position, the following spellings were used for these phonemes:

/tˢ/	*c* or *ç*:	*decir/deçir* 'to descend', *alçar* 'to raise', *caça* 'hunt'
/dᶻ/	*z*:	*dezir* 'to say', *pozo* 'well'
/s/	*ss*:	*espesso* 'thick', *passo* 'step'
/z/	*s*:	*espeso* 'spent', *casa* 'house'
/ʃ/	*x*:	*fixo 'fixed'*, *dixo* 'he said', *caxa* 'box'
/ʒ/	*j* or *g*:	*fijo* 'son', *mejor/meior* 'better', *mugier* 'woman'

It is possible that the phoneme /ʒ/, here classified as fricative, was affricate in at least some of its realizations (e.g. after a pause or after certain consonants).

This subsystem underwent a series of three changes:

1 The affricates /tˢ/ and /dᶻ/ (together with any affricate realizations of /ʒ/) were weakened to fricatives. Similar changes affect most other Western Romance

Table 2.24 *The early sixteenth-century Spanish sibilant system*

	Voiceless	Voiced
Dento-alveolar fricative	/s̪/	/z̪/
Alveolar fricative	/s/	/z/
Prepalatal fricative	/ʃ/	/ʒ/

languages and may be regarded as cases of economy of effort, affricates being rather more 'expensive' in terms of energy than other consonants. It is uncertain when this weakening occurred in Spanish, since, owing to the previous absence of dental fricatives from Spanish and the consequent impossibility of any merger resulting, it has no effect on the Spanish phonological system and is therefore not reflected in spelling. It seems likely, however, that the change was accomplished by the fifteenth century at latest, so that by the end of the Middle Ages, the sibilant subsystem of Spanish comprised six fricatives (see table 2.24).

2 The three voiced phonemes came to be devoiced and therefore merged with their voiceless counterparts. Neutralization of voiced and voiceless phonemes in syllable-final position had probably always been the norm in Spanish (see 2.5.3.2.4–6), a feature reflected in the fact that in this position there was no spelling contrast in Old Spanish between *c*/*ç* and *z*, between *ss* and *s* or between *x* and *j*/*g;* only *z*, *s*, and *x*, respectively, were used, e.g. *faz̪*, singular of *faces* (< FASCĒS) 'bundles', *cas̪car* (< *QUASSICĀRE) 'to split' (vs *passo* 'step' < PASSU), *linax̲* (a variant of *linage*) 'lineage', *relox̲* (< OCat. *relotge*, where *tg* indicates a voiced phoneme) 'clock'.

In syllable-initial position, the contrast of voice is lost (in favour of voiceless values) in the standard Spanish of the sixteenth century. Absence of voiced sibilants had probably been a feature of extreme northern varieties of Castilian (and of other northern dialects) for some centuries and some scholars have seen influence from the neighbouring Basque language (which also lacks voiced sibilants) as the cause (e.g. Martinet 1974: 448–61, Jungemann 1955: 318–35). Now, with the establishment of Madrid as the capital of Spain in the 1560s and the influx of northerners into the new capital, the merger of the voiced sibilants with the voiceless spreads south and becomes the norm in the standard language (see Alonso 1967, 1969). Speakers in Toledo and further south for some time adhered to the older system, a territorial distinction which is referred to in the much-quoted statement of Fray Juan de Córdoba (published in Mexico in 1578, but referring to the linguistic situation in Spain several decades earlier): 'Los de Castilla la Vieja dizen *haçer* y en Toledo *hazer*, y (los de Castilla la Vieja) dizen

Table 2.25 *The late sixteenth-century Spanish sibilant system*

	Voiceless	Examples
Dental fricative	/s̪/	*caça* /kás̪a/ (previously /kát^{s}a/)
		dezir /des̪íɾ/ (previously /ded^{z}íɾ/)
Alveolar fricative	/s/	*passo* /páso/ (no change)
		casa /kása/ (previously /káza/)
Prepalatal fricative	/ʃ/	*caxa* /káʃa/ (no change)
		mejor /meʃóɾ/ (previously /meʒóɾ/)

xugar, y en Toledo (dizen) *jugar'*, where the (non-standard) spellings with *ç* and *x* represent the new voiceless articulation, typical then of the northern half of the Peninsula, by contrast with *z* and *j*, which reflect the traditional voiced pronunciation, still found from Toledo southwards.

Evidence also comes from misspelling. While most writers continue to make the graphical distinction set out at the beginning of this section, the more careless are betrayed by their pronunciation into confusion of *c/ç* with *z*, *ss* with *s*, and *x* with *j/g*. Thus, Santa Teresa (b. Avila, 1515) spells *açer*, *reçar*, *deçir* (for the then correct *hazer*, *rezar*, *dezir*), *tuviese*, *matasen*, etc. (for *tuviesse*, *matassen*, etc.), *dijera*, *ejerçiçio*, *teoloxia* (for *dixera*, *exercicio*, *teología*).

As a result of the devoicing (and the consequent mergers) discussed here, minimal pairs like

hoçes 'sickles' < FALCĒS
hozes 'throats, ravines' < FŌCĒS (CL FAUCĒS)
osso 'bear' < URSU
oso 'I dare' , *AUSŌ (CL AUDEŌ)
coxo 'lame' < COXU
cojo 'I seize' < COLLIGŌ

were reduced to pairs of homonyms (now spelt *hoces, oso, cojo*). The sibilant subsystem of sixteenth-century Spanish therefore showed only three voiceless fricative phonemes (table 2.25).

3 The dental and prepalatal phonemes changed locus, because of the great functional load placed upon the contrast of locus which separated /s̪/, /s/ and /ʃ/. There had always been some interchange between alveolar and prepalatal fricatives (e.g. the Old Spanish competition between *tisera*(*s*) (<TŌNSŌRIĀS) and its eventually successful competitor *tijeras* 'scissors'), but by the late sixteenth century there were many pairs (even triplets) of words whose meanings were distinguished by the locus of the relevant consonant. A case in point is provided by the words *caça* 'hunt', *casa* 'house' and *caxa* 'box': meaning is now

Table 2.26 *Sibilant readjustment in early Modern standard Spanish*

	interdental	dento-alveolar	alveolar	palatal	velar
pre-sixteenth century		/t^s/ /d^z/	/s/ /z/	/ʃ/ /ʒ/	
sixteenth century		/s̺/	/s/	/ʃ/	
from 1650	/θ/		/s/		/x/

crucially dependent upon the correct production and perception of, respectively, the dental, alveolar and prepalatal locus of the intervocalic consonant. The potential confusion could only be avoided by making more perceptible the acoustic difference between the phonemes and this was achieved (for the most part) by exaggerating the contrasts of locus: /s̺/ was moved forwards (away from /s/) and became interdental /θ/, while /ʃ/ was moved backwards (also away from /s/) and became velar /x/. Thus, words like *caça, alçar, dezir, pozo* achieved their modern pronunciation /θ/, and *dixo, caxa, hijo, mugier*, etc., acquired their current pronunciation, /x/ (although the modern spellings of such words only emerged as a result of eighteenth- and nineteenth-century reforms).

These changes of locus were spreading through society from the late sixteenth century and became normal by about the middle of the seventeenth (see Alonso 1967, 1969), although it is evident that the educated pronunciation of the early seventeenth century still preferred prepalatal /ʃ/, since the French and Italian adaptations of the name *Don Quixote* (*Don Quichotte*, and *Don Chisciotto*, respectively) show that the Spanish word was still pronounced /kiʃóte/ by at least some speakers.

The changes discussed in this section (2.6.2) are summarized in table 2.26.

2.6.3 The sibilants in Andalusian and American Spanish

In Seville and, as a result, much of Andalusia and all of America, the sibilants were affected by a slightly different sequence of changes from that just examined (2.6.2) in the standard language. In southern texts of the fifteenth and sixteenth centuries, *ss* and s are occasionally replaced by *ç* and *z* respectively (e.g. *paço* for *passo*, *caza* for *casa*) and vice versa. Contemporary observers, because of their preoccupation with spelling (rather than sound), gave the name **çeçeo** (i.e. 'abuse of the letter *ç*') to cases like *paço* for *passo* and used the term **zezeo** ('abuse of the letter *z*') for cases like *caza* for *casa*. Such spelling errors are motivated by phonological changes which were in progress in the south of Spain, namely the merger of the alveolar sibilants with the dentals, in favour of the dentals:

Although full merger of these pairs of phonemes begins, as we have noted, in the fifteenth century, neutralization of /s̪/ with /s/, and of /z̪/ with /z/ is observable in syllable-final position rather earlier, and not only in Andalusia, as can be seen in misspellings like *azno* for *asno*, *diesmo* for *diezmo*, and in the occasional standard form like *mezclar* 'to mix' (< OSp. *mesclar* < *MISCULĀRE).

Rather than by a change of locus of alveolar /s/ and /z/ to dental /s̪/and /z̪/, this merger may have been motivated by the absence from medieval Andalusian speech of the alveolars /s/ and /z/. Corresponding to standard /s/ and /z/, southern speech may have had the dentals /s̪/ and /s̪/ (perhaps due to influence from Mozarabic or Arabic), so that the reduction of the (dento-alveolar) affricates /t^s/ and /d^z/ to fricatives (see 2.6.2(1)) caused immediate merger with pre-existing /s̪/ and /z̪/:

Whichever of these two accounts of the merger is correct, the two products of the merger (/s̪/ and /z̪/) were themselves merged in /s̪/. This merger of voiced /z̪/ with voiceless /s̪/ occurs for the same reasons and at the same time as the general devoicing of sibilants in Spanish (see 2.6.2(2)), so that four medieval sibilants (/t^s/, /d^z/, /s/ and /z/) are reduced in most Andalusian (and all American) speech to a single phoneme (/s̪/). Thus OSp. *caça*, *dezir*, *passo* and *casa* have come to share the phoneme /s̪/ in the areas named (/kás̪a/, /des̪íɾ/, /pás̪o/, /kás̪a/), a process which has brought about a number of homonymic collisions such as those between *caza* 'hunt' and *casa* 'house', or between *cocer* 'to cook' and *coser* 'to sew'.

Since its emergence from /t^s/, /d^z/, /s/ and /z/, the phoneme /s̪/ has come to be realized in two distinctive manners in Andalusian Spanish. In much of central Andalusia (including the cities of Seville and Córdoba) and also in the Canaries and throughout America, /s̪/ is realized as a dental sibilant (not dissimilar to English or French /s/); this dental result of the merger is referred to as **seseo**. In other areas (particularly the coastal areas of Andalusia, including the cities

Table 2.27 *Sibilant readjustment in Andalusian and American Spanish*

	dento- alveolar	alveolar	palatal	laryngeal
to c. 1400	/t^s/ /d^z/	/s/ /z/	/ʃ/ /ʒ/	/h/
to c. 1500	/s̪/ /z̪/	/s/ /z/	/ʃ/ /ʒ/	/h/
16th century	/s̪/ /z̪/		/ʃ/ /ʒ/	/h/
17th century	/s̪/		/ʃ/	/h/
late 17th century on	/s̪/			/h/

of Huelva, Cádiz, Málaga and Granada), a fronted variety of /s̪/ has come to be preferred. Although not identical to standard interdental /θ/, its acoustic effect is somewhat similar, and where this fronted variant is used, the local speech is described as showing **ceceo**. For *seseo* and *ceceo*, see Lapesa (1980: 283–4, 374–6, 508–9, 562–8).

The remaining sibilants behave in southern and American speech in a similar, but not identical, way to that seen in the standard. Devoicing of medieval /ʒ/ brings merger with /ʃ/ (see 2.6.2(2)), and this phoneme is then retracted to avoid confusion with /s/ (see 2.6.2(3)). However. whereas in the standard the result of this retraction is velar /x/, the process was more extreme in the regions now under consideration, resulting in laryngeal or glottal /h/; thus, OSp. *caxa* and *mejor* (MSp. *caja*, *mejor*) are pronounced in these areas /káha/ and /mehóɾ/, a result which had the result of causing merger with the /h/ descended from Lat. F- in areas where the latter survived (chiefly rural western Andalusia and rural American varieties). The Andalusian and American development of the sibilants, in which seven medieval phonemes are reduced to just two, can therefore be summarized as in table 2.27.

2.6.4 *The phonologization of /f/ and /h/*

We have seen (2.5.6) that in the Middle Ages, Spanish lacked a phoneme /f/, although in urban (including standard) Spanish, the sound [f] had come into existence, as one of the allophones of a phoneme here arbitrarily designated /h/:

/h/: [f] before [w] and /ɾ/: ['fweɾte], ['fɾio];
[h] elsewhere (i.e. before syllabic vowels and [j]): [ha'ɾina], ['horno], ['hjero]

all such words being written with a single letter, *f*, as befitted the monophonemic status of their initial consonant: *fuerte, frío, farina, forno, fierro*.

This case of complementary distribution of allophones was changed by the increasing introduction in Old Spanish of borrowings from Latin and Old

Gallo-Romance. In the case of borrowings of words spelt with *f* in the source-language, the Spanish sound [f] was used, in the first case because this was now the sound used in reading aloud Latin F and in the second case directly imitated from speakers of French or Occitan. In this way, [f] came to be used in environments from which it had previously been excluded (namely, before syllabic vowels and [j]) and could thereby come into meaningful contrast with [h]. Thus, the learned word *forma* 'shape', pronounced ['forma], contrasted with the popular word ['horma] 'shoemaker's last' (also spelt *forma*). From this stage onwards, Spanish is best described as having two phonemes /h/ and /f/, and at the very end of the fifteenth century, the spelling system of Spanish comes to reflect the phonological reality through the use, for the first time, of *h* to indicate /h/, leaving *f* to indicate the newly phonologized /f/; this spelling contrast is clearly seen in the works of Antonio de Nebrija, where words with /h/ receive their modern spelling (e.g. *horma* 'shoemaker's last') and only words with /f/ are spelt with *f* (e.g. *forma* 'shape'). For further discussion, see Penny (1990b).

2.6.5 *Learned consonant groups*

Many groups of consonants which had existed in Latin had been reduced to single phonemes during the development from Latin to Old Spanish. Thus the groups represented in Latin by the spellings CT, GN, X, MN, PT, PS, etc., had been resolved in the following ways (see 2.5.2.4, 2.5.3.2):

CT > /tʃ/: FACTU > *hecho* 'done'
GN > /ɲ/: PUGNU > *puño* 'fist'
X > /ʃ/: DIXI > *dixe* (later *dije*) 'I said'
MN > /ɲ/: SCAMNU > *escaño* 'bench'
PT > /t/: APTĀRE > *atar* 'to tie'
PS > /s/: IPSA > *essa* (later *esa*) 'that'

However, many learned words that were borrowed in the late Middle Ages and (increasingly) in the Golden Age, were adaptations of Latin words which contained such groups, and these groups now posed a phonological problem for Spanish. At this stage of the language's development, velar consonants and /p/ were impermissible in syllable-final position; that is, the orally inherited word-stock showed no instances of such phonemes in this position. Similarly, syllable-final /m/ could not occur before /n/, and although syllable-final /b/ did occur in some words (only before /d/), it was already being replaced by /u/ or /Ø/ (as in OSp. *cabdal* > *caudal*, OSp. *dubda* > *duda*; see 2.5.5 (end)). The problem posed by learned words containing impermissible groups was solved in two ways: by simplifying the group, usually through loss of the first consonant; or by attempting to pronounce both (or all three) consonants, thus introducing new phonotactic possibilities to Spanish. In the large majority of

Table 2.28 *Golden Age treatment of learned consonant groups*

group	reduced form	full form	etymon
CT	*efeto*	*efecto*	EFFECTU
CT (+ I + vowel)	*lición*	*lección*	LĒCTIŌNE
GN	*sinificar*	*significar*	SIGNIFICĀRE
X	*examen* /ʃ/	*examen* /ks/	EXĀMEN
	exercer /ʃ/	*exercer* /ks/	EXERCĒRE
XC	*ecelente*	*excelente*	EXCELLENTE
MN	*solene*	*solemne*	SOLLEMNE
MPT	*acetar*	*aceptar*	ACCEPTĀRE
NPT	*pronto*	*prompto*	PROMPTU
BST	*astener*	*abstener*	ABSTINĒRE

relevant learned words, both processes were applied, so that in late Old Spanish and in Golden Age Spanish, many such words had two written and pronounced forms (see table 2.28).

In the case of syllable-final /p/ and /b/ (and sometimes /k/), there was a third possibility in Golden Age Spanish: modification to the glide [u̯], like the treatment accorded to OSp. syllable-final /b/ (e.g. *cabdal* > *caudal*). Thus alongside *acetar* and *aceptar*, *afeto* and *afecto* we find spellings like *aceutar*, *afeuto*.

This variety of forms was eventually resolved (by the Real Academia Española in the late eighteenth century) in favour of the full (i.e. more Latinate) forms (those with the consonant group intact): *efecto*, *significar*, etc. As a result, the phonology of Spanish had come to accept syllable-final /k/, /g/, /p/ and /b/ (although with neutralization of /k/ and /g/, as of /p/ and /b/; see Alarcos 1965: 184–5). There are only two exceptions to this statement: on the one hand, many non-standard varieties of Spanish have not accepted these syllable-final consonants and continue to prefer forms like *efeto* or *efeuto*, and, on the other hand, even in the standard there is a minority of individual learned words which have passed into the modern language in reduced form (sometimes alongside an unreduced form, with different meaning), e.g.

CT *luto* 'mourning' < LŪCTU (cf. *luctuoso* 'mournful')
plática 'chatter' < PRACTICA (cf. *práctica* 'practice')
afición 'liking' < AFFECTIŌNE (cf. *afección* < AFFECTIŌNE)

GN *sino* 'fate' < SIGNUM (cf. *signo* 'sign')

X *ejercer* (now with /x/ < /ʃ/) 'to exercise' < EXERCERE (cf. *examen* (with /gs/) 'examination')

PT *setiembre* 'September' < SEPTEMBER (cf. *septiembre*, also pronounced without /p/)

2.6.6 *Yeísmo*

This term refers to the merger of the palatal lateral /ʎ/ and the midpalatal fricative /ǰ/, usually with non-lateral results:

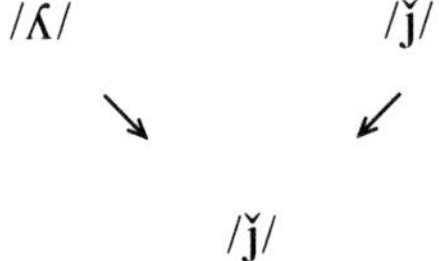

The opposition between /ʎ/ and /ǰ/ was probably never very productive and the merger gives rise to few cases of homonymic collision (*pollo* 'chicken' vs *poyo* 'stone bench', *mallo* 'mallet' vs *mayo* 'May', *malla* 'mesh' vs *maya* 'May Queen; Mayan', etc.). Although not attested in Spain until the eighteenth century, this merger probably began in late Old Spanish, since all varieties of Judeo-Spanish (separated from Peninsular Spanish in 1492) and most varieties of American Spanish witness its accomplishment. Today, almost the whole southern half of the Peninsula lacks /ʎ/ and uses only /ǰ/; this includes the capital, where the immense majority are *yeísta*. In the northern half of the Peninsula, most sizeable towns also show the merger, although intervening rural areas often maintain the traditional opposition.

Among speakers who have merged the two phonemes, various pronunciations are in use (see Penny 2000: 120–1, 147–8, 186):

[dǰ] ~ [ǰ] is usual in educated and urban Spanish in most areas of Spanish speech
[ʒ] occurs in parts of Andalusia and America
[dʒ] is associated with Extremadura, Argentina and Uruguay
[tʃ] occurs in urban speech in the River Plate area
[ʃ] appears in some varieties of Buenos Aires speech

2.6.7 *Weakening of syllable-final /s/ and /θ/*

Like *yeísmo*, this phenomenon is typical of the southern half of the Peninsula. However, although a few northern Peninsular districts are also affected (see Penny 1983a; 2000: 122–5, 148-50), weakening of /-s/ does not affect all American Spanish (most of Mexico and the Andean areas of South America are exempt) or any variety of Judeo-Spanish. Note that in those Peninsular areas (such as New Castile, Extremadura, Murcia) where /θ/ exists as a separate phoneme from /s/ and where weakening of /-s/ takes place, syllable-final /-θ/ is similarly weakened.

This weakening process can be regarded as showing increasing degrees of intensity. These will be considered in turn, beginning with the least intense grade:

1 /-s/ is realized as fricative [ɹ], before /d/, a pronunciation typical of many northern rural areas: *desde*: [déɹðe], *desdeñar*: [deɹðe'ɲaɾ].
2 A more intense degree of weakening affects most of the southern Peninsula, together with the northern areas mentioned and most (but not all) of Spanish America; it consists of the realization of syllable-final /s/ (and of /-θ/ where this is a separate phoneme) as an aspirate [^{h}], whether before a consonant or a pause. It will be noted that this aspiration implies neutralization of syllable-final /s/ and /θ/ in the areas affected. E.g.: *este*: ['e^{h}te], *asno*: ['a^{h}no], *la tos*: [la 'to^{h}], *los viernes*: [lo^{h}'βjeɾne^{h}], *hazte acá*: ['a^{h}te aká], *diezmo*: ['dje^{h}mo], *la voz*: [la 'βo^{h}].
3 The next most intense form of weakening of /-s/ is typical of Andalusia, but is also found in other areas where weakening occurs. It consists of various assimilations between the aspirate (see 2, above) and the following consonant. Usually the syllable-final phoneme takes on some of the features of the following phoneme, but when the second unit is /b/, /d/ or /g/ the latter is also affected, often becoming devoiced: *estos perros*: ['e^{t}to^{p}'pero^{h}], *las botas*: [la^{ɸ}'ɸota^{h}], *disgusto*: [di'hu^{t}to], *asno*: ['afino], *las manos*: [lafi'mano^{h}].
4 The next most severe form of weakening, found especially in western Andalusia and much of America (but also elsewhere, alongside less intense grades), consists of the total loss of final /s/ before a pause: *los perros*: [lo^{h}'pero], *las caras*: [la^{h}'kaɾa].
5 Finally, the most acute form of weakening of /-s/, total elimination in all environments, may be heard in eastern Andalusia: *las olas:* [la 'ola], *las manos:* [la 'mano].

This most intense form of weakening understandably has important phonological consequences, because of the hitherto vital grammatical role played by final /-s/ (as the marker of plural number in nouns, adjectives, etc., and as the marker of the second person in the verb). In areas where final /-s/ has been eliminated (i.e. in much of eastern Andalusia), the grammatical functions of this phoneme have been transferred to other phonemes, namely the preceding vowel. A vowel which belongs to a syllable ending in a consonant (such as /s/) often in Spanish has a slightly different quality from a vowel which is syllable-final, the syllable-final vowel usually being a little more close than its non-final counterpart (see Navarro Tomas 1961: 46–64). This difference of quality has been exploited by some of the dialects concerned, in such a way that, as final /-s/ was lost, the slightly open quality of the preceding (non-syllable-final) vowel was phonologized, so that such a vowel came into phonemic contrast with the corresponding word-final vowel, whose aperture had always been closer. In this way, the information originally carried by presence or absence of final /-s/ comes to be carried by the open or close aperture of the preceding vowel (and often of the other vowels of the word), e.g.:

vienes: ['bjɛnɛ] vs *viene*: ['bjene]
bolos: ['bɔlɔ] vs *bolo*: ['bolo]

In the case of the lowest vowels, it is not aperture which fulfils this role. The contrast is between fronted [æ] (where /-s/ previously followed) and [ɑ] (where the vowel was syllable-final):

las palas: [læ 'pælæ] *vs* *la pala*: [lɑ 'pɑlɑ]
cantas: ['kæntæ] *vs* *canta*: ['kɑntɑ]

Since these vowel contrasts are evidently meaningful, one must conclude that in these (eastern Andalusian) varieties of Spanish the vowel system consists of at least the following eight phonemes:

/i/ /u/
/e/ /o/
/ɛ/ /ɔ/
/æ/ /ɑ/

2.7 Chronology of phonological change

An attempt has been made throughout this chapter to give a rough dating for each change considered. Such a dating has to be extremely approximate, since all change takes a very long period to spread through the society concerned, and we can usually only assign a change to a relatively extensive period (e.g. 'late spoken Latin', 'early Old Spanish', 'Golden Age', etc.). However, although an absolute chronology of each change cannot be achieved, it is possible to establish, with some precision, a relative chronology of change, indicating the order in which changes occur in a given language. Such a relative chronology is attempted here of the various phonological changes which, occurring in spoken Latin, in Western Romance generally, in Hispano-Romance, and specifically in Castilian, have produced the phonological system of Modern Spanish. In some cases (e.g. metaphony), greater chronological precision is attempted here than in the relevant earlier section. For alternative approaches to the chronological sequence of phonological change in Spanish, see Menéndez Pidal (1958: 171–4), Hartman (1974) and Pensado Ruiz (1984).

1 Loss of final M (2.5.4) and initial H (2.5.2).
2 Pitch-accent replaced by stress-accent (2.3.2).
3 Vowel changes:
 (a) tonic (2.4.2.6)

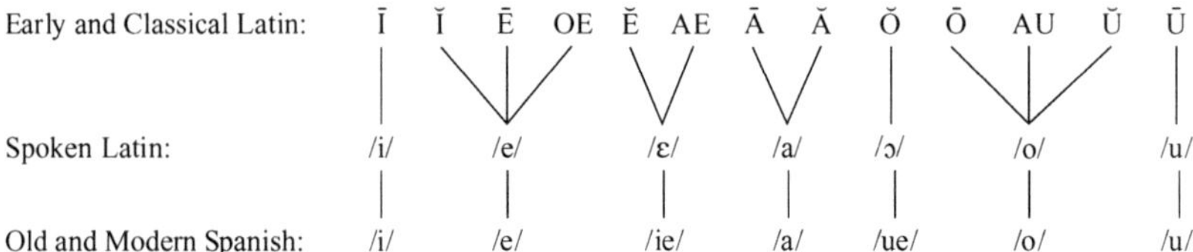

(b) atonic (2.4.3.1)

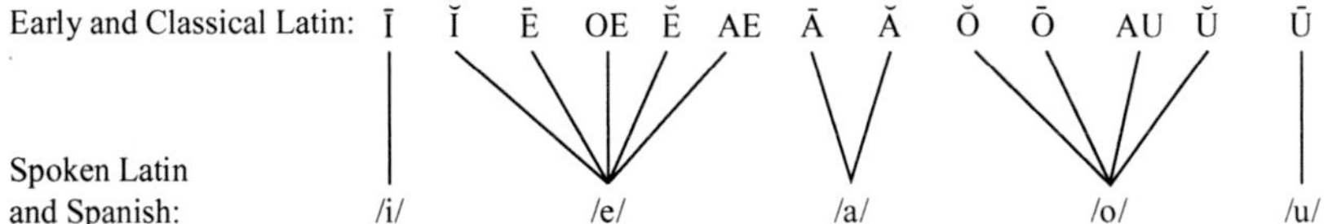

4 V fricatized to /β/ (2.5.3.1); non-syllabic I > /ǰ/ (2.5.2.1).
5 Intervocalic B and V merge in /β/ (2.5.3.1).
6 Atonic E or I in hiatus with a following vowel > palatal glide [j] (2.4.3.4).
7 Palatalization of T + [j] and C + [j] > /t^{s}/ and of TT + [j], CC + [j], etc. > /tt^{s}/ (2.5.2.2(1)).
8 Palatalization of syllable-initial C (+ E/I) and G(+ E/I) (2.5.2.3).
9 First loss of intertonic vowels (any, except A, in contact with R or L, sometimes S or N) (2.4.3.3).
10 Palatalization of syllable-final velars: CT > [i̯t], X > [i̯s], GN > [i̯n], CL/GL > [i̯l] (2.5.2.4).
11 Assimilation of consonant groups: PT > /tt/, RS > /ss/, PS > /ss/, NS > /s/, MN > /nn/, MB > /mm/ (2.5.3.2).
12 Raising of /o/ to /u/ when immediately followed by [i̯] or by N + [j]; raising of /e/ > /i/ and /o/ > /u/ when followed by M or B/V + [j] or by a group + [j] (2.4.2. 1).
13 Raising of /ɛ/ > /e/ and /ɔ/ > /o/ by any following palatal glide (2.4.2.1).
14 Palatalization of L > /ʎ/ and N > /ɲ/ when followed or preceded by a palatal glide (2.5.2.2(2–3), 2.5.2.4) and of D + [j] and G + [j] > /ǰǰ/ (2.5.2.2(4)).
15 Diphthongization of /ɛ/ > /ie/ and /ɔ/ > /ue/ (2.4.2.2).
16 Palatalization of T > /tʃ/ and S > /ʃ/ when preceded by a palatal glide (2.5.2.4).
17 F- realized as [h] in many environments (could be placed earlier; 2.5.6).
18 Metathesis of R + [j] > [i̯ɾ] and P + [j] > [i̯p] (2.5.2.2(6)).
19 /ʎ/ (resulting from 9 and 14) > /ʒ/ (2.5.2.2(2), 2.5.2.4).
20 Lenition (see 2.5.3.2 for the chronological relationship between (a), (b), (c) and (d)):
(a) geminate > simple (and sonorants are additionally modified: LL > /ʎ/, NN > /ɲ/, RR > /r/);
(b) voiceless > voiced (e.g. -T- > /d/, -S- > /z/, /t^{s}/ > /d^{z}/);
(c) voiced plosives > fricatives (and are often eliminated);
(d) /ǰ/ > /Ø/.
21 PL-, CL-, FL- > /ʎ/ (2.5.2.6).
22 Loss of surviving intertonic vowels (see 9), except /a/ (2.4.3.3); creates secondary consonant groups (2.5.6).

23 Metathesis s + [j] > [i̯s] (2.5.2.2(6)).

24 /au/ > /ou/ > /o/, and /ei/ (from earlier /ai/ and /ei/, which arose through change 9) > /e/ (2.4.2.3, 2.4.2.4).

25 Merger of final /i/ and /e/ in /e/ (2.4.3.2).

26 Loss of final /e/ after ungrouped dental and alveolar consonants (except /t/) (2.4.3.2).

27 Modification of secondary consonant groups (see 22), by assimilation, dissimilation, etc. (2.5.6).

28 Loss of /h/ (except in SW, W and NW varieties of Peninsular Castilian and in some American varieties; 2.6.4).

29 OSp. /b/ and /β/ merge in /b/ (2.6.1).

30 Syllable-final /b/ > [u̯] (2.5.5 (end)).

31 Deaffrication of /t^s/ > /s̺/ and /d^z/ > /z̺/ (2.6.2).

32 Devoicing of voiced sibilants and merger with voiceless counterparts: /s̺/ and /z̺/ merge in /s̺/; /s/ and /z/ merge in /s/; /ʃ/ and /ʒ/ merge in /ʃ/ (2.6.2).

33 Shift of locus /s̺/ > /θ/ (except in much of Andalusia and all America) and /ʃ/ > /x/ or /h/ (2.6.2).

3 Morpho-syntax

3.1 General concepts

Morphology studies the forms of words, and in particular the relationship between grammatical function and the various segments into which words can be divided from the point of view of such grammatical function. The basic units of morphological analysis are **morphemes**, segments which are capable of conveying grammatical function (such as 'plural', 'past', etc.), or lexical meaning ('clock', 'fish', 'think', etc.); the latter are also known as **lexemes**. Morphemes may consist of one or more phonemes, but may not be subdivided without losing their ability to convey grammatical information. Thus, the word *pequeñitos* may be analysed into four morphemes: a root morpheme (or lexeme) *pequeñ-*, which carries the lexical meaning of the word, *-it*, which conveys an affectionate or diminutive value, *-o-*, which indicates masculine gender, and *-s*, which is the exponent of plural number. Similarly, *cantaban* may be morphologically divided into four morphemes: a root morpheme *cant-*, a conjugation marker *-a-*, a tense/aspect/mood indicator (here, 'past' + 'imperfective' + 'indicative') *-ba-* and a person/ number morpheme *-n*.

Such morphological (or morphemic) analysis immediately reveals that the words of all languages are organized into closed sets (or paradigms). Two examples of paradigms in Spanish are

buen-o	buen-os
buen-a	buen-as

(in which morphemes of gender and number are applicable to a large number of noun and adjective root morphemes) and

cant-o	cant-amos
cant-as	cant-áis
cant-a	cant-an

(where morphemes indicating both tense/mood/aspect and person/number are applied to a large class of verbal roots).

Syntax is concerned with discovering and stating the rules which govern the combination of words into sentences. However, since morphological and syntactical change are often intimately related, it is convenient, from a historical viewpoint, to consider morphology and syntax in conjunction. Such simultaneously morphological and syntactical analysis of language is termed **morpho-syntax**.

The interrelationship between morphological and syntactical change is best expressed by saying that information which at one stage is expressed by morphological processes may come at a later stage to be expressed by syntactical processes, and vice versa. In the course of the development from Latin to Spanish, morphologically expressed information has frequently come to be syntactically expressed, while the reverse is rare. For example, while such information as 'sentence subject', 'direct object', 'indirect object', etc., was expressed in the Latin noun, adjective and pronoun systems by means of morphemes of case (and number), bound to a root morpheme, these notions came to be expressed in the descendants of Latin by syntactical means (word-order, number-agreement between subject and verb, presence or absence of prepositions, etc.). Languages like Latin, which have large numbers of bound morphemes (case-endings, verbal inflections, etc.) are sometimes categorized as **synthetic**, while languages like English, in which free morphemes (invariable words) predominate, can be called **analytic**. While Spanish is more synthetic than English (particularly in its verbal system), it is less synthetic than its parent, so that the morpho-syntactical development from Latin to Spanish (and the other Romance languages) can be broadly characterized as one in which there has been a drift in favour of syntactical rather than morphological means of conveying the same information.

3.1.1 Morphological change

Morphological change is brought about principally by the operation of two forces, phonological change and analogical adjustment. Conditioned phonological change (the normal type) frequently has a disruptive effect upon paradigms, since some forms of a given paradigm may exhibit the conditions required for a change to occur, while other forms of the same paradigm may lack this conditioning factor. Thus the present indicative paradigm of the Latin verb DĪCERE 'say' has the same phoneme, /k/, at the end of the root morpheme, whatever the following phoneme:

DĪCŌ = /diːkoː/
DĪCIS = /diːkis/, etc.

Now we have seen (2.5.2.3) that Lat. /k/ came to be palatalized before front vowels, but remained velar before non-front vowels. Bearing in mind other changes (see 2.5.3.2 and 2.6.2), we can therefore predict that the /k/ of DĪCŌ will yield Sp. /g/, while the /k/ of DĪCIS will give /θ/, a prediction which in this case proves accurate:

DĪCŌ > *digo*
DĪCIS > *dices*

Phonological change has in this case made the paradigm less coherent; it has introduced alternation between two phonemes where Latin showed a single phoneme, reducing the similarity between members of the same paradigm.

On the other hand, **analogy** often serves to restore or maintain the similarity between members of the same paradigm. Analogy is the process whereby forms which are related in grammatical function come to have a similar form. (Analogy also operates in the case of semantically related words, but this type of analogy does not concern us here.) Examples of grammatically motivated analogy can be seen in the present indicative paradigm of verbs like Lat. SENTĪRE 'feel, hear'. The tonic /ɛ/ of first person SENTIŌ, before the [j] of the final syllable, can be expected to provide Sp. /e/ (2.4.2.1), while, in the absence of [j], the tonic /ɛ/ of second-person SENTĪS and third-person SENTIT can be expected to yield Sp. /ie/ (2.4.2.2). Similarly, the /t/ + [j] sequence of words structured like SENTIŌ normally provides Sp. /θ/ (see 2.5.2.2), while such a result cannot arise in forms like SENTĪS, SENTIT, which lack [j]. In the development of SENTIŌ, neither of these two phonological changes took place (or, if they took place, they were reversed before the appearance of written Spanish) and the Spanish reflexes of the Latin forms are the familiar

SENTIŌ > *siento*
SENTĪS > *sientes*
SENTIT > *siente*

That is, owing to the similarity of function ('present indicative') between SENTIŌ and SENTĪS/SENTIT, the form of the first has remained or become similar, through analogy, to the form of other members of the paradigm, and phonological change has been resisted or reversed. Similarly, analogy may operate between paradigms; the present subjunctive of verbs like PLICĀRE 'fold', later 'arrive' (PLICEM, PLICĒS, PLICET, etc.) does not show the otherwise expected palatalization of Lat. /k/ (contrast DĪCIS > *dices*, above), but maintains the velar phoneme, later voiced to /g/:

PLICEM > *llegue*
PLICĒS > *llegues*
PLICET > *llegue*

Morphological change, then, may be viewed as (in part) the result of competitive struggle between phonological change (which normally operates without regard to the meaning or function of the words it affects and leads to disruption of paradigms) and analogical adjustment (which maintains or restores phonological similarity between forms which have a related function). It is difficult to predict, in a given case of morphological development, which of these two forces will gain the upper hand, but it can be seen that the success of one force rather than the other is correlated (at least weakly) with the frequency of the words concerned. The more frequent a set of forms, the less likely it is to be affected by analogy, and (it follows), the more likely it is to show the disruptive effects of phonological change. Thus the present indicative paradigm *digo*, *dices*, etc., of the very frequent verb *decir* 'say' is morphologically 'irregular' (although 'regular' from the point of view of historical phonology), while the corresponding paradigm (*siento*, *sientes*, etc.) of the somewhat less frequent *sentir* 'feel' is morphologically more regular (although phonologically 'irregular' from a historical viewpoint). However, it cannot be argued that frequency is the only relevant factor here; frequency may be countered by other, less easily identifiable, factors.

Other types of morphological change are not excluded from the history of Spanish. Certain words may lose their independent status, be reduced to an auxiliary role, and finally become inflectional morphemes. This is the case of HABĒRE, which came to be used with an infinitive to form a periphrastic future and conditional in spoken Latin (CANTĀRE HABEŌ/HABĒBAM). At a later stage, reduced forms of the auxiliary combined with the infinitive to form single words (*cantaré/cantaría;* see 3.7.8.4).

3.2 The noun

The Latin noun consisted of a root morpheme followed by a single bound morpheme which indicated case and number (3.2.1). Gender (3.2.2) was in part indicated by the same (principally case/number) morphemes, but can be regarded as inherent in the root. The noun was originally organized into five form classes (3.2.3).

3.2.1 Case and number

Each Latin noun had in principle twelve separate endings, by which were indicated the role of the noun in the sentence (i.e. its case) and its number. Using traditional terminology (where nominative = subject case, vocative = case for direct address, accusative = direct-object case, genitive = case indicating possession, etc., dative = indirect-object case, ablative = case expressing a variety of sentence relations, often in combination with a preposition), such endings may be exemplified by means of an *a*-class noun such as MENSA 'table' (table 3.1).

It will be seen that these nouns have only seven distinct endings and in this they are typical of Latin nouns; none had more than eight distinct endings. As a result, form alone sometimes (perhaps often) did not unambiguously specify the role of the noun in a given sentence. In order to understand the function of, say, MENSAE, in a particular sentence, the hearer would need to have recourse to other clues such as word-order, verbal endings, the endings of other nouns, etc. This source of potential misunderstanding was compounded by another

Table 3.1 *Case-endings of Latin* a-*class nouns*

	singular	plural
Nominative	MENSA	MENSAE
Vocative	MENSA	MENSAE
Accusative	MENSAM	MENSĀS
Genitive	MENSAE	MENSĀRUM
Dative	MENSAE	MENSĪS
Ablative	MENSĀ	MENSĪS

ambiguity inherent in the system: certain cases, especially the accusative and ablative, each had several different functions.

Although the system of case-endings described here could function reasonably well in written language, where re-reading will often resolve what is at first an ambiguity, this system was probably always inadequate at the spoken level, where immediate comprehension is required for communication to take place. Where the literary language (until about the first century AD) continued to rely on the unassisted case-endings, there is evidence that spoken Latin, from the earliest times, used additional devices, principally prepositions, to disambiguate the confusing noun-endings. Already in the popular drama of writers like Plautus (end of the third century BC) and even, occasionally, in the more 'serious' works of later writers, we find that certain noun functions are not indicated by the noun form alone, but by a combination of preposition and noun. The cases most frequently involved are the genitive, dative and ablative. Instead of the genitive, we occasionally find the preposition DE followed by an ablative: DĪMIDIUM DE PRAEDĀ (Plautus), DE MARMORE TEMPLUM (Virgil), PAUCĪ DE NOSTRĪS (Caesar). This analytic construction is inherited directly by Spanish in the form of *de* + noun (*la mitad del botín*, *un templo de mármol*, *pocos de los nuestros*).

The indirect object in spoken Latin was often expressed by means of IN or AD together with the accusative, while Classical Latin used an unqualified dative. The same construction (eventually *a* + noun) was used in Spain and other areas to express a personal direct object, rather than the accusative. Spanish (*se lo dio*) *a su amigo*, and (*vio*) *a su amigo* are the linear descendants of spoken Latin AD + accusative. In Old Spanish, this personal *a* construction was still not grammaticalized, but served to disambiguate propositions in which two nouns or pronouns were clustered with a verb of the same number (singular or plural). Under these circumstances, the relatively free word-order of Spanish (which frequently allows the subject to follow its verb) could give rise to doubt as to which of the nouns was to be interpreted as the subject and which as the object, but the appearance of *a* before one of the (pro)nouns implied that the other was to be construed as the subject. This potential ambiguity most frequently arose in the case of *personal* nouns, since such nouns are more likely to function as the subject of the sentence. It was only at the end of the Golden Age that the 'personal *a*' became an obligatory particle, although frequent examples of its former disambiguating role can be seen in contemporary sentences like *mordió el perro al gato* 'the dog bit the cat', where neither noun is personal, but where, without the preposition, it is impossible to determine which of the nouns is the subject.

The Classical Latin 'ablative of comparison' corresponded in spoken Latin to the construction DE + ablative, a construction which continues into early Old Spanish (e.g. *De Judas mui peor* (Berceo) 'much worse than Judas'), but was then ousted by the familiar *que* construction, one which has its roots in Latin QUAM. Similarly, the notion of the 'instrumental ablative' came to be expressed by means of expressions like *con* or *por medio de*. However, most values of the Latin ablative required the presence of a preposition even in the literary language. So, A(B) + ablative was used to express 'the person by whom (an action is carried out)', a construction which persists into early Old Spanish (e.g. *Poema de mio Cid* (*PMC*): *A los judios te dexaste prender* 'you let yourself be taken in by the Jews'), although it was then rapidly replaced by *de* + noun (e.g. *PMC: dexadas seredes de nos* 'you will be abandoned by us'), the expression of agency which is normal until the sixteenth century, when *de* is largely, but not in all cases, replaced by *por* in this function; the older use continues after certain participles, e.g. *amado de todos*. The 'ablative of company' also required the presence of a preposition (CUM), whose descendant is Spanish *con*.

This trend towards prepositional phrases was irreversible; although case-endings and prepositions perform the same function, the fact that the number of prepositions was larger than that of case-endings meant that prepositions performed this function more efficiently and the case-endings became mere redundant exponents of values better expressed by the accompanying prepositions. Such redundancy does not by itself imply that case-endings were bound to be abandoned (since all languages permit a large measure of redundancy), but it does mean that, should the case-endings be threatened with phonological convergence, such convergence is scarcely likely to be resisted. And phonological convergence is precisely what did overtake many pairs of endings. The relevant phonological convergences and their consequences for the case system were the following:

1 Loss of final -M (2.5.4) frequently caused the merger of accusative singular with ablative singular (e.g. acc. MONTE(M)= abl. MONTE).
2 Merger of Ă and Ā (see 2.4.1), together with loss of -M, made distinction impossible between nom. MENSA, acc. MENSAM and abl. MENSĀ.
3 Merger of Ō and Ŭ, together with the other back vowels in final position (see 2.4.3.2), additionally made accusative singulars like DOMINUM indistinguishable from dative/ablative singulars like DOMINŌ.

Table 3.2 *Case system of late spoken Latin*

		singular	plural
1 (*a*-class)	Nominative	/rósa/	/rósas/
	Oblique	/rósa/	/rósas/
2 (*o*-class)	Nominative	/ánnos/	/ánni/
	Oblique	/ánno/	/ánnos/
3a (*e*/cons.-class)	Nominative	/léo/	/leónes/
	Oblique	/leóne/	/leónes/
3b (*e*/cons.-class)	Nominative	/núβes/	/núβes/
	Oblique	/núβe/	/núβes/

4 Convergence of Ē and Ĭ, together with the other front vowels in final position (see 2.4.3.2), caused merger of nom./acc. plur. MONTĒS with gen. sing. MONTIS.

Note that it is not being argued here that phonological change caused morphological merger and the consequent replacement of case-endings by prepositions, as is often argued, but rather that the inadequate distinctions existing in early Latin between one case and another led to the use of prepositions in a disambiguating function, a development which made the case-endings largely redundant and allowed further merger, as a result of phonological change, to go ahead unchecked.

By the fourth or fifth century AD, the phonological changes just discussed led to a considerable reduction in the case forms of all singular Latin nouns, while the plural forms were similarly reduced by analogy with the singular. In the east and in some parts of the west, there may have been as many as three surviving case forms for some nouns (see Dardel 1964), but in most of the west (including Spain) by this period there was probably a maximum of two case forms (a nominative or subject case, in contrast with an oblique, which was used in all roles except that of subject) in both singular and plural. Even this distinction was no doubt lacking in some parts of the noun system. In the late spoken Latin of Spain and other areas, then, the noun system probably showed the pattern presented in table 3.2 (see Penny 1980).

The system posited here makes two assumptions which have not so far been discussed. Unimportant for present purposes is the assumption that in final syllables (see 2.4.3.2) /i/ (< Ī) and /e/ (< Ĭ, Ē, Ĕ) were still separate phonemes. More significant is the statement that the nominative plural ending of *a*-class nouns was /-as/. There is good evidence (see Aebischer 1971) that in the spoken Latin of most areas this was the case from early times, by contrast with the literary dialect, which showed analogical -AE.

This two-case system survived, in French and Provençal, with minor changes, until the twelfth or thirteenth century. In other areas, there was an early further reduction to invariable singular and plural noun forms, as the result of a series of analogical adjustments. It will be noted that *a*-class nouns already in late spoken Latin lacked any case-inflection, and that the same was true in the plural of the third declension in spoken Latin. The fact that no case distinction was possible in a large number of instances undoubtedly set the pattern for the obliteration of such distinction elsewhere. The analogical processes by which this obliteration was carried out were the following:

1 Final /s/ occurs in almost all plural forms, but in only some singular forms. This morpheme probably therefore came to be analysed as a marker exclusively of number and no longer of case. Crucially, this pattern (/-s/ = plur., /Ø/ = sing.) was already established in the first declension in spoken Latin. Analogical extension of this pattern no doubt led to the loss of /-s/ in those (usually nominative) singular instances where it hitherto occurred, bringing immediate further convergence of nom. sing. /ánno/, /núβe/ (previously /ánnos/, /núβes/) with the oblique singular.

2 Many nouns of group 3a (which are imparisyllabic nouns, ones in which the nominative singular has one syllable fewer than the other forms; see 3.2.3) suffered analogical levelling by means of the expansion of their short nominative singular forms. The *Appendix Probi* condemns expanded GLĪRIS, GRŪIS and recommends traditional GLĪS, GRŪS, while in non-literary Latin we find MENTIS for MENS, CARNIS for CARŌ, BOVIS for BŌS, etc. This levelling was limited in spoken Latin to nouns with non-personal sense, but must have been extended to personal nouns in the following period. Taken together with the loss of sing. /-s/ just discussed, this change implies merger of nom. sing. /leóne/ (< *LEŌNIS < LEŌ) with obl. sing. /leóne/.

3 The operation of the previous two changes leaves morphological contrast between nominative and oblique only in the plural of *o*-class nouns (/ánni/ vs /ánnos/). Even leaving aside the universal constraint that plurals may not show a greater degree of morphemic contrast than the corresponding singulars, it is evident that the internal analogical pressures to level out the contrast between /ánni/ and /ánnos/ must have been practically irresistible. But which was to survive? In Spain and other western areas, where the plural of most nouns was marked by the addition of /s/ to the same vowel as occurred in the singular, it is clear that /ánnos/ was bound to be preferred, and /ánni/ disappeared, perhaps after a period of free variation with /ánnos/ in both nominative and oblique roles. (In central Italy and other eastern areas, where /s/ was regularly lost and where most plurals differed from their corresponding singulars by means of a vowel alternation (sing. /rósa/, plur. /róse/), structural pressure would evidently lead to preference for /ánni/ over /ánnos)/.)

As a result of these adjustments, all traces of case distinction are lost from the system of the three major form classes that Spanish inherits: (1) *rosa*/*rosas*, (2) *año*/*años*, and (3) *león*/*leones*, *nube*/*nubes*. In the last category, the presence or absence of /-e/ is a matter of phonological history (see 2.4.3.2) rather than of morphology.

Traditional accounts of the development of the noun system (e.g. Menéndez Pidal 1958: 205–9) state that the Latin accusative case form survives at the expense of the other cases, taking over their functions. While it is true that the surviving Spanish noun-forms more closely resemble the Classical Latin accusative than any other case, the traditional account cannot explain why a form (accusative) which in Latin signals the direct object of a transitive verb should come to indicate also the subject of the sentence, as well as other functions. That is, the traditional argument, while morphologically adequate, is syntactically inadequate. The account given here, which depends upon phonological and analogical levelling of originally distinct endings, does not have to face this syntactical difficulty, since it argues that the Spanish (and other Romance) noun-forms inherit both the functions and (to a large extent) the forms of a wide variety of Latin cases.

3.2.2 Gender

In the development of the noun from Latin to Spanish, the category of gender undergoes two major modifications. On the one hand, there is the change from a three-gender system (masculine~feminine~neuter) to a two-gender system (masculine~feminine), with the consequent reassignment of surviving neuter nouns to one or other of the remaining genders. On the other hand, there were changes which brought about an increasingly close correspondence between gender and noun-endings.

3.2.2.1 Neuter nouns

It can be argued that the class of Latin neuter nouns was insufficiently distinctive both in form and semantic content and that this lack of distinctiveness ultimately caused its demise. The only formally distinctive characteristics of the neuters were the identity of nominative and accusative endings and the fact that the nominative and accusative plural always ended in /a/. On the semantic side, although the neuters may once have exclusively indicated the class of 'inanimates' (while the masculines and feminines together indicated the 'animates'), by the first century BC this relationship had become extremely blurred; many inanimates had masculine or feminine gender, and some animates were to be found among the neuters. The result of this indeterminacy of the neuter class was a large measure of interchange, in spoken Latin, between neuters and (especially) masculines; neuters are frequently found with masculine endings and traditionally masculine nouns sometimes occur with the neuter plural ending /a/. The general principle underlying the reallocation of the neuters is that, if the Latin noun had a back vowel in its final syllable, it was assigned to the masculine class, although those (relatively few) neuters which evolved through their plural form (in /-a/) acquired feminine gender. Where the final vowel was neither /-o/ nor /-a/ (that is, in those neuters with a final consonant or /-e/), the new gender appears to have been arbitrarily assigned, although in specific cases it appears that association of the neuter noun with a masculine or feminine noun of related meaning has been responsible for the assignment of masculine or feminine gender.

Latin neuters of the second declension (e.g. PRĀTUM, VĪNUM) differed in form from masculine nouns of the same class only in the nominative singular (-UM vs -US), the nominative plural (-Ā vs -Ī) and accusative plural (-Ā vs -ŌS). Even this degree of distinction would eventually have been lessened, when the nom. sing. /-s/ was lost from masculine nouns (see 3.2.1). However, even before this, such neuters had become identical with masculine nouns like ANNUS, DOMINUS, abandoning their plurals in /-a/ and adopting masculine endings. Such neuters therefore appear in Spanish as masculine:

PRĀTUM, PRĀTA > *prado, prados* 'meadow(s)'
VĪNUM > *vino* 'wine'

(It will be noted that VĪNUM and *vino*, as mass-nouns, do not have plural forms, except in the specialized sense of 'classes of wine'.)

Neuters of the fourth declension merged in the same way with masculines of the same class and later became identical to the previous group (*prado*, *vino*, etc.) when the fourth declension merged with the second (see 3.2.3). Thus

CORNU, CORNUA > *cuerno, cuernos* 'horn(s)'

Those neuters of the third declension whose nominative/accusative singular was in -US (TEMPUS, CORPUS, PECTUS, PIGNUS, OPUS; plur. TEMPORA, CORPORA, PECTORA, PIGNORA, OPERA; LATUS, plur. LATERA) were also eventually absorbed into the masculine class in *-o*, *-os*. However, there is some evidence that in pre-literary Spanish these nouns had an invariable /-os/ ending for both singular (where presence of /-s/ in the accusative as well as the nominative no doubt enabled the consonant to resist the analogical elimination which affected this consonant in masculine nouns (see 3.2.1)) and plural (where the ending was purely analogical). The evidence comes from early Old Spanish, where in certain phrases these nouns end in *-os* but have apparently singular meaning: *en tiempos de* 'in the time of', *en cuerpos* 'in body', *en pechos* 'on the breast', *huebos me es* 'it is necessary for me' (a continuation of the Latin phrase OPUS EST MIHĪ), *al lados de* 'beside'. But apart from such fossilized phrases, these nouns had by the Old Spanish period been fully assimilated to the masculine *-o*/*-os* group:

TEMPUS, TEMPORA > *tiempo*, *tiempos* 'time(s)'
CORPUS, CORPORA > *cuerpo*, *cuerpos* 'body, -ies'
PECTUS, PECTORA > *pecho*, *pechos* 'breast(s)'
PIGNUS, PIGNORA > *peño* 'pledge', later *empeño* 'id., etc.'
LATUS, LATERA > *lado*, *lados* 'side(s)'

The plural PIGNORA had an independent development (> *prenda*), as did the plural OPERA; see below.

Neuters of the third declension were, in form, a somewhat heterogeneous group, but a substantial subgroup consisted of imparisyllabic nouns (see 3.2.3) whose nominative/accusative singular ended in /n/ or /ɾ/ (e.g. NŌMEN, plur. NŌMINA, RŌBUR, plur. RŌBORA). In Spain, these nouns were treated like other imparisyllabics (see 3.2.1 (end)), suffering expansion of the nominative singular, and (since neuters had a short accusative singular) of the accusative singular too, in order to equalize the number of syllables in these forms with the number of syllables in the remaining forms of the paradigm. Since the expanded singular form ended in /e/ (e.g. NŌMEN > *NŌMINE, RŌBUR > *RŌBORE), these nouns were assimilated to the third Spanish noun class, replacing their -A plurals with /-es/. And since the class into which these nouns moved was shared by masculine and feminine nouns, the ultimate gender of the newcomers was arbitrarily assigned, although in some cases association of meaning with a pre-existing masculine or feminine noun may have played a role in assigning the new gender; thus LŪMEN becomes feminine (*lumbre*), perhaps by association with fem. LŪX (> *luz*). The nouns belonging to this group are:

NŌMEN/NŌMINA > *NŌMINE/NŌMINA > *nombre(s)* (masc).
VĪMEN/VĪMINA > *VĪMINE/VĪMINA > *mimbre(s)* (masc).
AERAMEN/AERAMINA > *AERAMINE/AERAMINA> *alambre(s)*(masc).
EXAMEN/EXAMINA > *EXAMINE/EXAMINA > *enjambre(s)* (masc).
LEGŪMEN/LEGŪMINA>*LEGŪMINE/LEGŪMINA> *legumbre(s)*(fem).
LŪMEN/LŪMINA > *LŪMINE/LŪMINA > *lumbre* (fem).
CULMEN/CULMINA > *CULMINE/CULMINA > *cumbre(s)* (fem).
RŌBUR/RŌBORA > RŌBORE/RŌBORA > *roble(s)* (masc).
ŪBER/ŪBERA > *ŪBERE/ŪBERA > *ubre(s)* (fem).
SULFUR > *SULFURE > *azufre* (masc).

Similarly expanded (i.e. by analogy with gen. LACTIS, dat. LACTI, etc.) is:

LAC > LACTE > *leche* (fem).

Other third declension neuters were rather disparate in form, and either did not require expansion (because they were already parisyllabic; see 3.2.3) or (for various reasons, sometimes obscure) resisted it:

FEL > *hiel* (fem).
MEL > *miel* (fem).
RĒTE (attested as f. RĒTIS in spoken Latin) > *red* (fem).
MARE > *mar* (masc. or fem. in Old Spanish, now usually masc.)

COCHLEĀRE > OSp. *cuchar* (masc. or fem.), with later preference for feminine gender and hypercharacterization (see 3.2.2.2), and movement to the *a*-class

CAPUT/CAPITA, with singular /-o/ in spoken Latin, was drafted into the *o*-class (therefore masc.), with analogical plural: *cabo(s)*

VAS/VASA had a spoken Latin competitor VASUM/VASA, which survives as Sp. *vaso(s)* (masc).

OS/OSSA similarly was ousted by spoken Latin OSSUM/OSSA, whence *hueso(s)*

Although most neuters suffered analogical restructuring of their plurals, a number of neuter plurals (in -A) were transferred to the *a*-class, naturally becoming feminine singular and acquiring a new plural in /-as/. Most such nouns were ones whose original plurals could be understood (sometimes loosely) as 'collective', a category in which the distinction between singular and plural becomes weakened. Thus, alongside CL neut. ARMUM/ARMA 'weapon(s)' (whose plural can be understood as a collective meaning 'weaponry' and therefore reinterpreted as a singular noun) we find attested fem. ARMA/ARMAE, ancestor of Sp. *arma(s)* 'weapon(s)'. Similarly, alongside CL OPUS/OPERA 'work(s)', we find OPERA/OPERAE, whence *obra(s)* 'id.' (for OPUS > OSp. *huebos*, see above).

Some of the neuter plurals which have in this way passed to the feminine *a*-class retain vestiges of collective sense (some continuing as mass-nouns and having no Spanish plural):

ARMA > *arma* 'weapon', but also 'weaponry'

BRACCHIA 'arms'> *braza* 'fathom (the length of two outstretched arms)' (compare singular BRACCHIUM > *brazo* 'arm')

FOLIA 'leaves'> *hoja* 'leaf' (but also collective: '(dead) foliage')

LIGNA '(pieces of)wood' > *leña* 'firewood'

*OVA (CL ŌVA) 'eggs' > *hueva* 'roe (of fish)' (compare *OVUM > *huevo* 'egg')

VŌTA 'vows' > *boda* 'wedding'

Others have entirely lost such collective sense:

MŌRA 'blackberries, mulberries' > *(zarza)mora* 'blackberry, mulberry'

OPERA > *obra* (see above)

PIGNORA 'pledges' > *prenda* 'pledge; garment'

PIRA 'pears' > *pera* 'pear'

Because of the amalgamation of the neuter nouns with masculines and feminines, there was a period of uncertainty in Latin over the gender of certain nouns, with the occasional effect that a masculine or feminine noun is found with the (originally neuter) plural ending /-a/. Even more rarely, such /a/-forms have survived, with feminine singular status, like ARMA > *arma*, OPERA > *obra*, etc.:

fruta '(piece of) fruit' < FRUCTA 'fruit(s)' ('incorrect' plural of FRUCTUS, whence *fruto* 'fruit, product')
rama 'branch' < *RAMA 'branches' ('incorrect' plural of RAMUS, whence *ramo*, now only 'twig, bouquet, etc.')

It can be seen, then, that in the reclassification of neuter nouns as either masculine or feminine, the form of the neuter noun determines its ultimate gender, with the rider that where form could not decide the matter (because the neuter noun ended in /e/ or a consonant), the ultimate gender is partly arbitrarily determined and partly determined by the gender of semantically related words.

3.2.2.2 Gender-marking of the noun

3.2.2.2.1 Masculine and feminine nouns in -US and -A. There was already in Classical Latin a strong correlation between gender and noun form; most nouns in -US (i.e. those of the second and fourth declensions) were masculine (leaving aside the neuters of these declensions, which rapidly acquired masculine gender), while the large majority of those in -A (those of the first declension) were feminine. In spoken Latin this correlation was strengthened (by the abandonment or by gender switch of feminines in -US and masculines in -A) and by the Old Spanish period the correlation was almost absolute. At that stage, probably the only aberrant forms were the fem. *mano* and the masc. *día*. In reaching this position, three groups of words, in particular, had required adjustment: tree-names, gem-names and kinship terms.

Tree-names, feminine in Latin, frequently ended in -US. The simplest solution to this 'anomaly', gender-switch, was adopted in numerous cases:

CERĀSIUS > *cerezo* 'cherry' POPULUS > *chopo* 'black poplar'
FRAXINUS > *fresno* 'ash' TAXUS > *tejo* 'yew'
PĪNUS > *pino* 'pine' ULMUS > *olmo* 'elm'

In other cases (especially, but not exclusively, where there was a need to distinguish between a tree-name and the name of the corresponding fruit), the tree-name continues to be feminine, but acquires an /a/ ending through replacement of the original noun by a related adjective which agrees with feminine ARBOR:

FĪCUS 'fig-tree' > (ARBOR) FICĀRIA > *higuera* 'id.' (NB FĪCUS 'fig' > *higo*)
FAGUS 'beech' > (ARBOR) FAGEA > *haya*

This process was also sometimes applied to tree-names with other endings, again especially to provide distinction between tree-name and fruit-name:

NUX 'walnut-tree' > (ARBOR) NUCĀLIS > *nogal*, or (ARBOR) NUCĀRIA > *noguera* (NB NUX/NUCE > *nuez* 'walnut')
ILEX 'evergreen oak' > (ARBOR) ILICĪNA > *encina*

Gem-names are not in all cases popular words; some were introduced to Old Spanish from written sources. However, among those that may have a continuous oral history in Spanish are to be observed some which were (at least sometimes) feminine in Latin but ended in -US. They were slower than tree-names to find a settled form and Old Spanish hesitated wildly over their form, while adhering to the pattern /-a/ = feminine, /-o/ = masculine:

AMETHYSTUS > OSp. *ametisto*/*ametista;* from the sixteenth century, *amatista*
SAPPHĪRUS > OSp. *çafir*; *zafiro* from the eighteenth century
SMARAGDUS > OSp. *esmeragde*/*esmeralda*, MSp. *esmeralda*
TOPAZIUS > OSp. *estopaçio*/*estopaza*/*estopazo* (later remodelled as *topacio*)

The kinship terms SOCRUS 'mother-in-law' and NURUS 'daughter-in-law' were of course feminine and therefore contravened the emerging spoken Latin rule of gender-marking. In this case, gender-switch is out of the question, so that change of form is the only available solution. That such change was already occurring in spoken Latin is attested by the *Appendix Probi* (NURUS NON NURA, SOCRUS NON SOCRA) and it is the condemned forms which have survived in Spanish as *nuera* and *suegra*.

There were, then, in Old Spanish perhaps only two exceptions (*mano* and *día*) to the rule that words in /-a/ were feminine and those in /-o/ masculine. However, from the late Middle Ages the force of this rule has been weakened and there are now large numbers of nouns which contravene it:

masculines in /-a/, borrowings of Greek neuters (often feminine in OSp.): *profeta*, *planeta*, *clima*, etc.
masculines in /-a/ originating, through metonymy (see 5.2.2), in feminine abstracts: *el cura* 'priest', *el corneta* 'cornet player', *guardia* 'policeman', *guarda* 'custodian', *centinela* (via Italian) 'sentinel', etc.
feminines in /-o/, created through metonymy, abbreviation, etc.: *la modelo* 'model', *la moto* 'motorcycle', *la foto* 'photograph', *la dinamo*, etc.

3.2.2.2.2 Masculine and feminine nouns in /e/ or a consonant. In these nouns there is, of course, no correspondence between gender and form. As a result, gender switch from masculine to feminine and vice versa is easy and relatively frequent, and affects both popular and learned words. Change of gender, usually from feminine to masculine, is particularly frequent in the case of nouns beginning with a vowel, since in Old Spanish the form of a preceding definite article or indefinite article was identical for the two genders (*el amor*, fem., *el origen*, fem., *un árbol*, fem.; see 3.5.3.2). In a minority of cases, the word may appear in Spanish with both genders, or there may be regional differences of gender. Examples of this hesitation of gender include:

amor, honor, masculine in Latin but found with both genders in Old Spanish, become masculine in early Modern Spanish

calor, color, masculine in Latin but most usually feminine in Old Spanish, revert to masculine after the Golden Age; still feminine in regional speech; note that *labor* retains feminine gender even in the standard

árbol, feminine in Latin; often still feminine in Old Spanish; now masculine

arte, feminine in Latin and in Old Spanish (usually meaning 'skill, trick'); now masculine in singular, feminine in plural

génesis, feminine as a common noun; masculine as referring to the first book of the Bible

linde, masculine in Latin; feminine in Old Spanish; now feminine in singular, masculine in plural

orden, masculine in Latin; gradually acquires feminine gender in some meanings (e.g. 'command')

origen, feminine in Latin and in Spanish until the Golden Age; now masculine

pirámide, borrowed in the Golden Age as masculine; now feminine

sal, masculine in Latin; now feminine except in the NW of Spain

valle, feminine in Latin; often still feminine in Old Spanish (*la val*, etc.); now masculine

From the Latin period onwards, there has been a tendency to switch nouns from the category in which gender is not overtly marked (those in /e/ or a consonant) into the categories in which there is correspondence between gender and form (the *a*-class and the *o*-class). This process of providing nouns with an overt sign of their gender (/-a/ or /-o/) is sometimes referred to as hypercharacterization of gender; for the process whereby feminine nouns originally ending in *-or, -és, -e, -ón* came to end in *-ora, -esa, -a, -ona* in the later Old Spanish period, see England (1984, 1987). Examples of hypercharacterization of feminine nouns include:

AMITES > OSp. *andes* > MSp. *andas* 'stretcher'

GRŪE > OSp. *grua* 'crane' (later *grulla* in ornithological sense)

INFANTE (fem.) > early OSp. *la infante* 'daughter of a noble family' > *infanta* 'princess'

PANTICE > *panza* 'belly'

PŪLICE > *pulga* 'flea'

PUPPE > *popa* 'poop, stern'

RESTE > *riestra* > *ristra* 'string (of onions), etc.'

SENIŌRE (fem.) > early OSp. *la señor* 'lady' > *señora* 'id.'
TURTURE > *tórtola* 'turtledove'

Examples of hypercharacterization of masculine nouns can be seen in:

CĪCERE > *chícharo* 'pea'
CORTICE > *corcho* 'cork'
CUCUMERE > OSp. *cogombro* > MSp. *cohombro* 'cucumber'
PASSARE (CL PASSER) 'sparrow' > *pájaro* 'songbird'
PULVERE > *PULVUS > early OSp. *polvos* > *polvo* 'dust'

3.2.3 Noun classes

The five noun classes of Latin were numerically unequal; the *a*-class (or first declension; e.g. MENSA, ROSA) was large, as were the *o*-class (or second declension; e.g. DOMINUS, MAGISTER) and the class characterized by a consonant or /i/ (the third declension; e.g. RĒX, NŪBIS), while the *u*-class (or fourth declension; e.g. MANUS, GRADUS) and the *e*-class (or fifth declension; e.g. DIĒS, RĒS) had few members.

Nouns of the third declension were divided between those that were imparisyllabic (with one syllable fewer in the nominative singular form than in the other cases (e.g. nom. sing. LEŌ, acc. sing. LEŌNEM, nom. acc. plur. LEŌNES), or in the case of neuter nouns, with one syllable fewer in both the nominative and the accusative singular (e.g. nom. acc. sing. NŌMEN, nom. acc. plur. NŌMINA)) and those that were parisyllabic (with the same number of syllables in all cases (e.g. nom. sing. NŪBIS, acc. sing. NŪBEM, nom. acc. plur. NŪBĒS)).

Nouns of the fourth declension shared many of their endings with those of the second, while fifth-declension nouns were in many respects identical to third-declension nouns. These similarities of structure were no doubt intensified as the system of case-endings was weakened (see 3.2.1), since the case forms which survived were precisely the ones in which the similarities between declensions were greatest. As a result of these similarities and of the numerical imbalance between classes alluded to above, there was a reduction of form classes, beginning in spoken Latin, from five to three. Before this merger, feminine nouns of the fifth declension generally moved to the first; thus MATERIĒS > MATERIA, RABIĒS > *RABIA. DIĒS, although only occasionally feminine in Classical Latin, and despite appearing in Spanish as masculine, was also modified to first-declension form: *DIA.

Bearing in mind these convergences of noun classes and previous discussion of the treatment of neuter nouns (3.2.2.1), Spanish comes to have three noun classes, the main contributors to each of which are the following groups of nouns:

1 Nouns in /a/:	nouns of the Latin first declension (e.g. *mesa*, *rosa*)
	fifth-declension feminines (e.g. *madera*, *rabia*)
	neuter plurals of any declension (e.g. *hoja*, *boda*)
	hypercharacterized feminines of the Latin third declension (e.g. *señora*, *pulga*)
2 Nouns in /o/:	masculines and neuters of the Latin second and declension (e.g. *dueño*, *vino*)
	masculines and neuters of the Latin fourth declension (e.g. *paso*) and the single fourth-declension feminine *mano*
	third-declension neuters whose nominative/accusative singular contained a back vowel (e.g. *cabo*, *tiempo*)
	hypercharacterized third-declension masculines (e.g. *pájaro*, *corcho*)
3 Nouns in /e/ or a consonant:	most Latin third-declension nouns (e.g. *nube*, *león*)
	those Latin fifth-declension nouns which did not pass to the *a*-class (e.g. *haz* 'face', *fe* 'faith')
	a few second-declension words, e.g. *cobre* 'copper' < CUPRU, *trébol* 'clover' < TRIFOL(I)U, whose endings were changed for obscure reasons

A very few Old Spanish nouns did not fit any of these declensional patterns. The main cases are *buei* '*ox*' (< BOVE), *lei* 'law'(< LĒGE), *rei* 'king' (< RĒGE), whose plurals were at first phonologically regular (but morphologically irregular): *bueis* (< BOVĒS), *leis* (< LĒGĒS), *reis* (< RĒGĒS). During the course of the Middle Ages, these aberrant nouns were accommodated to the *e*/cons.-class, through the remodelling of their plurals to *bueyes*, *leyes*, *reyes*.

3.3 The adjective

The function of the adjective remains unchanged in the course of the development of Latin to Spanish, and the syntactical rules governing its appearance remain essentially similar. Only position-rules appear to have been modified: whereas subclassifying or restrictive adjectives could appear before the noun in Latin, such adjectives now appear only after the noun, while the only adjectives that normally precede are a small class of very frequent words (*un buen amigo*), together with non-restrictive adjectives (*la verde hierba, las blancas casas de Andalucía*) and a few adjectives with determiner-like functions (*la próxima estación*). We shall therefore be concerned here only with the form of the simple adjective and with comparatives and superlatives.

3.3.1 Adjective endings

Latin had two major classes of adjectives. On the one hand, there were those like ALTUS,-A,-UM, in which there were separate sets of endings for all three genders, with endings identical to those of first- and second-declension nouns, and, on the other hand, there were adjectives like FORTIS, -E, in which one set of endings served for both masculine and feminine reference and the other for reference to neuter nouns, the endings of FORTIS, etc., being similar to those of third-declension nouns. A subclass of the latter type, e.g. POTĒNS, showed no contrast between the genders. With the reclassification of neuter nouns between the other two genders (see 3.2.2.1), there was no longer a requirement for neuter endings in the adjective and they fell out of use. Similarly, as the case-endings of the noun were merged, first to two endings then to one (see 3.2.1), it followed that the case-endings of the adjective would be similarly reduced. Thus, from the multiplicity of forms that adjectives could assume in Latin, those of the ALTUS class emerge in Spanish with only four distinct endings (*alto, alta, altos, altas* 'high'), while those of the FORTIS class have only two (*fuerte, fuertes* 'strong').

The loss of the final vowel of a few masculine singular adjectives (*buen, mal, primer, tercer*) and the reduction of *grande* to *gran* when these words immediately precede a noun referent is the result of the weakening process which affected intertonic and final vowels in pre-literary and early Old Spanish (see 2.4.3.2–3). Whereas analogy has ensured that this irregularity has been eliminated from the large majority of adjectives, the frequency of *bueno, malo, grande*, etc., has allowed them to preserve irregular singular forms (see 3.1.1).

Another form of adjectival 'irregularity' which was eliminated during the Old Spanish period was that which originally existed in adjectives like (masc.) *antigo*(*s*), (fem.) *antigua*(*s*) 'old, former', where differential phonological development of /kw/ before /o/ and /a/ (see 2.5.3.2.8) leads to the Old Spanish alternation. However, by the late fifteenth century (Nebrija), this alternation has been levelled in favour of the feminine form: *antiguo, antigua*.

As in the case of nouns (see 3.2.2.2), spoken Latin showed a tendency to shift adjectives from the class in which masculine or feminine gender was not explicitly marked in the ending (e.g. FORTIS) into the class in which this distinction was formally marked (e.g. ALTUS). Such hypercharacterization of gender is condemned by the *Appendix Probi* (PAUPER MULIER NON PAUPERA MULIER, TRISTIS NON TRISTUS), but clearly gained ground in many varieties of Romance. The process was weaker in Spain than in most other areas (note that the descendants, *pobre* and *triste*, of the two Latin adjectives just quoted show no gender contrast, while Lat. FIRMUS, whence semi-learned *firme*, loses this contrast), but during the Old Spanish period certain groups of adjectives came to be affected (see Malkiel 1957–8 and England 1984, 87):

1 Adjectives in *-or* were invariable for gender at first in Old Spanish (e.g. *alma sentidor*, *espadas tajadores*), but from the late fourteenth century gender-contrast is made overt by the introduction of feminine forms in *-ora: loadora, sabidora, traidora*, etc. This process does not extend to the comparatives *mejor*, *peor*, *mayor*, *menor*, *interior*, *inferior*, etc., unless nominalized (e.g. *superiora* 'mother superior'), although Old Spanish texts from the eastern area show examples of *menora*, etc., a tradition continued in modern Aragonese dialects.
2 Adjectives in *-ón* were, like the preceding group, unmarked for gender in early Old Spanish (e.g. *gentes españones*; cf. modern Judeo-Spanish *lengua espaniol*). Adjectives of this class are found in later Old Spanish with fem. *-ona* (*ladrona*, *bretona*), as are those in *-ol* (*española*) and *-án* (*alemana*, *holgazana*, etc.).
3 Adjectives in *-és* show occasional hypercharacterized forms in early Old Spanish, although usually in adjectives functioning as nouns (e.g. *PMC: burgesas*, feminine of *burgeses*). In later Old Spanish, fem. *-és* is challenged by hypercharacterized *-esa*, first in the East (e.g. *cortesa* [*Razón de amor*, 1205]), although fem. *-és* can still occasionally be found in the sixteenth century (e.g. *la leonés potencia*, *la provincia cartaginés*). Thereafter, fem. *-esa* becomes obligatory in adjectives denoting national or regional origin (i.e. in *gentilicios: francesa, leonesa, cordobesa*, etc.), and in some related words (*burgués*, fem. *burguesa*). However, other adjectives generally preserve invariability of form: *cortés*, *montés* (beside rare *montesa*).

3.3.2 Comparison of adjectives

The system of comparison applied to most adjectives in Classical Latin was synthetic (for this term, see 3.1):

FORTIS 'brave'
FORTIOR 'braver'
FORTISSIMUS 'bravest'/'very brave'

However, this system had an analytic competitor, at first applied only to adjectives whose final and penultimate vowels were in hiatus (for hiatus, see 2.4.3 4):

ARDUUS 'harsh'
MAGIS or PLŪS ARDUUS 'harsher'
MAXIME ARDUUS 'harshest'

In spoken Latin there was a clearly attested tendency to apply this analytic system to the large majority of adjectives; probably only the most frequent adjectives escaped. This tendency towards analysis was no doubt encouraged by the fact that the two senses (relative and absolute) of the superlative could thereby be distinguished:

FORTIS 'brave'
MAGIS or PLŪS FORTIS 'braver'
MAXIME FORTIS 'bravest'
MULTUM or VALDE FORTIS 'very brave'

It seems that in later spoken Latin the distinction between comparative and relative superlative (e.g. between 'braver (of two)' and 'bravest (of three or more)') was abandoned and the comparative form (e.g. MAGIS or PLŪS FORTIS) was used in both senses. This distinction was later reintroduced into different Romance languages (in Spanish, only partially) by the addition of the definite article in the case of the superlative. Thus Sp. *el más fuerte de todos* 'the strongest (man) of all', but *el hombre más fuerte* 'the stronger/strongest man'.

VALDE fell out of use, and MAGIS was preferred to PLŪS in most parts of Spain, so that in the late spoken Latin of these areas it is likely that the system of comparison was

FORTIS 'brave, strong'
MAGIS FORTIS 'braver, stronger; bravest, strongest'
MULTUM FORTIS 'very brave, very strong'

from which the Spanish system directly descends:

fuerte
(el) más fuerte
muy fuerte

Only the most frequent synthetic comparatives (and no synthetic superlatives) maintained their synthetic form. Thus, having added the role of the relative superlatives OPTIMUS, PESSIMUS, MAXIMUS, MINIMUS to their comparative function, MELIOR, PEIOR, MĀIOR, MINOR give Sp. *mejor*, *peor*, *mayor*, *menor*, although the last two compete with analytic *más grande* and *más pequeño*. With regard to their form, nom. MELIOR, PEIOR, MĀIOR, MINOR no doubt underwent expansion, like that of imparisyllabic nouns (see 3.2.1), and the expanded forms then merged with obl. MELIŌRE, PEIŌRE, MAIŌRE, MINŌRE. Other apparently synthetic comparatives like *inferior*, *superior*, *interior*, *exterior*, *ulterior*, etc., and superlatives like *óptimo, ínfimo, máximo, mínimo* are learned borrowings made from Latin in the medieval or post-medieval period. The comparative SENIOR (whose base form is SENEX 'old') lost all comparative value and gave *señor*.

The superlative ending *-ísimo* is also learned. Occasional instances of its use in Old Spanish (sometimes with the form *-ismo*) reveal relative sense. It was only in the sixteenth century that this form became usual in Spanish, henceforth only with absolute sense. The learned nature of this formation is revealed by the learned form adopted by some adjectives to which it is applied (*fuerte, fortísimo; antiguo, antiquísimo; cruel, crudelísimo*, etc.), although recent trends show a preference for a simpler form of derivation: *fuertísimo, buenísimo*, etc.

3.4 The adverb

Classical Latin derived adverbs from adjectives in a large variety of ways, of which the commonest were the following three: addition of the ending -E to adjectives of the BONUS type (e.g. MALE 'badly'), addition of the ending -ITER to adjectives of the GRANDIS type (e.g. FORTITER 'bravely'), and simple use of the neuter singular (nominative/accusative) of the adjective (e.g. MULTUM 'much', FACILE 'easily'). There are few survivals in Spanish of these derivational types:

1 BENE > *bien* 'well', MALE > *mal* 'badly', TARDE > *tarde* 'late', LONGE > OSp. *lueñe* 'in the distance', ROMANICE 'in the Roman manner', as in FABULĀRE ROMANICE, whence OSp. *fablar romançe* 'to speak the vernacular (= Castilian, etc.)'; the adverb was then substantivized with the sense 'vernacular speech', eventually also 'vernacular writing (by contrast to Latin)', and 'verse composition in the vernacular'.
2 -ITER leaves no descendants in Spanish.
3 MULTUM > *mucho*, and the comparatives LAXIUS 'more amply' > *lejos* 'far away', and MAGIS > *más*. It is possible that constructions like *hablar fuerte, ver claro*, etc., contain adverbs descended from Latin neuter adjectives.

An additional, and informal, means of marking adverbial function in Old Spanish, as in other Romance languages, was by means of final /s/. This so-called 'adverbial *s*' has its origins in a number of Latin adverbs which, for a variety of reasons, ended in /s/: the comparatives MAGIS, LAXIUS, etc., just mentioned, FORAS (> OSp. *fueras* 'outside'), POS(T) (> *pues, después*), etc., together with a number which did not leave descendants, like GRĀTIS, ALIĀS. This /s/ was extended to other Old Spanish adverbs, although it does not survive further in all cases: NUMQUAM > *nunca(s)*, ANTE > *antes*, IN TUNC > *entonz* > *entonces*, DUM INTERIM > *domientre* > *demientre* > *(de)mientras*. The same element is also visible in the Old Spanish adverbs *c(i)ertas* 'certainly' and *primas* 'for the first time'. However, 'adverbial *s*' is at all times too irregularly applied to constitute a genuine derivational suffix.

A genuine adverbial suffix (for adverbs of manner) was created in spoken Latin, from the noun MENS, MENTIS 'mind'. The Latin expressions concerned were at first adverbial phrases in which the noun (in ablative case) was accompanied by an agreeing adjective: DEVOTĀ MENTE 'in a devout frame of mind', i.e. 'devoutly'. It will be noted that the feminine gender of MENS requires a feminine form of the adjective. An indication that MENTE is moving towards the status of a derivational suffix comes in late Latin texts in which MENTE is accompanied by adjectives whose meaning is incompatible with the literal meaning of MENTE: LENTĀ MENTE, already at this stage, can only be glossed as 'slowly', the notion of 'mind' having been lost. The addition of MENTE to a feminine adjective remains the only productive means of creating adverbs in Spanish, although it will be noted that relics of the former independent status of *-mente* are to be found in the accentual pattern of the words concerned (these adverbs have two full stresses, unlike any other 'word'), and in the fact that where more than one such adverb occur in coordination and adjacent, *-mente* appears only with the last: *lenta y cuidadosamente*.

In Old Spanish, the ending *-mente* alternated with *-miente* and *-mientre* (e.g. *fuertemiente*, *fuertemientre*), forms conceivably modified under the influence of *(do)mientre* (< DUM INTERIM; see above). A further, occasional, source of adverbial expressions in Old Spanish was the juxtaposition of a feminine adjective with the noun *guisa* 'manner': *fiera guisa* 'boldly'.

Other adverbs form a heterogeneous group, with varied forms and origins:

Aquí < ECCUM HĪC, *ahí* < *a* + OSp. *y* 'there' < IBĪ (with loss of -B- under the influence of HĪC), *allí* < AD ILLĪC, *acá* < ECCUM HĪC, *allá* < AD ILLĪC, OSp. *end(e)* 'thence, for that reason' < INDE, OSp. *o* 'where' < UBĪ, *do* 'whence', later 'where' < *de* + *o*, OSp. *ond(e)* 'whence' < UNDE, OSp. *dond(e)* 'whence', later 'where' < *de* + *ond(e)*, *encima* < *en* + *cima* 'top', OSp. *suso* 'above' < SURSUM, *arriba* < *a* + OSp. *riba* 'riverbank', *debajo*, *abajo* < *de*/*a* + *bajo*, OSp. *(a)yuso* 'below' < DEŌRSUM (with the tonic vowel of SURSUM).

Ahora < OSp. *agora* < HAC HORĀ, *entonces*, OSp. *entonz*, *estonz* (see above), *luego* 'at once', later 'next', < (IN) LOCŌ, for ILICŌ, *aún* < ADHŪCINE (Apuleius; cf. Wolf 1988), *ya* < IAM, *jamás* < IAM MAGIS, *nunca* (see above), *cuando* < QUANDŌ, *hoy* < HODIE, *ayer* < *a* + HERĪ, OSp. *cras* 'tomorrow' < CRAS, *mañana* OSp. 'early', then 'tomorrow' < (HORA) *MĀNEĀNA, for MĀNE.

Así < *a* + OSp. *si* 'thus', later 'yes' < SĪC; *no*, OSp. *no(n)* < NŌN; *como*, OSp. *cuemo*/*como* < QUOMO, CL QUOMODO.

Note that the discussion above (3.3.2) concerning comparison of adjectives also applies, *mutatis mutandis*, to the comparison of adverbs. Thus, FORTITER–FORTIUS–FORTISSIME (as well as showing replacement of the simple adverbial ending by *-mente;* see this section) gives way to *fuertemente* – *más fuertemente* – *(lo) más fuertemente*. Again, only the commonest synthetic comparatives escape the analytic process. In the case of adverbs, there is only one surviving synthetic form: MINUS > *(lo) menos*.

3.5 The pronoun

The Latin pronouns had final morphemes which, like those of nouns and adjectives, indicated case and number, and which, like those of adjectives, indicated gender. These endings were for the most part phonologically the same as those

Table 3.3 *Development of the personal pronouns*

	Tonic		Atonic	
	Subject	Post-prepositional	Direct object	Indirect object
1 sing.	EGŌ > *yo*	MIHĪ > *mí*	MĒ > *me*	MĒ > *me*
2 sing.	TŪ > *tú*	TIBĪ > *ti*	TĒ > *te*	TĒ > *te*
3 sing. masc.	ILLE > *él*	ILLE > *él*	ILLUM > *lo*	ILLĪ > *le*
fem.	ILLA > *ella*	ILLA(M) > *ella*	ILLAM > *la*	ILLĪ > *le*
neut.	ILLUD > *ello*	ILLUD > *ello*	ILLUD > *lo*	ILLĪ > *le*
1 plur.	NŌS > *nos(otros)*	NŌS > *nos(otros)*	NŌS > *nos*	NŌS > *nos*
2 plur.	VŌS > *vos (otros)*	VŌS *vos (otros)*	VŌS > (*v*)*os*	VŌS > (*v*)*os*
3 plur. masc.	ILLŌS > *ellos*	ILLŌS > *ellos*	ILLŌS > *los*	ILLĪS > *les*
fem.	ILLĀS > *ellas*	ILLĀS > *ellas*	ILLĀS > *las*	ILLĪS > *les*
3 sing./plur. (reflexive)		SIBĪ > *sí*	SĒ > *se*	SĒ > *se*

of nouns and adjectives and were subject, in general, to the same processes of merger and loss (see 3.2.1–2, 3.3.1). However, personal and demonstrative pronouns have retained neuter singular forms (*ello*, *esto*, *eso*, etc.) separate from those of the masculine and feminine; these came to be used not to refer to the class of neuter nouns (which disappeared in spoken Latin), but to refer to ideas and propositions not reducible to a single noun. Likewise, although sentence-function ('case') is no longer signalled in the form of Spanish nouns, adjectives and most pronouns (as a result of the merger of the Latin case-endings), the personal pronouns have retained certain morphemes of case (e.g. nominative or subject-case *ella*, vs accusative or direct-object-case *la*, vs dative or indirect-object-case *le*).

3.5.1 Personal pronouns

Latin had specifically personal pronouns only for the first and second grammatical persons; for the third person, Latin used any of the demonstratives (IS, HIC, ISTE, ILLE), although ILLE came to be preferred in this new role and provides the Spanish pronouns of the third person.

Except as the subject of a verb or as the object of a preposition, the Latin personal pronouns lost their stress (in cases where they had stress in Latin) and became clitics (i.e. they came to form a single phonological word together with some preceding or following stressed word, usually a verb). As a result of this change, the personal pronoun system of Spanish is best described as divided into stressed (or tonic) forms and unstressed (or atonic) forms (see table 3.3).

1 The subject forms of Spanish listed in table 3.3 descend in almost all cases from a Latin nominative form (for popular Latin nominative plural feminine in -ĀS, see 3.2.1 and Aebischer 1971). The exception is masc. plur. ILLŌS; in

this instance, for similar reasons to those operating in the noun (preservation of /-s/ as a marker of plurality, etc.), originally accusative ILLŌS additionally acquires nominative role. The expanded form *vosotros*, introduced in late Old Spanish to distinguish the plural pronoun from frequently singular *vos*, will be considered in 3.5.1.1. The contemporary expansion *nos* > *nosotros* is an analogical imitation of the latter process.

It will be noted that those forms of the personal pronouns which retain their stress retain also the same number of syllables as their Latin antecedents (except for the regular loss of final -E in ILLE; see 2.4.3.2). Similarly, stressed forms alone show regular development of -LL- > /ʎ/; the apparent exception ILLE > *él* is accounted for in 2.5.3.2.9). Malkiel (1976) shows that EGŌ> EŌ > *yo* involves a regular development of the spoken Latin diphthong observable in this pronoun.

The pronouns *usted* and *ustedes* will be considered in 3.5.1.1.

2 The pronominal forms which follow prepositions descend for the most part from Latin accusative forms, but can be seen to have become identical, in most cases, to the subject forms. Such identity already existed in Latin in some cases (ILLUD, NŌS, VŌS, probably also ILLŌS), or came about through phonological change (acc. ILLAM, abl. ILLĀ merge with nom. ILLA), or through extension of nominative function to an accusative form (ILLĀS). Also implied is the same merger of accusative and ablative (and sometimes dative) forms we have observed in the development of the late spoken Latin oblique case of the noun (see 3.2.1).

The first- and second-singular forms, like the third-person reflexive pronoun *sí* (< SIBĪ), descend from the Latin dative (with raising of tonic /e/ due to metaphony ascribable to final -Ī; see 2.4.2.1). The use of the dative in this role (rather than acc./abl. MĒ, TĒ, SĒ) is an early innovation of obscure motivation. The fact that only in the first and second singular do the post-prepositional forms differ from the subject forms has led the non-standard speech of some areas (e.g. Aragon, parts of America) to use *yo*, *tú* after prepositions (*para yo*, *por tú*, etc.). Even in the standard, the contrast between reflexive *sí* and non-reflexive *él/ella/usted/ellos/ellas/ustedes* is often lost, usually in favour of the non-reflexive form (e.g. *por él* for *por sí*).

The appearance of a post-prepositional form (*él* < ILLE) descended from a nominative (rather than the expected accusative/ablative) is in part due to an extension of the substantial identity between subject and post-prepositional forms already commented on and in part to a need to preserve contrast between masculine and neuter forms, a problem we shall meet again in the case of the demonstrative (3.5.3).

The prepositional forms *conmigo*, *contigo*, *consigo* require special comment. Latin CUM, unlike other 'prepositions', followed certain personal pronouns (which took ablative form): MĒCUM, TĒCUM, SĒCUM, NŌBĪSCUM, VŌBĪSCUM. Owing to the general convergence of accusative and ablative in spoken Latin, the latter two forms were replaced in spoken Latin by NŌSCUM, VŌSCUM (cf. *Appendix Probi:* NOBISCUM NON NOSCUM, VOBISCUM NON VOSCUM). The anomaly of post-posed CUM was then partially remedied, by anteposing CUM to the phrase, but (oddly) without deleting it from final position, so that the 'preposition' came to be expressed twice: CUM MĒCUM, CUM TĒCUM, CUM SĒCUM, CUM NŌSCUM, CUM VŌSCUM. These phrases are inherited directly by Old Spanish, but with raising by one degree of the tonic (in the singular forms by analogy with *por mí, de ti*, etc., and in the plural forms perhaps by analogy with the vocalic pattern of the singular forms, namely /o/-/í/-/o/, but with retention of a high tonic back vowel appropriate to the plural forms): *comigo*, *contigo*, *consigo*, *con(n)usco*, *convusco*. The two plural forms were replaced before the end of the Middle Ages by restructured *con nos(otros)*, *con vos(otros)*, but the singular forms survive (with remodelling of *comigo* > *conmigo* on the basis of *co<u>n</u>tigo*, *co<u>n</u>sigo*).

3 As noted above, the direct-object forms (which descend from the Latin direct-object (i.e. accusative) case forms) have become atonic and, where not already so, monosyllabic. In addition, they come to form, together with a verb, a single phonological word (i.e. they become cliticized). It will be noted that because of the loss of tonicity of this class of words, direct (and, for that matter, indirect) object forms of ILLE show early reduction of -LL- to /l/, and therefore escape the palatalization of -LL- > /ʎ/ which occurs, regularly, in subject and other tonic forms.

The forms listed here, including the late Old Spanish reduction of *vos* > *os*, continue with direct-object function in many varieties of Spanish (principally Andalusian and American), but it will be noted that, in the Peninsular standard, certain interferences have taken place between direct- and indirect-object forms (see comments on *leísmo* and *laísmo* in the following section).

4 The indirect-object forms descend in part from Latin indirect-object (i.e. dative) forms (ILLĪ, ILLĪS), but also show spoken Latin replacement of dat. MIHĪ, TIBĪ, SIBĪ, NŌBĪS, VŌBĪS by acc. MĒ, TĒ, SĒ, NŌS, VŌS, and therefore convergence in these instances with the direct-object forms. The descendants of these forms have all become cliticized in the same way as the direct-object forms have been. Like the latter, they have become monosyllabic and show early reduction of -LL- > /l/.

The form *le* is the first to show change of function. Already in early Old Spanish (e.g. *PMC* 655: *al bueno de mio Cid en Alcoçer le van çercar*), *le* is being used as a direct-object form in the case of masculine personal referents (just as in the modern Peninsular standard). Northern dialects go further and use *le* as a direct-object form for masculine countable referents (whether personal or non-personal; e.g. *este vaso no hay que romperle*), but not for non-countable (or mass) referents (e.g. *heno*, *aire*, *machismo*). Such extension of the role of *le* is referred to as *leísmo*, while the retention of *lo* in its traditional, etymological function as a personal (as well as a non-personal) masculine pronoun is labelled *loísmo*. The latter term is also used for the very occasional extension of *lo* to indirect-object function.

The counterpart of *leísmo* is *laísmo*, the use of *la* in (feminine) indirect- as well as direct-object role (e.g. *la di el papel a tu madre*). This (non-standard but frequent) usage perhaps represents a further step (beyond that represented by *leísmo*) towards a system of pronoun reference in which case distinctions are suppressed and gender distinctions are enhanced.

Use of *les* for *los* (i.e. as (masculine) direct as well as indirect object) is less common than singular *leísmo*, and is today regarded as less than fully acceptable. Plural *laísmo* (*las* for *les*) is rare. (For *leísmo*, *laísmo* and *loísmo*, see Lapesa 1968, Fernández-Ordóñez 1994.)

When a clause contained both a third-person indirect object pronoun (ILLĪ) and a third-person direct object pronoun (ILLUM, ILLAM, ILLUD, ILLŌS, ILLĀS), results different from those listed above are observable. After normal spoken Latin vowel development and reduction of -LL- to /l/, the sequences ILLĪ ILLUM, ILLĪ ILLAM, etc., became /eljelo/, /eljela/, etc. Thereafter, normal Castilian treatment of the /l/ + /j/ cluster (see 2.5.2.2(2)) and elision of /e-/ (as in all other atonic personal pronouns) account for the appearance of the Old Spanish forms *gelo*, *gela*, etc. These forms also subsume the descendants of ILLĪS ILLUM, i.e. where the indirect object was plural and where the /s/ of ILLĪS might have been expected to prevent the formation of the glide [j] (only possible in cases of hiatus; see 2.4.3.2) and therefore of OSp. /ʒ/ (spelt *g*). That is, OSp. *gelo*, *gela*, etc., allow both singular and plural indirect-object referents; *digelo* means 'I gave it to him/her/it/them'. This indeterminacy of number is inherited by the Modern Spanish descendants of these words (*se lo*, *se la*, etc.), and since this *se* is often referentially equivalent to *le* (both mean 'to him, to her'), *le* may be found also with plural value (e.g. *le di la carta* 'I gave them the letter') in modern non-standard usage.

The replacement of OSp. *gelo* by *se lo* is in part a phonological matter (confusion in the sixteenth century between /ʃ/(< /ʃ/, /ʒ/) and /s/; see 2.6.2(3)) and in part a syntactical one (merger of *gelo* with pre-existing OSp. and MSp. *se lo*, in which *se* is (quasi-)reflexive, so that *su amigo gelo tomó* 'his friend took it from him' becomes identical with *su amigo se lo tomó* 'his friend took it (for himself)').

In Old Spanish, the atonic personal pronouns were essentially enclitic (i.e. they normally formed a single phonological word with a preceding stressed word, usually but not exclusively a verb). As a result, the /e/ of *me*, *te*, *le*, *se* was subject to loss, like any other final /e/, when the preceding word ended in a vowel (see 2.4.3.2). This apocopation was most frequent in the case of *le* and *se* (e.g. *metiól en el mayor az, antes quel prendan, pagós mio Cid, nos van* 'no se van') and occasional examples are to be found still in the fifteenth century. Apocopation of *me* and *te* was always less frequent (e.g. *déxem ir en paz, nom lo aviedes rrogado, veot aguijar, éstot lidiaré aquí*) and does not survive the thirteenth century.

The positioning of Old Spanish atonic pronouns followed rules different from those of the modern language, where such pronouns may follow only the infinitive, the gerund or a positive imperative. In Old Spanish, the pronoun(s) followed the verb (finite or non-finite), unless the verb was preceded, in the same clause, by another tonic word (noun, adverb, tonic pronoun, etc.). Thus: *e tornós pora su casa, ascóndense de mio Cid*, but *non lo desafié, aquel que gela diesse*. This position-rule does not give way to the modern rule until the Golden Age, when it is still observed by many seventeenth-century writers. It should be noted that if the first tonic word of an Old Spanish clause was a future or conditional verb or a compound verbal form consisting of participle + some form of *aver* (normally in this order under these circumstances), then any atonic pronoun(s) were positioned between the two elements which make up such verbal forms (for the compound nature of the future and conditional, see 3.7.7.4.1): *dargelo he* (MSp. *se lo daré*), *dargelo ia/ie* (MSp. *se lo daría*), *dado gelo ha* (MSp. *se lo ha dado*), etc. The Old Spanish constituent order continues into the Golden Age, but apart from occasional seventeenth-century examples like Gracián's *escusarse ia* (see Lapesa 1980: 392), the two elements which comprise the future and conditional are inseparable from the end of the sixteenth century.

For the changing values of the Spanish third-person clitics, see Klein-Andreu (1991, 2000), Fernández-Ordóñez (1994).

3.5.1.1 Forms of address

In the second person of the pronoun system, Latin at first made distinctions only of number, TŪ being used whenever a single individual was addressed, whatever his or her status *vis-à-vis* the speaker, and VŌS used for addressing more than one person. In later Latin, VŌS was used, in addition, for deferential address of a single person, apparently beginning with the Emperor, but then becoming extended to other circumstances where deference or formality of address was appropriate. This system, in which VŌS has both singular (deferential) and plural (deferential and non-deferential) values continues in early Old Spanish, as it still does in modern French. In the *Poema de mio Cid*, the king is addressed as *vos*, as is the Cid (by the king and others); the Cid addresses Ximena and most of his relatives as *vos*, but uses *tú* to his younger kinsmen. The young Infantes de Carrión are always addressed as *tú*. At this stage, the system of forms of address can be described as follows:

	non-deferential	deferential
sing.	*tú*	*vos*
plur.	*vos*	*vos*

However, in later Old Spanish, it is evident that *vos* has widened its range of reference in such a way that it is used for many social relationships, and thus has lost much of its deferential value. By the fifteenth century, *vos* has become so close in value to informal *tú* that new deferential forms of address are experimented with, based on abstract nouns such as *merced* 'grace', *señoría* 'lordship', etc. Although occasional examples of *tu merced* are found, it was *vuestra merced* that found favour, together with *vuestras mercedes*, representing an entirely new plural deferential category. In the same (late Old Spanish) period, plural *vos*, restricted to non-deferential value by the creation of *vuestras mercedes*, was regularly expanded to *vosotros*. The combination *vos* + *otros* had previously been available with contrastive value (cf. Fr. *vous autres*), but now becomes the unmarked plural form, in opposition to singular *vos*. Perhaps by imitation of *vosotros*, *nos* is also regularly replaced by *nosotros* in the fourteenth and fifteenth centuries.

At the beginning of the Golden Age, the system of forms of address had therefore become:

	non-deferential	deferential
sing.	*tú* ~ *vos*	*vuestra merced*
plur.	*vosotros*	*vuestras mercedes*

During the Golden Age and the eighteenth century, the competition between *tú* and *vos* was resolved in favour of *tú* throughout the Peninsula and in those parts of America (Peru, Bolivia, Mexico) in closest contact with cultural developments in Spain. At the same time, the cumbersome form of address *vuestra merced* underwent a series of contractions, at first disallowed in cultured speech, which gave rise to *vuesarced*, *voacé*, *vucé*, *vuced*, *vested*, etc., and finally *usted*. Likewise, *vuestras mercedes* was eventually reduced to *ustedes*. As a result, the modern system of pronominal address emerges:

	non-deferential	deferential
sing.	*tú*	*usted*
plur.	*vosotros*	*ustedes*

In western Andalusia and in the whole of America, the distinction between deferential and non-deferential plural forms has again been lost, but in favour of the originally deferential form *ustedes*, which in these areas is now therefore the equivalent (in non-deferential cases) of standard Peninsular *vosotros*. Meanwhile, the competition in America between *tú* and *vos* for singular non-deferential use is differently resolved in different areas: we have seen that Mexico, Peru and Bolivia came to prefer *tú*, as did the Caribbean islands and most of Venezuela; it can now be added that in those areas most culturally 'distant' from Spain (e.g. Argentina, Uruguay, Paraguay, the Central American states) *vos* came to dominate, while in other areas the two forms of address continue to compete, in complex sociolinguistic relationship (e.g. Chile, Ecuador, Colombia) (see Penny 2000: 151–6). Simplifying somewhat the complexity of the relationship between the two singular non-deferential forms, the forms of address used in American Spanish can be said to be:

	non-deferential	deferential
sing.	*tú* ~ *vos*	*usted*
plur.	*ustedes*	*ustedes*

It should be noted that whichever of the two subject pronouns, *tú* or *vos*, is used as the form of non-deferential address, the associated object pronoun (direct and indirect) is *te* and that the associated possessive forms are *tu* and *tuyo*. Where the expressed or unexpressed subject form is *vos*, we therefore find such constructions as the following: (*Vos*) *quedáte aquí* '(you) stay here' (imper.), (*Vos*) *te quedás aquí* 'you stay here' (indic.), (*vos*) *indicáme tu casa* '(you) show me your house', (*vos*) *siempre salís con lo tuyo* 'you always get your own way', etc. (For the verbal forms used in conjunction with *vos*, see 3.7.3, and Penny 2000: 156.)

3.5.2 The possessive

Although the possessive functions not solely as a pronoun (it can also be adjectival), it will be considered at this point, since its similarities with other adjectives are more superficial than fundamental.

Latin possessive pronouns are listed in table 3.4.

These forms were fully inflected (by means of endings identical to those of adjectives), each showing agreement with its noun referent in terms of case, number and gender.

The form VESTER had a spoken Latin competitor VOSTER. The latter was perhaps an older form, without assimilation (displaced by VESTER in the standard);

Table 3.4 *Latin possessive pronouns*

	singular possessor	plural possessor
1st person	MEUS	NOSTER
2nd person	TUUS	VESTER
3rd person (reflexive)	SUUS	SUUS

alternatively, it may have arisen through analogy with NOSTER, aided by the similarity of structure of the related personal pronouns NŌS, VŌS.

The form SUUS was used only when the possessor was the subject of the clause containing the possessive; it was therefore, at first, solely a reflexive form. When reference was to a possessor other than the clause-subject, Latin used invariable EIUS (lit. 'of him/her/it') or EŌRUM (lit. 'of them'). However, this distinction between reflexive and non-reflexive possessive was lost in spoken Latin, SUUS being used in both instances. By contrast, a distinction came to be made, in some varieties of spoken Latin, between the third-person possessive appropriate to a singular possessor and that used when the possessor was plural. In these varieties of spoken Latin, which did not include the Latin spoken in most of the Peninsula, SUUS was reserved for singular possessors and ILLŌRUM (lit. 'of them') came to be used in the case of a plural possessor (e.g., Fr. *son* 'his/her', *leur* 'their').

Each of the forms listed above could function *adjectivally* (i.e. in connection with an expressed noun; e.g. FRATER MEUS 'my brother'), or *pronominally* (i.e. in isolation from a noun, whether expressed or not; e.g. NOSTRĪ 'our ones' (masc.)). As we shall see, this dual function is retained, in essence, by the Old Spanish possessive, but only partially by the modern language.

With the reassignment of neuter nouns to the masculine and feminine genders (see 3.2.2.1), the neuter endings of the possessive fell from use. Similarly, as distinctions of case came to be expressed by means other than word-endings (see 3.2.1), so the various case-endings of the possessive merged (or were lost), in exactly the same way as occurred in the noun. As a result, Old Spanish retains only four forms of each possessive: masculine singular, feminine singular, masculine plural and feminine plural, which have descended into early Old Spanish in the manner shown in table 3.5.

The forms in parentheses (*tua(s)*, *sua(s)*) are rare.

Whether their function was adjectival (either before or after a noun) or pronominal, all the Old Spanish forms appear to have been fully tonic, like their Latin antecedents, but unlike some of their modern descendants, e.g. *el mio fiel vassallo*, *mios yernos*, *la mi muger*, *mis fijas; se fará lo to*, *las tus mañas*, *el so* ('el suyo'), *fue so criado*, *todos los sos*, *a sus dueñas*.

Table 3.5 *Development of the possessives*

		singular	plural
Singular	1st person (masc. referent)	MEU > *mio*	MEŌS > *mios*
	1st person (fem. referent)	MEA > *mia/mie/mi*	MEŌS > *mias/mies/mis*
	2nd person (masc. referent)	TUU > *to*	TUŌS > *tos*
	2nd person (fem. referent)	TUA > (*tua*)/*tue/tu*	TUĀS > (*tuas*)/*tues/tus*
	3rd person (masc. referent)	SUU > *so*	SUŌS> *sos*
	3rd person (fem. referent)	SUA > (*sua*)/*sue/su*	SUĀS > (*suas*)/*sues/sus*
Plural	1st person (masc. referent)	NOSTRU > *nuestro*	NOSTRŌS > *nuestros*
	1st person (fem. referent)	NOSTRA > *nuestra*	NOSTRĀS > *nuestras*
	2nd person (masc. referent)	VOSTRU > *vuestro*	VOSTRŌS > *vuestros*
	2nd person (fem. referent)	VOSTRA > *vuestra*	VOSTRĀS > *vuestras*

Masc. *mio/mios* are the regular reflexes of MEU/MEŌS; this sequence of vowels normally produces /ió/ (see Malkiel 1976). These forms were at first monosyllabic (*mió/miós*), but rhyme and assonance reveal that they were gradually replaced by disyllabic *mío/míos*, no doubt by analogy with the feminine forms, which almost always show forms with tonic /i/.

The feminine forms (singular possessor) descend from spoken Latin forms in which raising of the tonic has taken place, by dissimilation from final /a/ in hiatus; thus MEA = /mɛa/ > /méa/, TUA = /tóa/ > /túa/, SUA = /sóa/ > /súa/, by contrast with the masculine forms, where simple merger of like vowels takes place. Indeed, the first-person feminine form has undergone such dissimilation *twice*, since spoken Latin /méa/ has its tonic vowel further raised to /mia/. These feminine forms also reveal the beginnings of a separation of pronominal from adjectival forms. When used pronominally or as an adjective *following* a noun, there is a preference for forms in /-a/: *mia(s)*, *tuya(s)*, *suya(s)* (for the latter two forms, see below). By contrast, the forms *mie/mi*, etc., are almost exclusively used adjectivally before a noun.

Full separation into two sets of possessive forms takes place in the late Old Spanish period. When used adjectivally before a noun, the possessives lose their tonicity, shed their final vowels and (in the case of *to(s)*, *so(s)*) suffer raising of their newly atonic vowels. In atonic position, as a result, the contrast of gender is lost. However, it should be noted that the forms *nuestro(s)*, *-a(s)*, *vuestro(s)*, *-a(s)* escape this loss of stress and the consequent merger of masculine and feminine forms. To summarize these late Old Spanish changes in pre-noun position:

mio(s)/mi(e)(s) > mi(s)
to(s)/tu(e)(s) > tu(s)
so(s)/su(e)(s) > su(s)

This loss of tonicity and reduction of form is accompanied by the loss of the definite article, which in Old Spanish frequently accompanied the possessive in pre-noun position (see examples above), so that such sequences as *la mi casa* are rare by the early sixteenth century.

When used pronominally or when adjectival after a noun, the possessives remain fully tonic, remain disyllabic (in the case of *mio(s) become* disyllabic), and in some cases are reinforced with an intervocalic consonant:

mio(s) > *mio(s)*
mia(s) > *mia(s)*
to(s) > *tuyo(s)*
tua(s) > *tuya(s)*
so(s) > *suyo(s)*
sua(s) > *suya(s)*

This expansion begins early in the feminine forms. We have seen that *tua(s)* and *sua(s)* were rare in Old Spanish; they were rapidly replaced by *tuya(s)* and *suya(s)* partly for phonological reasons (to provide a sharper syllabic boundary than existed while /u/ and /a/ were in hiatus) and partly for analogical reasons (the possessives are in close semantic relationship with the interrogative pronoun meaning 'whose', i.e. OSp. *cuyo, -a* (e.g. *¿Cúyo es?* 'whose is it?'; see 3.5.4), and the form of the interrogative word influenced the form of its frequent (possessive) reply). Since this restructuring appears to have occurred first in the feminine, it follows that, for a time, the second- and third-person possessives showed the following alternation: masc. *to(s), so(s)*, fem. *tuya(s), suya(s)*. However, this alternation was levelled in the fourteenth century by the appearance of masc. *tuyo(s), suyo(s)*.

The lack of precision of the forms *su(s), suyo(s), -a(s)* has led to modifications, in the modern period, to many noun phrases containing a possessive. We have seen that Lat. SUUS was already appropriate to both singular and plural possessors and that this duality is inherited by Spanish; we have also seen that as well as being a reflexive possessive, SUUS additionally became non-reflexive in spoken Latin. With the late medieval appearance of *vuestra(s) merced(es)* (see 3.5.1.l), the forms *su(s), suyo(s), -a(s)* came to be used not just as third-person, but as second-person (deferential) possessives. This burden of values has come to be relieved by the optional addition of, or replacement by, genitive phrases (*de él, de ella, de ellos, de ellas, de Vd.*, etc.), so that, e.g. *su casa* may be clarified as *su casa de él, su casa de Vd.*, etc. (Note the similarity of this development with the Latin use of EIUS, EŌRUM and, later in some areas, ILLŌRUM; see above.) Particularly in American Spanish, these genitive phrases may become obligatory, to such an extent that *su(s)* becomes redundant and is replaced by the definite article: *su casa de él* > *la casa de él;* similarly, phrases like *es suyo* are often entirely displaced by *es de él*, etc. The final step (replacement of other possessives by genitive phrases, e.g. *nuestra casa* >

Table 3.6 *Development of demonstrative and related pronouns*

	anaphoric	personal	demon-strative 1	demon-strative 2	demon-strative 3	emphasis	identity
CL	IS	ILLE	HIC	ISTE	ILLE	IPSE	IDEM
spoken Latin	ILLE	ILLE	ISTE	IPSE	*ACCU ILLE	*MEDIPSISSIMUS	
Spanish	*el (que)*	*él*	*este*	*ese*	*aquel*	*mismo*	

la casa de nosotros) has been taken only by some (non-standard) varieties of Spanish.

3.5.3 Demonstratives and articles

We shall see in 3.5.3.2 that the Spanish definite article descends from the Latin third-person demonstrative, so that it is convenient to deal together with these categories, even though the indefinite article develops from a different category, the numeral (for which, see 3.6).

3.5.3.1 The demonstratives

The Latin demonstratives were fully inflected, like other pronouns and adjectives, in accordance with the case, number and gender of the referent concerned. Case distinctions were merged or lost in the ways discussed in 3.2.1–2 and 3.3.1. However, whereas the neuter forms of most other adjectives and pronouns were lost (for lack of neuter referents, once neuter nouns had been reclassified as masculine or feminine), the demonstratives retain a separate neuter form (see 3.5, and below), used to refer to ideas and propositions not reducible to a single noun.

Latin used the same demonstrative forms in both adjectival and pronominal function. The Classical Latin forms concerned, HIC, ISTE and ILLE, constituted a three-place system, in which each demonstrative was related to one of the three grammatical persons. HIC was thus applied to referents near to or concerned with the speaker, ISTE to referents near to or concerned with the person spoken to, while ILLE was used in the case of referents near to or associated with neither the speaker nor the person addressed. This system has been inherited intact by Spanish, although the Spanish exponents of the system (*este*, *ese*, *aquel*) do not descend from the corresponding forms of the Latin system (except, partially, in the case of *aquel*). The Latin demonstratives (and certain related forms) underwent a series of changes of function which can be represented as in table 3.6.

1 The phonological weakness of HIC, especially after the early loss of /h/ (2.5.2), is no doubt a major factor in its almost entire elimination from Latin speech, although there is evidence that, prior to its disappearance, it became a competitor of IS, in largely anaphoric role (i.e. it functioned mostly as the antecedent of a relative: IS QUĪ ... 'he who ... ', etc.), a role from which both IS and HIC were anyway displaced by ILLE.

2 Loss of HIC was accompanied by transfer of ISTE from second-person to first-person demonstrative role (the role still played by the Spanish descendant of ISTE, namely *este*). The Latin demonstrative system was in this way reduced from a three-place system to one of two places, a type which persisted into such Romance languages as Old French.

3 However, in more conservative areas such as Spain, the three-place system was restored by transfer of IPSE from its emphatic role (e.g. IPSE RĒX, originally 'the king himself)' to second-person demonstrative role. It is thus from IPSE that the Spanish second-person demonstrative (*ese*) descends.

4 It will be seen from table 3.6 that ILLE was over-worked. Not only was it a third-person demonstrative, but it also functioned as an anaphoric and as a personal pronoun (see also 3.5.1). Additionally, ILLE came to be used as a definite article (see 3.5.3.2). To avoid ambiguity, ILLE was reinforced, when it functioned as a demonstrative, by means of various deictic (pointing) particles. Spoken Latin ECCE ILLE, ATQUE ILLE, ECCU ILLE are attested in many areas; in Spain, the prefix took the form *ACCU (*ACCU ILLE > *aquel*).

5 When IPSE passed into the demonstrative system, its emphatic role was expressed by an expanded form *MEDIPSISSIMUS (a variant of attested METIPSISSIMUS), which additionally took over the role of IDEM; that is, RĒX *MEDIPSISSIMUS came to mean not only 'the king himself', 'the very king', but also 'the same king'. The Spanish descendants of *MEDIPSISSIMUS maintain this dual role, although the different senses may be distinguished by word-order: *el mismo rey* 'the king himself' or 'the same king', *el rey mismo* 'the king himself'. Spanish shows a number of competing descendants of *MEDIPSISSIMUS: an attested MEDIPSIMUS, representing a form (/medíssimos/ or /medéssimos/) reduced via haplology from *MEDIPSISSIMUS (pronounced /medissíssimos/), provides early OSp. *meísmo* and *me(e)smo*. From the fourteenth century *mesmo* is more frequent than *mismo* (< *meísmo*), and this continues to be the case in the Golden Age, but by the seventeenth century *mismo* is the preferred form in the standard, and in the following century *mesmo* comes to be restricted to rural use.

In the phonological development of ISTE, IPSE and *ACCU ILLE, only the masculine singular forms require comment, since it might be expected that, according to what we observe in the case of nouns and adjectives (see 3.2.1, 3.3.1), nom. ISTE, acc. ISTUM and dat./abl. ISTŌ would merge as **esto*, while **eso* and **aquello* would be the predicted outcomes of the second- and third-person masculine singular demonstratives. The emergence of *este*, *ese*, *aquel* must be due to the need to distinguish the masculine singular forms from neuter *esto*, *eso*, *aquello* (< ISTUD, IPSUM, *ACCU ILLUD). In Old Spanish, the masculine singular forms often lose their final /e/ (*est*, *es*), in accordance with 2.4.3.2.

Although the distinguishing prefix *ACCU was strictly required only in the third person, it was often applied to the other demonstratives, in medieval and Golden Age Spanish; *est(e)* and *es(se)* therefore alternated with *aquest(e)* and *aques(se)*, although the longer alternants were then rejected.

3.5.3.2 The articles

Latin originally lacked (and in its Classical form continued to lack) both definite and indefinite articles. Perhaps through the frequent bilingual use of Latin with Greek, both in Rome and in the east, speakers of Latin came to feel the need for such determiners and used pre-existing Latin particles to supply the newly felt need.

The essential function of the indefinite article is to refer to an individual (thing or person) not present before the participants in a dialogue and so far unknown to the hearer(s); e.g. 'Once upon a time there was a king . . . '. Since the singularity (not to say the uniqueness) of the individual is important in such a speech-situation, it is not surprising that spoken Latin should have used the numeral ŪNUS 'one' to fulfil this newly required role.

Masc. ŪNUS loses its final /o/ (> *un*; see 2.4.3.2), while fem. ŪNA > *una*, except that in Old Spanish, final /a/ was elided when the following word began with a vowel (*un escoba*, *un onda*) and not solely before word-initial /á/, as happens in the modern language. The plurals *unos, -as* are not articles in any real sense, and are best considered together with other quantifiers.

The most basic function of the definite article is to refer to an individual or individuals (things or persons) not present before the participants in a dialogue but already known to the hearer(s); e.g. 'Once upon a time there was a king. The king had three daughters.' Under these speech circumstances, it is understandable that an adjective of emphasis or emphasis/identity (IPSE RĒX 'the king himself') or a demonstrative appropriate to an absent individual (ILLE RĒX 'that king') should be pressed into service as a definite article by speakers of Latin. IPSE was preferred in this function in part of the Latin-speaking world (Sardinia, Balearic Islands, Costa Brava), but ILLE was elsewhere used as the spoken Latin definite article.

Just as happened when ILLE was used as an atonic personal pronoun (see 3.5.1), loss of tonicity on the part of ILLE, when used as an article, caused the reduction of -LL- to /l/ (rather than /ʎ/). However, the occasional medieval and early modern spelling *ell* of the masculine singular and feminine singular article, when the word it determined began with a vowel, suggests that the change -LL- > /ʎ/ *did* occur in this form of the article, perhaps at first only when -LL- was immediately followed by a tonic vowel (*ell omne*, *ell alma*), but later before atonic vowels too (*ell ermano*, *ell ermana*).

In pre-literary Spanish, the definite article was still disyllabic (*ela* < ILLA, *elos* < ILLŌS, *elas* < ILLĀS, although the masculine singular form is not unambiguously attested at the same stage), but lack of stress allowed elision of the initial vowel of the plural form (> *los*, *las*). In the singular forms, lack of stress led to the loss of one or other of the vowels (and, in some dialects, before a vowel, to loss of both). Thus masc. **elo* > *el* (and, in Old and early Modern Spanish, sometimes *ell* (see above) before a vowel, conditions under which northern Castilian dialects today allow reduction to /l/). Pre-literary fem. *ela* is reduced, in Old Spanish, either to *la* (where the following word begins with a consonant) or to *el* (when the next word had vocalic onset). Fem. *el* competes with occasional *ell*. This distribution of feminine forms continues until the sixteenth century, when fem. *ell* is lost and *el* is replaced by *la* except before /á/ (*el arpa*, *el hambre*).

Like other medieval Romance languages, Old Spanish saw the extension of the use of the definite article from the circumstances described above to an increasingly wide range of other groups of nouns. Nouns used generically (in the singular) or collectively (in the plural) did not in Old Spanish normally carry an article (*miseria de omne*, *cristianos e moros*); nor did abstracts (*vedar compra*). The article also frequently did not appear in prepositional phrases where today it is present (*en campo*, *en mano*); nor did it appear with river-names (*cruzar Arlanzón*). In all these cases (and some others), the definite article only gradually came to be used, in most cases by the early Golden Age.

3.5.4 *Relatives and interrogatives*

The Latin interrogative QUIS merged entirely with relative QUĪ and three members of the merged paradigm survive in Spanish: QUĪ > *qui*, QUEM > *quien*, QUID > *que*, although it is possible that other forms of the Latin interrogative/relative (e.g. QUAE) contribute to the form of *que*.

In Old Spanish, *qui* alternates with *quien*, with personal reference, both as subject of the clause (interrogative or relative) and as the object of a preposition: *a qui*..., etc. *Qui* is also occasionally found in combination with certain determiners, e.g. *aquel qui*. In this latter instance, *que* was always commoner, and in its other functions, *qui* was entirely displaced by *quien* before the end of the Middle Ages, even though in the thirteenth and fourteenth centuries *qui* is extremely frequent in circumstances where the modern language requires *quienquiera que* or *cualquier persona que* (e.g. OSp. *qui lo fiziere* 'anyone who does so').

The diphthong /ie/ of *quien* (< QUEM) suggests that this form emerged first in interrogative role only, where it would be fully tonic. However, even before the emergence of literary Old Spanish, *quien* had already acquired the relative value it still has (restricted then as now to personal reference), and had extended its role from accusative to nominative, as well as coming to be used as the object of a preposition (*a quien*, etc.), and as a plural (as well as a singular) form. Plur. *quienes* arises only in the Golden Age, although most writers prefer plur. *quien* until at least the eighteenth century.

In interrogative function, *qué* has always been restricted to non-personal use, except in adjectival role, where its more frequent competitor is *qual* (< QUALIS; later *cual*), a form which has always been present in Spanish as an interrogative pronoun. However, relative *que* has always been capable of personal as well as non-personal reference, as subject or object of a relative clause, singular or plural. In other words, although *que* inherits its form predominantly from neut. QUID, it inherits also the functions of masc. nom. QUĪ, fem. nom. QUAE, masc. acc. QUEM, and fem. acc. QUAM (as well as all the nominative and accusative plural forms QUĪ, QUŌS, etc.).

The pre-Classical Latin interrogative/relative adj. CUIUS 'whose', although falling out of use in literary and non-literary Latin in the central parts of the Empire, continued to be used in the spoken Latin of Sardinia and Spain, where it survives as *cuyo* (cf. Port. *cujo*) (see 1.2.1). In Old and early Modern Spanish, this form could still function as an interrogative (e.g. *¿cúyo es?* 'whose is it?'), a value it retains in the Spanish of the Canaries and parts of America (see Lapesa 1980: 587).

Lat. QUALIS 'of which kind?' loses its notion of 'quality' and provides the Spanish interrogative *¿cuál?* and the relative *el cual*, although it is to be noted that in Medieval Spanish relative *qual* was not normally accompanied by the definite article (e.g. *a qual dizen Medina* (*PMC* 2879)).

3.5.5 *Indefinites*

The Latin indefinite pronouns (and adjectives) were inherited by Spanish only in rare cases: TŌTUS (acquiring also the value of OMNIS) > *todo;* ALTER (combining the sense of ALTER and ALIUS) > *otro* (from which were derived OSp. *otri*, *otrie* and *otrien* 'somebody else'); *cierto* (< CERTUS) incorporates also the meaning of QUĪDAM; NŪLLUS > OSp. *nul*, *nulla* (ousted by *ningun(o)*, *-a*, see below); ALIQUOD > *algo;* pre-Classical ALID (CL ALIUD) > OSp. *al* 'something else'.

- NĒMŌ was replaced by NEC ŪNUS (> *ningun(o)*, 'nobody' as well as 'none' in Medieval and Golden Age Spanish) or by HOMINE NĀTU 'a man born', i.e. 'anyone at all', then 'nobody' (> early OSp. *omne nado*, whence later OSp. *nado*). OSp. *nado* competed with OSp. *nadi* (most probably *nado* modified under the influence of the Old Spanish interrogative *qui* (see 3.5.4), *pace* Corominas and Pascual 1980–91, s.v. *nacer*), and later with *nadie*, whose final syllable arguably shows interference from *quien*. In parallel fashion, NIHIL was replaced by REM NĀTA(M), which gave the occasional OSp. *ren* (Berceo), but was more usually contracted to NĀTA(M), whence Spanish *nada*.

- ALIQUIS was expanded to ALIQUIS ŪNUS, whence *algun(o)*, the normal Old Spanish expression for both 'some/any' and 'someone' until the fifteenth century introduction of its competitor *alguién* (stressed thus) – a form of *alguno* modified under the influence of *quien* – which later displaced *alguno* in the sense 'someone' and suffered accent-shift to *alguien*, perhaps in imitation of the accentual pattern of *algo* 'something'.
- QUISQUE gave way in spoken Latin to /káta/ (borrowed from Greek), whence *cada (uno)*.
- QUĪLIBET, etc., were replaced by new constructions in which *quien*, *cual*, *cuando*, etc., were compounded with the present subjunctive of *querer: quienquiera*, *cualquier(a)*, *cuandoquiera*, etc.

3.6 The numeral

3.6.1 Cardinal numerals

The forms of the Latin cardinal numerals were invariable except in the case of ŪNUS, DUO, TRĒS, and the hundreds from DUCENTĪ to NONGENTĪ, and MĪLLE (plur. MĪLIA). With the merger of case-endings in the noun (3.2.1), distinction of case is also lost from ŪNUS, etc. Similarly, with the reassignment of neuter nouns to other genders (3.2.2.1), the neuter form of these numerals also had to be abandoned. However, distinction of gender does survive in the members of this group of numerals, except in the case of TRĒS, which already lacked distinction between masculine and feminine forms in Latin. The distinction between MĪLLE 'one thousand' and DUO MĪLIA, etc. 'two thousand', etc., was also abandoned, in favour of invariable MĪLLE.

Because each numeral obviously forms part of an extensive series of numbers, semantic analogy (see 3.1) is especially likely to affect the development of any member of the series. In the following list, predictable phonological change is accounted for by cross-reference to the appropriate discussion elsewhere, and only analogical and other similar changes are commented upon.

ŪNU > *uno/un* (2.4.3.2).

ŪNA > *una/un*. (For the loss of final /a/ in *un espada*, *un onda*, etc., see 3.5.3.2.)

DUŌS = */dóos/ > *dos*.

DUĀS = */dúas/ > OSp. *duas*, more usually *dues*. The raising of spoken Latin tonic /o/ > /u/ in hiatus with final /a/ appears to be a (minor) regular change of Spanish, similar to that which raises spoken Latin /e/ > /i/ under the same circumstances (e.g. DIA > /déa/ > Sp. *día*. and the regular imperfect endings of *-er* and *-ir* verbs (see 3.7.8.3.1)).

TRĒS > *tres*.

QUATTUŌR = */kwattor/ (2.4.3, with reduction of two adjacent identical vowels to one) > OSp. *quatro* (2.5.4), later respelled *cuatro*.

QUĪNQUE = spoken Latin CĪNQUE, through dissimilation (2.1.1.2) /kw/ . . . /kw/ > /k/ . . . /kw/. The final /o/ of OSp. and MSp. *cinco* is probably due to analogy with *cuatro;* Corominas and Pascual 1980–91, s.v. *cinco*, quote cases of analogy between the numerals 'four' and 'five' in various languages.

SĒX > *seis* (2.4.2.1). The final /s/ is not palatalized, in accordance with 2.5.2.4 (end), although the retention of the glide [i̯] (by contrast with FRAXINU > *fresno*) is unexplained.

SEPTEM > *siete* (2.4.2.2).

OCTO > *ocho*.

NOVEM > *nueve* (2.4.2.2), beside occasional OSp. *nuef* (2.4.3.2) with devoicing of /β/ in word-final position.

DECEM > *diez* (2.4.2.2, 2.4.3.2).

ŪNDECIM, also attested as ŬNDECIM, whence OSp. *onze* (2.5.5) > MSp. *once*.

DUŌDECIM = spoken Latin /dódeke/ (through analogy with the tonic /o/ of DUŌS, and reduction of two identical spoken Latin vowels to one) > OSp. *dodze*/*doze* (2.5.5) > MSp. *doce*, where retention of /-e/ is probably due to analogy with *once*, *catorce*, *quince*, whose final vowel must be retained because it follows a consonant group.

TRĒDECIM > OSp. *tredze*/*treze* > MSp. *trece* (for /-e/ see *doce*).

QUATTUŌRDECIM > OSp. *catorze* (2.5.5), with reduction of UŌ > /o/ probably on the pattern of *once*, *doce*.

QUĪNDECIM > OSp. *quinze* (2.5.5) > MSp. *quince*.

SĒDECIM > OSp. *sedze*/*seze*, replaced by analytic *dizeseis*/*diezeseis* whence MSp. *dieciséis*/*diez y seis*.

SEPTENDECIM, OCTŌDECIM, NOVENDECIM were early replaced by the analytic type *DECEM ET SEPTEM, etc., whence OSp. *dizesiete*, *dizeocho*, *dizenueve*, MSp. *diecisiete*, etc.

VĪGINTĪ > OSp. *veínte* (with dissimilation of initial /i/ from tonic /i/, whose close aperture is due to metaphony exercised by final Ī; see 2.4.2.1) > MSp. *veinte* (with movement of accent from the higher to the lower of two vowels in hiatus; cf. REGĪNA > OSp. *reína* > MSp. *reina*).

TRĪGINTĀ > OSp. *treínta* (with /e/ analogical upon that of *tres* and /i/ on the pattern of OSp. *veínte*) > MSp. *treinta* (with accent-shift as in *veinte*).

QUADRĀGINTĀ = spoken Latin QUARĀGINTĀ > OSp. *quaraenta*. After palatalization and loss of $G^{e,i}$ (2.5.2.3 (end)), the accent in

Hispano-Latin was retained on the /e/ (< ĭ) and was not retracted to the preceding /a/, as occurred in the majority of varieties of Romance; cf. Fr. *quarante*, It. *quaranta;* during the thirteenth century the ending *-aenta* was reduced to *-enta* (see Craddock 1985). Thus MSp. (respelled) *cuarenta*.

QUĪNQUĀGINTĀ = spoken Latin CĪNQUĀGINTĀ, via the same dissimilation evident in CĪNQUE (> *cinco*), whence OSp. *cinquaenta*, MSp. *cincuenta*.

SEXĀGINTĀ > OSp. *sessaenta* (with /-s-/ due to analogy with *seis*) > MSp. *sesenta*.

SEPTUĀGINTĀ > OSp. *setaenta* (with loss of U on the analogy of certain other tens (e.g. *ochaenta*), which can be analysed as 'simple numeral stem' (*och-*) + suffix, but with avoidance of diphthongization of /ɛ/ or subsequent reduction of /ie/ to /e/ appropriate to atonic syllables) > MSp. *setenta*.

OCTŌGINTĀ > OSp. *ochaenta* (with replacement of intertonic /o/ by /a/ on the pattern of the other numerals 40–90) > MSp. *ochenta*.

NONĀGINTĀ > OSp. *nonaenta*, beside *novaenta* (the result of an analogical restructuring based on *nueve*, but with avoidance of diphthongization of /ɔ/ or subsequent replacement of /ue/ by /o/ appropriate to atonic syllables) > MSp. *noventa*.

CENTUM > *ciento*, reduced in Old Spanish before a noun or adjective to *cient* or *cien*, the latter especially where the following word began with a consonant. Only this (originally pre-consonantal) form could survive into the modern language, once the possibility of word-final consonant groups was rejected by Castilian (see 2.4.3.2).

DUCENTŌS, -ĀS > OSp. *dozientos*, *-as*, with normal treatment of intervocalic $C^{e,i}$ (2.5.2.3, 2.5.3.2.6), replaced in early Modern Spanish by *doscientos*, which, although written as a single word, reveals the treatment appropriate to initial $C^{e,i}$ (2.5.2.3) and is therefore a compound of *dos* and *ciento(s)* which imitates *cuatrocientos*, *ochocientos*, etc.

TRECENTŌS > OSp. *trezientos*, replaced by *trescientos* at the same time and for the same reasons as in the case of *doscientos*.

QUADRINGENTŌS does not leave a descendant in Spanish, but was early replaced by a type *QUATTUŌR CENTŌS, whence OSp. *quatrocientos*, later respelled *cuatrocientos*.

QUĪNGENTŌS survives in synthetic form as OSp. *quinientos/quiñentos*, showing one of the Castilian treatments of $\text{-NG}^{e,i}$- (> /ɲ/; the other produces OSp. /nd^z/). However, the palatal glide of the diphthong [je] either causes dissimilatory depalatalization of /ɲ/ > /n/, or is assimilated by it and is absorbed: [ɲj] > [ɲ]. Of the alternative forms thus produced, *quinientos* alone survives into the modern language, no doubt because its ending *-ientos* is shared by the remaining hundreds.

SEXCENTŌS was already analytic in Latin, and remains so in Spanish: *seiscientos.*

SEPTINGENTŌS, OCTINGENTŌS, NONGENTŌS were all replaced, before the emergence of Old Spanish, by analytic *setecientos*, *ochocientos*, *novecientos*.

MĪLLE > OSp. *mil*, *mill*. Both forms must represent /mil/, at least before a consonant, since Old Spanish (like the modern language) did not permit palatals in syllable-final position (see 2.5.3.2.8). However, it is conceivable that, before a vowel, *mill* indicated /miʎ/ (e.g. *mill ombres*), even in the Golden Age. If this pre-vocalic pronunciation existed, it was analogically replaced by /mil/. No trace is found of the Latin plur. MĪLIA (e.g. DUŌ MĪLIA). In Old Spanish, we find only *dos mil(l)*, etc., or *dos vezes mil(l)*, etc., of which only the former survives beyond the Middle Ages.

The term *millón is* a late fifteenth-century borrowing from Italian. Before that time, and later, *cuento* was used in this sense.

3.6.2 Ordinal numerals

Few of the Latin ordinal numerals have been inherited, as numerals, by Spanish, although rather more have survived in Spanish as nouns (e.g. SEXTA (HORA) > *siesta* 'siesta', DECIMU > *diezmo* 'tithe'). PRĪMUS (which survives as the noun *primo* 'cousin') was in much of Western Romance replaced by PRĪMĀRIUS, originally 'of the first rank', whence *primer(o)*, *-a*. SECUNDUS > *segundo*. TERTIUS was replaced by TERTIĀRIUS (> *tercer(o)*, *-a*). QUARTUS > *quarto*, later *cuarto*. QUĪNTUS > *quinto*.

The remaining ordinals of Spanish are learned: *sexto*, *séptimo*, *octavo*, etc., although Old Spanish also possessed a series in *-eno* (*sesseno*, *seteno*, *ocheno*, etc.), of which only *noveno* (together with the nominalized *decena*, *docena*, *cuarentena*) survives. However, especially from 'eleventh' onwards, Spanish more frequently uses cardinal numerals in ordinal function.

3.6.3 Multiples and fractions

The only Latin multiple numeral to be inherited by Spanish is *doble* (< DUPLUS, which Corominas and Pascual (1980–91, s.v. *dos*) suggest was subject to dissimilation /ó/ . . . /o/ > /ó/ . . . /e/). Other forms (e.g. *simple*, *duplo*, *triple*, *cuádruplo*, *múltiple*/*-o*) are learned.

Among the partitive numerals, only *mitad* (< MEDIĒTĀTE) is inherited. *Tercio* is learned and in the remaining cases, Spanish uses an ordinal numeral, sometimes in combination with *parte* (*un cuarto, la cuarta parte*, etc.), although in technical language the denominator of a fraction is characterized by the suffix *-avo: dos dozavos*, etc.

3.7 The verb

3.7.1 General developmental features

Certain aspects of verbal development are not restricted to a particular category (for example, the expression of time, grammatical person, or verbal mood), but in principle affect all relevant verbal forms. In some cases, the processes concerned are not even limited to verbal forms. When we consider the tendencies towards analytic and synthetic expression (3.7.1.1), the relationship between phonological and analogical change (3.7.1.2), the verbal accent (3.7.1.3), or apocope (3.7.1.4), we face problems which also belong to other linguistic fields. However, they have to be considered here in detail because they have special relevance to the development of verbal morphology.

3.7.1.1 Analytic and synthetic developments

The morphology of Classical Latin was notably more synthetic that that of Spanish (which is equivalent to saying that the morphology of Spanish is more analytic than that of literary Latin). That is to say that what was expressed in Latin by bound morphemes (e.g. the suffix {r} which was the exponent of voice in AMĀTUR 's/he is loved'), is often expressed in Spanish by independent morphemes (in this case, the various words which make up expressions like *es amado* or *se le ama*). This tendency towards analytic expression is much less marked in the verb than in the noun (compare 3.2), but we shall find important examples of its effect upon verbal morphology, not only in the expression of voice (3.7.2), but also in that of aspect (3.7.4).

Despite this partial drift towards analytic verbal expression, Spanish nevertheless occasionally displays the reverse tendency, towards synthesis. This kind of change can be seen, principally, in the case of the future and conditional paradigms (3.7.8.4), whose medieval forms were often of analytic type (e.g. *contar telo é*, where the infinitive and the auxiliary (*é*) are partially independent and can be separated by one or more clitic pronouns). From the medieval period onwards, there has been a synthetic tendency to convert the semi-independent auxiliary into a bound morpheme, which accordingly cannot be separated from the other morphemes which constitute the future or conditional verbal forms (*contar (telo) é* > *(te lo) contaré*).

3.7.1.2 Phonological and analogical change

Morphological change can be seen to be the outcome of two opposing processes. On the one hand, phonological change takes place without any regard for the sense or the grammatical value of the forms it affects. It applies blindly to verbs, just as it does to other word classes. In this way the phoneme /k/ of the Latin verb DĪC̲ERE obeys the 'rules' of Castilian phonological change and becomes OSp. /d^z/ when followed by a front vowel (e.g. DĪC̲ERE > *dez̲ir*, DĪC̲IS > *diz̲es*) but retains its velar place of articulation when followed by a non-front vowel (e.g. DĪC̲Ō > *digo*, DĪC̲AM > *diga*). (In both cases the consonant becomes voiced, because of its intervocalic positions; see 2.5.3.2.) Consequently, it can be said that phonological change, by applying 'regularly', nevertheless introduces irregularity into morphological paradigms.

On the other hand, analogy strives to reduce morphological irregularity by re-establishing a direct or iconic relationship between morphemes and their meanings. For example, the medieval verb *cozer* (< COQ(U)ERE) shows the same consonantal alternation as *dezir* (because its stem ends with the same /k/, after the early loss of the following U): *cuego~cuezes*, like *digo~dizes* (see 3.7.8.1.3.(1)). However, whereas *dezir* (> *decir*) maintains the alternation down to the present, *cozer* (> *cocer*) later underwent analogical readjustment, so that the stem consonant is now invariably /θ/: *cuezo~cueces*.

As with all cases of linguistic change, we are not in a position to predict exactly when analogy will defeat phonological change or when the latter will win the contest, but it can often be noted that the outcome is dependent upon the frequency of the lexeme in question. If *digo/dizes* has retained its consonantal alternation, which is the result of phonological change, while *cuego/cuezes* has been regularized (to *cuezo/cueces*), as the result of analogy, this outcome is almost certainly due to the much higher frequency of the first verb in comparison with the second. It is the most frequent words which resist analogical reconstruction, thereby allowing free rein to phonological change. Another way of noting this correlation is to observe that the most frequent words are almost always the most morphologically irregular, while the less frequent a word is in speech, the more it is subject to the operation of analogical restructuring, so that morphological regularity is seen in all but the most frequent words.

3.7.1.3 The verbal accent

The position of the accent in a Latin verbal form was determined by the application of the same rules that applied to the accentuation of all other word classes (see 2.3.1). As in the case of nouns, adjectives, etc., the position of the accent has remained highly stable over the centuries and today almost always falls on the same syllable it fell on in Latin. Thus the accent fell on the penultimate syllable if that syllable was long, either because it contained a long vowel, as in CANTĀ́MUS (whence *cantámos*), or because it ended in a consonant (and despite containing a short vowel), as in TIMÉNDŌ (> *temiéndo*); by contrast, if the penultimate syllable was short (i.e. if it ended in a short vowel), the accent fell on the antepenultimate (SÓLŬTU > *suelto*). Spanish verbal forms continue to have their accent on the syllable determined by this Latin rule, except in the few cases which are discussed in the following sections (3.7.1.3.1–4).

3.7.1.3.1 The third conjugation. Four forms of each Latin third-conjugation verb (those with infinitives of the type VĒNDĔRE) differed in their accentual pattern from the corresponding forms of verbs belonging to other conjugations. In the case of the large majority of verbs, and in accordance with the rule just discussed (3.7.1.3), the accent fell on the penultimate in the infinitive (CANTÁRE, TIMÉRE, AUDÍRE), in the first person plural of the present indicative (CANTÁMUS, TIMÉMUS, AUDÍMUS), in the second person plural of the present indicative (CANTÁTIS, TIMÉTIS, AUDÍTIS), and in the plural imperative (CANTÁTE, TIMÉTE, AUDÍTE). However, the same rule stipulated that in the corresponding forms of third-conjugation verbs the short penultimate syllable could not bear the accent, which fell on the antepenultimate (VÉNDERE, VÉNDIMUS, VÉNDITIS, VÉNDITE).

In Spanish, the analogical pressure exerted by the accentual pattern of the majority of verbs (assisted by further analogical pressure coming from the first- and second-person-plural forms of the present subjunctive, which were penultimate-stressed in all verbs (VĒNDÁMUS, VĒNDÁTIS like CANTÉMUS, CANTÉTIS, TIMEÁMUS, TIMEÁTIS, AUDIÁMUS, AUDIÁTIS)), was instrumental in shifting the accent of VÉNDERE, VÉNDIMUS, VÉNDITIS, VÉNDITE to the penultimate. As a result of this change of stress, and of the merger in spoken Latin of the vowels Ē and Ĭ (both pronounced /e/; see 2.4.2), verbs of the third conjugation became identical in their morphology with those of the second (as also happened in Portuguese, by contrast with the other Romance languages):

VÉNDĔRE > /βendére/ = /temére/ < TĬMĒRE
VÉNDĬMUS > /βendémos/ = /temémos/ < TĬMĒMUS
VÉNDĬTIS > /βendétes/ = /temétes/ < TĬMĒTIS
VÉNDĬTE > /βendéte/ = /teméte/ < TĬMĒTE

This analogical accentual shift is therefore largely responsible for the reduction of the four Latin verbal classes to three in Spanish.

3.7.1.3.2 The fourth conjugation. Certain verbs of the fourth Latin conjugation, namely those which had four or more syllables in the first person singular of the present indicative and in persons 1–3 and 6 of the present subjunctive, and which had a short penultimate syllable, carried the accent on the antepenultimate, in accordance with the normal accentuation rule (e.g. APÉRĬO, APÉRĬAM, APÉRĬĀS, APÉRĬAT, APÉRĬANT). By contrast, in persons 2–3 and 6 of the present indicative (where there was no palatal glide; see 3.7.8.1.1), the accent regularly fell on the preceding syllable (ÁPĔRĬS, ÁPĔRIT, *ÁPĔRENT). The pattern represented by these latter forms (from which *abres, abre, abren* descend) was applied analogically to the remaining root-stressed present-tense forms, where, following regular loss of the glide (3.7.8.1.1), the result in Spanish is *abro, abra, abras, abran*.

3.7.1.3.3 First- and second-person-plural forms. In the first and second persons plural of all Latin paradigms, apart from the preterite (3.7.8.6.1) and certain present indicative forms (3.7.1.3.1), the accent fell on the penultimate syllable, because it contained a long vowel (3.7.1.3). However, in all these forms the accent was analogically shifted to the antepenultimate, so that it would occupy the same position, in relation to the root, as the remaining forms of each paradigm. For example, in the imperfect indicative of *-ar* verbs,

CANTĀ́BAM > *cantaba*
CANTĀ́BĀS > *cantabas*
CANTĀ́BAT > *cantaba*
CANTABĀ́MUS > *CANTÁBAMUS > *cantábamos*
CANTĀ́BĀ́TIS > *CANTÁBATIS > *cantabais*
CANTĀ́BANT > *cantaban*

In the same way, the accent position was regularized in the following cases, so that it no longer shifted in respect to the root, but in every form of the paradigm fell on the syllable immediately following the root:

the imperfect indicative verbs in *-er* and *-ir*:
TIMĒBĀ́MUS > *temíamos*
TIMĒBĀ́TIS > OSp. *temíades*> MSp. *temíais*

the pluperfect indicative (later conditional and imperfect subjunctive):
CANTĀ(VE)RĀ́MUS > *cantáramos*
CANTĀ(VE)RĀ́TIS > *cantárades* > *cantarais*

the pluperfect (later imperfect) subjunctive:
CANTĀ(VI)SSḖMUS > *cantássemos* > *cantásemos*
CANTĀ(VI)SSḖTIS > *cantássedes* > *cantaseis*

the perfect subjunctive/future perfect indicative (later future subjunctive):
CANTĀ(VE)RĪ́MUS > *cantáremos*
CANT(VE)RĪ́TIS > *cantáredes* > *cantareis*

3.7.1.3.4 Learned verbs. As a consequence of the phonological development of verbs inherited orally from Latin (especially as a result of the loss of intertonic vowels (2.4.3.3)), no popular verb in Old Spanish had a singular or third-plural present-tense form with the accent in any position except on the last syllable of the root. Thus SE VINDĬCAT, with the accent on the first of the two root syllables, was reduced to *se venga*, with the accent on the last (and in this case the only) root syllable. However, learned verbs (introduced, by definition, through the medium of writing; 2.2.2), retained all their vowels and therefore offered the possibility of bearing the accent on a root syllable other than the last. In the thirteenth century, we find examples of this kind of verbal accentuation; in Berceo's poetry, the metre assures us that *significa* (a learned adaptation of SIGNÍFĬCAT) was accentuated *signífica*. However, learned verbs were soon adapted to the accentual rule which had emerged in popular verbs, which prohibited accentuation on any other than the last root vowel; in this way, *signífica* and its like were changed to *significa*, etc. Consequently, a different structural contrast was created between certain popular verbs and their learned counterparts; contrast popular CÓMPĂRAT > *CÓMPĔRAT > *compra* 'he buys' with learned CÓMPĂRAT > **cómpara* > *compara* 'he compares'.

3.7.1.4 Apocope of *-e*

Latin verbal forms whose final syllable contained a front vowel preceded by a dental or alveolar consonant should lose this final vowel in accordance with regular phonological development (2.4.3.2), provided the previous syllable was open (i.e. ended in a vowel). This rule of apocope is indeed frequently applied to the Old Spanish verb, so that we can observe the following medieval forms (although they were never obligatory, and are found alongside unapocopated forms):

3rd pers. sing. pres. indic.: *tien, vien, sal, val, quier, plaz, pid*
1st pers. sing. strong preterite: *vin, fiz, quis*
3rd pers. sing. imperf. subj.: *dixiés, toviés, llegás*
3rd pers. sing. fut. subj.: *estovier, tomar*
sing. imperative: *ten, ven, sal, faz*

Such apocope also appears, less frequently, in the first person of the imperfect subjunctive, but is practically never seen in the present subjunctive, where (in *-ar* verbs) it might theoretically appear (*pare* > **par*). Forms without *-e* persisted longest in the future subjunctive, but reached the present day only in the singular imperative of a few very frequent verbs. The reason for this near-disappearance of apocope lies in the analogical pressure exerted by the respective verbal paradigms, where in the overwhelming majority of forms the person/number marker consists of at least one vowel. Only the imperatives, which do not belong to the normal six-member paradigms, were able to partially escape this pressure and keep a few apocopated forms.

Medieval Spanish phonology additionally allowed the loss of final /e/ after consonants other than dentals and alveolars, and after certain consonant groups. Although these phonotactic possibilities have not survived into the modern language, they could affect the medieval verb, so that we find apocopated forms like *vinist, llegast, amanezient, adux* (= modern *aduje*), beside the full forms which later displaced them.

3.7.1.5 Root vowels

As in present-day rural varieties of Spanish, the medieval language showed a certain instability with regard to the aperture of atonic vowels, especially to the contrast between /e/ and /i/ (e.g., *cevil~civil, iglesia~eglesia*) and between /o/ and /u/ (e.g. *jogar~jugar, logar~lugar, sospirar~suspirar*). This hesitation in principle affected all classes of words, but in the verb it was exploited to increase the morphological contrast between *-er* and *-ir* verbs. The differences between the endings of these classes were minimal, being limited to only four cases: the infinitive (*temer* vs. *sentir*), the first-person-plural present indicative (*tememos* vs. *sentimos*), the second-person-plural present indicative (*temedes* vs. *sentides*), and the plural imperative (*temed* vs. *sentid*). However, the high vowels /i/ and /u/ were excluded from the root of *-er* verbs, both when the root received the stress and when it was atonic; in these verbs, the root could contain only mid vowels, /e/ or /o/ (*temer*, *comer*) or the open vowel /a/ (*valer*). By contrast, the root of *-ir* verbs *could* contain high vowels (*bivir*, *subir*), while mid vowels were excluded from tonic roots; only forms like *bive, sube* were permissible in these verbs, never ***beve,* ***sobe*, etc. However, mid vowels could occur in the atonic roots of *-ir* verbs (*bevir*, *sobir*), and /a/ appeared both tonically and atonically (*sale, salir*).

The key issue is that, in the atonic roots of *-ir* verbs, the variability between /e/ and /i/ or between /o/ and /u/ was never associated with any difference of meaning. This fact allowed speakers to increase the morphological contrast between *-er* and *-ir* verbs (which was otherwise threatened) by preferring, for *-ir* verbs, those root vowels which could not appear in *-er* verbs (namely /i/ and /u/). It should be made clear that the preference for high vowels in these roots cannot have a phonetic or phonological cause; for example, it cannot be caused by metaphony before [j] (2.4.2.1). On the one hand, although *-ir* verb forms with [j] heavily prefer a high root vowel in Old Spanish (*escriviendo, subiendo, escrivió, subió, escrivieron, subieron, escriviera, subiera,* etc.), such forms coexisted with others which had a mid vowel (*escreviendo, sobiendo,* etc.) (see López Bobo 1998). But the opposite was not true of *-er* verbs; in these verbs only mid or low vowels could appear in the root: *temiendo, comiendo, temió, comió, temieron, comieron, temiera, comiera*, etc., but never ***timiendo*, etc.

Especially significant are the medieval future and conditional forms. We shall see (3.7.8.4.3(4)) that many *-er* and *-ir* verbs had contracted forms in these paradigms; that is, the infinitival /e/ or /i/ was eliminated when the auxiliary (*(h)e, (h)as*, etc.) was added directly to the verb (without intervening clitic): *prendrá, combrá, repintrá, subrá*. Under these circumstances, where the conjugation marker (the /e/ or /i/ of the infinitive) was lacking, high root vowels were obligatory in *-ir* verbs and mid vowels were impermissible. We do not find such forms as ***escrebrá,* ***sobrá*, etc. This polarization of root vowels clearly shows that choice of vowel is determined by conjugational class and not by any phonological factor.

In the case of *-ir* verbs with a back vowel in the root, the mid variant /o/ was successfully eliminated towards the end of the Middle Ages or in the early part of the sixteenth century. Very few verbs escaped this avoidance of root /o/: *podrir* (currently giving way to *pudrir*), *abolir* (and a handful of other learned verbs, all defective), and *oír*, the only true exception to this process, which perhaps maintained /o/ in order to avoid homonymic collision with *huir*, which in the sixteenth century was finally losing its initial aspirate in the standard (see 2.5.6). (For the two *-ir* verbs which additionally maintained root /ue/, see 3.7.8.1.4(2).)

In the case of verbs whose root shows a front vowel, the modern results are more complex, since the preference for high vowels in the root of *-ir* verbs was at odds with the process of vowel dissimilation /i/. . . /í/ > /e/. . . /í/. That is, when the verbal ending contained tonic /í/, it became impossible for the root to contain /i/ (in verbs inherited from Latin and which belonged to the standard from the sixteenth century on). The same happened in those forms (future and conditional) in which the conjugation-marker (/i/), previously tonic, had lost its stress in the synthesizing process (3.7.8.4) involved in the creation of these paradigms. The forms affected by this dissimilatory process were:

OSp. *pedir/pidir* > MSp. *pedir*
OSp. *pedimos/pidimos* > MSp. *pedimos*
OSp. *pedides/pidides* > MSp. *pedís*
OSp. *pedí/pidí, pediste(s)/pidiste(s)* > MSp. *pedí, pediste, pedisteis*
OSp. *pedía/pidía*, etc. > MSp. *pedía,* etc.
OSp. *pedido/pidido* > MSp. *pedido*
OSp. *pediré/pidiré/pidré*, etc. > MSp. *pediré*, etc.
OSp. *pediría/pidiría/pidría*, etc. > MSp. *pediría*, etc.

By contrast, in their other forms (i.e. those which lacked tonic /í/ in the ending), these verbs maintained or imposed a high root vowel:

OSp. *pido/pides/pide/piden* > MSp. *pido/pides/pide/piden*
OSp. *pedió/pidió/pedieron/pidieron* > MSp. *pidió/pidieron*
OSp. *pediera/pidiera*, etc. > MSp. *pidiera*, etc.
OSp. *pediesse/pidiesse*, etc. > MSp. *pidiese*, etc.
OSp. *pediere/pidiere*, etc. > MSp. *pidiere*, etc.
OSp. *pediendo/pidiendo* > MSp. *pidiendo*

Only certain learned verbs, borrowed from Latin through the written medium, escaped this pattern and could offer the sequence /i/. . . /í/ (*permitir, delinquir, distinguir*, etc.), together with a few popular verbs which in the Middle Ages behaved like *pedir*, etc., hesitating between root /e/ and /i/ (*escrevir/escrivir, bevides/bivides, recebían/recibían*, etc.). From the Golden Age onwards, these three verbs followed the learned vocalic pattern with /i/. . . /í/ (*escribir, escribía, vivís, vivido, recibían, recibir*, etc.), possibly because users of standard Spanish were aware that the etyma of these verbs had I in the root (SCRI̱BERE, VI̱VERE, RECI̱PERE). (For the few verbs which, additionally, maintained a root diphthong /ié/, see 3.7.8.1.4(2).)

In the case of the strong preterites (3.7.8.6.2) and related paradigms, there developed a similar preference for high root vowels except where these were prevented by dissimilation from following /í/. But in this case no distinction arose among the verb classes, since *-ar, -er* and *-ir* verbs were treated alike. Those medieval irregular preterites which had /ó/ in the first and third person singular (e.g. *estove/-o, tove/-o, troxe/-o*) showed a strong preferences for the same root vowel where the latter was atonic (*estoviste(s), estovimos, estovieron, estoviera*, etc.). However, a high vowel occasionally appeared (*estuviste(s), estuvimos, estuvieron, estuviera*, etc.), and this solution became the norm towards the end of the fifteenth century, in keeping with the process which at that time affected the regular *-ir* preterites (see above). And the preference for high root vowels went so far as to impose /u/ even in the strong forms of the paradigm (*estove/-o* > *estuve/-o*, etc.).

Those irregular preterites which had tonic /ú/ in the first and third person singular (e.g. *pude, puse, aduxe*) only occasionally allowed /o/ to appear in the unstressed root (*podiste, posieron, adoxiera*, etc.). These minority variants with /o/ were suppressed at the end of the Middle Ages; thereafter these verbs could show only root /u/, and a single pattern was established for all irregular preterites with a back vowel in the root (*pudiste* = *estuviste*, etc.).

Medieval irregular preterites do not include any with root /é/ (except the very infrequent *trexe* < TRAXĪ, see 3.7.8.6.2(1–2)), and verbs with root /í/ (e.g. *dixe, fize, vine*) only occasionally allowed /e/ when the root was atonic (*dexiste/dixiste, fezieron/fizieron, veniera/viniera*, etc.). The root vowel /e/ became impermissible before the end of the fifteenth century, making /i/ the only front vowel possible in the root of irregular preterites, and also making these forms the only ones (apart from the few learned verbs mentioned above) not subject to the dissimilatory process /i/.../í/ > /e/.../í/ (e.g., *dijiste, hicimos, vinisteis*).

3.7.2 *Voice*

The contrast between active and passive voice was expressed in Latin in two different ways. In the *infectum* (present indicative and subjunctive, imperfect indicative and subjunctive, future), passive voice was expressed synthetically, by the addition of the morpheme {-(u)r} to the active forms: pres. indic. AMAT vs. AMĀTUR, pres. subj. AMET vs. AMĒTUR, imperf. indic. AMĀBAT vs. AMĀBĀTUR, imperf. subj. AMĀRET vs. AMĀRĒTUR, fut. AMĀBIT vs. AMĀBITUR. By contrast, in the *perfectum* (perfect indicative and subjunctive, pluperfect

Table 3.7 *Non-preterite person/number markers*

1st pers. sing.	-Ō > /o/ (e.g. CANTŌ > *canto*)
	-M is lost (e.g. CANTĀBAM > *cantaba*)
2nd pers. sing.	-S > /s/ (e.g. CANTĒS > *cantes*)
3rd pers. sing.	-T survives until the twelfth century (e.g. VENIT > *vinet* (*ARM* 19) = *vienet*), and is then lost (*viene*)
1st pers. plur.	-MUS > /mos/ (e.g. CANTĀMUS > *cantamos*)
2nd pers. plur.	-TIS > OSp. /des/ (e.g. CANTĀTIS > *cantades*)
3rd pers. plur.	-NT > /n/ (e.g. CANTĀBANT > *cantaban*)

indicative and subjunctive, future perfect) the passive forms were analytic, consisting of the participle and an appropriate form of the auxiliary ESSE: AMĀVIT vs. AMĀTUS EST, AMĀVERIT vs. AMĀTUS SIT, AMĀVERAT vs. AMĀTUS ERAT, AMĀVISSET vs. AMĀTUS ESSET, AMĀVERIT vs. AMĀTUS ERIT. In spoken Latin, the analytic pattern gradually spread to the paradigms of the *infectum*, through a reinterpretation of the tense-value of the auxiliary. On the basis of attributive phrases like CARUS EST ('he is dear (to me)', i.e. with present value), Latin speakers began to assign present-tense value ('he is loved') to AMĀTUS EST, in place of its traditional value ('he was/has been loved'). Similarly, the meaning of AMĀTUS ERAT was shifted from 'he had been loved' to 'he was loved', and so on. This change required the creation of new forms to express what had previously been conveyed by AMĀTUS EST, AMĀTUS ERAT, AMĀTUS ERIT, etc.; the use of AMĀTUS FUIT to mean 'he was/has been loved', of AMĀTUS FUERAT to mean 'he had been loved', etc., is well attested in late Latin.

Although this type of passive (now *ser* + participle) was inherited by Spanish and has always existed in the language, it has always been subject to certain semantic and stylistic restrictions. Not only does it have competitors (*se* constructions, the indefinite third plural), but from the Golden Age onwards its semantic field has become limited to dynamic situations (those that express change, such as *fue hecho*), while a state resulting from an earlier action is now conveyed by the structure *estar* + participle (*está hecho*).

3.7.3 *Person and number*

In the Latin verb, morphemes expressing grammatical person cannot be disentangled from those expressing number; the same morphemes expressed both categories. In their development from Latin to Spanish, these elements have undergone no changes other than those determined by regular phonological change. Since person and number were and are marked somewhat differently in the preterite, when compared with other paradigms, we shall first examine the morphemes applied to these other paradigms (see table 3.7).

The preterite endings differed from those of table 3.7 only in the following respects:

1st pers. sing. -Ī (see 3.7.8.6)
2nd pers. sing. -STĪ > /ste/ (e.g., CANTĀVISTĪ> *cantaste*)
2nd pers. plur. -STIS > OSp. /stes/ > MSp. /steis/ (e.g. CANTĀVISTIS > *cantastes* > *cantasteis*)

Occasionally in Old Spanish, an /-s/ was added to the second-person-singular preterite ending (e.g. *cantastes*), no doubt in imitation of all other second-person-singular endings, which are marked with this morpheme. However, this analogical change created identity of ending with the second-person-plural ending; as a result, *(Tú) cantastes* was never frequent until the modern period, when the change *(Vos) cantastes* > *(Vosotros) cantasteis* (see below) resolved the homonymy, allowing *(Tú) cantastes* to become extremely common in all varieties except the standard.

Further comment is required only on the second-person-plural forms. Except in the preterite, the -T- of this morpheme was intervocalic in Latin and so became voiced to /d/ in Old Spanish (2.5.3.2.4). OSp. /d/ from this source is predicted to pass unchanged into the modern language (cf. AETĀTE > *edad*), but in the second-person-plural verb-ending this /d/ was eliminated, from the fourteenth century onwards, perhaps because of the increased frequency of such verb forms, which were increasingly used to indicate a singular as well as a plural subject, at first denoting deference on the part of the speaker, but increasingly without such a nuance. The result of this loss of /d/ was the formation of various cases of hiatus, each of which was reduced to a single syllabic nucleus in a variety of ways. The chronology of these reductions depends upon the accentual pattern of the verb form in question; the following discussion will therefore deal separately with penultimate stressed, antepenultimate stressed and final-syllable stressed forms. (See also Líbano Zumalacárregui 1991.)

3.7.3.1 Paroxytonic forms of the second person plural

In the present indicative, present subjunctive and simple future paradigms of Old Spanish, the *Vos* form was stressed on the penultimate (i.e. it was paroxytonic): *cantades, temedes, sentides, sodes; cantedes, temades, sintades; cantaredes*, etc. These forms began to lose their /d/ towards the end of the fourteenth century, first in the case of *-edes*, where the resulting hiatus (/ée/) was resolved either as /é/, through assimilation, or as /éi/, through dissimilation: *temedes* > *temées* > *temés* or *teméis, cantedes* > *cantées* > *cantés/ cantéis, cantaredes* > *cantarées* > *cantarés/cantaréis*. Almost at once, and by imitation of this change, the other proparoxytonic forms suffered similar reductions: *cantades* > *cantáes* > *cantás/cantáis, temades* > *temáes* > *temás/temáis, sintades* > *sintáes* > *sintás/sintáis, sentides* > *sentís* (in this case a dissimilated result **/íi/ was impermissible in Spanish), *sodes* > *soes* > *sos/sois*.

Table 3.8 *Chronology of the paroxytonic forms of the second person plural*

Latin	CANTĀTIS
Spanish to 1400	*cantades*
1400–1470	*cantades, cantáes*
1470–1550	*cantáes, cantáis, cantás*
1550 onwards	In Spain: *cantáis*
	In America: *cantás, cantáis*

The chronology of these changes is summarized in table 3.8.

From the mid-sixteenth century, it can be seen, Peninsular Spanish opted for the dissimilated forms (e.g. *cantáis*, except in the case of *salís*, where this option was not available), now only with plural value. In those American regions where *voseo* (use of subject *Vos* with singular non-deferential value) is used (3.5.1.1), the assimilated forms (e.g., *cantás*) were for the most part preferred, although assimilated forms continued to have some use, as they still do today, especially in Central America (see Penny 2000: 151–7).

3.7.3.2 Proparoxytonic forms of the second person plural

As we have seen (3.7.1.3.3), the second-person-plural forms of a number of paradigms, despite being paroxytonic in Latin, appear as proparoxytonic in Old Spanish (CANTĀBĀ́TIS > OSp. *cantávades*, etc.). These forms maintained their /d/, and therefore remained proparoxytonic until the Golden Age, contrasting in that period with the originally paroxytonic forms, which had lost their /d/ and become final-stressed (*cantades* > *cantáis/cantás*; 3.7.3.1) two centuries earlier. Only in the sixteenth century (occasionally) and in the seventeenth (frequently) was /d/ lost from these forms, whereupon the resulting hiatus was reduced either to a diphthong (via dissimilation) or to a monophthong (via assimilation) (table 3.9).

Out of the forms which emerged in the late seventeenth century, only the dissimilated ones (*cantabais*, etc.) survived in the Peninsula, always with plural value, just as happened with the originally paroxytonic forms (*cantáis*, etc.). The assimilated forms were identical to those which belonged to subject *Tú* (so that *Tú cantabas* = *Vos cantabas*), a fact which no doubt assisted the increasing merger of the two modes of address, at this stage barely distinguished, into a single type, to express the speaker's solidarity with a single interlocutor. At all events, in America, where the historically second-person-plural forms survived with exclusively singular value, it was the assimilated forms (*cantabas*, etc.) which continued in use, while the dissimilated forms were lost.

Table 3.9 *Proparoxytonic forms of the second person plural*

	Old and Golden Age Spanish	Modern Spanish
Imperfect indicative	*cantávades*	*cantabais* or *cantabas*
	temíades, etc.	*temíais* or *temías*
Conditional	*cantaríades*, etc.	*cantaríais* or *cantarías*
Pluperfect/conditional/	*cantárades*	*cantarais* or *cantaras*
imperfect subjunctive	*temiérades*	*temierais* or *temieras*
Imperfect subjunctive	*cantássedes*	*cantaseis* or *cantases*
	temiéssedes	*temieseis* or *temieses*
Future subjunctive	*cantáredes*	*cantardes, cantareis, cantares*
	temiéredes	*temierdes, temiereis, temieres*

In the future subjunctive (OSp. *cantáredes*), early Modern Spanish not only had forms without /d/ (*cantareis, cantares*), but also frequent variants in which the post-tonic /e/ had been syncopated, allowing /d/ to survive, newly grouped as it was with /r/ (*cantardes*). These latter forms did not survive the eighteenth century.

3.7.3.3 Oxytonic forms of the second person plural

The Latin imperative plurals (CANTĀTE, TIMĒTE, /βendéte/ (< VENDĬTE; 3.7.1.3.1), AUDĪTE) gave rise to oxytonic forms in Old Spanish. Although there is some early evidence of penultimate-stressed antecedents (*cantade*, etc.), the latter appear to have developed rapidly in two directions: firstly, final /e/ was lost after /d/, as is normal in Spanish (2.4.3.2), giving *cantad, comed, oíd*; alternatively, early loss of /d/ (see 3.7.3) allowed assimilation of the resulting hiatus (*cantade > *cantae > cantá, comede > *comee > comé, oide > *oíe > oí*). These developments leave aside certain forms with early loss of /d/ and dissimilation of the resulting hiatus (*cantai, comei*), which rapidly became confined to peripheral regions (Asturias, León, Cantabria, etc.), where they survive in rural use. Both series of frequent forms (*cantad, comed, oíd; cantá, comé, oí*) continued to be used in the Golden Age (see Anipa 2000), during which period the forms with /d/ were finally selected for the standard, except when the imperative was followed by the reflexive clitic *os* (< *vos*): *levantaos, meteos.*

3.7.4 Aspect

Aspect is the verbal category whose forms allow the speaker to distinguish between various ways of envisaging the organization of an action or a situation over time; in this way, the different internal structures of actions and situations may be expressed. The category of aspect is independent of tense, so that the speaker is in principle able to discriminate between the internal structures of situations whether they belong to the present, the past, or the future (Comrie 1976). Spanish, through its verbal morphology, allows the speaker, to distinguish between *perfective, imperfective* and *perfect* aspects, and additionally between *progressive* and *non-progressive* aspects (Rona 1973).

Perfective aspect: the situation described is either momentary (its beginning and end are simultaneous) (e.g. *cayó al suelo*), or it belongs to a period of time which is explicitly or implicitly delimited by the speaker. If the temporal point of reference is the moment of speaking, the situation concerned occupies a segment of time whose beginning and end belong to a period of time which has already fully elapsed (e.g. *cené con ellos (anoche)*), or whose beginning (but not its end) belongs to such an earlier period (*conocí a mi mujer en Madrid*). Alternatively, the (temporally limited) situation may be linked to a reference-point which is earlier than the moment of speaking (e.g. *habían cenado (cuando yo llegué)*), or to a later reference-point (e.g. *habrán cenado (antes de que llegues)*).

Imperfective aspect: the speaker is not concerned either with the beginning or with the end of the situation, but only with its development over time (e.g. *ya cenaban (cuando yo llegúe)*).

Perfect aspect: the situation may or may not be concluded, but it takes place in a period of time which the speaker considers to be still current. This period may be long (e.g. *la ley escrita ha existido en España durante dos mil años*) or short (*me has fastidiado mucho con lo que me acabas de decir*), but it always includes the moment of speaking.

Progressive aspect: the speaker may choose to insist upon the development of the situation concerned, whether between (explicit or implicit) time limits (e.g. *estuvieron cenando durante tres horas, estuvieron mucho tiempo esperando*), or without such time limits (e.g. *estaban paseando por ahí cuando los vi*). (It can be seen from these examples that progressive aspect can be expressed simultaneously with perfective and imperfective aspect.) It is also compatible with perfect aspect, as when the speaker insists upon the duration of a situation which has developed within a period of time which the speaker regards as still current (e.g. *han estado jugando todo el día*).

The Latin verb allowed a distinction, through its morphology, only between perfective and imperfective aspects. Depending on whether the situation described was conceived as belonging to the moment of speaking (the present), to some future or past period, or to a period before some anterior reference-point, the Latin contrast between perfective and imperfective aspects was conveyed by the verbal forms listed in table 3.10.

Leaving aside the question of the absence of future subjunctive forms (for which see 3.7.8.4.4), it can be seen that Latin lacked the means to distinguish between perfective and imperfective aspects in the *anterior* temporal category.

Table 3.10 *The Latin aspectual system*

	Indicative		Subjunctive	
	Imperfective	Perfective	Imperfective	Perfective
Anterior	CANTĀVERAM		CANTĀVISSEM	
Past	CANTĀBAM	CANTĀVĪ	CANTĀREM	CANTĀVERIM
Present	CANTŌ	CANTĀVĪ	CANTEM	CANTĀVERIM
Future	CANTĀBO	CANTĀVERŌ		

Nor was there any morphological means of distinguishing between perfect and perfective aspects; with reference to past time, both were expressed by the forms CANTĀVĪ and CANTĀVERIM, respectively indicative and subjunctive. However, this aspectual difference could on occasion be marked syntactically, since the Latin sequence of tense rules required a present-tense subordinate verb where a main verb of the type CANTĀVĪ included the moment of speaking in its time-frame (i.e. when it had perfect aspect), and a past-tense subordinate verb when CANTĀVĪ referred to a period of time deemed by the speaker to be already concluded (i.e. when it had perfective aspect). In terms of English translation equivalents, this implies that CANTĀVĪ/CANTĀVERIM meant both 'I have sung' and 'I sang'.

3.7.4.1 Changes in the aspectual system of spoken Latin

The great aspectual innovation of spoken Latin was the introduction of forms that could unambiguously indicate perfect aspect. This process began among the transitive verbs and consisted of the structure HABEŌ 'I have' + participle. An example is HABEŌ CULTELLUM COMPARĀTUM (roughly 'I have the knife, which I bought'), in which the direct object of the verb (CULTELLUM) had a participle agreeing with it (COMPARĀTUM) which indicated an earlier action (here the 'purchase'). Since current possession (expressed by HABEŌ) implied that the action (contained in COMPARĀTUM) belonged to a period of time still current, this structure was close to conveying 'I have bought the knife', hitherto one of the meanings of COMPARĀVĪ CULTELLUM. Consequently, the introduction of HABEŌ COMPARĀTUM made possible a perfect/perfective distinction between HABEŌ COMPARĀTUM 'I have bought' and COMPARĀVĪ 'I bought'.

However, the idea of possession expressed by HABEŌ was not completely lost for centuries. The first stage in the semantic weakening of HABEŌ can be seen when this structure begins to be used with participles which were logically incompatible with the notion of possession, e.g. HABEŌ ILLUD AUDĪTUM, approximately 'I have heard it'. And when we find examples of HABEŌ + participle without an overt direct object (i.e. without anything expressly 'possessed'), as in HABEŌ INTELLECTUM for INTELLĒXĪ 'I have understood', we can conclude that HABEŌ has been grammaticalized as a morpheme expressing perfect aspect and that the notion of possession has been lost.

But speakers did not forget for centuries that the participle in this structure was dependent upon a direct object, often overt, and that it therefore had to agree in number and gender with that object. Thus the spoken Latin structure HABEŌ VACCĀS COMPARĀTĀS continued in early Old Spanish as *he compradas unas vacas*, although already in the thirteenth century this agreement was no longer obligatory and it was gradually abandoned between the thirteenth and the fifteenth centuries (Menéndez Pidal 1964b: 360–1, Pountain 1985).

Nor was it forgotten that the structure *he comprado* (< HABEŌ COMPARĀTUM) belonged exclusively to transitive verbs (the only ones capable of having a direct object); throughout the Middle Ages, this structure could not be used in the case of intransitives, which expressed perfect aspect by means of a different syntagma, e.g. *son idos* 'they have gone'. The origin of this structure is unclear, but it may descend from the perfect of the Latin deponent verbs (intransitives whose morphology was the same as the passive endings of transitive verbs, but whose meaning was active; e.g., MORTUUS EST 'he (has) died'). Be that as it may, the perfect of Old Spanish intransitives always adhered to the pattern *ser* + participle, a structure in which the participle normally agreed with the verbal subject: *salida es, venidos son, llegadas son*. Although intransitive examples of *haber* + participle (e.g. *han ido*) can be found before the sixteenth century, it is only at this stage that the modern structure becomes the norm for the perfect of all intransitives, and therefore of all Spanish verbs (England 1982, Pountain 1985).

Once the structure HABEŌ + participle was established in spoken Latin as the means of expressing perfect aspect in transitives, and SUM + participle was established for intransitives, speakers were free to extend these structures to other tenses and moods. But whereas the creation of HABEŌ CANTĀTUM, HABEAM CANTĀTUM, etc., had enlarged the Latin aspectual system, contrasting the new structures with existing CANTĀVĪ, CANTĀVISSEM, etc., and introducing a new distinction, between perfect and perfective aspect, the extension of this pattern to other tenses did not involve any further aspectual complication, since the new structures had the same values as existing forms (HABĒBAM CANTĀTUM = CANTĀVERAM, HABUISSEM CANTĀTUM = CANTĀVISSEM, etc.), and the latter gradually disappeared. This replacement process was evidently slow and in Spain had still not been completed by the end of the fifteenth century, since CANTĀVERAM could still then be used as a pluperfect (under the form *cantara*) beside analytic competitors (*ove cantado/avía cantado*, later *hube cantado/había cantado*). This development of compound verbal forms is summarized in table 3.11.

The Old Spanish forms *avría cantado, sería venido* (conditional perfect) and *oviere cantado, fuere venido* (future perfect subjunctive) had no Latin

Table 3.11 *Development of the Spanish compound verb forms*

Classical Latin		Old Spanish		Modern Spanish
Transitive	Intransitive	Transitive	Intransitive	All
CANTĀVĪ	VĒNĪ	*(h)e cantado*	*so venido*	*he cantado/venido*
CANTĀVERAM	VĒNERAM	*avía/ove cantado* *cantara*	*era venido* *viniera*	*había/hube cantado/venido*
CANTĀVERŌ	VĒNERŌ	*avré cantado* *avría cantado*	*seré venido* *sería venido*	*habré cantado/venido* *habría cantado/venido*
CANTĀVERIM	VĒNERIM	*aya cantado*	*sea venido*	*haya cantado/venido*
CANTĀVISSEM	VĒNISSEM	*oviesse cantado* *oviere cantado*	*fuesse venido* *fuere venido*	*hubiese/hubiera cantado/venido* *hubiere cantado/venido*

antecedents and were created as counterparts of the simple conditional and future subjunctive paradigms (see 3.7.8.4.2, 3.7.8.4.4, respectively).

3.7.4.2 The Old Spanish verbal system

Although in most cases the perfective forms of the Latin verbal system (table 3.10) were replaced by compound structures (table 3.11), certain perfective forms avoided this process. In each case, these forms became morphologically simplified, losing the marker of perfectivity -V(E/I)-. This simplification had already occurred in standard Latin, in certain perfective forms of the -ĪRE conjugation, where loss of -V- between identical vowels was phonologically regular: AUDĪVI > AUDĪI, AUDĪVISSEM > AUDĪISSEM, etc. This change was then spread to the remaining perfective forms of -ĪRE verbs (AUDĪVERAM > AUDĪERAM, etc.), and to -ĀRE verbs, so that reduced forms such as CANTĀĪ (< CANTĀVĪ), CANTĀRAM (< CANTĀVERAM), CANTĀSSEM (< CANTĀVISSEM), CANTĀRŌ (< CANTĀVERŌ), etc., were frequent in non-standard Latin. The relevant Romance forms descend from these reduced Latin forms.

The verb forms of this type which survived into Old Spanish without being replaced by compound forms were the following:

1 CANTĀVĪ (whence *canté*) came to be restricted to having perfective value, losing its perfect sense.
2 CANTĀVERAM (> CANTĀRAM > *cantara*) kept its pluperfect value until the Golden Age, and may even keep it today in certain written registers and in certain clauses (i.e. relative clauses) (e.g. *el libro que* ***escribiera*** *(= había escrito) en su juventud*). However, already in late Latin this form could have conditional or conditional perfect value (in the protasis of conditional sentences which expressed improbability or impossibility of outcome), and this value was common in Old and Golden Age Spanish (e.g. *si viniera/viniese, se lo* ***diera***), but becoming limited, in the modern language, to certain very

Table 3.12 *The Old Spanish verbal system*

	Indicative			Subjunctive		
	Imperfective	Perfective	Perfect	Imperfective	Perfective	Perfect
Anterior		*ove cantado/ avía cantado/ cantara*			*oviesse cantado*	
Past	*cantava*	*canté*	*he cantado*	*cantasse*		*aya cantado*
Present	*canto*			*cante*		
Future	*cantaré*	*avré cantado*		*cantare*	*oviere cantado*	
Conditional	*cantaría*	*avría cantado*				

frequent verbs (*quisiera, debiera, hubiera,* occasionally *pudiera*). From the fourteenth century, this *-ra* form acquired a third value, namely that of imperfect subjunctive, a change which made it equivalent, in some types of clauses, to *cantase* (see 3.7.6, 3.7.8.3.2(2)). (For the history of *cantara*, see Wright 1932.)

3 CANTĀVISSEM (> CANTĀSSEM > *cantasse* > *cantase*) had already lost its pluperfect subjunctive value, in most varieties of spoken Latin, and had acquired imperfect subjunctive function, replacing CANTĀREM (see 3.7.8.3.2).

Bearing in mind these changes of value, the Old Spanish verbal system which emerged from the Latin system was as shown in table 3.12.

3.7.4.3 The modern Spanish verbal system

The changes which lead from the medieval to the modern system are few. The system continues unchanged in its overall structure, although certain verbal forms occupy a different position in the modern scheme:

1 *Ove cantado* (now *hube cantado*) has become increasingly rare, and is now limited to the most formal registers and to certain types of clause (subordinate temporal clauses) (e.g. *apenas hube llegado, cuando...*).

2 *Cantare* and *oviere cantado* have abandoned their syntactical role to the present and perfect subjunctive forms (*cante, haya cantado*), or, in the protasis of 'open' conditional sentences, to the present and perfect indicative (e.g. *si viniere, se lo daré > si viene, se lo daré*). This change can be seen to be under way in the seventeenth century and the future subjunctive now survives only in certain formulaic expressions (e.g. *sea lo que* ***fuere***).

3 *Cantara* has moved definitively into the subjunctive mood (see 3.7.8.3.2), losing its older pluperfect and conditional (perfect) values.

In the light of these changes, the modern Spanish verbal system can be presented as in table 3.13.

Table 3.13 *The Modern Spanish verbal system*

<table>
<tr><th></th><th colspan="3">Indicative</th><th colspan="3">Subjunctive</th></tr>
<tr><th></th><th>Imperfective</th><th>Perfective</th><th>Perfect</th><th>Imperfective</th><th>Perfective</th><th>Perfect</th></tr>
<tr><td>Anterior</td><td></td><td colspan="2">(ove cantado)/
había cantado</td><td></td><td colspan="2">hubiera/hubiese cantado</td></tr>
<tr><td>Past</td><td>cantaba</td><td>canté</td><td>he cantado</td><td colspan="2">cantara/cantase</td><td>haya cantado</td></tr>
<tr><td>Present</td><td>canto</td><td></td><td></td><td>cante</td><td></td><td></td></tr>
<tr><td>Future</td><td>cantaré</td><td colspan="2">habré cantado</td><td>(cantare)</td><td colspan="2">(hubiere cantado)</td></tr>
<tr><td>Conditional</td><td>cantaría</td><td colspan="2">habría cantado</td><td></td><td></td><td></td></tr>
</table>

The distinction between *canté* and *he cantado*, as exponents of perfective and perfect aspect respectively, is not identical in all parts of the Spanish-speaking world. In the northwest of the Peninsula and in practically the whole of Spanish America, the perfect forms are used to refer only to situations which are capable of being prolonged into the future (e.g. *Siempre ha sido muy amigo mío* 'he has always been a good friend of mine'). In these areas, the perfect is not used for situations which come to an end in the current period of time (as conceived by the speaker). So, whereas a speaker from the centre or south of the Peninsula might say *Han llegado hoy*, where *hoy* denotes a period of time still current, by contrast with *Llegaron ayer*, where the period of time envisaged has concluded, speakers from the northwest or from America will say *Llegaron hoy/llegaron ayer* using the same verb form for both situations. (For further details and for the extent of this phenomenon, see Penny 2000: 158–61; for discussion of the general nature of this contrast, see Mackenzie 1995, 1999: 63–72.)

3.7.4.4 Progressive aspect

In recent centuries, Spanish has developed a series of verbal structures which serve to emphasize that the situation described is a developing one. This structure, which consists of a form of the verb *estar* + gerund, is compatible with any tense (*está esperando, estaba esperando, estará esperando, estaría esperando*), and with the other aspects already discussed (imperfective, perfective and perfect). It might be said that the use of progressive aspect in conjunction with imperfective aspect (e.g. *estaba esperando* vs *esperaba*) does not indicate a view of the situation which is markedly different from that indicated by the imperfective marker alone. However, this is not the case when progressive aspect is combined with perfective or perfect aspect: *estuvo esperando* and *ha estado esperando* add to *esperó* and *ha esperado* a nuance of extended duration (see 3.7.4) which is difficult to express by other means. (For the form of the gerund, see 3.7.9.)

3.7.5 Tense

Although there have been substantial changes in the aspectual system as the verb developed from Latin to Spanish (see 3.7.4), the tense system has hardly been changed over the same period. Latin contrasted past with non-past time-reference, and allowed the possibility of contrasting the future with the present, although this was never obligatory and a present-tense form could often have future time-reference. As can be seen from tables 3.10 and 3.11, the only structural changes which took place between Latin and Old Spanish, with regard to tense, were the creation of a category of conditional forms (for which, see 3.7.8.4.2), and the extension of the subjunctive category to include future forms (3.7.8.4.4).

3.7.6 Mood

The contrast between indicative and subjunctive moods (for the forms, see table 3.10, and 3.7.8.1.1–6, 3.7.8.3.2) carried the same fundamental meaning contrast in Latin as in Spanish. That is, the contrast of moods allowed the speaker to attach different truth-values to the propositions contained in the clauses concerned. Although the use of one or other mood has become automatic in some sentence types (e.g. the subjunctive in *Te prohíbo que salgas*), Spanish offers the same possibility as Latin did to change the meaning of a clause by substituting one mood for the other. Thus, in relative clauses, Spanish has inherited from Latin the ability to express contrasts of the following kind:

Los que han terminado pueden irse
Los que hayan terminado pueden irse

In the first (indicative) case, the speaker asserts the existence of such people (that is, the speaker already knows that such people exist), while in the second case we infer that the speaker cannot assert such a reality (that is, the speaker does not know if such people exist). This inherited contrastive ability is not limited to relative clauses, but to many other types of Spanish sentences (those containing dependent noun clauses, adverbial clauses, etc.).

The only verbal form which has changed its mood value in the history of Spanish is the form *cantara* (< CANTĀRAM < CANTĀVERAM). Its Latin pluperfect indicative value had been preserved in Old Spanish (see 3.7.4.2(2), 3.7.8.3.2(2)), together with the conditional (or conditional perfect) value which it had acquired in late Latin. But from the fourteenth century *cantara* began to be used as an imperfect subjunctive, coming into competition with *cantas(s)e*, and eventually ousting this form in many varieties of Spanish (3.7.4.3(3)).

For some scholars, the imperative constitutes a third mood. We leave this matter aside and study the imperative forms in 3.7.8.2.

Table 3.14 *Present indicative and subjunctive forms of Classical Latin verbs in -ĒRE and -ĔRE*

Verbs in -ĒRE		Verbs in -ĔRE	
Present indicative	Present subjunctive	Present indicative	Present subjunctive
TÍM(E)O	TÍM(E)AM	VĒNDO	VĒNDAM
TÍMES	TÍM(E)ĀS	VÉNDIS	VÉNDĀS
TÍMET	TÍM(E)AT	VÉNDIT	VÉNDAT
TIMÉMUS	TIM(E)ÁMUS	VÉNDIMUS	VENDAMUS
TIMÉTIS	TIM(E)ÁTIS	VÉNDITIS	VENDATIS
TÍMENT	TÍM(E)ANT	VÉNDUNT	VÉNDANT

3.7.7 Verb classes

Among the four Latin verb classes (or conjugations), only those with infinitive in -ĀRE or -ĪRE were genuinely productive, while additions were rarely made to those with infinitive in -ĒRE and -ĔRE (except in the case of the inceptive subgroup in -ĒSCĔRE). Although in most Romance languages a contrast was maintained (sometimes only in the infinitive itself) between the types in -ĒRE and -ĔRE, in the centre and west of the Peninsula these two classes were reduced to one as a result of two series of changes, which affected the vowels of their endings and their accentual patterns. The present indicative and subjunctive forms of verbs belonging to these two classes can be exemplified as in table 3.14.

3.7.7.1 Reduction from four classes to three

In order to understand this change, three regular phonological processes must be taken into account:

1 the loss of the palatal glide [j] (here represented by -E-) from the ending of -ĒRE verbs (see 3.7.8.1.1);
2 the merger in spoken Latin of Ē and Ĭ under all stress conditions (see 2.4.2, 2.4.3.2);
3 the accent shift discussed in 3.7.1.3.1.

As a result of these processes, the only difference between these two verb classes lay in the third person plural of the present indicative (TIMENT vs. VENDUNT). The analogical adjustment of VENDUNT to the rest of the paradigm (giving *VENDENT) is occasionally attested in the Latin of Spain, so that by the end of the Roman period a single present indicative paradigm and a single present subjunctive paradigm had developed for these two verb classes (table 3.15).

As a result of this merger of endings, and of the fact that the endings of the Latin -ĒRE and -ĔRE conjugations did not differ in any other surviving paradigm, the four Latin conjugations were reduced to three before the emergence of the earliest Spanish texts.

Table 3.15 *Present indicative and subjunctive forms of verbs in* -ere *(< -ĒRE and -ĔRE) in the late Latin of Spain*

Present indicative	Present subjunctive
/témo/ = /βéndo/	/téma/ = /βénda/
/témes/ = /βéndes/	/témas/ = /βéndas/
/témet/ = /βéndet/	/témat/ = /βéndat/
/temémos/ = /βendémos/	/temámos/ = /βendámos/
/temétes/ = /βendétes/	/temátes/ = /βendátes/
/témen(t)/ = /βénden(t)/	/téman(t)/ = /βéndan(t)/

Only a handful of verbal forms from the -ĔRE class escaped accent-shift, because of their high frequency. Early Spanish literary texts show *femos, feches* (< FÁCIMUS, FÁCITIS), together with plural imperative *fech* (< FÁCITE; later adjusted to the regular ending: *fed, fet*), and the infinitives *fer* and *far* (< FÁCERE). However, all these forms compete with the regularized forms *fazemos, fazedes, fazed, fazer*. We also find unshifted *tred* (< TRÁHITE), beside *traed* (with accent shift). Similarly, it is possible to argue that the present indicative forms *vamos, vades* are products of proparoxytonic VÁDIMUS, VÁDITIS. However, on the basis of VÁDIMUS, VÁDITIS, we would predict the outcome ***vemos*, ***vedes*, and it is more probable that *vamos, vades* are originally subjunctive forms (< VADAMUS, VADATIS; see 3.7.8.1.5 (1, *ir*)), which came to compete with indicative *imos, ides* and which then displaced these forms because they were structurally better integrated with the remaining forms of the paradigm: *vo, vas, va, van*.

3.7.7.2 Changes of verb class

No -ĀRE verb moves to another conjugation; on the contrary, the -ĀRE class is the main recipient of verbs from other sources. Firstly, the number of *-ar* verbs is increased by a few migrants from other Latin verb classes: TORRĒRE > Golden Age and dialectal *turrar*; FIDĔRE > *fiar*; MINUĔRE > *menguar*; MEIĔRE (already attested as MEIĀRE) > *mear*. Secondly, almost all verbal borrowings from non-Romance languages move into this class (e.g. Germanic RAUBÔN > *robar*, WARDÔN > *guardar*), as do most verbs derived from nouns, adjectives, etc.

Most Latin -ĒRE and -ĔRE verbs which survive remain within the *-er* class. However, this conjugation scarcely increased the number of its members; the only newcomers are: a single -ĪRE verb (TUSSĪRE > *toser*); a considerable number of verbs in *-ecer* derived from nouns (*anochecer*, etc.), from adjectives (*enriquecer*, etc.), or from *-ir* verbs (*guarnecer* < *guarnir*, *ofrecer* < *ofrir*);

and a number of latinisms (*defender*, etc.). On the contrary, the *-er* class lost members to the *-ir* conjugation.

The *-ir* class retained all surviving -ĪRE verbs (except TUSSĪRE), and was increased by Germanic loans in -JAN (SKARNJAN > *escarnir*, later *escarnecer*), and by a large number of learned borrowings (*definir, infundir*, etc.). This class was also expanded by the addition of numerous verbs which moved from the -ĒRE and -ĔRE classes. This movement took place for either or both of the following reasons:

1 The root vowels /i/ or /u/, which were very rare in -ĒRE and -ĔRE verbs but frequent in the -ĪRE class, came to be a morphological markers of the *-ir* class. Consequently, the few -ĒRE and -ĔRE verbs which had root Ī or Ū moved to the latter conjugation. Thus, DĪCERE, RĪDERE, LŪCĒRE, etc., became *decir, reír, lucir*.
2 The fact that all -ĒRE and some -ĔRE verbs had a palatal glide in certain endings (see 3.7.8.1.1), namely in the very endings where a glide occurred in *-ir* verbs, led to the movement of a number of -ĒRE and -ĔRE verbs into the *-ir* class, where the glide was preserved for longer.

Consequently:

COMPLĒRE > *cumplir* 'to fulfil'
FERVĒRE > *hervir* 'to boil'
FLORĒRE > *florir* (later *florecer*) 'to flower'
IMPLĒRE > *henchir* 'to fill out'
MONĒRE > OSp. *muñir* 'to summon'
PUTRĒRE > *pudrir* 'to rot'
RE-PAENITĒRE > *arrepentirse* 'to repent'
CONCIPĔRE > *concebir* 'to conceive'
FUGĔRE > *huir* 'to flee'
*MORĔRE (CL MORĪ) > *morir* 'to die'
PARĔRE > *parir* 'to give birth'
RECIPĔRE > *recibir* 'to receive'
SUCCUTĔRE > *sacudir* 'to shake'

However, this movement towards the *-ir* class was not limited to verbs with high root vowels or with a palatal glide, but included other -ĔRE verbs, some of which appear in medieval texts with both *-er* and *-ir* forms:

CON-BATTUĔRE > *combatir* (also OSp. *combater*) 'to fight'
CONFUNDĔRE > *confundir* (also OSp. *cofonder*) 'to confuse'
EX-CON-SPUĔRE > *escupir* 'to spit'
*IN-ADDĔRE > *añadir* (also OSp. *eñader*) 'to add'
PETĔRE > *pedir* 'to ask for'
REDDĔRE > *rendir* (also OSp. *render*) 'to give back'
*SEQUĔRE (CL SEQUĪ) > *seguir* 'to follow'
*SUFFERĔRE (CL SUFFERRE) > *sufrir* 'to suffer'

3.7.8 Verb paradigms

Each of the major verbal paradigms is discussed below (3.7.8.1–6).

3.7.8.1 Present indicative and subjunctive

The most important developmental features of the present tenses are examined in the following sections (3.7.8.1.1–5).

3.7.8.1.1 The palatal glide [j]. The pronunciation of Latin reveals a palatal glide (also called a yod, symbolized here as [j] and spelt E or I in Latin), between the verbal root and certain person/number morphemes. It occurred only in some verbal classes, specifically all -ĒRE and -ĪRE verbs and a subclass of -ĔRE verbs (those of the 'mixed' conjugation). The verbal forms in which this glide appeared were: the first person singular of the present indicative (e.g. DĒBEO, AUDIO, CAPIO); the third person plural of the same paradigm, except in the case of -ĒRE verbs (e.g. AUDIUNT, CAPIUNT); and in all forms of the present subjunctive paradigm (e.g. DEBEAM, AUDIAM, CAPIAM, etc.).

This yod was gradually lost from pronunciation, in the early centuries AD, probably for analogical reasons. The models for this analogical restructuring were: the absence of yod from all -ĀRE verbs (e.g. CANTŌ) and from most -ĔRE verbs (e.g. MOLŌ), and its absence from the second and third persons singular and the first and second persons plural of the verbs discussed in the previous paragraph (DEBĒS, DEBET, DEBĒMUS, DEBĒTIS, AUDĪS, AUDIT, AUDĪMUS, AUDĪTIS, CAPIS, CAPIT, CAPIMUS, CAPITIS, etc.). However, before it was lost from pronunciation, this yod had certain assimilatory (i.e. metaphonic) effects on the root vowel of *-ir* verbs (see 2.4.2.1, 3.7.8.1.4(2)). By contrast, it had little effect on the root-final consonant with which it was normally grouped. When the root ended, for example, in /k/ or /t/ (e.g. FACIŌ, MĒTIŌ(R)), assimilation between the consonant and the following yod might be expected (cf. ERĪCIU > *erizo*, PUTEU > *pozo*; see 2.5.2.2). However, it can be seen that, in most cases, the yod ceased to be pronounced before it could have this effect. Thus FACIŌ > *hago*, MĒTIŌ(R) > *mido*, rather than ***hazo* or ***mizo*, although some would argue that Port. *faço, jaço* < FACIŌ, IACEŌ suggest that the glide *did* palatalize root-final /k/ in pre-literary Spanish, and that **fazo* was then replaced by *fago* (later *hago*) by analogy with *digo*, etc. Only three groups of verbs clearly show the assimilatory effect of the glide contained in the verbal ending; these are discussed in 3.7.8.1.1(1–3).

1 Verbs in /dj/, /gj/ and /bj/. Those verbs which combine root-final /d/ or /g/ with a following glide, together with an occasional form with root-final /b/, show the normal development of these groups (see 2.5.2.2(4–5)). That is, the group becomes the mid-palatal fricative /ǰ/, which is then eliminated after a front vowel (/e/ o /i/):

VIDEŌ, VIDEAM, etc. > *veo, vea*, etc.
RĪDEŌ, RĪDEAM, etc. > *río, ría*, etc.
AUDIO, AUDIAM, etc. > OSp. *oyo, oya*, etc. (later *oigo, oiga*; see 3.7.8.1.3)
SEDEAM, etc. > *sea*, etc.
FUGIŌ, FUGIAM, etc. > *huyo, huya*, etc.
HABEAM, etc. > *haya*, etc.

A number of verbs with root-final /d/ in spoken Latin, but which belonged to the third conjugation and therefore lacked the palatal glide, analogically acquired this pattern:

CADŌ, CADAM, etc. > OSp. *cayo, caya*, etc. (later *caigo, caiga*; see 3.7.8.1.3)
RADŌ, RADAM, etc. > *rayo, raya*, etc.
RODŌ, RODAM, etc. > *royo, roya*, etc.
VADAM, etc. > *vaya*, etc.
TRADŌ, TRADAM, etc. (CL TRAHŌ, TRAHAM, etc.) > OSp. *trayo, traya*, etc. (later *traigo, traiga*; see 3.7.8.1.3)

Among these medieval verbs with root-final /ǰ/, those which had a preceding back vowel (/o/ or /u/) extended the /ǰ/ to all those present indicative forms which would otherwise have had the unprecedented hiatus /óe/, /úe/ between root and ending. Thus, AUDĪS > **oes* > *oyes,* AUDIT > **oe* > *oye,* *AUDENT (for AUDIUNT) > **oen* > *oyen,* FŪGIS > **fúes* > *fuyes* > *huyes,* FŪGIT > **fúe* > *fuye* > *huye,* *FŪGENT (for FŪGIUNT)> **fúen* > *fuyen* > *huyen.* This rejection of /óe/, /úe/ was later applied to learned verbs in *-uir*, whence *contribuye, instruyes, confluyen,* etc.

2 Verbs in /pj/. The glide was also preserved after root-final /p/, maintaining the voiceless feature of this phoneme, and then being transferred to the previous syllable:

CAPIŌ, CAPIAM, etc. > *quepo, quepa*, etc.
SAPIAM, etc. > *sepa*, etc.

A single verb in /kj/ (PLACEAT > *plega*) adopts this pattern in Old Spanish, unlike FACIŌ, FACIAM, IACEŌ, IACEAM, etc., which became *fago, faga, yago, yaga*, etc. in the medieval language (see 3.7.8.1.1).

3 Verbs in /nj/. Judging by cognate Romance forms (Ptg. *venho, tenho*, Gal. *veño, teño*, OItal. *vegno, tegno*), the glide which followed root-final /n/ was kept long enough in pronunciation to palatalize this consonant. The result was a consonantal alternation (/ɲ/ vs /n/) which was unprecedented in Spanish: **veño* (< VENIŌ) vs *vienes*, etc. (< VENĪS, etc.). This alternation was therefore replaced, as also occurred in Italian, by another (namely, /ng/ vs /n/) which was already established in the language (see 3.7.8.1.3). Consequently, in the

Table 3.16 *Regular present-tense endings of* -ar, -er *and* -ir *verbs*

Present indicative	Present subjunctive
CANTŌ > *canto*	CANTEM > *cante*
CANTĀS > *cantas*	CANTĒS > *cantes*
CANTAT > *canta*	CANTET > *cante*
CANTĀMUS > *cantamos*	CANTĒMUS > *cantemos*
CANTĀTIS > *cantades* > *cantáis*	CANTĒTIS > *cantedes* > *cantéis*
CANTANT > *cantan*	CANTENT > *canten*
DEB(E)Ō > *debo*	DEB(E)AM > *deba*
DEBĒS > *debes*	DEB(E)ĀS > *debas*
DEBET > *debe*	DEB(E)AT > *deba*
DEBĒMUS > *debemos*	DEB(E)ĀMUS > *debamos*
DEBĒTIS > *devedes* > *debéis*	DEB(E)ĀTIS > *devades* > *debáis*
DEBENT > *deben*	DEB(E)ANT > *deban*
APER(I)Ō > *abro*	APER(I)AM > *abra*
APERĪS > *abres*	APER(I)ĀS > *abras*
APERIT > *abre*	APER(I)AT > *abra*
APERĪMUS > *abrimos*	APER(I)ĀMUS > *abramos*
APERĪTIS > *abrides* > *abrís*	APER(I)ĀTIS > *abrades* > *abráis*
APER(I)UNT > *abren*	APER(I)ANT > *abran*

earliest Spanish texts we already find *vengo, venga, tengo, tenga*, etc. (< VENIŌ, VENIAM, TENEŌ, TENEAM, etc.), and the occasional example of *remanga*, etc. (< REMANEAT). Another verb which soon adopted this pattern is PONŌ, PONAM, etc., although it had never had /nj/ in Latin: *pongo, ponga*, etc.

3.7.8.1.2 The present-tense endings. Keeping in mind what has been said about the verbal accent (3.7.1.3), about apocope of *-e* (3.7.1.4), and about changes affecting the second person plural (3.7.3.1), the development of the present-tense endings of the three Spanish verbal classes is otherwise phonologically regular. They are set out in table 3.16. The only additional point worthy of note is the adaptation of the form APER(I)UNT (> *APERENT > *abren*), in which the back vowel is replaced by /e/, thus extending to the third person plural the equivalence of ending already established in the remaining root-stressed forms of the paradigms of the verbs in *-er* and *-ir* (*deb<u>o</u>* = *abr<u>o</u>*, *deb<u>es</u>* = *abr<u>es</u>*, *deb<u>e</u>* = *abr<u>e</u>*, *deb<u>a</u>* = *abr<u>a</u>*, etc.). See also 3.7.7.1.

3.7.8.1.3 Consonantal alternation. Almost all the consonantal alternations that are found in the root of Spanish verbs are due to the double phonological development of the Latin velar consonants. The latter became palatalized before front vowels (/e/ or /i/) but remained velar before other vowels (2.5.2.3). Since, in the Latin verbal endings, front vowels alternated with back vowels, the root-final consonant of a given verb could appear in Spanish in either of two shapes.

However, the predicted consonantal alternation is limited to *-er* and *-ir* verbs. No *-ar* verb displays this effect. This is probably due to the fact that in *-ar* verbs the minority alternant was to be found only in the present subjunctive forms, which were too infrequent to preserve a contrasting morphological shape. For example, in the form PLICĀRE, the root-final /k/, being intervocalic and standing before a non-front vowel, gives Spanish /g/: PLICĀRE > *llegar*. The same happens in the large majority of the forms of this verb: PLICŌ > *llego*, PLICĀS > *llegas*, PLICĀVIT > *llegó*, etc. Only in the present subjunctive, where the ending contains a front vowel (PLICEM, PLICĒS, etc.), does one predict a palatalized result (theoretically PLICĒS > **lleces*, etc.). However, all the *-ar* verbs with a stem-final velar have been regularized, bringing the present subjunctive in line with the other paradigms: *llegue, llegues*, etc.

This process of analogical levelling in the verb can be usefully exemplified with the identical sequences PACEM /pákem/ and PACĒS /páke:s/. When these forms function as present subjunctives (of the verb PACĀRE 'to pay'), we have just seen that the velar is retained (as voiced /g/): *pague, pagues*. But when the identical forms correspond to the noun PAX 'peace', the consonant undergoes regular change (PACEM > *paz,* PACĒS > *paces*).

Such analogical levelling is considerably less powerful in the case of *-er* and *-ir* verbs, so that many Spanish verbs of these classes show the predicted consonantal alternation. In these verbs, once the glide had been eliminated from the ending (3.7.8.1.1), and once the third-person-plural endings of -ĔRE and-ĪRE verbs had been adjusted ((-I)UNT > -ENT; see 3.7.7.1, 3.7.8.1.2), the root-final consonant was followed by a non-front vowel (/a/ or /o/) in seven forms (the first-person-singular present indicative and the six forms of the present subjunctive), while in all other forms it was followed by a front vowel. If the root-final consonant was velar, it is predicted to be assimilated to such a front vowel, becoming palatalized, whereas if the ending contained /o/ or /a/ the consonant should maintain its velar place of articulation.

We find three groups of Latin verbs with a velar root-final consonant and which have descendants in Spanish: those with /k/ preceded by a vowel (e.g. DICERE); those whose root ends in /rg/ or /ng/ (e.g. SPARGERE); and those with root-final /sk/ (e.g. COGNŌSCO). Each of these types will be discussed in turn, although it will be seen the first two lead to a single Spanish type.

1 Verbs in vowel + /k/. In keeping with regular consonantal change in Spanish (2.5.2.3), the two following results are predicted:

1 (vowel +) /k/ (+ /o/, /a/) > OSp. and MSp. /g/ (e.g. IOCU > juego)
2 (vowel +) /k/ (+ /e/, /i/) > OSp. /d^z/ (spelt *z*) > MSp. /θ/ (e.g. VĪCĪNU > *vezino* > *vecino*)

Table 3.17 *Development to Old Spanish of verbs with root in vowel + /k/*

1st sing. pres. indic.	Pres. subj.	2nd–3rd sing., 1st–3rd plur. pres. indic.	Infinitive, etc.
DĪCŌ > *digo*	DĪCAM > *diga*	DĪCIS > *dizes*	DĪCERE > *dezir*
FAC(I)Ō > *fago*	FAC(I)AM > *faga*	FACIS > *fazes*	FACERE > *fazer*
COQ(U)Ō > *cuego*	COQ(U)AM > *cuega*	COQ(U)IS > *cuezes*	COQ(U)ERE > *cozer*
ADDŪCŌ > *adugo*	ADD ŪCAM > *aduga*	ADDŪCIS > *aduzes*	ADDŪCERE > *aduzir*
IAC(E)Ō > *yago*	IAC(E)AM > *yaga*	IACĒS > *yazes*	IACĒRE > *yazer*

The first result can be predicted to appear in seven forms of *-er* and *-ir* verbs: the first-person-singular present indicative (with ending in /o/), and the six forms of the present subjunctive (with endings in /a/). The remaining verbal forms (with /e/ or /i/ in the ending) are predicted to show the second result. A good number of Old Spanish verbs show the predicted morphological shape as given in table 3.17.

Although some of these verbs later adopted other morphological patterns, the most frequent among them (*decir* and *hacer*) kept this alternation, which became indistinguishable from the following type (3.7.8.1.3(2)). This combined pattern was then extended to many other verbs (see below).

2 Verbs in /ɾg/ and /ng/. When the root of a Latin verb ends in /ɾg/ or /ng/, we can predict that the velar will remain unchanged when a non-front vowel follows (i.e. in the first person singular of the present indicative and in all the present subjunctive):

1 /ɾg/, /ng/ (+ /o/, /a/) > OSp. and MSp. /ɾg/, /ng/ (e.g. VIRGA > *verga*, FUNGU > *fongo* > *hongo*)

But the velar will be palatalized when it is followed by a front vowel (as occurs in all remaining verbal forms), with two possible results in the case of /ng/:

2 /ɾg/ (+ /e/, /i/) > OSp. /ɾd^z/ > MSp. /ɾθ/ (e.g., ARGĪLLA > *arzilla* > *arcilla*) /ng/ (+ /e/, /i/) > OSp. /nd^z/ or /ɲ/ > MSp. /nθ/ or /ɲ/ (e.g. GINGĪVA > *enzía* > *encía*, LONGE > OSp. *lueñe*; in Modern Spanish, /ɲ/ < /ng/ can only be seen in verbal examples).

A number of Old Spanish verbs reveal that they have evolved in keeping with this model (see table 3.18).

The alternating verbs so far discussed, although they have different phonological structures in Latin, form a single type in Old Spanish, characterized by having /g/ at the end of the root in seven forms (first-person-singular present indicative, plus the six forms of the present subjunctive), alternating with another consonant (which may be /d^z/ or /ɲ/) in the remainder. This pattern, because

Table 3.18 *Development to Old Spanish of verbs with root in /ɾg/, /ng/*

1st sing. pres. indic.	Pres. subj.	2nd–3rd sing., 1st–3rd plur. pres. indic.	Infinitive, etc.
SPARGŌ > *espargo*	SPARGAM > *esparga*	SPARGIS > *esparzes*	SPARGERE > *esparzir*
ER(I)GŌ > *yergo*	ER(I)GAM > *yerga*	ERIGIS > *yerzes*	ER(I)GERE > *erzer*
TANGŌ > *tango*	TANGAM > *tanga*	TANGIS > *tañes*	TANGERE > *tañer*
PLANGŌ > *plango*	PLANGAM > *planga*	PLANGIS > *plañes*	PLANGERE > *plañir/plañer*
FRANGŌ > *frango*	FRANG AM > *franga*	FRANGIS > *frañes*	FRANGERE > *frañir/ frañer/franzir*

it had originated in a number of frequent verbs, became attractive to Spanish speakers and began to be spread to verbs whose Latin root had not ended in a velar. The extension of the pattern, which consists of the addition of /g/ to the seven relevant forms of new verbs, can be seen from earliest times in those whose root ended in /n/ (see 3.7.8.1.1(3)), and gradually affects those with root /ɾ/ or /l/:

VENIŌ/VENIAM: *vengo/venga*
TENEŌ/TENEAM: *tengo/tenga*
PONŌ/PONAM: *pongo/ponga*
FER(I)Ō/ FER(I)AM: *fiergo/fierga* (beside *fiero/fiera* > *hiero/hiera*)
SAL(I)Ō/ SAL(I)AM: *salgo/salga* (beside *salo/sala*, later lost)
DOL(E)AT: *duelga* (later only dialectal, beside *duela*)
TOLLŌ/TOLLAM: *tuelgo/tuelga* (infinitive *toller*, a verb later lost)
SOL(E)Ō: *suelgo* (later only dialectal, beside *suelo*)

This model continued to expand during the Golden Age, as /g/ was added to the root of another verb in /l/, several in /ǰ/ (see 3.7.8.1.1(1)), and a single verb in /s/:

VAL(E)Ō/VAL(E)AM > OSp. *valo/vala* > GA *valgo/valga*
AUDIŌ/AUDIAM > *oyo/oya* > *oigo/oiga*
CADŌ/CADAM > *cayo/caya* > *caigo/caiga*
TRAHŌ/TRAHAM > *trayo/traya* > *traigo/traiga*
FUGIŌ/FUGIAM > *fuyo/fuya* > *huyo/huya~huigo/huiga*
VĀDAM > *vaya* > *vaya~vaiga*
HABEAM > *haya* > *haya~haiga*
(derivative of ANSA) > *aso/asa* > *asgo/asga*

However, although this alternation was extended in these cases, a number of other verbs which displayed the alternation in Old Spanish (and which were usually less frequent than the verbs just listed) lost it in the later Middle Ages. Almost always the more frequent of the two alternants was extended to all forms of the verb concerned, so that the /g/ which marked the first-person-singular

Table 3.19 *Development to Old Spanish of verbs with root in /sk/*

1st sing. pres. indic.	Pres. subj.	2nd–3rd sing., 1st–3rd plur. pres. indic.	Infinitive, etc.
*MERĒSCŌ > *meresco*	*MERĒSCAM > *meresca*	*MERĒSCIS > *mere(s)çes*	*MERĒSCERE > *mere(s)çer*
COGNŌSCŌ > *conosco*	COGNŌSCAM > *conosca*	COGNŌSCIS > *cono(s)çes*	COGNŌSCERE > *cono(s)çer*
*NĀSCŌ > *nasco*	*NĀSCAM > *nasca*	*NĀSCIS > *na(s)çes*	*NĀSCERE > *na(s)çer*

present indicative and the six forms of the subjunctive was replaced by its competitor:

OSp. *cuego/cuezes/cozer* > MSp. *cuezo/cueces/cocer*
OSp. *espargo/esparzes/esparzer* > MSp. *esparzo/esparces/esparcir*
OSp. *tango/tañes/tañer* > MSp. *taño/tañes/tañer*
OSp. *plango/plañes/plañir* > MSp. *plaño/plañes/plañir*
OSp. *cingo/ciñes/ceñir* > MSp. *ciño/ciñes/ceñir*

However, in a single, unexplained case, the less frequent alternant, with /g/, was spread to the remaining forms of the verb:

OSp. *yergo/yerzes/erzer* > MSp. *yergo/yergues/erguir.*

The forms *huigo/huiga, vaiga, haiga* never became established in the standard language, but the last two continue to be frequently used in popular varieties of Spanish.

3 Verbs in /sk/. Verbs with root-final /sk/ are particularly frequent because this group formed part of the Latin infix which lent inceptive value (a notion of 'beginning') to the verb to which it was added (e.g. FLORĒRE 'to be in bloom' vs FLORĒSCERE 'to come into bloom'). Depending on the locus of the following vowel, Latin /sk/ is predicted to have either of the following results in Spanish:

1 /sk/ (+ /a/, /o/) > OSp. and MSp. /sk/ (cf. MUSCA > *mosca*)
2 /sk/ (+ /e/, /i/) > OSp. $/t^s/$ > MSp. /θ/ (cf. PISCĒS > *peçes* > *peces*)

This double outcome is in fact seen in a large number of verbs at the Old Spanish stage (see table 3.19).

Towards the end of the fifteenth century, spelling reveals a small adjustment in this alternation: $/t^s/$, characteristic of the majority of the forms of each of these verbs, replaces the /s/ of the minority. Later, this $/t^s/$ (spelt *z* in this syllable-final position) is regularly changed to /θ/:

OSp. *conosco/conosca/cono(s)ces* > MSp. *conozco/conozca/conoces*

At the same time, this highly frequent alternation was spread analogically to a considerable number of other verbs which did not have /sk/ in Latin but whose majority root-final consonant ($/d^z/$) was closely related to that ($/t^s/$) of the group of verbs under consideration here:

OSp. *adugo/aduzes/aduzir* > MSp. *aduzco/aduces/aducir*
OSp. *condugo/conduzes/conduzir* > MSp. *conduzco/conduces/ conducir*
OSp. *yago/yazes/yazer* > MSp. *yazco/yaces/yacer*
OSp. *plego/plazes/plazer* > MSp. *plazco/places/placer*
OSp. *lugo/luzes/luzir* > MSp. *(re-)luzco/luces/lucir*

For the Old Spanish form of these verbs, see 3.7.8.1.3(1).

3.7.8.1.4 Vocalic alternation. Alternation of root vowels is very frequent in Spanish (often under the name of 'radical-changing verbs'), and is due to two phonological processes:

1 Metaphony of the root vowel caused by a palatal glide in those verbal endings that contained such a sound (see 2.4.2.1, 3.7.8.1.1).
2 Diphthongization undergone by the tonic vowels /ɛ/ (= CL Ĕ) and /ɔ/ (= CL Ŏ), by contrast with their retention as monophthongs in unstressed positions (see 2.4.2.2).

The first of these processes cannot apply to *-ar* or *-er* verbs. The *-ar* class never had a glide at the beginning of the verbal ending; if, in a given verb, a glide appeared at the end of the root (e.g. *CAPTIĀRE) it formed part of the root and appeared in all forms of the verb, and could not therefore give rise to alternations (thus, *CAPTIĀRE > *cazar*, as *CAPTIŌ > *cazo*, etc.). In *-er* verbs, the glide was rapidly eliminated, before it could raise the tonic vowel (3.7.8.1.1). However, in *-ir* verbs the glide persisted long enough to have this effect, and we have to take it into account (see 3.7.8.1.4(2)).

In order to gain a clear understanding of vowel alternation, we must also take into account the position of the accent in verbal forms (see 2.3.1, 3.7.1.3). To summarize: in the spoken Latin of Spain the accent fell on the root of nine verbal forms (leaving aside the strong preterites; see 3.7.8.6.2): the first, second and third person singular and the third person plural of the present indicative; the same persons of the present subjunctive; and the singular imperative. In the remaining forms, the accent fell on the ending.

1 Vocalic alternation in *-ar* and *-er* verbs. Alternation is only predicted in the case of those verbs whose Latin ancestor contained the root vowel /ɛ/ or /ɔ/ (= CL Ĕ or Ŏ). If the accent fell on the /ɛ/ or /ɔ/, it became a diphthong, but if the root was atonic (i.e. when the accent fell on the ending) the root vowel remained undiphthongized. The following list summarizes these predictions:

stressed /ɛ/ > /ie/ (cf. PĔTRA > *piedra*)
unstressed /ɛ/ > /e/ (cf. *PĔTRĀRIA > *pedrera*)
stressed /ɔ/ > /ue/ (cf. BŎNU > *bueno*)
unstressed /ɔ/ > /o/ (cf. BŎNITĀTE > *bondad*)

Table 3.20 *Vocalic alternation in* -ar *and* -er *verbs due to diphthongization/non-diphthongization of /ɛ/ and /ɔ/*

Stressed root	Unstressed root
NĔGŌ > *niego*	NĔGĀMUS > *negamos*
NĔGĀS > *niegas*	NĔGĀTIS > *negáis*
NĔGAT > *niega*	
NĔGANT > *niegan*	
NĔGEM > *niegue*	NĔGĒMUS > *neguemos*
NĔGĒS > *niegues*	NĔGĒTIS > *neguéis*
NĔGET > *niegue*	
NĔGENT > *nieguen*	
NĔGĀ > *niega*	
MŎV(E)Ō > *muevo*	MŎVĒMUS > *movemos*
MŎVĒS > *mueves*	MŎVĒTIS > *movéis*
MŎVET > *mueve*	
MŎVENT > *mueven*	
MŎV(E)AM > *mueva*	MŎV(E)ĀMUS > *movamos*
MŎV(E)ĀS > *muevas*	MŎV(E)ĀTIS > *mováis*
MŎV(E)AT > *mueva*	
MŎV(E)ANT > *muevan*	
MŎVĒ > *mueve*	

Indeed, many of the verbs with root /ɛ/ or /ɔ/ which survive in Spanish as members of the *-ar* and *-er* classes show the expected alternations (see table 3.20).

Verbs whose Latin etyma contained other root vowels should not in principle show this alternation. However, some verbs which descend from Latin antecedents with root /e/ or /o/ (= CL Ē/Ĭ or Ō/Ŭ) came to share the same root vowel (/e/ or /o/) as the verbs we have been studying. Since there was no contrast in spoken Latin between unstressed /ɛ/ and /e/ or between unstressed /ɔ/ and /o/, bearing in mind the merger of atonic Ĕ, Ē and Ĭ, on the one hand, and between Ŏ, Ō and Ŭ, on the other (see 2.4.3.1), Spanish could not distinguish between the unstressed root vowels of verbs like the following:

NĔCĀRE, NĔCĀMUS, NĔCĀTIS > *negar, negamos, negades*, etc.
SĒMINĀRE, SĒMINĀMUS, SĒMINĀTIS > *sembrar, sembramos, sembrades*, etc.

or

RŎGĀRE, RŎGĀMUS, RŎGĀTIS > *rogar, rogamos, rogades*, etc.
MŌNSTRĀRE, MŌNSTRĀMUS, MŌNSTRĀTIS > *mostrar, mostramos, mostrades*, etc.

Because of this identity of root vowel among the forms which bore the stress on the ending (i.e. the large majority), identity of root vowels could be extended to the nine forms which were root-stressed. This analogical process consists of the introduction, at various periods, of a diphthong where it was not historically justified, as in:

sembro, sembras, sembren, etc. > *siembro, siembras, siembren,* etc. 'I sow'

**mostro,* **mostran,* **mostre,* etc. > *muestro, muestran, muestre,* etc. 'I show'

A large number of verbs whose Latin antecedents had root Ē/Ĭ or Ō/Ŭ have followed this path:

FRĬCĀRE/FRĬCŌ > *fregar/friego* 'to scrub' (although *fregar/frego* survives in rural varieties)

PĒNSĀRE/PĒNSŌ > *pensar/pienso* 'to think' (cf. *pesar/peso* 'to weigh', without alternation)

PLĬCĀRE/PLĬCŌ > *plegar/pliego* 'to fold'

RĬGĀRE/RĬGŌ > *regar/riego* 'to water'

FĒTĒRE/FĒTEŌ > *heder/hiedo* 'to stink'

FĬNDERE/FĬNDO > *hender/hiendo* 'to split'

CŌLĀRE/CŌLŌ > *colar/cuelo* 'to filter'

CŌNSŌLĀRĪ/CŌNSŌLŌ(R) > *consolar/consuelo* 'to console'

CŌNSTĀRE/CŌNSTŌ > *costar/cuesto* 'to cost'

FŬLLĀRE/FŬLLŌ > *hollar/huello* 'to dent'

Other verbs have sometimes adopted this alternation, but without being consolidated in the standard language: CŌNS(U)ERE/CŌNS(U)Ō > *coser/cueso* 'to sew' and CŬRRERE/CŬRRŌ > *correr/cuerro* 'to run'.

By contrast with this extension of the diphthong, a number of verbs which showed alternation in the medieval period (and sometimes still in the Golden Age), because they descended from Latin verbs with root Ĕ or Ŏ, later lost it and appear in the modern language with forms levelled in favour of the undiphthongized root. Among them we find:

ĒNĔCĀRE/ĒNĔCŌ > *anegar/aniego* > *anegar/anego* 'to flood'

INTĔGRĀRE/INTĔGRŌ > *entregar/entriego* > *entregar/entrego* 'to hand over'

PRAESTĀRE/PRAESTŌ > *prestar/priesto* > *prestar/presto* 'to lend'

TEMPĔRĀRE/TEMPĔRŌ > *temprar/tiempro* > *templar/templo* 'to cool'

VĔTĀRE/VĔTŌ > *vedar/viedo* > *vedar/vedo* 'to forbid'

PRAETĔNDERE/PRAETĔNDŌ > *pretender/pretiendo* > *pretender/pretendo* 'to aspire'

AD-PŎRTĀRE/AD-PŎRTŌ > *aportar/apuerto* > *aportar/aporto* 'to contribute'

ASŎLĀRE/ASŎLŌ > *asolar/asuelo* > *asolar/asolo* 'to raze'

CONFŎRTĀRE/CONFŎRTŌ > *confortar/confuerto* > *confortar/conforto* 'to console'

Table 3.21 *Development of the present indicative of* llevar

Latin	13th–14th centuries	15th centuries	16th centuries on
LĔVĀRE	*levar*	*levar*	*llevar*
LĔVŌ	*lievo*	*llevo*	*llevo*
LĔVĀS	*lievas*	*llevas*	*llevas*
LĔVAT	*lieva*	*lleva*	*lleva*
LĔVĀMUS	*levamos*	*levamos*	*llevamos*
LĔVĀTIS	*levades*	*leváis*	*lleváis*
LĔVANT	*lievan*	*llevan*	*llevan*

der. *RŎCCA > *derrocar/derrueca* > *derrocar/ derroca* 'to overthrow'
SŎRBĒRE/SŎRBEO > *sorber/suerbo* > *sorber/sorbo* 'to sip'

Less frequently, levelling has occurred in the opposite direction, spreading the diphthong to all the forms of an originally alternating verb. This type of analogical levelling is normally limited to cases where the verb is transparently related to a diphthongized noun or adjective, and where the verb was (or was thought to be) derived from that noun or adjective:

OSp. *atesar/atieso* > MSp. *atiesar/atieso* 'to stiffen' (cf. *tieso*)
OSp. *despezar/despiezo* > MSp. *despiezar/despiezo* 'to break up' (cf. *pieza*)
OSp. *dezmar/diezmo* > MSp. *diezmar/diezmo* 'to decimate' (cf. *diezmo*)
OSp. *desossar/des(h)uesso* > MSp. *deshuesar/deshueso* 'to bone' (cf. *hueso*)
OSp. *encorar/encuero* > MSp. *encuerar/encuero* 'to strip' (cf. *cuero*)
OSp. *encovar/encuevo* > MSp. *encuevar/encuevo* 'to hatch' (cf. *cueva*)
OSp. *engrossar/engruesso* > MSp. *engruesar/engrueso* 'to get fat' (cf. *grueso*)

Until the Middle Ages, the verb LĔVĀRE underwent a development which was typical of those with root Ĕ, that is, in Old Spanish it had the alternation /e/~/ie/. Nevertheless, in its nine diphthongized forms, the initial group [lj] became [ʎ], a sporadic change that can also be seen (in the fifteenth and sixteenth centuries) in *callente* < *caliente*, etc. This caused the verb to show an alternation of initial consonants (between /l/ and /ʎ/), an unprecedented circumstance in Spanish. No doubt because of its isolation, this alternation was then levelled, in favour of /ʎ/ (see table 3.21).

Another verb which shows regular alternation in Old Spanish, but which, in this case, is now irregular, is OSp. *jogar* (e.g. *juego~jogamos* < *IŎCŌ, *IŎCĀMUS, CL IŎCOR, IŎCĀMUR). The change /o/ > /u/ in the unstressed root (similar to other cases of occasional change like *logar* > *lugar*, which are unsatisfactorily explained) produced an alternation /ué/~/u/ (*juego~jugamos*), which is unique in Spanish.

Table 3.22 *Algorithm of* -ir *root-vowel development*

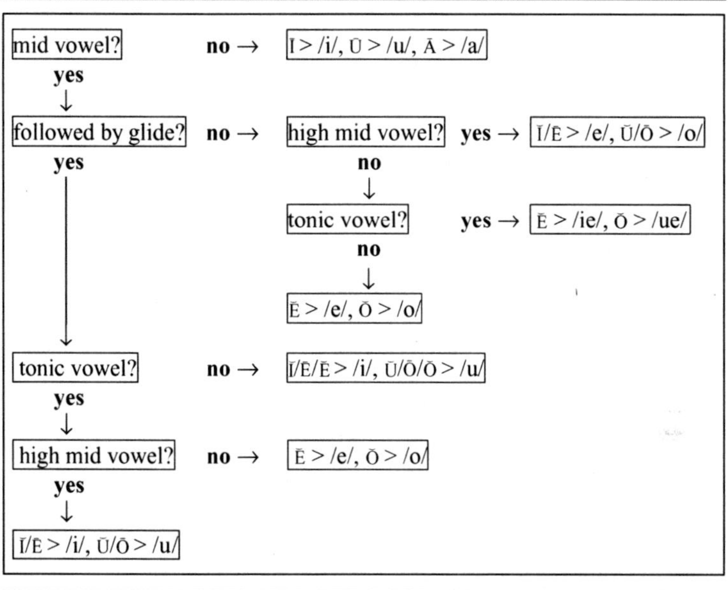

2 Vocalic alternation in *-ir* verbs. As we mentioned in 3.7.8.1.4, *-ir* verbs must have retained the palatal glide (which appeared between the root and the person/number morpheme; see 3.7.8.1.1) for longer than verbs of other classes. This yod remained long enough to have a metaphonic effect upon the root vowel. Metaphony (2.4.2.1) is an assimilatory process comprising the raising of a vowel (in our case, the root vowel) under the influence of a close element in the same or following syllable (in our case, the palatal glide of the ending). Since the high vowels /i/ and /u/ cannot be further raised, they are immune from metaphony, as is /a/ in verbal forms. As can be seen from tables 3.22 and 3.23, metaphony is felt by both stressed and unstressed vowels, each being raised one degree during the process. However, it should be borne in mind that, at the time metaphony took place (in late spoken Latin?), the atonic vowel system (with three degrees of aperture, there being no contrast between /ɛ/ and /e/ or between /ɔ/ and /o/) differed from that of tonic vowels (which showed four degrees of aperture). Furthermore, since metaphony took place before diphthongization, one of its effects was to prevent the diphthongization of the vowels /ɛ/ and /ɔ/, raising them to /e/ and /o/ respectively before they could be diphthongized. Taking into account the combined effects of metaphony and diphthongization, the algorithm in table 3.22 summarizes the predicted

Table 3.23 *Development of tonic and atonic vowels in Spanish affected and unaffected by metaphony exercised by [j]*

Latin vowel	Conditions	Spanish	Example
Ī	+ stress, + [j]	/i/	VĪNEA > *viña*
	+ stress, − [j]	/i/	FĪLU > *hilo*
	− stress, + [j]	/i/	(none)
	− stress, − [j]	/i/	HĪBERNU > *invierno*
Ē/Ĭ	+ stress, + [j]	/i/	VINDĒMIA > *vendimia*
	+ stress, − [j]	/e/	PLĒNU > *lleno*
	− stress, + [j]	/i/?	(none)
	− stress, − [j]	/e/	PLĬCĀRE > *llegar*
Ĕ	+ stress, + [j]	/e/	MATĔRIA > *madera*
	+ stress, − [j]	/ie/	PĔTRA > *piedra*
	− stress, + [j]	/i/	RĔNIŌNE > *riñón*
	− stress, − [j]	/e/	LĔNTICULA > *lenteja*
Ū	+ stress, + [j]	/u/	(none)
	+ stress, − [j]	/u/	FŪMU > *humo*
	− stress, + [j]	/u/	(none)
	− stress, − [j]	/u/	SŪDĀRE > *sudar*
Ō/Ŭ	+ stress, + [j]	/u/	RŬBEU > *rubio*
	+ stress, − [j]	/o/	CŬPPA > *copa*
	− stress, + [j]	/u/	MŬLIĒRE > *mujer*
	− stress, − [j]	/o/	NŌMINĀRE > *nombrar*
Ŏ	+ stress, + [j]	/o/	ŎSTREA > *ostra*
	+ stress, − [j]	/ue/	BŎNU > *bueno*
	− stress, + [j]	/u/	CŎCHLEĀRE > *cuchara*
	− stress, − [j]	/o/	CŎRTICEA > *corteza*

development of the various Latin vowels under the conditions which applied to the roots of *-ir* verbs.

Table 3.23 presents the same data, showing the predicted outcome of each Latin vowel under each of four sets of conditions (stressed and unstressed, with and without following glide), with a non-verbal example of each development, where available.

It can be seen that for each root vowel four sets of conditions have to be considered, which apply to the named forms of the *-ir* verbs:

1 Stressed root, with following glide: first-person-singular present indicative (e.g. SERVIŌ), first, second and third-person-singular and third-plural present subjunctive (e.g., SERVIAM, SERVIĀS, SERVIAT, SERVIANT).
2 Stressed root, without following glide: second- and third-person-singular and third-plural present indicative (e.g. SERVĪS, SERVIT, *SERVENT, singular imperative (e.g. SERVĪ).
3 Unstressed root, with following glide: first- and second-person-plural present subjunctive (e.g. SERVIĀMUS, SERVIĀTIS)

Table 3.24 *Development of front root vowels in* -ir *verbs*

Root vowel	1 + stress, + [j]	2 + stress, − [j]	3 − stress, + [j]	4 − stress, − [j]
Ī	RĪDEŌ > *río*	RĪDĒS > *ríes*	RĪDEĀMUS > *riamos*	RĪDĪMUS > *reímos*
Ē/Ĭ	MĒTIO(R) > *mido*	MĒTIS > *mides*	MĒTIĀMUS > *midamos*	MĒTĪMUS > *medimos*
Ĕ	SĔRVIŌ > *sirvo*	SĔRVĪS > *sirves*	SĔRVIĀMUS > *sirvamos*	SĔRVĪMUS > > *servimos*
	SĔNTIŌ > *siento*	SĔNTĪS > *sientes*	SĔNTIĀMUS > *sintamos*	SĔNTĪMUS > *sentimos*

4 Unstressed root, without following glide: first- and second-person-plural present indicative (e.g. SERVĪMUS, SERVĪTIS), plural imperative (e.g. SERVĪTE), infinitive (e.g. SERVĪRE).

In tables 3.24 and 3.25, each of these four categories is exemplified by a single form (respectively, by the first-person-singular present indicative, the second-person-singular present indicative, the first-person-plural present subjunctive, and the infinitive). Where the development of the root vowel conforms to the expected phonological outcome (tables 3.22, 3.23), the Spanish example appears in italics; when analogical processes intervene, the example is underlined and arrows indicate the source(s) of the analogical influence. Front vowels are examined first (table 3.24).

1 In the forms with tonic root and following yod (column 1), it can be seen that the /i/, predictable in roots with Ī and Ĭ/Ē (*río, mido*), has been spread to many verbs with root Ĕ (*sirvo*), with the analogical assistance of the forms in column 3, where /i/ is expected and found throughout. *Siento* represents the minority of verbs with Ĕ which have remained independent of this tendency towards root /i/, although the diphthong of *siento* is also analogical, an imitation of *sientes*, etc. In Old Spanish, there are relics of other Ĕ verbs which maintained their autonomy: *siervo, sieguen, vieste, riendo* (Malkiel 1966). By contrast, some modern dialects (e.g. those of Cantabria) have gone further than the standard language, preferring /i/ in all front-vowel roots: *sinto, minto, hirvo*, etc.

2 Among the forms of column 2, root /i/ is expected only in verbs with Ī in Latin (*ríes*), but /i/ has been spread to the verbs in Ĭ/Ē (*mides*), and to the majority of those with Ĕ (*sirves*), once again with the assistance of the column 3 forms (*riamos, midamos*, etc.), but on this occasion also in accordance with the pattern seen in *mido* (column 1).

3 In column 3, root /i/ is expected in Spanish whatever the Latin vowel. The only verb which escapes this regularity is *venir*: *vengamos, vengáis* (< VĔNIĀMUS, VĔNIĀTIS), forms which are perhaps due to influence from *tener* (*tengamos, tengáis*), since *venir* and *tener* show an almost exact parallelism in their development.

It can be seen, on the basis of the forms so far examined (columns 1–3), that the vowel /e/ has come to be excluded from the root of all these forms of the *-ir* verbs. The only root vowels we find are /i/ and /ie/, with the result that root /e/ has come to belong exclusively in Spanish to *-er* (and *-ar*) verbs.

4 In the forms of column 4, we expect root /i/ in those verbs with Ī in Latin. However, two forces have combined to impose /e/ here (*reímos*). First, analogy is exercised by Ĭ/Ē verbs (*medimos*) and Ĕ verbs (*servimos, sentimos*). Second, account must taken of the powerful effect of the dissimilation /i/. . . /í/ > /e/. . . /í/ (e.g. VĪCĪNU > *vecino*). Although in modern times /e/ has become the norm in all these forms (except in learned verbs (*dirigimos*, etc.) and in *escribimos, vivís, recibir* (influenced since the Renaissance by the root I of the Latin spelling: SCRIBIMUS, VIVITIS, RECIPERE), /i/ can frequently be seen in medieval forms, not only in Ī verbs (*dizimos*, beside *dezimos*), but also in verbs with other root vowels (*midimos, sintir, mintides*, beside *medimos, sentimos, mentides*, etc.).

As a result of the changes examined here, the contrast between Latin root vowels Ī and Ĭ/Ē has been eliminated, and many Ĕ verbs have become indistinguishable in their roots from Ī and Ĭ/Ē verbs. The verb *erguir* (< ĔRIGERE) is a good example of the double treatment of the Ĕ verbs, since on the one hand it may show the attraction of the Ĭ/Ē verbs (*irgo, irgues*), while on the other hand it also has forms which are independent of this effect (*yergo, yergues*). If the standard language has failed to carry through this process to its conclusion (by eliminating /ie/ from all Ĕ verbs), some non-standard varieties have been more thoroughgoing (see above).

We come now to those *-ir* verbs whose root contains a back vowel (table 3.25).

We have just seen that, in the case of *-ir* verbs with a front vowel in the root, the mid vowel /e/ was not entirely eliminated (table 3.24), since the forms of column 4 resisted the adoption of /i/. By contrast, among the *-ir* verbs whose root contains a back vowel, the mid vowel /o/ has been all but eliminated in favour of /u/ (see table 3.25); the high vowel has become universal except in two verbs (*dormir* and *morir*). The only exception verb is *oír* (< AUDĪRE), where root /o/ is maintained throughout, perhaps to avoid homonymic clash with *huir* = /uír/ (< FUGERE) in Old Castile, where initial /h/ (< F-) had earlier been lost.

1 The forms of column 1 are exactly parallel with those of the verbs with a front vowel in the root, since root /u/, originating among the Ū and Ŭ/Ō verbs

Table 3.25 *Development of back root vowels in* -ir *verbs*

Root vowel	1 + stress, + [j]	2 + stress, − [j]	3 − stress, + [j]	4 − stress, − [j]
Ū	*ADDŪCIŌ > *aduzco*	ADDŪCIS > *aduces*	*ADDŪCIĀMUS > *aduzcamos*	*ADDŪCĪMUS > *aducimos*
Ō/Ŭ	SŬBEŌ > *subo*	SŬBĪS > *<u>subes</u>*	SŬBEĀMUS > *subamos*	SŬBĪMUS > *<u>subimos</u>*
Ŏ	MŎLLIŌ > *<u>mullo</u>*	MŎLLĪS > *<u>mulles</u>*	MŎLLIĀMUS > *mullamos*	MŎLLĪMUS > *<u>mullimos</u>*
	DŎRMIŌ > *<u>duermo</u>*	DŎRMĪS > *duermes*	DŎRMIĀMUS > *durmamos*	DŎRMĪMUS > *dormimos*

(*aduzco, subo*), has been spread to the great majority of verbs in Ŏ (*mullo*), except that preference for the high vowel has been even stronger among the back-vowel verbs. Only two verbs (*duermo, muero*) resist this process, although it should be noted that their diphthong is due to intraparadigmatic analogy with the forms of column 2 rather than to regular phonological development.

2 Again in the case of forms with stressed root and no following glide (column 2), we note complete similarity of development between back-vowel and front-vowel verbs. That is, high /u/ is spread from the Ū verbs (*aduce(s), aducen*) to those with Ŭ/Ō (*sube(s), suben*), and to the majority of those with Ŏ (*mulle(s), mullen*), although the latter forms owe their shape in part to intraparadigmatic analogy on the pattern *aduzcamos*: *aduces* :: *mullamos*: *x*, where $x =$ *mulles*. Again the only forms which escape this analogical pressure are *duerme(s), duermen* and *muere(s), mueren*.

3 The forms in column 3 show /u/ in the case of all the Latin root vowels, in keeping with the predictions of tables 3.22 and 3.23, the high vowel again showing parallelism with the /i/ of the corresponding forms of front-vowel verbs. The invariability of the /u/ in *subamos*, etc., no doubt lent powerful support to the spread of the high vowel to the other forms with a back vowel in the root (columns 1, 2 and 4).

4 In the column-4 forms, there was no constraint upon preference for root /u/, which spread from the Ū verbs (*aducimos*) to those with Latin Ŭ/Ō and Ŏ (*subimos, mullimos*). In this set of forms, then, the parallel between back-vowel and front-vowel verbs is broken, since the dissimilatory process /i/... /í/ > /e/... /í/, which imposed a mid vowel in the root of the latter group, has no counterpart among the verbs with a back vowel in the root. Consequently, root /u/ appears in all but two back-vowel verbs (*dormimos, morimos*), both with Ŏ. However, this near-unanimity is relatively recent, and until the

sixteenth century many verbs allowed variation between /u/ and /o/. Although *bullir, confundir, escurrir, incurrir, urdir* (with Latin Ŭ/Ō) rarely allow /o/, the majority of Ŭ/Ō verbs and all Ŏ verbs preferred /o/, beside less frequent /u/: *cobrir, complir, escopir, foir, mollir, nozir, sobir, sofrir, recodir* (beside *cubrir, cumplir*, etc.). Even Ū verbs could appear with /o/ in Old Spanish (*adozir*, etc.), but during the sixteenth century /u/ became the only permissible root vowel, with the sole exception of *dormir* and *morir* (which occasionally allowed root /u/ in the Middle Ages) and of *podrir~pudrir* (which has maintained this variability down to the present).

This preference for root /u/ cannot be considered separately from the preference (similarly established in the sixteenth century) for the same vowel in the gerund, in the third person of the preterite, and throughout the paradigms related to the preterite; the medieval variability of the type *fuyendo~foyendo, cubrió~cobrió, subieron~sobieron, sufriera~sofriera*, etc., was at that stage resolved in favour of the forms with the high vowel (see 3.7.8.3.2, 3.7.8.4.4, 3.7.8.6.1, 3.7.9.2). It should be noted that preference here for /u/ cannot be ascribed to metaphony (2.4.2.1, 2.4.3.1), despite the appearance of a glide in the ending of all these forms, since the *-er* verb forms which have a glide in the corresponding endings never raise their root vowel from /o/ to /u/ (*comiendo, comió, comieron, comiera,* etc.). For further discussion of this point, see Penny (forthcoming).

The preference for high vowels in the root of *-ir* verbs cannot have phonological causes, as we have just noted, but must be due to morphological and semantic factors. Because of the rarity of contrast between the endings of the *-er* and the *-ir* verbs (limited to no more than four forms: *-er/-ir, -emos/-imos, -edes/-ides* (> *-éis/-ís*), *-ed/-id*), Medieval Spanish speakers probably sought alternative ways of establishing a morphological contrast between the two verb classes. The absence of high vowels from the roots of *-er* verbs provided a means of marking this distinction, by gradually expelling the mid vowels /e/ and /o/ from the root of *-ir* verbs (replacing them with /i/ and /u/). Only the dissimilatory process /i/ . . . /í/ > /e/ . . . /í/ prevented this polarization of root vowels between the two conjugations from becoming total. It is also likely that this morphological polarization was caused, at least in part, by an increasing semantic contrast between the verb classes under consideration; verbs with stative meaning were concentrated in the *-er* class, while those with active meaning were to be found predominantly in the *-ir* conjugation. See Montgomery (1975–6, 1978, 1979, 1980, 1985) and Penny (1972b and forthcoming).

3.7.8.1.5 Irregular present-tense paradigms. A distinction should be drawn between those paradigms which were irregular in Latin, from a synchronic point of view (and which may have maintained some irregularity in Spanish), and those which through regular phonological change, or through analogical adjustment, have acquired their irregularity at a later stage.

1 Verbs with irregularities in Latin.

Ser. Only some of the forms of the present indicative of *ser* descend from the corresponding forms of ESSE, which were:

SŬM SŬMUS
ĔS ESTIS
ĔST SŬNT

In Spanish, *somos* (< SŬMUS) and *son* (< SŬNT) show normal phonological development, while OSp. *so* (< SŬM) shows irregular loss of -M (already attested in a late Latin inscription SO, although -M is normally preserved as /n/ in monosyllables, e.g. TAM > *tan*; see 2.5.4), probably because its retention would have created an unprecedented first-person ending: ***son*. Elsewhere in the paradigm, following the regular reduction of -ST > /s/ (compare POST > *pues*), the second- and third-person-singular forms became identical, and the need to distinguish between these persons (which are distinct in all other paradigms) gave rise to the replacement of second-person ĔS by the corresponding member of the future paradigm (ĔRIS), and the continuation of ĔS(T), despite the fact that this form had an ending (-/s/) which is not found in other third-person forms.

As copular verbs (and therefore fully stressed forms), ĔRIS and ĔS(T) could be expected to undergo diphthongization of their root vowel Ĕ (> /ie/). However, because they had a frequent auxiliary function (shared with the rest of their paradigm, and demanding less than full stress) in the perfect of intransitives (*es llegado*) and in the passive (*es amado*), ĔRIS and ĔS(T) remained undiphthongized (as *eres* and *es*) in all their values.

The form ESTIS did not survive in the Latin of Spain, but was replaced by *SŬTIS, modelled analogically on SŬMUS and SŬNT.

As a result of these changes, the Old Spanish paradigm of the verb *ser* was as follows:

so *somos*
eres *sodes*
es *son*

The change *sodes* > *sois/sos* (later only *sois* in standard Peninsular Spanish) follows the normal rule (see 3.7.3.1), but the change *so* > *soy* has received no definitive explanation. This latter change, which began in the fourteenth century, is inseparable from the changes *do* > *doy, estó* > *estoy, vo* > *voy*, and is similar to the development of *ha* > *hay*, although in the case of *hay* the added element can be positively identified as the adverb *y* (< ĬBĪ) 'there', just as happens in the equivalent French expression *il y a*. Many explanations have been given for this change, but none is totally convincing. However, Paul Lloyd reasonably concludes, after a minute discussion of the theories on offer (1993: 565–70), that the addition of *-y* (probably < ĬBĪ) served to clarify the distinction between the *-ó* of the preterite and these present-tense forms, which also ended in *-ó* (by contrast with other present-tense forms, where the *-o* was atonic).

The present subjunctive of ESSE (SIM, SIS, etc.) does not survive in Romance, and is replaced by the corresponding forms of SEDĒRE 'to be (seated)', a verb which in some contexts was synonymous with ESSE, and which is the source of several paradigms which competed with those of ESSE, or which (as in this case and in that of the infinitive *ser* < SEDĒRE) replaced those of ESSE. The present subjunctive of SEDĒRE (SEDEAM, SEDEAS, etc. > *sea, seas*, etc.) develops regularly (see 3.7.8.1.1(1)).

Ir. The various present-tense forms of ĪRE suffered from the disadvantage of having no consonant in the root:

EŌ	ĪMUS	EAM	EĀMUS
ĪS	ĪTIS	EĀS	EĀTIS
IT	EUNT	EAT	EANT

This fact must have made these forms difficult to separate from adjacent words in normal speech, and which caused the majority of them to be replaced by longer forms, drawn from other verbs. The verb which most frequently provided these longer forms was VADERE 'to go, hurry', so that in the spoken Latin of Spain, the paradigms which expressed the notion of 'go' were probably

VADO	ĪMUS	VADAM	VADĀMUS
VADIS	ĪTIS	VADĀS	VADĀTIS
VADIT	VADUNT/*VADENT	VADAT	VADANT

The forms VADO, VADIS, VADIT, VADUNT/*VADENT were remodelled (probably on the pattern seen in *do, das, da, dan, estó, estás, está, están*), in such a way that, following loss of -D-, the root was maintained separated from the person/number marker (that is, without vowel-reduction of the type VADIS > /βáes/ > /βais/ > **/βes/, etc.). The subjunctive forms were attracted to the CADEAM > *caya* type (see 3.7.8.1.1(1)), except that in the first and second persons plural there were also phonologically regular reflexes of VADĀMUS, VADĀTIS, such that the Old Spanish paradigms were:

vo	*imos*	*vaya*	*vamos/vayamos*
vas	*ides*	*vayas*	*vades/vayades*
va	*van*	*vaya*	*vayan*

The subjunctive forms *vamos, vades* (< VADĀMUS), VADĀTIS) began to be used in Old Spanish as indicatives, since they chimed better with the indicative paradigm (*vo, vas, va, van*) than with the other forms of the subjunctive paradigm (*vaya, vayas*, etc.). This was a slow change, and although *imos, ides* ceased to be used before the sixteenth century, *vamos, vais* continued to appear with occasional subjunctive value in the Golden Age, and still today *vamos* keeps its optative sense (*¡Vamos!, ¡Vámonos!*). Thus emerged the modern paradigms:

vo	*vamos*	*vaya*	*vayamos (vamos)*
vas	*vais*	*vayas*	*vayáis*
va	*van*	*vaya*	*vayan*

The expansion *vo* > *voy* is discussed above under *ser*, and the non-standard forms *vaiga, vaigas*, etc., at 3.7.8.1.3(4).

Dar, estar. DĀRE and STĀRE were irregular in the Latin present tenses only because many of these forms were monosyllabic, and therefore received the stress on a vowel (their only vowel) which in other verbs was atonic (and belonged to the person/number marker). This characteristic was retained in Spanish, even after the regular Romance addition of /e/ to the initial group ST- of STĀRE:

DŌ > *do* > *doy*	DEM > *dé*
DĀS > *das*	DĒS > *des*
DAT > *da*	DET > *dé*
DĀMUS > *damos*	DĒMUS > *demos*
DĀTIS > *dades* > *dais*	DĒTIS > *dedes* > *deis*
DANT > *dan*	DENT > *den*
STŌ > *estó* > *estoy*	STEM > *esté*
STĀS > *estás*	STĒS > *estés*
STAT > *está*	STET > *esté*
STĀMUS > *estamos*	STĒMUS > *estemos*
STĀTIS > *estades* > *estáis*	STĒTIS > *estedes*> *estéis*
STANT > *están*	STENT > *estén*

The expansion *do* > *doy, estó* > *estoy* is discussed above under *ser*

Poder. The Latin verb POSSE showed most of the irregularities of ESSE, since it originated in a compound expression POTIS ESSE. However, this verb became regular in spoken Latin, no doubt because some of its forms were identical to those of regular -ĒRE verbs: pres. indic. POTES, perf. POTUĪ, POTUISTĪ, etc., pluperf. POTUERAM, future perf. indic. POTUERŌ, future perf. subj. POTUERIM. Judging by the later Romance paradigms, forms like *POTĒRE, *POTET, *POTĒMUS, etc., were rapidly created, whose Spanish descendants were indistinguishable, bearing in mind the expected diphthongization of Ŏ > /ue/ when the root was stressed, from those of verbs like *mover* (see 3.7.8.1.4(1)).

2 Spanish verbs with irregularities. Regular phonological change may lead to morphological irregularity, an effect which can also be brought about by analogy, which sometimes spreads an irregularity from one group of lexemes to other lexemes (see 3.7.1.2). This is true of the verbs which are now considered, all of which have regular present paradigms in Latin.

Haber. The Latin verb HABĒRE 'to have' acquired new auxiliary values in spoken Latin, where it served, in conjunction with the participle, as a marker of perfect aspect in transitive verbs (see 3.7.4.1), where it also became the prime means of forming the future, in conjunction with the infinitive (see 3.7.8.4.1).

Table 3.26 *The twofold evolution of the present indicative of* HABĒRE

	Lexical verb	Auxiliary verb
HABEŌ	*(he)e*	*(h)e*
HABĒS	*aves*	*(h)as*
HABET	*ave*	*(h)a*
HABĒMUS	*avemos*	*(h)emos*
HABĒTIS	*avedes*	*(h)edes*
HABENT	*aven*	*(h)an*

However, this verb did not at once lose its lexical value, and in most Romance areas never did. In Spain, its descendant, *aver*, was restricted to auxiliary use in the fifteenth century, as its lexical role was taken over by *tener*. The double value of *aver* is what explains its double form in Old Spanish: as a grammatical marker, HABĒRE enormously increased its frequency in Latin, which led to its dramatic phonological reduction, which consisted in the total loss of the root, while as a lexical verb it maintained its full form for some time. We must therefore distinguish two partly overlapping present-tense paradigms in Old Spanish (table 3.26).

The development HABEŌ > *(h)e* can only be explained as occurring in a partly proclitic form. After the change [bj] > /ǰ/ (see 3.7.8.1.1(1)), whence /áǰo/, the final /o/ can have been lost only when this form was used as an auxiliary before a participle or infinitive, a loss which is comparable to that which occurs in a number of frequent words under similar circumstances: *bueno* > *buen, malo* > *mal, uno* > *un*, when they precede a noun, etc. (see 2.4.3.2). As a lexical verb, HABEŌ would not be expected to undergo this apocope, so that the form *(h)e*, in this function represents a first example of confusion between the two paradigms, a confusion which gradually spreads to other forms of the paradigms.

In reality, apart from *avemos, avedes*, the full forms were infrequent in Old Spanish; that is, *ave, -s, -n* were increasingly replaced by *(h)a, -s, -n* as lexical verb forms. The long forms of the first and second persons plural continued to be used (with the shape *havemos, havéis*) until the Golden Age (although *havemos* was already in competition with *hemos*), when they were pushed out by *tenemos, tenéis*.

When this verb had auxiliary function, it was always the short forms that were used to form the future (see 3.7.8.4.1), although in the perfect (see 3.7.4.1) the full form *avedes* was used almost exclusively and *avemos* was very frequent, beside *(h)emos*. In Modern Spanish, the reflex of *avedes* (i.e. *habéis*) has become exclusive in the perfect, while *avemos/habemos* has become restricted to non-standard, especially rural, varieties.

The present subjunctive, HABEAM, HABEĀS, etc., has a single development (> *haya, hayas*, etc.), whether its value was lexical or auxiliary. The form *haiga* is discussed in 3.7.8.1.3(2, end).

For *hay* (< *ha* + *y* < HABET + IBĪ), see 3.7.8.1.5(1, *Ser*)

Ver. The Old Spanish result of the Latin paradigms of this verb is entirely regular, since, despite the loss of root-final -D- (2.5.3.2) and of /ǰ/ (from earlier [dj]) after a front vowel (2.5.2.2(4)), the boundary between root and ending is maintained, by means of the hiatus /ee/ or /ea/:

VIDEŌ > *veo*	VIDEAM > *vea*
VIDĒS > *vees*	VIDEĀS > *veas*
VIDET > *vee*	VIDEAT > *vea*
VIDĒMUS > *veemos*	VIDEĀMUS > *veamos*
VIDĒTIS > *veedes*	VIDEĀTIS > *veades*
VIDENT > *veen*	VIDEANT > *vean*

Later, this verb did not resist the reduction /ee/ > /e/ (unlike *leer, creer, poseer*, rather less frequent verbs which maintained the hiatus at the root/ending boundary), so that its present indicative paradigm (except for *veo*) became similar to that of *dar, estar, ir*, whose tonic vowel straddles the morpheme boundary.

Saber, caber. The development of SAPIŌ and CAPIŌ seems to be entirely regular (2.5.2.2(6)), except that there are few, if any, other words which show the sequence ['apj]. The preservation of the voiceless feature of /p/, in those cases where it was followed by a glide, and the vowel change ['ai̯] > /é/ (2.4.2.1) introduce an alternation which is new to Spanish, but limited to these verbs:

CAPIŌ > *quepo*	CAPIAM > *quepa*
CAPIS > *cabes*	CAPIĀS > *quepas*
CAPIT > *cabe*	CAPIAT > *quepa*
CAPIMUS > *cabemos*	CAPIĀMUS > *quepamos*
CAPITIS > *cabéis*	CAPIĀTIS > *quepáis*
CAPIUNT > *CAPENT > *caben*	CAPIANT > *quepan*

The same alternation is seen in *saber*, except that in this verb there was complete remodelling of the first person singular of the present indicative. The form *sé* must be due to an analogy, probably with *he* (< HABEŌ) (see 3.7.8.1.5 (2, under *Haber*)), since the verbs *saber* and *haber*, both highly frequent, share many morphological features (especially in their vowel structure), although they differ in their root consonant in Old Spanish (*saber* vs. *aver*).

Oír. From the regular Latin AUDIŌ, we find in Old Spanish a verb with double irregularity. Firstly, the appearance of root /ó/ is unprecedented in a verb of the -*ir* class (see 3.7.8.1.4(2)); secondly, this verb has extended root-final /ǰ/ from the first person singular (*oyo* < AUDIŌ) to the other present indicative forms

Table 3.27 *Development of the regular imperative*

	Singular	Plural
-ĀRE verbs	CANTĀ > *canta*	CANTĀTE > *cantad*
-ĒRE verbs	TĬMĒ > *teme*	TĬMĒTE > *temed*
-ĔRE verbs	VĒNDĔ > *vende*	VĒNDĬTE > *vended*
-ĪRE verbs	APERĪ > *abre*	APERĪTE > *abrid*

with tonic /ó/ in the root (*oyes, oye, oyen*), probably to reinforce the syllabic and morphological boundary: /óe/ > /óǰe/ (see 3.7.8.1.1(1)). The addition of /g/ (*oyo* > *oigo, oya* > *oiga,* etc.) is discussed in 3.7.8.1.3(2, end).

Hacer. Like other very frequent verbs, *hacer* undergoes little analogical restructuring (see 3.7.1.2). Therefore, phonological change has given it its irregular form (*hago/haga* vs. *haces/hacen*; see 3.7.8.1.3(1)). In Old Spanish, this verb showed even greater irregularity, since it was one of the few which preserved the accentual pattern typical of Latin verbs in -ĔRE (see 3.7.1.3.1, 3.7.7.1); in the thirteenth century one finds the forms *femos, feches* (< FÁCIMUS, FÁCITIS), later regularized (> *fazemos, fazedes*, then *hacemos, hacéis*) to conform with the predominant accentual pattern of the Spanish conjugation.

3.7.8.2 Imperative

The regular forms of the Latin imperative show the development in Spanish summarized in table 3.27.

It can be seen that the singular endings are reduced to two, by the merger of final -Ē, -Ĕ, and -Ī in /e/. In the case of the plural forms, see 3.7.1.3.1 for the accent-shift in VĒNDĬTE, etc., and 3.7.3.3 for the development of the endings. Root vowels (+ stress, -[j] in the singular; −stress -[j] in the plural) are discussed in 3.7.8.1.4(1) (*-ar* and *-er* verbs) and 3.7.8.1.4(2) (columns 2 and 4 in tables 3.24 and 3.25).

In the case of VĔNĪ > *ven*, the high final vowel engenders metaphony of the tonic, thus circumventing diphthongization. Because of the close structural resemblance between *venir* and *tener* (see also 3.7.8.1.4(2)), this metaphonic treatment is spread to *ten*, although such an outcome is not expected in a form ending in -Ē (TĔNĒ).

In Old Spanish *-er/-ir* verbs, when the root ended in a vowel (as in *creer, leer, seer, veer, traer*), the singular imperative ending was often /-i/: *crey, ley, sey, vey, tray*. These forms were later brought in line with the majority: *cree, lee, sé, ve, trae*.

Many singular imperatives were open to apocope of *-e* (see 2.4.3.2 and 3.7.1.4), and could therefore appear without ending in Old Spanish: *ix/ex* (imperative of *exir* 'to go out'), *promed* (MSp. *promete*). Only the most frequent verbs (and, among these, only those whose root ended in an ungrouped dental or alveolar) were resistant to the analogical reintroduction of final *-e*: MSp. *pon, ten, ven, sal, haz*.

The irregular Latin imperatives DĪC and FAC have been treated differently. Loss of final -C is predicted (cf. ILLĪC > *allí*), and this indeed occurs in DĪC > *di* (and in OSp. *adu* < ADDŪC). However, the form *haz* does not descend from FAC; its root has been remodelled on the pattern of regular verbs (although it does not acquire the *-e* of the majority).

The singular imperatives of ĪRE and ESSE did not survive in Spanish. Similarly to what happened in the present indicative and subjunctive (3.7.8.1.5(1, under *Ir*), the form Ī was replaced by the corresponding form of VADERE: VADĔ. By contrast with the present indicative, where VADIT was reduced analogically to *va*, VADĔ at first kept both vowels (**vai*), which were later regularly combined (/ái/ > /é/): *ve*. In the case of ESSE, as happened in the present subjunctive, ES was replaced by the corresponding form of SĒDĒRE, i.e. SĒDĒ, whence *sé*.

The plural imperative forms are regular without exception. We have noted (3.7.3.3) that until the Golden Age there was free alternation between forms with and without final *-d*, and that the latter have been preserved when a reflexive pronoun followed: *callaos*, etc. The only form which keeps *-d* under all circumstances is *id*: *idos*. Although /d/-less forms were preserved in American areas of *voseo* (3.5.1.1), Peninsular forms like *cantá* must have increasingly been felt to be informal variants of the *cantad* imperatives, as word-final /d/ acquired weaker and weaker realizations (including zero articulation) in recent centuries. Such a development would have ensured that *cantá* was excluded from careful (above all, written) styles, just as participles with zero realization of /d/ (*cantao*, etc.) are excluded from careful Spanish.

In the medieval and Golden Age periods, imperative *-d* could undergo metathesis with the initial consonant of a following clitic (*lo, nos*, etc.). Thus, in the *Poema de mio Cid* we find *dandos, tenendos, yndos* (= *dadnos, tenednos, idnos*), and in Classical Spanish combinations of the type *poneldo, dalde* (= *ponedlo, dadle*) are very frequent. No doubt this change occurred because in those periods internal syllable-final /d/ was very rare. This phonotactic 'rule' only changed upon the introduction of so many learned words like *adquirir, admirar*, etc.

Another type of mutual adaptation between imperative and pronoun is the assimilation noted in medieval forms like *avello, prendellas* (MSp. *tenedlo, tomadlas*).

3.7.8.3 The imperfect

The following sections discuss predominantly morphological aspects of the development of the imperfect. In 3.7.4, we examined the aspectual contrasts which distinguish the imperfect from other past tenses.

Table 3.28 *Development of the imperfect indicative of* -ar *verbs*

Latin	Old Spanish	Modern Spanish
CANTĀBAM	*cantava*	*cantaba*
CANTĀBĀS	*cantavas*	*cantabas*
CANTĀBAT	*cantava*	*cantaba*
CANTĀBĀMUS	*cantávamos*	*cantábamos*
CANTĀBĀTIS	*cantábades*	*cantabais*
CANTĀBANT	*cantavan*	*cantaban*

3.7.8.3.1 The imperfect indicative. The first-person-singular endings of the various Latin verb classes were:

-ĀRE verbs: -ĀBAM
-ĒRE verbs: -ĒBAM
-ĔRE verbs (CADŌ type): -ĒBAM
-ĔRE verbs (CAPIŌ type): -IĒBAM
-ĪRE verbs: -IĒBAM

However, in the last two classes -ĪBAM had also existed from archaic Latin onwards; this was the form which passed into Hispanic Latin and which underlies the imperfect forms of Peninsular Romance. Leftward accent-shift has to be borne in mind in the first and second persons plural: CANTĀBĀMUS, CANTĀBĀTIS > *cantábamos, cantabais* (see 3.7.1.3.3).

Latin intervocalic -B- is normally preserved in Spanish (e.g. HABĒRE > *aver* > *haber*, AVE > *ave*), and this regular development is seen in the imperfect of -ĀRE verbs (table 3.28).

By contrast, in other verb classes, -B- is lost, for reasons that are not totally clear. It is possible that the starting point for this loss was a dissimilation which happened in certain -ĒRE, -ĔRE and -ĪRE verbs, some of them highly frequent, whose root ended in -B- or -V- (which were pronounced identically in spoken Latin):

HABĒBAM > */aβéa/
DEBĒBAM > */deβéa/
BIBĒBAM > */beβéa/
VIVĒBAM > */βeβéa/
*SUBĪBAM > */suβía/

At all events, Spanish shows no trace of the -B- marker in the imperfect of *-er* and *-ir* verbs. As a separate matter, the endings of these classes merged into forms with tonic /í/, an outcome due to the regular development of the sequence /éa/ > /ía/ (cf. VĬA > spoken Latin /βéa/ > Sp. *vía*; (MĔA >) /méa/ > *mía*; 3.5.2).

Table 3.29 *Development of the imperfect indicative of* -er *and* -ir *verbs*

Latin	Old Spanish			Modern Spanish
DĒBĒBAM	*devía*			*debía*
DĒBĒBĀS	*devías*	*devíes*	*deviés*	*debías*
DĒBĒBAT	*devía*	*devíe*	*devié*	*debía*
DĒBĒBĀMUS	*devíamos*	*devíemos*	*deviémos*	*debíamos*
DĒBĒBĀTIS	*devíades*	*devíedes*	*deviédes*	*debíais*
DĒBĒBANT	*devían*	*devíen*	*devién*	*debían*
SUBĪBAM	*sobía*			*subía*
SUBĪBĀS	*sobías*	*sobíes*	*sobiés*	*subías*
SUBĪBAT	*sobía*	*sobíe*	*sobié*	*subía*
SUBĪBĀMUS	*sobíamos*	*sobíemos*	*sobiémos*	*subíamos*
SUBĪBĀTIS	*sobíades*	*sobíedes*	*sobiédes*	*subíais*
SUBĪBANT	*sobían*	*sobíen*	*sobién*	*subían*

In Old Spanish, the *-ía* endings competed (except in the first person singular) with endings in *-íe* (with occasional loss of *-e*: *fazí* 'hacía') and especially *-ié*. Malkiel (1959a) argues that the *-ié* forms (particularly frequent in the first and second persons plural: *vendiemos, vendiedes*) were transferred from the Old Spanish preterite (e.g. *vendiemos, vendiestes*; see 3.7.8.6.1(3)). Imperfects with /e/ appear already in the eleventh century and are the dominant forms in the twelfth and thirteenth centuries. They begin to decline in the fourteenth, but there are frequent examples in the fifteenth and some (e.g. in Santa Teresa) in the sixteenth century. The eventual preference for forms in /a/ is probably due to analogical pressure from the first person singular (which rarely showed *-ie*), and from the *-ar* verbs, where the imperfect always included an /a/ marker.

These changes are summarized in table 3.29.

With regard to root vowels, it is noteworthy that while *-er* verbs allow only /a/, /e/ or /o/ in the root, *-ir* verbs allow the full range of root vowels in Old Spanish. By consulting column 4 of tables 3.24 and 3.25 and the related commentary in 3.7.8.1.4(2), it will be seen that in a given Old Spanish *-ir* verb there was variation between /e/ and /i/ and between /o/ and /u/ in those forms which lacked root stress and which did not have a glide in the ending. As is mentioned there, this variation belonged as much to the imperfect as to the present tenses (*servía~sirvía~servíe~sirvíe*; *sobía~subía~sobíe~subíe*), and it is especially the case that the high root vowel was preferred when the ending was *-ié* (*sirvié, subié*). Later, root /e/ became standard in all verbs with a front root vowel (*servía, medía*), except in a few orally transmitted verbs (*escribía, recibía, vivía*), and in some learned verbs (*dirigía*, etc.), for the same reasons as in the present (namely, dissimilation /i/.../í/ > /e/.../í/, which was only ineffective when there was awareness that the Latin etymon of the verb concerned should be written with root I). In the case of *-ir* verbs with a back vowel in the root, /u/ became the norm (*subía, sufría, cubría*, etc.), with the same three exceptions as in the present (*dormía, moría, oía*), and for the same reasons as in that case (the need to distinguish *-ir* verbs from the *-er* class, from which high root vowels were totally excluded). The contrast with the *-er* verbs lies in the fact that the latter never show a high root vowel in Old (or Modern) Spanish (*devía~devíe, tenía~teníe, comía~comíe, molía~molíe*), not even before *-ié* (*devié, tenié, comié, molié*).

The verb HABĒRE, beside its regular imperfects (OSp. *avía~avíe, avié*, MSp. *había*) – previously used in the sense now expressed by *tenía*, and still used as the pluperfect auxiliary (*avía fecho*, etc.) – had a paradigm of reduced forms, used with auxiliary value, together with the infinitive, to form the conditional (see 3.7.8.4.2). As in the case of the reduced present forms (3.7.8.1.5(2), under *Haber*), the reduced imperfect forms result from the complete loss of the root, leaving only the ending: (HAB)ĒAS, (HAB)ĒAT, etc. > *ías, ía*, etc. In Old Spanish, these conditional endings showed the same variation as those of the imperfect (e.g. *cantarían~cantaríen~cantarién, conbidar le ien* (*PMC* 12), MSp. *le convidarían*), with the same later preference for the *-ía, -ías* forms.

The imperfect which descended from VĪDĒBAM had two forms in Old Spanish. On the one hand, following loss of -D-, the Ī of the root combined with the /í/ of the ending: VĪDĒBAM > **vidía* > *viía* > *vía/víe/vié*. On the other hand, at the **vidía* stage the familiar dissimilation /i/.../í/ > /e/.../í/ occurred: **vidía* > **vedía* > *veía/veíe/veié*. Eventually the standard language imposed the second type, *veía*, despite the fact that it matched less well with the other forms of this verb, which either always lacked a root vowel (*vi, viste, viera, viese, viere, visto*) or could allow its non-appearance and lost it definitively during the Middle Ages (*ves, ve, vemos, veis, ven, viendo*) (see 3.7.9.1).

The Latin imperfect of ĪRE (namely, ĪBAM, ĪBĀS, etc.) was irregular in the Classical language by having Ī(BAM) rather than IĒ(BAM), although it was regular with regard to archaic and regional Latin (which had AUDĪBAM, etc.). In Spanish, the irregularity of the descendant of ĪBAM (*iba*) lies in the preservation of -B-, which was lost from other *-er* and *-ir* verbs but kept in this verb alone, which, had it followed the rule, would have become dangerously short for effective communication.

The irregular imperfect of ESSE, Latin ĔRAM, preserved its irregular shape in Spanish, but did not undergo diphthongization of its tonic Ĕ, no doubt for the same reasons as those which prevented diphthongization in ĔST and ĔRIS (see 3.7.8.1.5(1), under *ser*), that is, because it was frequently used as an auxiliary, without full stress. Beside *era, eras*, etc., there existed in the Middle Ages the form *se(d)ía~se(d)íe*, etc., descended from SEDĒBAM, the imperfect of SEDĒRE 'to be seated', a verb which (in this paradigm as in others) overlapped in meaning with ESSE, especially in the locative sense now expressed by *estar* (e.g. *En Valençia seí mio Çid con todos sos vassallos*, *PMC* 2278).

3.7.8.3.2 The imperfect subjunctive

1 The imperfect subjunctive in *-se*. The Classical Latin imperfect subjunctive forms (CANTĀREM, DĒBĒREM, VĪVEREM, AUDĪREM) have scarcely any reflexes in the Romance languages. They were replaced by pluperfect subjunctive forms (CANTĀVISSEM, DĒBUISSEM, VĪXISSEM, AUDĪVISSEM) already in non-standard Latin. This replacement seems to have its origins in conditional sentences expressing improbability of fulfilment (e.g. 'If I could, I would do it (but I fear I won't be able to)'), where the temporal distance associated with the pluperfect appears to have enhanced the sense of improbability expressed by such clauses. In this way, Classical sentences of the type SĪ POSSET, ID FACERET 'If I could, I would do it', with imperfect subjunctives, were replaced by the type SĪ POTUISSET, ID FĒCISSET, which had previously only expressed impossibility of outcome ('If I had been able to, I would have done it'). Thereafter, the Romance descendants of SĪ POTUISSET, ID FĒCISSET expressed both notions, improbability and impossibility, although with a pluperfect indicative or a conditional in the apodosis: in Old Spanish, *si pudies(se), fiziéralo/ferlo ia* meant both 'If I could do it, I would' and 'If I had been able to, I would have done it'. Only towards the end of the Middle Ages were these two types of conditional sentences partially distinguished, with the introduction of the type *si hubiese podido, lo habría hecho* to express impossibility. (For the semantic and syntactical history of conditional sentences, see Harris 1971, 1986, Porcar Miralles 1993, Rojo and Montero 1983.)

With regard to the morphological development of -ĀRE verbs, we have seen (3.7.4.2) that CANTĀVISSEM, etc. (like other paradigms), had already lost the mark of perfectivity (-VI-) in Latin, and that there was a consequent contraction of the ending (CANTĀVISSEM > CANTĀSSEM). Bearing in mind the stress shift in the first and second persons plural (CANTĀSSĒMUS, CANTĀSSĒTIS > *cantássemos, cantássedes*) (see 3.7.1.3.3), and the occasional apocope of final /e/ in Old Spanish (see 3.7.1.4), the development of the Spanish imperfect subjunctive of *-ar* verbs can be summarized as in table 3.30.

There was also contraction in the case of -ĪRE verbs (SUBĪVISSEM > SUBĪSSEM), although the contracted form SUBĪSSEM, well attested in Latin, cannot explain the Spanish forms (*sobiesse*, later *subiese*). The /ie/ diphthong of these forms must come from the tonic Ĕ of the type *VENDĔSSEM (a form which arose through reduction, via haplology, of *VENDĔDISSEM, which in its turn came from Classical VENDIDISSEM, when this was remodelled on the pattern of

Table 3.30 *Development of the imperfect subjunctive of* -ar *verbs*

Classical Latin	Non-Classical Latin	Old Spanish	Modern Spanish
CANTĀVISSEM	CANTĀSSEM	*cantas(se)*	*cantase*
CANTĀVISSĒS	CANTĀSSĒS	*cantasses*	*cantases*
CANTĀVISSET	CANTĀSSET	*cantas(se)*	*cantase*
CANTĀVISSĒMUS	CANTĀSSĒMUS	*cantássemos*	*cantásemos*
CANTĀVISSĒTIS	CANTĀSSĒTIS	*cantássedes*	*cantaseis*
CANTĀVISSENT	CANTĀSSENT	*cantassen*	*cantasen*

DĔDISSEM, the imperfect subjunctive of DĀRE, with which VENDIDISSEM was in close derivational relationship). (For the role of the verb VENDERE in the development of the preterite and related paradigms, see 3.7.8.6.1(2–3)).

The endings of the regular *-er* verbs (e.g. *debiese, temiese*) must also have been taken from *VENDĔSSEM, since the standard Latin forms (DEBUISSEM, TIMUISSEM) cannot explain the /ie/ which characterizes their Spanish reflexes.

It should be remembered that the imperfect subjunctive paradigms descend from Latin paradigms (those of the pluperfect subjunctive) which shared their stem with the Latin perfect. The consequence is that those Old Spanish verbs which preserved or acquired an irregularity in their preterite (see 3.7.8.6.2) showed the same stem irregularity in the imperfect subjunctive. So, in the same way that the perfect of, for example, HABĒRE (e.g. HABUIMOS) became *ov(imos)/ov(iemos)*, so also HABUISSEM became *ov(iesse)*, and both paradigms maintain this identity of root down to the present (*hub(imos), hub(iese)*, etc.).

With regard to the root vowel of the imperfect subjunctive of regular *-er* verbs, it should be noted that the high vowels /i/ and /u/ are impermissible, just as they are in other *-er* paradigms. Only /a/, /e/ or /o/ may appear there (*saliese, temiese, comiese*). By contrast, the Old Spanish *-ir* verbs showed almost free variation between /e/ and /i/, on the one hand, and between /o/ and /u/ on the other: *sentiesse~sintiesse, serviesse~sirviesse, mediesse~midiesse; escopiesse~escupiesse, sobiesse~subiesse, foyesse~fuyesse, dormiesse~durmiesse*, etc. This variation was resolved in favour of the high vowel (*sintiese, subiese*, etc.) only at the end of the Middle Ages and in the early sixteenth century, at the same time as the parallel variation in the preterite and related paradigms was being resolved. The different treatment undergone by the root vowels of *-er* and *-ir* verbs, respectively, shows clearly that the eventual selection of high root vowels in *-ir* verbs (*sirviese, midiese, subiese, durmiese*, etc.) cannot have been determined phonologically (metaphony caused by [j] in the ending), since the element which allegedly caused this change (the glide [j])

Table 3.31 *Development of the* -ra *form of* -ar *verbs*

Classical Latin	Non-Classical Latin	Old Spanish	Modern Spanish
CANTĀVERAM	CANTĀRAM	*cantara*	*cantara*
CANTĀVERĀS	CANTĀRĀS	*cantaras*	*cantaras*
CANTĀVERAT	CANTĀRAT	*cantara*	*cantara*
CANTĀVERĀMUS	CANTĀRĀMUS	*cantáramos*	*cantáramos*
CANTĀVERĀTIS	CANTĀRĀTIS	*cantárades*	*cantarais*
CANTĀVERANT	CANTĀRANT	*cantaran*	*cantaran*

occurs in both the *-er* and *-ir* classes. As in other paradigms, the conclusion must be that the reason for preferring high root vowels in *-ir* verbs is the need to increase the morphological contrast between the two classes, a contrast which was otherwise maintained by only four endings (*traer, traemos, traéis, traed* vs. *salir, salimos, salís, salid*). See 3.7.8.1.4(2), end).

2 The imperfect subjunctive in *-ra.* The forms of the paradigm considered in 3.7.8.3.2(1) (*temiese, durmiese*, etc.) were the only Old Spanish forms with imperfect subjunctive value. The *-ra* forms which today share this value with the *-se* forms had other values in the medieval period, which we are about to examine.

The *-ra* forms descend from the Latin pluperfect indicative (CANTĀVERAM, DĒBUERAM, VĪXERAM, AUDĪVERAM), and the forms with the perfective marker -VE- underwent in Latin the same contraction as that suffered by other paradigms with this marker: CANTĀVERAM, AUDĪVERAM > CANTĀRAM, AUDĪRAM (see 3.7.4.2). The development of the *-ar* paradigm was exactly parallel to that of the *-se* imperfect subjunctive of the same class (see table 3.31).

The Spanish *-ir* paradigm (*durmiera, durmieras*, etc.) is not a reflex of the Latin contracted forms, since these could only provide such non-existent forms as ***durmira,* ***durmiras*, etc. To explain the /ie/ diphthong, we must refer once again to the effect of the verb VENDERE and other derivatives of DĀRE on the regular preterite and related tenses. The Classical pluperfect of VENDERE (VENDIDĔRAM), must have become *VENDĔDĔRAM, on the analogy of the corresponding paradigm (DĔDĔRAM) of its base verb DĀRE, and then (like DĔDĔRAM > *DĔRAM, whence *diera*) would have been reduced through haplology to *VENDĔRAM. The parallelism with *DĔRAM (< DĔDĔRAM) would have served to keep the stress on the Ĕ, which later diphthongized normally to /ie/: VENDIDĔRAM > *VENDĔDĔRAM > *VENDĔRAM > *vendiera*. The ending which thus originated in the group of verbs centred upon VENDERE served as the model for all -ĒRE, -ĔRE and -ĪRE verbs: *temiera, moliera, durmiera.*

We refer to 3.7.8.6.1 for the general effect of the verb VENDERE on the regular endings of the preterite and related paradigms, and to 3.7.8.6.2 for the irregular roots (*hubiera, dijera, hiciera*, etc.) shared by the preterite and the imperfect subjunctive.

With regard to the root vowels of the *-ra* forms, what has been said in 3.7.8.3.2(1) about the *-se* forms applies equally here: only *-ir* verbs allow variation /e/~/i/ and /o/~/u/ in Old Spanish (*serviera~sirviera, mediera~midiera, dormiera~durmiera, sobiera~subiera*, etc.), with imposition of the high vowel at the end of the Middle Ages and in the early sixteenth century (*sirviera, midiera, durmiera, subiera*). By contrast, and as usual, *-er* verbs never allowed high vowels in the root; we only find such forms as *temiera, debiera, moliera, comiera*. As in other paradigms (see 3.7.8.1.4(2), 3.7.8.3.2(1), 3.7.8.6.2, 3.7.8.4.3), this increasing contrast of root vowels served to distinguish more clearly the *-er* and *-ir* verb classes, which were threatened with merger because of the minimal contrast between their endings. Only in the case of irregular *-er* verbs may high vowels appear in the root (OSp. *presiera~prisiera, oviera~(h)uviera, sopiera~supiera*; see 3.7.8.6.2).

When we consider the semantic value of the *-ra* forms, we note gradual but profound changes: this paradigm has its origins in the Latin pluperfect indicative (1), later acquiring conditional value (2), and finally becoming an equivalent of the *-se* imperfect subjunctive (3). (See Wright 1932, Ridruejo 1982, Pountain 1983, Lapesa 2000: 845–56.)

1 The Latin pluperfect indicative value was frequently maintained in the Old Spanish *-ra* forms, in competition with the newer compound paradigms, created in spoken Latin (see 3.7.4.1). Thus *cantara* 'I had sung' was approximately equivalent in meaning to *avía/-ie cantado, ovo cantado* (e.g. *Fizo enbiar por la tienda que dexara allá* '... that he had left there', *PMC* 624; see Menéndez Pidal 1964b: 276–7, 356–7). Although pluperfect *cantara* was almost completely displaced by *había cantado* in the early Golden Age, the *-ra* forms have preserved down to the present a vestige of their former use, limited to relative clauses and only in literary registers; e.g. *la casa que construyera diez años antes* 'the house he had built...'.

2 There is good evidence that, already in late Latin, verbal forms in -RAM had acquired conditional sense. That is, we find them used in the apodosis of conditional sentences expressing improbability or impossibility of fulfilment: SĪ POTUISSET, ID FĒCERAT 'If I could, I would do it' or 'If I had been able to, I would have done it' (for more usual SĪ POTUISSET, ID FĒCISSET, see 3.7.8.3.2 (1)). This type of conditional sentence continued to be used in Spanish throughout the Middle Ages (e.g. *si ellos le viessen, non escapara* 'If they had seen him, he would not have escaped', *PMC* 2774), and still quite frequently in the Golden Age (alongside the then dominant type *si hubiese podido, lo habría hecho*). During the last five hundred years, the use of the *-ra* forms with conditional

or conditional perfect value has become less and less frequent, although it can be argued that present-day Spanish continues to assign this value to *-ra* forms, although only in the case of a handful of highly frequent verbs: *quisiera, debiera* and *hubiera*. These forms keep their equivalence to conditional forms (*querría, debería, habría*) and are indeed more frequent than the latter when used with modal sense, as was also true of *pudiera* (= *podría*) until the twentieth century.

3 It is only towards the end of the Middle Ages that we find cases of *-ra* forms with imperfect subjunctive value. Once again, the origins of this change are to be found in conditional sentences expressing improbability or impossibility. We have just seen that a frequent Old Spanish sentence-type to express these meanings was *si ellos le viessen, non escapara* (i.e. the type *si pudiesse, fiziéralo*). However, beginning in the fourteenth century, we come across examples of a new type, with a *-ra* form in both protasis and apodosis (*si pudiera, fiziéralo*), a type which possibly owes its origins to a universal tendency to give similar forms to the two verbs in conditional sentences, a tendency clearly visible in Latin (see examples in 3.7.8.3.2(1)). In the Golden Age, this is the preferred type for expressing conditions whose fulfilment is improbable or impossible, although it coexisted with other types (those with an *-se* form in the protasis, those with an *-ía* form in the apodosis: *si pudiese/pudiera, lo hiciera/haría*, etc., as well as compound forms, which were beginning to be used more systematically to distinguish impossible conditions from improbable ones: *si hubiese/hubiera podido, lo habría/hubiera hecho*). For the first time, although only in these conditional sentences, the *-ra* forms had become equivalent to the *-se* forms, and it can be concluded that the *-ra* paradigm had acquired imperfect subjunctive value. But this equivalence between *-ra* and *-se* forms took centuries to be accepted in other types of sentences. For example, in the Golden Age, the *-ra* form is not found in final clauses, where *-se* is exclusive (e.g. *para que lo supiese/**supiera*), and total interchangeability of the two paradigms is only achieved in the nineteenth century. Now the tables have been turned, and many Spanish speakers, especially those in Spanish America, scarcely use the *-se* forms, which are becoming increasingly restricted to written varieties of the language.

3.7.8.4 The future and the conditional

Since the historical morphology and syntax of the future and of the conditional have much in common, we discuss in 3.7.8.4.1 those features which belong exclusively to the future paradigms, and in 3.7.8.4.2 those which are specific to the conditional. Those matters which pertain to both paradigms are postponed until 3.7.8.4.3.

3.7.8.4.1 Origins of the future indicative. The Latin future forms (CANTĀBŌ, TIMĒBŌ, VENDAM, AUDIAM) have no descendants in any Romance language; they were replaced by new constructions in spoken Latin. A series of reasons for this loss are habitually cited, the most important of which are:

1 The lack of formal similarity between -ĀBŌ, -ĒBŌ, on the one hand, and -IAM, -AM, on the other.
2 In the first person singular, -IAM, -AM, functioned as a marker of both future and present subjunctive.
3 In the -ĀRE conjugation, the futures CANTĀBIT and CANTĀBIMUS could be confused with the corresponding perfect forms (CANTĀVIT and CANTĀVIMUS), following the regular merger of intervocalic -B- and -V-. Nevertheless, it is possible that this confusion never arose, since the contraction of the perfects (CANTĀVĪ> CANTĀĪ; see 3.7.8.6.1(1)) may have occurred before the merger of -B and -V.
4 Following the merger in /e/ of Ĕ, Ē and Ĭ in final syllables (2.4.3.2), it was impossible to distinguish in speech the highly frequent third-person-singular forms of the future (VENDĔT) and present (VENDĬT) in the -ĔRE conjugation.

None of these considerations is crucial for CANTĀBŌ, etc., but it should be noted that many languages lack specifically future forms, and also that those languages that do have them often avoid them, using present-tense forms to include future time, with or without adverbs to clarify the future reference. It is clear that spoken Latin could function perfectly well without paradigms devoted to the expression of future time.

Nevertheless, for special purposes, Latin speakers could make use of other constructions, originally without future reference, to emphasize that the situation concerned did not belong to the present. Among these constructions, some of which, in various parts of the Romance-speaking world, became regular future paradigms, were the following:

1 EŌ 'I go' [or an equivalent] (± preposition) + infinitive: *VADO (AD) CANTĀRE. This construction, used by all Romance languages, never became regular in any of them, although in many varieties of Modern Spanish the type *voy a hacerlo* is in the process of replacing *lo haré*.
2 VENIŌ 'I come' (± preposition) + infinitive: *VENIŌ (AD) CANTĀRE.
3 VOLŌ 'I wish' + infinitive: VOLŌ CANTĀRE. This type provided the regular Romanian future (*vóiu cînta*).
4 DĒBEŌ 'I owe, I must' + infinitive: DĒBEŌ CANTĀRE. This construction accounts for the Sardinian future forms (*deppo cantare*).
5 HABEŌ 'I have' (± preposition) + infinitive: HABEŌ (DE/AD) CANTĀRE/ CANTĀRE HABEŌ. These structures are the ones which enjoyed greatest success, and provided the basis of the future forms of French, Occitan, Rhaeto-Romance, Italian, Catalan, Spanish, and Portuguese.

With the order infinitive + auxiliary (CANTĀRE HABEŌ), the last of these constructions accounts for the Spanish future. In this structure, HABEŌ rarely kept its most basic sense ('I possess'), but gave the clause a nuance of 'intention'

Table 3.32 *Development of the future indicative*

Classical Latin	Spoken Latin	Old Spanish	Modern Spanish
CANTĀBŌ	CANTĀRE HABEŌ	*cantar (h)e/cantaré*	*cantaré*
CANTĀBIS	CANTĀRE HABĒS	*cantar (h)as/cantarás*	*cantarás*
CANTĀBIT	CANTĀRE HABET	*cantar (h)a/cantará*	*cantará*
CANTĀBIMUS	CANTĀRE HABĒMUS	*cantar (h)emos/cantaremos*	*cantaremos*
CANTĀBITIS	CANTĀRE HABĒTIS	*cantar (h)edes/cantaredes*	*cantaréis*
CANTĀBUNT	CANTĀRE HABENT	*cantar (h)an/cantarán*	*cantarán*

('I intend to sing'), then of obligation ('I must sing'), and finally (since intentions and obligations are necessarily directed towards the future) a notion of simple futurity ('I shall sing'). These successive meanings can be seen in written Latin. Cicero (first century BC) expresses intention (with some trace of the idea of possession) when he writes: DĒ RĒ PUBLICĀ NIHIL *HABEŌ* AD TE *SCRĪBERE* ('I have nothing to tell you about politics', = 'I don't propose to say anything about politics'?). If Seneca (first century AD) could express obligation, in the past, by asking QUID *HABUĪ FACERE?* ('What should I have done?'), this implies the possibility of a question *QUID *HABEŌ FACERE?*, with the meaning 'What must I do?'. When it can be seen that this construction is being used with impersonal grammatical subjects, it becomes clear that the notions of possession, intention or obligation are absent, since they are only compatible with human subjects. Thus, when St Augustine (fourth to fifth centuries AD) writes TEMPESTĀS ILLA *TOLLERE HABET* TŌTAM PALEAM DE ĀREA, with an inanimate subject, there is no other way of interpreting this construction than as a future ('the storm will carry away all the straw from the threshing-floor'). We also note that the order of the elements is beginning to be fixed as infinitive + auxiliary.

We have seen (3.7.8.1.5(2), under *Haber*) that HABEŌ underwent radical shortening when it had auxiliary function (as is the case in this construction). In principle, each member of the paradigm was reduced to its tonic vowel, followed by the appropriate person/number marker. Anticipating what will be said in 3.7.8.4.3(1) about the unmarked nature of the order infinitive + auxiliary, we can summarize the development of the Spanish future forms in table 3.32.

The use of the various medieval forms (*cantar (h)e* vs *cantaré*) will be discussed in 3.7.8.4.3(2).

For the future perfect indicative (HABĒRE HABEŌ CANTĀTUM > *avré cantado* > *habré cantado*, etc.), see 3.7.4.1.

3.7.8.4.2 Origins of the conditional. The conditional paradigm (*cantaría*, etc.) today has two principal functions. Firstly, it is used in the apodosis of conditional sentences which express improbable or impossible fulfilment (*Si viniera esta noche, se lo daría* 'If he were to come tonight, I would give it to him'; *Si fuera rico, me lo compraría* 'If I were rich, I would buy it'). Secondly, it belongs to subordinate clauses of sentences in indirect speech, where the *verbum dicendi* is in a past tense (*Me comunicó que no iría ese día a casa* 'He informed me that he would not go home that day'; *Me preguntó si iría allí al día siguiente* 'He asked me if I would go there the next day'). In the first case, Latin used the imperfect or pluperfect subjunctive (see 3.7.8.3.2(1)), later the pluperfect indicative (3.7.8.3.2(2)), and it was only in the Middle Ages that the conditional began to be used in these circumstances. It was probably in indirect speech that the conditional paradigm was created.

To convey indirect speech, Classical Latin used the 'accusative + infinitive' construction. For example, when the *verbum dicendi* was in the present:

(1)	CRĒDŌ	EUM	VĒNTŪRUM	ESSE
	think+pres.indic+1 sing.	*him*+acc.	*come*+fut.+acc.	*be*+infin.
	'I think he will come'			

The same subordinate construction was used when the main verb was in a past tense:

(2)	CRĒDĒBAM	EUM	VĒNTŪRUM	ESSE
	think+imperf.indic.+1sing.	*him*+acc	*come*+fut.+acc.	*be* +infin.
	'I thought he would come'			

In spoken Latin, sentence-type (1) began to be replaced by constructions with a finite subordinate verb, a future form following the conjunction QUOD. In those Latin-speaking regions, including Spain, where the future was expressed by an infinitive + HABEŌ (see 3.7.8.4.1), the new indirect speech construction was as in (3):

(3)	CRĒDŌ	QUOD	VĒNĪRE	HABET
	think+pres.indic.+1sing.	subord.	*come*+infin.	*have*+pres.
	'I think he will come'			indic.+3sing.

As a result of the Latin sequence-of-tenses rule, whenever the main verb was in a past tense the subordinate verb took the same past form. Thus:

(4)	CRĒDĒBAM	QUOD	VĒNĪRE	HABĒBAT
	think+imperf.indic.+1sing	subord.	*come*+infin.	*have*+imperf.
	'I thought he would come'			indic.+3sing.

In principle, if the main verb was preterite (the Latin perfect), the subordinate verb also took preterite form:

Table 3.33 *Development of the conditional*

Spoken Latin	Old Spanish	Modern Spanish
CANTĀRE HABĒBAM	*cantar (h)ía* *cantaría*	*cantaría*
CANTĀRE HABĒBĀS	*cantar (h)ías/yes* *cantarías/-ies*	*cantarías*
CANTĀRE HABĒBAT	*cantar (h)ía/ye* *cantaría/-ie*	*cantaría*
CANTĀRE HABĒBĀMUS	*cantar (h)íamos/yemos* *cantaríamos/-iemos*	*cantaríamos*
CANTĀRE HABĒBĀTIS	*cantar (h)íades/yedes* *cantaríades/-iedes*	*cantaríais*
CANTĀRE HABĒBANT	*cantar (h)ían/yen* *cantarían/-ien*	*cantarían*

(5) CRĒDIDĪ QUOD VĒNĪRE HABUIT
think+pret.+1sing. subord. *come*+infin. *have*+pret.+3sing.
'It struck me that he would come'

However, this contrast between preterite and imperfect subordinate verbs was lost in Romance and in each area either VENĪRE HABĒBAT or VENĪRE HABUIT was selected whenever the main verb was in any past tense. VENĪRE HABUIT was chosen in parts of Italy (e.g. standard Italian *verrebbe*), but in the Peninsula it was VENĪRE HABĒBAT that was chosen in all such cases: *(Yo) creí/creía que (él) vendría.*

The development of the conditional paradigm can be summarized as in table 3.33.

In the development of this paradigm, the evolution of the auxiliary HABĒBAM (for which see 3.7.8.3.1) showed the same kind of contraction as HABEŌ underwent in the future; that is, forms were reduced to the tonic vowel, followed by the person/number ending. It should also be borne in mind that the conditional endings, being descendants of the imperfect indicative of HABĒRE, in the Middle Ages showed the same variation as other *-er* and *-ir* imperfects, namely between /ía/, /íe/, /í/ and /ié/ (see 3.7.8.3.1). (Forms with /í/ (e.g. *cantarí*) are omitted from table 3.33, because of their infrequency.) Furthermore, the Old Spanish conditionals could either be analytic, with insertion of a pronoun (*cantarlo (h)ía*) or synthetic (*cantaría*) (see 3.7.8.4.3(2)).

For the conditional perfect (HABĒRE HABĒBAM CANTĀTUM > *avría cantado* > *habría cantado*, etc.), see 3.7.4.1.

3.7.8.4.3 Morphology and syntax of the Old Spanish future and conditional. In the following four sections we discuss those matters which concern the morphology of the future/conditional root (the morphology of the endings is dealt with in 3.7.8.4.1–2), and the relation between the components of these compound forms.

1 Order of components. We have seen that in Latin the order of the components of the new future was not fixed (and we can assume that the same was true of the conditional). The auxiliary HABĒRE may precede or follow its infinitive, although a certain preference for postposition can be deduced, a perception that is confirmed by the near-unanimity of the Romance languages on this matter. However, there are relics in Old Spanish of the preposed auxiliary (*hemos cantar*).

The Latin HABEŌ + infinitive structure also allowed the insertion of a preposition (see 3.7.8.4.1(5)). A descendant of this possibility is *he de cantar*, which has modal sense very close to that of the future, although sometimes retaining the notion of 'intention' which we have seen was an intermediate stage in the semantic development of the more typical variant of this structure (i.e. infinitive + HABEŌ).

2 Analytic and synthetic forms. The medieval future and conditional forms were frequently written as single words (and had, we conclude, a single stress, on the auxiliary): *cantaré, veremos, andaríamos, tañeríades, comeríen*, etc. However, the possibility of separating the two elements (with double stress, on infinitive and auxiliary) persisted until the early seventeenth century. This separation occurred when one or more atonic pronouns accompanied the verb: *enpeñar gelo he; pedir vos a poco; mereçer no'lo hedes* (= *nos lo*); *auer la yemos nos* (= MSp. *la tendríamos nosotros*); *buscar nos ye el rey* (= MSp. *nos buscaría el rey*); etc. (examples taken from the *PMC* 92, 133, 197, 2663, 528). This analytic form of the future and conditional was not only frequent in the Middle Ages, but was obligatory when the verb headed its clause or was preceded by certain atonic words (*e, mas*). When the verb followed a tonic word belonging to the same clause, the pronoun(s) preceded the verb, which therefore adopted synthetic form: *non nos osariemos; que nos ayudarán; quel buscarie mal; dellos nos serviremos* (*PMC* 44, 640, 509, 622).

By the sixteenth century, the large majority of future and conditional forms were synthetic, even though an atonic pronoun was still prohibited from appearing in clause-initial position. In that period, and much later, we find sentences like *harélo mañana* (but *mañana lo haré*), *daríaselo a su hermano*, etc. The last examples of synthetic forms are seen in the seventeenth century, when they appear, albeit infrequently, in texts like *Don Quijote*.

It should be emphasized that some scholars claim a semantic and pragmatic opposition between the analytic and synthetic forms. See, for example, Company Company and Medina Urrea (1999).

3 Syncope of synthetic forms. It has been seen in 3.7.8.4.3(2) that synthetic future and conditional forms had a single stress, which fell on the auxiliary. This implies that the theme vowel of the infinitive (_cantaré, deberé, sentiré_) had become atonic and was now in pretonic position, a circumstance which may lead to elimination, or syncope, of the vowel (see 2.4.3.3). Since the low vowel /a/ is exempt from this loss, the stress-pattern of synthetic forms has no consequences for _-ar_ verbs. However, the infinitival /e/ and /i/ of _-er_ and _-ir_ verbs were subject to syncope in Old Spanish, when the preceding consonant allowed this loss (the following consonant, always /ɾ/, favours syncope). Only when the theme vowel is in hiatus with the root vowel (e.g. _oiré, fuiré, caeré, traeré_) is such syncope impossible; in other cases, the theme vowel could be eliminated, with or without modification of the preceding consonant.

The simplest and most frequent cases of Old Spanish syncope were those in which the new consonant group was identical to an already existing group. So, in the future of _poder_, the group /dɾ/ which results from syncope of /e/ (_*poderá > podrá_) posed no articulatory problems, since /dɾ/ appeared in many long-established Spanish words (_padre, madre_, etc.). In other cases, it was necessary to modify the group resulting from the syncope, either by strengthening the /ɾ/ that followed the lost vowel (_salirá > salrrá_, etc.), or by a more fundamental adaptation, such as the epenthesis of a transitional consonant (_comerá > combrá_), metathesis of the two consonants (_*ponerá > porná_), total or partial assimilation of the first consonant (_*dezirá > dirá, *ponerá > porrá_). (See 2.5.5 for these processes.)

In table 3.34 are presented typical cases of syncopated futures and conditionals, together with the analytic form of each verb, the latter exemplified with an intercalated pronoun.

We have seen that verbs whose root ended in a vowel were not open to syncope, so that the normal futures and conditionals of verbs like _caer, oír, roer, traer_, etc., were _caeré, oirien, roerán, traeriemos_, etc. However, in earlier Old Spanish texts we find forms like _cadrán, odredes, rodré_, where we can hypothesize that a Romance /d/, descended from Latin -D- (CADERE > _*cader_, AUDĪRE > _*odir_, RODERE > _*roder_), was preserved long enough to allow syncope (_*caderá > cadrá, *odirá > odrá, *roderá > rodrá_), despite being regularly lost in the infinitive (_*cader > caer, *odir > oír, *roder > roer_) (see 2.5.3.2(4)).

An apparent exception to what has just been said is seen in the verbs _creer, seer, veer_ (< CREDERE, SEDĒRE, VIDĒRE), which never appear in Old Spanish with futures and conditionals in /dɾ/. When Romance /d/ (< -D-) was between

Table 3.34 *Syncopated future and conditional forms of Old Spanish*

Consonants brought into contact	Result	Adaptive process	Syncopated form	Analytic form
/b/.../ɾ/	/bɾ/	(none)	*cabrá*	*caberme a*
			concibrán	*concebirlo an*
			recibré	*recebirlo e*
			sabríades	*saberlo yedes*
/β/.../ɾ/	/βɾ/	(none)	*avrién*	*averlo yen*
			bevremos	*beverlo emos*
			bivríades	*biviríades*
			movrá	*moverlo ha*
/m/.../ɾ/	/mbɾ/	epenthesis	*combré*	*comerlo he*
(cons)/t/.../ɾ/	(cons)/tɾ/	(none)	*consintrá*	*consentirmelo a*
			mintrién	*mentirme yen*
			partrié	*partirlo ie*
			repintrían	*repentirse ian*
			vistrá	*vestirse a*
(cons)/d/.../ɾ/	(cons)/dɾ/	(none)	*ardrá*	*arderá*
			comidrán	*comedirlo han*
			enadrán	*enadirlo an*
			perdrás	*perderlo as*
			pidrá	*pedirmelo a*
			podriedes	
			prendrás	*prenderlo as*
(cons)/t^{s}/.../ɾ/	(cons)/t^{s}ɾ/	(none)	*creçremos*	*creçerle hemos...*
			pareçrá	*pareçerle a*
			vençrán	*vençerlos han*
	/t^{s}tɾ/	epenthesis	*falleztrá*	*falleçerme a*
			conoztrán	*conosçerlos an*
/d^{z}/.../ɾ/	/d^{z}ɾ/	(none)	*luzrá*	*luzirme a*
			yazredes	
	/ɾ/	assimilation	*adurá*	*aduzirlo a*
			diriades	*dezirlo iades*
	/d^{z}dɾ/	epenthesis	*yazdrá*	
/n/.../ɾ/	/nr/	reinforcement	*venr(r)án*	*venirnos han*
	/ɾn/	metathesis	*terné*	*tenerlo he*
			vernie	*venirle ie*
	/ndɾ/	epenthesis	*remandrán*	*remanirnos han*
			tendrá	*tenerlo a*
	/r/	assimilation	*porrá*	*ponerlo a*
			verrán	*venirle han*
/l/.../ɾ/	/lr/	reinforcement	*salrrá*	*salirá*
			valrá	*valerle ha*
	/ldɾ/	epenthesis	*doldrié*	*dolerle ie*
			moldrié	*molerlo ie*
			saldredes	
			valdrá	*valerle ha*

Table 3.34 (*cont.*)

Consonants brought into contact	Result	Adaptive process	Syncopated form	Analytic form
/ɾ/.../ɾ/	/r/	(none?)	*conquerrá*	*conquerirlos a*
			ferredes	*ferirlos edes*
			morremos	*morirnos emos*
			parrá	*parirlo ha*
			querrá	*quererle a*
/ʎ/.../ɾ/	/ldɾ/	epenthesis	*faldrá*	*fallirme a*
			toldrié	*tollerlo ie*
/g/.../ɾ/	/gɾ/	(none)	*consigrá*	*conseguirlo a*

identical vowels (*creder,* **seder,* **veder*), we can conclude that it was lost earlier than when it separated unlike vowels, so that syncope of the kind **crederé* > ***credré* was impossible. On the contrary, following loss of /d/ the sequence /ee/ was contracted to /e/ in the synthetic future and conditional forms of these verbs (*crerán, seré, veriedes*, etc.), by contrast with what happened when the accent fell on the second /e/, as occurred in the analytic future, and in the infinitive (see 3.7.9.1). In the latter case, Old Spanish shows both outcomes, contraction (*verlo an*) or retention of the hiatus (*veerlo han*, etc.).

The future and conditional of the verb *fazer* (that is, *feré, feremos, farán, faria, ferie*, etc.), is formed upon the infinitives *fer* or *far*, rather than upon an assimilated form of *fazer* (see 3.7.9.1). This can be deduced from the analytic futures and conditionals of this verb, which in the earliest Spanish texts take the form *fer lo han, far melo ien*, etc., and never ***fazer lo han*, etc.

Despite the frequency of syncopated futures in Old Spanish, they were never the only forms in use; unsyncopated forms are fairly frequent, especially in verbs where the root ended in a consonant group: *perderá, partirá, prenderá, vestirá* (Schede 1987: 535, 546, 573, 753). Few syncopated forms survived beyond the sixteenth century; from then onwards, we find them only in the case of the most frequent verbs (*habrá, sabrá*, which carries *cabrá* in its wake; *querrá; pondrá, tendrá, vendrá, saldrá, valdrá; dirá*), although there was still some hesitation in the Golden Age between the syncopated and full forms of one or two further verbs (e.g. *devrá*~*deverá*, now *deberá*). Of the Old Spanish forms *fará* and *ferá*, the first was selected, now *hará*. The reason for the loss of so many syncopated futures is twofold analogical pressure: on the one hand, the *-ar* futures were never syncopated and therefore provided a model in which the full infinitive was clearly audible (*cantar : cantará :: comer : x; x* = *comeré*, a form which displaces *combré*); on the other hand, all syncopated forms coexisted with full forms, that is with analytic futures (*luego lo combré* = *comerlo e luego*), which also helped to impose the unsyncopated model on syncopated forms.

For further details of Old Spanish future and conditional morphology, see Saralegui (1983), Schede (1989).

4 Root vowels. As in other paradigms (see 3.7.1.5, 3.7.8.1.4(2), 3.7.8.3.2, 3.7.8.6.1(2), 3.7.9.2), a certain polarization of root vowels was established in Old Spanish between *-er* futures and those of *-ir* verbs. Since the infinitives of *-er* verbs did not allow root /i/ or /u/, these vowels could not occur in the root of future and conditional forms of these verbs; there was no root-vowel variation in *bevrá*~*beverá, comeré*~*combré*, etc. By contrast, in *-ir* verbs not only were the high vowels /i/ and /u/ allowed in atonic roots (beside /e/ and /o/: *servir*~*sirvir, complir*~*cumplir*), but the mid vowels were excluded from tonic roots (*sirvo, cumplo*, never ***servo,* ***complo*).

As an extension of this contrast between the two conjugations, and as in other cases where a conjugation marker was lacking from the ending (that is, in forms other than *servir, servimos, servides, servid, complir, complimos, complides, complid*, where /í/ marks verbal class), there was a strong Old Spanish tendency to prefer /i/ and /u/ in the atonic roots of *-ir* verbs. We shall see (or have seen) that *sirvió, sirvieron, sirviera, sirviese, cumplió, cumplieron, cumpliera, cumpliese*, etc., were much more frequent than *servió, servieron, serviera, serviese, complió, complieron, compliera, compliese*, etc., and that *sirvía, sirvido, cumplía, cumplido*, etc., coexisted with *servía, servido, complía, complido*, etc. This tendency towards high root vowels became the norm, in the case of /u/, in the fifteenth and sixteenth centuries, and in the case of /i/ it was thwarted, in the majority of relevant verbs, only in those forms which had tonic /í/, as a result of dissimilation /i/. . . /í/ > /e/. . . /í/ (*servir, servimos, servía, servido*, etc.).

This same polarizing tendency can be seen in the roots of Old Spanish syncopated futures and conditionals (that is, in those forms in which the conjugation-identifying vowel was absent), even when the ending contained tonic /í/ (as frequently happened in conditionals). Thus, on the one hand, /i/ and /u/ could not occur in the root of *-er* verbs (as was predictable), and, on the other, a high vowel was obligatory in the large majority of *-ir* verbs: *adurá, bivrá, bivría, comidrán, concibrán, consigrá, consintrá, dirá, mintrién, pidrá, pidría, recibré, repintrían, vistrá; recudrá* (never ***bevrá* (this form functioned only as the future of *bever*), ***comedrán*, ***recodrá*, etc.). Only in very few *-ir* verbs were /e/ or /o/ permitted in the root of syncopated futures and conditionals: *conquerrá, ferrá, morrá, verrá*~*verná*~*vendrá*. It can be seen at once that this exception, in most cases (*conquerrá, ferrá, morrá, verrá*), has phonological causes: the well-known lowering effect of /r/ upon preceding vowels. In the case of *venir*, the forms with /e/ must be placed alongside *vengamos, vengades*, which are

Table 3.35 *Development of the future subjunctive of* -ar *verbs*

Classical Latin	Latin of Spain	Old Spanish	Modern Spanish
CANTĀVERŌ CANTĀVERIM	CANTĀRŌ, -RIM	*cantaro, -r(e)*	*cantare*
CANTĀVERIS CANTĀVERĪS	CANTĀRIS	*cantares*	*cantares*
CANTĀVERIT	CANTĀRIT	*cantar(e)*	*cantare*
CANTĀVERIMUS CANTĀVERĪMUS	CANTÁRIMUS	*cantáremos*	*cantáremos*
CANTĀVERITIS CANTĀVERĪTIS	CANTÁRITIS	*cantár(e)des*	*cantareis*
CANTĀVERINT	CANTĀRINT	*cantaren*	*cantaren*

also exceptional in having root /e/ (see 3.7.8.1.4(2)). In both cases, the probable reason for the appearance of /e/ is the mutual influence between this verb and *tener*, an influence frequently seen in the morphology of these two verbs.

3.7.8.4.4 The future subjunctive. As we saw in 3.7.4.2, the Latin of Spain saw the creation of a future subjunctive (and later a future perfect subjunctive), which had no equivalent in Classical Latin, but which developed from Latin paradigms with other values. These paradigms were the future perfect indicative (CANTĀVERŌ) and the perfect subjunctive (CANTĀVERIM). In both cases, as happened in the majority of the Latin perfective paradigms, the values expressed in Latin by these forms came to be expressed by new compound forms (respectively, HABĒRE HABEŌ CANTĀTUM and HABEAM CANTĀTUM, whence *habré cantado* and *haya cantado*) (see 3.7.4.1–3).

The paradigms CANTĀVERŌ and CANTĀVERIM, abbreviated to CANTĀRŌ and CANTĀRIM in the way examined in 3.7.4.2, differed morphologically only in the first person singular (-ĀRŌ vs. -ĀRIM), in the second person singular (-ĀRIS vs. -ĀRĪS, a contrast eliminated by the regular development of final vowels), and in the accentuation of the first and second persons plural (-ÁRIMUS, -ÁRITIS vs. -ARÍMUS, -ARÍTIS, a difference which disappeared when speakers adopted the system of always stressing the theme vowel, here -ÁRIMUS, -ÁRITIS, in such cases; see 3.7.1.3.3). Consequently, the two paradigms were reduced to one in Old Spanish, with the occasional survival, in the first person singular, of *-ro* (*cantaro*), beside *-re* (*cantare*), or *-r*, if we take account of apocope of *-e* (see 3.7.1.4).

The development of the future subjunctive of *-ar* verbs can be seen in table 3.35.

The corresponding paradigms of Latin -ĪRE verbs also underwent contraction, but the resulting forms (AUDĪRŌ, AUDĪRIM) cannot, because of their Ī, explain the diphthong of the Spanish endings (*oyer(e)*, etc.). As in the case of the imperfect subjunctive in *-se* (see 3.7.8.3.2(1)) and in *-ra* (see 3.7.8.3.2(2)), and the preterite (3.7.8.6.1), the influence of the verb VENDERE and related verbs was decisive. The relevant paradigm of VENDERE (VENDIDERŌ/-ERIM) was restructured as *VENDĔDERŌ/-ERIM on the model of DĔDERŌ/-ERIM, and then reduced to *VENDĔRŌ/-ĔRIM through haplology. This form accounts for the endings of *-er* verbs, which adapted to the *vender* model, and of *-ir* verbs, whose endings were remodelled, as in other cases, on the *-er* verbs.

It should also be noted that the verbs which in Old Spanish have some kind of strong preterite (see 3.7.8.6.2(1–4)) appear with the same root in the future subjunctive, a root shared also with the imperfect subjunctive in *-se* and in *-ra*, because all these paradigms descend from Latin paradigms formed from the Latin 'perfect' stem. Thus, for example, *ovier(e)* shows the same root as *ove, oviesse* and *oviera*.

What will be said about the behaviour of the root vowels of regular *-er* and *-ir* preterites (3.7.8.6.1(2–3)) and of irregular preterites (3.7.8.6.2) applies *pari passu* to the development of the root vowels of the future subjunctive.

Despite the long survival of the Spanish future subjunctive, this paradigm had scarcely any exclusive functions. It was used in 'open' conditional clauses (those that express neutral probability as to whether the condition will be satisfied): *si assí lo* ***fiziéredes****, mando a vuestro altar buenas donas* (*PMC* 223), *si* ***vençiéremos*** *la batalla, creçremos en rictad* (*PMC* 687). However, under these circumstances a present indicative could also appear: *si non das consejo, a Teca e a Ter[rer] perderás* (*PMC* 632).

The future subjunctive also appeared in temporal clauses which referred to the future (*mientra que* ***visquiéredes****, bien se fará lo to* (*PMC* 409)), although such clauses could alternatively contain a present subjunctive (*ante que anochesca, pienssan de cavalgar* (*PMC* 432)), or a future indicative (*quando los gallos cantarán* (*PMC* 316)).

Perhaps the most important use of the future subjunctive was in relative clauses which had an indefinite antecedent and which were oriented towards the future: *el que assí lo* ***fizier***. This use, which is highly frequent in legal texts to convey hypothetical future situations, was the one that persisted longest in Spanish and is still occasionally found, in certain highly restricted legal registers. In other registers, this use of the future subjunctive has been replaced by that of the present subjunctive (*el que no* ***prestare*** *atención a la ley* > *el que no preste atención a la ley*). The same is happening in the few set phrases like *sea lo que* ***fuere***, which are increasingly being replaced by others containing a present subjunctive (*sea lo que sea*).

For the future perfect subjunctive (HABĒRE HABUERŌ/HABUERIM CANTĀTUM > *ovier(e) cantado* > *hubiere cantado*, etc.), see 3.7.4.1. This compound paradigm has shared the fate of its simple counterpart, becoming increasingly restricted to legal style and disappearing from normal use after the eighteenth century.

3.7.8.5 The perfect

The Latin perfect forms (e.g. AMĀVĪ, AUDĪVĪ, DĪXĪ, FĒCĪ) were exponents of two values (see 3.7.4.1). On the one hand, they were used to express perfect aspect, that is, to indicate that the situation envisaged by the speaker belonged to a period of time which was still in force at the moment of speaking (SEMPER ILLAM AMĀVIT 'he has always loved her (and continues to love her)'). On the other hand, these forms expressed perfective aspect, that is, they were used to show that that the situation discussed belonged to a period of time which concluded before the moment of speaking (MULTŌS ANNŌS ILLAM AMĀVIT 'he loved her for many years (but no longer)'). The first of these values came to be expressed in spoken Latin and its descendants by means of compound verb forms consisting of a present indicative of HABĒRE plus participle (HABEŌ AMĀTUM, whence *he amado*) (see 3.7.4.1). The perfective value continued to be expressed by traditional AMĀVĪ, etc. (see 3.7.8.6).

3.7.8.6 The preterite

Here we discuss essentially the morphology of the Spanish preterite. In 3.7.4 we considered the aspectual contrasts which opposed the Latin imperfect to the perfect (the morphological ancestor of the Spanish preterite), and the creation of the new contrast between perfect and perfective aspects.

From a morphological standpoint, two broad classes of Latin perfects should be distinguished. One the one hand, a large majority of -ĀRE and -ĪRE verbs had endings which always bore the accent (*weak* or *arrhizotonic* perfects, e.g. AMĀVĪ, AUDĪVĪ, etc.). On the other hand, almost all -ĒRE and -ĔRE verbs bore the accent on the root in some forms of their paradigms; this type of paradigm is called *strong*, including as it does various *rhizotonic* forms (those stressed on the root): HABUĪ, DĪXĪ, FĒCĪ, DEDĪ, etc. Historically the weak preterites have deeply influenced the strong type, an influence which has a number of effects:

1 Many verbs which were strong in Latin, and which have continued to be used in the Romance languages, have become weak. Thus, TIMUĪ, MOLUĪ, APERUĪ, DEBUĪ; ARSĪ, SPARSĪ; CŌNCĒPĪ, LĒGĪ, MOVĪ, VĪCĪ; CECIDĪ, MOMORDĪ, CUCURRĪ, etc., changed to the weak type (*temí, molí, abrí, debí; ardí, esparcí, concebí, leí, moví, vencí, caí, mordí, corrí*, etc.). Only a minority of very frequent verbs preserved their strong accentuation (see 3.7.8.6.2(1–4)).

2 The Latin strong perfects could be rhizotonic in a maximum of four forms; only the second-person forms never carried the accent on the root FḖCĪ, FḖCIT, FḖCIMUS, FḖCERUNT vs FĒCÍSTĪ, FECÍSTIS. However, under the influence of the weak paradigm (and of FĒCÍSSEM, etc., which was always ending-stressed), only the first and third persons singular of the strong paradigm kept the accent on the root (*hice, hizo*), while the other members of the paradigm were or became arhizotonic (*hiciste, hicimos, hicisteis, hicieron*). The change of accent involved here affected not only the preterite (FḖCIMUS, FḖCERUNT >

FĒCÍMUS, FĒCÉRUNT), but also the remainder of the Latin paradigms that shared the same root as the preterite. There is therefore also an accentual shift in the *-ra* paradigm and in the future subjunctive (FḖCERAM, FḖCERO > FĒCÉRAM, FĒCÉRO, whence, with further vowel-changes, *hiciera, hiciere*).

3 The endings of the strong preterites have been taken, in certain cases, from the weak paradigm. The endings of *hizo, hicimos*, etc., cannot be explained on the basis of FĒCIT, FĒCIMUS, etc., where the short Ĭ should give /e/, but through the influence of *cantó, oyó; oímos, salimos*, etc. In the case of the third person singular of most strong preterites (*dixo*, etc.), the replacement of /e/ by /o/ has the advantage of distinguishing this form from the first person singular, where the final Ī also becomes /e/ (DĪXĪ > *dixe*). It is true that the diphthong /ie/ of *hicieron, hiciera, hiciese, hiciere* may be the regular result of the short Ĕ of the Latin ending, but this can only be the case after the analogical shift of the accent onto this vowel: FḖCĔRUNT > FĒCÉRUNT > *hicieron*, etc.

We shall first discuss the regular or weak preterites (3.7.8.6.1), and then the irregular or strong types (3.7.8.6.2).

3.7.8.6.1 The weak preterite. To the weak types belonging to the Latin first and fourth conjugations (AMĀVĪ, AUDĪVĪ), which give the regular *-ar* and *-ir* paradigms, was added a third weak type, whose origin lay in the perfect of verbs like VENDĔRE, and which provided the paradigm adopted by the many second- and third-conjugation verbs which changed from strong to weak accentuation. There was a series of mutual influences between the preterite endings of these last two classes (the *-er* and *-ir* verbs), the result of which was a single paradigm of mixed origins.

1 Verbs in *-ar*. We have seen (in 3.7.2 and 3.7.8.3.2(1)) that non-standard Latin lost the aspect marker from the endings -ĀVĪ, -ĀVISTĪ, etc., which became contracted (AMĀVĪ, AMĀVISTĪ, etc., > AMĀĪ, AMĀSTĪ, etc.). In the case of the third person singular, there were various contractions in different parts of the Latin-speaking world, with preference for -ĀUT in the centre and west of the Peninsula. In table 3.36 can be seen the Old and Modern Spanish preterite forms and their Latin antecedents.

The Spanish forms are direct descendants of the non-Classical Latin forms, by regular phonological change, except in the following cases (which are underlined in table 3.36). The medieval forms *cantest(e), cantemos, cantestes* borrowed their tonic vowel from first-person-singular *canté* as a result of an analogical imitation of the *-ir* preterite, where the same tonic vowel occurred in all the corresponding forms. Thus, *oí : oíste :: canté : x* (*x* = *canteste*), etc. These forms with /é/, although frequent in Old Spanish, were later restricted to rural varieties of the language.

Table 3.36 *Development of the preterite of* -ar *verbs*

Classical Latin	Non-Classical Latin	Old Spanish	Modern Spanish
CANTĀVĪ	CANTĀĪ	*canté*	*canté*
CANTĀVISTĪ	CANTĀSTĪ	*cantast(e)*	*cantaste*
		cantest(e)	*cantastes*
CANTĀVIT	CANTĀUT	*cantó*	*cantó*
CANTĀVIMUS	CANTĀMUS	*cantamos*	*cantamos*
		cantemos	
CANTĀVISTIS	CANTĀSTIS	*cantastes*	*cantasteis*
		cantestes	
CANTĀVERUNT	CANTĀRUNT	*cantaron*	*cantaron*

Table 3.37 *Development of the preterite of* -ir *verbs*

Classical Latin	Non-Classical Latin	Old Spanish	Modern Spanish
AUDĪVĪ	AUDĪĪ	*oí*	*oí*
AUDĪVISTĪ	AUDĪSTĪ	*oíst(e)*	*oíste*
		oyest(e)	*oístes*
AUDĪVIT	AUDĪUT	*oyó*	*oyó*
AUDĪVIMUS	AUDĪMUS	*oímos*	*oímos*
		oyemos	
AUDĪVISTIS	AUDĪSTIS	*oístes*	*oísteis*
		oyestes	
AUDĪVERUNT	AUDĪRUNT	*oyeron*	*oyeron*

The final *-s* of the modern form *cantastes* arose through analogy with the second-person-singular forms of other paradigms, all of which are marked by *-s*. Although this ending has been rejected by the standard, it remains very frequent in informal styles in many Spanish-speaking areas. *Cantasteis* (< OSp. *cantastes*) owes its diphthong to an analogy with the other second-person-plural forms, all of which, from the seventeenth century, have been marked by a diphthong in the final syllable (see 3.7.3.2).

2 Verbs in *-ir*. The loss of the perfective aspect marker (see 3.7.4.2, 3.7.8.3.2(1)) and the consequent contraction AUDĪVĪ, AUDĪVISTĪ, etc. > AUDĪĪ, AUDĪSTĪ, etc., was even earlier in the -ĪRE verbs than in the first conjugation. As in the case of the *-ar* verbs, there were various contractions in the third-person-singular form (-ĪT, -ĪUT, etc.), with -ĪUT coming to be preferred in the centre and west of the Peninsula. In table 3.37 are set out the medieval and modern forms of this paradigm, with their Latin antecedents.

Some scholars believe that contraction of the plural forms of this paradigm led to forms with ĪĬ or ĪĒ (AUDĪVIMUS, AUDĪVISTIS, AUDĪVERUNT > *AUDĪĬMUS, *AUDĪĬSTIS, *AUDĪĒRUNT), a hypothesis elaborated to explain the diphthong of the Old Spanish forms *oyemos, oyestes, oyeron* (Lapesa 2000: 768), on which basis singular *oyest(e)* was analogically restructured. However, there is no evidence of such Latin forms and they contradict the Latin rule that imposes a single long vowel when two front vowels combine (e.g. SĪ VIS > SĪS). In our view, *oyest(e), oyemos, oyestes, oyeron* have endings borrowed from the *-er* paradigm (see 3.7.8.6.1(3)), although it also possible that they were modelled on such strong preterites as that of *dar*, where *diemos, diestes, dieron* were the commonest Old Spanish forms (3.7.8.6.2(4)).

The *-s* of Modern (non-standard) Spanish and the diphthong of *oísteis* are explained in the same way as the corresponding forms of the *-ar* paradigm (3.7.8.6.1(1)).

As in other paradigms of the *-ir* conjugation (3.7.8.1.4(2), 3.7.8.3.1, 3.7.8.3.2), the Old Spanish *-ir* preterite showed great instability in its root vowels. In the case of front vowels, although there was preference for root /e/ when the ending contained tonic /í/ (*sentí, sentist(e), sentimos, sentistes*), and although a high root vowel was more frequent than mid /e/ when the ending contained a diphthong (*sintiest(e), sintió, sintiemos, sintiestes, sintieron*), we also find some examples with high /i/ before /í/ (*sintí, sintist(e), sintimos, sintistes*), and there are frequent cases of root /e/ before a diphthong (*sentiest(e), sentió, sentiemos, sentiestes, sentieron*). As in the case of the present and imperfect paradigms, the modern rule only emerged in the sixteenth century: root /i/ was selected and /e/ abandoned, in order to mark more sharply the contrast between *-ir* and *-er* verbs (from which root /i/ was excluded), except when the dissimilation /i/... / í/ > /e/... /í/ prevented such a choice. In this way the modern paradigm was established: *sentí, sentiste, sintió, sentimos, sentisteis, sintieron*. The only verbs to escape this rule are *escribí, recibí, viví*, and certain learned verbs (*adquirí, distinguí*, etc.), whose root /i/, supported by Latin spelling, resisted the force of dissimilation.

With regard to back root vowels, Old Spanish showed the same variation between mid /o/ and high /u/, but since in this case there was no dissimilatory process parallel to /i/... /í/ > /e/... /í/, both root vowels are found with the same frequency before /í/ (*sobí~subí, sobist(e)~subist(e), sobimos~subimos, sobistes~subistes; dormí~durmí, dormist(e)~durmist(e), dormimos~ durmimos, dormistes~durmistes*) as before a diphthong (*sobiest(e)~subiest(e), sobió~subió, sobiemos~subiemos, sobiestes~subiestes, sobieron~subieron; dormiest(e)~durmiest(e), dormió~durmió, dormiemos~durmiemos, dormiestes~ durmiestes, dormieron~durmieron*). At the end of the Middle Ages and in the early sixteenth century, once again as in other paradigms (present and imperfect indicative and subjunctive, etc.), root /u/ was selected in almost all these

Table 3.38 *Development of the preterite of* -er *verbs*

Classical Latin	Spoken Latin	Old Spanish	Modern Spanish
VENDIDĪ	*VENDḖDĪ	*vendí*	*vendí*
VENDIDISTĪ	*VENDEDISTĪ	*vendist(e)*	*vendiste*
		(*vendiest(e)*)	*vendistes*
VENDIDIT	*VENDḖDIT	*vendió*	*vendió*
VENDIDIMUS	*VENDEDIMUS	*vendimos*	*vendimos*
		vendiemos	
VENDIDISTIS	*VENDEDISTIS	*vendistes*	*vendisteis*
		vendiestes	
VENDIDERUNT	*VENDEDERUNT	*vendieron*	*vendieron*

verbs: *subí, subiste, subió, subimos, subisteis, subieron*. In this way the contrast between the *-ir* and the *-er* classes was reinforced, since *-er* verbs did not permit root /u/. The only three verbs which escaped this rule were the same ones which escaped it in other paradigms: *dormir, morir* and *oír*, together with an occasional learned verb, e.g. *abolir*. *Dormir* and *morir* imposed /u/ only before a diphthong (*durmió, murieron*), but, by contrast with all other verbs of their pattern (perhaps because of their high frequency), they (like *abolir*) selected /o/ before /í/ (*abolí, dormiste, morimos, moristeis*). *Oír* maintained /o/ in all its forms (*oí, oyeron*, etc.), as in other paradigms, probably to avoid homophony with *huir*, once the latter lost its initial consonant.

3 Verbs in *-er*. Only a handful of Latin second-conjugation verbs had weak perfects (e.g. DELĒRE: DELĒVĪ), and none of these survived in Romance. Furthermore, all third-conjugation verbs had strong perfects. The question therefore arises of why the large majority of Spanish *-er* verbs have weak preterites. The view of Heinrich Lausberg (1966: 345–8), a very attractive one, is that these verbs adopted a paradigm which had its origins in a group of frequent third-conjugation verbs. These verbs (VENDERE, CREDERE, PERDERE, REDDERE), were derivatives of DĀRE, and, like DĀRE, had strong perfects of the reduplicative type (see 3.7.8.6.2(4)): VENDIDĪ, CREDIDĪ, PERDIDĪ, REDDIDĪ. However, these perfects became weak (*VENDḖDĪ, *CREDḖDĪ, *PERDḖDĪ, *REDDḖDĪ) to make their morphological structure more similar to that of the perfect of DĀRE (namely, DḖDĪ), in line with a frequent process of spoken Latin, which tended to restructure derivatives to make them more similar to their bases (e.g. CADERE 'to fall': RECIDERE 'to fall again' > CADERE: *RECADERE > *caer, recaer*).

VENDIDĪ and its congeners evolved as in table 3.38.

The first-person-singular *vendí* is the regular result of *VENDḖDĪ, with loss of intervocalic -D- (2.5.3.2), metaphony /ɛi/ > /ei/ (2.4.2.1) and resolution of /éi/

to /í/. In the second person singular, the same loss of -D- and metaphony caused by final Ī (2.4.2.1), followed by resolution of /eí/ to /í/, allow *VENDĔDISTĪ to evolve regularly to *vendiste*. *VENDĔDIMUS, *VENDĔDISTIS and *VENDĔDĔRUNT lost a whole syllable through haplology (the elimination of one two similar successive syllables, in this case /dɛ́dɛ/ or /dɛdɛ́/ > /dɛ́/), after which tonic /ɛ́/ was regularly diphthongized: *vendiemos, vendiestes, vendieron*. The rather rare form *vendiest(e)* is to be explained by the analogical extension of /ié/ from these forms to the second person singular.

The remaining medieval and modern forms are analogical: since *vendí* and *vendiste* showed the same endings as *oí* and *oíste*, other endings from the *-ir* paradigm could be applied to *-er* verbs, whence *vendió, vendimos, vendistes*. However, analogy based on the identity of endings between *vendí, vendiste* and *oí, oíste* could also operate in the opposite direction, introducing into the *-ir* paradigm endings which had developed first among *-er* verbs. This is no doubt how *oyest(e), oyemos, oyestes* and *oyeron* arose (3.7.8.6.1(2)).

Following these interchanges of endings, the endings of *-er* verbs could not be distinguished from those of *-ir* verbs. The Modern Spanish paradigm represents a selection from among the medieval forms, with preference for the forms with /í/, in those cases where such forms were available (*vendí, vendiste, vendimos, vendisteis; oí, oíste, oímos, oísteis*). This selection of forms with /í/ was in part due to the unvarying appearance of /í/ in the first-person-singular *vendí, oí*, and in part to the need to distinguish adequately between preterite and imperfect indicative forms, a need finally felt after several centuries in which the first-person-plural forms *vendiemos, oyemos* could function with both values (see 3.7.8.3.1). The remaining forms of these paradigms (*vendió, vendieron, oyó, oyeron*) had no competitors in /í/ and passed unchallenged into the modern language.

The modern *-s* of *vendistes* and the diphthong of *vendisteis* are to be explained in the same way as the corresponding forms of *-ar* and *-ir* verbs (3.7.8.6.1 (1–2)).

It remains to be emphasized that, despite the identity of endings between the *-er* and *-ir* preterite paradigms, these paradigms did not merge totally, owing to the vowel contrast established in the root. While high vowels were frequent in the root of medieval *-ir* verbs and while, among those verbs with a velar root vowel, /u/ became universal in the Golden Age (see 3.7.8.6.1(2)), high vowels were always rigorously excluded from the root of *-er* verbs. Thus, in the Middle Ages *vendió, vendieron* were opposed to *sentió~sintió, sentieron~sintieron*, and *molió, molieron* contrasted with *sobió~subió, sobieron~subieron*, and in the modern language this opposition has been consolidated with the abandonment of *sentió, sentieron, sobió, sobieron*. This polarization of root vowels, as has been several times underlined, served to compensate for the almost complete absence of contrast between the endings of these two Spanish verb classes. (For further discussion, see Penny forthcoming.)

Table 3.39 *Development of the endings of strong preterites*

Classical Latin	Spoken Latin	Old Spanish	Modern Spanish
	DĪ́XĪ	*dix(e)*	*dije*
	DĪXÍSTĪ	*dixist(e)*	*dijiste*
		dixiest(e)	*dijistes*
	DĪ́XIT	*dixo*	*dijo*
DĪ́XIMUS	*DĪXÍMUS	*diximos*	*dijimos*
		dixiemos	
	DĪXÍSTIS	*dixistes*	*dijisteis*
		dixiestes	
DĪ́XERUNT	*DĪXÉRUNT	*dixieron*	*dijeron*

3.7.8.6.2 The strong preterite. In Spanish, this type of paradigm came to belong only to a minority of verbs, although all very frequent ones, by contrast with Latin, where it was applied to all -ĔRE verbs and the vast majority of those of the -ĒRE class (see 3.7.8.6). Also, we have seen there that strong accentuation was maintained only in the first and third persons singular, whereas in Latin this type of accentuation also occurred in the first person plural, and sometimes in the third plural (e.g. Latin FḖCIMUS, FḖCERUNT, Spanish *hicimos, hicieron*). (For such effects of analogical pressure exercised by the weak preterites, see 3.7.8.6. For the possible exception represented by FŬIMUS, FŬERUNT, see 3.7.8.6.2(3, 3).)

It should be borne in mind, also, that accent-shift towards the ending affected not only the first and third persons plural of the preterite, but also all the forms of many of the paradigms which shared their roots with the preterite. Thus, there was accent-shift in the *-ra* paradigm (FḖCERAM > *hiciera*) (see 3.7.8.3.2(2)), and in the future subjunctive (FḖCERIM, FḖCERŌ > *hiciere*) (see 3.7.8.4.4).

With regard to the endings of the strong preterite forms, we have seen in 3.7.8.6 that few descend directly from their Latin counterparts. If we examine the endings of a typical strong preterite (table 3.39), we can see that, even taking into account the accent-shift that occurred in several forms, the development of the endings cannot be explained on the basis of the regular development of the Latin phonemes, but only through analogy with the weak preterites.

As can be seen from table 3.39, the only medieval forms whose endings are the phonological product of their Latin antecedents are *dix(e)* (with regular treatment of -Ī > /e/, and the frequent loss of this vowel when it followed certain consonants; 3.7.1.4), *dixiste* (showing the regular metaphonic effect of final -Ī on preceding tonic Ĭ; 2.4.2.1) and *dixieron* (with regular diphthongization of tonic Ĕ; 2.4.2.2). The forms *dixiest(e), diximos, dixiemos, dixistes, dixiestes* have endings taken from those of the weak *-er* and/or *-ir* preterites (see tables 3.37, 3.38), while the ending of *dixo* was probably also extracted (see Craddock 1983) from that of the weak preterites, at the stage *CANTĀUT, *IMPLĒUT, *AUDĪUT (see 3.7.8.6.1(1–2), whence *DĪXUT, etc. This acquisition of /-o/ brings the advantage, in almost all strong verbs, of providing a morphological distinction between the third and the first persons singular, which was otherwise obscured by the merger of -Ī and -IT in /-e/ or /-i/.

If we examine the root vowels of strong preterites, we can see that (by contrast with what applies to the weak preterites and all other regular paradigms) there is no contrast in the treatment of *-er* and *-ir* verbs. That is, *-er* verbs allow high vowels in the root (by contrast with what is the case outside the strong preterite and related paradigms). Because of the absence of root /e/ (beyond a few examples of *trexe* (MSp. *traje*), and early cases of *fezo, veno*, which rapidly gave way to *fizo, vino* (see below)), four groups of Old Spanish verbs can be distinguished:

1 with root /a/ in all forms: *nasco* (inf. *na(s)cer* 'to be born'), *raxo* (inf. *raer* 'to scrape'), *remase* (inf. *remanir* 'to remain'), *tanxe* (inf. *tañer* 'to touch'), *traxe* (inf. *traer* 'to bring').

2 with root /i/ in the two rhizotonic forms and with heavy preponderance of /i/ in other forms: *andido* (inf. *andar* 'to walk'), *aprise/aprisiste* (inf. *aprender* 'to learn'), *cinxo* (inf. *ceñir* 'to gird'), *dixe/dixiste* (inf. *dezir* 'to say'), *escrise/escrisiste* (inf. *escrevir* 'to write'), *estide* (inf. *estar* 'to be'), *fize/fiziste* (inf. *fazer* 'to do'), *mise/misiste* (inf. *meter* 'to put'), *prise/prisiste* (inf. *prender* 'to take'), *quise/quisiste* (inf. *querer* 'to wish'), *rise/risiste* (inf. *reír* 'to laugh'), *tinxe/tinxiste* (inf. *teñir* 'to dye'), *vine/viniste* (inf. *venir* 'to come'), *visque* (inf. *bevir* 'to live'), *yxo* (inf. *exir* 'to go out'). Some of these forms descend from Latin perfects with Ī (throughout the paradigm) (DĪXĪ, SCRĪPSĪ, MĪSĪ, RĪSĪ), and in such forms one would predict root /i/ in all Spanish forms. In other cases, the Latin etymon had a non-high vowel (FĒCĪ, QUAESĪĪ, VĒNĪ), and in these instances we might expect some examples of root /e/. In the first person singular of both subgroups /e/ is unknown, as it is in the third person singular of the large majority of verbs; we only find *fezo* and *veno*, in very early Spanish texts (see 3.7.8.6.2(3)). In the arrhizotonic forms, we frequently find root /e/ in the second subgroup (*feziste, fezimos, fezistes, fezieron, quesiste, veniste, venimos*, etc.), together with more frequent forms with /i/ (*fiziste*, etc.), while root /e/ is rare but not absent in the first subgroup (*dexiste, presiste*, etc.). From the sixteenth century, those verbs which pass into the modern language show only root /i/, despite the strength of the dissimilatory tendency /i/. . . /í/ > /e/. . . /í/ which has been noted on other occasions (3.7.1.5, 3.7.8.1.4(2), 3.7.8.3.1, 3.7.8.6.1(2)): *dije/dijiste, hice/hiciste, quise/quisiste, vine/viniste*.

3 with root /o/ throughout the paradigm: *andove/andoviste* (inf. *andar* 'to walk'), *atrovo* (inf. *atreverse* 'to dare'), *cope/copiste* (inf. *caber* 'to fit'),

crove/croviste (inf. *creer* 'to believe'), *estove/estoviste* (inf. *estar* 'to be'), *ove/oviste* (inf. *aver* 'to have'), *plogue/ploguiste* (inf. *plazer* 'to please'), *sope/sopiste* (inf. *saber* 'to know'), *sove/soviste* (inf. *s(e)er* 'to be'), *tove/toviste* (inf. *tener* 'to have'), *troxe/troxiste* (inf. *traer* 'to bring'), *yogue/yoguiste* (inf. *yazer* 'to lie'). This group retains its separate identity from the following group until the end of the Middle Ages, although not without the occasional example of root /u/ in the fifteenth century, especially before /ie/ (*supieron, tuviestes, uviera*). In the first half of the sixteenth century, root /u/ was imposed throughout the paradigm of those verbs which survived into Modern Spanish (*anduve, cupe, estuve, hube, supe, tuve*), so that the preterites of this group then became identical with those in 4, which had always had root /u/.

4 with root /u/ throughout the paradigm: *aduxe* (inf. *aduzir* 'to bring'), *conuvo* (inf. *cono(s)cer* 'to know'), *fuxe* (inf. *fuir* 'to flee'), *respuso* (inf. *responder* 'to reply'), *pude* (inf. *poder* 'to be able'), *puse* (inf. *poner* 'to put'). These verbs show exclusively /u/ in the first and third persons singular, and scarcely any other possibility in the arrhizotonic forms. Only very rarely does one find /o/, most usually before /í/ (*posimos, podiste, adoxistes*), a possibility which is eliminated before the end of the Middle Ages.

For discussion of the cohesion and convergence among the patterns represented in the strong preterite, see Maiden (2001).

With regard to the typology of the Latin strong perfects, four classes can be distinguished, each of which has descendants in Modern Spanish. They are examined in the following sections (3.7.8.6.2(1–4)).

1 Strong preterites in -UĪ. Almost all verbs of the -ĒRE conjugation, whatever their root vowel, had this type of preterite (TIMĒRE: TIMUĪ, DEBĒRE: DEBUĪ, etc.), but relatively few Spanish verbs (all from etyma with root A or Ŏ) continue this pattern. However, several other verbs, most belonging to the *-er* class, adopted the patterns which descended from these preterites in A-UĪ and Ŏ-UĪ. In both cases, the Ŭ of the ending, pronounced as [w] in spoken Latin, was moved to the end of the preceding syllable, becoming [u̯] and combining, with different outcomes, with the A or Ŏ which formed the nucleus of that syllable.

In the verbs with root /a/, the sequence [au̯] was regularly simplified (2.4.2.3) and appeared in Old Spanish as /o/:

HABUĪ > OSp. *ove*
SAPUĪ > *sope*
IACUĪ > *yogue*
PLACUĪ > *plogue*

The first two of these forms served as models for the preterite of other verbs which in Latin did not show this pattern. Thus, in the case of *tener*, instead of a descendant of TENUĪ, we find *tove*, on the pattern of *ove*. Other preterites which are remodelled in this way are: *andove*, *atrovo* (CL TRIBUIT), *crove* (CRĒDIDĪ), *estove* (STĒTĪ, see 3.7.8.6.2(4)), *sove* (SĒDĪ) 'I was (seated)'. In similar fashion, *sope* served as a model for *cope* (CL CĒPĪ, although this analogical shift may have been earlier, since CAPUIT is attested in the first century AD). By contrast, the form *troxe* 'I brought' (CL TRAXĪ) only partly adopted this model, showing the vowel of *ove, sope*, etc., but keeping the consonant /ʃ/ which is the expected outcome of -X- (see 2.5.2.4, 3.7.8.6.2(2)).

In the preterites in -UĪ whose root vowel was Ŏ, this vowel was doubly raised to /u/ by the joint effect of the following glide [w] and the final -Ī. The glide was presumably transferred to the preceding syllable and absorbed by /u/, so that the earliest Spanish forms of these preterites already show the vocalic pattern /u/. . . /e/. There are only two cases of this development:

PŎSUĪ > OSp. *puse*
PŎTUĪ > *pude*

Again, these forms provided a model for the preterite of other verbs. Modelled on the first, we find *respuse* 'I replied' (CL RESPONDĪ), and on the second *andude* and *estude* (see also *estove*, above, and *estide* 3.7.8.6.2(4)). Judging by the rare *tudiere* (future subjunctive), there must have also have existed a form **tude*, modelled on *pude*. On the other hand, it is possible that the form *conuve* 'I knew', with the same vowel as *puse* and *pude*, is an independent reflex of COGNŌVĪ, with metaphony /ó/ > /ú/ due to final -Ī.

For the development of the root vowels of these two groups of preterites, which came to be merged in a single type with root /u/, see 3.7.8.6.2.

Of the preterites discussed in this section, only a few have survived into Modern Spanish with the forms cited above: *hube, anduve, estuve, tuve, supe, cupe, puse, pude*. The other preterites with this pattern were lost, either replaced by a weak form, which was often already in existence in the Middle Ages (*atrovo, crove, conuve* were in competition with *atrevió, creí, conocí*), or pushed out by an alternative strong form (*sove, troxe, andude, estude, *tude* were ousted by *fui, traje, anduve, estuve, tuve*). *Respuse* also seems to survive, in certain narrative styles, confused with the preterite of *reponer* but with its traditional sense: *repuso* 'he replied'.

2 Strong preterites in -SĪ. The Latin preterites marked by this ending (or by -XĪ when the ending combined with a velar consonant at the end of the root: DĪC-SĪ= DĪXĪ), often called *sigmatic* preterites, belonged especially to the -ĔRE conjugation and descended in some numbers into Old Spanish:

AD-, CON-DŪXĪ > OSp. *a-, con-duxe* (inf. *aduzir* 'to bring', *conduzir* 'to lead')
COXĪ > *coxe* (inf. *cozer* 'to cook')
DESTRŪXĪ > *destruxe* (inf. *destruir* 'to destroy')
DĪXĪ > *dixe* (inf. *dezir* 'to say')
MĪSĪ > *mise* (inf. *meter* 'to put')
QUAESIĪ > *quise* (inf. *querer* 'to wish')

REMANSĪ > *remase* (inf. *remanir* 'to remain')
RĪSĪ > *rise* (inf. *reír* 'to laugh')
SUBRĪSĪ > *sonrise* (inf. *sonreír* 'to smile')
SCRĪPSĪ > *escrise* (inf. *escrevir* 'to write')
TRAXĪ > *traxe* (inf. *traer* 'to bring')

It should be noted that neither *quise* nor *traxe* show regular development of the root vowel. In Old Spanish, we would expect /e/ in both cases (in QUAESIĪ through metaphony of AE (= Ĕ), caused by final -Ī, cf. VĒNĪ > *ven*; in TRAXĪ from the combination of /a/ with the [i̯] from syllable-final /k/, cf. AXE > *eje* 'axle'), a vowel not elsewhere found in strong preterite roots. The vowel of *quise* is due to analogy with *mise*, etc., and that of *traxe* to analogy with the root of the present tenses, etc. (*trae*, etc.).

Preterites with root-final /s/ or /ʃ/ inherited from Latin served as models, as in other cases we have examined, for other verbs, which in Latin did not have this type of preterite:

(DISPENDĪ) OSp. *despise* (inf. *despender* 'to spend')
(FŪGĪ) *fuxe* (inf. *fuir* 'to flee')
(PREHENDĪ) *prise* (inf. *prender* 'to take')
(APPREHENDĪ) *aprise* (inf. *aprender* 'to learn')
(TETIGĪ) *tanxe* (inf. *tañer* 'to touch, play')
(CINXĪ) *cinxe* (inf. *ceñir* 'to gird')
(TINXĪ) *tinxe* (inf. *teñir* 'to dye')

The forms *cinxe*, *tinxe* cannot be direct descendants of CINXĪ, TINXĪ, since the group /nks/ cannot develop to /nʃ/. For /ʃ/ to appear, the pre-Romance /s/ has to be grouped with preceding [i̯], which can only result from /k/ if this velar is post-vocalic (see 2.5.2.4: TRAXĪ = /tráksi/ > *traxe*, etc.). The presence of /n/ makes this development of /k/ impossible. Therefore, *cinxe, tinxe*, like *tanxe*, must have been formed on the basis of their present-tense root (*ciñ(-es), tiñ(-es), tañ(-es)*) plus *-xe* taken from *aduxe, dixe, destruxe*, etc.

In Old Spanish there sprang up a type of sigmatic preterite of semi-learned origin, probably inspired by a Church pronunciation of VĪXĪ (perfect of VĪVERE). Apparently, the group /ks/ was reversed and VĪXĪ came to be pronounced /βíski/~/βíske/, a form which was borrowed by Spanish as *visque* (a preterite which coexisted with the weak form *beví~biví*) 'I lived'. On the model of *visque* were created *nasque* 'I was born', and *trasqui* 'I brought'.

For the development of the root vowels of this class of preterites, see 3.7.8.6.2.

Of the many Latin sigmatic perfects, only some survived into Old Spanish (see above). The majority were replaced by weak forms before the emergence of the earliest Spanish texts; thus ARSĪ, SENSĪ, SPARSĪ, etc., were lost and Old Spanish has only *ardí, sentí, esparzí*, etc. Of the sigmatics that survived, almost all had weak competitors in Old Spanish; thus, beside *mise, rise, coxe*, etc., we find *metí, reí, cozí*, etc., which alone pass into the modern language. As a result of this and of the abandonment of some of the verbs which had sigmatic preterites in Old Spanish (*despender, remanir*), Modern Spanish is left with only the following irregular preterites of this type: *conduje* (and, with other prefixes, *aduje, reduje*, etc.), *dije, traje* and *quise*.

3 Strong preterites with change of root vowel. A good number of Latin verbs, belonging to the -ĒRE, -ĔRE and -ĪRE conjugations, marked the contrast between present and perfect through an alternation of the root vowel, without any marker in the ending. Only four verbs with this kind of perfect have passed into Spanish, although it cannot be claimed that they any longer form a distinctive morphological class. They are:

FACĔRE: perf. FĒCĪ
VĔNĪRE: perf. VĒNĪ
VĔDĒRE: perf. VĪDĪ
ESSE: perf. FŬĪ

FŬĪ is only grouped with the other verbs for reasons of Latin morphological history.

1 FĒCĪ and VĒNĪ, because of their identical vowel structure and parallel history, can be considered together. In both cases, the only constant is the root /i/ in the first person singular (arrived at by metaphony exercised upon the stressed Ē by the final Ī). In the third person singular, where the Latin ending had -Ĭ, metaphony could not occur, and consequently the earliest Spanish texts (twelfth to thirteenth centuries) show *fezo, veno*, although the analogical pressure exerted by the first person soon led to the introduction of root /i/ (*fizo, vino*). In the remaining forms of the paradigm, root /e/ and /i/ alternated, with a slight preference for /i/ when the ending contained a diphthong. For the question of accentuation and for the endings of this paradigm, see 3.7.8.6.2 and table 3.40.

It can be seen that, as happens in other strong preterites (3.7.8.6.2(2, 2)), medieval root /e/ has been rejected, /i/ becoming the norm from the sixteenth century.

2 In the perfect VĪDĪ, the regular loss of -D- (slower in VĪDĪ, VĪDIT than in the other forms of the paradigm) leads to loss of distinction between the strong and the weak preterite, since fusion takes place between the vowel of the root and the first vowel of the ending, rendering otiose the difference between stem-stress and ending-stress. This fusion was not complete in Old Spanish, since the stem-final /d/ was sometimes preserved, especially in the first and third persons singular: *vide, vido* are found with some regularity, and there are occasional examples of *vidiest(e), vidiemos, vidieste, vidieron* in early texts. In the case of the third person singular, it seems that the accent remained for some time on the root even after the loss of /d/, since we find *vío* in rhyme with *río*, etc. These developments are summarized in table 3.41.

Table 3.40 *Development of the preterite of* hacer *and* venir

Classical Latin	Non-Classical Latin	Old Spanish	Modern Spanish
FĒCĪ		*fiz(e)*	*hice*
VĒNĪ		*vin(e)*	*vine*
FĒCISTĪ		*fezist(e)~fizist(e)*	*hiciste(s)*
VĒNISTĪ		*feziest(e)~fiziest(e)*	
		venist(e)~vinist(e)	
		veniest(e)~viniest(e)	*viniste(s)*
FĒCIT		*fezo > fizo*	*hizo*
VĒNIT		*veno > vino*	*vino*
FĒCIMUS	*FĒCÍMUS	*fezimos(~fizimos)*	*hicimos*
VĒNIMUS	*VĒNÍMUS	*feziemos~fiziemos*	
		venimos~vinimos	*vinimos*
		veniemos~viniemos	
FĒCISTIS		*fezistes~fizistes*	*hicisteis*
VĒNISTIS		*feziestes~fiziestes*	
		venistes~vinistes	*vinisteis*
		veniestes~viniestes	
FĒCERUNT	*FĒCÉRUNT	*fezieron~fizieron*	*hicieron*
VĒNERUNT	*VĒNÉRUNT	*venieron~vinieron*	*vinieron*

Table 3.41 *Development of the preterite of* ver

Classical Latin	Non-Classical Latin	Old Spanish	Modern Spanish
VĪDĪ		*vide~vi*	*vi*
VĪDISTĪ		*(vidieste(e)~)vist(e)*	*viste(s)*
VĪDIT		*vido~vío > vio*	*vio*
VĪ́DIMUS	*VĪDÍMUS	*(vidiemos~)*	*vimos*
		vimos~viemos	
VĪDISTIS		*(vidiestes~)*	*visteis*
		vistes~viestes	
VĪ́DERUNT	*VĪDÉRUNT	*(vidieron~)*	*vieron*
		vieron	

Following the elimination of /d/ and the consolidation of the accentuation of *vió* (< *vido*), the preterite of this verb had become identical, before the end of the Middle Ages, with that of a regular *-er* or *-ir* verb: *vi, viste, vio, vimos, vistes, vieron*. Speakers no doubt perceived these forms as corresponding most closely with a monosyllabic infinitive, i.e. with *ver*, a perception which led to preference for *ver* over its disyllabic rival *veer* (see 3.7.9.1). A different choice was made in the case of *creer, leer*, etc., whose preterites (*creí, leí, creyó, leyó*, etc.) always displayed a boundary between root and ending.

Despite the loss of /d/ in the standard preterite of this verb, *vide* and *vido* were not lost is other varieties of Spanish. They were spread to America, where they continue to be used in rural speech, as also happens in certain Peninsular areas.

3 Beside Classical FŬĪ, with short root vowel, FŪĪ existed in early Latin texts and was apparently transmitted to the spoken Latin of Spain. It also seems that this was the only verb which resisted accent-shift, in the first and third persons plural, from the root to the ending (see 3.7.8.6(2) and 3.7.8.6.2), with the consequence that the post-tonic Ĭ was lost (FŬĬMUS > *FŬMUS, FŪĬMUS > *FŪMUS, FŬĔRUNT > *FŬRUNT, FŪĔRUNT > FŪRUNT). The variation between root Ŭ and Ū would have been eliminated in the first person singular (FŬĪ/FŪĪ both > *fue*) through the metaphonic raising of Ŭ > /u/ by final -Ī, and a similar merger also happened when the Spanish ending contained /é/, since */oé/ is normally resolved as /ué/ (FŬĬMUS/FŪĬMUS, etc. > *fuemos*, etc.). Furthermore, we never find root /o/ where the ending has /í/, as occurred through metaphony in the second person singular; there **foíste* (<FŬISTĪ) was modified to *fuiste*, perhaps to avoid collision with *foiste* the weak preterite of Old Spanish *foír/fuir* 'to flee', bearing in mind that both preterites were pronounced with initial /h/ in Old Spanish (2.5.6).

Taking into account the changes so far considered, the descendants of FŬĪ can be set out as in table 3.42, where the Old Spanish forms are divided between those which result from phonological change and those which are due to analogical readjustment.

The forms without diphthong (*foste(e), fust(e), fo, fomos, fumos, fostes, fustes, foron, furon*), although frequent in the thirteenth century, especially in Berceo's works, were gradually abandoned in the centre of the Peninsula and eventually rejected by the standard. First-person-singular *fue* continued to be used throughout the Middle Ages and was only lost in the sixteenth century. Among the analogical forms, some (*fost(e), fust(e), foron, furon*) were due to intraparadigmatic restructuring (on the basis of *fo, fomos, fumos, fostes, fustes*), while the remainder (*fui, fuimos, fuistes*) were due to the influence of the weak *-er/-ir* paradigm, an influence supported by *fuist(e)*, which through its phonological development had come to have the same ending as these weak verbs.

The paradigm recommended at the end of the fifteenth century by Antonio de Nebrija (1980/1492: 238) represents a logical selection from among the medieval forms: *fue, fueste, fue, fuemos, fuestes, fueron*. However, this paradigm never took root in the standard, which could not abandon the forms with /í/, which appeared not only in this verb but also in all other strong preterites and in the weak *-er/-ir* paradigm. Consequently, the modern paradigm presents an uncomfortable alternation between /é/ (*fue, fueron*) and /í/ (*fui, fuiste, fuimos, fuisteis*).

Table 3.42 *Development of the preterite of* ser *and* ir

Latin	Old Spanish		Modern Spanish
	Phonological forms	Analogical forms	
FŬĪ FŪĪ	*fu, fúe > fue*	*fui*	*fui*
FŬĬSTĪ FŪĬSTĪ	*fuist(e)*	*fuest(e), fost(e), fust(e)*	*fuiste*
FŬIT	*fo*		*fue*
FŪIT	*fu, fúe > fue*		
FŬIMUS FŪIMUS	*fuemos*	*fuimos*	*fuimos*
FŬ(I)MUS	*fomos*		
FŪ(I)MUS	*fumos*		
FŬISTES FŬISTES	*fuestes*	*fuistes*	*fuisteis*
FŬ(I)STES	*fostes*		
FŪ(I)STES	*fustes*		
FŬĒRUNT FŪĒRUNT	*fueron*	*foron, furon*	*fueron*

All other surviving Latin verbs which had this type of perfect (e.g. CONCĒPĪ, FŪGĪ, LĒGĪ, MŌVĪ, VĪCĪ) replaced it with the weak type (or by another strong type) before the appearance of the earliest Spanish texts, where we find *concebí, foí* (beside *fuxe*), *leí, moví, vencí*, etc.

4 Strong preterites with consonant reduplication. Two Latin verbs whose perfect showed reduplication of a root consonant (and change of root vowel) were inherited by Old Spanish with this type of preterite, namely DĔDĪ (perfect of DĀRE) and STĔTĪ (perfect of STĀRE). Considering that these Classical Latin perfects could only give ***dei*, ***stei* (since the metaphonic effect of -Ī on tonic Ĕ could only lead to /é/), it has been suggested that the Spanish forms descend from *DĒDĪ, *STĒTĪ, forms which imitate the vowel-structure of FĒCĪ, VĒNĪ, etc. This analogy, although highly possible, could only apply to the first person singular, since third-person *dio* (like the attested form *estiedo* (*Alexandre*, 546)) can only be explained on the basis of forms with Ĕ (DĔDIT, STĔTIT).

Table 3.43 *Development of the preterite of* dar

Classical Latin	Non-Classical Latin	Old Spanish	Modern Spanish
DĔDĪ	*DĒDĪ	*di*	*di*
DĔDISTĪ		*dist(e), diest(e)*	*diste(s)*
DĔDIT		*dio*	*dio*
DĔDIMUS		*diemos, dimos*	*dimos*
DĔDISTIS		*diestes, distes*	*disteis*
DĔDERUNT		*dieron*	*dieron*

If this hypothesis is correct (although simple imitation of *vi* by *di* should not be overlooked), the reflexes of DĔDĪ can be explained as in table 3.43.

Following regular loss of -D-, the development of *di, diste* can be regarded as regular, both forms showing metaphony of the tonic vowel caused by final -Ī, and with an intermediate form **deíste* in the case of the second person. *Dio* is probably also regular, via **dieo* (cf. MĔU > **mieo* > *mio*), its final *-o* being due to analogy with the weak *-er/-ir* paradigm (*comió, salió*). The tonic vowels of *diemos, dieron* probably arose from regular diphthongization of Ĕ following haplology: DĔ(DI)MUS > *diemos*, DĔ(DE)RUNT > *dieron*, while *diestes* and relatively rare *diest(e)* are due to analogy with the latter. On the other hand, *dimos* and *distes* (less common in Old Spanish than *diemos, diestes*) were arrived at through imitation of the weak *-er/-ir* paradigm, where the endings *-iemos*~*-imos, -iestes*~*-istes* alternated (3.7.8.6.1(2–3)).

The corresponding forms of *estar* (*estide, estido* (which imitates the root vowel of *estide*; cf. *fezo, veno* > *fizo, vino*, 3.7.8.6.2(3)), *estidieron*, etc.) did not survive beyond the Middle Ages, but nevertheless served as a model for the creation of other strong preterites in Old Spanish. This analogy occurred in certain *-ar* verbs whose root ended, like that of *estar*, in a dental (/t/, /d/), giving rise to the occasional medieval forms *andido, demandido, entrido, catido*, all in competition with other forms (*andove, demandé, entré, caté*) which were later preferred in the standard.

Other reduplicative Latin perfects did not even survive into Old Spanish. Typical of these are CECIDĪ, CUCURRĪ, MOMORDĪ, etc., all replaced by weak preterites (*caí, corrí, mordí*, etc.).

3.7.9 *Non-finite verbal forms*

Here we discuss the history of those forms which are unmarked for tense, aspect, mood, or grammatical person. The infinitive (3.7.9.1) and the gerund (3.7.9.2) are also unmarked for gender and number, although the participle (3.7.9.3) may carry such markers.

3.7.9.1 The infinitive

The four types of regular Latin infinitives (e.g. CANTĀRE, TIMĒRE, VENDĔRE, AUDĪRE) were reduced to three before the emergence of Spanish, through the adaptation of third-conjugation infinitives to the second-conjugation model (VENDĔRE > *VENDĒRE, whence *vender*, whose form is identical to that of *temer* < TIMĒRE). This change of accentuation and theme-vowel is analogical, an extension of the identity of many third-conjugation forms with their second-conjugation counterparts in spoken Latin (see 3.7.7).

A single -ĔRE verb, FACĔRE, partly escaped this change of structure, keeping its rhizotonic form. Following regular syncope of post-tonic Ĕ (FÁCĔRE > /fákre/), and the expected vocalization of /k/ > [i̯] in syllable-final position (2.5.2.4), FÁCĔRE was reduced to OSp. *fer*. (Some object that the /k/ of /fákre/ was in syllable-initial position and therefore could not become vocalized, in which case we should argue for an analogical restructuring on the model of *femos* < /fákmos/ (< FÁCĬMUS), where /k/ was indubitably in syllable-final position.) However, in the earliest Spanish texts *fer* coexisted with *fazer*, a form which follows the normal path for third-conjugation infinitives, and with *far*, a reflex of spoken Latin *FĀRE, probably an analogical imitation of DĀRE and STĀRE. Although the competition between *fer, far* and *fazer* was resolved in favour of the latter (whence *hacer*) before the end of the Middle Ages, the form *far* continued to be used as the root of the future and conditional of this verb: *haré*, etc. (see 3.7.8.4.3(3)).

In Medieval and Golden Age Spanish, the final /ɾ/ of the infinitive could be assimilated to the /l/ of a postposed clitic, whence /ʎ/: *acogello, vedallo, cantallas*, etc., forms confirmed by rhyme (*esperallo*//*gallo*, etc.). Still frequent in the standard language of the seventeenth century, these forms were displaced in the eighteenth by the corresponding analytic forms (*cantarlas*, etc.). Another type of medieval assimilation, that of *–r + se > -se* (*tornasse = tornarse*) did not survive into Golden Age and Modern Spanish.

Among the Old Spanish infinitives with /e-é/ at the boundary between root and ending (a hiatus due to the loss of -D- or -G-: *seer, veer, creer, leer, posseer* < SEDĒRE, VIDĒRE, CREDERE, LEGERE, POSSIDĒRE), some always showed the hiatus (*creer, leer, poseer*), while others hesitated between keeping it (*seer, veer*) and reducing it (*ser, ver*). We have seen (3.7.8.4.3(3)) that in the Old Spanish synthetic futures and conditionals of these two verbs there was not normally a hiatus in the segment which was supplied by the infinitive (*será, verie*, etc.), and we know that in the modern language *creer*, *leer* and *poseer* keep their hiatus, while *seer~ser* and *veer~ver* have lost it. Why were there these two contrasting outcomes? It would seem that it depended on speakers' consciousness of whether the verb concerned had (or did not have) a vowel in the root. In the case of *creer*, *leer* and *poseer*, a root vowel is always present (*creo, creía, creyó, creyesse; leamos, leí, leyeron, leyendo; posseo, possea, posseía, posseí, posseyera*; etc.), while in the case of *veer~ver* the root /e/ is obligatorily present in only a few forms (first-person-singular present indicative *ve-o*; present subjunctive: *ve-a*), and is normally lacking in many forms (second and third persons singular and all plural forms of the present indicative: *ve-es~v-es, ve-emos~v-emos*; imperfect indicative: *ve-ie~v-ie*: gerund: *ve-yendo~v-iendo*). By contrast, a root vowel never appears in other forms (all preterite forms: *v-i, v-iste~v-ieste, v-io, v-imos~v-iemos, v-istes~v-estes, v-ieron*; imperfect subjunctive: *v-iesse*; pluperfect: *v-iera*; future subjunctive: *v-iere*; participle *v-isto*). The lack of root /e/ in so many forms implies that the phonological tendency to reduce the hiatus (/eé/ > /é/) met no morphological resistance from most other forms of the verb and *ver* became the norm (just as happened in *ves, ve, vemos, vedes > veis, ven, viendo*, while *veo, veía*, which lacked /eé/, retained the root vowel).

The double form of OSp. *seer/ser* (< SEDĒRE) was reduced to monosyllabic *ser* in a manner similar to the reduction of *veer/ver* to *ver*. However, *seer/ser* lacked forms which corresponded to most of the forms of *ver* we have just examined, in which roots with vowels competed with others that lacked them (*ve-es* vs. *v-es*, etc.). The only forms which might have suggested a disyllabic infinitive were the present subjunctive *sea* and imperfect indicative *seía*, etc., a form that was always less frequent than *era*, and which had a narrower semantic range than that of *era* (see 3.7.8.3.1). We must therefore assume that the process of hiatus-reduction (/e-é/ > /é/) met no structural opposition, so that monosyllabic *ser* became the norm. (For the medieval and Golden Age treatment of vowel-final verbal roots, see López Bobo 1999.)

The irregular Latin infinitive ESSE was remodelled in many varieties of spoken Latin, on the pattern of the regular third-conjugation infinitives, becoming *ESSĔRE. With the accent-shift typical of the Latin of central and western Spain, *ESSĔRE would have become *ESSÉRE there. It is at least possible that such a form existed, and that, through loss of its first syllable (*/essér/ > /sér/), it merged with the product of SEDĒRE to form OSp. *ser/seer*.

Among the irregular Latin infinitives, POSSE, SUFFERRE and OFFERRE were inherited in regularized form by Spanish. POSSE was modified analogically to *POTĒRE, on the basis of its perfect POTUĪ, and the related paradigms POTUERAM, POTUISSE, POTUERIM, POTUERŌ, all forms which likened this verb to the regular second-conjugation verbs (e.g. TIMĒRE, perf. TIMUĪ, with related tenses TIMUERAM, TIMUISSE, TIMUERIM, TIMUERŌ; see 3.7.8.1.5 (1), under *Poder*). From *POTĒRE, the regular outcome is *poder*.

When the highly irregular FERRE was lost from spoken Latin, replaced by PORTĀRE, LEVĀRE, etc., the derivatives of FERRE were remodelled on the pattern of regular -ĪRE verbs. Thus, SUFFERRE > *SUFFERĪRE, OFFERRE > *OFFERĪRE. The Old Spanish reflexes of these forms (*sofrir, ofrir*) then developed regularly, except that *ofrir* became a member of that group of *-ir* verbs which shifted to the *-ecer* class: *ofrir > ofrecer* (see 3.7.7.2).

With regard to the root vowels of infinitive forms, Spanish *-ar* and *-er* verbs have undergone no changes in their history, with the rare exception of an occasional verb like OSp. *jogar* > MSp. *jugar* 'to play' (where the resulting /u/∼/ué/ alternation is unprecedented in Spanish; see 3.7.8.1.4(1), end). It should be noted, as in other contexts, that *-er* verbs never allowed root /i/ or /u/, but that the Old Spanish *-ir* verbs showed frequent hesitation between root /e/ and /i/, and between root /o/ and /u/, irrespective of the original Latin root vowel. Thus, in Old Spanish we find, beside *dezir*, the less frequent *dizir* (Latin root vowel Ī: DĪCERE), *midir* beside *medir* (Ē: MĒTĪRĪ), *sintir* beside *sentir* (Ĕ: SĔNTĪRE). As we saw in 3.7.8.1.4(2), the first of these variations was resolved in favour of /e/ (through the dissimilatory process /i/.../í/ > /e/.../í/, standardized at the beginning of the sixteenth century), except in the case of *recibir, escribir, vivir*, where the received pronunciation appears to have been imposed through awareness of the spelling I of the relevant Latin etyma (RECI̱PERE, SCRI̱BERE, VI̱VERE). Other exceptions were certain learned words like *adquirir, distinguir*, etc. Similarly, but with eventual preference for the high vowel, the /o/∼/u/ variation was resolved at the same time: *adozir/aduzir* (Ū: ADDŪCERE), *sobir/subir* (Ŭ: SŬBĪRE), *complir/cumplir* (Ō: CŌMPLĒRE) > *aducir, subir, cumplir*, etc. The only exceptions to this preference for /u/ were an occasional learned word like *abolir*, and the verb *oír* (AUDĪRE), which only shows /u/ in Old Spanish in forms which also preserve the root consonant (*udir*); when the /d/ is lacking, we never find ***uír*, but always an infinitive with /o/, probably to maintain a phonological contrast between this verb and *fuir* (< FUGERE), which in certain central Castilian varieties had lost its initial consonant and was pronounced /uír/. In the case of the *-ir* verbs with root vowel descended from Latin Ŏ, we find the usual /o/∼/u/ variation in Old Spanish: *dormir/durmir* (DŎRMĪRE), *morir/murir* (*MŎRĪRE). However, the only two verbs of this subclass that survived into Modern Spanish (namely, *dormir, morir*) preferred the mid vowel, as also happened in the other arrhizotonic forms of *dormir, morir* which lacked a palatal glide in the ending (see 3.7.8.1.4(2)). This preference for /o/ is no doubt due to the fact that these two verbs are the only members of the *-ir* class to keep the diphthong /ué/ in the root (*duermo, muero*, etc.), combined with the fact that the alternation /ué/∼/o/ is so frequent in Spanish.

3.7.9.2 The gerund

The Spanish gerund descends from the ablative of the Latin gerund (CANTANDŌ, TIMENDŌ, VIVENDŌ, AUDIENDŌ), which expressed, among other things, the manner in which the action conveyed by the main verb is achieved (e.g. HOMINIS MENS DISCENDŌ ALITUR 'man's mind is nourished by studying'). The Latin use of IN + ablative of the gerund (e.g. VIRTŪTES CERNERE IN AGENDŌ 'virtues are recognized through actions') was preserved in Spanish until recently, although only with temporal sense (e.g. *en llegando, te lo doy* 'when I arrive, I shall give it to you'), but this use of the gerund has practically fallen out of use in the standard language. (For the semantic development of the gerund, see Lausberg 1966: 288–94.)

The forms of the Latin ablative gerund and its Spanish reflexes are: CANTANDŌ > *cantando*, TIMENDŌ > *temiendo*, VENDENDŌ > *vendiendo*, SENTIENDŌ > *sintiendo*. There is some indication that the fourth-conjugation forms (and those of verbs like SAPIŌ: SAPIENDŌ, belonging to the third) were simplified in spoken Latin (SENTIENDŌ > *SENTENDŌ, SAPIENDŌ > *SAPENDŌ), through loss of the glide which was also lost in the present-tense forms of these verbs (see 3.7.8.1.1). The regular diphthongization of tonic Ĕ accounts for the ending of the *-er* and *-ir* verbs (*temiendo, vendiendo, sintiendo*).

As in other paradigms (see 3.7.1.5, 3.7.8.1.4(2), 3.7.8.3.2(1-2), 3.7.8.4.3(4), 3.7.8.6.1(2)), the nature of the root vowel in the gerund is determined in part by the need to distinguish morphologically between the *-er* and *-ir* classes. Thus, high vowels never appear in the root of *-er* gerunds, which only show mid or low vowels (*vendiendo, temiendo, comiendo, moliendo, sabiendo*), despite the potential raising effect exercised by the palatal glide in the ending (/e/, /o/. . . /ié/ > /i/, /u/. . . /ié/) which in principle might affect these forms. Both in the Middle Ages and today, *-er* gerunds reject root /i/ and /u/ (*pace* Alvar and Pottier 1983: 254, who do not state the source of the forms they cite). By contrast, the root of Old Spanish *-ir* gerunds shows variation between /e/ and /i/ and between /o/ and /u/ (*veniendo~viniendo, sentiendo~sintiendo, compliendo~cumpliendo, dormiendo~durmiendo*), with later preference for the high root vowel, a preference which become categorical in the sixteenth century. This solution is exactly congruent with the root morphology of other paradigms, and shows the same few exceptions: *oyendo* (to avoid homonymic collision with *huyendo*), *agrediendo, aboliendo*, and a number of other latinisms).

The Old Spanish verbs whose root ended in a vowel (e.g. *caer, traer, raer; seer~ser, veer~ver; creer, leer, poseer, proveer; roer; reír, freír; destruir, fuir*) have gerunds which behave in accordance, for the most part, with what was said in the previous paragraph: (*cayendo, trayendo, rayendo; creyendo, leyendo, poseyendo, proveyendo; royendo; reyendo~riendo, friendo; destroyendo~destruyendo, foyendo~fuyendo*). It can be seen that in verbs like *reír* and *freír*, root /i/ may merge with the /i/ (= [j]) of the ending, so that the hiatus which in other forms marks the boundary between root and ending is submerged. In the case of Old Spanish verbs which could appear with or without hiatus (*seer~ser* and *veer~ver*), there are also two morphological patterns for the gerund: *seyendo~siendo, veyendo~viendo*. This variation was resolved at the same time and for the same reasons as in the infinitive (see 3.7.9.1), in favour of the forms without root vowel (*siendo, viendo*).

Very occasionally in Old Spanish one finds gerunds based upon the preterite root (see 3.7.8.6.2(1–4)): *toviendo~tuviendo*, beside *teniendo*; *fuxendo* beside *fuyendo*, etc., a type of gerund which continues to have some use in Aragonese, Leonese and Spanish-American areas (*dijiendo, trajiendo, pusiendo*, etc.). The only case which has survived in the modern standard language is *pudiendo*, which coexisted with *podiendo* in Old Spanish. *Pudiendo* cannot be considered a regular form of the gerund of *poder*, since we have seen that other *-er* gerunds do not allow root /u/.

The Spanish reflexes of the Latin present participle (CANTANS, TIMENS, etc.) have not been orally inherited, but are learned, each borrowed as a noun or adjective (*cantante, amante, hirviente*, etc.). The verbal value expressed by the Latin present participle was transferred to the infinitive or the gerund (e.g. *la vi fumar/fumando un cigarrillo*), although in Old Spanish we find a few rare cases of forms in *–nt(e)* with verbal value, which are probably imitations of Latin syntax and display one of the values of the present participle in that language: *Un sábado esient, domingo amanezient / vi una grant visión en mio leio [= lecho] dormient* 'As Saturday departed and Sunday dawned, I saw a great vision as I slept in my bed' (*Disputa del alma y el cuerpo*, verses 3–4).

3.7.9.3 The participle

As in the case of the Latin perfect (see 3.7.8.6), a distinction should be drawn between weak and strong participles. As in the perfect, the large majority of -ĀRE and -ĪRE verbs had weak (ending-stressed) participles (CANTĀTUS, AUDĪTUS, whence *cantado, oído*), while a high proportion of participles belonging to -ĒRE and -ĔRE verbs bore the accent on the root (TEMĬTUS, MISSUS, DICTUS, etc.). A further similarity with the perfect is that the majority of verbs which in Latin had strong participles, and which have survived in Spanish, now have weak participles (e.g. CURSUS, HABĬTUS, MISSUS > *corrido, habido, metido*).

A small groups of Latin verbs in -ŬĔRE (where the Ŭ belonged to the verbal root: BATTŬĔRE, MINŬĔRE, etc.) had perfects in -UĪ and weak participles in -ŪTUS: BATTŪTUS, MINŪTUS, etc. This type of participle became popular in spoken Latin and was spread to many other verbs whose perfect was in -UĪ, but where the Ŭ belonged to the ending (e.g. TENĒRE, TENUĪ, TENTUS > TENĒRE, TENUĪ, *TENŪTUS). The spread of this type of participle was more vigorous in the centre of the Latin-speaking world, and in Romania, areas where it became the regular ending for -ĒRE and -ĔRE verbs. It was less successful in the Peninsula and was limited to certain *-er* verbs: *conosçudo, metudo, perdudo, sabudo, tenudo, vençudo*, etc. (which coexisted with *conoscido, metido, perdido, sabido, tenido, vencido*, etc.). The ending *-udo* was not extended to all *-er* verbs and from the earliest texts was in competition with *-ido*, as we have seen.

The adoption of the ending *-ido* was not due solely to spread of the ending belonging to *-ir* verbs (*oído, sentido, dormido*, etc.), but in part to the development of verbs like VENDĔRE, whose participle continued to be VENDĬTUS in the Latin of Spain. When VENDĔRE changed its stress-pattern and came to form a single conjugation with TIMĒRE, etc. (see 3.7.7.1), its participle must also have changed its accentuation: VÉNDĬTUS > VENDĬ́TUS. Now if this change took place before the merger of Ĭ and Ē, as is likely (Lausberg 1966: 359), the newly accentuated ending would have been associated with that of the -ĪRE verbs, giving *vendido* as the Spanish result, a form then imitated by other *-er* verbs.

Participles in *-udo* were fairly frequent until the thirteenth century, but then rapidly declined and disappeared almost entirely in the fourteenth, replaced by forms in *-ido*, thereby contributing to the loss of contrast between *-er* and *-ir* verbs.

The root vowels of the weak participle in *-ido* were treated in exactly the same way as those of the infinitive and of other verbal forms with tonic /í/ in the ending; *-er* verbs allowed only root /e/, /a/ or /o/ (*metido, salido, roído*), but there was hesitation, in the case of *-ir* verbs, between /e/ and /i/ (e.g. *servido~sirvido*), and between /o/ and /u/ (*sobido~subido, dormido~durmido*). This variation was resolved by the end of the Middle Ages in favour of /e/ and /u/ respectively (but with the same exceptions as in other cases: *recibido, vivido, dormido, oído*, and a few other cases, all latinisms: *dirigido, abolido*, etc.).

Verbs with root-final vowels (e.g. *caer, traer, raer; seer~ser, veer~ver; creer, leer, poseer, proveer; roer; reír, freír; destruir, fuir*), leaving aside those with strong participles (*visto, provisto, frito*, for which see below), appeared in Old Spanish with the participial ending *-ido* (never, it would seem, with *-udo*), and with the expected hiatus between root and ending: *caydo, traydo, creydo, leydo, reydo, destroydo~destruydo, foydo~fuydo*). In the case of *seer~ser*, we find the same kind of variation (here *seydo~sido*) as in the infinitive and gerund. This hesitation was resolved in favour of *sido*, for the same reasons as the infinitive was reduced to *ser* and the gerund to *siendo* (see 3.7.9.1–2).

Despite the replacement of many strong participles by the weak forms found in Spanish, the medieval language retained a more extensive series of strong participles than are now in use. The large majority of these descended from Latin participles in -TUS, although (by contrast with what happened in the weak endings) the /t/ often remained voiceless, either because it was preceded by another consonant in Latin (APERTUS) or because early syncope (2.4.3.3, 2.5.5) brought it into contact with a consonant which had headed the preceding syllable (e.g., POSITUS > *POSTUS > *puesto*). In both cases, /t/ was not intervocalic at the time of voicing of intervocalics, and so remained voiceless. The main examples are:

APERTUS > *abierto* 'open(ed)'

CINCTUS > *cinto* 'girded' (later lost; participle of *ceñir*, beside *ceñido*)

COOPERTUS > *cubierto* 'covered'

IUNCTUS > *junto* (rare participle of *uncir* 'to yoke', etc.; later only adjectival: 'next to')

MORTUUS > *muerto* 'dead'

NATUS > *nado* 'born'(later lost; it coexisted with *nacido*)

POSITUS > *puesto* 'put'

RUPTUS > *roto* 'broken'(still in competition with *rompido*)

SCRĪPTUS > *escrito* 'written'

TINCTUS > *tinto* 'dyed' (participle of *teñir*, beside *teñido*; now only adjectival: 'red')

TORTUS > *tuerto* 'twisted' (participle of *torcer*, beside *torcido*; now only adjectival: 'one-eyed')

In imitation of these strong participles with /t/, inherited from Latin, others were analogically created:

conquisto 'conquered' (CL CONQUISĪTUS), participle of *conquerir*, beside *conquerido*; *conquisto* gave rise to a new verb *conquistar*, part. *conquistado*

quisto 'beloved' (CL QUAESĪTUS), beside *querido*; later restricted to the compounds *bienquisto, malquisto*, replaced by *bienquerido, malquerido*

suelto 'released' (CL SOLŪTUS), at first the participle of *solver* (cf. *resolver: resuelto*), it formed the basis of a new creation *soltar*, part. *soltado*

tuelto 'taken away' (CL SUBLĀTUS), participle of *toller* (also *tullir*), beside *tollido*~*tullido*; the verb was lost, except for now adjectival *tullido* 'crippled'

visto 'seen' (CL VĪSUS), beside weak *veído* (only in the *Auto de los reyes magos*)

vuelto 'turned round' (CL VOLŪTUS)

The Latin participles in -CTUS, preceded by a vowel, developed in different ways. The syllable-final /k/, in accordance with the regular change (2.5.2.4), became the glide [i̯], a sound which combined with /t/ to give /tʃ/, except when preceded by Ī, a vowel which absorbs the glide before it can palatalize the /t/:

ADDUCTUS > *aducho* 'brought' (later lost; participle of *aduzir*, beside *aduzido*)

COCTUS >*cocho* 'cooked' (only retained in the compound *bizcocho*; participle of *cozer*, beside *cozido*)

COLLECTUS > *cogecho* 'gathered' (at first, the participle of *coger*, from which it borrows its root consonant; it only survives as the noun *cogecha*, later *cosecha* 'harvest')

DICTUS > *dicho* 'said' (via **decho* (cf. STRICTU > *estrecho*), with root vowel taken from other strong forms of this verb: *digo, dizes, dixo*, etc.)

FRĪCTUS > *frito* 'fried' (now in competition with *freído*)

SATISFACTUS > *satisfecho* 'satisfied'

TRACTUS > *trecho* (in Old Spanish, a rare participle of *traer* 'to bring'; later preserved only as a noun and in adjectival compounds: *maltrecho* 'in a bad way', etc.)

Latin had inherited some strong participles in -SUS, a few of which survived into Old Spanish:

DEFĒNSUS > *defeso* 'defended, forbidden' (participle of *defender*, beside *defendido*)

EXPĒNSUS > *despeso* (participle of later abandoned *(d)espender* 'to spend (money)')

INCĒNSUS > *enceso* 'ignited' (participle of *encender*, beside *encendido*)

PRĒNSUS > *preso*, sometimes *priso* 'seized' (participle of *prender* 'to take', only retained as a participle in passive structures, e.g. *fueron presos* 'they were captured')

These strong participles in /s/, which belonged to verbs whose roots ended in /nd/, formed the model for occasional analogical imitations:

repiso 'repented' (CL PAENITUS), participle of *rependirse*; more usual was *repentirse* (part. *repentido*), now *arrepentirse* (part. *arrepentido*).

It has been noted that a number of Old Spanish participles survived in Modern Spanish only with nominal or adjectival value (*junto, tinto, tuerto, suelto, (mal)trecho*, etc.). The same observation can be made about an earlier period, since many Latin strong participles passed into Old Spanish without participial function: CORRĒCTUS (CORRIGERE) > *correcho* 'correct', DUCTUS (DUCERE) > *ducho* 'expert', EXPERGITUS (EXPERGERE) > *despierto* 'awake', FALSUS and *FALLITUS (FALLERE) > *falso* 'false', *falto* 'lacking' (whence *faltar*), FĪCTUS (Old Latin, for FĪXUS) (FIGERE) > *fito* 'fixed'> *hito*, RĀSUS (RĀDERE) > *raso* 'flat', TĒNSUS (TENDERE) > *teso* (later remodelled as *tieso*) 'stiff', etc.

For some time there existed in Spanish a small number of truncated strong participles, belonging to *-ar* verbs (e.g. *canso, pago*), forms which continue to be used in some Peninsular and American areas of Spanish speech. The explanation for these forms probably lies in certain Old Spanish participles. We have just seen that *conquisto* and *suelto* at first belonged to the verbs *conquerir* and *solver*, but when these verbs fell out of use their participles continued to be used and served as the basis for new creations, *conquistar* and *soltar*. For some time, *conquisto* and *suelto* continued to function as the participles of these new verbs: *conquistar*: *conquisto*; *soltar*: *suelto*. This was the model for the creation of other 'short' participles (*cansar*: *canso*; *pagar*: *pago*), although the verbs *conquistar*, *soltar* later came to have regular participles: *conquistado*, *soltado*.

3.8 Other word classes

3.8.1 The preposition

The prepositions of Spanish, like those of other languages, have values which are organized in a way which is much looser than that observable in the case of other categories (for example, the categories of gender in the noun, or tense in the verb). Prepositions are 'organized' in open systems which are similar to those found in the lexical component of languages, but since their function can be described as primarily grammatical (e.g. they have much in common with other, purely grammatical, markers of 'case'; see 3.2.1), and only secondarily lexical, it is convenient to consider them here, rather than in the section on lexis (chapter 4).

Historically, prepositions have a close relationship with adverbs, in the sense that adverbs (either in combination with preexisting prepositions (e.g. Sp. *más allá de*, *fuera de*) or alone (e.g. Sp. *bajo*)) may come to have prepositional value; for the adverbs concerned, see 3.4. Certain nouns too have contributed to the creation of prepositions (e.g. *frente a*, *arriba de*, *al lado de*), and it is evident that there is a close relationship between many prepositions and conjunctions (e.g. *para*/*para que*, *después*/*después* (*de*) *que*).

It can be seen from some of the above examples that no attempt will be made to distinguish, in this discussion, between simple prepositions (*con*, *por*, *de*, etc.) and prepositional phrases (i.e. groups of words which function in the same way as a simple preposition: *alrededor de*, *cerca de*, *detrás de*, etc.).

For a fuller account of the development of prepositions in Spanish, see Alvar and Pottier (1983: 285–319).

AD 'to' was inherited by Spanish as *a*, although *para* (see PER, below) in part also expresses this concept. In the sense 'towards' (also expressed by VERSUS), AD (like VERSUS) was replaced by expressions derived from FACIĒ 'face': pre-literary OSp. *faz a*, later *faza*, *fazia* (now *hacia*). In the same sense, Old Spanish occasionally used the form *cara a* (based on *cara*, also 'face'), often modified to *carra* and *carria* (under the influence of *fazia*); however, forms based on *cara* now survive only in non-standard Spanish. In the sense 'as far as' (also conveyed by TENUS), AD was superseded by Ar. *hátta*, borrowed in various guises (*adta*, *ata*, *hata*, *fata*, *fasta*) by early Old Spanish. From the thirteenth century, we find only *fasta*, eventually respelled *hasta*. For *a* as a marker of indirect objects and of personal direct objects, see 3.2.1.

AB 'away from' could scarcely survive, since it would have become identical to the product of AD. Its content came to be expressed by *de* or *desde*. We have seen (3.2.1) that to express the agent of a passive verb, Latin AB did survive tenuously into Old Spanish, as *a*, but was soon replaced entirely by *de*, the preposition used until the early modern period, when it was largely replaced by *por*.

DE 'away from, after' expanded its range of reference (absorbing the values of AB and EX) and survived as *de*. It could be combined with EX in the OSp. *des* (e.g. *des allí*), a form later found only in the further expanded *desde*.

CUM '(together) with' > *con*.

SINE 'without' > *sin*. The expected form is *sen*, which occurs only rarely in the medieval period. *Sin* (together with occasional OSp. *sines*) may owe its form to influence from OSp. *nin* or *sino*, perhaps to avoid confusion with *en* after words ending in /s/.

IN 'to, into, in, at' > *en*, which continued in Old Spanish to be compatible with expressions of movement (e.g. *allá las subie en el más alto logar* (*PMC* 1611)) as well as with 'static' expressions. The former pattern is now almost entirely restricted to *entrar en* (*casa*, etc.), and the preposition *a* (< AD) has replaced *en* in almost all cases where motion is involved.

EX (and its variant Ē) 'away from, out of' has left little trace in Spanish. Combined with DE (DE + EX), it survives in OSp. *des*, later *desde* (see DE, above), but it has been generally replaced by DE alone (e.g. *salir de casa*), or by expressions based on FORAS (an adverbial variant of FORIS 'outside', used in spoken Latin already as a preposition), whence *fuera de*, as in *llevar a alguien fuera de su país*. It can be seen that as well as replacing EX, *fuera de* also replaces Lat. EXTRA 'outside'.

INTER 'between, during' survives as *entre* (for metathesis of -R, see 2.5.4), although the Spanish form retains only some of the meanings of its ancestor ('between', 'among', occasionally 'during', e.g. *entre tanto* 'meanwhile'). To express 'within', it has been replaced by *dentro de* (see INTRO), and the meaning 'during' is now most commonly expressed by *durante*, originally a present participle, used in absolute phrases like *durante la comida*, whose literal sense was at first 'while the meal lasted'.

INTRO 'within' survives only as part of the originally compound form *dentro* (< DE + INTRO). *Dentro* could function in Old Spanish as a simple preposition (e.g. *dentro la villa*), but was more frequently found in combination with *en* (e.g. *dentro en Sevilla*). Later, it entered into combination with *de* (*dentro de*), the only prepositional form now used by Spanish.

EXTRA 'beyond, outside of' is largely replaced by *fuera de* (see EX, above).

PER 'through, during, by means of' coalesces, probably in spoken Latin, with PRO 'in front of, on behalf of, in place of', providing OSp. *por*, a form which expresses almost all the senses of the two Latin prepositions, together with those of OB and PROPTER 'because of', although 'in front of' was already at that stage expressed by the descendants of ANTE (see below). As an alternative to *por*, in some of its senses, Old Spanish used the combination *por a*, more usually written *pora*, which is normal (in the senses today expressed by *para*) until the late thirteenth century, when it is replaced by the modern form, *para*. This change is unsatisfactorily explained, but may be due to influence from an independent Old Spanish descendant of PER, namely *par*, used only in oaths and exclamations (e.g. *par Dios*). *Para* has increased its range of reference over the centuries, and has encroached on the territory of other prepositions, for example *hacia* (see AD, above), coming to mean 'towards'. On the other hand, *por* has suffered competition, in some senses, from new creations, including *a través de* 'through, across', first recorded in the Golden Age (in the form *al través de*).

TRANS 'across, beyond' retains this sense only in certain place-names (*Trasmiera*, etc.). When used in expressions of movement, it is replaced by *por* (< PER /PRO) and by *a través de*; in static expressions (where it competed with ULTRA (see below), TRANS was superseded by *más allá de*, *del otro lado de*, or, in Old Spanish only, *allén de* (< ILLINC 'from there'), later felt to be a single word, *allende* (e.g. *allende mar* 'beyond the sea') which could suffer loss of its final vowel: *allend* ~ *allent* ~ *allén*. TRANS is retained, as *tras*, only in the (static) sense 'behind'.

SUPER 'over, above, during, besides' > *sobre*, a form almost entirely restricted to locative sense, in which it is in close relationship with *en* and expressions derived from nouns such as *arriba de* (< RĪPA '(river-)bank'), *encima de* (< late OSp. *cima* 'summit' < CYMA 'shoot (of a plant)'). In temporal sense, *sobre* conveys only 'at about' (e.g. *sobre las seis*) and has otherwise been replaced by *durante* (see INTER, above). The sense 'besides' came eventually to be expressed by the compound preposition *además de*.

SUB 'under' > *so*, the commonest form in Old Spanish, but antiquated by the sixteenth century. Its competitors, *baxo de* (later *bajo de*, and *bajo* only since the seventeenth century) and *debaxo de* (later *debajo de*), are adaptations of the adjective *baxo* 'low' < BASSUS, with internal consonant modified under the influence of *baxar* 'to go down, to lower' < *BASSIĀRE.

RETRO 'behind' and POST 'id.' (for the temporal sense of POST, see below) are replaced by descendants of TRANS (originally 'across, etc.'; see above): *tras*, *detrás de*. For the descendant of RETRO, see CIRCA, below.

ANTE 'before, in front of, faced with' provides OSp. *ante*, a form which continues all the Latin meanings (of time, place, etc.). A competitor *(antes (de))* with 'adverbial *s*' (see 3.4) is only gradually preferred in temporal sense, while in locative sense *ante* had competitors derived from combinations of ANTE with other prepositions: *desante* < DE EX ANTE, *enante* < IN ANTE, *denante* < DE IN ANTE. From the last of these descends *delante*, through dissimilation /n/ . . . /n/ > /l/ . . . /n/, and non-standard *delantre*, with addition of /ɾ/ perhaps through influence from OSp. *mientre* 'while', etc. Descendants of ANTE have therefore absorbed the values of PRAE 'in front of'.

Other prepositional expressions of place are created in Spanish on the basis of nouns: *al lado de*, *enfrente de*, *frente a*.

POST 'after, behind' does not survive in simple form, except as an adverb (*pues*). In temporal sense, it is expanded to OSp. *empués*, *empós* (< IN POST), *depués* (< DE POST), *después* (< DE EX POST), and *después de*, of which only the last survives into the modern language, or is replaced by *desde* (see DE and EX, above). In locative sense, POST is replaced by descendants of TRANS (see above): *tras*, *detrás de*.

ULTRA 'on the far side of' does not survive, and its values are expressed by descendants of TRANS (*tras*, *detrás de*, see above), by new creations based on LATUS 'side' (*del otro lado de*, etc.), and by originally adverbial *más allá de*, *allén de* (see TRANS, above).

CITRA 'on this side of' is likewise lost, its content expressed by *de este lado de*, *más acá de*, or, in Old Spanish only, by *aquén de* (< *ACCU HINC 'from here'), which, like *allén de* (see TRANS, above) could be treated as a single word, *aquende*.

SECUNDUM 'following, next to, in accordance with' survives, with the last sense only, as *según* (OSp. also *segund*, *segunt*).

CONTRA 'against, contrary to, opposite' appears in Old Spanish in a variety of forms, occasionally displaying diphthongization (*cuentra*), or combining with other prepositions (*escontra*, *encontra*), most usually in what is now its only shape (*contra*).

CIRCA 'around, near' maintains the second of these senses (also expressed in Latin by PROPE, which does not survive) in its descendant *cerca*, at first found in simple form (e.g. OSp. *cerca el pueblo*), later only in combination with *de*. The same meaning is also expressed by OSp. *cabo*, *cab(e)* (abbreviations of *(al) cabo de* 'beside', an expression based on *cabo* 'extremity' < CAPUT 'head') and by *junto a* (< IUNCTU, participle of IUNGERE 'to join'). In the sense 'around', CIRCA is replaced by descendants of RETRO (see above): OSp. *redor (de)*, later combining with other prepositions (*aderredor*, *enderredor (de)*). *Aderredor* was modified to *alderredor* (perhaps because at this stage *-derredor* was interpreted as a noun), and finally, through metathesis, to *alrededor*.

LONGE 'in the distance, far away' functioned in Latin only as an adverb (which survives as OSp. *lueñe* 'id.'). *Lueñe* is ousted, in later Old Spanish, by its competitor *lexos* (< LAXIUS 'more broadly, more separately'), and it is from this adverb that Spanish derives its most frequent preposition meaning 'far from': *lejos de*.

3.8.2 *The conjunction*

The coordinating conjunctions of Spanish are largely inherited from Latin.

ET 'and', being atonic, is generally represented in Old Spanish by *e*, although *i/y* also appears in early texts. The latter form probably arose in cases where the conjunction preceded a vowel (*e esto* > *y esto*), but both forms are found in all environments until the early sixteenth century, when *e* gives way to *y* except before /i/, even though some writers use *y* before /i/ until the eighteenth century. The common Old Spanish spelling *et* is an imitation of Latin ET and reflects the pronunciation /e/, just as *e* does.

AUT 'or' > *o*. The form *u* probably arose in prevocalic position, and has only in the modern period come to be restricted to use before words beginning with /o/ (e.g. *uno u otro*).

NEC 'and not, nor' appears in Old Spanish as *ni*, or as *nin* (until the fifteenth century), a form arrived at by imitation of the Old Spanish alternation between *no* and *non*. The vowel /i/ is difficult to explain, and cannot be due simply to development in prevocalic position (as applies in the case of *y* < ET (see above)) since *ne* is very rare in Medieval Spanish. Corominas and Pascual (1980–91, s.v. *no*) postulate primitive **nei*, in which the final glide is the product of -C before a consonant (see 2.5.2.4), with subsequent reduction to *ni*.

SED 'but' was generally replaced in spoken Latin by MAGIS, whence early OSp. *maes*, quickly replaced by its competitor *mas*. The synonym *pero* descends from post-Classical PER HOC, which, especially in negative clauses, came to mean 'nevertheless', a sense still attached to OSp. *pero*, but eventually weakened to that of 'but', after which *pero* succeeded in restricting *mas* to literary registers. *Pero* could be used after negatives until the seventeenth century, but thereafter is entirely replaced by *sino*. The latter form represents a coalescence of *si* and *no* (OSp. variant *sinon*) whose medieval meaning was 'except' (e.g. *nadi, sinon dos peones* (*PMC* 686)), from which the modern value (already occasionally visible in Old Spanish: *non se faze assi, sino...*) then emerges.

Few subordinating conjunctions are inherited by Spanish from Latin. *Si* (occasionally *se* in early Old Spanish) continues SĪ 'if', although its negative counterpart NISI leaves no descendant, but is replaced by *si...no* or by new creations based on MINUS 'less': *a menos que*. Apart from SĪ, the only frequent survivor is the prime marker of subordination *que*, < QUID (the replacement of CL QUOD), which clearly already had this subordinating role (amongst other functions; for its relative value, see 3.5.4). It is likely that *que* (alongside an Old Spanish variant *ca*) also descends from an atonic variant of QUIA 'because' (although loss of -A is difficult to account for), since OSp. *que* frequently has this value. Similarly, *que* has acquired the value of QUAM 'than' (again, beside *ca*, although *ca* with this meaning is rare and restricted to early texts). Another descendant of a Latin subordinating conjunction is *quando*, later *cuando* < QUANDO.

OSp. *que* expressed a wide range of meanings, now associated with other conjunctions: 'in such a way that', 'in order that', 'because', etc. This multivalency, which marks early texts, continues at least until the fourteenth century. Until well after Spanish began to be used as the vehicle of history, science, philosophy, etc., kinds of writing in which complex subordination is used, *que* is used with multiple values, provided the context makes it sufficiently clear which particular value is intended.

However, during this time and earlier, Spanish was enriched with a new range of conjunctions, from a variety of sources, sometimes used in combination with the subordinator *que*, sometimes without.

An addition to the stock of conjunctions in spoken Latin was the Greek borrowing μακάριε (voc. of μακάρος 'happy, fortunate'), whence OSp. *maguer(a)* 'although'. At first this form functioned only as an adverb, with a similar sense to that of *enhorabuena*. Lapesa (1980: 62) exemplifies the change of sense by noting the approximate equivalence of meaning between a phrase such as *hágalo enhorabuena; no lo aprobaré* and others such as *no lo aprobaré aunque lo haga. Maguer(a)*, sometimes combined with *que*, declines in the face of *aunque, puesto que* during the fourteenth and fifteenth centuries and is rarely found in the sixteenth. A later addition, this time found only in Peninsular Romance, is OSp. *oxalá*, now *ojalá* < Ar. *wa šā llâh* 'and may God will'.

Other subordinating conjunctions are created from words belonging to other classes. Adverbs are a frequent source. DUM INTERIM 'while' > early OSp. *domientre* (whose diphthong results from the influence of the Old Spanish adverbial ending *-mientre* < MENTE; see 3.4). *Domientre* was modified to *demientre* (since many other conjunctions, adverbs and prepositions had *de-* as their first syllable (*de(s)pués, debajo, detrás*, etc.) and then to *mientre* for similar reasons (the fact that *de-* often functioned as a detachable prefix: *debajo, detrás*, beside *bajo, tras*, etc.). The change of the final syllable, to *mientra(s)*, comes about through attraction exerted by other Old Spanish particles ending in *-a(s)* (*fuera(s), nunca(s), contra*, etc.). From earliest times, *mientras* appears either with or without *que*, and it is only in recent times that the form without *que* has come to be preferred in the temporal sense ('during the time that'), while the form with *que* is now preferred where a contrastive sense ('whereas'). Other conjunctions created from adverbs include *aunque, ya que* (frequent from the Golden Age), and *como* < QUOMO (CL QUOMODO) 'in what way'. In Old Spanish, *como* competed with *cuemo/quemo*, a form which probably arose where the word was used under conditions of full stress, by analogical extension of the frequent Castilian pattern in which /ue/ was the tonic counterpart of atonic /o/.

Conjunctions created from prepositions include *pues* (< POST, already used in late Latin in place of POSTQUAM 'after, since'; in the latter sense *pues* was later challenged by *puesto que*, originally 'although' (see below)), *pues que, antes que, porque* (which in Old Spanish meant both 'because', when followed by an indicative verb, and 'in order that', when followed by a subjunctive, a duality which persists into Golden Age Spanish and marginally into the modern literary language), and *para que* (the form which has almost entirely replaced *porque* to introduce final clauses).

Subordinating conjunctions are sometimes created from nouns. Such new formations include *de manera que, de modo que*, OSp. *de guisa que* (based upon a medieval synonym (< Gmc. WĪSA) of *manera* and *modo*), *a pesar de que*.

Additionally, conjunctions have been formed from other classes of words: OSp. *como quier(a) que* 'although', *puesto que*, which also meant 'although' until the seventeenth century, when the modern sense 'since' emerges, perhaps because of the similarity of form between *puesto que* and *pues*.

3.9 Conditional sentences

Conditional sentences require special consideration owing to the fact that the relationship between the two clauses of such sentences is far closer than the relationship between 'principal' and 'subordinate' clause in other types of complex sentences. The unitary nature of conditional sentences is demonstrated in particular by the fact that the conditional clause (or protasis) and the clause expressing the consequence (or apodosis) in such sentences frequently display verbs with the same tense/mood marker, a parallelism which frequently involves the use of subjunctive verb forms in the principal clause, a characteristic which is rare outside conditional sentences.

Conditional sentences in Latin and in Spanish can be conveniently divided into three types. Firstly, there are those sentences in which the speaker leaves open the question of whether or not the condition stated will be or will not be fulfilled (or was or was not fulfilled); these sentences will be labelled *open conditional sentences*. Secondly, the speaker may wish to imply that the condition stated is (or was) unlikely to be fulfilled; these sentences will be called *improbable conditional sentences*. Finally, the sentence may express the fact that the condition definitely was not (or could not) be fulfilled; such sentences will be called *impossible conditional sentences*.

It is implied in the foregoing discussion that it is often necessary to distinguish between conditions which arose in the past, on the one hand, and those which arise in the present or will arise in the future, on the other. This sixfold system can be illustrated by means of the following Classical Latin conditional sentences, to which an English gloss (together with other explanatory detail) is added:

	past	non-past
1 (open)	SĪ FĒCIT, IMPRUDENS FUIT (pret. + pret.) 'If he did that (and I don't know), he was unwise'	SĪ POTEST~POTERIT, ID FACIET (pres. indic. ~ future + future) 'If he can, he will do it' SĪ POTEST, ID FACIT (pres. indic. + pres indic.) 'If he can, he does it'
2 (improbable)	SĪ POSSET, ID FACERET (imperf. subj. + imperf. subj.) 'If he was able (but I don't think he was), he would have done it'	SĪ POSSIT, ID FACIAT (pres. subj. + pres. subj.) 'If he were to be able (but I don't think he is/will be), he will/would do it'

3 (impossible)	SĪ POTUISSET, ID FĒCISSET (pluperf. subj. + pluperf. subj.) 'If he had been able to (but he wasn't), he would have done it'	SĪ POSSET, ID FACERET (imperf. subj. + imperf. subj.) 'If he were to be able (but he definitely isn't/won't be), he would do it'

3.9.1 Open conditional sentences

These sentences are characterized, in Latin and in Spanish, by the indicative verb-forms which appear in both the protasis and the apodosis, in sentences which refer both to past and non-past time. In past open conditions, Latin and Spanish can employ any past indicative verb form, such as the preterite (SĪ FĒCIT, IMPRUDENS FUIT > *Si lo hizo, fue imprudente*), the imperfect (SĪ POTERAT, FACIĒBAT > *Si podía, lo hacia*), etc. Where reference is to present time, the Latin present indicative of both protasis and apodosis is directly inherited by Spanish (SĪ POTEST, FACIT > *Si puede, lo hace*), but in the case of future conditions, where Latin allowed a future indicative (POTERIT) or a present indicative (POTEST) in the protasis, Spanish allows only the present, while at both stages the verb of the apodosis is in the future indicative (although at a colloquial level Spanish allows a present indicative here too: *Si viene, se lo doy* 'if he comes, I'll give it to him'). Thus SĪ POTEST ~ POTERIT, ID FACIET > *Si puede, lo hará*. It should of course be noted that the exponents of 'future indicative' differ widely between Latin and Spanish; for the replacement of FACIET by FACERE HABET (whence *hará*), see 3.7.8.4.1.

An exception to the statement that open conditional sentences allow only indicative verb forms can be seen in those that refer to future time. Throughout the medieval and Golden Age periods, such sentences often displayed a future subjunctive (alternating apparently freely with the present indicative) in the protasis (*Si pudiere, ferlo ha*, later *Si pudiere, lo hará*). This tense, whose form represents an amalgam of the Latin future perfect indicative (POTUERŌ) and the perfect subjunctive (POTUERIM) (see 3.7.7.4.3), has been ousted in recent centuries from these sentences by its present indicative competitor, just as in other sentences it was ousted by the present subjunctive (see 3.7.8.4.4).

3.9.2 Improbable and impossible conditional sentences

These types of sentences need to be discussed jointly because, for much of its history, Spanish has shown no distinction between the two types, and there continues to be identity (as in Latin) between past improbable conditions and non-past impossible conditions. From the table above, it can be seen that Latin improbable and impossible conditional sentences are characterized (in contrast to open conditional sentences) by the presence of subjunctive verb forms, in both protasis and apodosis, whether present (SĪ POSSIT, ID FACIAT), imperfect (SĪ POSSET, ID FACERET), or pluperfect (SĪ POTUISSET, ID FĒCISSET).

In late spoken Latin (see Harris 1978: 239), the difference between impossible and improbable conditions, and between past and non-past types, was obscured, perhaps obliterated, by the incursion of the type SĪ POTUISSET, ID FĒCISSET into non-past impossible sentences and into all improbable sentences. As a result of this change, the present subjunctive (as in non-past improbable sentences of the type SĪ POSSIT, ID FACIAT) everywhere ceases to be used in conditional sentences. We have already noted (3.7.8.3.2) that the general replacement of the imperfect subjunctive by the pluperfect subjunctive probably began in the types of sentences now under scrutiny (SĪ POSSET, ID FACERET giving way to SĪ POTUISSET, ID FĒCISSET), perhaps because the temporal remoteness of a pluperfect form was felt to enhance the notion of improbability of outcome, even at the expense of removing the distinction between impossible and improbable conditions. To summarize these changes in late spoken Latin, we can say that at that stage the commonest exponents of improbable and impossible conditional sentences were as follows:

	past	non-past
(improbable)	SĪ POTUISSET, ID FĒCISSET 'If he was able (but I don't think he was), he would have done it'	SĪ POTUISSET, ID FĒCISSET 'If he were to be able (but I don't think he is/will be), he will/would do it'
(impossible)	SĪ POTUISSET, ID FĒCISSET 'If he had been able to (but he wasn't), he would have done it'	SĪ POTUISSET, ID FĒCISSET 'If he were to be able (but he definitely isn't/won't be), he would do it'

A further Latin change, which was not to become universal, but which was fully accomplished in Spain, was the replacement of FĒCISSET (in the apodosis of improbable and impossible conditional sentences) by FĒCERAT. This use of the 'pluperfect indicative' for the 'pluperfect subjunctive' was at first, naturally, limited to past impossible conditions (e.g. Cicero, PRAECLĀRĒ VĪCERĀMUS, NISI (. . .) LEPIDUS RECĒPISSET ANTŌNIUM 'We should have won a famous victory, if Lepidus had not recaptured Antony'), but, as FĒCISSET moved into the apodosis of other impossible and all improbable conditional sentences, so FĒCERAT accompanied it, and, in Spain, completely ousted FĒCISSET from this niche, giving rise to the following system in the Latin of Spain (and some other areas):

	past	non-past
(improbable)	SĪ POTUISSET, ID FĒCERAT 'If he was able (but I don't think he was), he would have done it'	SĪ POTUISSET, ID FĒCERAT 'If he were to be able (but I don't think he is/will be), he will/would do it'
(impossible)	SĪ POTUISSET, ID FĒCERAT 'If he had been able to (but he wasn't), he would have done it'	SĪ POTUISSET, ID FĒCERAT 'If he were to be able (but he definitely isn't/won't be), he would do it'

Bearing in mind the regular changes associated with the development in Spanish of the 'pluperfect subjunctive' and 'pluperfect indicative', this system evolves directly into the main early Old Spanish (pre-fourteenth-century) system, a system which still, therefore, lacked distinction between improbable and impossible conditional sentences and between past and non-past types:

	past	non-past
(improbable)	*Si pudies(se), fizieralo* 'If he was able (but I don't think he was), he would have done it'	*Si pudies(se), fizieralo* 'If he were to be able (but I don't think he is/will be), he will/would do it'
(impossible)	*Si pudie(se), fizieralo* 'If he had been able to (but he wasn't), he would have done it'	*Si pudies(se), fizieralo* 'If he were to be able (but he definitely isn't/won't be), he would do it'

It should be noted that those cases of Old Spanish conditional sentences which are quoted (e.g. by Harris 1978) with *-se* forms in both clauses are not descendants of the Latin type SĪ POTUISSET, ID FĒCISSET. In every case I have examined of such Old Spanish sentences the *-se* form of the apodosis appears there because the apodosis is in turn subordinated to another verb which requires a past subjunctive, e.g. *PMC* 163–4: *Ca assil' dieran la fe e ge lo avien iurado/ que si antes las catassen que fuessen periurados*, where the form *fuessen* is determined by the expression *dieran fe que* 'they had sworn that'.

The main competitor of this early Old Spanish type is that in which the Romance conditional tense (developed from infinitive + HABĒBAT, e.g. *feria, ~ie, faria, ~ie*, or with inserted pronoun *fer~farlo ia~ie*; see 3.7.8.4.2–3) replaces the verb form of the apodosis. This innovation undoubtedly began in late spoken Latin, and is occasionally attested in writing (e.g. St Augustine, *Serm. app.* 253, 4: SĀNĀRE TĒ HABĒBAT DEUS, SĪ(...) FATĒRĒRIS 'God would cure you, if you confessed'). As a result, we find in early Old Spanish, alternating with the type already discussed (*Si pudies(se), fizieralo*), and surpassing it in frequency (Montero Cartelle 1989: 120, 129, 1310), the following sentence type:

	past	non-past
(improbable)	*Si pudies(se), ferlo ie~ia* 'If he was able (but I don't think he was), he would have done it'	*Si pudies(se), ferlo ie~ia* 'If he were to be able (but I don't think he is/will be), he will/would do it'
(impossible)	*Si pudies(se), ferlo ie~ia* 'If he had been able to (but he wasn't), he would have done it'	*Si pudies(se), ferlo ie~ia* 'If he were to be able. (but he definitely isn't/won't be), he would do it'

It will be noted that in past contexts, the 'conditional' verb form has what would now be regarded as 'conditional perfect' sense.

From the fourteenth century, a further element of variation is introduced into the sentences under consideration, namely the introduction into the protasis of the *-ra* form. The motive was no doubt the (possibly universal) tendency, already observed in Latin, for the same verb form to appear in both the apodosis and the protasis of conditional sentences. As a result, in all the categories of conditional sentences under consideration here, we find the type *Si pudiera, fizieralo*. Although never the exclusive late Old Spanish type (as already seen, we also find the types *Si pudies(se), fizieralo* and, most frequently, *Si pudies(se), ferlo ia~ie*, beside innovatory *Si pudiera, ferlo ia~ie*), the type *Si pudiera, fizieralo* became more frequent in the late medieval period and became the most frequent type in the Golden Age (then superficially changed to *Si pudiera, lo hiziera*).

It has been noted above that, throughout the Old Spanish period, there was normally no distinction made between improbable and impossible conditional sentences, nor between conditions which arose in the past and those which arise in the present or future. However, with the spread of compound verb forms (consisting of *aver* or *ser* + participle) from one tense to another and from one mood to another (see 3.7.4), the means were increasingly available to introduce (more precisely, to reintroduce) a more subtle discrimination between conditional sentence types. The notion of completion expressed by the participle of compound verb forms was particularly appropriate to past impossible conditions, where, by definition, the speaker knows that the possibility of the condition being fulfilled has come to an end. Perhaps for this reason, we find occasional cases in Old Spanish of compound verb-forms occurring in one or both of the clauses of past impossible conditional sentences. The verb forms concerned are *ovies(se) podido* or (from the fourteenth century) *oviera podido* in the protasis, and *oviera fecho* or *avria~-ie fecho* in the apodosis. For late Old Spanish, then, the complete range of conditional clause types can be stated as follows:

	<u>past</u>	<u>non-past</u>
(improbable)	*Si pudies(se)/pudiera, fizieralo/ferlo ie~ia* 'If he was able (but I don't think he was), he would have done it'	*Si pudies(se)/pudiera, fizieralo/ferlo ie~ia* 'If he were to be able (but I don't think he is/will be), he will/would do it'
(impossible)	*Si pudies(se)/pudiera// ovies(se)/oviera podido, fizieralo/ferlo ie~ia//ovieralo fecho/avria~-ielo fecho* 'If he had been able to (but he wasn't), he would have done it'	*Si pudies(se)/pudiera, fizieralo/ferlo ie~ia* 'If he were to be able (but he definitely isn't/won't be), he would do it'

This system remains fundamentally unchanged during the sixteenth and seventeenth centuries, although with minor changes of spelling, phonology and morphology. Thus, to use typical Golden Age spelling, the forms appropriate to past impossible conditional sentences were as follows: *Si pudies s e/pudiera// huvies s e podido/huviera podido, lo hiziera/lo haria//lo huviera hecho/lo havria hecho.*

However, during the Golden Age and in the eighteenth century we can perceive the two changes which were to bring about the modern system. On the one hand, simple forms are gradually excluded from both clauses of past impossible sentences, leaving only compound forms. On the other hand, *-ra* verb forms are increasingly excluded from the apodosis of all types of conditional sentences. This exclusion appears to operate verb-by-verb, so that in current Peninsular Spanish, only in the case of a handful of common verbs does the *-ra* form have 'conditional' sense (i.e. can appear in the apodosis of conditional sentences): *hubiera*, *quisiera*, *debiera*, and occasionally *pudiera*. As a result, the verb forms which can occur in the various types of Modern Spanish conditional sentences are the following:

	<u>past</u>	<u>non-past</u>
(improbable)	*Si pudiese/pudiera, lo haría* 'If he was able (but I don't think he was), he would have done it'	*Si pudiese/pudiera, lo haría* 'If he were to be able (but I don't think he is/will be), he will/would do it'

(impossible)	*Si hubiese podido/hubiera podido, lo hubiera hecho/lo habría hecho* 'If he had been able to (but he wasn't), he would have done it'	*Si pudiese/pudiera, lo haría* 'If he were to be able (but he definitely isn't/won't be), he would do it'

The occasional appearance, in the modern language, of compound *-se* forms (e.g. *hubiese hecho*) in the apodosis of past impossible conditional sentences would appear to be a hypercorrection, due to the fact that in many varieties of spoken Spanish the *-se* is declining in frequency while the *-ra* form increasingly becomes the only 'spontaneous' form of the past subjunctive. Under these circumstances, the *-se* form is felt to be a more prestigious or more literary variant than *-ra* and may therefore replace the latter in pretentious styles, even in the case of clauses (the apodosis of past impossible conditional sentences) from which the *-se* form has traditionally been excluded in Spanish.

For further discussion of conditional sentences in Spanish, see Harris (1978: 234–46, 1986), Mendeloff (1960), Porcar Miralles (1993), Pountain (1983), Rojo and Montero (1983), Wright (1932).

4 Lexis

By contrast with phonological, morphological and syntactical systems, the lexical systems of language are inherently open-ended, and it is not intended here to attempt an exhaustive treatment of the Spanish lexis (such a treatment is, in any case, by definition impossible) or to account in detail for the cultural conditions which were responsible for borrowings from various sources. Partial discussion of these matters will be found in the various sections of the Introduction (1.1–5); in the sections that follow, the intention is to examine in outline the main sources of the vocabulary of Spanish, using a minimum of exemplification.

4.1 Vocabulary inherited from Latin

The core vocabulary of Spanish, including many hundreds of the most frequent words, as well as many less frequent items, has descended from spoken Latin, passed on orally in unbroken succession from generation to generation, and undergoing the various phonological changes detailed in chapter 2. Such words have already been defined (see 2.2.1) as popular words.

However, it should be noted that semi-learned words (see 2.2.3), over which there has been much controversy, are here regarded also as orally inherited, differing from popular words only to the extent that semi-learned words have undergone one or more modifications of form due to the influence exerted upon them by the pronunciation with which related Latin words were read aloud at various periods, either as part of the offices of the Church or in legal/administrative circles.

4.2 Words of pre-Roman origin

As the use of Latin spread across the Peninsula, in the centuries following the first Roman involvement in Spain (218 BC), Latin came to be used bilingually with other, pre-existing, languages. Since the linguistic map of pre-Roman Spain was complex, the nature of this bilingualism differed from area to area, but it is evident that the conditions existed for the borrowing of lexical items by the Latin of Spain from a variety of other languages. Such borrowing does not appear to have been extensive, since the languages spoken bilingually with Latin mostly enjoyed low prestige and no doubt exhibited the more restricted vocabulary associated with the less-developed cultures they served. However, in some instances there would be no Latin term to express some concept (usually related to local flora or fauna, to local life-styles or techniques) and the remedy was to borrow the local term for the concept. On other occasions, despite the prior existence of a Latin word, the borrowing of a local word (to replace its Latin counterpart) could remedy some Latin lexical defect. Such a defect might be that the Latin term had acquired in some contexts a negative value (e.g. SINISTER 'sinister'); borrowing of a non-Latin word (in this case, the Basque word which gives rise to *izquierdo),* to replace the Latin term in its primary sense ('left'), solved a problem of potential ambiguity.

Celtic was widely spoken in central and western parts of the Peninsula in pre-Roman and Roman times and has provided a number of loans to the Latin of Spain. The following can be included among such borrowings, with varying degrees of certainty: *álamo* 'poplar', *berro* 'watercress', *bota* 'leather wine-bottle', *brezo* 'heather', *brío* 'verve', *engorar* 'to addle', *gancho* 'hook', *greña* '(greasy) lock of hair', *lama* 'silt', *légamo* 'slime', *losa* 'flagstone', *serna* 'ploughed field'. However, rather more words of Celtic origin were borrowed outside the Peninsula (mostly from the Gaulish speech of France) and became part of the word-stock of popular Latin wherever it was used, including Spain. Spanish words arguably inherited in this way from Celtic have cognates in other Romance languages and include *abedul* 'birch', *alondra* 'lark', *arpende* 'unit of land-measurement', *braga* 'breeches', *cabaña* 'shack', *camino* 'road, path', *camisa* 'shirt', *carpintero* 'carpenter', *carro* 'cart', *cerveza* 'beer', *legua* 'league', *saya* 'skirt', *vasallo* 'vassal'.

Basque provides a number of borrowings in Spanish, many of which were no doubt introduced into the Latin of Spain in the period following the Roman conquest of the northern Peninsula. However, since Basque, alone among the pre-Roman languages of Spain, has continued to be spoken down to the present, this language has at all times constituted a potential source of borrowing. Especially frequent are personal names (e.g. *García*, *Ínigo*, *Javier*, *Gimeno*, *Sancho*, although the last may be from Lat. SANCTULUS; see Lapesa 1988), but a certain number of other words (especially nouns) have often been claimed to have Basque origin, including: *aquelarre* 'witches' sabbath', *boina* 'beret', (*caer*) *de bruces* '(to fall) headlong', *cachorro* 'whelp', *cencerro* 'animal bell', *chaparro* 'dwarf oak', *izquierdo* 'left', *laya* 'spade', *legaña* 'rheum', *narria* 'sledge', *pizarra* 'slate', *socarrar* 'to scorch', *urraca* 'magpie', *zurdo* 'left-handed'. However, it should be noted that R. L. Trask (1997a: 415–21) rejects this origin for all these (and other) words, except *izquierdo*.

It is probably therefore wise to include most of the words just mentioned among a somewhat larger group of Spanish terms which in all probability were borrowed from unidentified pre-Roman sources (in some cases, perhaps Basque). Cognates of these words are sometimes to be found in Portuguese and/or Gascon, but they do not appear to be related to any known Latin or Celtic word. The following may be included (with varying degrees of certainty) in this portion of the Spanish vocabulary: *abarca* 'sandal', *aliso* 'alder', *alud* 'avalanche', *arroyo* 'stream', *ascua* 'live coal', *balsa* 'pool', *barro* 'clay, mud', *becerro* 'calf', *bruja* 'witch', *cama* 'bed', *chamorro* 'close-cropped', *charco* 'puddle', *garrapata* 'tick', *gazapo* 'young rabbit', *gusano* 'maggot, caterpillar', *madroño* 'strawberry tree', *manteca* 'lard', *nava* 'marshy valley', *páramo* 'moor', *pestaña* 'eyelash', *sapo* 'toad', *sarna* 'scabies', *sarro* 'plaque (on teeth)', *vega* 'river-plain', *zarza* 'bramble'.

4.3 Latinisms

From the Middle Ages onwards, Spanish has made lexical borrowings from Latin; this element of the Spanish vocabulary is often referred to as that of 'learned words' (see 2.2.2), although some scholars do not equate the two terms, and define 'learned' in terms of stylistic value, whatever the source of the words concerned. Latinisms have been transferred to Spanish from written Latin sources, and with minimal change (usually limited to the final syllable, to fit the latinism to the morphological patterns of Spanish). The requirement which Spanish has continually had for new vocabulary (chiefly, but by no means exclusively, relating to non-material aspects of life) could often be met by borrowing from Latin, whether from the Latin of the Church, the law or administration, or, especially from the Renaissance onwards, from Classical Latin sources. Because of the prestige associated with the Latin language, over the centuries and still today, the Latin lexicon has usually been the first source to which Spanish speakers and writers have turned to provide labels for new concepts.

There is no period in which latinisms have not been introduced abundantly into written Spanish, and although a proportion of those introduced were subsequently abandoned, it has been calculated (Alvar and Mariner 1967: 21–2) that such loans comprise between 20 and 30 per cent of the vocabulary of Modern Spanish (although, if the calculation is made on the basis of the frequency of words in Spanish, the proportion is much smaller).

Before the development of reasonably consistent vernacular spelling (in the later twelfth century), it is impossible to distinguish latinisms from archaically spelt popular or semi-learned words. Thus, an early spelling like *desiderio* (Silos gloss 132: see e.g. Menéndez Pidal 1964a: 16) may be interpreted as a rendering of a borrowing from Latin pronounced /desidério/ (which failed to become established or later fell out of use) or (more probably) of a noun pronounced /deséo/ (derived from the verb *desear* < DĒSIDIARE, for DĒSĪDERĀRE). However, from the early thirteenth century onwards, following the adoption of spelling norms based upon phonological principles (Wright 1982), latinisms can be clearly distinguished from inherited vocabulary, so that, for example, we are safe in interpreting *vision* (*Disputa del alma y el cuerpo*, 4) as a learned borrowing pronounced [βi'zjon] (< VĪSIŌ, VĪSIŌNIS), later pronounced [bi'sjon]. And from this point on, borrowings from Latin can be identified in every period, in greater or lesser quantities according to the cultural climate. In periods of literary development in which translation from Latin or adherence to Latin literary models is frequent (as in the later thirteenth century, the fifteenth century, much of the Golden Age and the eighteenth century), latinisms are numerous. Similarly, borrowing from Latin has satisfied part of the requirement for new scientific and commercial terminology, especially in the nineteenth and twentieth centuries, although a substantial proportion of the latter borrowings were probably not made directly from Latin, but via other modern European languages.

A selection of Latin borrowings made by Spanish at various periods can be made as follows:

By the thirteenth century: *actoritat* (later *auctoridat*, *autoridad*) 'authority', *alfabeto* 'alphabet', *alva* (later *alba*) 'dawn', *ángel* 'angel', *argumento* 'argument', *ascensión* 'ascent, ascension', *bendiçión* 'benediction, blessing', *caridat* (later *-dad*) 'charity', *castidat* (later *-dad*) 'chastity', *claridat* (later *-dad*) 'clarity', *cocodrilo/crocodilo* (later only *cocodrilo*) 'crocodile', *comendaçión* 'commendation', *condición* 'condition', *confortar* 'to comfort', *contrición* 'contrition', *criatura* 'creature' (later 'child'), *crucificado* 'crucified', *diluvio* 'flood', *ébano* 'ebony', *fastidio* 'annoyance', *monumento* 'monument', *perturbar* 'to perturb', *término* 'end', *título* 'title'.

By the fourteenth century: *adversario* 'adversary', *alteración* 'alteration', *ánima* 'soul, spirit', *apellido* '(sur)name', *ceremonia* 'ceremony', *colegio* 'college, etc.', *comparar* 'to compare', *conceder* 'to concede', *constante* 'constant', *continuo* 'continuous', *cotidiano* 'daily', *defender* 'to defend', *despacio* 'slowly', *e(n)mendar* 'to put right', *fragoso* 'rocky', *girar* 'to revolve', *herencia* 'inheritance', *imaginar* 'to imagine', *injuriar* 'to curse', *intención* 'intention', *manifestar* 'to show', *patrimonio* 'patrimony', *precepto* 'precept'.

By the fifteenth century: *afeitar* 'to shave' (formerly also 'to apply makeup'), *afeite* 'makeup' (now antiquated), *cicatriz* 'scar', *comprimir* 'to compress', *cóncavo* 'concave', *ebúrneo* 'made of ivory', *epitafio* 'epitaph', *férreo* 'made of iron, iron-like', *fulgente* 'brilliant', *globo* 'globe' (later also 'balloon'), *húmido* (later *húmedo*) 'damp', *ínclito* 'illustrious', *ingente* 'enormous', *inteligente* 'intelligent', *intentar* 'to attempt', *jerarquía* 'hierarchy', *máquina* 'machine', *mente* 'mind', *naufragio* 'shipwreck', *necesitar* 'to need', *perplejo* 'perplexed', *poema* 'poem' (taken by Latin from Greek), *principiar* 'to begin', *rito* 'rite', *sórdido* 'squalid', *súbito* 'sudden', *terror* 'terror', *trémulo* 'tremulous', *veloz* 'swift', *vestigio* 'vestige', *vital* 'vital' (plus many subsequently abandoned: *nequicia* 'evil-doing', *nubífero* 'cloud-bearing', *vanîloco* 'boastful', etc.).

By the sixteenth century: *ambición* 'ambition', *cómodo* 'comfortable', *contagioso* 'contagious', *decidir* 'to decide', *decoro* 'decorum', *dócil* 'docile', *ecepción* (later *excepción*) 'exception', *foca* 'seal', *foro* 'forum', *frecuente* 'frequent', *fuga* 'flight', *fugaz* 'fleeting', *hispánico* 'Hispanic', *horror* 'horror', *inerte* 'inert', *objeto* 'object', *pretender* 'to try', *pálido* 'pale', *precisión* 'precision', *presidir* 'to preside', *purpúreo* 'purple', *superstición* 'superstition', *temeridad* 'temerity', *tenaz* 'tenacious', *tétrico* 'gloomy' (again together with some latinisms later abandoned, such as *flamígero* 'fiery', *horrísono* 'dreadful sounding', etc.).

By the seventeenth century: *aplausos* 'applause', *cándido* 'white, candid', *capacidad* 'capacity', *cerúleo* 'azure', *cólera* 'anger, cholera', *concepto* 'concept', *crepúsculo* 'twilight', *ejecución* 'execution', *emular* 'to emulate', *erigir* 'to erect', *esplendor* 'splendour, *evidencia* 'evidence', *exhalación* 'exhalation', *fábrica* 'factory', *fugaz* 'fleeting', *funesto* 'disastrous', *inmóvil* 'motionless', *instante* 'moment', *mísero* 'miserable', *nocturno* 'nocturnal', *oficina* 'workshop' (later 'office'), *ostentar* 'to flaunt, show off', *prodigio* 'prodigy', *rústico* 'rustic', *tedio* 'tedium', *trémulo* 'tremulous'.

By the eighteenth century: *amputación* 'amputation', *caries* 'tooth decay', *conmiseración* 'commiseration', *excavación* 'excavation', *excreción* 'excretion', *proyección* 'projection', *undulación* 'undulation'.

In the case of the latinisms of the nineteenth and twentieth centuries, it is often the case that the words concerned entered Spanish through the medium of some other modern language, at first usually French, now usually English. Such words should therefore be regarded strictly as gallicisms or anglicisms. At all events, we are dealing here with forms it would be pointless to list, since they have cognate forms (usually with identical meaning) in a variety of other languages.

For the problem of phonological adaptation posed by some latinisms, and the resolution of this problem in the Golden Age, see 2.6.5. For the definition and general discussion of latinisms in Spanish, see Clavería Nadal (1991), and the introduction to Castro (1936). For latinisms introduced up to and including the sixteenth century, see Herrero Ingelmo (1994–5).

4.4 Hellenisms

Apart from a handful of place-names, the language spoken in the Greek settlements along the east coast of the Peninsula in pre-Roman (and possibly in Roman) times has left no legacy in Spanish. All the hellenisms in Spanish found their way into the language as a result either of being first incorporated into the Latin of Rome or of being borrowed directly from literary Greek. Three separate strands of such Greek borrowings can be recognized in Spanish.

Firstly, popular Latin borrowed a considerable number of words from Greek, owing to contact between Greek speakers and Latin speakers at all levels of Roman society and over a period of several centuries. Such borrowings became part of the popular Latin word-stock and in many cases were inherited orally by Spanish (that is to say that, once borrowed by Latin, such words are treated identically to words of native Latin origin and in the process of their inheritance they undergo all the changes which affect orally inherited Latin words, although a number have been subjected to semi-learned remodelling, again in the same way as many inherited Latin words). The hellenisms of this first stratum typically refer to aspects of everyday life, and include names of tools and domestic items (*ampolla* 'flask', *ancla* 'anchor', *baño* 'bath', *cesta* 'basket', *cuévano* 'basket (carried on the back)', *cuchara* 'spoon', *cuerda* 'rope', *espada* 'sword', *espuerta* '(non-rigid) basket', *estopa* 'tow', *lámpara* 'lamp', *linterna* 'lantern', *sábana* 'sheet', *saco* 'bag'), items referring to the house and to building (*bodega* 'wine-cellar', *cal* 'lime', *cámara* 'chamber', *mármol* 'marble', *piedra* 'stone', *plaza* 'square', *torre* 'tower', *yeso* 'plaster'), terms relating to the land (*greda* 'chalk', *yermo* 'wasteland'), botanical names (*ajenjo* 'absinthe', *caña* 'cane', *cánamo* 'hemp', *cereza* 'cherry', *cima* '(tree)top', *cizaña* 'darnel', *codeso* 'laburnum', *espárrago* 'asparagus', *esparto* 'esparto', *olivo* 'olive tree', *rábano* 'radish', *regaliz* 'liquorice', *tallo* 'stem (of plant, etc.)', animal names (*concha* 'shell', *esponja* 'sponge', *morena* 'moray (eel)', *ostra* 'oyster', *perdiz* 'partridge', *pulpo* 'octopus', *púrpura* 'purple (originally extracted from the murex)'), words related to man (*golpe* 'blow', *huérfano* 'orphan', *lágrima* 'tear', *pena* 'grief', *talento* 'talent', *tío, -a* 'uncle, aunt'), as well as a small number of grammatical particles (*cada* 'each' (see 3.5.5), OSp. *maguer* 'although' (see 3.8.2)).

Secondly, since the language of the Church, even in the Western Empire, was at first Greek, ecclesiastical Latin was full of hellenisms, many of which have passed into Spanish. However, since ecclesiastical Latin (with its Greek lexical component) continued to be heard in church down to the twentieth century, vernacular Spanish words of Greek origin relating to Christianity and the Church (like their purely Latin-derived counterparts) were especially open to latinizing influences, so that, on the one hand, much of the vocabulary concerned reveals semi-learned transmission, while, on the other, some ecclesiastical hellenisms are fully learned. Words of this group include: *abismo* 'abyss', *bautismo* 'baptism', *bautizar* 'baptize', *biblia* 'bible', *blasfemar* 'blaspheme' (and, via a modified Latin form of the same hellenism, *lastimar* 'harm, pity'), *canónigo* 'canon', *cátedra* '(bishop's) chair', later also 'university chair' (contrast the early borrowing *cadera* 'hip', from the same etymon; see 5.2.2), *catedral* 'cathedral', *católico* 'catholic', *celo* 'zeal', *cementerio* 'cemetery', *cisma* 'schism', *clérigo* 'cleric', *coro* 'choir, chorus', *diablo* 'devil', *diácono* 'deacon', *ermita* 'hermitage', *himno* 'hymn', *iglesia* 'church', *lego* 'lay(man)', *limosna* 'alms', *mártir* 'martyr', *misterio* 'mystery', *monaguillo* 'altar boy', *monasterio* 'monastery', *palabra* originally 'parable', then 'word', *papa* 'pope', *paraíso* 'paradise', *parroquia* 'parish (church)', *Pascua* 'Easter, Christmas', *patriarca* 'patriarch', *profeta* 'prophet', *salmo* 'psalm'.

Thirdly, Greek has served, throughout the history of Spanish, as a source of technical and scientific vocabulary. Most such words are ones which have first passed into Latin, as Latin expanded its own lexical resources, and should therefore be regarded as a subset of the learned words discussed in 4.3. However, a number of words from this stratum (especially medical terms) passed sufficiently early into everyday speech to undergo the phonological changes typical of the vernacular and must therefore be regarded as popular words, while other hellenisms of this stratum which passed into the vernacular were subject to partial remodelling (particularly from the period of the humanists onwards) and therefore constitute examples of semi-learned transmission.

As in the case of latinisms, a small selection of technical and scientific borrowings from Greek is given, organized by approximate period of adoption.

By the thirteenth century: *anatomía* 'anatomy', *apoplejía* 'apoplexy', *catarro* 'catarrh', later 'common cold', *cólera* 'bile, anger', *estómago* 'stomach', *flema* 'phlegm', *lepra* 'leprosy'; *alabastro* 'alabaster', *diamante* 'diamond', *esmeralda* 'emerald', *jaspe* 'jasper', *tesoro* 'treasure', *topacio* 'topaz' (see 3.2.2.2.1); *carta* 'charter, letter', *crónica* 'chronicle', *escuela* 'school', *filosofía* 'philosophy', *gramática* 'grammar', *historia* (at first also *estoria*) 'history', *lógica* 'logic', *pergamino* 'parchment', *poeta* 'poet', *teatro* 'theatre', *teología* 'theology'; *caramillo* 'flute', *música* 'music', *órgano* 'organ', *zampoña* 'Pan pipes'; *aire* 'air', *aritmética* 'arithmetic', *astrólogo* 'astrologer', *astrónomo* 'astronomer', *astronomía* 'astronomy', *clima* 'climate', *átomo* 'atom', *esfera* (at first also *espera*) 'sphere', *geometría* 'geometry', *hora* 'hour, time', *planeta* 'planet', *ballena* 'whale', *búfalo* 'buffalo', *cocodrilo* 'crocodile', *dragón* 'dragon', *elefante* 'elephant', *gigante* 'giant', *grifo* at first 'griffin', later 'gargoyle', now 'tap'.

By the fifteenth century: *arteria* 'artery', *cardíaco* 'cardiac', *cólico* 'colic', *diarrea* 'diarrhoea', *epilepsia* 'epilepsy', *gangrena* 'gangrene', *pronóstico* 'prognosis', *tísico* 'consumptive'; *academia* 'academy', *alfabeto* 'alphabet', *armonía* 'harmony', *biblioteca* 'library', *coma* 'comma', *comedia* 'comedy, play', *diptongo* 'diphthong', *etimología* 'etymology', *melodía* 'melody', *metro* 'metre', *ortografía* 'orthography', *prólogo* 'prologue', *ritmo* 'rhythm', *sintaxis* 'syntax', *tragedia* 'tragedy'; *ártico* 'Arctic', *caos* 'chaos', *cilindro* 'cylinder', *cono* 'cone', *cubo* 'cube', *eclipse* 'eclipse', *matemáticas* 'mathematics', *océano* 'ocean', *período* 'period', *polo* 'pole', *trópico* 'tropic', *zona* 'zone'; *acacia* 'acacia', *celidonia* 'celandine', *narciso* 'daffodil', *peonía* 'peony'; *arpía* 'harpy', *bisonte* 'bison', *delfín* (at first also *dolfín*) 'dolphin', *hiena* 'hyena', *lince* 'lynx', *sátiro* 'satyr', *sirena* 'mermaid', *tigre* 'tiger'.

By the seventeenth century: *antídoto* 'antidote', *ántrax* 'anthrax', *cráneo* 'cranium', *disentería* 'dysentery', *dosis* 'dose', *embrión* 'embryo', *epidemia* 'epidemic', *erispela* 'erysipelas', *esqueleto* 'skeleton', *laringe* 'larynx', *náusea* 'nausea', *síntoma* 'symptom', *terapéutica* 'treatment', *tráquea* 'trachea'; *catálogo* 'catalogue', *crítico* 'critic(al)', *dialecto* 'dialect', *drama* 'drama', *enciclopedia* 'encyclopaedia', *epigrama* 'epigram', *epíteto* 'epithet', *escena* 'stage', *filología* 'philology', *frase* 'phrase, sentence', *hipótesis* 'hypothesis', *idea* 'idea', *idioma* 'language', *metáfora* 'metaphor', *museo* 'museum', *paradoja* 'paradox', *paréntesis* 'parenthesis', *problema* 'problem', *símbolo* 'symbol', *sinónimo* 'synonym', *teoría* 'theory', *tesis* 'thesis', *tomo* 'volume'; *ábaco* 'abacus', *catástrofe* 'catastrophe', *cometa* 'comet', *diámetro* 'diameter', *elipse* 'ellipse', *éter* 'ether', *fósforo* 'phosphorus', *geografía* 'geography', *horizonte* 'horizon', *máquina* 'machine', *meteoro* 'meteor', *paralelo* 'parallel', *topografía* 'topography'; *achicoria* 'chicory', *crisantemo* 'chrysanthemum', *menta* 'mint', *mirto* 'myrtle', *opio* 'opium'; *anfibio* 'amphibious', *fénix* 'phoenix', *foca* 'seal', *hipopótamo* 'hippopotamus', *rinoceronte* 'rhinoceros'; *anarquía* 'anarchy', *aristocracia* 'aristocracy', *democracia* 'democracy', *déspota* 'despot', *economía* 'economy', *monarca* 'monarch'; *esfinge* 'sphinx', *quimera* 'chimera'; *ateo* 'atheist', *místico* 'mystic'.

By the eighteenth century: *asfixia* 'asphyxia', *autopsia* 'autopsy', *hemorragia* 'haemorrhage', *miope* 'short-sighted'; *antología* 'anthology', *bibliografía* 'bibliography', *criterio* 'criterion', *heterodoxo* 'heterodox', *homónimo* 'homonym(ic)', *lema* 'motto', *parodia* 'parody', *sinfonía* 'symphony', *sistema* 'system', *táctica* 'tactic(s)'; *base* 'base', *ciclo* 'cycle', *farmacia* 'pharmacy', *fase* 'phase', *hélice* 'helix', later also 'propeller', *magnético* 'magnetic', *periferia* 'periphery', *prisma* 'prism', *simetría* 'symmetry'; *autonomía* 'autonomy', *crisis* 'crisis', *dinastía* 'dynasty'.

The words borrowed from Greek during the nineteenth and twentieth centuries are almost all international words (and in many cases probably reached Spanish from other modern European languages, rather than directly from Greek or Latin). They include a number of words which combine Greek lexemes in ways not observed in Greek. Only a small selection of the many recent hellenisms will be given: *anemia* 'anemia', *anestesia* 'anaesthesia', *clínico* 'clinical', *neumonía* 'pneumonia', *psiquiatría* 'psychiatry', *quirófano* 'operating theatre', *quiste* 'cyst', *raquitismo* 'rickets'; *autógrafo* 'autograph manuscript', *biografía* 'biography', *fonética* 'phonetics', *taquígrafo* 'stenographer'; *asteroide* 'asteroid', *cosmos* 'cosmos', *cráter* 'crater', *sismo* 'earthquake'; *arcaico* 'archaic', *arqueología* 'archaeology', *laico* (beside *lego*, see above) 'lay', *programa* 'programme'.

For Greek words which passed to Spanish via Arabic, see 4.6, and, for further discussion of hellenisms in general, see Fernández Galiano (1967) and Eseverri Hualde (1945).

4.5 Germanic borrowings

Words of Germanic origin, from which we arbitrarily exclude recent anglicisms (discussed in 4.10), constitute a relatively small proportion of the Spanish vocabulary, although a few members of the group have quite high frequency. Like some other groups of borrowings, loans from Germanic languages have reached Spanish by a number of routes.

Firstly, a certain number of germanisms entered spoken Latin as a result of the centuries-long contact between Latin speakers and speakers of Germanic languages along an extensive frontier. A proportion of such loans became part of the normal vocabulary of spoken Latin and were used in all the territories where Latin was established as the vernacular, although usually with the exception of Dacia, which was largely cut off from the spread of western neologisms after it was abandoned by Rome in AD 271. The borrowings of this group were made, by definition, before the political fragmentation of the Empire, probably in the fourth and fifth centuries, and it follows that the Spanish words which descend from these loans have cognates in other Western Romance languages, but not usually in Romanian. Examples of Spanish words descended from this first stratum of Germanic loans include: *banco* 'bench', *brasa* 'ember', *espuela* 'spur', *fresco* 'fresh, cool', *guadañar* 'to scythe', *guarda* 'watchman', *guardar* 'to keep', *guarir* (later *guarecer*) 'to protect', *guarnir* (later *guarnecer*) 'to adorn', *guerra* 'war', *guiar* 'to guide', *guisa* 'manner', *jabón* 'soap', *rico* 'rich', *robar* 'to steal', *tapa* 'lid, cover', *tejón* 'badger', *tregua* 'truce', *yelmo* 'helmet'.

Secondly, a number of terms of Germanic origin can be observed to occupy only the Peninsula and southern France, or the Peninsula alone. These borrowings were taken from the Gothic language of the tribe (the Visigoths) who were allowed by the Roman authorities to settle in southwestern Gaul in the early fifth century and who established there a semi-autonomous kingdom, with its capital at Toulouse (see map 1.2, p. 15). During the fifth century, the Visigoths expanded their territory to embrace considerable portions of the Iberian Peninsula, so that the earliest loans from Gothic are to be found not only in Occitan, but also in Catalan, Spanish and Portuguese. Examples of Spanish words which descend from Gothic borrowings made in this early period include: *arenga* 'harangue', *banda* 'group of soldiers, etc.', *bramar* 'to roar', *brote* 'bud', *escullirse* 'to overflow', *espía* 'spy', *espiar* 'to spy', *estaca* 'stake', *guadaña* 'scythe', *hato* 'clothing; herd', *parra* (?) 'climbing vine', *rapar* 'to crop (hair)', *ropa* 'clothing', *rueca* 'distaff', *sacar* 'to extract', *sera* 'esparto basket', and perhaps *sitio* 'place'. However, the Visigoths were driven out of southern France by the Franks in the later fifth century, and the final borrowings made by Romance from Visigothic survive only in the Peninsular languages, e.g. Spanish *ataviar* 'to adorn', *casta* (?) 'breed', *cundir* (?) 'to be abundant', *espeto* 'roasting spit', *escanciar* 'to pour wine', *esquilar* 'to shear', *frasco* 'bottle', *gana* 'desire', *ganar* to earn', *ganso* 'goose', *gavilán* 'sparrow hawk', OSp. *taxugo*/texugo 'badger', *triscar* 'to stamp, gambol'.

Thirdly, the vocabulary passed to Spanish from French and Occitan (especially in the twelfth and thirteenth centuries, but also in subsequent periods (see 4.8)), and also from Catalan (see 4.11), contained a considerable proportion of words which in turn had earlier been borrowed from varieties of Germanic (principally Frankish). Such loans include the following cases: *adobar* 'to prepare', *afanar* 'to harass', *albergue* 'hostel', *ardido* 'bold', *arenque* 'herring', *arpa* 'harp', *bala* 'bale', *banda* 'strip', *bando* 'edict', *barón* 'baron' and *varón* 'male', *blanco* 'white', *blandir* 'to brandish', *botar* 'to bounce, launch' (orig. 'throw'), *bruñir* 'to burnish', *buque* 'ship', *cañivete* 'small knife', *dardo* 'spear', *desmayar* 'to faint', *escarnir* (later *escarnecer*) 'to scorn, mock', *esgrimir* 'to fence', *esmalte* 'enamel', *esquila* 'cattle-bell', *esquina* 'external corner', *estandarte* 'banner', *estribo* 'stirrup', *falda* 'skirt', *fieltro* 'felt', *flecha* 'arrow', *flete* 'charter price', *fruncir* 'to gather (fabric)', *gerifalte* 'gerfalcon', *guante* 'glove', *guinda* 'morello cherry', *hucha* 'chest', *jardín* 'garden', *marta* 'pine-marten', *orgullo* 'pride', *sala* 'room', *toldo* 'awning'.

The processes of phonological adaptation of Germanic loans differ according to the period of borrowing. Borrowings of the third group suffer most of the phonological changes typical of French and/or Occitan before passing into Spanish, at which stage the modification required is relatively slight, since the phonemic systems of Old French/Occitan and Old Spanish were considerably more similar than those of their modern descendants. Thus, for example, Frankish *HERIALD > OFr. *hiraut/héraut*, in which the initial aspirate is maintained. The second of these forms (/*heráut*/) was borrowed by Old Spanish, again maintaining the aspirate, but with addition of /e/ after the now-impermissible final /t/: *faraute* 'ambassador, interpreter'. It will be noted that the initial letter of *faraute* is merely the normal Medieval Spanish spelling of /h/ (thus *faraute* = /haráute/), while Golden Age *faraute* (where *f-* = /f/) indicates that the Old French word may have been transmitted to Spanish also via a second channel, namely Occitan or Catalan, where OFr. /h/ was replaced by /f/.

Germanic loans made in the Latin and Visigothic periods were apparently readily adapted to the phonology of the recipient language and occurred sufficiently early for them to be subject to all the regular phonological changes typical of spoken Latin, Hispano-Romance and Spanish. Only in the case of a few Germanic phonemes was there no near equivalent in Latin, a situation requiring more radical processes of adaptation; thus Germanic /h/, /w/ and /θ/, and the intervocalic plosives /p/, /t/, /k/ gave rise to certain problems.

Since Latin /h/ had been eliminated by the first century BC (see 2.5.2), Germanic /h/ was problematic for Latin speakers and words containing it were adapted by simply dropping the /h/: HARPA > *arpa* 'harp', HELM > *yelmo* 'helmet', *HRAPÔN > *rapar* 'to crop (hair, etc.)', *SPAIHA > *espía* 'spy'. Similarly, since spoken Latin had no syllable-initial [w] (early [w], spelt V, had rapidly become [β] or [v]; see 2.5.3.1), Germanic /w/ was replaced by [gw] (which was familiar in traditional Latin words like LINGUA, by this stage pronounced ['leŋgwa]). This adapted pronunciation has survived in Spanish where the following vowel is /a/, but, where a front vowel followed, [gw] was later reduced to /g/, although the same spelling (*gu-*) continues to be used with both values: WAITH- (+ suffix) > *guadaña* 'scythe', WARDÔN > *guardar* 'to guard, put away'; WERRA > *guerra* 'war', WĪSA > OSp. *guisa* 'manner, way'.

Latin and its successors had no /θ/ (Spanish /θ/ arises only in the seventeenth century; see 2.6.2), and in Germanic words containing this phoneme, /θ/ is replaced by /t/: THRISKAN > *triscar* 'to gambol', *THAHSUS > late Latin TAXŌ, -ŌNIS > *tejón* 'badger'. Similarly, it seems likely that the Germanic intervocalic voiceless plosives differed from their nearest Latin counterparts, perhaps in that the Germanic phonemes were aspirated (like English initial /p/, /t/, /k/: [pʰ], [tʰ], [kʰ]), and were sometimes equated with Latin /pp/, /tt/, /kk/, rather than with /p/, /t/, /k/. As a consequence (see 2.5.3.2), Germanic intervocalic /p/, /t/, /k/ often appear in Spanish as /p/, /t/, /k/, rather than as /b/, /d/, /g/: *RAUPA > *ropa* 'clothes', SPITU > *espeto* '(roasting) spit', REIKS (whence *RĪCUS) > *rico* 'rich'.

4.6 Arabisms

From the eighth to the fifteenth century, Arabic was the official language of a considerable (but eventually shrinking) portion of the Peninsula, and within this area (i.e. within Al-Andalus) all inhabitants would have at least some familiarity with that language, whether as native speakers or as second-language users. However, the multilingual nature of Al-Andalus cannot by itself explain the host of arabisms incorporated into the Spanish lexicon, since the forms of Romance (the Mozarabic dialects) spoken bilingually with Arabic in Islamic Spain were, of course, not forms of Castilian, but independent descendants of spoken Latin, which became extinct in the later Middle Ages. The Castilian dialect, from which standard Spanish descends, originated outside Al-Andalus, so that the loans it made from Arabic (the large majority of which were made in the period up to the tenth century, before the substantial expansion of Castile and its dialect into Arabic-speaking territory) were loans made from a neighbour rather than from a language spoken in the same territory. The reasons for the heavy borrowing of Arabic words by Castilian must therefore be sought in factors other than extensive bilingualism, and can probably be reduced to two: firstly, the need for names applicable to the many new concepts (both material and non-material) which reached Castile from Al-Andalus, and which it was most convenient to name by means of words borrowed from the dominant language used in that area, and secondly, the very high prestige associated with Arabic in the early Middle Ages, owing to the fact that Arabic was the vehicle of a culture which was considerably more advanced than that of Christian Spain, and indeed than that of the rest of Christian Europe. The first of these factors is responsible for the numerous additions to the Spanish vocabulary from Arabic sources, while the second factor is responsible for the less frequent replacement of existing Castilian words by Arabic synonyms. However, other factors must be borne in mind in conjunction with those just mentioned. On the one hand, even in the period up to the tenth century, there was a certain influx into Castile (as into other Christian territories) of southern Christians (Mozarabs) already familiar with Arabic and perhaps speakers of it. On the other hand, from the tenth century on, through the southward expansion of Castile and the movement of Castilian-speaking population into newly reconquered Arabic-speaking territory, there would have come into existence for the first time a certain body of bilingual Castilian–Arabic speakers, who would have been responsible for the borrowing of at least some Arabic lexical items.

A very high proportion of the arabisms in Spanish are nouns, an even higher proportion than that observable in other cases of heavy inter-language borrowing, where nouns normally predominate. These loans very frequently begin with the syllable *a(l)-*, owing to the fact that the Arabic definite article *al*, etc. (which was invariable for gender and number) was interpreted by speakers of Romance (where the definite article varied in form) as an integral part of the noun and therefore borrowed together with the noun it accompanied. The Spanish vocabulary contains many hundreds of arabisms, some of which are among the most frequently used words of the language, spread across most semantic fields. The semantic fields selected for discussion here are those in which borrowing from Arabic was particularly frequent, usually because of the large number of new concepts, introduced to Spanish speakers, which belonged to those fields.

As Castilian speakers adopted Moorish weaponry and tactics during the Reconquest, they often adopted the associated Arabic terminology: *adarga* 'shield', *alfanje* 'scimitar', *alférez* 'second lieutenant', *alforjas* 'saddlebag', *alarde* 'review, display', *almirante* 'admiral', *jinete* 'horseman', *rehén* 'hostage', *tambor* 'drum', *zaga* 'rearguard'. Closely related are terms relating to fortification: *alcaide* 'governor of fortress', *alcázar* 'citadel', *almenas* 'battlements', *atalaya* 'watchtower'.

Civil life too was affected by new arrangements, borrowed from Moorish Spain together with the necessary vocabulary: *alcalde* 'mayor', *aldea* 'village', *alguacil* 'bailiff', *almacén* 'warehouse, department store', *arrabal* 'suburb', *barrio* 'district (of town)'.

The development of commerce and trade which took place in medieval Spain under the influence of the Moors is likewise reflected by Castilian borrowings: *aduana* 'customs', *ahorrar* 'to save (money)', *almoneda* 'auction', *alquiler* 'renting, rental', *maravedí* 'a former coin', *tarifa* 'tariff'. Until the introduction of the metric system (and still in rural areas in Spain and Spanish America), the names of weights and measures were mostly arabisms: OSp. *adarme* 'dram', *arroba* '11.5 kilos', *azumbre* '2.016 litres', *cahiz* '666 litres; 690 kilos', *fanega* '1.58 bushels; 1.59 acres', *maquila* 'multure', *quilate* 'carat', *quintal* '46 kilos'. Similarly, the names of certain trades are borrowed from Arabic: OSp. *alarife* 'architect', *albañil* 'builder', *albardero* 'packsaddle-maker', *albéitar* 'veterinary surgeon', *alfarero* 'potter'; as are certain names of tools and instruments: *alfiler* 'pin', *alicates* 'pliers', *almadía* 'raft', *almohaza* 'currycomb'.

As a result of the imitation of building styles and techniques, Castilian acquired considerable numbers of arabisms related to house-building and decoration: *adobe* 'sun-dried brick', *albañal* 'drain', *alcantarilla* 'sewer', *alcoba* 'bedroom', *aldaba* 'bolt, doorknocker', *andamio* 'scaffolding', *azotea* 'flat roof', *azulejo* 'ceramic tile', *rincón* '(interior) corner', *zaguán* 'vestibule'. For similar reasons, the contents of the house often have Arabic-derived names: *ajuar* 'household furnishings', *alacena* 'larder', *alfombra* 'carpet', *almirez* 'mortar', *almohada* 'pillow', *jarra* 'jug, mug', *jofaina* 'washbasin', *taza* 'cup'.

The introduction by the Moors of new techniques and sometimes new species of plants revolutionized the agriculture of the Peninsula. New products (and some already known) which reached the Castilian north often brought their Arabic names: *aceite* '(olive) oil', *aceituna* 'olive', *acelga* 'chard', *albaricoque* 'apricot', *albérchigo* '(clingstone) peach', *alcachofa* '(globe) artichoke', *alfalfa* 'alfalfa', *alfónsigo* 'pistachio tree', *algarroba* 'carob bean', *algodón* 'cotton', *alubia* 'kidney bean', *arroz* 'rice', *azafrán* 'saffron', *azúcar* 'sugar', *berenjena* 'aubergine', *chirivía* 'parsnip', *limón* 'lemon', *naranja* 'orange', *zanahoria* 'carrot'. As Castilian came to be spoken in territories previously cultivated by the Moors, it adopted some words related to agricultural techniques (*almazara* 'oil-mill', *almocafre* 'hoe'), and the majority of its vocabulary relating to irrigation (e.g. *acequia* 'irrigation channel', *alberca* 'reservoir', *aljibe* 'cistern', *azuda* 'sluice', *noria* 'chain pump'), although these words remain typical only of the southern half of the Peninsula.

Gardening (including the herb-garden) was a further area of skill in which the Moors had much to offer, and as Castilians became familiar with Moorish gardens, they adopted many names of plants and related notions: *albahaca* 'basil', *alerce* 'larch', *alhelí* 'wallflower', *alheña* 'privet, henna', *alhucema* 'lavender', *almáciga* 'seedbed', *almez* 'nettle tree', *almoraduj* 'marjoram', *altramuz* 'lupin', *arrayán* 'myrtle', *azahar* 'orange blossom', *azucena* 'white lily'.

Words referring to the natural world which were borrowed by Castilian from Arabic are not numerous, but a small number of such terms has remained frequent: *alacrán* 'scorpion', *alcaraván* 'stone curlew', *alcatraz* 'gannet', *bellota* 'acorn', *garra* 'claw', *jabalí* 'wild boar'.

A number of new foods found their way into the Spanish diet, bringing their Arabic names: *albóndiga* 'meat ball', *alfeñique* 'sugar paste', *almíbar* 'syrup', *fideos* 'vermicelli', *jarabe* 'syrup', *mazapán* 'marzipan'.

Because Arabic science, during much of the Middle Ages, was considerably more advanced than that of Christian Spain (and indeed of Europe generally), Castilian speakers acquired almost the whole of their scientific vocabulary from Arabic. A good number of these medieval scientific terms persist in Spanish: *alambique* 'retort', *alcanfor* 'camphor', *alcohol* 'alcohol', *álgebra* 'algebra', *almanaque* 'almanac', *alquimia* 'alchemy', *azogue* 'quick-silver', *cénit* 'zenith', *cero* 'zero' (via Italian; see 4.1.3), *cifra*, at first 'zero', now 'figure', *nadir* 'nadir'.

It has already been said that arabisms have penetrated almost all fields of the Spanish lexicon. In addition to those considered above, the following terms may serve to illustrate the degree of penetration of the Spanish vocabulary by Arabic and the persistence there of the Arabic-derived words: *ajedrez* 'chess' (and the related *alfil* 'bishop'), *albornoz* 'bathrobe', *alcurnia* 'ancestry', *alhaja* 'jewel', *alquitrán* 'tar', *añil* 'indigo', *asesino* 'murderer', *ataúd* 'coffin', *azafata* 'stewardess', *azul* 'blue', *carmesí* 'crimson', *dado* (?) 'dice', *fonda* (?) 'inn', *fulano* 'what's-his-name', *gandul* 'good-for-nothing', *hasta* 'as far as; even', *hazaña* 'feat', *joroba* 'hunchback', *marfil* 'ivory', *melena* 'mop (of hair)', *mezquino* 'wretched; paltry', *mengano* 'what's-his-name', *mezquita* 'mosque' (together with *alminar* 'minaret', *almuédano* 'muezzin'), *nuca* 'nape', *ola* 'wave', *ojalá* 'if only!', *recamar* 'to embroider (in relief)', *tabaco* (?) 'tobacco', *tarea* 'task', *zagal* 'youth'.

With the decline in prestige of Arabic culture in the late Middle Ages and in the Spanish Golden Age, some losses did occur from among the arabisms of Castilian. In a number of cases, an arabism was replaced by a borrowing from a source at that stage perceived as more prestigious, or by a term created by means of the derivational resources of Spanish. Thus *albéitar* gave way to *veterinario* (from Latin), *alfageme* 'barber' disappeared in the face of *barbero* (a derivative of pre-existing *barba* 'beard'), *alfayate* 'tailor' was replaced by *sastre* (from Occitan), *alarife* was displaced by *arquitecto* (from Greek, via Latin).

Not all of the arabisms which appear in Spanish are borrowings of words which belong to the native Arabic word-stock. Because Arabic, after the seventh century, was the language of a cultural zone which stretched from India to the Atlantic, it was in contact with many other languages, some of which had great prestige, and from which Arabic consequently borrowed numbers of words. Such words were in some cases passed on to Spanish (and to other European languages). Examples of such complex transmission include Sp. *ajedrez* and *alcanfor* (from Sanskrit), *alfalfa*, *alfeñique*, *almíbar*, *añil*, *azul*, *jazmín*, *naranja* (from Persian), and *acelga*, *adarme*, *alambique*, *alquimia*, *arroz* (from Greek). In addition, before its expansion out of the Arabian peninsula, Arabic came into contact with Latin, sometimes directly, sometimes via Greek, and borrowed from that source a number of words which were subsequently passed to Spanish. These include *albaricoque* (Lat. PRAECOQUU '(early) peach'), *albérchigo* (Lat. PERSICU, whence also Sp. *prisco* 'apricot', by normal descent), *alcázar* (Lat. CASTRU, from a diminutive form of which, CASTELLU, descends *castillo*, by direct transmission), *almud* (Lat. MODIU) 'measure for grain'.

The incorporation of arabisms into the Spanish vocabulary posed considerable problems of phonemic adaptation (unlike the incorporation of Germanic loans; see 4.5). At the time of intense borrowing from Arabic (eighth to tenth centuries), and later, Arabic contained a fair number of phonemes with no near equivalent in Romance. These phonemes were for the most part velar and laryngeal consonants, but the Arabic dental fricatives and Arabic /w/ were also problematical for Romance speakers. In addition, there were problems of distribution (phonemes similar to those of Romance but in unfamiliar positions in the word) to be overcome.

The Arabic velars and laryngeals were occasionally replaced by Castilian /h/ (spelt *f*), as in *ḥinna* > *alfeña* (later *alheña*) 'privet, henna', *ḥanbal* > OSp. *alfamar*, later *alhamar* 'carpet'. However, the Spanish velars /k/ and /g/ were also used as replacements for the 'difficult' Arabic phonemes: *ʿarabiya* > *algarabía* 'hubbub', *manâḫ* > *almanaque* 'almanac', *šaix* > OSp. *xeque*, MSp. *jeque* 'sheikh', *ḥuršûfa* > *alcachofa* 'artichoke', *ḫarrûba* > *algarroba* 'carob bean'. A further solution was to omit the Arabic phoneme: *ʿaqrab* > *alacrán* 'scorpion', *ʿarif* > *alarife* 'architect', *ʿard* > *alarde* 'display', *ʿazʿár* > *alazán* 'chestnut(-coloured)', *háu̯la* > *ola* 'wave', *ṭaríḥa* > *tarea* 'task'. Where /f/ appears in Modern Spanish in correspondence with an Arabic velar or laryngeal (e.g. *ḥorğ* > *alforja* 'saddlebag'), it is probably the case that the Arabic word was first borrowed by a non-Castilian variety of Romance (where no /h/ was available as a replacement for the problematic phoneme) and that the word was then passed to Castilian at a relatively late date (see Penny 1990b).

The Arabic dental fricatives represented by *s* (*sin*) and *z* (*zay*) (both unvelarized) and by *ṣ* (*sad*) (velarized) did not correspond closely to Romance /s/ and /z/, which were apico-alveolar. The Arabic phonemes were consequently replaced by the nearest Romance *dental* phonemes: voiceless *s* and *ṣ* by the Old Spanish affricate /t^s/ and voiced *z* by the afficate /d^z/. These phonemes were spelled *ç*~*c* and *z* respectively in the medieval period, and merge to provide /θ/ in the modern language (see 2.6.2): *sékka* > *ceca* 'mint', *ṣifr* > *cifra* 'figure', *safunariya* > OSp. *çahanoria* > MSp. *zanahoria* 'carrot', *sâqa* > *zaga* 'rearguard'. A special problem arose in the case of the Arabic group /ṣt/. The sibilant was first replaced, as we have just seen, by Romance /t^s/, and then the resulting group /t^st/ was simplified to /t^s/ (/θ/ since the seventeenth century): *ʿusṭuwân* > OSp. *açaguán* > MSp. *zaguán* 'vestibule', *mustaʿrib* > *moçarabe* > *mozárabe* 'Mozarab'.

Arabic syllable-initial [w] was modified in more than one way during the borrowing process. On the one hand, it was sometimes replaced by /g/ + [w] (just as had happened in the case of Germanic words in [w]): *'usṭuwân* > *zaguán* 'vestibule', *wazîr* > *alguacil* 'constable, etc.', *sarāwîl* > *zaragüelles* 'wide-legged breeches', *wadî* > *Guad-* (*Guadiana*, *Guadalquivir*, *Guadarrama*, etc.) 'river'. Secondly, [w] could be interpreted as [β] (OSp. *v*): *karawân* > *alcaraván* 'stone curlew', *mugāwir* > *almogávar* 'frontier-soldier', *wasīya* > *alvacea* > *albacea* 'executor'. A further treatment of [w] was retention, when, through loss of a preceding vowel, [w] comes to occupy second position in a syllable: *šuwâr* > *ajuar* 'trousseau', *diwân* > *aduana* 'customs (house)'.

Words borrowed from Arabic which ended in a single labial or velar consonant or in /t/, /tʃ/ or /dʒ/ offered a structure which was impermissible in Spanish (at least, in Spanish before the twelfth and after the thirteenth century; see 2.4.3.2). The solutions adopted were (1) to add a final /e/, (2) to replace the impermissible consonant with a dental or alveolar, or (3) to omit it. Examples of these three adaptation processes can be seen in: (1) *a'rab* > *árabe* 'Arab', *'arif* > *alarife* 'architect', *'anbiq* > *alambique* 'alembic, retort', *laqqâṭ* > *alicate(s)* 'pliers', *zabáğ* > *azabache* 'jet'; (2) *'aqrab* > *alacrán* 'scorpion', *muḫtasáb* > *almotacén* 'inspector of weights and measures', *rabáb* > *rabel* 'rebec', *muqáddam* > *almocadén* 'commander'; (3) *rabâb* > *rabé* 'rebec'.

Arabic words ending in a consonant cluster were adapted either by adding a final /e/ or by anaptyxis (addition of a vowel between the consonants): *'ard* > *alarde* 'display', *ṯumn* > *azumbre* 'liquid measure' (for Romance M'N > /mbr/, see 2.5.5); *qaṣr* > *alcázar* 'fortress', *quṭn* > *algodón* 'cotton', *rahn* > *rehén* 'hostage', *baṭn* > *badén* 'furrow drain'.

Medieval Spanish had few if any nouns and adjectives ending in a tonic vowel, so that Arabic words with this pattern (or ones which had lost a final consonant following a tonic vowel) were sometimes modified when borrowed by Spanish, usually by addition of one of the permissible word-final consonants: *waqî* > *aloquín* 'mould', *kirâ'* > *alquiler* 'rent', *qabâ'* > *gabán* 'overcoat', *bannâ'* > *albañil* 'builder'. However, in other instances the final tonic was retained, thus extending the phonemic possibilities of Spanish: *ḫairî* > *alhelí* 'wallflower', *qarmazî* > *carmesí* 'crimson', *habalî* > *jabalí* 'wild boar'.

In other respects, arabisms usually appeared early enough in Hispano-Romance to undergo the same phonological changes undergone by words of Latin origin. Thus, the intervocalic voiceless phonemes of Arabic are subject to lenition (see 2.5.3.2): *quṭn* > Hispano-Arabic *quṭún* > *algodón* 'cotton', *sâqa* > *zaga* 'rearguard'. Similarly, Ar. /ll/ and /nn/ underwent palatalization: *ġulla* > *argolla* '(metal) hoop', *ḥinna* > *alheña* 'privet, henna', *bannâ'* > *albañil* 'builder' (see 2.5.2.5). Likewise, /ai/ and /au/ were generally reduced to /e/ and /o/ (*dáị'a* > *aldea* village', *máịs* > *almez* 'lotus', *háụla* > *ola* 'wave', *sáut* > *azote* 'blow, lash'; see 2.4.2.3–4), although there is a residue of arabisms in which the first diphthong survives, as /ai/ or /ei/: *ǧufáịna* > *jofaina* 'wash-basin', *qâ'id* > *alcaide* 'prison governor', *záịt* > *aceite* 'oil', *báịtar* > *albéitar* 'vet'. The latter forms may be suspected of being passed from Mozarabic to Castilian (having earlier been borrowed by Mozarabic from Arabic) only after the termination of the processes /au/ > /o/ and /ai/ > /e/.

It is clear that the palatalization of syllable-initial velars (see 2.5.2.3) had ceased to occur before the incorporation of arabisms into Spanish, since Arabic velars before front vowels remain velar in Spanish: *miskîn* > *mezquino* 'poor, wretched'.

4.7 Mozarabisms

Castilian displays a number of borrowings from Mozarabic, the vernacular speech of Christians (but also of many Muslims and Jews) in Al-Andalus, that is, in those areas of medieval Spain which were under Islamic rule. With reference to language history, the term 'Mozarabic' indicates a series of descendants of Latin, spoken until at least the thirteenth century (and perhaps as late as the fifteenth in Andalusia) in the southern two-thirds of the Peninsula. These southern Hispano-Romance varieties were eventually replaced by Catalan, Castilian and Portuguese, as the latter, northern, varieties of Hispano-Romance expanded in the wake of the Christian Reconquest of Islamic Spain. In New Castile, Murcia and Andalusia, Castilian was spoken alongside Mozarabic, no doubt often by the same individuals, for considerable periods of time after the conquest of each city. It is known, for example, that in the case of Toledo, reconquered in 1085, Mozarabic still enjoyed some use in the early thirteenth century (see González Palencia 1926–30, Galmés 1983), in part because its speakers were often more cultured than the incoming Castilian speakers, owing to their ancestors' participation in the culture of Al-Andalus, which until the eleventh century was more culturally and economically developed than the Christian north. Until the creation of literary Castilian (beginning in the late twelfth century) and until Castilian came to be used as a national language of administration (in the later thirteenth century), Mozarabic no doubt enjoyed considerable social prestige in reconquered areas and was therefore in a position to exert influence upon Castilian. This influence, as we have seen (4.6), often resulted in the transmission to Castilian of arabisms previously adopted by Mozarabic, but also accounts for the borrowing by Castilian of certain Mozarabic words of Latin origin (in some cases, perhaps, replacing traditional Castilian forms). Among such borrowings, words referring to agriculture and the living world were particularly frequent, as can be seen from the following selection of probable mozarabisms in Spanish: *cagarruta* '(animal) dropping', *campiña* 'area of cultivated land', *cangilón* 'jug, bucket of chain-pump, etc.', *capacho* '(shopping) basket', *capuz* 'hood, hooded cloak', *corcho* 'cork', *chícharo* 'pea' (in Andalusia, Galicia, Cuba,

Mexico, etc.), *chinche* 'bedbug', *chirivía* 'parsnip', *fideos* 'noodles', *gazpacho* 'id.', *guisante* 'pea', *habichuela* 'bean', *jibia* 'cuttlefish', *judía* 'bean', *macho* 'mallet', *marisma* 'salt marsh', *mastranzo* 'variety of mint', *muchacho* 'boy', *muleto* 'young mule', *nutria* 'otter', *pleita* 'plaited esparto', *rodaballo* 'turbot', *semilla* 'seed', *testuz* 'forehead'.

For further discussion of mozarabisms, see Corominas and Pascual (1980–91), Galmés (1967: 316–23, 1983).

4.8 Gallicisms and occitanisms

Although there are arguably a few gallicisms which passed into Spanish in the early Middle Ages, almost all have entered the language since the eleventh century. The reasons for the very frequent medieval borrowing from French and Occitan lie, naturally, in the cultural importance of northern and southern France in the later Middle Ages, and can be seen to be related, in particular, to four spheres of life, political, religious, literary and commercial.

French involvement in the Reconquest and in the settlement of reconquered areas is well known, as is their role (particularly that of the monks of Cluny and Cîteaux) in monastic and other religious reform and in the pilgrimage to Santiago (the majority of pilgrims were French and many French men and women were permanently established along the pilgrim routes). The indebtedness of Medieval Spanish literature to French and Occitan writing is well established, as is the growing commercial importance of France from the late Middle Ages. Many of these general motives for borrowing have persisted into the modern period (although religious influence has perhaps been slight in recent centuries).

In some cases, it is difficult to establish whether a borrowing has been taken from French or from Occitan, and this will not be attempted here. However it should be noted that occitanisms are almost entirely restricted to the medieval period, since before the end of that period Occitan culture was in severe decline, dominated by that of northern France. For Germanic words passed to Spanish via French, see 4.5.

In the following discussion, mention will be made only of words which have survived to the present (sometimes with changed meaning); we shall pass over the many borrowings, some of them very frequent in their day, which have become obsolete.

Contacts with territories north of the Pyrenees became increasingly important from the eleventh century, owing to the greater political stability of the Christian kingdoms of Spain. This increased stability attracted French and Occitan immigrants both of a temporary kind, such as pilgrims, and of a more permanent kind, like monastic reformers and settlers of newly reconquered territories. In this first period of frequent borrowings from French and Occitan (eleventh to thirteenth centuries), we observe the most remarkable loan of all, *español*

'Spanish', replacing native *españón*. Borrowed military terms, reflecting French participation in the Reconquest, include *aliar* 'to ally', *blandir* 'to brandish', *corcel* 'steed', *dardo* 'spear', *esgrimir* 'to wield', *estandarte* 'banner', *flecha* 'arrow', *galopar* 'to gallop', *maestre* 'master (originally of a chivalric order)', *malla* 'chainmail', *trotar* 'to trot', together with the more general *emplear* 'to use'. Religious terminology is also well represented: *capellán* 'chaplain', *capitel* 'capital (of a column)', *deán* 'dean', *fraile* 'friar, monk', *hereje* 'heretic', *hostal* 'hostelry (originally a religious foundation)', *preste* 'priest' (archaic). Terms related to the feudal system and to a leisured lifestyle are relatively frequent: *bachiller* 'holder of certificate of secondary education' (originally 'young knight'), *doncel* 'squire', *doncella* 'maiden', *duque* 'duke', *homenaje* 'homage', *linaje* 'lineage'; *bailar* 'to dance', *danzar* 'to perform a dance', *rima* 'rhyme', *trobador* 'poet, troubadour', *vihuela* 'viol', *deleite* 'pleasure', *vergel* 'orchard'; *joya* 'jewel', *granate* 'garnet', *estuche* 'small box, case', *cascabel* 'small bell (on clothing, a hawk's leg, etc.)', *polaina* 'gaiter', *palafrén* 'palfrey'. A number of words refer to the household and to food: *arenque* 'herring', *jamón* 'ham', *jengibre* 'ginger', *manjar* '(fine) food', *vianda* 'food'; *antorcha* 'torch', *chimenea* 'chimney', *jaula* 'cage', *mecha* 'wick'. A few terms belong to the natural world: *baya* 'berry', *laurel* 'laurel', *papagayo* 'parrot', *ruiseñor* 'nightingale'. Others, including abstracts, cover a wide field: *desdén* 'contempt', *desmayar* 'to faint', *enojar* 'to annoy', *esquila* 'handbell, cattlebell', *gris* 'grey', *jornada* '(period of a) day', *jornal* 'day's wage', *ligero* 'light (in weight)', *mensaje* 'message', *tacha* 'blemish'.

In the fourteenth and fifteenth centuries, borrowing from French and Occitan had passed its apogee but was still reasonably frequent. In this period we continue to find military and related (including naval) terms: *baluarte* 'bastion', *botín* 'booty', *heraldo* 'herald', *pabellón* 'pavilion; flag'; *amarrar* 'to moor', *cable* 'cable', *quilla* 'keel'. The courtly life continues to be reflected, for example in: *dama* 'lady', *paje* 'pageboy', *gala* 'elegant dress; elegance', *galán* 'gallant', *jardín* 'garden', *patio* 'courtyard'; *balada* 'ballade', *chirimía* 'shawm', *flauta* 'flute', *refrán* 'refrain; proverb'. The material and natural worlds are reflected in: *cordel* 'cord, rope', *correo* 'courier; post', *despachar* 'to dispatch, settle', *forjar* 'to forge', *maleta* 'suitcase', *perfil* 'outline, profile', *pinzas* 'pincers', *trinchar* 'to carve'; *avestruz* 'ostrich', *faisán* 'pheasant', *salvaje* 'wild'. Other borrowings of this period include: *ardite* 'farthing', *burdel* 'brothel', *desastre* 'disaster', *embajada* 'mission; embassy', *jerigonza* 'gibberish', *lisonja* 'flattery', *parlar* 'to chat'.

In the Golden Age, the conflict between France and Spain led to many borrowings in the military and naval spheres, including: *arcabuz* 'arquebus', *asamblea* 'assembly', *barricada* 'barricade', *batallón* 'battalion', *batería* 'battery', *bayoneta* 'bayonet', *brecha* 'breach', *calibre* 'calibre', *carabina* 'carbine', *cartucho* 'cartridge', *coronel* 'colonel', *jefe* 'head, leader', *marchar* 'to march', *piquete* 'picket', *rancho* 'communal meal', originally 'billet, etc.', *trinchera* 'trench', *tropa* 'troop'; *babor* 'port side', *estribor* 'starboard', *borde* 'edge', originally 'side (of ship)', *convoy* 'convoy', *izar* 'to hoist', *pilotaje* 'pilotage', (*echar*) *a pique* 'to sink'. Words concerning elegant living continue to be borrowed: *banquete* 'banquet', *billete* 'note, ticket', *carmín* 'crimson', *conserje* 'porter', *damisela* 'damsel', *etiqueta* 'etiquette; label', *galón* 'braid', *moda* 'fashion', *ocre* 'ochre', *parque* 'park', *peluca* 'wig', *servilleta* 'napkin', *sumiller* 'chamberlain'. Words concerning the house, including food, are also frequently represented among these borrowings: *barrica* 'barrel', *baúl* 'trunk', *claraboya* 'skylight', *dintel* 'lintel', *hucha* 'chest', *marmita* 'cooking pot', *paquete* 'packet', *taburete* 'stool'; *bacalao* 'cod', *clarete* 'rosé wine', *crema* 'cream', *fresa* 'strawberry'. Other gallicisms of this period include: *farándula* 'wandering theatre company', *frenesí* 'frenzy', *peaje* '(road) toll', *placa* 'plate, plaque', and *tacha*, later *tachuela* 'hobnail'.

The eighteenth century is usually regarded as the period of most intense borrowing from French, but many eighteenth-century gallicisms failed to establish themselves permanently in the language, partly as a result of purist reaction among certain prestigious Spanish writers. This period can nevertheless be seen as one in which particularly large numbers of French words passed into Spanish. Military and naval terms continue to form a significant proportion of loans: *brigada* 'brigade', *brigadier* 'brigadier', *cadete* 'cadet', *comandar* 'to command', *desertar* 'to desert', *fusil* 'rifle', *obús* 'shell', *retreta* 'retreat; tattoo'; *corbeta* 'corvette', *equipar* 'to fit out'. Loans relating to fashion and to dress are particularly frequent: *bisutería* 'dress jewellery', *boga* 'fashion', *bucle* 'ringlet', *corsé* 'corset', *jade* 'jade', *modista* 'dressmaker', *pantalón* 'trousers', *satén* 'sateen', *tisú* 'lamé'. Words concerning the house, domestic activities, and food, are well represented: *chalé* 'detached house', *hotel* 'hotel'; *botella* 'bottle', *buró* 'bureau', *cacerola* 'saucepan', *sofá* 'sofa'; *croqueta* 'croquette', *frambuesa* 'raspberry', *galleta* 'biscuit', *grosella* '(black)currant', *merengue* 'meringue'. Words relating to the practical world, to work, etc., are present for the first time: *bisturí* 'scalpel', *control* 'check', *engranaje* 'gear(s)', *hulla* 'coal', *lingote* 'ingot', *resorte* 'spring', *útiles* 'tools'. The natural world is represented by: *avalancha* 'avalanche', *chacal* 'jackal', *pingüino* 'penguin'. Other borrowings of this period include: *abonar* 'subscribe', *billar* 'billiards', *coqueta* 'coquette', *detalle* 'detail', *esternón* 'breastbone', *favorito* 'favourite', *galante* 'gallant', *galimatías* 'nonsense', *interesante* 'interesting', *intriga* 'intrigue', *rango* 'rank', *silueta* 'silhouette'.

During the nineteenth and twentieth centuries, borrowing from French continued apace, slackening in frequency only in the last few decades, in the face of the onslaught of anglicisms (see 4.10). Words relating to the financial and commercial world were borrowed in this period: *bolsa* 'stock exchange', *cotizar* 'to quote', *cupón* 'coupon', *endosar* 'to endorse', *explotar* 'to exploit', *ficha* 'counter, filing card', *financiero* 'financial', *finanzas* 'finance(s)', *garantía* 'guarantee', *letra de cambio* 'bill of exchange', *lote* 'lot, share', *postal* 'postal'. Technical vocabulary was frequently drawn from French: *aterrizaje* 'landing', *aviación* 'aviation; air force', *avión* 'aircraft', *bicicleta* 'bicycle', *biela* 'connecting rod', *bloque* 'block', *bobina* 'spool', *bujía* 'candle; spark plug', *camión* 'lorry', *cremallera* 'rack; zip fastener', *descapotable* 'convertible (car)', *garaje* 'garage', *rodaje* 'running-in (of car)'. We also find words referring to political and related matters: *burocracia* 'bureaucracy', *comité* 'committee', *complot* 'conspiracy', *debate* 'debate', *parlamento* 'parliament', *patriota* 'patriot', *personal* 'staff', *reportaje* 'report', *rutina* 'routine', *tomar acta* 'to take notes'. Words concerning clothes and personal appearance are frequent, as in previous periods: *babucha* 'slipper, mule', *beige* 'beige', *blusa* 'blouse', *canesú* 'bodice, yoke', *chaqueta* 'jacket', *frac* 'dress coat', *levita* 'frock coat', *maquillaje* 'makeup', *maquillarse* 'to put on makeup', *marrón* 'brown'. Vocabulary related to domestic life and food continued to be borrowed from French in this period: *bidé* 'bidet', *damajuana* 'demijohn', *ducha* 'shower', *parqué* 'parquet', *quinqué* 'oil lamp', *somier* 'spring mattress', *vitrina* 'display cabinet'; *besamel(a)* 'béchamel sauce', *consomé* 'consommé', *coñac* 'cognac', *cruasán* 'croissant', *champán* 'champagne', *champiñón* 'button mushroom', *escalope* 'escalope', *flan* 'caramel custard', *paté* 'paté', *restaurant(e)* 'restaurant', *suflé* 'soufflé'. Borrowings in the field of entertainment include: *acordeón* 'accordion', *clisé* 'photographic negative', *debut* 'début', *debutar* 'to make one's debut', *doblaje* 'dubbing', *film* 'film', *filmar* 'to film', *ruleta* 'roulette'. Borrowings reflecting urban life include: *boutique* 'boutique', *bulevar* 'boulevard', *quiosco* 'kiosk'. Words concerning nature include: *begonia* 'begonia', *buganvilla* 'bougainvillaea', *chimpancé* 'chimpanzee', *morsa* 'walrus'. However, gallicisms are found which belong to a wide variety of other spheres: *bebé* 'baby', *braza* 'breaststroke', *camuflaje* 'camouflage', *carné* 'card, licence', *entrenar* 'to train', *esquí* 'ski(ing)', *gripe* 'flu', *pelotón* 'squad', *turismo* 'tourism', *turista* 'tourist'.

For further details of borrowing from French and Occitan, see Colón (1967a), Lapesa (1980), Pottier (1967).

4.9 Amerindianisms

The first European contact with the New World (as a result of Columbus's voyages of discovery) took place in the West Indies and the major West Indian islands became an indispensable staging-post for the later conquest of the northern and southern continents. The first contact of Spanish with Amerindian languages was thus with the languages of the Caribbean (Carib and Arawak, the latter including Taíno, the variety of Arawak spoken in the major Caribbean islands), followed by contact with the main language of Mexico (Nahuatl) and that of the Inca Empire (Quechua). The majority of loans to Spanish were made from these languages, although numbers of borrowings were made (and continue to be made) from other Amerindian sources, including Maya (southern Mexico and the northern isthmus), Chibcha (Ecuador, Colombia and the southern isthmus), Tupí-Guaraní (the major river-basins of the southern continent, including Paraguay), Araucanian or Mapuche (central Chile and the Pampa area of Argentina). However, very few words borrowed from languages other than Carib, Arawak, Nahuatl and Quechua have become universal in Spanish or have even become general in American Spanish.

There follows a selection of words which Spanish has borrowed from a variety of Amerindian sources. The words selected are those which show a significant geographical spread, having become universal in the Spanish-speaking world, or being used throughout Spanish America or in several major Spanish American countries. The origin of the words indicated with (?) is still the subject of dispute, either as to the precise Amerindian source-language or as to whether they are Amerindian borrowings at all.

Borrowings from Arawak (including Taíno) comprise, among others, *ají* 'chilli', *batata* 'sweet potato', *bejuco* 'liana, rattan', *bohío* 'cabin, hut', *cacique* 'Indian chief, local political boss', *canoa* 'canoe', *caoba* 'mahogany', *cayo* 'low island, key', *comején* 'termite', *enaguas* 'petticoat', *guacamayo* 'macaw', *hamaca* 'hammock', *huracán* 'hurricane', *iguana* 'iguana', *maguey* 'agave', *maíz* 'maize', *maní* 'peanut', *sabana* 'savannah', *tuna* 'prickly pear', *yuca* 'cassava'.

Loans from Carib include *batea* (?) 'flat pan for separating gold from sand', *butaca* '(easy) chair', *caníbal* 'cannibal', *curare* 'curare', *loro* 'parrot', *mico* 'monkey', *piragua* 'wooden canoe'.

A few amerindianisms borrowed in the Caribbean area may be from Arawak or from Carib: *aje* 'kind of yam', *guasa* 'joke', *guateque* 'party', *guayaba* 'guava'.

Among the many loans made to Spanish by Nahuatl are *aguacate* 'avocado', *cacahuete* 'peanut', *cacao* 'cocoa', *coyote* 'prairie wolf', *chicle* 'chewing-gum', *chile* 'chilli', *chocolate* 'chocolate', *galpón* 'shed', *guajolote* 'turkey', *hule* 'rubber', *jícara* 'cup (for chocolate)', *nopal* 'prickly pear', *ocelote* 'ocelot', *petaca* 'tobacco pouch, cigarette case', *petate* 'palm matting', *sinsonte* 'mockingbird', *tiza* 'chalk', *tocayo* (?) 'namesake', *tomate* 'tomato', *zopilote* 'buzzard'.

Loans from Quechua include *alpaca* 'alpaca', *cancha* 'open space; (tennis) court, etc.', *coca* 'coca', *cóndor* 'condor', *guanaco* 'guanaco', *guano* 'guano', *llama* 'llama', *mate* 'Paraguayan tea', *palta* 'avocado', *pampa* 'pampas', *papa* 'potato', *puma* 'puma', *puna* 'high plateau, altitude sickness', *soroche* 'altitude sickness', *vicuña* 'vicuña'.

From Tupí-Guaraní have been borrowed *ananá(s)* 'pineapple', *cobaya, -o* (?) 'guinea-pig', *jaguar* 'jaguar', *mandioca* 'manioc', *ñandú* 'rhea, American ostrich', *petunia* 'petunia', *tapioca* 'tapioca', *tapir* 'tapir', *tiburón* 'shark', *tucán* 'toucan', *zarigüeya* 'opossum'.

In addition, there are a number of frequent words, like *caucho* 'rubber', whose origin is Amerindian but whose precise linguistic source is unknown.

When speakers of Spanish travelled or settled in the New World, their new experiences were often interpreted as we have just seen, by means of words borrowed from native languages. The earliest of these (*canoa*, *cacique* and the disputed borrowing *niames* 'yams') are recorded in Columbus's shipboard log of 1492–93. However, it should not be forgotten that borrowing is not the only means of giving linguistic labels to new concepts; a pre-existing word may extend its sense to encompass the new experience. Thus, the jaguar, the puma, and the pineapple were at first named by means of the Old World terms *tigre*, *león* and *piña*, words which eventually came to have competitors of Amerindian origin (*jaguar*, *puma*, *ananá(s)*), and this competition may survive through the centuries. In the cases mentioned, *jaguar* and *puma* became part of the Old World Spanish, while *tigre* and *león* continue in use (at least in popular speech) in much of the area where these animals have their habitat; on the other hand, the borrowing *ananá(s)* is not used in Peninsular Spanish or in large regions of Spanish America (where only *piña* occurs).

On other occasions, a New World concept may be labelled by competing amerindianisms. A well-known case is that of the avocado; the term *aguacate* (from Nahuatl, as noted above) is used in Spain, in North and Central America and in the northwestern region of the southern continent (Colombia and Venezuela), while in territories further south (Ecuador, Peru, Bolivia) the Quechua loan *palta* is used.

For further discussion of Amerindian loans, including those whose distribution is limited to part of the American continent, see Buesa (1967).

4.10 Anglicisms

Until the middle of the twentieth century, almost all English words borrowed by Spanish were of British English origin, and were usually transmitted through writing, often via French. From the 1950s onwards, the main source of such borrowing has been American English, and anglicisms have been transmitted partly through written media (especially newspapers, translation of scientific works, etc.), but increasingly through the oral media (dubbing of American films, TV programmes, etc.).

The term 'anglicism', like others referring to interlanguage borrowing, is poorly defined. The definition adopted here is that of Pratt (1980) (from whom many examples are taken); 'anglicisms' are loans whose immediate etymon is an English word or expression, irrespective of the source of the English word (whose ultimate etymon is often a word or expression of a third language). By this criterion, it is appropriate to include among the anglicisms of Spanish such items as the following, whose ultimate etymology is indicated in parentheses: *anorak*, *kayak* (Eskimo), *kindergarten* (German), *kimono~quimono*, *judo*, *karate* (Japanese), *géiser* (Icelandic), *gongo* (Malay), *caqui*, *pijama* (Persian). Similarly, it will be necessary to exclude from the list of anglicisms in Spanish such terms as the following, whose ultimate etymon is an English word, but which have reached Spanish through the medium of another language (usually French): *auto-stop* 'hitch-hiking', *camping* 'campsite', *dáncing* 'dance-hall', *footing* 'jogging', *parking* 'car-park', *récordman* 'record-holder', *(espejo) retrovisor* 'rear-view (mirror)', *smoking* 'dinner jacket', *en directo* 'live (e.g. TV programme)'. The items quoted should be considered to be gallicisms, since they are attested earlier in French than in Spanish and often reveal French processes of semantic adaptation.

The most frequent (but by no means the only) manifestation of the influence of English upon Spanish is lexical loan. Anglicisms of this kind generally reflect the need to label new concepts (although some are introduced for non-linguistic reasons such as snobbery) and affect a very wide range of semantic fields. The language of almost every aspect of urban, sophisticated life reveals borrowings from English, but the language of the media, fashion, business, science and sport are particularly affected. In the vocabulary of the communications media, which naturally intersects with the terminology of the technological world, we find: *bestséller*, *cámera*, *cameraman*, *cassette*, *cinemascope*, *clip*, *copyright*, *disc-jockey*, *fading*, *film(e)*, *flas(h)*, *hit*, *interviewar~interviuvar*, *interviú*, *LP~elepé*, *mass-media*, *monitor*, *offset*, *off* (e.g. *una voz en off*), *pick-up*, *playback*, *pop*, *póster*, *rol*, *scriptgirl*, *show*, *sketch*, *speaker~espíquer* 'newsreader', *spot* 'advertising spot', *suspense*, *trailer*, *transistor*, *video*, *videocassette*. Lexical borrowings from English in the field of fashion and cosmetics and clothing include such items as: *anorak*, *bikini*, *coldcream*, *cosmético*, *champú*, *cheviot*, *eslip~slip*, *jersey*, *jumper*, *kilt*, *kimono~quimono*, *loción*, *minifalda*, *nylon~nailon*, *overol*, *panty*, *pijama*, *pullover*, *raglán*, *rímel*, *shetland*, *shorts*, *suéter~sweater*, *tweed*. The language of commerce and finance provides examples such as: *actuario*, *boom*, *boutique*, *broker*, *cartel*, *chárter*, *deflación*, *devaluación*, *dumping*, *factoring*, *holding*, *inflación*, *leasing*, *manager*, *marketing*, *self(-service)*, *stock*, *ténder*, *turismo*. In the world of science and technology (including medicine) we note many anglicisms, including: *acrílico*, *aeropuerto*, *aerosol*, *ameba*, *analgesia*, *baquelita*, *cibernética*, *ciclamato*, *colesterol*, *coma*, *contáiner*, *cracking*, *detergente*, *ecología*, *esquizofrenia*, *fobia*, *fuel-oil*, *gasoil*, *polución*, *quántum*, *quark*, *radar*, *robot*, *síndrome*, *spray* 'aerosol', *stress~estrés*, *trolebús*. Sporting language has long shown a particular openness to anglicisms, which can be exemplified by: *bantam, béisbol, bob, bobsleigh, boxes, bunker, caddie, córner, crawl~crol, croquet, cross country, chutar, doping, dribbling, fútbol, gol, golf, groggy~grogui, handicap, hockey~jóquey, jockey, judo, júnior, karate, karting, kayak, knock-out~nocaut, lob, match, off-side, par, penalty, ping-pong, pony, record, ring, round, rugby, set, slam, smash, sparring, sprint, tándem, tenis, volleyball~volibol, wélter*.

English can also be seen to have affected the morphology and syntax of Spanish (see Pratt 1980). The semantic influence of English upon Spanish, extending the sense of pre-existing Spanish words, has also been considerable; this latter phenomenon is examined and exemplified in 5.1.5.

4.11 Catalanisms

Considerable numbers of words have passed from Catalan to Castilian, especially in a number of fields in which the inhabitants of Catalonia, Valencia and the Balearic Islands were perceived by Castilian speakers to be pre-eminent. In some cases, these words were earlier borrowed from other sources, including Occitan, Old French, Italian and Arabic.

Food is one semantic field in which such borrowing is common. We find names of fish, such as *anguila* 'eel', *calamar* 'squid', *jurel* 'horse mackerel', *mujol* 'mullet', *rape* 'monkfish', together with many other culinary terms including *anís* 'aniseed', *butifarra* 'Catalan sausage', *entremés* 'hors d'oeuvre; short comedy', *escalfar* 'to poach (eggs)', *escarola* 'endive', *horchata* (?) 'drink made of almonds or chufas', *paella* 'id.', *sémola* 'semolina', *vinagre* 'vinegar', *vinagreta* 'vinaigrette'.

Other domestic terms borrowed from Catalan are not infrequent: *barraca* 'cabin, stall', *delantal* 'apron', *fogón* 'kitchen range, stove', *patio* 'courtyard', *picaporte* 'doorlatch, -knocker', *reloj* 'clock, watch', *retrete* 'lavatory', *convite* 'invitation, banquet'. Much of the terminology of card-playing is also of Catalan origin, including *naipe* 'playing card', *sota* 'knave (in cards)'.

The Catalans were the predominant sea-faring group in the Peninsula until the end of the Middle Ages and this predominance is reflected in the many Castilian borrowings belonging to this semantic field, such as *aferrar* 'to grapple, anchor, grasp', *betún* 'bitumen', *buque* 'ship', *calafatear* (?) 'to caulk (a ship)', *esquife* 'skiff', *galera* 'galley', *gobernalle* 'helm', *golfo* 'gulf', *muelle* 'dock, pier', *nao* 'sailing ship', *socaire* 'lee', *surgir* 'to anchor', *timonel* 'helmsman'. Closely related are catalanisms relating to trade, which include *a granel* 'in bulk', *mercader* 'merchant', *oferta* 'offer', *tarifa* (from Ar.) 'tariff'.

Many other borrowings reflect the practical skills of the Catalans: *avanzar* 'to advance', *avería* 'breakdown, damage', *caja* 'box', *cañivete* 'small knife', *cartel* 'poster', *cordel* 'cord', *cotejar* 'to compare', *crisol* 'crucible', *doblegar* (?) 'to fold, bend, twist', *escayola* 'plaster of Paris, stucco', *esmalte* 'enamel', *faena* 'task', *farol* 'lantern, street-lamp', *forcejar* 'to struggle', *gafa(s)* 'hook; spectacles', *grúa* '(mechanical) crane', *maestre* 'master of order of chivalry', *metal* 'metal', *molde* 'mould, cast', *nivel* 'level', *paleta* 'trowel, shovel', *pantalla* 'lampshade', *sastre* 'tailor', *traste* 'fret (of guitar)', *trasto* 'piece of junk', *viaje* 'journey'. Some of the terminology of printing and writing is also of Catalan origin: *imprenta* 'printing', *papel* 'paper', *prensa* 'press', *tilde* 'tilde, accent'.

A number of words relating to the natural world are borrowings from Catalan, including *becada* 'woodcock', *bosque* 'wood, forest', *caracol* 'snail', *clavel* 'carnation', *dátil* 'date', *follaje* 'foliage', *palmera* 'palm tree'.

Some military terms, of more distant ultimate origin, probably passed to Castilian via Catalan; these include *capitán* 'captain', *coronel* (?) 'colonel', *cuartel* 'barracks'. The same is probably true of the following terms related to dress, etc.: *falda* (from Gmc.) 'skirt', *guante* (from Gmc.) 'glove', *palafrén* (from OFr.) 'palfrey', etc. A number of verbs and abstract nouns of Catalan origin can be exemplified by *añorar* 'to miss', *congoja* 'anguish', *retar* 'to challenge', *trajinar* 'to transport, bustle', *ultraje* 'outrage'.

Finally, the following miscellaneous list of catalanisms reflect the somewhat broad range of semantic fields affected: *borracho* (?) 'drunk', *cohete* 'rocket', *esqueje* 'cutting (of plant)', *follón* 'arrogant, cowardly', *pila* 'pile', *plantel* 'seedbeds', *pólvora* 'gunpowder', *quijote* 'cuisse (of armour)', *ristre* 'lance-socket (in armour)', *sardana* 'Catalan dance', *seo* 'cathedral', *sor* 'sister (in religious titles)', *retablo* 'altarpiece', *verdete* 'verdigris'.

The best source of information on the Catalan borrowings made by Castilian continues to be Corominas and Pascual (1980–91), together with the indexes of the earlier edition (Corominas 1954–7). Also to be consulted is Colón (1967b).

4.12 Lusisms

Under this term we include words borrowed from either Portuguese or Galician, since it is usually impossible, on grounds of form, to distinguish between loans from these sources. Lusisms have passed into Spanish with some facility since the Middle Ages; the use, in medieval Castile, of Galician–Portuguese as the language of the love-lyric is responsible for some of the earliest, such as *coita* 'sorrow', *coitado* 'sorrowful', *ledo* 'joyful', although the first two terms were replaced by *cuita*, *~-ado* and the last later fell from use. Later medieval borrowings include words referring to the emotions, such as *enfadarse* 'to become angry', *desenfadar* 'to quieten', *desenfado* 'carefree', *enfadoso* 'irksome'.

The largest group of Portuguese borrowings refers, unsurprisingly, to the world of the sea and ships, since Portuguese expertise in these fields anteceded that of Spain. Such loans include *angra* 'creek', *balde* 'pail, bucket', *buzo* 'diver', *callao* 'pebble beach' (restricted to seaman's language, except in the

Canaries), *cantil* and *acantilado* 'cliff', *carabela* 'caravel', *chubasco* 'squall', *estela* 'wake', *garúa* 'drizzle' (chiefly used in American Spanish), *laja* 'flat stone' (restricted to Andalusia and America), *marejada* 'swell' (unless it is a catalanism), *monzón* 'monsoon', *pleamar* 'high tide', *tanque* 'water tank', *vigía* 'lookout', *virar* 'to tack'. Closely related are names of fish and other sea creatures: *almeja* 'clam', *cachalote* 'sperm whale', *chopa* 'black bream', *mejillón* 'mussel', *ostra* 'oyster', *perca* 'perch', *sollo* 'sturgeon'.

The establishment of Portugal's maritime empire allowed borrowing by Portuguese of words from many oriental languages. Some of this originally exotic vocabulary was then passed on to Spanish: *bambú* 'bamboo', *biombo* 'folding screen', *cacatúa* 'cockatoo', *carambola* 'cannon (in billiards)', *catre* '(camp) bed', *cha* 'tea' (ousted, after the seventeenth century, by *té*, which probably entered via French), *charol* 'varnish; patent leather', (*juegos*) *malabares* 'juggling', *pagoda* 'pagoda'.

Other words borrowed, or probably borrowed, from Portuguese or Galician include: *barullo* 'confusion', *basquiña* 'skirt', *bicho* 'creature', *brincar* 'to gambol', *caramelo* 'sweet', *corpiño* 'sleeveless bodice', *despejar* 'to clear', *laya* 'type, quality', *macho* 'mule', *mequetrefe* 'whippersnapper', *mermelada* 'jam', *sarao* 'soiree', *traje* 'suit; costume', *vaivén* 'swaying, bustle'.

For further discussion of borrowings from Portuguese, see Salvador (1967), and Corominas and Pascual (1980–91).

4.13 Italianisms

The earliest borrowings made by Spanish from Italian are found towards the end of the Middle Ages, but it is in the sixteenth and seventeenth centuries that such loans reach their apogee, owing principally to the prestige of concepts emanating from Renaissance Italy and to the military involvement of Spain in the Italian Peninsula. Borrowing has continued, particularly in the field of music, down to the present, but became relatively infrequent after the eighteenth century. It should be noted that not all italianisms originate in Tuscan; some (particularly maritime terms) are borrowings from Genoese, Venetian, Milanese, etc., or from southern Italian or Sicilian varieties.

Adaptation of italianisms to Spanish is, as might be expected, generally straightforward. However, there is a small number of words which in the fifteenth century and in the Golden Age appear in Spanish with final /e/ following an ungrouped dental or alveolar consonant (contrary to the normal Spanish developmental process, for which see 2.4.3.2), and which are usually described as latinisms, but which may in fact more reasonably be described as italianisms: *felice* 'happy', *infelice* 'unhappy', *interese* 'interest'. This /e/ is later lost, bringing these words into line with the regular pattern of Spanish words: *feliz, infeliz, interés*, etc.

Words relating to the arts constitute one of the largest groups of italianisms in Spanish. In the vocabulary of literature and philosophy, we find *esdrújulo* 'proparoxytonic', *novela* 'novel', *soneta* 'sonnet', *terceto* 'tercet'; *folleto* 'pamphlet', *humanista* 'humanist', *parangón* 'comparison'. In the language of the theatre are to be found *bufón* 'buffoon', *comediante* 'actor', *payaso* 'clown', *saltimbanqui* 'acrobat', and in that of art, *acuarela* 'water colour', *arabesco* 'arabesque', *caricatura* 'caricature', *cartón* 'cartoon', *claroscuro* 'chiaroscuro', *destacar* 'to highlight', *diseño* 'design', *encarnado* 'red', *esbelto* 'slender', *esfumar* 'to tone down', *fresco* 'fresco', *grotesco* 'grotesque', *grupo* 'group', *lápiz* 'pencil', *miniatura* 'miniature', *modelo* 'model', *pintoresco* 'picturesque', *temple* 'tempera', *ultramarino* 'ultramarine'. The following architectural terms are also borrowed from Italian: *apoyar* 'to support', *balaústre* 'banister', *balcón* 'balcony', *casino* 'small house' (later 'casino'), *cúpula* 'cupola', *escayola* 'stucco', *fachada* 'façade', *fontana* 'fountain', *pedestal* 'pedestal' (via French), *pórtico* (?) 'portico', *terraza* 'terrace', *zócalo* 'plinth', while in sculpture we find *busto* 'bust', *medalla* 'medal, plaque', *relievo* 'relief', *terracota* 'terracotta'. As in the case of all European languages, borrowing by Spanish of Italian musical terms is extremely frequent; such loans include *alto* 'alto', *bajo* 'bass', *barítono* 'baritone', *contralto* 'contralto', *soprano* 'soprano', *tenor* 'tenor'; *mandolina* 'mandolin', *piano* 'piano', *viola* 'viola', *violín* 'violin', *violoncelo, -chelo* 'cello', *violón* 'double bass'; *aire* 'melody', *aria* 'aria', *batuta* 'baton', *cantata* 'cantata', *cavatina* 'cavatina', *compositor* 'composer', *concierto* 'concert, concerto', *dúo* 'duet', *fantasía* 'fantasia', *fuga* 'fugue', *fusa* 'demisemiquaver', *libreto* 'libretto', *madrigal* 'madrigal', *ópera* 'opera', *serenata* 'serenade', *solista* 'soloist', *solo* 'solo', *sonata* 'sonata', *sordina* 'mute', *tempo* 'tempo', *tocata* 'tocata'. Names of dances include *pavana* 'pavane', and *tarantela* 'tarantella'.

Italian military terms were borrowed in profusion by Spanish in the sixteenth and seventeenth centuries, although one or two of the following items are first attested in Spanish earlier or later than the Golden Age: *alerta* 'alert', *asalto* 'assault', *atacar* 'to attack', *batallón* 'battalion', *bombarda* 'bombard', whence *bombardear* 'to bomb', *canjear* 'to exchange (prisoners, etc.)', *cañón* 'cannon', *centinela* 'sentinel', *colina* 'hill', *coronel* 'colonel', *destacar* 'to detach (soldiers)', *duelo* 'duel', *embestir* 'to attack', *emboscada* 'ambush', *emboscar* 'to ambush', *escolta* 'escort', *escopeta* 'shotgun', *escuadrón* 'squadron', *generalísimo* 'supreme commander', *granada* 'grenade', *guardia* 'guard', *infante* 'infantryman', *marchar* (?) 'to march, go', *mosquete* 'musket', *mosquetero* 'musketeer', *penacho* 'plume', *saquear* 'to plunder', *zapar* 'to sap'. Words referring to defensive building are particularly well represented: *bastión* 'bastion', *ciudadela* 'citadel', *cuneta* 'cunette, ditch', *escarpa* 'escarpment', *muralla* 'defensive wall', *parapeto* 'parapet', *reducto* 'redoubt'.

Italian is one of the languages, together with Portuguese, Catalan and various Germanic languages, which have contributed substantially to the maritime vocabulary of Spanish. This semantic field is represented by the following loans, among others: *bogavante* 'stroke, first oarsman' (unless from Catalan), *brújula* 'compass', *corsario* 'corsair', *chusma* 'gang of galley slaves', later 'rabble', *dársena* 'dock', *escollo* 'reef', *fragata* 'frigate', *góndola* 'gondola', *mesana* 'mizzenmast', *piloto* 'pilot', *zarpar* 'to weigh anchor'.

Significant numbers of italianisms relate to commerce and industry, reflecting the Italian domination of these fields in the early modern period. Among others we find: *avanzar* 'to be in excess (over a calculated amount)' (later 'to advance'), *balance* 'balance (in accounts)' (possibly a catalanism, ultimately from Italian), *bancarrota* 'bankruptcy', *banco* 'bank', *en bruto* 'gross', *cero* 'zero', *contrabando* 'contraband', *crédito* 'credit', *débito* (?) 'debit, debt', *depósito* 'deposit', *factura* 'bill', *letra de cambio* 'bill of exchange', *mercancía* 'merchandise', *mercante* 'merchant', *millón* 'million', *monte de piedad* 'pawnshop', *montepío* 'pawnshop', *negociante* (?) 'businessman, -woman', *neto* 'net', *póliza* '(insurance) policy', *saldar* 'to liquidate', *saldo* 'bargain sale'. Particular commodities whose names are of Italian origin include *brocado* 'brocade', *cartulina* 'Bristol board', *granito* 'granite', *índigo* 'indigo', *porcelana* 'porcelain', *tafetán* 'taffeta' (or from Catalan).

A number of italianisms can be observed in the wider fields of social life, reflecting to some extent the imitation of Italian manners, principally in Spain's Golden Age. Words relating to general human characteristics and activities include *aguantar* 'to hold back, endure', *aspaviento* 'fuss', *bizarro* 'gallant, dashing', *bravata* 'piece of bravado', *brusco* (?) 'abrupt', *campeón* 'champion', *canalla* 'rabble; swine', *capricho* 'caprice', *cortejar* 'to woo', *cortejo* 'retinue', *cortesano* 'courtly', *chanza* 'joke', *charlar* 'to chat', *charlatán* 'garrulous', *chulo* 'swaggering, flashy', *desfachatado* 'insolent', *estafar* 'to swindle', *estrafalario* 'eccentric', *farsante* 'charlatan', *fogoso* 'spirited', *garbo* 'gracefulness', *mafia* 'Mafia', *rufián* 'pimp; villain', *superchería* 'fraud'. In the field of games and similar activities, we find *cucaña* 'greasy pole', *empatar* 'to tie, draw', *regata* 'regatta', *trucos* 'billiards', *tute* 'tute (the card game)'. The fields of education and transport produce *gaceta* 'gazette', *pedante* 'pedant'; *carroza* '(horse-drawn) carriage', *esguazar* 'to ford', *ferroviario* 'railway (adj.); railwayman', *pista* 'track', *valija* 'suitcase'. In the field of religion we observe *camposanto* 'churchyard', *carnaval* 'Carnival', *plebe* (?) 'people', *sotana* 'cassock'.

In the fields relating to private life, we find terms relating to the house, such as *cantina* 'wine cellar, bar', *celosía* 'lattice window', *chaveta* 'securing peg', *pérgola* 'pergola', *toalla* (?) 'towel', some referring to dress and adornment, including *capucho* 'hooded cloak', *corbata* '(neck)tie', *filigrana* 'filigree', *perla* (?) 'pearl', *recamar* 'to embroider in relief' (taken by Italian from Arabic), *turbante* 'turban', some related to food, like *café* 'coffee', *caviar* 'caviar', *macarrones* 'macaroni', *menestra* 'mixed vegetables', *salchicha* 'sausage', and some which refer to the body and illness, such as *belleza* 'beauty', *caricia* 'caress', *chichón* (?) 'bump (on the head)', *malaria* 'malaria', *pelagra* 'pellagra'.

The physical world is apparently less well represented than others are. We find some names relating to the natural world, *anchoa* 'anchovy' (probably via Catalan), *carroña* 'carrion', *pichón* 'young pigeon', *tarántula* 'tarantula', *pistacho* 'pistachio', *remolacha* 'beet', and some topographical terms, *cascada* 'waterfall', *golfo* 'gulf (but, more probably, this is a catalanism, see 4.11), *gruta* 'cavern', *pantano* 'marsh; reservoir'.

In addition, a small number of rather general terms has been borrowed by Spanish from Italian: *bagatela* 'trifle', *estropear* 'to spoil', *fiasco* 'fiasco', *flamante* 'splendid', *fracasar* 'to fail', *manejar* 'to handle', *pillar* 'to grasp, steal', *premura* 'urgency'.

The main sources of further information on italianisms in Spanish are Terlingen (1943, 1967) and Corominas and Pascual (1980–91).

4.14 Word-formation

The vocabulary of Spanish can be said to consist of three components. In addition to words inherited from Latin (popular and semi-learned words, see 4.1), and to words borrowed from other languages (4.2–13), the Spanish lexicon includes items which have been created, through word-formation, by means of the language's internal resources. The term 'word-formation' includes reference to prefixation (4.14.1), derivation (4.14.2) and composition (4.14.3).

4.14.1 Prefixation

Latin prefixes were in close relationship with the prepositions of the language (see the discussion at 3.8.1), in that many particles which functioned as prepositions also functioned as prefixes, usually with similar sense. However, not all the particles that have survived as prepositions have also survived as prefixes.

Many prefixed Latin words ceased at an early stage to be analysed by speakers as consisting of {prefix + base morpheme} and developed thereafter as unitary words. This is exemplified by cases like PROFECTU > *provecho* 'advantage', where Latin /f/ has been given the treatment normally accorded to this phoneme in intervocalic position (i.e. /-f-/ > OSp. /β/, MSp. /b/; see 2.5.3.2.2). Similarly, DECOLLĀRE > *degollar* 'to cut the throat', where /k/ is given intervocalic treatment (> /g/). Where speakers continued to perceive the morphological complexity of a word, any consonant or consonant group which follows the prefix (and therefore stands at the beginning of the base morpheme) is treated in the same way as if it were in word-initial position. Thus, DEFĒNSA 'forbidden (land)' must for some centuries have continued to be perceived as a complex word, since it develops to *dehesa* 'unenclosed pasture', showing the Latin /f/ is here given word-initial treatment (becoming /h/, later /Ø/, as in FŪMU > *humo* 'smoke', etc.; see 2.5.6, 2.6.4). In a small but crucial number of cases, the complex structure of the prefixed Latin word has continued to be perceived as such throughout its history, as in APPREHENDERE 'to seize' (in relation with PREHENDERE 'id.') > *aprender* 'to learn' (still in relationship with *prender* 'to seize').

It is cases like APPREHENDERE > *aprender* which provided the model (in spoken Latin or at any later stage including the present) for the creation of new words by the addition of a prefix to a pre-existing verb, noun, adjective or adverb (examples of prefixed adverbs can be seen at 3.4). The prefixes which have a continuous history from Latin to Spanish (and which served and serve to create new words) are discussed below. No distinction is made, in the examples, between simple prefixation and parasynthesis, in which a prefix and a suffix are simultaneously added to a root (as in *des-* + *alm-* + *ado* → *desalmado* 'heartless') and where the parasynthetic nature of the structure is recognizable by the absence from Spanish of words consisting of the same prefix and the same stem, or of the same stem and the same suffix (in this case, by the absence of such words as **desalma* or **almado*). It should also be noted that, whereas in Classical Latin sequences of two or more prefixes were rare (e.g. COMPRŌMITTŌ), spoken Latin and its successors (including Spanish) expand this possibility considerably.

AD- The Latin meaning ('to, towards', etc.) has been almost entirely lost from this prefix, and its descendant *a-* is generally void of sense. It is used above all to create verbs from nouns or adjectives (e.g. *agrupar* 'to group', *amontonar* 'to pile up', *apaciguar* 'to pacify', *atormentar* 'to torment', *agravar* 'to aggravate', *amortecer* 'to deaden'), but may appear in other formations (e.g. *adiós* 'goodbye'). The form *ad-* appears in a number of prefixed forms borrowed from Latin: *adaptar* 'to adapt', *adherir* 'to adhere', *admirar* 'to admire, wonder at', etc.

DIS- The notion of 'separation' inherent in the Latin prefix was later expanded to include 'away from' (absorbing DE-) and 'out of', so that it came into competition with EX-, and in particular with the compound prefix DE + EX-, which (at least before stems beginning with a consonant) shared the same phonetic outcome as DIS-, namely *des-*. The competition with EX-, whereby Spanish came to have two prefixes, *des-* and *es-*, of identical meaning and similar structure, explains the frequent alternation in Old Spanish and modern non-standard speech between these two prefixes (e.g. *destender*~*estender* 'to spread, extend'). However, the modern standard language has resolved these cases of alternation, usually on etymological grounds (so that *estender* is preferred, and is erroneously respelled *extender*, on the basis of EXTENDERE). Examples of *des-* include: *desconfiar* 'to distrust', *descoser* 'to unsew', *desdecir* 'to retract', *desechar* 'to discard', *deshacer* 'to undo', *deshonrar* 'to dishonour', *desmentir* 'to deny', *desviar* 'to deflect'.

Forms in *dis-*, *di-*, or *de-* betray their learned origins: *discernir* 'to discern', *disforme* 'deformed', *divertir* 'to amuse', *denegar* 'to refuse'.

IN- This prefix retains the Latin sense 'in(to), on', and its form in Old Spanish is generally *en-*, even before /p/ and /b/ (reflecting the neutralization of /m/, /n/ (and /ɲ/) in syllable-final position), although modern spelling distinguishes *en-* from *em-*, in imitation of the Latin alternation between IN- and IM-. *En-*~*em-* is used to create verbs from nouns or adjectives: *embarrar* 'to cover with mud', *emborrachar* 'to make drunk', *empapelar* 'to paper', *empeñar* 'to pledge, pawn', *encabezar* 'to lead', *enganchar* 'to hook'; *engordar* 'to fatten', *enloquecer* 'to go or drive mad', *enrasar* 'to make level'. Occasionally it is used to create new verbs from existing verbs: *embeber* 'to soak up', *encoger* 'to shrink', etc.

In a few instances, IN- was compounded with EX-, producing the sequences *ens-* or OSp. *enx-*, MSp. *enj-*: *ensalzar* (< *IN EX ALTIĀRE) 'to exalt', *ensanchar* 'to widen', *enjalbegar* (< *IN EX ALBICARE) 'to whitewash', *enjuagar* (< *IN EX AQUĀRE) 'to rinse, *enjugar* (< *IN EX SŪCĀRE) 'to dry'.

The learned descendant of IN-, Spanish *in-*, has two values, the first of which is indistinguishable from that of popular *en-*: *inmiscuir* 'to mix', *innato* 'inborn', *inspirar* 'to inspire'. The second, negative, value of Latin IN- is also widely imitated in Spanish, not only under the form *in-*~*im-*, but under forms which imitate the Latin assimilation of N before L and R: *insensato* 'senseless', *impiedad* 'impiety', *impopular* 'unpopular', *ilegítimo* 'illegitimate', *ilimitado* 'unlimited', *irreal* 'unreal', *irrespetuoso* 'disrespectful'.

EX- The popular descendant of EX- is OSp. *es-* (sometimes now respelled *ex-* but without phonological change). It has been seen (DIS-, above) that *es-* has since Latin times been in competition with *des-* in the sense 'out of'. Forms with this prefix include *escapar* 'to escape', *escardar* 'to weed', *escoger* 'to choose', *extender* 'to spread'.

Learned use of this prefix, in the form *ex-*, extends from borrowings of forms which already displayed this prefix in Latin (in which case we also find examples of *e-*: *emanar* 'to emanate', *exhibir* 'to exhibit', *extirpar* 'to eradicate'), to the addition of the prefix to stems not found in Latin with EX- (*excéntrico* 'eccentric', *excarcelar* 'to release from prison'), and its semi-independent use before certain nouns (*ex primer ministro* 'ex-prime minister', *ex presidente* 'ex-president').

INTER- The popular descendant of this prefix, *entre-*, appears in relatively few forms, but shows considerable development of sense from the Latin 'between' (as in *entrecomillar* 'to place in inverted commas') to 'partially' (*entreabrir* 'to half open', *entresacar* 'to thin (the hair, etc.)'), 'reciprocally' (*entreayudarse* 'to help one another', *entrecruzar* 'to inter-twine'), or 'intermediate' (*entrecano* 'greying (hair)', *entrefino* 'of medium quality').

Words which display the learned form of this prefix, *inter-*, are most frequently borrowings or calques from other languages, typically French or English (e.g. *interferir* 'to interfere', *intermuscular* 'intermuscular'), although some are borrowings made directly from Latin by Spanish (e.g. *interrumpir* 'to interrupt').

TRANS- The Latin sense 'across' rarely appears in the popular reflex of this prefix, *tras-* (e.g. *trasvolar* 'to fly across'). Instead we find other meanings such as 'behind' (*traslapar* 'to overlap', *trastienda* 'back room (behind a shop))', 'during' (*trasnochar* 'to stay up late'), or 'excessively' (*trastornar* 'to disrupt').

No doubt because of the frequent reduction (at least in conversational style) of syllable-final /ns/ to /s/ (see Navarro 1961: 112), the learned form of this prefix, *trans-*, is in many cases interchangeable with the popular form, both forms appearing with the same stem (e.g. *trasmitir*~*transmitir* 'to transmit').

SUB- Although the popular reflex of the preposition SUB has now all but disappeared, that of the prefix SUB-, *so-*, is reasonably well represented in Spanish. Most frequently it retains the Latin sense 'under': *sobarba* 'double chin', *socavar* 'to undermine', *solapar* 'to overlap', *solomillo* 'sirloin', *someter* 'to subdue', *soterrar* 'to bury'. Occasionally, this prefix is used to attenuate the action indicated by the stem: *soasar* 'to roast lightly', *sofreír* 'to fry lightly'.

The learned form of the same prefix, *sub-*, may indicate location, as in *subsuelo* 'subsoil', *submarino* 'submarine', *subrayado* 'underlining', but more often has the metaphorical value of 'less than' the notion expressed by the stem, e.g. *subdesarrollado* 'underdeveloped', *subvalorar* 'to underrate'.

SUPER- The relatively frequent popular descendant of this prefix, *sobre-*, appears with the senses 'above' (e.g. *sobrecama* 'bedspread', *sobrenadar* 'to float'), 'after' (e.g. *sobremesa* 'after-dinner chat', *sobrevivir* 'to survive'), and 'in excess' (e.g. *sobrecargar* 'to overload', *sobremanera* 'exceedingly', *sobresueldo* 'bonus').

Probably under the influence of English, the learned form of the prefix, *super-*, has enjoyed an enormous productivity in recent decades. It shows the same range of meanings as the popular form, but with the sense of 'excess' being by far the most frequent: *superestructura* 'superstructure', *supervivencia* 'survival', *supercompresión* 'super-charging', *superpoblación* 'over population'.

RE- In the case of this prefix, it is impossible to distinguish popular and learned reflexes, on the basis of form; both types of transmission of course produce *re-*. However, on the basis of meaning it may be possible to make some distinction, since it seems likely that the repetitive sense now sometimes associated with *re-* is a recent development, due to influence from Latin or from other modern languages which commonly display the repetitive meaning of this prefix (e.g. French or English). Examples of this development include *reanudar* 'to renew', *reaparecer* 'to reappear', *rehacer* 'to remake'. Traditional senses include reference to place (e.g. *recámara* 'dressing room' (i.e. 'a place beyond a bedroom'), *recocina* 'scullery', *rebotica* 'room behind a chemist's shop'), and occasionally to time (e.g. *redolor* 'discomfort remaining after an accident'), but most usually the prefix simply emphasizes the notion expressed by the stem: *rebién* 'very well indeed', *rebuscar* 'to search thoroughly', *recalentar* 'to overheat', *remoler* 'to grind up', *repudrir* 'to rot completely', *retemblar* 'to shake (violently)'.

Other prefixes derived from Latin are almost exclusively learned. PER- and PRO-, whose prepositional correlates merge as *por* (see 3.8.1), only in one instance behave in parallel fashion, in the development PERFĪDIA > *porfía* 'stubbornness'. *Per-* is found, with intensifying value, in the language of the rustic characters of Renaissance drama (probably reflecting the rural speech of the Salamanca area; see Penny 1990a), and with similar value in the rural speech of present-day Asturias, but is absent from standard Castilian except in learned formations like *perdurar* 'to last', *perjurar* 'to commit perjury', but also 'to curse repeatedly'. *Pro-* is always learned (e.g. *promedio* 'average', *prometer* 'to promise').

All of the following, ultimately of Latin origin, have entered Spanish through writing, their frequency increased today by the many anglicisms which display them: *pos(t)-* (< POST-), *ante-* (< ANTE-), *pre-* (< PRAE-), *com-*~*con-*~*co-* (< COM-, the correlate of the preposition CUM), *retro-* (< RETRŌ-), *contra-* (< CONTRĀ-), *extra-* (< EXTRĀ-), *intra-* (< INTRĀ-), *infra-* (< INFRĀ-), *supra-* (< SUPRĀ-), *circun-* ~ *circum-* (< CIRCUM-), *ultra-* (< ULTRĀ-); e.g. *posguerra* 'post-war period', *anteponer* 'to antepose', *preindustrial*

'preindustrial', *condueño* 'joint owner', *contraproducente* 'counterproductive', *retroceder* 'to move back', *extraterrestre* 'extraterrestrial', *intranuclear* 'intranuclear', *infraestructura* 'infrastructure', *supranacional* 'supranational', *circunlocución* 'circumlocution', *ultramarinos* 'groceries'. A particularly productive subset of learned prefixes comprises quantifying expressions, exemplified by the following: *bisabuelo* 'great-grandfather', *bipolaridad* 'bipolarity', *maxifalda* 'maxi-skirt', *minifundio* 'small farm', *multicolor* 'multicoloured', *pluriempleo* 'moonlighting', *semi-final* 'semi-final', *sesquióxido* 'sesquioxide', *vicetiple* 'chorus girl'.

The stock of Spanish prefixes has similarly been enriched by the introduction of a number of forms whose origin is ultimately Greek but whose current frequency is again probably due to the influence of English, where these prefixes are especially numerous in scientific and journalistic language (see Pratt 1980: 185–91). The prefixes concerned are exemplified by the following selection of words: *antioxidante* 'antirust', *autopromoción* 'self-promotion', *hipertensión* 'hypertension', *macroeconómico* 'macro-economic', *microorganismo* 'micro-organism', *pericráneo* 'pericranium', *polivalencia* 'polyvalence', *protohistoria* 'protohistory' (see also 4.14.3).

4.14.2 Derivation

The addition of suffixes to pre-existing stems in Spanish serves two contrasting purposes: first, the creation of a word which refers to a different concept (albeit a related one) to that referred to by the original word, and second, the addition of a nuance which reveals the speaker's attitude to the concept concerned. In the latter case, no new concept is involved; the original word and the derived word refer to the same concept. To exemplify the two processes we may consider, first, the relationship between *vaca* 'cow' and *vacada* 'herd of cows'. It is evident that the derived form *vacada* indicates a concept which is different from (but related to) the concept indicated by the base-word. However, if one compares, secondly, the word *gordo* 'fat' with its derivative *gordito* 'nice and fat, chubby', it is clear that the concept referred to is essentially the same in each case, but that in the case of *gordito* the speaker's attitude to the concept is approving and affectionate.

However, these two derivational processes are not always as sharply distinguished as this discussion suggests; they overlap in two ways. On the one hand, the 'same' suffix may serve both derivational purposes. The ending *-ito* which conveys overtones of affection in *gordito* expresses no such nuance in *carrito;* in this case, the concept referred to ('trolley') is a different one from that indicated by *carro* (namely 'cart', 'car', etc.). Similarly, the *-azo* which appears in *vinazo* 'coarse wine' (or, sometimes, 'magnificent wine'!) clearly carries emotive value but does not alter the basic reference (to 'wine'), while the 'same' element in *cabezazo* invokes reference to a different concept ('head-butt') from that of the base-word *cabeza* ('head'). On the other hand, the emotive nuance added to a concept by the addition of a suffix may be closely related to an element of objective meaning. Thus, there is often a correlation between the affectionate response of the speaker and relative smallness of the referent (e.g. *gatito* 'kitten'), or between the repugnance expressed by the speaker and the relative bigness or coarseness of the referent (e.g. *novelón* 'long boring novel').

Despite the difficulties posed by the overlaps between these two derivational processes, it is useful to keep them separate in discussion. Further, the standpoint taken here is that where emotive nuances are associated with a given suffix, such nuances predominate over any element of objective meaning which may also be present. This view is in accordance with that expressed in a fundamental study of the suffixes concerned (Alonso 1935) and can further be justified by reference to Gooch (1970). In what follows, we shall distinguish the two types of derivation by using the label *lexical* for the type which produces new names for new concepts, and *affective* for the type which expresses the speaker's attitude towards the concept evoked.

4.14.2.1 Lexical derivation

Suffixes may be used to create new nouns, adjectives and verbs. Each of these categories will be considered in turn. A derived noun may have as its base another noun, an adjective or a verb. In table 4.1 are listed the main suffixes (i.e. those which remain productive or which at some stage have been so) which may be applied to each type of base, together with the source of each suffix and representative examples of each combination.

It can be seen that in a number of cases, the form of the suffix has not been arrived at through regular phonological change. That is, a number of suffixes have passed into Spanish as a result of the borrowing of Latin words which contained the suffixes concerned, after which the suffix could become available for application to inherited stems. The learned suffixes concerned are: *-ía*, *-ismo*, *-ista*, *-ante*, *-(i)ente*, *-ancia*, *-(i)encia*, *-orio*, *-mento*, *-ción*. In a few cases, such learned forms compete with inherited forms of the same Latin suffix; this can be seen in the case of *-anza/-ancia*, *-ero/-orio*, *-mento/-miento -zón/-ción*. In some of these cases, the learned form (e.g. *-ancia*, *-ción*) is today more productive than the popular form; in the remaining cases (*-ero*, *-miento*) the reverse is true. Similarly, *-aje* results from the borrowing of French words from the Middle Ages onwards, and coexists with inherited *-adgo*, later *-azgo*, the latter now unproductive.

Certain of the suffixes used to derive nouns from verbs, namely *-ero*, *-or*, *-ura*, descend from Latin suffixes which were applied to participles. This structural feature continues to characterize Spanish, so that in the cases concerned we find participial *-ad-*, *-ed-*, or *-id-* between stem and suffix.

Table 4.1 *Derived nouns*

Base	Suffix MSp. (OSp.)	Source	Example
Noun	*-ada*	-ĀTA	*puñalada* 'stab'
	-ado	-ĀTU	*bocado* 'mouthful'
	-aje	Fr. *-age* (<-ĀTICU)	*aprendizaje* 'apprenticeship'
	-al~-ar	-ĀLE	*trigal* 'cornfield'
			olivar 'olive grove'
	-azgo (-adgo)	-ĀTICU	*noviazgo* 'courtship'
	-azo	-ĀCEU,-ĀTIO	*vistazo* 'glance'
	-ero	-ĀRIU	*joyero* 'jeweller'
	-ía	-ĪA (< Gk.-ια)	*abadía* 'abbey'
	-ismo	-ĪSMU (<-ισμός)	*espejismo* 'mirage'
	-ista	-ĪSTA (<-ιστα)	*modista* 'dressmaker'
	-o, -a	-U, -A	*manzano* 'appletree'
Adjective	*-dad*	-TĀTE	*tenacidad* 'tenacity'
	-dumbre	-TŪMINE	*reciedumbre* 'strength'
	-era	-ĀRIA	*cojera* 'lameness'
	-ez	-ITIE	*vejez* 'old age'
	-eza	-ITIA	*rareza* 'rarity'
	-ismo	-ĪSMU (<-ισμός)	*humanismo* 'humanism'
	-ista	-ĪSTA (<-ιστα)	*izquierdista* 'leftist'
	-or	-ŌRE	*grosor* 'thickness'
Verb	*-ada, -ida*	-ĀTA, -ĪTA	*huida* 'flight'
	-ado, -ido	-ĀTU, -ĪTU	*alumbrado* 'lighting'
	-aje	Fr. *-age* (<-ĀTICU)	*tatuaje* 'tattoo'
	-ando	-ANDU	*graduando* 'graduand'
	-ante, -(i)ente	-ANTE, -(I)ENTE	*amante* 'lover'
	-anza~-ancia, -(i)encia	-ANTIA, -(I)ENTIA	*alabanza* 'praise'
			ganancia 'profit'
			creencia 'belief'
	-e, -o, -a		*derrumbe* 'demolition'
			derribo 'demolition'
			marcha 'progress'
	-ero (-uero) ~		*atracadero* 'quay'
	-orio	-ŌRIU	*lavatorio* 'washing'
	-mento~-miento	-MENTU	*pulimento* 'shine'
			llamamiento 'appeal'
	-ón, -ona	-ŌNE	*tumbona* 'deckchair'
	-or	-ŌRE	*pensador* 'thinker'
	-ura	-ŪRA	*armadura* 'armour'
	-zón, -ción	-TIŌNE	*hinchazón* 'swelling'
			turbación 'confusion'

Table 4.2 *Derived adjectives*

Base	Suffix	Source	Example
Adjective	*-ado*	-ĀTU	*azulado* 'bluish'
	-enco	?	*azulenco* 'bluish'
	-iento	-ENTU	*avariento* 'miserly'
	-ino	-ĪNU	*blanquecino* 'whitish'
	-ista	-ĪSTA (< -ιστα)	*socialista* 'socialist'
	-izo	-ĪCIU	*rojizo* 'reddish'
	-oide	Gk. - οειδης	*negroide* 'Negroid'
	-oso	-ŌSU	*verdoso* 'greenish'
	-usco	-ŪSCU	*pardusco* 'greyish'
	-uzco	-ŪSCU	*blancuzco* 'whitish'
Noun	*-al~-ar*	-ĀLE~-ĀRE	*invernal* 'wintry'
			seglar 'secular, lay'
	-ano	-ĀNU	*mediano* 'average'
	-ense	-ĒNSE	*ateniense* 'Athenian'
	-eño	-INEU	*panameño* 'Panamanian'
	-ero	-ĀRIU	*playero* 'beach'
	-és	-ĒNSE	*montés* 'wild'
	-esco	-ISCU	*gigantesco* 'gigantic'
	-ico	-ICU	*borbónico* 'Bourbon'
	-í	Ar. *-î*	*iraní* 'Iranian'
	-il	-ĪLE	*estudiantil* 'student'
	-ino	-ĪNU	*cristalino* 'crystalline'
	-ón	-ŌNE	*narizón* 'long-nosed'
	-oso	-ŌSU	*miedoso* 'fearful'
	-udo	-ŪTU	*orejudo* 'big-eared'
Verb	*-able, -ible*	-ĀBILE, -ĪBILE	*inoxidable* 'stainless (steel)'
			movible 'movable'
	-ado, -ido	-ĀTU, -ĪTU	*apagado* 'dull, weak'
			aburrido 'boring'
	-ante, -(i)ente	-ANTE, -(I)ENTE	*titubeante* 'shaky'
	-ero	-ĀRIU	*decidero* 'mentionable'
	-ivo	-ĪVU	*impulsivo* 'impulsive'
	-izo	-ĪCIU	*olvidadizo* 'forgetful'
	-ón	-ŌNE	*mirón* 'nosy'
	-or	-ŌRE	*embriagador* 'intoxicating'

Derivation of nouns in *-o* from others in *-a*, and vice versa, is a relatively unproductive process, but accounts historically for such pairs in Spanish as *manzano* 'appletree'/*manzana* 'apple', *cesto* '(small) basket'/*cesta* '(large) basket', etc. On the other hand, deverbal nouns in *-e*, *-o*, *-a* are quite frequent and the process continues to be productive.

Derived adjectives may be based, similarly, on nouns, verbs, or on other adjectives, as listed in table 4.2.

Table 4.3 *Derived verbs*

Base	Suffix	Source	Example
Verb	*-ear*	-IDIĀRE (< -ιζειν)	*toquetear* 'to finger'
	-ecer	-ĒSCERE	*embebecer* 'to delight'
Noun	*-ar*	-ĀRE	*salar* 'to salt'
	-ear	-IDIĀRE (< -ιζειν)	*cabecear* 'to nod'
	-ecer	-ĒSCERE	*anochecer* 'to grow dark'
	-ificar	-IFICĀRE	*glorificar* 'to glorify'
	-izar	-IDIĀRE (< -ιζειν)	*tapizar* 'to carpet'
Adjective	*-ar*	-ĀRE	*igualar* 'to make equal'
	-ear	-IDIĀRE (< -ιζειν)	*blandear* 'to weaken'
	-ecer	-ĒSCERE	*blanquecer* 'to whiten'
	-ificar	-IFICĀRE	*amplificar* 'to amplify'
	-guar	-IFICĀRE	*santiguar* 'to bless'
	-izar	-IZĀRE	*fecundizar* 'to fertilise'

It will be seen that adjectives derived from other adjectives for the most part denote colours related to those denoted by the base. Adjectives in *-ista* function also as nouns.

As in the case of derived nouns, we find cases of competition between popular and learned descendants of the same Latin suffix; thus popular *-és* coexists with learned *-ense*. Again as in the case of derived nouns, some deverbal adjectives have a participle as their base; this is generally so in the case of *-ero*, *-izo* and *-or*.

Derived verbs are again based upon nouns, adjectives or verbs. The principal productive types of derivatives are listed in table 4.3.

It can be seen that both the suffixes *-ear* and *-izar* descend ultimately from the same Greek causative suffix -ιζ ειν. The latter was adapted, as it passed into early spoken Latin by oral transmission, to -IDIARE whose later development to Spanish *-ear* is regular (see 2.5.2.2(4)). The suffix *-ear* is applied straightforwardly to nouns and adjectives, but to verbs usually by means of an infix (e.g. *toqu* + *et* + *ear*, *freg* + *ot* + *ear*, *gim* + *ot* + *ear*) which generally has 'repetitive' value.

Gk -ιζειν was borrowed a second time by (later literary) Latin, in the form -IZARE, which was later taken through writing into Medieval Spanish as *-izar*. Perhaps under the influence of other modern languages, where the corresponding suffix (*-ise*, *-ize*) is very productive, *-izar* has become one of the most frequent means of creating new verbs.

Latin -IFICĀRE also shows dual development. Via popular transmission, it shows the expected regular changes Ĭ > /e/, voicing of intervocalic -F- and -C- to [β] and [ɣ] respectively, and loss of pretonic Ĭ: *[-eβˈɣar]. At this stage,

/β/ was modified to a closing glide (as in the case of OSp. /βd/; 2.5.5 end), but then metathesized with the following consonant: *[-eβ'ɣar] > *[-eu̯'ɣar] > [-e'ɣwar]. Pretonic /e/ was then raised to /i/ by assimilation to the following glide (cf. AEQUĀLE > OSp. *egual* > *igual* 'equal'): *-iguar*. When transmitted through writing, -IFICĀRE shows the usual minimal change to *-ificar*.

It will be noted that all the productive verbal suffixes belong to the *-ar* class, with the exception of *-ecer*, which usually appears in parasynthetic derivatives. In the Middle Ages, this type often competed with non-derived verbs in *-ir* (*escarnir*~*escarnecer*, *gradir*~*agradecer*, *guarnir*~*guarnecer*, *resplandir* ~*resplandecer*, etc.), eventually ousting the simple verb in each case.

4.14.2.2 Affective derivation

In 4.14.2 we defined affective derivation as the process of adding suffixes which reveal the speaker's attitude towards the concept denoted by the base. The view was also expressed that the affective content of the suffixes concerned was more salient than any objective meaning (such as 'smallness', 'largeness', 'coarseness', etc.) the suffixes might also convey. Each of the main affective suffixes of Spanish will be discussed here, with comments on emotive and objective content, whether the suffix lends itself to lexicalization (the denotation of a concept different from that of the base and with loss of affective value), and with consideration of its origin. The suffixes may be applied to nouns, adjectives and participles, or adverbs.

-ito denotes approval/affection and is diminutive in value: *osito* 'teddy bear', *librito* 'nice (little) book', *crecidito* 'nice and tall (of child)', *bajito* 'small but nice'. Its Latin origins are hazy; it may have been extracted from certain personal names (JŪLITTA, BONITTA, SALVITTUS), but must have acquired frequent use in spoken Latin, since it is well represented in Romance (Fr. *-et, -ette*, It. *-etto*, *-etta*, Cat. *-et -eta*, etc.). The form of the Latin suffix appears to have alternated between *-ĪTTU, whence Sp. *-ito*, and *-ĬTTU, from which the remaining Romance forms descend, including Fr., Occ., Cat. *-et*, borrowed by Castilian as *-ete* (see below). The suffix *-ito* is infrequently represented in thirteenth- and fourteenth-century texts (there is only one example in Berceo, who makes frequent use of other affective suffixes, and one in Juan Manuel) but gains in frequency in those fifteenth-century writers who most closely reflect the spoken language (the Archpriest of Talavera, Fernando de Rojas, etc.). Its frequency grows among similar writers of the Golden Age (especially Santa Teresa), whereafter it gradually displaces competitors (chiefly *-illo* and *-ico*) until it achieves its present dominance. Only in Andalusia does *-illo* retain its status as the preferred affectionate suffix.

-ico is also affectionate and also has diminutive value: *besico* 'sweet little kiss', *malico* 'poorly', *un tantico* 'a wee bit'. Its origins are unknown, it has few Romance cognates, and its history until the Golden Age closely parallels that of *-ito*. But since that period, *-ico* has retreated from Castilian (being used now only in a limited range of forms) and remains frequent only in Navarre, Aragon, Murcia and eastern Andalusia, and parts of Spanish America, where it is often the preferred affectionate form.

-ín plays a similar role to that of *-ito* and *-ico* (it is affectionate and diminutive): *pajarín* 'sweet little bird', *pequeñín* 'tiny, wee (fellow)'. However, it lends itself to numerous lexicalizations: *comodín* 'joker (in cards)', *futbolín* 'table football', etc. It may represent a development of the Latin suffix -ĪNUS, used to indicate the young of certain animals (e.g. PALUMBĪNUS (PULLUS) 'young dove') and throughout its history has been commonest in the western half of the Peninsula (Ptg. *-inho*, Gal. *-iño*, Ast. *-ín*, León and Extremadura *-ino*). It has always had some frequency in Castilian, but cannot be freely applied to any base.

-illo although affectionate (and diminutive) for most of its history, this suffix now often has a slightly pejorative tone: *asuntillo* 'an unimportant piece of business', *empleíllo* 'rotten little job', *novelilla* 'piffling novel', *envidiosillo* 'pettily envious'. It also gives rise to frequent lexicalizations: *camilla* 'stretcher', *casilla* 'pigeonhole', *molinillo* 'coffee grinder', *pitillo* 'cigarette, fag'. It is the first of the suffixes considered here which has a clear Latin antecedent, -ELLUS, which was certainly diminutive and probably affectionate. Its descendant, *-iello*, was the commonest Old Spanish affectionate diminutive, and was gradually replaced by *-illo*, spreading from the Burgos area (see 2.4.2.5). In the Golden Age, *-illo* is still dominant (and still affectionate) but since that time has been challenged by *-ito* as the 'normal' Castilian diminutive form and has acquired its current slightly pejorative tone (except in Andalusia).

Lat. -ELLUS was applied directly to nouns and adjectives in -US and -A, but in the case of nouns and adjectival with other endings an infix -(I)C- was inserted. Since the /k/ of this infix was commonly intervocalic, it evolves to OSp. /d^z/, MSp. /θ/: *PAUPERCELLU (for PAUPERCULU) > OSp. *pobreziello* > MSp. *pobrecillo*. The extension of the use of this infix is dealt with at the end of this section.

-ejo This suffix is generally pejorative in value and has diminutive sense when applied to nouns: *animalejo* 'wretched creature', *calleja* 'alley', *lugarejo* 'tin-pot village', *medianejo* 'poor to middling'. It gives rise to a certain number of lexicalizations: *candilejas*

'footlights'. The Latin antecedent of *-ejo*, -ULUS, was attached directly to nouns in -US and -A (e.g. FLAMMA → FLAMMULA) but to other nouns by means of the infix -(I)C- (PAUPER → PAUPERCULUS). In this respect, -ULUS was like -ELLUS (see *-illo* above) and the two suffixes were probably also similar in their affectionate/diminutive value. However, unlike -ELLUS, -ULUS was atonic (see 2.3.1), and in the case of nouns in -US and -A there was a strong tendency in spoken Latin to replace atonic -ULUS with tonic -ELLUS: ROTA → ROTULA 'little wheel' > ROTELLA (> *rodilla* 'kneecap' > 'knee'). Where -ULUS continued to be productive (i.e. when combined with the infix -IC-: -ICULUS), it lent itself to frequent lexicalization, including cases where the suffixed form displaced the original base-form, which thus lost all affectionate/diminutive value: OVICULA (for OVIS) 'sheep', AURICULA (for AURIS) 'ear', APICULA (for APIS) 'bee' (whence *oveja*, *oreja*, *abeja*). The change in value, from affectionate to derogatory, is already apparent in Old Spanish, where *-ejo* has a value similar to that which it has in the modern language.

-uelo is now most frequently pejorative in tone and may have diminutive value: *autorzuelo* 'insignificant writer', *ojuelos* 'mean little eyes', *gentezuela* 'petty riffraff', *gordezuelo* 'nastily small and fat'. It easily lends itself to lexicalization: *habichuela* 'French bean', *hoyuelo* 'dimple'. Its Latin antecedent, -OLUS, was at first inherently atonic (see 2.3.1) and was applied to forms which displayed hiatus between the two final syllables: FILIUS → FILIOLUS, FLUVIUS → FLUVIOLUS. Under such phonological conditions, spoken Latin transferred the stress from the antepenultimate to the penultimate syllable (see 2.3.1, end), thus converting the suffix from atonic to tonic and ensuring its continued identity (FILIOLU > *hijuelo* 'offspring'). The suffix *-uelo* was very frequent in Old Spanish and apparently retained the affectionate value of its Latin ancestor. During the Golden Age, it continues to be well represented, but then declines in frequency and acquires its current predominantly pejorative tone. It has already been remarked that *-uelo is* often attached to its base by means of the infix *-(e)z*, borrowed from structures like OSp. *simpleziello*: *ladronzuelo* 'little thief'.

-ete has above all a jocular tone (making it especially open to ironic use) and generally diminutive value: *comedieta* 'insubstantial little play', *curete* 'jolly old priest', *pillete* 'young rascal', *tacañete* 'pretty stingy'. It appears particularly frequently in lexicalized forms: *boquete* 'hole', *camioneta* 'van', *chincheta* 'drawing pin', *salmonete* 'red mullet'. This suffix has the same (obscure) origin as *-ito*

but has reached Spanish as a result of borrowing of French/Occitan/ Catalan words in *-et*. It may appear with the infix which originated in -ICELLUS (*trenecete* 'a joke of a train'), but may not be applied to bases with absolute freedom.

-uco has pejorative tone and diminutive value, where it appears (albeit infrequently) in the standard language: *casuca* 'mean little house', *frailuco* 'petty little friar'. It gives rise to occasional lexicalized forms: *hayucos* 'beech mast'. By contrast, in the Cantabria region, this suffix is the commonest affectionate morpheme. Its origin is uncertain, but it may be a variant of *-ico,* on the pattern of other suffixes which share the same consonantal pillar combined with different vowels (e.g. *-azo*, *-izo*, *-uzo*).

-ucho is (like *-uco*) pejorative in tone and often diminutive in value: *aldeúcha* 'miserable little village', *animalucho* 'wretched creature', *feúcho* 'rather ugly', *medicucho* 'tenth-rate doctor', *tabernucha* 'grotty little bar'. It provides only occasional lexicalizations: *aguilucho* 'eaglet'. Its origin is unclear, as is its history in Spanish.

-ón As applied to words denoting or referring to people, this suffix is generally pejorative, and augmentative in the sense that it implies an 'increase' or 'excess' of some quality: *feón* 'very ugly', *maricón* 'pansy', *mujerona* 'hefty great woman', *sargentona* 'bossy woman', *valentón* 'boastful', *zampón* 'very greedy'. As applied to non-personal concepts, *-ón* still implies 'excess' and is pejorative in tone, except where 'excess' can be interpreted as desirable: *caserón* 'great big house', *gotón* 'big drop', *novelón* 'boringly long novel'. There are many cases of lexicalization of words containing *-ón*: *abejón* 'drone', *pimentón* 'paprika', *velón* 'oil lamp'; however, a number of lexicalized cases show that *-ón* may have diminutive value: *cordones* 'shoelaces', *ratón* 'mouse', *tapón* 'plug, stopper', *terrón* 'clod of earth; sugar lump'.

The notion of 'excess' was present in the Latin antecedent, -ŌNE, of this suffix (e.g. NĀSŌ, NĀSŌNIS 'big-nosed') and probably also the pejorative tone which springs from the notion of excess. However, we have already seen (4.14.2.1) that *-ón* extended its role to form lexical derivatives of various types. As an affective suffix, *-ón* may now be added with considerable (but not complete) freedom to a wide range of bases.

-azo is similar to *-ón* in its derogatory tone and its 'augmentative' value: *acentazo* 'heavy, unpleasant accent', *broncazo* 'big row', *olaza* 'threatening wave'. Again like *-ón*, its pejorative note may be replaced by an approving tone where 'excess' is seen as desirable: *bodaza* 'slap-up wedding', *torazo* 'fine big bull'. There are

significant numbers of lexicalizations: *barcaza* 'barge', *espinazo* 'backbone'.

As Malkiel (1959b) shows, this suffix originates in Lat. -ĀCEU and is to be regarded as historically separate from the homophonous *-azo* 'blow', which descends from -ĀTIO (see 4.14.2.1). As the examples given show, derogatory/augmentative *-azo* has a feminine counterpart *-aza*, whereas *-azo* 'blow' does not. However, both suffixes have been frequent throughout the history of Spanish and remain fairly highly productive.

-ote is almost always pejorative in tone and 'augments' the concept expressed by the base to which it is attached: *frescote* 'cheeky devil', *machote* 'tough guy', *palabrota* 'swear-word', *seriote* 'glum'. It gives rise to frequent lexicalizations: *barrote* 'bar (of cage, etc.)', *camarote* 'cabin (in ship)', *capota* '(woman's) bonnet; hood (of car)'. The suffix *-ote* appears to have entered Spanish by borrowing from Gallo-Romance (or was extracted from individual borrowings of French/Occitan words ending in *-ot*). If it indeed has Gallo-Romance origins, we should note the change of sense from 'diminutive' in Gallo-Romance to 'pejorative/ augmentative' in Spanish.

-aco is pejorative in tone and appears to convey no connotation of size: *libraco* 'rotten old book', *pajarraco* 'ugly bird'. It is a relatively unproductive suffix whose obscure origins may lie, like those of *-uco*, in vocalic variation on the theme represented by *-ico*.

-acho is similarly pejorative and only occasionally connotes 'increase' of the concept indicated by the base: *covacha* 'nasty cave', *poblacho* 'dump of a village', *populacho* 'common herd', *ricacho* 'filthy rich'. The suffix *-acho* may have the same origin as pejorative *-azo* but have entered Spanish via the Mozarabic dialect (where ĀTIŌ > /-átʃo/). At all events, it is today relatively infrequent and unproductive.

-ajo is strongly pejorative: *cintajo* 'tawdry ribbon', *latinajos* 'dog Latin', *pequeñajo* 'runtish', *trapajo* 'tatter'. It frequently gives rise to lexicalizations: *cascajos* 'rubble', *estropajo* 'scourer', *rodaja* '(round) slice'. It probably descends from -ACULUS, where -A- originally belonged to the base and -C- is the infix which in Latin linked certain bases to diminutive suffixes (see *-ejo*, and *-illo* above). Alternatively, *-ajo* may represent a variant of *-ejo* and/or *-ujo*.

-ujo is always pejorative and occasionally diminutive: *blandujo* 'soggy', *ramujo*, *ramuja* 'dead wood', *tapujos* 'jiggery-pokery'. It is of limited productivity and its origins are similar to those of *-ajo*.

Spanish has a considerable number of other pejorative suffixes, but which are quite unproductive, in some cases appearing with no more than a single base.

These include *-ángano* (*curángano* 'wretched priest'), *-ango* (*querindango* 'pathetic lover'), *-astre* (*pillastre* 'miserable young scoundrel'), *-astro* (*camastro* 'miserable bed'), *-engue* (*blandengue* 'contemptibly feeble (person)'), *-ingo* (*señoritingo* 'contemptible young gentleman'), *-orio* (*papelorios* 'rubbishy papers'), *-orrio* (*villorrio* 'tenth-rate village'), *-orro* (*chistorro* 'crude joke'), *-ute* (*franchute* 'Frog (= Frenchman)'), *-uza* (*gentuza* 'rabble, scum').

It should be noted that affective suffixes (and, to a much lesser extent, the suffixes responsible for lexical derivation (4.14.2.1)) may appear in sequences of two or more items joined to a single base. Such sequences usually consist of suffixes with the same or similar affective quality: *chiquitillo* 'little boy', *chiquitín* 'tiny', *riachuelo* 'insignificant stream', *valentonazo* 'utterly boastful man'. Where there is an apparent conflict of affective values, it is usually the case that the first suffix combines with the base to form a lexicalization and only the second retains affective value: *saloncito* 'attractive little room', *caperucita* 'charming little hood'.

The appearance (and origin) of the infix *-(e)c/z-* has been noted (see *-illo*, *-ejo*, above). Although the morpheme from which it descends was originally placed between -ELLUS and a base which ended otherwise than in -US or -A, and continues in such forms (e.g. *florecilla*), this infix has extended its use in the course of time in two ways; firstly, there are cases where the infix has come to be used before other appreciative suffixes (*ladronzuelo*, *florecita*); and secondly, there are many cases in which the infix has come to be used with bases ending in /o/ or /a/: *manecita*, *huertecillo*, *pueblecito*, *viejecito*, etc. The latter forms are often ones in which the base displays a diphthong in either the final or the penultimate syllable, but are far from universal in the Spanish-speaking world; in general, American and Canarian Spanish prefers forms without infix (*manita*, *huertito*, *pueblito*, *viejito*).

For further discussion of the history of the 'diminutives' from the Middle Ages, see González Ollé (1962) and Náñez (1973). For additional detail on the current value of the suffixes considered here, see Alemany (1920), Alonso (1935), Alvar and Pottier (1983: 363–80) and Gooch (1970), from the last of whom a number of glosses have been taken.

4.14.3 Composition

Creation of new vocabulary by compounding two or more lexemes is today a relatively frequent process in Spanish. Such composition reveals differing degrees of fusion between the contributing elements, ranging from simple juxtaposition (where the second element modifies the first, e.g. *tren correo* 'mailtrain', *ciudad dormitorio* 'dormitory town, bedroom community') through union without modification (e.g. *sordomudo* 'deaf and dumb', *abrelatas* 'tin opener', *tocadiscos* 'record-player'), union via modification to /i/ of the final vowel of the first element (e.g. *machihembra* 'tongue and groove', *rojiblanco* 'red and white'), to parasynthetic composition, in which two lexemes are compounded at the same time as a suffix is added (e.g. *estadounidense* 'American', *sietemesino* 'seven-month'). The classification adopted here is based upon the grammatical function of the words which enter into the compound and examples will be drawn from the various types of compounding just mentioned.

Noun + noun. It is normal for the second noun to modify the first: *perro guardián* 'guard dog', *hombre rana* 'frogman', *buque-hospital* 'hospital ship', *aguamiel* 'mead', *telaraña* 'spider's web', *zarzamora* 'blackberry (bush)'. In *aguanieve* 'sleet', *machihembra* 'tongue and groove', *puerco espín* 'porcupine', the two elements are co-ordinated rather than showing subordination of one (the second) to the other. Parasynthetic composition can be seen in *salpimentar* 'to season'.

Noun + adjective. This combination produces, on the one hand, co-ordinated nominal expressions (e.g. *aguardiente* 'eau-de-vie', *camposanto* 'cemetery', *guardia civil* 'civil guard', *Nochebuena* 'Christmas Eve') and, on the other, a wide range of adjectival expressions in which the second element is syntactically subordinated to the first (e.g. *barbirrojo* 'red-bearded', *cariancho* 'broad-faced', *cejijunto* 'bushy-browed', *corniabierto* 'wide-horned', *cuellilargo* 'long-necked', *maniabierto* 'open-handed', *ojinegro* 'black-eyed', *patizambo* 'knock-kneed', *peliagudo* 'thorny (problem)', *puntiagudo* 'pointed', *rabicorto* 'short-tailed'; *cabizbajo* 'crestfallen' no doubt represents a modification of earlier **cabezibajo*, which accords with this pattern).

Adjective + noun. In this case, we find co-ordinated expressions which function as nouns: *bajamar* 'low tide', *cortocircuito* 'short circuit', *cortometraje* 'short film', *extremauncion* 'extreme unction', *mediodía* 'midday'.

Adjective + adjective. The result of composition (inevitably of co-ordinating type) between two adjectives may give rise to a new adjective (*agridulce* 'bitter-sweet', *rojiblanco* 'red and white (striped)', *sordomudo* 'deaf and dumb', *verdinegro* 'dark green'), or to a noun (*altibajos* 'vicissitudes', *claroscuro* 'chiaroscuro').

Verb + noun. This combination, in which the verb is imperative or present indicative and the noun functions as its direct object, has always constituted a frequent type of composition in Spanish: *abrelatas* 'tin opener', *aguafiestas* 'spoilsport', *cortaplumas* 'penknife', *cortafuego* 'fire-break', *espantapájaros* 'scarecrow', *guardacostas* 'coastguard', *guardarropa* 'wardrobe', *hincapié* 'firm footing', *pasatiempo* 'pastime', *picamaderos* 'woodpecker', *portaaviones* 'aircraft carrier', *portavoz* 'spokesperson', *rompecabezas* 'puzzle', *rompehielos* 'icebreaker', *sacacorchos* 'corkscrew', *saltamontes* 'grasshopper', *tragaperras* 'fruit machine'. Less frequently, the noun of the compound does not function as direct object of the verb, but has one of a variety of other roles: *cortafrío* 'cold chisel', *girasol* 'sunflower', *trotaconventos* 'go-between'.

Pronoun + verb. This type is rare, but appears in the very common expression *quehacer* 'chore'.

Verb + verb. Such co-ordinated combinations, with or without the copula /i/, provide new nouns: *duermevela* 'the state of being half-asleep', *pasapasa* 'sleight of hand', *de quitaipón* 'detachable', *vaivén* 'swaying; bustle'.

Syntagmatic compounds. These compounds, all with nominal function, originate in a variety of sequences of words, as they occur in connected speech: *ciempiés* 'centipede', *correveidile*~*correvedile* 'gossip', *hazmerreír* 'laughingstock', *metomentodo* 'busybody', *padrenuestro* 'Lord's Prayer', *tentemozo* 'prop', *tentempié* 'snack'.

In addition to the types of composition discussed, we find a further type, which is of recent origin and now relatively frequent, and which represents a position intermediate between composition and prefixation. A 'prefixoid' (an element typically ending in /o/, but also in /i/ or /e/, and usually derived through writing from a Greek or Latin noun or adjective) is combined with a second element, which may be an inherited or borrowed word. It has been suggested (Pratt 1980: 186–9) that the profusion of such formations is one manifestation of the influence of English on the modern Spanish language. The 'prefixoids' involved include *aero-* (*aerofotografía* 'aerial photography'), *ambi-* (*ambigenérico* 'ambigeneric'), *archi-* (*archiconocido* 'known by all'), *auto-* (*autorretrato* 'self-portrait'), *bio-* (*biomecánica* 'biomechanics'), *electro-* (*electrodomésticos* 'electrical household appliances'), *euro-* (*eurocomunista* 'Euro-communist'), *ferro-* (*ferroníquel* 'ferronickel'), *filo-* (*filosoviético* 'admiring of the Soviet Union'), *hidro-* (*hidroelectricidad* 'hydroelectricity'), *macro-* (*macroempresa* 'big business'), *micro-* (*microfilm* 'microfilm'), *mono-* (*monocarril* 'monorail'), *moto-* (*motosegadora* 'motor scythe'), *multi-* (*multigrado* 'multigrade'), *núcleo-* (*nucleo-electricidad* 'nuclear energy'), *poli-* (*polideportivo* 'sports hall'), *proto-* (*prototipo* 'prototype'), *radio-* (*radiofaro* 'radio beacon'), *semi-* (*semidesnudo* 'half-naked'), *tele-* (*teledirigido* 'remote controlled', *telediario* 'TV news bulletin'), *termo-* (*termonuclear* 'thermonuclear'), *tri-* (*tricolor* 'three-coloured'), *zoo-* (*zoogeografía* 'zoogeography').

5 Semantics

The development of the meaning of words is an important part of the history of a language, and it can be argued that of all the elements of language, meaning is least resistant to change. Yet the semantic history of Spanish words has received relatively little attention from scholars. An important source of information is Corominas and Pascual (1980–91), but etymological dictionaries such as this do not give systematic and consistent detail on the developing meaning of the words of the language, let alone of the causes of change. In the absence of a full-scale historical dictionary of Spanish (the Spanish Academy's *Diccionario histórico de la lengua española* (Real Academia Española 1972–) has not yet reached the letter B-), any discussion of its semantic development is inevitably incomplete and is likely to be at least partially inaccurate.

Existing historical grammars of Spanish lack chapters dealing exclusively or predominantly with semantic development and what follows is an (admittedly provisional) attempt to fill this identifiable gap. It should also be made clear that there are no 'rules' of semantic development which might be comparable with statements of, say, phonological development; examples of semantic change remain just that: examples. The structure of the discussion follows Ullmann's (1962) account of meaning-change, distinguishing between its causes, its nature and its consequences.

5.1 Causes of semantic change

Since the appearance of Ogden and Richards's now classic treatment of meaning (1923), it has been accepted that there is no direct relationship between the words (or symbols) of language and the things and events of the 'real world'. This relationship is indirect and mediated by the mental constructs (or concepts) by which we represent the world to ourselves. It is the interrelationship between symbol and concept (wherein lies the essence of 'meaning') that falls within the domain of linguistics and any change in this relationship constitutes an instance of semantic change. The relationship between symbol and concept is possibly more unstable than other aspects of language and its disruption may be caused by any of a number of factors, of which Ullmann (1962) distinguishes the following six.

5.1.1 Linguistic causes

Changes of meaning may be occasioned by the frequent collocation of two or more words. That is, if words frequently occur together in the same speech-context, (part of) the meaning of one may be transferred to the other, and eventually this transferred sense may come to belong to the 'receiving' word even in the absence of the 'donating' word. It is well known that many of the negative words of Romance were originally positive in sense but acquired their negative value by frequent collocation with the negative particle NŌN and its descendants. In the Latin of Spain and some other areas, the phrase HOMINE NĀTU, literally 'a man born', first acquired the sense 'anyone (at all)'; in combination with NŌN, it therefore meant 'no one (at all)', and this sense eventually predominated even in the absence of NŌN. Early Old Spanish shows examples of *omne nado* in the sense 'no one', but through ellipsis (see 5.2.4) *nado* alone is then found with this meaning. Subsequent modification of the form of *nado* (see 3.5.5) produces OSp. and MSp. *nadie.*

More widely in spoken Latin, a parallel phrase REM NĀTA (for the persistence of final -M here, see 2.5.4) meant at first 'anything (at all)'. At first only in conjunction with NON, but eventually even in the absence of NŌN, it meant 'nothing (at all)', and from this now negative phrase descend the various Old Spanish words with this meaning: ellipsis of REM produces OSp. and MSp. *nada*, but the alternative ellipsis of NATA produced *ren* in the Navarro-Aragonese region. In general, Lat. RĒS (acc. REM) 'thing' was replaced in spoken Latin by CAUSA, and this replacement intermittently included the phrase REM NĀTA, producing *CAUSA NĀTA, whence OSp. *cosa (nada)*, with the same transfer of negative sense as in the case of (REM) NĀTA > *nada*. In recent Spanish, the phrase *en absoluto* has undergone similar negative development, so that its most frequent meaning is now 'not at all'.

5.1.2 Historical causes

Any change of a concept which is not accompanied by a corresponding change of symbol constitutes a semantic change. Since all concepts (whether they refer to things, institutions, abstract notions, etc.) are subject to at least gradual change, and since the symbols (or words) which reflect these concepts are slower to be replaced (or may not be replaced at all), it follows that any (non-linguistic) historical development is likely to provoke a semantic change. Many examples of this kind of shift are trivial or well known (thus, the symbol *coche* continued to be used (at least in Spain) even though the concept it represented evolved from 'horse-drawn vehicle' to '(motor-propelled) car'), but others may be less easy to reconstruct, often because of the remoteness in time of the change concerned. Examples of semantic change motivated by evolution of the concepts concerned (and ultimately by the evolution of their referents, the things and events of the 'real world' to which the concepts correspond) include the following:

- Latin created the form *CALCEA (derived from CALCEUS 'shoe') to indicate 'stockings', newly adopted from the Germanic north. During the Middle Ages, the garment became longer and longer until it stretched from feet to waist; the descendant of Lat. *CALCEA (OSp. *calça*) now therefore meant approximately 'tights', and this sense can be seen in *PMC* 3085–6: *calças de paño en sus camas metió, / sobr' ellos unos çapatos que a grant huebra son*. Later development of the garment, its sixteenth-century division into two parts, did necessitate certain changes of name: the lower portion, from thighs to feet (approximately 'hose') was specified as *medias calças*, later abbreviated to *medias*, a label which continues to be applied to 'stockings', although now only to a women's garment; meanwhile the upper part, from waist to thighs, continued to be labelled by means of the term which once indicated the undivided garment, although the term now meant 'breeches' and had a more specific equivalent (*calçones*). For these changes in the sense of *calzas*, see Jaberg (1926).
- In accordance with its etymon (Ar. *qâḍī*), Sp. *alcalde* when first borrowed meant 'judge (according to Islamic law)'. The functions of the post were subsequently broadened to include administrative activities, so that in Golden Age Spanish the term *alcalde* indicates an official who is both magistrate and mayor. Since that time, the judicial functions of the post have been lost and the term now means exclusively 'mayor'.
- *alférez* (< Ar. *fâris* 'horseman') OSp. 'horseman' > 'best horseman (of a squadron)' > GA Sp. 'standard bearer' > MSp. 'second lieutenant'.
- *alguacil* (< Ar. *wasîr* 'chief minister') OSp. 'governor of a town in Islamic Spain' > OSp. 'magistrate' > GA 'constable' > MSp. 'minor court official; town-hall messenger'.
- *barbero* (a late medieval derivative of *barba* 'beard'), like corresponding words elsewhere in Europe, indicates a 'barber/surgeon/dentist' until at least the eighteenth century, later becoming limited to the sense 'barber'.

5.1.3 Social causes

A change in a word's meaning may take place when the word ceases to be part of the vocabulary of all or most speakers of the language concerned and becomes restricted to the technical vocabulary of a particular social group (typically a trade, a profession or an interest-group). When this happens, there is normally an accompanying restriction of the word's meaning. Thus a form

*ORDINIĀRE 'to organize' came to be restricted to farming language and its sense was restricted (via 'organizing the chores of the cow-shed'?) to that of 'to milk'. Similarly, *afeitar* (a borrowing from Latin AFFECTĀRE 'to devote oneself') was restricted first to the Old Spanish sense 'to adorn, beautify', then to the Golden Age sense 'to beautify with makeup; to shave', and later to the latter sense only. *Botar*, a medieval borrowing from Old French, at first has the general sense 'to throw', which the verb retains in some varieties of Spanish (including most American varieties); however, Peninsular Spanish has seen its restriction to the meaning 'to launch', no doubt as the word ceased to be part of the common vocabulary and became limited to that of boat-builders. However, some other (metaphorical) senses of *botar* also survive, as well as intransitive 'to bounce'.

The reverse process, by which a word broadens its meaning as it passes from the language of a social subgroup into that of the whole community, is also widely attested. From the language of gaming, where Sp. *azar* (< Ar. *zahr* 'dice') meant at first an 'unfortunate throw of the dice', the word has passed into more general use, widening its sense to that of 'misfortune' or 'chance (lucky or unlucky)'. *Armario*, when first borrowed from Latin in the Middle Ages, maintained its connection with *arma* and meant 'armoury'; its sense was soon widened to its current value of 'cupboard'.

5.1.4 Psychological causes

Changes of meaning which spring from the mental state of particular speakers, who have creatively extended the sense of words by using them metaphorically, are manifold in language and this process will be considered in more detail in 5.2.1. However, there is a specific psychological cause of semantic change which is particularly powerful (and which has been studied in detail): **taboo**. 'Taboo' is a term which indicates a prohibition on the mention of a particular word, for a variety of reasons which vary from culture to culture but which show some inter-cultural constants (see, for example, Meillet 1921). Since the concept related to a tabooed word nevertheless has to be referred to in some fashion, a frequent solution is to resort to a **euphemism**, that is, to a word or expression which for some reason can replace the tabooed item. It follows that a word used euphemistically undergoes semantic change in the form of an addition to its earlier sense or senses, but it is also probably the case that once a word's 'euphemistic' sense comes to be widely used, this fact prevents (or at least militates against) the word's use in its earlier sense, since speakers are likely to be unwilling to risk their non-euphemistic intention being interpreted in a euphemistic way. In other words, an expression which has acquired a new, euphemistic, sense is likely to rapidly lose its earlier, non-euphemistic, sense or senses.

Examples of euphemism are frequently due to one or other of three types of taboo: fear taboo (5.1.4.1), delicacy taboo (5.1.4.2), or decency taboo (5.1.4.3).

5.1.4.1 Fear taboo

The fear which forbids use of certain words in a particular culture (and which brings about a change of sense in their euphemistic replacements) is often of a religious or superstitious kind. It is well known that the prohibition placed upon the Jews against the use of the name of God led to the use of euphemisms such as that translated into English as 'Lord', or into Spanish as 'Señor'. But it is not solely the names of supernatural beings which are subject to taboo; the names of perfectly 'worldly' concepts may be similarly tabooed if there is an association in speakers' minds between some 'worldly' referent and some feared supernatural referent. The classic case is that of the weasel, which in some cultures, including many Western European ones, is seen as endowed with certain supernatural forces, mostly evil. In most of the Romance-speaking world, the Latin name of the weasel, MUSTĒLA, has been replaced by euphemisms, which have consequently undergone dramatic meaning-change. Within the Peninsula (see Menéndez Pidal 1964a: 396–405), *mustela* remains in Catalan and in one area of southern Galicia, together with (originally) affectionate derivatives of the same base in northern Leon and western Santander (*mostolilla*). Elsewhere, we find similarly propitiating terms: affectionate derivatives of DOMINA 'lady' in the west (Ptg. *doninha*, Gal. *don(oc)iña*, *donicela*, Leonese *donecilla*, etc.), *paniquesa* (no doubt referring to the animal's colouring) in the northeast (NE Castile, Navarre, Aragon), *comadreja* (an originally affectionate derivative of *comadre* 'neighbour') in most of Castile, Murcia and Andalusia (whence its introduction to Spanish America), together with many other forms in Asturias and Santander.

Taboos on animal names are not infrequent. Lat. VULPES 'fox' scarcely survives; in Spain it is replaced by a derivative VULPĒCULA, originally affectionate and no doubt propitiatory, but soon lexicalized and surviving as *gulpeja* until the fourteenth century. Its first euphemistic replacement (*raposa*~*rabosa*), referring to the animal's bushy tail, was itself largely displaced by *zorra*, possibly a nominalization of a borrowing from Basque meaning 'lazy'. In Andalusia we find euphemistic use of personal names, such as *juanica*, *maría*, *maría garcía*, *mariquita*.

Other fear taboos include avoidance of the words meaning 'left', owing to the popular association between this concept and evil or the Devil. Of the Latin terms for 'left', LAEVUS, SCAEVUS, SINISTER, only the latter survives, partially, in Romance; in Old Spanish it appears as *siniestro* (with /ie/ under the influence of its antonym *diestro*). Thereafter, it is retained only in the sense 'sinister', reflecting the association just mentioned, and in the sense 'left' is replaced by another borrowing from Basque, namely *izquierdo*. It will be noted that foreign borrowings may serve the same purpose as euphemisms in providing replacements for tabooed words.

5.1.4.2 Delicacy taboo

The tendency to avoid words referring to concepts considered disagreeable may also lead to the use of euphemisms. The concepts concerned include those associated with disease, death, mental or physical infirmity, crime, etc. Examples of Spanish words which have acquired their current sense through the effects of delicacy taboo include the following:

- *cretino* 'cretin' is a borrowing from French and originates in a dialectal form of Fr. *chrétien* 'Christian', used euphemistically.
- *tullido* 'crippled' is the only surviving Modern Spanish part of the Old Spanish verb *toller~tullir* 'to take away, deprive'.
- *matar* 'to kill' may owe its origin to the euphemistic use of a verb whose original meaning was different. Late Lat. MATTUS 'stupid, stupefied' may have served as the base of a derived verb *MATTĀRE 'to stun, stupefy', which then underwent meaning-change through its euphemistic use.

Modern Spanish has a host of expressions which may be used euphemistically to express the notion 'to kill': *cargarse a uno*, *dar el pasaporte*, *dar el paseo*, *liquidar*, *eliminar*, some of which may be calques of similar English euphemisms. Similarly, we find many terms used as euphemisms for 'to steal, rob': *coger*, *pillar*, *apañar*, *aliviar*, *trabajar*, *raspar*. Expressions which in the same way may mean 'to die' include *reventar*, *estirar la pata*, etc. For these euphemisms, see Beinhauer (1968).

5.1.4.3 Decency taboo

The motive for semantic change in this case is the avoidance of mention of words related to sex, and to certain parts of the body and their functions. The following cases illustrate the semantic consequences of this kind of taboo:

- *manceba* and *barragana* 'concubine' originally meant 'young woman', as can be seen by reference to their masculine counterparts *mancebo* 'youth' and OSp. *barragán* 'id.'
- *fulana* 'lover, concubine, prostitute' (cf. *fulano* 'so-and-so').
- *ramera* 'prostitute' probably earlier meant 'inn-keeper's wife; (female) innkeeper'.
- *buscona* 'prostitute' and *buscón* 'thief' are probably euphemistic derivatives of *buscar* 'to seek' whose original sense was 'seeker'.
- *amiga* and *querida* 'mistress'.
- *parir* 'to give birth' is increasingly avoided, when reference is to humans, in favour of euphemistic *dar a luz*, *alumbrar*.
- *embarazada* originally 'encumbered' or *en estado* (a reduction of *en estado interesante*) often replace *preñada* 'pregnant'.

- *aseo, baño* and *servicio(s)* have euphemistically extended their sense as replacements for *retrete* 'lavatory'.

Religious and sexual oaths may also be subject to decency taboo, with the effect that another word (usually one which shares a syllable or more of its form with the tabooed item) may change its sense to enable it to replace the original oath. Thus *¡caracoles!* (lit. 'snails') may replace *¡carajo!* (lit. 'penis').

Further exemplification of the effects of taboo can be seen in Kany (1960).

5.1.5 Foreign influences which cause semantic change

Coexistence between two languages (typically in the form of their use by substantial numbers of bilingual individuals or in the form of frequent translation between them) may lead to modification of the meanings of words in either or both of the languages concerned. Where two words (one belonging to each of the languages concerned) are approximate translation equivalents, any additional meaning belonging to one of the words may be transferred to the other. **Semantic loan** of this kind has no doubt taken place in some degree between Spanish and each of the languages with which it has been in contact over the centuries, but two particular instances of foreign influence on the meaning of Spanish words (that of Arabic and English) have received particular attention and will be considered here.

Although, in the early centuries (the eighth to the tenth) of the Reconquest, bilingualism between Arabic and Castilian must have been limited to small numbers of individuals, the following period (the late eleventh to the fourteenth centuries) saw the expansion of Castile into territories where substantial numbers of Arabic speakers continued to use their traditional language at the same time as learning Castilian. In the same period, translation of Arabic works, at first into Latin via the vernacular and then definitively into Castilian, became extremely frequent. The conditions for semantic loan were therefore more than satisfied and a good number of cases have been identified. Not all are beyond dispute, but there is reasonable evidence that the following words, all of Latin origin, acquired their sense through influence from Arabic (see Lapesa 1980: 154–7):

- *adelantado* 'placed in front' > 'military governor of an overseas territory' in imitation of Ar. *muqáddam* 'placed in front; chief'.
- OSp. *casa* 'house' > 'town' through the influence of Ar. *dār* 'house; town' (although the sense 'town' has now been lost from *casa*).
- OSp. *correr* 'run' > 'depredate'; cf. Ar. *gāwara* 'run; depredate' (again, the acquired sense was later lost).
- *criar* 'to feed, rear, educate' > 'to grow (hair, fur, feathers)'; cf. Ar. *rabba* 'id.'
- *hidalgo* 'noble' < OSp. *fijodalgo* 'noble' (lit. 'son of wealth'), by imitation of Arabic expressions containing *ʿibn* 'son of' and having metaphorical value (e.g. *ʿibn ad-dunyâ* 'son of wealth; rich man').

- *infante* (< INFANTE 'child') 'son of the king', until the thirteenth century also meant 'son of a nobleman'; cf. Ar. *walad* 'child; son of the king'. In this case, after the semantic extension, the original sense ('child') was entirely lost.
- *plata* 'silver' (< *PLATTA 'flat') may have acquired its sense by semantic loan from Ar. *luğayn* or *wáraqa*, both 'lamina (i.e. a thin plate); silver'. The later, American-Spanish, development of the sense of this word to 'money' is a more 'normal' case of semantic development, through association of ideas.
- OSp. *poridat* 'secrecy, intimacy' (< PŪRITĀTE 'purity') perhaps acquired this sense by loan from derivatives of Ar. *ḫalasa* 'to be pure'.

Semantic influence of English on Spanish is widely attested (see Pratt 1980: 160–76), and often condemned by purists. It is particularly evident in the case of paronyms (pairs of words, one belonging to each of the two languages, which are obviously related in form but which have different meanings), the 'false friends' of the unwary translator. In this case, semantic loan can be said to turn 'false friends' into 'true friends' or at least 'truer friends'. The following instances of semantic loan due to paronymy (not all equally frequent, but most now well established) are among the many that have been identified. Where there is a traditional term, with which the new form has entered into competition, it is given in square brackets: *administración [gobierno]* 'administration, government', *agenda [orden del día]* 'agenda', *apartamento [piso]* 'flat, apartment', *arruinar [dañar, estropear]* 'to ruin', *ataque* 'attack (e.g. heart)', *base* '(military) base', *cereales* 'cereals (as generic)', *círculo [sector, ambiente]* 'circle', *complejo* 'complex (in the psychological and industrial sense)', *congelar* 'to freeze' (e.g. prices or salaries), *crucial [crítico]* 'crucial', *duplicar [copiar]* 'to duplicate', *editor [redactor]* '(newspaper) editor', *estudio* '(film or TV) studio', *factoría [fábrica]* 'factory', *fatiga* '(metal) fatigue', *firma [empresa]* 'firm', *flota* 'fleet (of cars)', *honesto [honrado]* 'honest', *humor [gracia]* 'humour', *ignorar [pasar por alto]* 'to ignore', *incidente [suceso]* 'incident', *liberar [libertar]* 'to liberate', *literalmente [al pie de la letra]* 'literally', *nativo [natural]* 'native', *permisivo* 'permissive', *planta* '(industrial) plant', the noun *plástico* 'plastic', *proceso [procedimiento]* 'process', *satélite* 'satellite (with reference to space technology, politics, or town planning)', *simple [sencillo]* 'simple', *soda [seltz]* 'soda(water)', *tanque* '(military) tank', *torpedo* '(naval) torpedo', *verificar [comprobar]* 'to verify'.

However, semantic loan from English is also evident in cases where no paronymy is involved, e.g. *cadena* 'chain (of shops)', *canal* '(TV) channel', *cumbre* 'summit (meeting)', *escoba* 'sweeper (in football)', *estrella* '(film, etc.) star', *mariposa* 'butterfly (in swimming)', *muestra* '(statistical) sample', *ventilar* 'to air (an issue)'.

Semantic loan from English may also take the form of **loan translation** (or **calque**), in which the separate words of an English expression are individually translated, giving rise to new compounds, some of which have already been considered in 4.14.3, since it is possible in some cases that an English model is not involved. Such loan translations include compounds consisting of:

nouns + noun: *buque escuela* 'training ship', *perro guardián* 'guard dog', *ciudad dormitorio* 'dormitory town, bedroom community', *encuentro [en la] cumbre* 'summit meeting', *hombre rana* 'frogman', *horas punta* 'rush hour', *madre patria* 'motherland', *cine club* 'cine club', *misión rescate* 'rescue mission', *año luz* 'light year', *hora cero* 'zero hour', *tiempo récord* 'record time', *tren miniatura* 'miniature train'

verb + noun: *calientaplatos* 'plate warmer', *cortacésped* 'lawnmower', *limpiaparabrisas* 'windscreen-wiper(s)', *portaaviones* 'aircraft carrier', *rompehielos* 'icebreaker'

noun + adjective: *caja fuerte* 'strongbox', *elefante blanco* 'white elephant', *guerra fría* 'cold war', *mesa redonda* 'round table', *perro caliente* 'hot-dog'

adjective + noun: *próximo oriente* 'Near East', *tercer mundo* 'Third World', *tercer programa* 'Third Programme'

Such loans may also include more complex structures, such as noun + *de* + noun: *beso de la vida* 'kiss of life', *cruce de cebra* 'zebra crossing', *fuera de juego* 'offside', *máquina de coser* 'sewing machine', *tubo de ensayo* 'test tube'.

5.1.6 *The need to name a new concept*

As new concepts become current in a linguistic community, there simultaneously arises an evident requirement for a means of expressing the new concept. The solution may be to borrow a word from another language (sections 4.2–13 are primarily concerned with this solution), to create a new term through word-formation (see 4.14.1, 4.14.2.1, 4.14.3), or to extend the sense of an existing word. In the case of Spanish (as with many languages), it is often difficult to distinguish between the latter process and semantic loan, that is, to know whether an extension of sense occurred spontaneously in Spanish or whether it is due to imitation of an extension of sense which took place in another language. The only firm guide here is the date of first attestation of the extended sense in the language concerned. Thus it is likely that *platillo volante* is a loan translation of Eng. *flying saucer*, rather than an independent creation within Spanish. By contrast, it is clear that the developments *león* 'lion' > 'puma', *piña* 'pine-cone' > 'pineapple', *tigre* 'tiger' > 'jaguar' are not due to foreign models (see 4.9).

5.2 Types of semantic change

Ullmann (1962, based on Roudet 1921) classifies semantic changes according to two criteria; on the one hand, a distinction is made between those changes

Table 5.1 *Types of semantic change*

Change based on:	Association of meanings	Association of word forms
Similarity	metaphor	popular etymology
Contiguity	metonymy	ellipsis

which originate in an association of meanings and those which originate in an association between word-forms; on the other hand, a contrast is drawn between those changes which are motivated by similarity (either of meaning or form) and those which stem from contiguity (either of meaning or form), where 'contiguity' indicates 'juxtaposition' in a broad sense, as when the meanings concerned refer to things which appear together in the real world or when the words concerned are frequently collocated. This classification may be stated (now adding labels to each of the four types of semantic change involved) as in table 5.1.

5.2.1 Metaphor

Many words have acquired their current sense (or one or more of their current senses) by having been used at one time or another as metaphors. The metaphor is fundamentally a comparison, in which one concept (the one which the speaker essentially has in mind) is compared with another (which the speaker sees as having some similarity with the first). If the name of the second concept, as a result of this metaphorical process, is used to replace the name of the first concept and the metaphor gains acceptance in the linguistic community concerned, it follows that a new sense has come to be associated with an existing word.

While the literal (or traditional) sense of a word continues to be present alongside the metaphorical sense, the metaphor concerned may be regarded as a 'living' metaphor, unless the two senses come to be regarded as unrelated, in which case one is simply faced with an instance of polysemy (more than one sense attached to a single word). By contrast, where the traditional sense is abandoned and only the metaphorical sense survives, the metaphor is best described as 'dead' and is only recognizable as a metaphor in the light of historical information not normally available to the speaker. Thus, it is likely that the sense 'mountain-range' which belongs to *sierra* is the result of metaphorical use of *sierra* 'saw' (< SERRA 'id.'). But whether native speakers regard *sierra* 'mountain range' as a (living) metaphor, rather than a case of polysemy, is open to dispute.

Many types of metaphor have been recognized, of which the most frequent will be exemplified here. 'Anthropomorphic' metaphors transfer names of parts of the body to inanimate objects: *boca* 'mouth (of river)', *entrañas* 'bowels (of the earth)', *manecillas* 'hands (of clock)', *ojo* 'eye (of needle)', *pata* 'leg (of table)', etc. The reverse process is also common: *caja* (*del pecho*) '(rib-) cage', *globo* (*del ojo*) 'eyeball', *nuez* (*de la garganta*) 'Adam's apple', etc. The same process can be seen in a number of dead metaphors: *pierna* 'leg' < PERNA 'ham', OSp. *tiesta* 'head' (like Fr. *tête*, etc.) < TESTA '(flower) pot', *yema* 'tip (of the finger)' < GEMMA 'shoot (of plant)'.

Animal metaphors, in which animal names are applied to plants or inanimate objects, can be seen in *diente de león* 'dandelion', *pata de gallo* 'goose foot'; *araña* 'chandelier', *gato* 'jack', *gatillo* 'trigger', *grúa* '(mechanical) crane' (< OSp. *grúa* 'crane (ornith.)', later changed to *grulla*).

The metaphorical use of originally concrete terms to convey non-concrete (e.g. abstract) notions can be exemplified by: *coz* 'kick' (< CALCE 'heel'), *depender* 'to depend' (also 'hang' < DĒPENDERE 'hang'), *fuente* (*de ingresos*) 'source (of income)', *pensar* 'think' (< PĒNSĀRE 'to weigh (up)'), *sembrar* (*odios*) 'to sow (discord)'.

'Synaesthetic' metaphors, which allow adjectives associated with one corporeal sense to be used in connection with another, are as frequent in Spanish as in other languages: *voz fría* 'cold voice', *voz dulce* 'sweet voice', *sonidos penetrantes* 'piercing sounds', *colores chillones* 'loud colours', *chillido agudo* 'shrill cry', etc.

5.2.2 *Metonymy*

Unlike metaphor, which forges links between previously unrelated concepts, metonymy exploits previously existing links between the names of things which are already linked in the 'real world'. It may be defined as the process of applying to a concept the name of an already related concept. The types of relationship involved (and therefore the types of metonymy) are several.

Spatial metonymy, where the name of an object is applied to another which is in physical contiguity with it, can be seen in: *acera* 'pavement, sidewalk' (< OSp. *façera* 'facade (of a row of buildings facing a street or square)'), *cadera* 'hip' <*'buttock' (< VL CATHEGRA (CL CATHEDRA) 'chair'), *asiento* 'backside' (< 'seat'), *boca* 'mouth' (< BUCCA 'cheek'), *mejilla* 'cheek' (< MAXILLA 'jaw'), *carrillo* '(lower) cheek' (earlier 'jaw'). For the facial terms mentioned, and others, see Wright (1985).

Temporal metonymy allows shifts of sense along the temporal axis: *ahora* 'now' may also mean 'soon, presently'; *verano* ('summer') until the Golden Age meant 'late spring' (by contrast with *estío* 'summer') but has become synonymous with *estío*, which is now restricted to literary register; *almuerzo* means 'breakfast' in Old and Golden Age Spanish (as it still does in American and regional Peninsular Spanish) but in urban Peninsular Spanish has come to mean 'lunch'; *cena* 'dinner' descends from CĒNA 'main meal (taken at about 3 pm)'.

Synecdoche, the application of the name of part of a larger concept to the whole of that concept, or vice versa, can be regarded as a kind of metonymy: *almiar* 'haystack' (< (PERTICA) MEDIĀLE 'central pole', around which haystacks in Spain are commonly built), *boda* 'wedding' (< *'marriage vows' < VŌTA 'vows'), *césped* 'lawn' (< CAESPITE '(piece of) turf'), *cimientos* 'foundations' (< CAEMENTŌS 'building stones'), *puerto* 'harbour' (< PORTU 'harbour entrance').

Other types of metonymy include the use of a name of a substance to indicate something made from that substance (*alambre* 'wire' < *'bronze wire' < AERĀMEN 'bronze(work)'), the use of proper nouns to indicate an associated product (*jerez, montilla, champán, coñac*, etc.), and the use of abstract terms to indicate some associated concrete notion (*cuenta* 'account, bill', *cura* 'priest', *encuadernación* 'binding (of a book)', *guardia* 'policeman').

5.2.3 *Popular etymology*

This process, which essentially changes the form of 'unmotivated' (i.e. structurally isolated) words in order to make them conform to pre-existing families of words to which they do not historically belong, may also result in some change of meaning, usually quite subtle. A well-known case is that of *vagabundo* 'tramp', which through popular etymology often appears in colloquial speech as *vagamundo*, thereby specifying its sense as 'one who wanders the world'. Similarly, when OSp. *berrojo* 'bolt' (< *VERRUCULU) was modified to *cerrojo*, by attraction to *cerrar* 'to close', its meaning was no doubt also modified, associating it exclusively with the closing of doors, etc. Other examples include *tinieblas* 'darkness' (< OSp. *tiniebras*), where association with *niebla* 'fog' has not only changed the form of the word but has arguably added the notion of 'fogginess' to that of 'darkness' in *tinieblas*, and *pulgar* 'thumb' (< OSp. *polgar*), where it may be that, as the form of the word became more like that of *pulga* 'flea', speakers have come to associate the meaning 'flea' with *pulgar* (perhaps envisaging the thumb as a suitable weapon for killing fleas).

5.2.4 *Ellipsis*

We have seen (5.1.1) that when two words are frequently collocated, the meaning of one may be added to that of the other. A further change is the deletion (or ellipsis) of one of the words, so that the other bears the whole semantic burden of the originally compound expression. A frequently observed effect of such change is that in a noun + adjective phrase the noun is deleted and the adjective thereby takes on the function and meaning of a noun: *ábrego* 'south wind' (< (VENTU) AFRICU 'African wind'), *aguijada* 'goad' (< (PERTICA) *AQUĪLEĀTA (for ACŪLEĀTA) 'sharpened pole'), *albérchigo* 'clingstone peach' (< (MĀLU) PERSICU 'Persian fruit'), *almiar* 'haystack' (< (PERTICA) MEDIĀLE ‘central pole’; see 5.2.2), *armiño* ‘stoat; ermine’ (< (MŪRE) ARMENIU ‘Armenian mouse’), *avellana* ‘hazelnut’ (< (NUCE) ABELLĀNA ‘nut from Abella (in Campania)’), *breva* ‘early fig’ (< (FĪCU) BIFERA ‘figtree bearing fruit twice per year’), *campana* ‘bell’ (< (VĀSA) CAMPĀNA ‘vessels from Campania’), *ciruela* ‘plum’ (< (PRŪNA) CĒREOLA ‘wax-coloured plums’), etc.

5.3 Consequences of semantic change

Irrespective of the cause of a semantic change or the general type to which it belongs, if one examines the meanings of words before and after a change, one can observe two broad semantic effects. On the one hand, there may be modification of the range and complexity of meaning of the word concerned, while on the other, it may undergo a change in any affective nuances which it possesses.

5.3.1 Change of semantic range

One consequence of meaning-change is a movement from greater generality to greater specificity or the reverse. It should be noted that the first of these movements is accompanied by an increase in the ‘amount’ of meaning conveyed, while the change towards greater generality is accompanied by a decrease in the ‘amount’ of meaning. In this context, ‘amount’ refers to the number of separately identifiable components which make up the total meaning of the word. Thus, as Lat. SECĀRE ‘to cut’ becomes more specific in sense and is restricted to the meaning ‘to reap’ (Sp. *segar*), additional components of meaning (‘with a scythe, machine, etc.’, ‘appropriate to grass, corn, etc.’) can be recognized in the word. By contrast, as STĀRE ‘to stand’ becomes more general in sense (> Sp. *estar*), it loses such components of its meaning as ‘in vertical position’. In the following examples of increase in specificity and complexity, it will be noted that where a Latin word has been transmitted to Spanish by more than one channel, the learned form concerned usually retains the unrestricted Latin meaning (see 2.2.4):

- *adobar* ‘prepare (meat for sausage); to tan (leather)’ < OSp. *adobar* ‘to prepare, provide with’
- *anegar* ‘to drown’ < ĒNECĀRE ‘to kill (especially by strangling or stifling)’
- *ánsar* ‘wild goose’ < OSp. *ánsar* ‘goose’ (cf. Juan Manuel: *ánsares bravos*) < VL ANSAR (CL ANSER) ‘goose’
- OSp. *arienço* ‘a medieval coin/weight’ < ARGENTEU ‘(made) of silver’
- *boda* ‘wedding’ < *‘marriage-vows’ < VŌTA ‘vows’
- *bruma* ‘mist, haze’ < OSp. *bruma* ‘winter’ < BRŪMA ‘id.’
- *cebo* ‘fodder; bait (for fishing)’ < CIBU ‘food’

- *colgar* 'to hang' < COLLOCĀRE 'to place' (cf. the unrestricted learned term *colocar* 'to place')
- *comulgar* 'to take communion' < COMMŪNICĀRE 'to communicate' (cf. the unrestricted learned term *comunicar* 'to communicate')
- *cuero* 'leather' < CORIU 'skin (of people and animals)' (although some varieties of Spanish, especially American, retain the unrestricted sense)
- *cuñado* 'brother-in-law' < OSp. *cuñado* 'relation by marriage' < COGNĀTU 'blood-relation'
- *dehesa* 'open pasture' < DĒFĒNSA 'forbidden land' (i.e. 'forbidden to huntsmen'?)
- *guisar* 'to cook' (or, with even further specialized sense, 'to casserole') < OSp. *guisar* 'to prepare, arrange' (derived from *guisa* 'manner')
- *ponzoña* 'poison' < PŌTIŌNE 'drink, potion'
- *rezar* 'to pray' < OSp. *rezar* 'to recite, say aloud' < RECITĀRE 'id.' (cf. the unrestricted learned term *recitar* 'to recite')
- *siesta* 'siesta' < OSp. *siesta* 'mid-day heat' < SEXTA (HŌRA) 'sixth (hour)' (cf. the unrestricted sense of the learned numeral *sexta* 'sixth')
- *tañer* 'to play (an instrument)' < OSp. *tañer* 'to touch; to play (a musical instrument)' < TANGERE 'to touch'

The reverse process, generalization of sense with loss of complexity, is probably rarer, but nevertheless provides frequent examples in the development of Spanish. Again, any learned correlates will normally retain the Latin sense, in this case a more specific sense:

- *asir* 'to grasp', as a derivative of *asa* 'handle', earlier meant 'to grasp by the handle'
- *barro* 'mud' until the Golden Age meant only '(potter's) clay', a specific sense also still available in the word
- *compañero* 'companion' < OSp. *compaño* 'id.' < Late Lat. COMPĀNIŌNE 'table-companion' (lit. 'one who eats bread with another')
- *cosa* 'thing' < CAUSA 'cause; matter, question' (cf. learned *causa* 'cause')
- *dinero* 'money' < DĒNĀRIU '(a specific) coin'
- *grande* 'large in size, morally great, etc.'< GRANDE 'large in size'
- *hallar* 'to find' < AFFLĀRE 'to breathe out', perhaps via the meanings 'to follow the scent' and 'to find the prey', with reference originally to hunting-dogs
- *lograr* 'to succeed' < OSp. *lograr* 'to enjoy the fruits of', perhaps via 'to enjoy, possess' and 'to acquire' (e.g. *lograr los deseos* 'to achieve one's desires', whence *lograr hacer*, etc.)
- *palabra* 'word' < PARABOLA 'comparison, allegory', probably via 'phrase, sentence'
- *parientes* 'relatives' < OSp. *parientes* 'parents' (< PARENTĒS 'id.')

A particular subgroup of cases of meaning-generalization is constituted by instances in which a proper noun has acquired the status of a common noun.

Some examples are trivial and well-known (e.g. *un donjuan, un quijote*), but others require historical information for their elucidation. Thus, the nineteenth-century expression *quevedos* 'spectacles' owes its origin to portraits of Quevedo wearing spectacles, while *asesino* 'murderer' descends from Ar. *ḥaššāšî*, lit. 'hashish-drinkers', the name of an eleventh-century Muslim sect with the reputation for butchering opponents.

5.3.2 *Change of affectivity*

The emotive overtones which accompany many words (revealing an attitude, on the part of the speaker, of hostility, contempt, approval, fondness, etc., towards the concept concerned) are as subject to change as any other semantic component, and in broad terms may show development of either pejorative or favourable sense.

Development of pejorative meaning may be the result of various processes, including use of the word as a euphemism (see 5.1.4), association of ideas, prejudice, etc. For example:

- *algarabía* 'gibberish; uproar' < Ar. *ʕarabîya* 'the Arabic language'
- *cautivo* (a semi-learned descendant of CAPTĪVU 'captive') underwent a series of changes, in adjectival use, of increasingly pejorative tone: 'captive' > 'wretched' > 'wicked, evil' (its commonest Golden Age sense, perhaps reinforced by Italian *cattivo* 'bad'), although the meaning 'captive' has alone survived
- *necio* 'foolish' < NESCIU 'ignorant'
- *simple* 'simple, half-witted' (alongside other senses) < SIMPLU 'simple'
- *siniestro* 'sinister' < OSp. 'left' < SINISTRU 'id.' (see 5.1.4.1)
- *villano* 'boorish' (derived from the descendant of VĪLLA 'farm') < 'rustic' < 'rural'

The opposite process, development of favourable sense, is again motivated by a wide range of factors, and can take the form of movement from unfavourable to less unfavourable meaning (usually through hyperbole, as in the case of *terrible, horrible* or in that of *lamentar* 'to regret' < 'to lament, grieve') or movement from derogatory to favourable meaning, as in the following cases:

- *caballo* 'horse' < CABALLU 'nag; workhorse'
- *calle* 'street' < CALLE '(cattle-)path'
- *casa* 'house' < CASA 'hut, cottage'
- *condestable* 'High Constable' < COMITE STABULĪ 'officer in charge of the stable'
- *corte* 'court'/*Cortes* 'Parliament' < COHORTE 'enclosure, farmyard', via 'division of a Roman military camp' > 'body of troops (belonging to that division)' > 'Imperial guard' > 'palace'. The originally rural sense survives in dialectal *corte* 'cow-shed'
- *ministro* 'minister' < MINISTRU 'servant'

A particular case of appreciative sense development can be seen in the so-called *voces mediae*, words whose tone is essentially neutral but which may take on favourable or unfavourable overtones in different contexts. Such words may eventually take on permanently pejorative or favourable sense. Many are concerned with the notion of 'luck':

- *accidente* 'accident' is now unfavourable despite its neutral origins (a borrowing of ACCIDENS, -TIS 'occurring')
- *fortuna* 'fortune' (< FORTŪNA 'id.' has acquired favourable overtones as can be seen more clearly in its derivative *afortunado* 'fortunate'
- *sino* 'fate' (< SIGNU 'sign, constellation') is normally interpreted as having unfavourable associations
- *suerte* 'luck' (< SORTE 'casting a lot') implies 'good luck' (e.g. in wishing someone *¡Mucha suerte!*), as can also be seen by the necessity to add an adjective (e.g. *mala suerte*) to indicate 'bad luck'

6 Past, present and future

6.1 The nature of language history

Almost all histories of highly standardized languages, including those of Spanish, treat the development of the language concerned as if that development were linear. That is to say, such histories adopt the convenient fiction that there has been an unbroken chain of events leading from the earliest phase examined down to the present. There are excellent presentational reasons for adopting this approach, and it has been adopted in this book.

However, there are good reasons for claiming that language history is not linear, but rather that it proceeds from one condition of variation, through other such conditions, down to the inherently varied present state of affairs (see Penny 1998). In particular, I have claimed elsewhere (Penny 2000) that the history of Spanish is particularly discontinuous, since the present-day language has emerged from a series of dialect-contact situations (e.g. in tenth-century Burgos, in twelfth-century Toledo, in thirteenth-century Seville, in sixteenth-century Madrid, not to mention sixteenth- and seventeenth-century Mexico City, Lima, etc.). At each stage, the creation of a new community, made up principally of immigrants who spoke noticeably different varieties of Peninsular Romance, led to a process of koineization: the creation of a new variety (a *koiné*) which typically preferred the linguistically simpler variants that were available to the community at large.

Nevertheless, although the formulations used in this book (e.g. ŏcŭlum > oclum > /ói̯lo/ > /óʎo/ > /óʒo/ > /óʃo/ > /óxo/ *ojo* 'eye') are necessarily a simplified representation of the historical reality (since each 'stage' cannot in fact be neatly separated from preceding and following stages, but overlaps with them, and usually with other variants which failed to survive in the language of the community concerned), it is hoped that the distortion they represent is not so great as to invalidate the historical claims they inadequately make.

6.2 World Spanish

No history of Spanish can do proper justice to the enormous variety of forms which comprise present-day Spanish, spoken natively by perhaps 350 million people in more than twenty-three countries (1.7), and as a second language in many more. Although the range of variation in Spanish is little greater, if any, than that of other world languages, such as English or Portuguese, this book has necessarily ignored, for the most part, all but the standard forms of Spanish. But 'standard' does not here mean 'Peninsular', since the modern standard is supranational and intercontinental. Accordingly, a historical account is given of such features as *seseo* (2.6.3), weakening of syllable-final /s/ (2.6.7), *voseo* (3.5.1.1) and the verb-forms associated with it (3.7.3.1–3), which, even if they are not all exclusively American, are typical of many, sometimes all, American regions. Rarely are the features discussed here exclusively European. If most of the changes discussed here occurred in Europe, that is because the vast majority of the changes which gave rise to the characteristic features of modern world Spanish took place before the spread of Peninsular varieties to the Americas.

6.3 Convergence and divergence

Will Spanish remain a single language or will it fragment into a number of mutually unintelligible languages? This issue was repeatedly raised in the twentieth century, with many scholars forecasting an outcome for Spanish that would be comparable with the fragmentation of Latin into the various Romance languages. On this prognosis, Mexican and Argentinian Spanish, say, would come to be separate codes from European Spanish, as different from the latter as French and Italian are from present-day Spanish.

However, from an early twenty-first-century perspective, this outcome seems much less likely. There are two broad reasons why the earlier pessimism now seems unfounded.

Firstly, the pressures towards divergence which fragmented the descendants of Latin are unlikely to be repeated in coming centuries. Over the centuries that stretch from the late Roman period to the twelfth century, communications between different parts of the Romance-speaking world were distinctly weak, while a relatively small segment of the population (the literate minority) was subject to the unifying pressure exerted by the then single standard language, namely Latin. As a result, local changes were likely to have only local spread, leading to increasing diversification of speech. From the twelfth century onwards, different forms of Romance could be associated with different medieval states, and could be promoted as national languages in those states with the resources required to carry out such an enterprise. The creation of these separate standard languages, within a territory where up to that point there had been a single prestige language, is now seen to require the establishment of new and distinct traditions of spelling and grammar in different portions of the territory concerned (see Wright 1982). Such revolutions did indeed occur in the Latin-speaking world of medieval Europe, usually resulting from the dedication of considerable resources to the project (as happened under Alfonso X, the Learned, king of Castile and Leon in the later thirteenth century; see 1.4), by contrast with what happened in the Chinese- or Arabic-speaking areas, where maintenance of a single written standard served to maintain the unity of those languages (despite considerable linguistic variation within the areas concerned). In the current Spanish-speaking world, there is no evidence of significant moves towards the adoption of separate spelling and grammatical codes in different countries. Nor is there evidence that any of the present-day states of the Spanish-speaking world (where, naturally, somewhat different forms of Spanish are in use) is motivated to promote its local variety as a national language distinct from the varieties used in other states.

Secondly, pressures towards convergence are today greater than in the past, especially the medieval past. Collaboration between the Academies (which exist in practically all Spanish-speaking countries) almost always ensures a single set of linguistic recommendations, enshrined in official publications, which are generally followed scrupulously by the press and publications media. Likewise, migration, travel and new types of communication between speakers of different varieties of Spanish provide unprecedented conditions for the face-to-face contact which promotes similarity of linguistic usage. This is not to deny the considerable variation (especially in lexis) which exists between one Spanish-speaking region and another, but speakers almost always handle this variation in such a way that it does not impede communication.

6.4 English and Spanish

These two languages are arguably the only two genuine world languages, in the sense that they are sponsored by a significant number of nation states in most continents, where they are the normal vehicle of education, administration and the media. The great difference between the two lies in the fact that English (but not Spanish) is used as a second language, by a very large numbers of non-native speakers, in an enormous range of countries. The future of English is consequently likely to be different from that of Spanish, since it is possible that the native English-speaking populations of the world, despite their size, may not be in a position to dominate the development of the language, with the result that variation within world English is likely to become more marked than variation within Spanish.

Currently it seems that English is ahead of Spanish in the competition, if that is what it is, to become the world's first global language (a language used in some measure by a majority of the world's population). This state of affairs is no doubt due to the overwhelming economic and political power of the core English-speaking countries, chiefly the United States. If there is room for a second global language (which some would say is unlikely), then Spanish is the main candidate to fill this role.

One way in which the balance between English and Spanish has shifted in the last half century is in the relationship between the two languages in the United States. We have noted (1.7) that some 10 per cent of the US population are native speakers of Spanish. Unlike other minority languages that have been and are used in the US, Spanish shows no sign there of failing to be passed on to the youngest generation in the communities concerned, and as a result the Spanish-speaking segment of the population continues to grow, even without the increase implied by constant immigration from Spanish-speaking countries. Rate of growth of the US Spanish-speaking community is notably greater than that of the English-speaking majority. Numbers alone do not confer high status, and up to the present Spanish in the US has been the language of a deprived and low-status sector of the nation. However, there are some signs of change in the appreciation accorded to Spanish; politicians no longer merely pay lip-service to Spanish speakers, with the purpose of gathering electoral support, but Spanish-speaking politicians are beginning to come to national prominence. Use of Spanish as a second language by native speakers of English has also increased markedly in recent decades, most notably in those areas with the greatest concentrations of native Spanish speakers: New York and some other northern cities, Florida, and the Southwest. The shift in the relationship between English and Spanish in the United States, if it continues in its present direction, is likely to enhance the use and status of Spanish in the rest of the world, assuming the continued power of the United States to influence the cultural patterns of the rest of the world.

Such an outcome would be paradoxical, in the light of the way in which contact between English and Spanish is generally viewed within the Spanish-speaking world. Although not as paranoid as speakers of some languages are about the 'deleterious' effects of English on their native language, some speakers of Spanish (typically those who see themselves as guardians of traditional culture) see the impact of English on Spanish as a highly undesirable process. We have noted the deep influence of English on the vocabulary of Spanish (4.10), and its lesser effect on the semantic value of Spanish words (5.1.5). But such influence rarely if ever is felt in the phonology, morphology or syntax of Spanish, and there is little evidence that the impact of English on Spanish is more than superficial.

The internal and external health of Spanish is reasonably assured for the foreseeable future.

Glossary of technical terms used in the text

Some definitions are taken from Trask (1997b).

ablative The case form which expresses the meaning 'out of' or 'away from', 'by means of', etc.

accusative The case form which is typically used to indicate the direct object of a verb.

allophone Any one of the phonetically different forms which can be assumed by a single phoneme.

analogy Also **analogical change**. Any type of language change in which forms are altered so as to make them more similar to other forms. See especially 2.1.4.

analytic A label applied to a grammatical form which is constructed by adding additional words to the word being inflected.

aperture The degree of openness of a vowel. Thus /a/ has greater aperture than /i/.

apico-alveolar A label applied to any speech sound in which the tip (apex) of the tongue is moved against or towards the teeth-ridge (alveolus).

apocope The loss or omission of one or more sounds from the end of a word.

apodosis In a sentence of the *If*... (*then*) type, the part that follows the *then*. See also **protasis**.

arrhizotonic A label applied to a verbal form which does not carry the accent on the root. (That is, a form in which the accent falls on the ending.)

aspect A grammatical category which deals with distinctions in the way in which an action or a situation is regarded as being distributed in time, that is, with the internal structure of the action or situation.

assimilation Any phonetic or phonological process (see especially 2.1.1.1) in which a particular sound becomes more similar to some other nearby sound.

atonic Also **unstressed**. A label applied to a vowel, syllable or word which does not carry primary stress.

calque Also **loan translation**. A word or phrase constructed by using a word or phrase in another language as a model and translating it piece by piece. See especially 5.1.5.

ceceo A style of pronunciation in which the dental fricative /s̪/ (corresponding to both /θ/ and /s/ of standard Peninsular Spanish, e.g. in *caz̲a* and *cas̲a*) is fronted to become /s̪^{θ}/, similar but not identical to standard Peninsular /θ/. See especially 2.6.3.

clitic A grammatical item which appears to be less than a word but more than an affix (e.g. *me, te, se, le, lo, la, nos, os, les, los, las*).

cognate A word in a particular language which is related to another word in a genetically related language, in that both represent continuations of a word in the common ancestor of both languages.

dative That case which is typically used to mark an indirect object.

derivative A word obtained from another word by adding an affix or affixes.

dissimilation Any phonetic or phonological process (see especially 2.1.1.2) in which a particular sound becomes more different from some other nearby sound.

doublet A pair of words in the same language which descend from the same source word. See especially 2.2.4.

enclitic A label applied to a **clitic** which is phonologically attached to what precedes it.

epenthesis The insertion of a segment into the middle of a word. See especially 2.1.1.3.

etymon (plural **etyma**) An ancestral form of a word. The opposite of **reflex**.

euphemism An expression used to replace another which is subject to **taboo**. See especially 5.1.4.

false friend See **paronym**.

final A label applied to a segment at the end of a word. If that segment is a vowel or a syllable, the term **final** implies that it is **atonic**.

finite A label applied to a verb which is fully marked for whatever tense and agreement is typical of the language to which it belongs. In Spanish, all verb forms other than the infinitive (e.g. *cantar*), the participle (e.g. *cantado*), and the gerund (e.g. *cantando*) are finite.

geminate A label applied to a consonant which is significantly longer than is normally the case. Thus, the /nn/ of Spanish *innegable* is geminate.

gender A grammatical phenomenon by which nouns are distributed among two or more classes requiring different kinds of agreement on other words which are connected, such as determiners or adjectives. Gender should not be confused with biological sex.

genitive That case which marks a possessor.

gentilicio A Spanish noun or adjective which indicates the place of origin of the person or thing to which it is applied (e.g. *gaditano* 'belonging to Cadiz').

glide A speech sound which patterns like a consonant (e.g. it is excluded from the syllabic nucleus), but has some of the characteristics of a vowel. The Spanish glides are characterized by an articulatory movement from a consonantal to a vocalic conformation of the vocal tract, or vice versa. They comprise [j] (*t<u>i</u>ene*), [i̯] (*ba<u>i</u>le*), [w] (*b<u>u</u>eno*), [u̯] (*ca<u>u</u>sa*). See **wau** and **yod**.

haplology The loss of one of two consecutive syllables which are similar or identical.

hiatus A juncture between two vowels which belong to separate syllables.

homonymy A condition in which two or more words (**homonyms**), each with its separate meaning, share an identical pronunciation.

imparisyllabic A label applied to certain Latin nouns (typically of the third declension) whose nominative singular form (nominative and accusative in the case of neuter nouns) has one syllable fewer than their other case forms. See **parisyllabic**.

initial A label applied to a segment at the beginning of a word. If that segment is a vowel or a syllable, the term **initial** implies that it is **atonic**.

intertonic A label applied to an **atonic** vowel or syllable which is internal within a word (i.e. it is neither **initial** nor **final**).

intervocalic A label applied to a single non-geminate consonant which is both preceded and followed by a vowel.

laísmo A non-standard system of pronoun reference in which the clitic *la* refers not merely to a feminine direct object (e.g. *A mi madre* ***la*** *vi anoche*), but also to a feminine indirect object (e.g. *A mi madre* ***la*** *di la carta*).

learned A label applied to a word borrowed into a language (via a written source) from an ancestral form of that language and which therefore does not show the normal phonological developments typical of the borrowing language. See especially 2.2.2.

leísmo A system of pronoun reference in which the clitic *le* refers not merely to indirect objects (e.g. *A mi padre **le** di la carta*), but also to masculine (usually personal) direct objects (e.g. *A mi padre **le** vi anoche*).

lenition A phonological process of weakening (typically one which affects **intervocalic** consonants) in which a speech sound is changed to another sound which involves a less complete blockage of the airstream. See especially 2.5.3.2.

lexeme A lexical item.

levelling A type of change in which the grammatical forms of certain words are changed so as to make the whole set of forms more regular.

loan translation See **calque**.

loísmo A system of pronoun reference (rare in Spanish) in which the clitic *lo* refers not merely to a (masculine) direct object (e.g. *A mi padre **lo** vi anoche*), but also to a masculine indirect object (e.g. *A mi padre **lo** di la carta*). [Some writers also use this term, confusingly, to refer to the normal Andalusian and American system of pronoun reference in which the clitic *lo* refers to all masculine direct objects (e.g. *A mi padre **lo** vi anoche, el pan **lo** dejé en la mesa*), by contrast with the ***leísmo*** of central and northern Spain.]

merger A type of change in which speakers cease to differentiate between two or more formerly distinct phonemes. See especially. 2.1.3.2.

metaphor The process of naming a concept by means of a term which refers to something imaginatively connected with that concept. See especially 5.2.1.

metaphony A process by which a vowel in a word is raised (typically by one degree) through **assimilation** to a later higher element (vowel or glide). See especially 2.4.2.1.

metathesis Any change in the form of a word in which one or more segments are moved to different places in the word. See especially 2.1.1.4.

metonymy The process of referring to a concept by means of a word which refers to a concept related to the first in the real world. See especially 5.2.2.

mood The grammatical category which expresses the degree or kind of reality the speaker assigns to a sentence.

morpheme The minimal grammatical unit; the smallest unit that plays any part in morphology or syntax.

neutralization The disappearance in certain positions of a contrast between two or more phonemes which exists in other positions.

nominative That case form which used to mark the subject of a sentence.

non-finite A label applied to any verb form which does not carry full marking for tense and agreement. See **finite**.

number The grammatical category which marks a grammatical distinction reflecting the number of countable things under discussion.

oblique A case form which marks any role other than that of sentence-subject.

palatalization Any change in which a non-palatal sound is replaced by a palatal or alveolo-palatal sound.

parasynthesis A process of derivation in which a prefix and a suffix are simultaneously added to the same root. See 4.14.1.

parisyllabic A label applied to Latin nouns (the large majority) all of whose case forms have the same number of syllables each. See **imparisyllabic**.

paronym A word which bears a resemblance to a second word, the latter belonging to a different language and having a different meaning. Also **false friend**. See especially 5.1.5.

person The grammatical category which distinguishes individuals and entities according to their role in the conversation. The first person is the speaker and possibly others associated with the speaker; the second person is the addressee(s) and possibly others associated with the addressee(s); the third person is everyone and everything else.

phoneme Any one of the minimal sound units of a language which (in contrast with another phoneme or phonemes) is capable of being correlated with a difference of meaning.

popular A label applied to words which have been transmitted orally from Latin to one or more of its descendants, and which have consequently undergone all the changes typical of that descendant. The counterpart of **learned**. See especially 2.2.1.

post-tonic A label applied to an **atonic** vowel or syllable which occurs between the **tonic** and the **final** syllable of a word.

pretonic A label applied to an **atonic** vowel or syllable which occurs between the **initial** and the **tonic** syllable of a word

proclitic A label applied to a **clitic** which is phonologically attached to what follows it.

protasis In a sentence of the *If*... (*then*) type, the part that follows the *If*.... See also **apodosis**.

reflex A word or form which is descended from an ancestral word or form which is under consideration. The opposite of **etymon**.

register A particular style of language which is appropriate in certain circumstances.

rhizotonic A label applied to a verbal form which carries the accent on the root.

rhotic Informally, any *r*-sound.

root In morphology, the simplest form of a lexical morpheme, which expresses the basic meaning of the word concerned and to which affixes may be added

semi-learned A much debated term, which in this text is an historical label applied to words which have been transmitted orally from Latin but which have undergone modification of their forms under the influence of the manner in which Latin was read aloud in the Middle Ages. See especially 2.2.3.

seseo A variety of Spanish pronunciation in which a single voiceless dental fricative /s̪/ corresponds to both /θ/ and /s/ of standard Peninsular Spanish (e.g. in *caza* and *casa*). See especially 2.6.3.

sibilant Informally, a hissing sound. More properly, a fricative or affricate consonant formed by constriction in the dental, alveolar or palatal areas. See especially 2.6.2.

split A type of phonological change in which the speech sounds that formerly belonged to one **phoneme** divide into two different phonemes. See especially 2.1.3.1.

stem In morphology, a form of a word which cannot stand alone but to which affixes may be added to produce grammatical word forms. Typically, a stem consists of a **root** plus some additional material (e.g. Lat. CANT-Ā-RE, where the root is CANT- and -Ā- is a **theme vowel**).

syncope The loss of a segment, especially a vowel, from the middle of a word.

synecdoche The application of the name of part of a larger concept to the whole of that concept, or vice versa. See 5.2.2.

synthetic A label applied to a grammatical form which is constructed entirely by affixing or modifying the word in question, without the use of any additional words. Thus, the preterite of Spanish *comer* is the synthetic form *comió*, while its perfect is the analytic *ha comido*. See **analytic**.

taboo A prohibition on the mention of a particular word or name. See especially 5.1.4.

tense	A grammatical category which correlates directly or approximately with time.
theme vowel	In Latin and the Romance languages, a vowel (immediately following the **root**) which marks the class or conjugation to which a verb belongs.
tonic	A label applied to a vowel or syllable which carries the main word stress.
toponym	A place-name.
vocative	A case form used to directly address the person indicated by the form concerned.
voice	In grammar, any one of the ways that may exist in a language for attaching the various participant roles (such as agent, patient, recipient) to the various grammatical relations (such as subject, direct object, indirect object). Spanish distinguishes active voice (e.g. *Este edificio lo construyó el Ayuntamiento*) from passive voice (e.g. *Este edificio fue construido por el Ayuntamiento*).
wau	A labiovelar **glide**, either opening [w] or closing [u̯].
yeísmo	A type of Spanish pronunciation in which the phonemes /ʎ/ and /ǰ/ have undergone **merger**, with some non-lateral result. See especially 2.6.6.
yod	A palatal **glide**, either opening [j] or closing [i̯].

Topics for discussion and further reading

1 INTRODUCTION

- On what basis can it be claimed that Spanish *is* Latin?
- What grounds are there for thinking that first-century AD Latin showed substantial internal variation?
- Assess the role of Alfonso X in the standardization of Spanish.
- Discuss the forces which propelled the dialect of Burgos towards the status of national and international language.
- Discuss the competition between Castilian and other Peninsular languages.

Further reading: Herman (2000), Lapesa (1980), Lleal (1990), Penny (2000), Rohlfs (1960), Väänänen (1968), Wright (1982).

2 PHONOLOGY

- Discuss the processes of *assimilation, dissimilation, analogy* and *hypercorrection* and give examples of their operation drawn from the history of Spanish.
- Discuss the development in Spanish of the Latin tonic vowels, making particular reference to the processes illustrated by the following cases:

SĔPTE	>	*siete*	MATĔRIA	>	*madera*
DĔCE	>	*diez*	LĔCTU	>	*lecho*
NŎVU	>	*nuevo*	NŎVIU	>	*novio*
NŎVE	>	*nueve*	LĔCTU	>	*lecho*

- How does the development of atonic vowels differ from that of tonic vowels in Spanish? Why is this?
- To what extent has Spanish repaired the earlier absence of labiodental phonemes from its inventory?
- In what ways does the development of secondary consonant groups differ from that of primary groups?
- What are the broad processes underlying the development of the Medieval Spanish sibilant phonemes (/ʃ/, /ʒ/, /s/, /z/, /t^s/, /d^z/) into their modern reflexes (/x/, /s/, /θ/)?

- What is meant today by the terms *seseo* and *ceceo*? What was meant by the term *çeçeo* in the sixteenth and seventeenth centuries?
- What are the effects (including grammatical effects) of the weakening of syllable-final /s/ in Spanish?

Further reading: Alarcos Llorach (1965), Lausberg (1965), Lloyd (1987), Pountain (2001).

3 MORPHO-SYNTAX

- Describe the development in Spanish of the various types of second-person address.
- Discuss the relationship between form and gender in Modern Spanish, and give an historical account of the patterns that can be observed.
- What is meant by the terms *leísmo, laísmo* and *loísmo*? What reasons can be given for the development of these patterns of clitic usage?
- How is the development of definite articles related to that of the demonstratives?
- Discuss some of the main competing views concerning the development of the Latin case-system in Spanish.
- Comment on the development Spanish future and conditional paradigms, in the light of the fact that while the Latin verbal system has in general become more analytic (i.e. less synthetic) in type, these paradigms exhibit exactly the opposite trend.
- Seek reasons for the fact that most of the Latin rhizotonic (strong) perfects have become arrhizotonic (weak) in Spanish.
- Identify the main factors which account for stem-vowel alternation in the present-tense paradigms of Spanish. In particular, account for the alternations visible in such cases as *pienso/pensamos, quieras/queráis, siento/ sentimos/ sintamos, vuele/volemos, mueles/moléis, duermo/dormís/durmáis*.
- Trace the development in Spanish of the paradigms characterized by the endings *-ra, -se* and *-re* (e.g. *cantara, cantase, cantare, comiera, comiese, comiere*).
- Discuss the aspectual contrasts between Spanish preterite, perfect and imperfect paradigms (e.g. *hizo, ha hecho, hacía*), together with the Latin antecedents of these contrasts.

Further reading: Alvar and Pottier (1983), Lapesa (2000), Lausberg (1966), Lloyd (1987), Pountain (2001).

4 LEXIS

- Trace the main paths by which Latin words have been transmitted to Spanish (popular, semi-learned and learned).

- Irrespective of the source of borrowing of foreign words, what are the broad motives for such borrowing?
- It used to be thought that the impact of Basque on Spanish was considerable. How can this view be challenged, on the basis of lexical borrowing?
- Why does Spanish contain far more words of Arabic origin than of Germanic origin (if English is excluded)?
- What do Spanish borrowings from Amerindian languages reveal about the nature of the contact between Europeans and native American peoples?
- Discuss the interchange of vocabulary between Spanish and the other Romance languages.

Further reading: Clavería Nadal (1991), Corriente (1999).

5 SEMANTICS

- Discuss the main motives for semantic change, as seen in the changing meaning of Spanish words.
- What is the role of euphemism in semantic change?
- Discuss the notion of *semantic loan.*
- Explain and illustrate the phenomenon known as *calque* or *loan translation.*
- Can it be claimed that *metaphor* is an everyday process of language development, or does it belong only to poetic registers?
- How do the effects of *metonymy* differ from those of *metaphor*?
- Discuss narrowing and broadening of the semantic range of Spanish words.

Further reading: Ogden and Richards (1923), Ullmann (1962).

6 PAST, PRESENT AND FUTURE

- What differences can be seen between the world roles of Spanish and of English?
- Compare the variation within the Romance language family with that observable within Spanish. Consider reasons for the different degree of variation in each case.
- This book claims that the internal and external health of Spanish is reasonably assured for the foreseeable future. Do you agree?

Further reading: Mar-Molinero (2000), Stewart (1999).

References

ArL	*Archivum Linguisticum*
ARM	*Auto de Los Reyes Magos*
BHS	*Bulletin of Hispanic Studies*
BRAE	*Boletín de la Real Academia Española*
CLHM	*Cahiers de Linguistique Hispanique Médiévale*
CQ	*Classical Quarterly*
HR	*Hispanic Review*
JHP	*Journal of Hispanic Philology*
L	*Language*
MR	*Medioevo Romanzo*
NRFH	*Nueva Revista de Filología Hispánica*
PMC	*Poema de mio Cid*
PMLA	*Publications of the Modern Language Association*
RF	*Romanische Forschungen*
RFE	*Revista de Filología Española*
RLiR	*Revue de Linguistique Romane*
RPh	*Romance Philology*
VKR	*Volkstum und Kultur der Romanen*
ZRP	*Zeitschrift für romanische Philologie*

Abercrombie, David. 1967. *Elements of General Phonetics*. Edinburgh University Press.

Adams, J. N. 1977. *The Vulgar Latin of the Letters of Claudius Terentianus*. Manchester: Manchester University Press.

Aebischer, Paul. 1971. 'Le pl. -ās de la 1ère decl. latine et ses résultats dans les langues romanes', *ZRP*, 87: 74–98.

Alarcos Llorach, Emilio. 1965. *Fonología española*, 4th edn. Madrid: Gredos.

Alemany Bolufer, José. 1920. *Tratado de la formación de palabras en la lengua castellana: la derivación y la composición: estudio de los sufijos y prefijos empleados en una y otra*. Madrid: Suárez.

Allen, Jr, J. H. D. 1976. 'Apocope in Old Spanish', in *Estudios ofrecidos a Emilio Alarcos Llorach*, ed. M. V. Conde et al., vol. I. Universidad de Oviedo. 15–30.

Alonso, Amado, 1935, 'Noción, emoción, acción y fantasía en los diminutivos', *VKR*, 8: 104–26; reprinted in his *Estudios lingüísticos: temas españoles*, 2nd edn. Madrid: Gredos, 1961. 161–89.

1943. *Castellano, español, idioma nacional: historia espiritual de tres nombres*, 2nd edn. Buenos Aires: Losada.

1947. 'Trueques de sibilantes en el antiguo español', *NRFH*, 1: 1–12.

1951. 'La "LL" y sus alteraciones en España y América', in *Estudios dedicados a Menéndez Pidal*, vol. II, Madrid: CSIC, 41–89; reprinted in his *Estudios lingüísticos: temas hispanoamericanos*, 3rd edn. Madrid: Gredos, 1967. 159–212.

1967. *De la pronunciación medieval a la moderna en español*, vol. I, 2nd edn. Madrid: Gredos.

1969. *De la pronunciación medieval a la moderna en español*, vol. II. Madrid: Gredos.

Alonso, Dámaso. 1962. *La fragmentación fonética peninsular*, published as *Enciclopedia lingüística hispánica*, vol. I (Supplement). Madrid: CSIC.

Alvar, Manuel. 1978. 'Para la historia de "castellano"', in *Homenaje a Julio Caro Baroja*, ed. A. Carreira et al. Madrid: Centro de Investigaciones Sociológicas. 71–82.

Alvar, Manuel, et al. (eds.). 1960. *Enciclopedia lingüística hispánica*, vol. I, *Antecedentes. Onomástica*. Madrid: CSIC.

1967. *Enciclopedia lingüística hispánica*, vol. II, *Elementos constitutivos y fuentes*. Madrid: CSIC.

Alvar, Manuel, and Sebastián Mariner. 1967. 'Latinismos', in Alvar 1967: 3–49.

Alvar, Manuel, and Bernard Pottier. 1983. *Morfología histórica del español*. Madrid: Gredos.

Anipa, Kormi, 2000. '*Tomad* and *tomá*, etc.: change and continuity in a morphological feature', *MLR*, 95: 389–98.

Baldinger, Kurt. 1972. *La formación de los dominios lingüísticos en la Península ibérica*. 2nd edn. Madrid: Gredos.

Beinhauer, Werner. 1968. *El español coloquial*, 2nd edn. Madrid: Gredos (German original: *Spanische Umgangssprache*. Bonn: Dummlers, 1958).

Blake, Robert J. 1987–8. '*Ffaro*, *faro* or *haro*?: f-doubling as a source of linguistic information for the Early Middle Ages', *RPh*, 41: 267–89.

1988. 'Aproximaciones nuevas al fenómeno [f] > [Ø]', in *Actas del I congreso internacional de historia de la lengua española*, ed. M. Ariza, A. Salvador and A. Viudas, vol. I. Madrid: Arco Libros. 71–82.

Blase, H. 1898. 'Zur Geschichte des Futurums und des Konjunctivs des Perfekts im Lateinischen', *Archiv für lateinische Lexicographie und Grammatik*, 2: 313–43; translated as 'De la historia del futuro y del perfecto de subjuntivo en latín', in *Introducción plural a la gramática histórica*, ed. Francisco Marcos Marín. Madrid: Cincel, 1982. 147–69.

Blaylock, Curtis. 1986. 'Notes on the chronology of a morpho-phonological change in Golden-Age Spanish: the loss of *-d-* in proparoxytonic forms of the second person plural verbs', *HR*, 54: 279–85.

Boyd-Bowman, Peter. 1956. 'The regional origins of the earliest Spanish colonists of America', *PMLA*, 71: 1152–72.

1964. *Índice geobiográfico de 40.000 pobladores españoles de América en el siglo XVI*, vol. I. Bogotá: Instituto Caro y Cuervo.

Buesa, Tomás. 1967. 'Elementos constitutivos: americanismos', in Alvar 1967: 325–48.

Bynon, Theodora. 1977. *Historical Linguistics* (Cambridge Textbooks in Linguistics). Cambridge: Cambridge University Press.

Canfield, D. Lincoln. 1981. *Spanish Pronunciation in the Americas*. Chicago: University of Chicago Press.

Castro, Américo. 1936. *Glosarios latino-españoles de la Edad Media (RFE, anejo* 22). Madrid: Centro de Estudios Históricos.

Clavería Nadal, Gloria. 1991. *El latinismo en español*. Barcelona: Universitat Autònoma de Barcelona.

Coleman, R. G. G. 1971. 'The origin and development of Latin HABEO + infinitive', *CQ*, n.s., 21: 215–32.

Colón Domènech, Germán. 1967a. 'Occitanismos', in Alvar 1967: 154–92.

1967b. 'Catalanismos', in Alvar 1967: 193–238.

Company Company, Concepción, and Alfonso Medina Urrea. 1999. 'Sintaxis motivada pragmáticamente: futuros analíticos y sintéticos en el español medieval', *RFE*, 79: 65–100.

Comrie, Bernard, 1976. *Aspect: An Introduction to the Study of Verbal Aspect and Related Problems*. Cambridge: Cambridge University Press.

Corominas, Joan. 1954–7. *Diccionario crítico etimológico de la lengua castellana*. Madrid: Gredos; Berne: Francke.

Corominas, Joan, and José A. Pascual. 1980–91. *Diccionario crítico etimológico castellano e hispánico*, 6 vols. Madrid: Gredos.

Corriente, Federico. 1999. *Diccionario de arabismos y voces afines*. Madrid: Gredos.

Craddock, Jerry R. 1980. 'The contextual varieties of yod: an attempt at systematization', in *Festschrift for Jacob Ornstein: Studies in General Linguistics and Sociolinguistics*, ed. Edward L. Blansin, Jr, and Richard V. Teschner. Rowley, MA: Newbury House. 61–8.

1983. 'Descending diphthongs and the regular preterite in Hispano-Romance', *BHS*, 60: 1–14.

1985. 'The tens from 40 to 90 in Old Castilian: a new approach', *RPh*, 38: 425–35

Dalbor, John B. 1980. *Spanish Pronunciation: Theory and Practice*, 2nd edn. New York: Holt, Rinehart and Winston.

Dardel, Robert de. 1964. 'Considérations sur la déclinaison romane à trois cas', *Cahiers Ferdinand de Saussure*, 21: 7–23.

De Gorog, Ralph. 1980. 'L'Origine des formes espagnoles *doy*, *estoy*, *soy*, *voy*', *CLHM*, 5: 157–62.

Dworkin, Steven N. 1978. 'Phonotactic awkwardness as an impediment to sound change', *Forum Linguisticum*, 3: 47–56.

1988a. 'The interaction of phonological and morphological processes: the evolution of the Old Spanish second person plural verb endings', *RPh*, 42: 144–55.

1988b. 'The diffusion of a morphological change: the reduction of the Old Spanish verbal suffixes *-ades*, *-edes* and *-ides*', *HR*, 13: 223–36.

England, John. 1982. '*Ser* and *aver* with the past participles of intransitive verbs in the works of Don Juan Manuel', *Don Juan Manuel: VII centenario*. Murcia: Universidad de Murcia y Academia Alfonso X el Sabio. 117–33.

1984. 'Observaciones sobre las nuevas formas femininas en el castellano del siglo XII', in *Estudios dedicados a James Leslie Brooks*, ed. J. M. Ruiz Veintemilla. Barcelona: Puvill, for University of Durham. 31–44.

1987. 'New feminine forms in Old Spanish: the fourteenth and fifteenth centuries', *BHS*, 64: 205–14.

Eseverri Hualde, Crisóstomo. 1945. *Diccionario etimológico de helenismos españoles* (Pampilonensia: Publicaciones del seminario diocesano de Pamplona, serie B. vol.1), Burgos: Aldecoa.

Fernández Galiano, M. 1967. 'Helenismos', in Alvar 1967: 51–77.

Fernández-Ordóñez, Inés, 1994. 'Isoglosas internas del castellano: el sistema referencial del pronombre átono de tercera persona', *RFE*, 74: 71–125.

Galmés de Fuentes, Álvaro. 1955–6. 'Influencias sintácticas y estilísticas del árabe en la prosa medieval castellana', *BRAE*, 35: 213–75, 415–51; 36: 65–131, 255–307.

1967. 'Dialectalismos', in Alvar 1967: 307–24.

1983. *Dialectología mozárabe*. Madrid: Gredos.

Gamillscheg, Ernst. 1967. 'Germanismos', in Alvar 1967: 79–91.

González Ollé, Fernando. 1962. *Los sufijos diminutivos en castellano medieval* (*RFE*, *anejo* 75). Madrid: CSIC.

González Palencia, Cándido. 1926–30. *Los mozárabes de Toledo en los siglos XII y XIII*, 4 vols. Madrid: Instituto de Valencia de Don Juan.

Gooch, Anthony. 1970. *Diminutive, Augmentative and Pejorative Suffixes in Modern Spanish: A Guide to their Use and Meaning*, 2nd edn. Oxford: Pergamon.

Harris, Martin B. 1971. 'The history of the conditional complex from Latin to Spanish: some structural considerations', *ArL*, n.s., 2: 25–33.

1978. *The Evolution of French Syntax: A Comparative Approach*. London: Longman.

1982. 'The "past simple" and the "present perfect" in Romance', in *Studies in the Romance Verb*, ed. N. Vincent and M. Harris. London: Croom Helm. 42–70.

1986. 'The historical development of conditional sentences in Romance', *RPh*, 39: 405–36.

Hartman, Steven Lee. 1974. 'An outline of Spanish historical phonology', *Papers in Linguistics*, 7: 123–91.

Henríquez Ureña, Pedro. 1932. *Sobre el problema del andalucismo dialectal de América* (Biblioteca de Dialectología Hispánica, 1). Buenos Aires: Instituto de Filología.

Herman, József. 2000. *Vulgar Latin*. Pennsylvania: Pennsylvania State University.

Herrero Ingelmo, José Luis, 1994–5. *Cultismos renacentistas: cultismos léxicos y semánticos en la poesía del siglo XVI*. Madrid: Real Academia Española [first published as five articles in *BRAE*, 74 (1994) and 75 (1995)].

Jaberg, Carl, 1926. 'Zur Sach- und Bezeichnungsgeschichte der Beinbekleidungen in der Zentralromania', *Wörter und Sachen*, 9 (2): 137–72.

Jungemann, Frederick H. 1955. *La teoría del sustrato y los dialectos hispanoromances y gascones*. Madrid: Gredos.

Kany, Charles E. 1960. *American-Spanish Euphemisms*. Berkeley: University of California Press.

Klein-Andreu, Flora, 1991. 'Losing ground: a discourse-pragmatic solution to a problem in the history of Spanish', in *Categories of the Verb in Romance: Discourse Pragmatic Approaches*, ed. S. Fleischman and L. Waugh. London: Routledge. 164–78.

2000. *Variación actual y evolución histórica: los clíticos le/s, la/s, lo/s* (LINCOM Studies in Romance Linguistics, 16). Munich: LINCOM.

Lapesa, Rafael. 1951. 'La apócope de la vocal en castellano antiguo: intento de explicación histórica', in *Estudios dedicados a Menéndez Pidal*, vol. II. Madrid: CSIC. 185–226.

1968. 'Sobre los orígenes y evolución del leísmo, laísmo y loísmo', in *Festschrift Walther von Wartburg zum 80. Geburtstag*, 2 vols. Tübingen: Niemeyer. 523–51 [reprinted in Lapesa 2000: 279–310].

1970. 'Las formas verbales de segunda persona y los orígenes del "voseo"', in *Actas del Tercer Congreso Internacional de Hispanistas*, ed. Carlos H. Magis. Mexico City: Colegio de México, for Asociación Internacional de Hispanistas. 519–31.

1975. 'De nuevo sobre la apócope vocálica en castellano medieval', *NRFH*, 24: 13–23.

1980. *Historia de la lengua española*, 8th edn. Madrid: Gredos.

1982. 'Contienda de normas lingüísticas en el castellano alfonsí', in *Actas del Coloquio hispano-alemán Ramón Menéndez Pidal*, ed. Wido Hempel and Dietrich Briesemeister. Tübingen: Niemeyer. 172–90.

1988. 'Sobre el origen de *Sancho*', in *Homenagem a Joseph M. Piel por ocasião do seu 85º aniversário*. Tübingen: Niemeyer. 79–83.

2000. *Estudios de morfosintaxis histórica del español*, ed. Rafael Cano Aguilar and M.ª Teresa Echenique Elizondo, 2 vols. (Biblioteca Románica Hispánica). Madrid: Gredos.

Lausberg, Heinrich. 1965. *Lingüística románica*, vol. I, *Fonética*. Madrid: Gredos.

1966. *Lingüística románica*, vol. II, *Morfología*. Madrid: Gredos.

Líbano Zumalacárregui, Ángeles. 1991. 'Morfología diacrónica del español: las fórmulas de tratamiento', *RFE*, 71: 107–21.

Lipski, John M. 1994. *Latin-American Spanish* (Longman Linguistics Library). London and New York: Longman.

Lleal, Coloma, 1990. *La formación de las lenguas romances peninsulares*. Barcelona: Barcanova.

Lloyd, Paul M. 1993. *Del latín al español*, vol. I, *Fonología y morfología históricas de la lengua española*. Madrid: Gredos; translation of *From Latin to Spanish: Historical Phonology and Morphology of the Spanish Language* (Memoirs of the American Philosophical Society, 173). Philadelphia: American Philosophical Society, 1987.

López Bobo, M.ª Jesús, 1998. *El vocalismo radical átono en la conjugación castellana: etapa medieval y clásica*. Oviedo: Departamento de Filología Española.

1999. '¡Quién lo *vido* y quién lo *vee*!', *Moenia*, 5 (Lingüística): 321–65.

Lyons, John. 1968. *Introduction to Theoretical Linguistics*. Cambridge: Cambridge University Press.

Mackenzie, Ian. 1995. 'The supposed imperfectivity of the Latin American perfect', *Hispanic Linguistics*, 6–7: 29–60.

1999. *Semantics of Spanish Verbal Categories*. Berne: Lang.

Macpherson, I. R. 1975. *Spanish Phonology: Descriptive and Historical*. Manchester University Press; New York: Barnes and Noble.

Maiden, Martin, 2001. 'A strange affinity: "perfecto y tiempos afines"', *BHS* (Liverpool), 78: 441–64.

Malinowski, Arlène. 1983. 'The pronouns of address in contemporary Judeo-Spanish', *RPh*, 37: 20–35.

Malkiel, Yakov. 1949. 'The contrast *tomáis-tomávades*, *queréis-queríades* in Classical Spanish', *HR*, 17: 159–65.

1957–8. 'Diachronic hypercharacterization in Romance', *ArL*, 9: 79–113, 10: 1–36.

1959a. 'Towards a reconsideration of the Old Spanish imperfect in *-ía*~*-ié*', *HR*, 27: 435–81.

1959b. 'The two sources of the Hispanic suffix *-azo*, *-aço*', *L*, 35: 193–258.

1963–4. 'The interlocking of narrow sound-change, level of transmission, areal configuration, sound symbolism: diachronic studies in the Hispano-Latin consonant clusters CL-, FL-, PL-', *ArL*, 15: 144–73, 16: 1–33.

1966. 'Diphthongization, monophthongization, metaphony: studies in their interaction in the paradigm of the Old Spanish -IR verbs', *L*, 42: 430–72.

1971. 'Derivational transparency as an occasional co-determinant of sound change: a new causal ingredient in the distribution of *-ç-* and *-z-* in ancient Hispano-Romance (I)', *RPh*, 25: 1–52.

1974. 'New problems in Romance interfixation (I): the velar insert in the present tense (with an excursus on *-zer/-zir* verbs)', *RPh*, 27: 304–55.

1976. 'From falling to rising diphthongs: the case of Old Spanish *ió* < **éu* (with excursuses on the weak preterite; on the possessives; and on *judío*, *sandío*, and *romero)'*, *RPh*, 29: 435–500.

1982. 'Interplay of sounds and forms in the shaping of three Old Spanish consonant clusters', *HR*, 50: 247–66.

Mańczak, W. 1976. 'Espagnol classique *tomáis*, *queréis* mais *tomávades*, *queríades'*, *Kwartalnik Neofilologiczny*, 23: 181–6.

Marcos Marín, Francisco. 1982. 'Observaciones sobre las construcciones condicionales en la historia de la lengua española', *NRFH*, 28: 86–105; reprinted in *Introducción plural a la gramática histórica*, ed. Francisco Marcos Marín. Madrid: Cincel. 186–204.

Mar-Molinero, Clare, 2000. *The Politics of Language in the Spanish-Speaking World*. London: Routledge.

Martinet, André. 1974. *Economía de los cambios fonéticos: tratado de fonología diacrónica*. Madrid: Gredos.

Meillet, Antoine. 1921. 'Quelques hypothèses sur des interdictions de vocabulaire dans les langues indo-européennes', in his *Linguistique historique et linguistique générale*. Paris: Klinksieck. I: 281–91.

Mendeloff, H. 1960. *The Evolution of the Conditional Sentence Contrary to Fact in Old Spanish*. Washington: The Catholic University of America Press.

Menéndez Pidal, Ramón. 1958. *Manual de gramática histórica española*, 10th edn. Madrid: Espasa-Calpe.

1960. 'Dos problemas iniciales relativos a los romances hispánicos', in Alvar 1960: lix–cxxxviii.

1964a. *Orígenes del español: estado lingüístico de la Peninsula Ibérica hasta el siglo XI*, 5th edn. Madrid: Espasa-Calpe.

1964b, ed. *Cantar de mio Cid*, vol. I, *Gramática*, 4th edn. Madrid: Espasa-Calpe.

Miller, Elaine R. 2000. *Jewish Multiglossia: Hebrew, Arabic and Castilian in Medieval Spain*. Newark, DE: Juan de la Cuesta.

Montero Cartelle, Emilio. 1989. *Gonzalo de Berceo y el Libro de Alexandre: aproximación al sistema verbal de la época desde los esquemas condicionales* (*Verba* anexo 30). Santiago de Compostela: Universidad.

Montgomery, Thomas. 1975–6. 'Complementarity of stem-vowels in the Spanish second and third conjugations', *RPh*, 29: 281–96.

1978. 'Iconicity and lexical retention in Spanish: stative and dynamic verbs', *L*, 54: 907–16.

1979. 'Sound-symbolism and aspect in the Spanish second conjugation', *HR*, 47: 219–37.

1980. 'Vocales cerradas y acciones perfectivas', *BRAE*, 60: 299–314.

1985. 'Sources of vocalic correspondences of stems and endings in the Spanish verb', *Hispanic Linguistics*, 2: 99–114.

Müller, Bodo. 1963. 'Span. *soy*, *estoy*, *doy*, *voy* im Lichte der romanischen Endungsneubildung mit flexionsfremden Elementen', *RF*, 75: 240–63.

Náñez Fernández, Emilio. 1973. *El diminutivo: historia y funciones en el español clásico y moderno*. Madrid: Gredos.

Navarro Tomás, Tomás. 1961. *Manual de pronunciación española*, 10th edn. Madrid: CSIC.

Nebrija, Elio Antonio de. 1492. *Gramática de la lengua castellana*, ed. Antonio Quilis (Clásicos para una Biblioteca Contemporánea). Madrid: Editora Nacional, 1980.

Ogden, C. K. and I. A. Richards. 1923. *The Meaning of Meaning: A Study of the Influence of Language upon Thought and of the Science of Symbolism*, 1st edn. London: Kegan Paul [the edition used is the 10th (1949)].

Penny, Ralph J. 1972a. 'The reemergence of /f/ as a phoneme of Castilian', *ZRP*, 88: 463–82.

1972b. 'Verb-class as a determiner of stem-vowel in the historical morphology of Spanish verbs', *RLiR*, 36: 343–59.

1976. 'The convergence of B-, V- and -P- in the Peninsula: a reappraisal', in *Medieval Studies Presented to Rita Hamilton*, ed. A. D. Deyermond. London: Tamesis. 149–59.

1980. 'Do Romance nouns descend from the Accusative?: preliminaries to a reassessment of the noun-morphology of Romance', *RPh*, 33: 501–9.

1983a. 'The Peninsular expansion of Castilian', *BHS*, 60: 333–8.

1983b. 'Secondary consonant groups in Castilian', *JHP*, 7: 135–40.

1987. 'Derivation of abstracts in Alfonsine Spanish', *RPh*, 41: 1–23.

1988. 'The Old Spanish graphs "i", "j", "g" and "y" and the development of Latin $G^{e,i}$- and J-', *BHS*, 65: 337–51.

1990a. 'The stage jargon of Juan del Encina and the castilianization of the Leonese dialect area', in *Golden Age Literature: Studies in Honour of John Varey by his Colleagues and Pupils*, ed. Alan Deyermond and Charles Davis. London: Queen Mary and Westfield College. 155–66.

1990b. 'Labiodental /f/, aspiration and /h/-dropping in Spanish: the evolving phonemic values of the graphs *f* and *h*', in *Cultures in Contact in Medieval Spain: Historical and literary essays presented to L. P. Harvey* (King's College London Medieval Studies, 3), ed. David Hook and Barry Taylor, London: King's College. 157–82.

1993. *Gramática histórica del español*. Barcelona: Ariel.

1998. '¿En qué consiste una historia del castellano?', in *Actas del IV Congreso Internacional de Historia de la Lengua Española (La Rioja, 1–5 de abril de 1997)*, 2 vols., ed. Claudio García Turza, Fabián González Bachiller and Javier Mangado Martínez. Logroño: Asociación de Historia de la Lengua Española, Gobierno de La Rioja, and Universidad de La Rioja. II: 583–94.

2000. *Variation and Change in Spanish*. Cambridge: Cambridge University Press.

forthcoming. 'Procesos de clasificación verbal española: polaridad de vocales radicales en los verbos en *-er* e *-ir*', in *Homenaje al Profesor Fernando González Ollé*, ed. María Victoria Romero, Manuel Casado, Carmen Saralegui, Claudio García Turza and Emili Casanova. Pamplona: Universidad de Navarra.

Pensado Ruiz, Carmen. 1984. *Cronología relativa del castellano* (Acta Salmanticensia, Filosofía y Letras, 158). Salamanca: Universidad de Salamanca.

1999. 'Frontera de prefijo, aspiración de "F" y procesos de nasalización en la historia del español', *RPh*, 47: 89–112.

Porcar Miralles, Margarita. 1993. *La oración condicional: la evolución de los esquemas verbales condicionales desde el latín al español actual*. Castellón: Universitat Jaume I.

Pottier, Bernard. 1967. 'Galicismos', in Alvar 1967: 127–51.

Pountain, Christopher J. 1983. *Structures and Transformations: The Romance Verb*. London: Croom Helm; Totowa, NJ: Barnes and Noble.

1985. 'Copulas, verbs of possession in Old Spanish: the evidence for structurally interdependent changes', *BHS*, 62: 337–55.

2001. *A History of the Spanish Language through Texts*. London: Routledge.

Pratt, Chris. 1980. *El anglicismo en el español peninsular contemporáneo*. Madrid: Gredos.

Quilis, Antonio. 1980. 'Le Sort de l'espagnol aux Philippines: un problème de langues en contact', *RLiR*, 44: 82–107.

Quilis, Antonio and Joseph A. Fernández. 1969. *Curso de fonética y fonología españolas*, 4th edn. Madrid: CSIC.

Real Academia. 1972–. Real Academia Española, *Diccionario histórico de la lengua española* [vols I-II, vol. III, fasc. 1–2 (*antigramatical-apasanca*), vol. IV, fasc. 1 (*b-bajoca*) so far published]. Madrid: RAE.

Renfrew, Colin, 1998. *Archaeology and Language: The Puzzle of Indo-European Origins*. London: Pimlico.

Ridruejo, Emilio. 1982. 'La forma verbal en *-ra* en español del siglo XIII (oraciones independientes)', in *Introducción plural a la gramática histórica*, ed. Francisco Marcos Marín. Madrid: Cincel. 170–85.

Robson, C. A. 1963. '*L'Appendix Probi* et la philologie latine', *Le Moyen Âge*, livre jubilaire, 39–54.

Rohlfs, Gerhard. 1960. *La diferenciación léxica de las lenguas románicas* (Publicaciones de la *Revista de Filología Española*, 14). Madrid: CSIC.

Rojo, Guillermo and Emilio Montero Cartelle. 1983 *La evolución de los esquemas condicionales (potenciales e irreales desde el poema del Cid hasta 1400)* (*Verba, anexo* 22). Santiago de Compostela: Universidad de Santiago de Compostela.

Rona, José Pedro. 1973. 'Tiempo y aspecto: análisis binario de la conjugación española', *Anuario de Letras*, 11: 211–23.

Roudet, L. 1921. 'Sur la classification psychologique des changements sémantiques', *Journal de Psychologie*, 18: 676–92.

Sala, Marius. 1979. 'Sobre el vocabulario del judeo-español', in *Festschrift Kurt Baldinger zum 60. Geburtstag*, ed. M. Höfler, H. Vernay and L. Wolf, vol. II. Tübingen: Niemeyer. 910–16.

Salvador, Gregorio. 1967. 'Lusismos', in Alvar 1967: 239–61.

Samuels, M. L. 1972. *Linguistic Evolution* (Cambridge Studies in Linguistics, 5). Cambridge: Cambridge University Press.

Saralegui, Carmen. 1983. 'Morfología del futuro y condicional castellanos: polimorfismo antiguo y fijación lingüística', *MR*, 8: 419–59.

Schede, Hildegard, 1989. *Die Morphologie des Verbes im Altspanischen*. Frankfurt, Bern, New York: Lang.

Stewart, Miranda, 1999. *The Spanish Language Today*. London: Routledge.

Terlingen, Johannes H. 1943. *Los italianismos en español desde la formación del idioma hasta principios del siglo XVII*. Amsterdam: N. V. NoordHollandsche Uitgevers Maatschappij.

Terlingen, Juan. 1967. 'Italianismos', in Alvar 1967: 263–305.

Togeby, Knud. 1963. *Mode, aspect et temps en espagnol*, 2nd edn. Copenhagen: Munksgaard.

Tovar, Antonio. 1952. 'Sobre la cronología de la sonorización de las sordas en la Romania Occidental', in *Homenaje a Fritz Krüger*, I. Mendoza: Universidad de Cuyo 9–15.

Trask, R. L. 1997a. *The History of Basque*. London and New York: Routledge.

1997b. *A Student's Dictionary of Language and Linguistics*. London: Arnold.

Trudgill, Peter. 1986. *Dialects in Contact* (Language in Society, 10). Oxford: Blackwell.

Ullmann, Stephen. 1962. *Semantics: An Introduction to the Science of Meaning*. Oxford: Blackwell.

Väänänen, Veikko. 1968. *Introducción al latín vulgar*. Madrid: Gredos.

Valesio, P. 1968. 'The Romance synthetic future pattern and its first attestations, I', *Lingua*, 20: 113–61.

Vincent, Nigel. 1982. 'The development of the auxiliaries HABERE and ESSE in Romance', in *Studies in the Romance Verb: Essays Offered to Joe Cremona on the Occasion of his 60th Birthday*, ed. Nigel Vincent and Martin Harris. London: Croom Helm, pp. 71–96.

Whinnom, Keith. 1954. 'Spanish in the Philippine Islands: a sociolinguistic survey', *Journal of Oriental Studies* (Hong Kong), 1: 129–94.

1956. *Spanish Contact Vernaculars in the Philippines*. Hong Kong: University Press; London: Oxford University Press.

Wilkinson, Hugh E. 1971. 'Vowel alternation in the Spanish *-IR* verbs', *Ronshu* (Aoyama Gakuin University, Tokyo), 12: 1–21.

1973–5. 'The strong perfects in the Romance languages', *Ronshu* (Aoyama Gakuin University, Tokyo), 14 (1973): 157–94, 15 (1974): 23–44, 16 (1975): 15–31.

1976. 'Notes on the development of -KJ-, -TJ- in Spanish and Portuguese', *Ronshu* (Aoyama Gakuin University, Tokyo), 17: 19–36.

Wolf, Heinz Jürgen. 1988. 'Aún', in *Homenagem a Joseph M. Piel por ocasião do seu 85º aniversário*. Tübingen: Niemeyer: 443–7.

Wright, Leavitt Olds. 1932. *The -ra Verb-form in Spain: The Latin Pluperfect Indicative Form in its Successive Functions in Castilian* (University of California Publications in Modern Philology, 15, no. 1). Berkeley: University of California Press.

Wright, Roger. 1976. 'Semicultismo', *ArL*, n.s., 7: 14–28.

1982. *Late Latin and Early Romance in Spain and Carolingian France* (ARCA Classical and Medieval Texts, Papers and Monographs). Liverpool: Francis Cairns.

1985. 'Indistinctive features (facial and semantic)', *RPh*, 38: 275–92.

Zamora Vicente, Alonso. 1967. *Dialectología española*, 2nd edn. Madrid: Gredos.

Word index

Words are cited as they appear in the text and the list includes both Old and Modern Spanish spellings, Latin forms (in small capitals), as well as some Arabic and Greek words.

Subject index

CPSIA information can be obtained at www.ICGtesting.com
Printed in the USA
243095LV00002B/1/P

9 780521 011846